Y0-BBW-407

Published in 2018 by Rockridge edu. enterprise & services. inc.

All inquiries should be addressed to:
Rockridge edu. enterprise & services inc.
869 SEYMOUR BLVD. NORTH VANCOUVER B.C. CANADA V7J 2J7
satvancouver@gmail.com

HOW TO USE THIS BOOK

Why Is It So Hard to Improve Reading and Writing Scores?

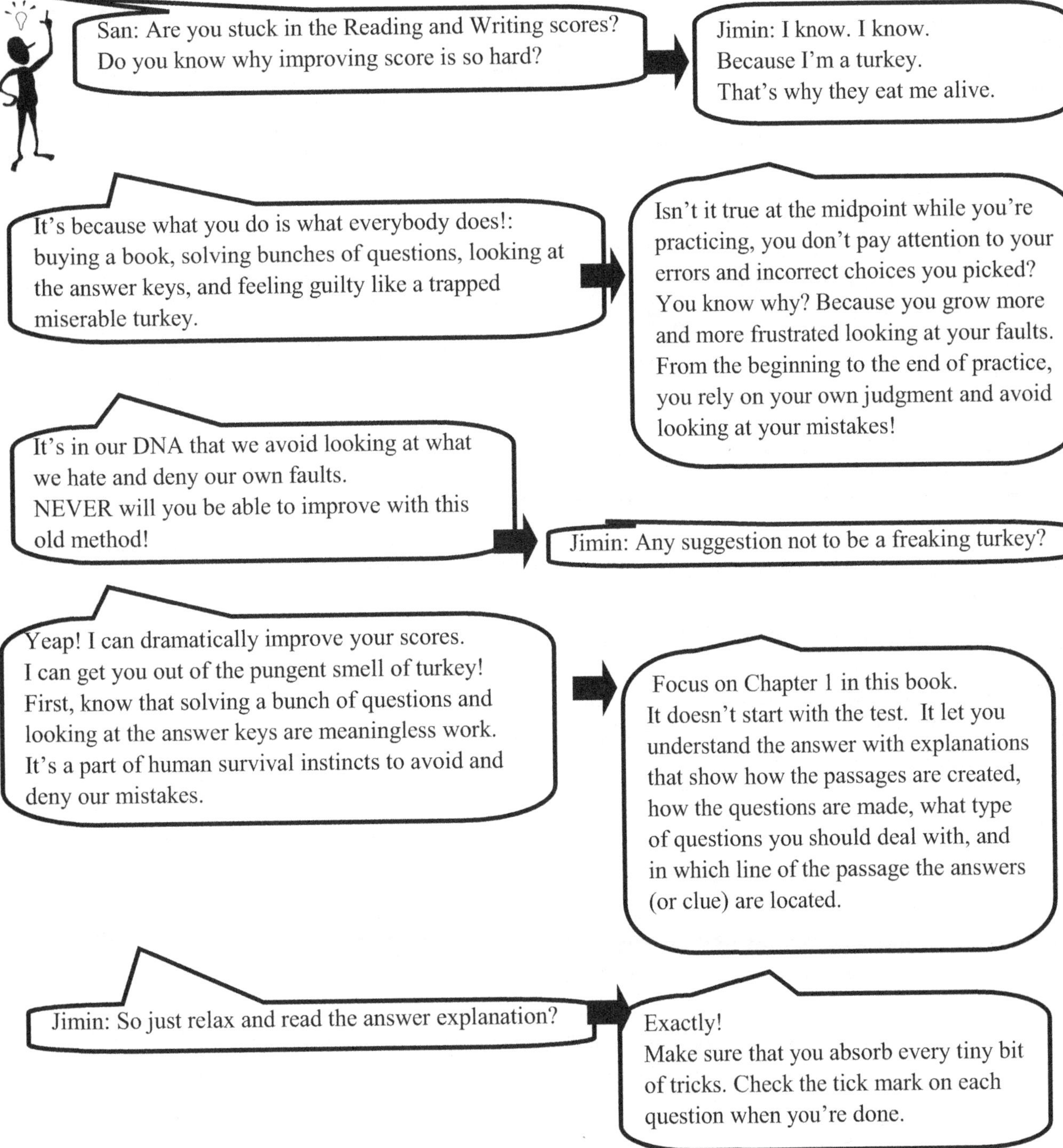

How to Use This Book

Why Is It So Hard to Improve Reading and Writing Scores?

Jimin: That makes sense!
Think I can cut myself off from doing the turkey business from now on.

Nice! At least you're reaching out something new. Once you completely understand the logic behind the questions, move onto the next page.

There you'll see the exactly same questions under the name of TEST 1. Try to finish it as fast as you can, and you must get them all . Your scores will improve at a head-spinning rate.

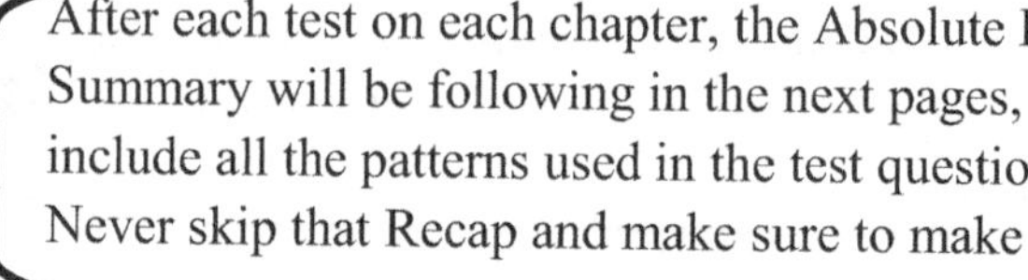

Jimin: I feel like I'm already doing great!

Yeap! You are and you will!

The following chapter 2, however, begins with the actual test 2.
If you still feel uncomfortable with your scores, it's your book, do the same process as you did in Chapter 1. Move onto the next Chapter 3, 4, 5,...until you feel confident about what you're doing.

Jimin: But, with all due respect, isn't it a cheating?

I know! When you do this you might feel a sort of wearing a brand-new underwear, a bit uncomfortable inside.
But soon will you find it comfortable like it becomes a part of your skin. You'll notice there's an Eagle in your sprit that can crush SAT.

How to Use This Book

How to Read the Chapter 1. Reading Answer Explanations

Do you know, Jimin, that every single reading question is created by a unique but repeating pattern?

Jimin: I feel guilty, but I don't. What are they like?

√ The entire Reading Section uses the unique but repeating patterns.

√ The official SAT creates the questions based on these patterns.

√ This book is created by focusing on this fact by categorizing the entire questions with Absolute Patterns:

-12 Reading Absolute Patterns

-20 Common Patterns for Incorrect Choices

Instead of practicing each individual question endlessly without knowing the patterns and logic behind it, please work with these hidden patterns. Memorize these Absolute Patterns in this book and check to see if you are following the patterns.

How to Use This Book

How to Read the Chapter 1. Reading Answer Explanations

Chapter 1: Test 1 Answer Explanations

Questions 11-21 are based on the following passage.

Obama's Disillusioned Doctrine Hope and change, by any means necessary By Shubhankar Chhokra, Harvard University © The Harvard Crimson
Reprinted with Permission

Each passage signify two critical information: Underlines (the questions); Boldfaces (the answer locations)

Goldberg's piece lays out The Obama Doctrine, the organizing principle behind the momentous foreign policy of a man (11C) **whose unlikely rise to the American presidency often overshadows his far more unlikely rise** to the seat of Commander in Chief. Here's a man who went from being the Illinois State Senator to the commander of our armed forces in a mere four years—quite a remarkable feat.

No less remarkable a feat than Goldberg's essay itself, "The Obama Doctrine" is not conjecture from historians poring through State of the Union transcripts decades later, but rather the words of a sitting president. The gravity of this essay cannot be overstated. In it, we see Obama reflect on specific decisions—not striking Assad, pivoting to Asia, intervening in Libya—(12C) **only in order to make broader claims about his presidency**, to situate himself historically among the liberal interventionists, the internationalists, the isolationists, and the realists.

Out of these schools, Obama says he is closest to the realists, believing that "we cannot, at any given moment, relieve all the world's misery." He says, "We have to choose where we can make a real impact." That is why, he says, he stood quietly as Putin invaded Crimea in 2014, a core interest for Russia but hardly one for the United States. That is why he reneged on his 2012 promise to intervene in Syria after Assad deployed chemical weapons on his own people.

(13D & 14A)**Throughout the interview, one observes an insuperable level of disillusionment in our president.** Obama deplores the Western allies who ride on American coat tails, a claim that would be understandable if he at least took part of the blame for his missteps.
In perhaps the most irritating line of the entire interview, Obama comments on the failure to stabilize Libya: "When I go back and I ask myself what went wrong, there's room for criticism,

By following these underlines and boldfaces can you avoid sharp swings between the lines without direction, while observing from where the questions and answers are created.

Q13. **Absolute Pattern 4: Example Question**
Understanding example sentence and the true purpose behind a specific name or idea.
Question Pattern: The author mentions **Russia and Syria** (lines 29-31) to suggest the

A) difficulty of controlling foreign affairs
B) extent to which real impact cannot be reached
C) extended examples of world's misery
D) degree of disappointment Obama rendered

D) Russia and Syria issues are mere examples that support the main idea. The answer can be found not in the example sentence, but in the topic or concluding sentence that hosts the example. That's why and where "the author mentions **Russia and Syria** (lines 29-31) to suggest the."

How to Use This Book

How to Read the Chapter 1. Reading Answer Explanations

Question Pattern is the Backbone of each question.
You know that backbone never changes! The number of these unchanging patterns is very limited. In fact, there are only twelve of them. These patterns will appear on your test by slightly modifying words in this book.

Jimin: Why are patterns so important?

Three reasons. First, you'll be familiar with tricky terms that always appear on the test so that you can save time and completely understand exactly what the question wants.

Second, you can guess where to find the answer even without reading the passage.
For instance, Informational graph question always asks you to read the passage (e.g., "Based on the passage….").
Did you know, however, that 50~70% of the graph questions is solely based on the info. found in the graph? Knowing this, you have no reason to waste your time and energy by re-reading the passage. Even worse, reading the passage could confuse you even more as you acquire unrelated information!

Third, you can avoid possible confusion or mistakes such as "EXCEPT" or "Unlike" questions.

Jimin: I do that a lot in EXCEPT question. Tell me more about the Keywords.

Inside the unique pattern in each question are Keywords added so that it become a unique question. You should have one or more keywords in each question. Quite often question keyword itself contains the answer.
Those top scorers often solve questions by simply reading questions.
Do you know how they do it?

They gather information from the previous questions and simply find whether the question is positive or negative tone, through which they follow and pick the same tone from the multiple choices. When I ask them how they got it, they can't tell the reason for the answer because they actually don't know for sure.

How to Use This Book

How to Read the Chapter 1. Reading Answer Explanations

Question Pattern can be divided into two parts: the question pattern,—which never changes in the actual test—and the keywords that make each question unique. The keywords are boldfaced.

Q12. **Absolute Pattern 8: Understanding the True Purpose** Finding the true purpose of the statement **Question Pattern:** In lines 19-22, the statement **"to situate himself …realists"** emphasizes the author's recognition of	
A) Obama as the liberal interventionists B) Obama as president who made spectacular efforts **C) Obama, not subject to any of the category** D) people's provocative reaction against Obama	**C) only in order to make broader claims about his presidency**, to situate himself historically among the liberal interventionists, the internationalists, the isolationists, and the realists. Only C), D) are negative that corresponds to the passage's tone. D) shifts the focus to people, an unrelated issue. D) Please refer to incorrect choice pattern # 4

Chapter 1. Reading Test 1

After reading the answer explanation, try to solve these identical questions as fast you can by relying on your memory. You will get close to, if not 100 percent, the perfect score. This process will give you in-depth, stress free training.

1 1

Questions 11-21 are based on the following passage.

Obama's Disillusioned Doctrine Hope and change, by any means necessary By Shubhankar Chhokra, Harvard University © The Harvard Crimson
Reprinted with Permission

Goldberg's piece lays out The Obama Doctrine, the organizing principle behind the momentous foreign policy of a man whose unlikely rise to the American presidency often overshadows his far more unlikely rise to the seat of Commander in Chief. Here's a man who went from being the Illinois State Senator to the commander of our armed forces in a mere four years—quite a remarkable feat.

11

The author's tone when he says "quite remarkable feat" in line 9 is one of

A) cynicism

B) limited approval

C) enthusiasm

D) appreciation

HOW TO USE THIS BOOK

How to Read the Chapter Summary: 12 Reading Patterns

12 Absolute Patterns for Reading are equally divided at the end of each chapter.
You may read and practice all of them at once.

Category A: Content Question has 6 patterns:

San: The Content question may also be called the local question.
Either with the line reference number (i.e., line 5) or without it, the content question normally asks localized, detailed information from only one or two sentences in the passage.

The question may ask explicitly stated keywords in the sentences, or, in more complex level, implicitly analogous (similar) situations within a sentence.

Neither of the cases requires the holistic understanding of the entire passage. Reading only the target sentence will save your precious time and mental horsepower.
Now. Let's talk about the Content Question Patterns.

Absolute Pattern 1: Main Idea Question

San: The main idea question asks either from an entire passage or a paragraph.

When question asks about the main idea of the entire passage, the answer is highly likely to be located in the concluding paragraph.—if not in the last sentence.

To get the answer, the best way is to skip the question and save it for last until you have solved all the other questions because you might need to know the general idea of the entire passage.

For instance, if you found choice (A) from the middle of the second paragraph while (B) from the concluding paragraph, the answer will be more likely (B) than (A) due to the unique characteristic of this question.

How to Use This Book

How to Read the Chapter Summary: 20 Common Patterns

Chapter 5

20 Common Patterns for *In*correct Choices in Reading

Jimin: This is what drives me nut. Out of four choices, My eagle eyes catch two incorrect ones. No doubt, hands down! I' m always stuck with these two remaining choices, and then I listen to my heart, which betrays me utterly.

Now, we know how the passages are created, how the questions art created, and how the answers are going to look like. So far so good. 75% accuracy you have achieved.

20 Common Patterns for Incorrect choices focus on the typical patterns found in incorrect choices. Once mastered, you won't be compromised. Trust me! You will say NO to incorrect choices.

1 Positive-Negative Tone (value)

This simple rule is the most powerful tool to isolate the incorrect choices. All you need is to identify the keywords—normally noun or verb—in each multiple choice.

Identify if the keywords in the multiple choices are positive or negative.

Then match them with the reading passage's keywords from the line you're supposed to read based on positive-negative value. Practically majority of the incorrect choices are checked and axed down through this process.

How to Use This Book

Please practice the official PSAT with the Absolute Patterns. You will notice how the Absolute Patterns actually work in the official PSAT and SAT test.

PSAT Reading Section Pattern Analyses

To download the test, please visit:
https://collegereadiness.collegeboard.org/pdf/psat-nmsqt-practice-test-1.pdf

Q12. Absolute Pattern 10: Understanding the Structure of the Passage		
Question Pattern: discussion primarily serves **Question Keyword (s):** 1960s		
Step 1	Step 2	Step 3
Keywords from the Text	Keyword from answer	Tones / Concepts
L6: Visitors to the Soviet Union in the 1960s…A vast informal economy driven by human relationships, dense networks of social connections through which people traded	(A) social networking	Positive
Incorrect Choices & Their Common Patterns		
Evidence	Incorrect keywords	Incorrect Patterns
1> The "social connections" is switched to "social networking" 2> This question asks the first sentence of the introduction paragraph, and asks how it primarily serves. Of course, it primarily serves (A) "to Introduce," "social connection (networking), " the main topic of the passage.	(B) technology (C) other countries (D) historical	Please refer to incorrect choice pattern #4 and #11.
As discussed in the previous question, the example sentence exists to support the topic or the main purpose of the paragraph found in the last sentence of the same paragraph.		

Q16. Absolute Pattern 8: Understanding Attitude (Point of View) Question [Category B]		
Question Pattern: author recognizes **Question Keyword (s):** counterargument		
Step 1	Step 2	Step 3
Keywords from the Text	Keyword from answer	Tones / Concepts
L85: Much has been written about how technology distances us …I think those are important concerns.	(A) acknowledge risks	Primary concept
Incorrect Choices & Their Common Patterns		
Evidence	Incorrect keywords	Incorrect Patterns
"much has been written," forebodes the author's counterargument. This type of concession appears very often in the actual test. The answer to this type of tone should always be either (A) "acknowledge" or (B) "admitting."	(B) spend time (C) 1960 (D) conceding	Please refer to incorrect choice pattern # 4,8.

How to Use This Book

Please practice the official PSAT with the Absolute Patterns. You will notice how the Absolute Patterns actually work in the official PSAT and SAT test.

Q 8. Absolute Pattern 5: Word-In-Context Question		
Question Pattern: most nearly means	**Keyword:** form	
Step 1	Step 2	Step 3
Keywords from the Text	Keyword from answer	Tones / Concepts
Akira came directly, breaking all tradition. Was that it? Had he followed form..	(B) custom	Synonym
Incorrect Choices & Their Common Patterns		
Evidence	Incorrect keywords	Incorrect Patterns
The clue word is "tradition," which he did not follow by "breaking all tradition" The passage suggests he should have followed form or not breaking all tradition. (B) custom means tradition	(A) appearance (C) structure (D) nature	A), C), and D) are unrelated and too literal usage. Please refer to incorrect choice pattern # 7

Q 47. Absolute Pattern 9: Relationships Question		
Question Pattern: central claim of passage 2,	**Keyword:** positive, but	
Step 1	Step 2	Step 3
Keywords from the Text	Keyword from answer	Tones / Concepts
Line 57: But its consequences requires, careful consideration.	(B) should be thoughtful	B) meets the central tone of the passage 2
Incorrect Choices & Their Common Patterns		
Evidence	Incorrect keywords	Incorrect Patterns
In almost all cases in SAT, Passage 2 views the same issue from the bigger picture and yields more concerns than P1.Therefore, B) is always the answer. The reasoning behind this logic...	(A) reckless (C) resources disappearing (D) commercial viability	A) Please refer to incorrect choice pattern #12. C) Please refer to incorrect choice pattern #4. D) Please refer to incorrect choice pattern #2

The reasoning behind this logic comes from the origin of passage. In most cases, the source contexts in both Passage 1 and Passage 2 are in fact a single article. Passage 1 places intro. and the first half of the article; second half of the article including conclusion goes into Passage 2. Passage 1 reveals more general concept while Passage 2 presents more reservation. Passage 2 always presents more limitations, concerns, counterarguments, opposition.

HOW TO USE THIS BOOK

How to Read the Chapter 1. Writing Answer Explanations

TEST 1

WRITING AND LANGUAGE SECTION PATTERN ANALYSES

Questions 1-12 are based on the following passage

Global Warning

Harvard University The Crimson
Reprinted with Permission

Just when I was starting to get used to the passionate debates [1] characterize meals in Annenberg, a recent dinner conversation threw me a curveball. Last week, I had the unique—and frustrating—privilege of dining with the last individual on earth who does not believe in global warming.

Or so I thought. Further research indicates that my acquaintance was far from alone; according to a 2008 Gallup poll, about 11 percent of Americans still think that global warming "will never happen." [2] Perhaps most

[The bottom line is that the scientific community has come to a clear consensus that the evidence of a warming trend is "unequivocal" and [7] It is thus troubling that one in five Americans remain unconvinced by the vast majority of the scientific community that we have an immediate obligation to change our behavior and to protect our planet.

Beyond the scientific evidence,[8] a plan of action that reduces carbon emissions based on our moral considerations alone can be achieved.

Next to the question number Q8 will you see the unique Pattern applied in each question. This pattern never changes and will appear on your actual SAT test.

Q8. Absolute Pattern 1: Adding, Revising, Deleting, Retaining Information	
Which choice **best combines the sentence** underlined?	
Beyond the **scientific evidence**, [8] a plan of action that reduces carbon emissions based on our moral considerations alone can be achieved. (1)	
	A) NO CHANGE
	B) one can support a plan of action to reduce carbon emissions based on our moral considerations alone.
	C) based on moral considerations alone, we can reduce carbon emissions
√	**D) carbon emissions** (2) can be **reduced** (3) **based on our moral** (4) considerations alone.

(D) First, "carbon emissions," the main subject, correctly pulls the modifier "Beyond the scientific evidence"
Second, it places the modifier "**based on our moral considerations alone**" as a reason for "**reduction**"

(A) (1) wordy: "a plan of action" and "can be achieved." (2) indirect and ambiguous expression (3) the misplaced modifier error: "Beyond the scientific evidence" must be connected to "carbon emissions", not "a plan" and "based on our moral considerations alone" next to "carbon emissions" is also misplaced.
(B) is wordy and inconsistently shifts the pronoun "our" to "one"
(C) The modifying phrase "Beyond the scientific evidence" should be carried out by the main clause, not by another modifier "based on moral considerations alone." because it will be confusing to which phrases the modifier is connected.

How to Use This Book

Chapter 1. Writing and Language Test 1

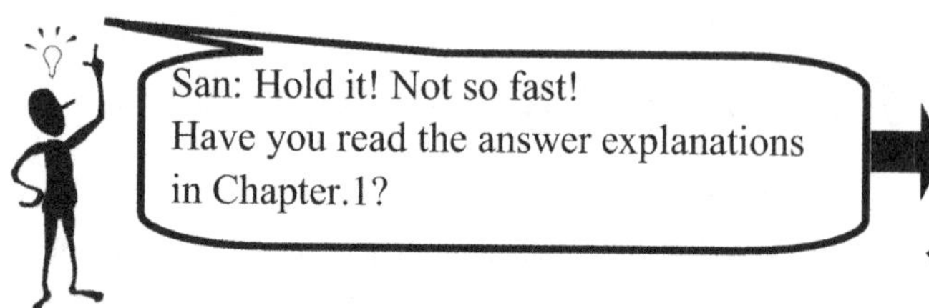

After practicing with the answer explanations, try to solve these identical questions as fast as you can by relying on your memory. You will get close to, if not 100 percent, the perfect scores.

-70 Writing and Language Absolute Patterns.

-24 CP (24 Common Patterns for Incorrect Options in Writing and Language)

2 2

Question 1-11 is based on the following passage.

An Imperfect Necessity
© Harvard university, The crimson
Reprinted with Permission

When it comes to the standardized college admissions tests [1] like the SAT and ACT, there's a lot to gripe about. Beyond bringing additional stress to the admissions process, [2] there is a unclear problem that standardized tests are really fair or measure actual aptitude. Indeed, studies [3] had shown that

Want optimum results super-fast?
Do 70 + 24 first. It can boost your understanding

I know you that you rely on your instinct when you deal with the Writing questions. Please analyze your instinct based on 70 + 24 Absolute Patterns.

3

A) NO CHANGE
B) have shown
C) showed
D) shows

HOW TO USE THIS BOOK

How to Read the Chapter Summary: 70 Writing Patterns

Jimin: For the Writing section,
I always listen to my heart.
I don't know why, but it works!

San: so does your gut always work, always?
I know what you mean. Master these 70 Absolute Patterns. You will know exactly why it works!
And also, why sometimes it doesn't.

The entire Writing Section uses unique but repeating patterns.
The official SAT creates the questions based on these patterns.
This book is created by focusing on this fact. It categorized the entire SAT questions into 70 Absolute Patterns.

70 Absolute Patterns for Writing Section are carefully selected and created to introduce the most important grammar rules for SAT Writing and Language Test.

70 Absolute Patterns for Writing Section

Question 1
Down the road from the school, my brother attend, Seven Eleven convenient store is always open, and some customers are always there.

A) NO CHANGE
B) school, my brother attends
C) school my brother attends
D) school, which is my brother attends,

RULE #1 Hint: Quick Interjection	**Restrictive Modifier** The correct answer is C. "the school" in the sentence is not any schools in general but the only one where "my brother attends that is located down the road near the Seven Eleven convenient store. Therefore, it is an essential part of the sentence and needs to be considered as a part of the main sentence without offsetting (Be careful. It's not upsetting) by a pair of commas.

How to Use This Book

How to Read the Chapter Summary

Chapter 5

24 Common Patterns for *In*correct Choices in Writing

Jimin: Same as Reading section, My gut feeling can easily remove two out of four choices! But I feel turkey when I'm stuck with another two choices.

San: Think of these 24 Common Patterns for Incorrect Choices in Writing.
They'll cross examine those two ahead of you.

1 Adding, Revising, Deleting, Retaining Information

This pattern contains a phrase such as "If the author…'deleted / wish to add / support / would lose..," The multiple choices normally carry 'YES' 'NO' or 'Keep', 'Delete'.

Keep in mind not to choose options with new information.
However tempting it may sound, insertion of new person, character, specific information is outright wrong.

Any new inserted conjunctions or conjunctive adverbs such as 'but,' 'because,' 'although,' 'since,' 'however,' 'Granted,' etc, steer the flow of sentences, paragraph, or the entire passage. Please be careful to those conjunction that suddenly arise between the sentences.

How to Use This Book

This is the official PSAT Writing and Language Section Analyses using the Absolute Patterns. Please download the test booklet from the website on your right.

https://collegereadiness.collegeboard.org/pdf/psat-nmsqt-practice-test-1.pdf

PSAT COLLEGE BOARD OFFICIAL GUIDE
WRITING AND LANGUAGE SECTION PATTERNS

Q1. Absolute Pattern 19: Redundant Error		
Passage keywords: yearly, annually		
	A) yearly, annually	Always Pick the Shortest One from the Multiple Choices! Not easy is making incorrect choice by reducing information. Adding a few words to make something wrong is a piece of cake. A), B), D) are all Redundancy error. Redundancy Error is harder than it may appear to be until looking at the answer. The easiest way to understand the Redundancy Error is to look for the shortest one.
	B) annually, each year	
√	**C) annually**	
	D) yearly, annually	

Q15. Absolute Pattern 9: Informational Graphs		
Passage keywords: exceeded 25%		
	A) exceeded 25%	70% of the Graph Questions Does Not Need a Passage Information 30% of the Graph Questions Needs a Passage Information All the graph questions in this PSAT Test required no passage information. B) This question does not need a reference from the passage.
√	**B) above, acceptable**	
	C) not changed	
	D) increased every year	A) 2011, Incorrect value (less than) C) Antonym or opposite perception D) Incorrect value (fluctuated every year)

Q32. Absolute Pattern 1: Adding, Revising, Deleting, Retaining Information		
Question keywords: reinforcing, also skepticism.		
	A) supporters, wait verified	(D) Negative 1> The question is seeking a negative answer 2> The preceding and the following sentences are also negative. 3> Therefore, the options containing a positive tone, however related and tempting, should not be the answer. (A), (C) Positive (B) is redundant error. The same statement is already mentioned in the previous sentence.
	B) no sound, data	
	C) continue, farming	
√	**D) not fact**	

How to Use This Book

San: This is the official SAT Writing and Language Section Analyses using the Absolute Patterns. Please download the test booklet from the website on your right.

To download the test, please visit: https://collegereadiness.collegeboard.org/pdf/sat-practice-test-1.pdf

SAT COLLEGE BOARD OFFICIAL GUIDE
WRITING AND LANGUAGE SECTION PATTERNS

Q13. Absolute Pattern 16: Precision, Concision, Style		
Passage keywords: evidence, thawing		
√	**A) following**	For this type of question, <u>(A) should be the answer— almost always</u>. <u>You do not even need to re-read the passage.</u> A) <u>doesn't use conjunction "and" while all the other options do</u>. (A) is concise and precise. B) and C) use "thawing" unnecessarily. D) uses "evidence" unnecessarily.
	B) thawing	
	C) thawing	
	D) evidence	

The quintessential concept of precision and concision is eliminating unnecessary words and keep the sentence simple.
B), C), D) are all Redundancy error.
1> Redundancy Error is harder than it may appear to be until looking at the correct answer.
2> The easiest way to understand the Redundancy Error is to look from the concision and precision of the sentence

Q17. Absolute Pattern 7: Conjunction Error		
Passage keywords: , some of it		
	A) of it	<u>If the choice contains "some of which" or "some of whom," that's the answer because the question asks the function of "which" as a conjunction that avoids comma splice error.</u> 1> The subject "tundra fires" and the verb "produced" make a complete independent sentence. 2> "Some of it" and "drifted" make it another clause. However, these two sentences are connected with a comma. This is called the Comma Splice error. 3> To avoid the comma splice error, the answer must contain a conjunction 4> Only (C) has the conjunction "which"
	B) soot	
√	**C) of which**	
	D) delete	

How to Use This Book

Almost all students preparing for the SAT put enormous intellectual effort to achieve their goals. However, when they receive the test results, they soon find themselves disappointing scores.
The Reading and Writing, most often than not, are the main culprits.
That's what delays your score improvement.
This book focuses on Reading and Writing sections.
Please practice with the ABSOLUTE PATTERNS until you thoroughly understand the logic behind each question. You will get the score you want on your upcoming test!

Can This Book Guarantee My Score?

Yes.
If you understand all the ABSOLUTE PATTERNS in this book and maintain the minimum vocabulary level.
But remember! There's no overnight scheme. You should work very hard to memorize essential SAT vocabulary and Solve this book completely and the entire Collegeboard Practice Tests.

What is The Minimum Vocabulary And Where to get Collegeboard SAT Tests?

SAT Nat'l Top 10% ....1680 vocabulary
SAT Nat'l Top 30% . ...800 vocabulary
SAT Beginners or Gr.8-9.....500 vocabulary
I made bunches of uninspiring, difficult-to-memorize SAT vocabularies into a pretty sexy Absolute Vocabulary book with photo descriptions. It will instantly increase your humble vocabulary greatly: email me for free copy: satvancouver@gmail.com

https://collegereadiness.collegeboard.org/pdf/sat-practice. You'll get several official SAT tests.

What If I Fail on My SAT, What Can I do? Suppose I Memorized All the Vocabulary and Understood All Patterns, But Still Failed.

If you failed on your SAT, you should try again! In fact, there are seven chances to try again every year!
Nobody reaches to the goal in just one shot!
Let's find out a solution.
Email me including your SAT or ACT or PSAT or even ISEE / SSAT scores, grade, duration of SAT practice, your realistic time left and goals: satvancouver@gmail.com

CONTENTS

CONTENTS

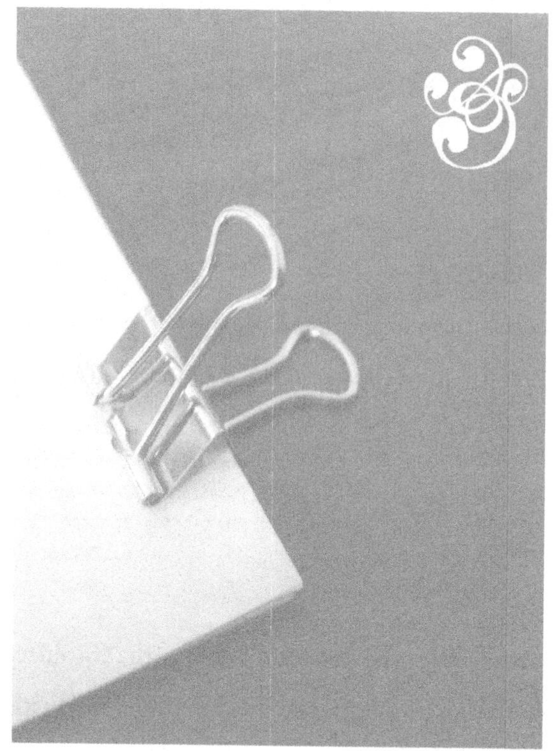

Chapter 1

1. **ANSWER EXPLANATIONS for TEST 1**

2. **TEST 1**

3. **CHAPTER SUMMARY**

SAT Reading Section Answer Explanations & Pattern Analyses for Test 1

Test 1 starts with the Answer Explanations using the Absolute Patterns

Please understand each question according to the Patterns

There's No Time Limit for this Practice.

ALL THE LOGIC AND RULES BEHIND EVERY SINGLE SAT QUESTION

Questions 1-10 are based on the following passage.

Lit.

(6C) **The family of Dashwood had long been settled in Sussex**, where, for many generations, they had lived in so respectable a manner as to engage the general good opinion of their surrounding acquaintance. The old Dashwood was a single man, who lived to a very advanced age, and who for many years of his life, had a (3D) **constant companion and house keeper in his sister.** But her death, which happened ten years before his own, produced a great alteration in his home; (1C &2A &4D) **for to supply her loss, he invited and received into his house the family of his nephew** (7C) **Mr. Henry Dashwood, the legal inheritor of the Norland estate, and the person to whom he intended to bequeath it.** But by his own marriage Mr. Henry added to his wealth. To him therefore the succession to the Norland estate was not so really important as to his Sisters, and could be (5D) **but small.** He was (8A) **neither so unjust, nor so ungrateful,** as to leave his estate to Mr. Henry Dashwood on such terms as **destroyed half the value of the bequest to his Sisters.**	He meant not to be unkind, however, and, as a mark of his affection for the three girls, he left them a thousand pounds a-piece. Mr. Dashwood's disappointment was, at first, severe; (9D) **but his temper was cheerful and sanguine**; and he might reasonably hope to live many years, and by living economically, lay by a considerable sum from the produce of an estate already large, and capable of almost immediate improvement. But the fortune, which had been so tardy in coming, was his only one twelvemonth. He survived his uncle no longer; and ten thousand pounds, including the late legacies, was all that remained for his widow and daughters. His son was sent for as soon as his danger was known, and to him Mr. Dashwood recommended, with all the strength and urgency which illness could command, the interest of his mother-in-law and sisters. (10B) **Mr. John Dashwood had not the strong feelings of the rest of the family; but he was affected by a recommendation** of such a nature at such a time.

Q1. **Absolute Pattern 2: Summary Question** Summarizing a sentence, or entire passage
Question Pattern: According to paragraph 2 (lines 6-15), **the old Dashwood invited Mr. Henry Dashwood for**

A) he had a contemptuous feeling to Mr. Henry B) Mr. Henry had some financial issue **C) he had more than one reason** D) he needed to repent his wrongdoings	C) for to supply her loss, he invited and received into his house the family of his nephew Mr. Henry Dashwood, the legal inheritor of the Norland estate, and the person to whom he intended to bequeath it.

Q2. **Absolute Pattern 11:** Textual Evidence Question Finding evidence for the previous question
Question Pattern: Which choice provides the best evidence for the answer to the previous question?

A) Lines 11-15 (for to supply...bequeath it) B) Lines 16-17 (But by his own...his wealth.) C) Lines 17-19 (To him therefore...but small.) D) Lines 20-23 (He was neither … to his sister)	A) Textual evidence question is a paired question with the preceding question. The question statement never changes: *"Which choice provides the best evidence for the answer to the previous question?"* Given that idea, we can certainly be ready to solve two questions simultaneously by referring to the four options already given in this textual evidence question.

Jimin: How do you know the answer is (C)? Did you get it right away? Maybe, the process of elimination?

San: Not right away! Apply 3:1 Rule, not the process of elimination, for the question like this.

San: The process of elimination finds errors under the assumption that every choice could possibly be correct. Remember you are looking at the four choices, 75% of which is wrong, either completely or insufficient to be the answer. If you approach every choice should be the answer, you might get trapped. Consider all four choices are absolutely incorrect. Find a keyword from each choice that makes the entire statement incorrect.

CONTINUED NEXT PAGE

In this process, one option that you can't find what's wrong is often the answer without knowing the exact reason.
A), B) can be eliminated simply because they are negative tone, which is direct opposite from the main positive tone of the passage. D) is a hard part as it tingles our common sense.
A), B) Please refer to incorrect choice pattern # 1, 2.
D) Please refer to incorrect choice pattern # 4.

Q3. **Absolute Pattern 2: Summary Question**
Question Pattern: According to paragraph 1 and 2, all of the following correctly **describe the Old Dashwood EXCEPT**

A) he lived in the parents' house B) his family was well respected from the neighbors C) he did not have a wife **D) he lived all alone as a single man**	D) The late owner of this estate was a single man, who lived to a very advanced age, and who for many years of his life, (D) had a constant companion and housekeeper in his sister.

"EXCEPT" or "NOT" questions are technically called the Negative Type Question; that is, the question asks an untrue statement. This Negative type question takes enormous time and energy and almost always difficult. Please use your time wisely. In other words, you should leave this question until the end and come back later if it's difficult .

Q4. **Absolute Pattern 7: Understanding Attitude (Tone) Question**
Finding a tone such as positive-negative, active-passive, mental-physical, subjective-objective
Question Pattern: Which word best summarizes the description of the **old Dashwood in the second paragraph** ?

A) acquisitive B) uneducated C) respectful **D) practical**	D) for **to supply her loss,** he invited and received into his house the family of his nephew Mr. Henry Dashwood, the legal inheritor of the Norland estate, and the person to whom he intended **to bequeath it.** A), B) Please refer to incorrect choice pattern # 1 C) Please refer to incorrect choice pattern # 8. It was mentioned in p1, not p2.

Q5. **Absolute Pattern 8: Understanding the True Purpose** Finding the true purpose of statement
Question Pattern: To **Mr. Henry, the succession to the Norland estate** mentioned in line 17 was

A) significant B) a gift to strengthen distinctive family tie C) important to satisfy his greed **D) insignificant**	D) To him therefore the succession to the Norland estate was not so really important as to his Sisters, and could be **but small.** A), C) are Opposite B) uses our common sense. B) Please refer to incorrect choice pattern # 4

Q6. **Absolute Pattern 10: Understanding the Structure of the Passage**
Finding the structure of the entire passage or organizational relations between the paragraphs
Question Pattern: The **primary function** of the passage is to

A) define a legal custom related to inheritance B) emphasize the benefits of having good neighbors **C) introduce the settings of the story** D) show a prolonged family feud	**C) The family of Dashwood had long been** settled in Sussex, where, for many generations, they had lived in so respectable a manner ... * The first sentence describes where the character lives, who he is,.... It describes the settings of the story.

The key point of this question is the question itself. "primary function" is what the question asks, not the content information. Think this way. The question asking the function of the house and what happens in the house is different. From this perspective, we can simply eliminate A), B), and D).

Q7. **Absolute Pattern 3: Inference Question** Finding an indirect suggestion (or guessing) **Question Pattern:** It can be inferred from line 23 that the **"Sisters"**	
A) had amassed great wealth B) had some difficulties with the Old Dashwood **C) were not the legal inheritors** D) were preferred inheritors to Mr. Henry Dashwood	C) Mr. Henry Dashwood, the legal inheritor of the Norland estate, and the person to whom he intended to bequeath it. destroyed half the value of the **bequest to his Sisters**
*The legal inheritor is Mr. Henry Dashwood. Therefore, sisters are not. A), B), D) Please refer to incorrect choice pattern # 2	

Q8. **Absolute Pattern 3: Inference Question** Finding an indirect suggestion (or guessing) **Question Pattern:** It can be inferred from lines 20-23 (He mean not...a piece) that **in his will, the Old Dashwood tried to?**	
A) balance and appease every heir B) condescend every heir C) defend his estate from every heir D) remove Mr. Henry from his family	A) He was **neither so unjust, nor so ungrateful,** as to leave his estate. *In other words, he tried to balance and appease every heir. B), C),D) are all Negative, contrary to the passage description about the character. Please refer to incorrect choice pattern # 1

Q9. **Absolute Pattern 3: Inference Question** Finding an indirect suggestion (or guessing) **Question Pattern:** In lines 27-32 (Mr. Dashwood's disappointment...immediate improvement.), **the author characterizes Mr. Henry Dashwood** as	
A) a maverick B) a dilettante C) a charlatan **D) an optimist**	D) Mr. Dashwood's disappointment was, at first, severe; **but** his temper was cheerful and sanguine **Pattern: Always Look for 'but,' or 'however' in the passage. That's the answer.** *Maverick: someone who does not follow rules. *Dilettante: amateur *Charlatan: con artist
Having a little trouble with these words? Allow me to improve your humble vocabulary. I made bunches of boring and difficult-to-memorize SAT words into a pretty sexy SAT Absolute Vocabulary with photo descriptions. Email me for FREE copy: satvancouver@gmail.com	

Q10. **Absolute Pattern 7: Understanding Attitude (Tone) Question** Finding a tone such as positive-negative, active-passive, mental-physical, subjective-objective **Question Pattern: Mr. John Dashwood's attitude** in lines 42-45 (Mr. John Dashwood...such a time) can be best characterized as	
A) appreciation **B) reluctance** C) ambivalence D) frustration	B) Mr. John Dashwood had not the strong feelings of the rest of the family; but he was affected by a recommendation of such a nature at such a time. A) Opposite B) Too Extreme C) Too Weak B) Please refer to incorrect choice pattern # 12 C) Please refer to incorrect choice pattern # 11

Questions 11-21 are based on the following passage.

Goldberg's piece lays out The Obama Doctrine, the organizing principle behind the momentous foreign policy of a man (11A) **whose unlikely rise to the American presidency often overshadows his far more unlikely rise** to the seat of Commander in Chief. Here's a man who went from being the Illinois State Senator to the commander of our armed forces in a mere four years—quite a remarkable feat.

No less remarkable a feat than Goldberg's essay itself, "The Obama Doctrine" is not conjecture from historians poring through State of the Union transcripts decades later, but rather the words of a sitting president. The gravity of this essay cannot be overstated. In it, we see Obama reflect on specific decisions—not striking Assad, pivoting to Asia, intervening in Libya—(12C) **only in order to make broader claims about his presidency**, to situate himself historically among the liberal interventionists, the internationalists, the isolationists, and the realists.

Out of these schools, Obama says he is closest to the realists, believing that "we cannot, at any given moment, relieve all the world's misery." He says, "We have to choose where we can make a real impact." That is why, he says, he stood quietly as Putin invaded Crimea in 2014, a core interest for Russia but hardly one for the United States. That is why he reneged on his 2012 promise to intervene in Syria after Assad deployed chemical weapons on his own people.

(13D & 14C)**Throughout the interview, one observes an insuperable level of disillusionment in our president.** Obama deplores the Western allies who ride on American coat tails, a claim that would be understandable if he at least took part of the blame for his missteps.

In perhaps the most irritating line of the entire interview, Obama comments on the failure to stabilize Libya: "When I go back and I ask myself what went wrong, there's room for criticism, (15C&16D) **because I had more faith in the Europeans,** given Libya's proximity, being invested in the follow-up."

"There's room for criticism because I had more faith in the Europeans"—no line better betrays this administration's gross misunderstanding of global power dynamics. In Brussels along with 34 civilians, in the deadliest act of terrorism in Belgian history.

Obama claims that "ISIS is not an existential threat to the United States," rather "climate change is a potential existential threat to the entire world if we do not do something about it." (17C &18A) **This is jaded Obama at work—recklessly allowing his Weltschmerz to loud his judgment, choosing more romantic, less controversial battles** like climate change and the favorite cause of his first term, the "pivot to Asia." This is not to discount Obama's likely genuine belief that climate change demands our attention more than terrorism. **But at the root of this claim is not logic, but a fatigue of the Middle East and a yearning for something new.** Obama explains to Goldberg about why he prefers to talk about Asia more than ISIS, "They are not thinking about how to kill Americans," he says. "What they're thinking about is 'How do I get a better education? How do I create something of value?'"

David Frum's takeaway from Goldberg's final essay is that (20C & 21A) **all of us have disappointed Barack Obama**—that **our Western allies are guilty of free-loading, that Americans are guilty of overestimating the threat of ISIS to the point that out fear devolves into bigotry, and that the entire world just** (19A) **needs to be more realistic**. President Obama is probably not wrong about any of this, but he is certainly wrong in expecting others to sympathize with his disappointment.

Q11. **Absolute Pattern 7: Understanding Attitude (Tone) Question**
Question Pattern: The author's tone when he says "**quite remarkable feat**" in line 9 is

A) cynicism B) limited approval C) enthusiasm D) appreciation	A) "The Obama Doctrine, the organizing principle behind the momentous foreign policy of a man whose unlikely rise to the American presidency often overshadows his far more unlikely rise to the seat. B) is incorrect because the author's cynicism is quite harsh, not limited C) or D) are opposite. Please refer to incorrect choice pattern # 2

<table>
<tr><td colspan="2">Q12. Absolute Pattern 8: Understanding the True Purpose
Question Pattern: In lines 19-22, the statement "to situate himself…realists" emphasizes the author's recognition of</td></tr>
<tr><td>A) Obama as the liberal interventionists
B) Obama as president who made spectacular efforts
C) Obama, not subject to any of the category
D) people's provocative reaction against Obama</td><td>C) only in order to make broader claims about his presidency, to situate himself historically among the liberal interventionists, the internationalists, the isolationists, and the realists.
Only C), D) are negative that correspond to the author's tone.
D), however, shifts the focus to people, unrelated issue.
Please refer to incorrect choice pattern # 1, 4</td></tr>
<tr><td colspan="2">Q13. Absolute Pattern 4: Example Question
Finding the true purpose behind a specific name or idea within a sentence
Question Pattern: The author mentions Russia and Syria (lines 29-31) to suggest the</td></tr>
<tr><td>A) difficulty of controlling foreign affairs
B) extent to which real impact cannot be reached
C) extended examples of world's misery
D) degree of disappointment Obama rendered</td><td>D) Russia and Syria issues are mere examples that support the main idea. The keywords for this answer can be found not in the example sentence, but in the topic or concluding sentence that hosts the example text because the author usually employs an example sentence to emphasize his main idea.</td></tr>
<tr><td colspan="2">Q14. Absolute Pattern 11: Textual Evidence Question
Question Pattern: Which choice provides the best evidence for the answer to the previous question?</td></tr>
<tr><td>A) Lines 14-15(The gravity of this essay...overstated.)
B) Lines 23-24 (Out of these schools...the realists.)
C) Lines 33-35 (Throughout the interview...president)
D) Lines 50-51 (Obama claims that...United States.)</td><td>C) Russia but hardly one for the United States. That is why he reneged on his 2012 promise to intervene in Syria after Assad deployed chemical weapons on his own people. Throughout the interview, one observes an insuperable level of disillusionment in our president.</td></tr>
<tr><td colspan="2">Q15. Absolute Pattern 7: Understanding Attitude (Tone) Question
Finding a tone such as positive-negative, active-passive, mental-physical, subjective-objective
Question Pattern: President's attitude toward the Western allies is best characterized as</td></tr>
<tr><td>A) open-minded
B) pragmatic
C) disillusioned
D) apathetic</td><td>C) "there's room for criticism <u>because I had more faith in the Europeans"</u> The president meant that he is disillusioned.
Pattern: Conjunction "because" always gives you the answer.</td></tr>
<tr><td colspan="2">Q16. Absolute Pattern 11: Textual Evidence Question Finding evidence for the previous question
Question Pattern: Which choice provides the best evidence for the answer to the previous question?</td></tr>
<tr><td>A) Lines 10-14 (No less...sitting president.)
B) Lines 14-15 (The gravity...cannot be overstated.)
C) Lines 33-35 (Throughout the interview… our president.)
D) Lines 41-43 (When I go back...faith in the Europeans,)</td><td>D) Please refer to the above question</td></tr>
</table>

Q17. **Absolute Pattern 8: Understanding the True Purpose** Finding the true purpose of statement
Question Pattern: The author's purpose of mentioning **"climate change"** (line 52) is to display the

A) problem the nation will ultimately encounter B) problem demands our attention more than terrorism **C) issue Obama exploited to gloss over other crisis** D) an important issue Obama failed to meet	C) Obama claims that "ISIS is not an existential threat to the United States," rather "climate change is a potential existential threat to the entire world. choosing more romantic, less controversial battles like climate change

Q18. **Absolute Pattern 4: Example Question**
Understanding example sentence and the true purpose behind a specific name or idea.
Question Pattern: The author mentions **ISIS** in lines 50 to

A) emphasize a naïve indifference of Obama B) describe the trivial subject C) elicit Obama's priority D) explain the uncertainty of Middle East	A) "ISIS is not an existential threat to the United States," rather "climate change is a potential existential threat to the entire world if we do not do something about it." This is jaded Obama at work—recklessly allowing his Weltschmerz to loud his judgment, **choosing more romantic, less controversial battles**.

Obama compares ISIS to climate change, prioritizing the latter.
B) is Obama's view, not the author's C) is Opposite

Q19. **Absolute Pattern 5: Word-In-Context Question**
Finding a clue word and the keyword from the sentence in question
Question Pattern: As used in line 74, **"bigotry"** most nearly means

A) discrimination B) impartiality C) adherence D) overlooked evaluation	A) Americans are guilty of overestimating the threat of ISIS to the point that out fear devolves into bigotry, and that the entire world just needs to be **more realistic.** Obama suggests that our reaction to ISIS is overstated based on our bigotry. Because the word "bigotry" is surrounded by negative tone, the answer should also be negative. Bigotry = discrimination

Q20. **Absolute Pattern 4: Example Question**
Question Pattern: The author mentions **David Frum** mainly to

A) de-emphasize Goldberg's argument B) cast aspersions on Goldberg's final essay **C) parody the words used by Barack Obama** D) rail against Western allies	C) that all of us have disappointed Barack Obama—that our Western allies are guilty of free-loading, that Americans are guilty of overestimating the threat of ISIS…

* David Frum's statement is made of derogatory tone to rail against Obama. When a scholar or a well-known figure is introduced as a part of the examples, it usually serves as a leverage to support the author's argument.
A), B) are Opposite Please refer to incorrect choice pattern # 2
D) Please refer to incorrect choice pattern # 5

Q21. **Absolute Pattern 7: Understanding Attitude (Tone) Question**
Question Pattern: The author's **attitudes toward Barak Obama and David Frum** are respectively

A) disappointment and acceptance B) indifference and mild concern C) praise and staunch advocacy D) refusal and veneration	A) David Frum's statement is a cynical parody to Obama, so we can assume that the author favors him, while opposing Obama. "veneration" in D) is too extreme word. Please refer to incorrect choice pattern # 12

Questions 22-31 are based on the following passage.

Passage 1

(22C) **Nothing would please me** more than writing an article chronicling mankind's fixation with the apple. That says a lot about me. Fortunately for you though, the apple is even more important as a commodity than an artifact, so this is the story of how one fruit might just determine the future of American agriculture.

Earlier this week, the United States Department of Agriculture announced that it is lifting its import restrictions on fresh apples from China. (Q31) **That means starting this month, China—the world's largest producer of apples—can freely enter American markets, selling cheap and low-quality fruit in direct competition with our nation's harvest.**

American officials are hoping this decision would persuade the Chinese—who only currently import red and golden delicious apples from a handful of states—to loosen their own trade restrictions in good faith. (23D & 24C) **As China's consumption of American apples is definitely nontrivial, this expectation of requital makes sense.**

Interestingly, according to President of the Washington Apple Commission Todd Fryhover, Chinese consumers are especially hungry for more Red Delicious apples (25C) **because their rich, crimson hue represents good fortune in their culture.**

But flooding American markets with Chinese apples in hope of the reverse is ultimately unfruitful triage for the more pressing problem, one that is closer to home: we just had the largest apple crop in American history and (26B) **need foreign buyers to compensate for** lackluster domestic demand. Even if they do, it won't amount to much. (27D & 31C) **If you've been following the Chinese's apple purchasing closely for the past couple years** (like, who hasn't?), you would notice that China doesn't really need American apples.

Passage 2

Apples are important. They are lodged in our throats and imprinted on our cell phones. They proxy in for the unspecified fruit Eve gave Adam, and pies made out of them are quintessentially American. My graduating class planted 14 trees of them at our high school, and 30 years from now, we hope to return with spouses and children, hungry for the fruits of our labor. And as I eat this apple, alternating bites with lines of prose, I savor all this historical, cultural, and personal significance even more than its sweet flavor.

This is all to say the USDA is either lying or kidding itself when it says that it expects China to contribute no more than 0.4% of apples consumed in America. There are reasons why we haven't welcomed Chinese apples in the past. China's atrocious food safety regulations and pollution problems pose a serious threat to American consumers. And the USDA initially barred Chinese apples because they carry invasive pests like the Oriental fruit fly that could destroy entire crops of American apples. (29D & 30C) **These dangers, unlike the government's attitude towards them, haven't changed.** The integrity of the American economy does not boil down to apple trade. But at its core, the apple is important. (28A) It **demystified gravity**. It has **kept doctor after doctor away**. It almost **killed Snow White**, for **Christ's sake**. And in a matter of months, it will be shipped by the ton from China to a supermarket near you, leaving an important American industry to rot.

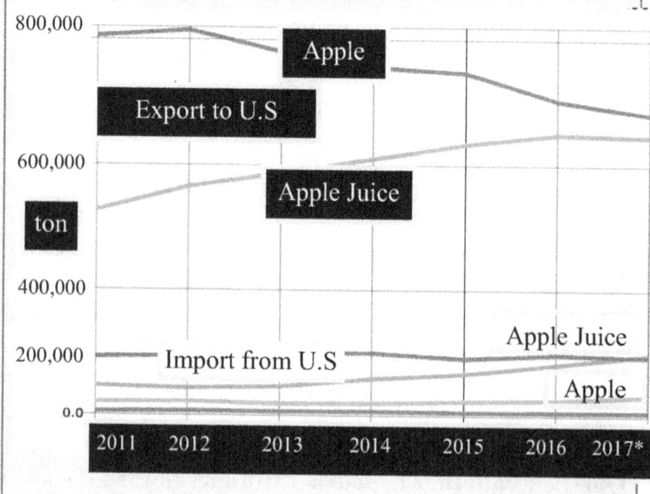

<table>
<tr><td colspan="2">Q22. Absolute Pattern 7: Understanding Attitude (Tone) + Understanding the Structure of the Passage
Question Pattern: In context, the author's tone in lines 1-15 ("Nothing … harvest") shifts from</td></tr>
<tr><td>A) awe to uncertainty
B) sadness to wonder
C) delight to concern
D) curiosity to frustration</td><td>C) Line 1 (Topic sentence) : Nothing would please me more …
Line 12 (Concluding sentence): That means...China...—can freely enter American Markets

The underlined portions of the texts show how the author's tone shifts from the positive to negative or delight to concern.)</td></tr>
<tr><td colspan="2">When one or two entire paragraphs are compared, it normally asks the structural organization and the relationships between the paragraphs. Please pay special attention to the topic and the concluding sentences of each paragraph.</td></tr>
<tr><td colspan="2">Q23. Absolute Pattern 2: Summary Question Summarizing a sentence, or an entire paragraph
Question Pattern: According to the author, cheap fruits importation from China in lines 14 makes sense because</td></tr>
<tr><td colspan="2">A) lifting its import restrictions on fresh apples from China prevents significant trade loss in other areas
B) fruit from China is different from ones the competitions produce in U.S.
C) Chinese to loosen their own trade restrictions can be guaranteed
D) China's consumption of American apples in return will not be marginal</td></tr>
<tr><td colspan="2">D) As China's consumption of American apples is definitely nontrivial, this expectation of requital makes sense.

Conjunction "because" or a sentence that implies the cause-and-effect always carries a clue word.
*nontrivial means significant or "not marginal."</td></tr>
<tr><td colspan="2">Q24. Absolute Pattern 11: Textual Evidence Question Finding evidence for the previous question
Question Pattern: Which choice provides the best evidence for the answer to the previous question?</td></tr>
<tr><td>A) Lines 3-7 (Fortunately … agriculture.)
B) Lines 16-20 (American officials, … faith)
C) Lines 20-23 (As China's…senses)
D) Lines 37-41 (If you've…apples)</td><td>C) Please refer to the above question</td></tr>
<tr><td colspan="2">Q25. Absolute Pattern 3: Inference Question Finding an indirect suggestion (or guessing)
Question Pattern: The statement lines 24-29 indicates that Chinese consumers</td></tr>
<tr><td>A) value aesthetically pleasing fruit
B) savor rich taste of American apple
C) tend to relate crimson hue with culture
D) think Chinese apple has no crimson hue</td><td>C) Chinese consumers are especially hungry for more Red Delicious apples because their rich, crimson hue represents good fortune in their culture."
A), B), and D) Please refer to incorrect choice pattern # 4</td></tr>
<tr><td colspan="2">Q26. Absolute Pattern 5: Word-In-Context Question
Finding a clue word and the keyword from the sentence in question
Question Pattern: In line 35, "lackluster" most nearly means</td></tr>
<tr><td>A) uninvolved
B) dwindling
C) lack of
D) diminishing</td><td>B) we just had the largest apple crop in American history and need foreign buyers to compensate for lackluster domestic demand.

D) is too extreme. Please refer to incorrect choice pattern # 12</td></tr>
</table>

<table>
<tr><td colspan="2">Q27. Absolute Pattern 8: Understanding the True Purpose Finding the true purpose of statement
Question Pattern: The parenthesis (like, who hasn't?) in line 39 in passage 1 primarily emphasizes</td></tr>
<tr><td>A) the importance of following the Chinese's apple purchasing trend
B) that everyone follows the Chinese's apple purchasing closely
C) the financial trade-off with China
D) tinged with humor to readers' reaction</td><td>D) If you've been following the Chinese's apple purchasing closely for the past couple years (like, who hasn't ?).

<u>In fact, hardly will any reader in reality pay any attention</u> to such an issue. Therefore, the author is giving a humorous remark by exaggerating the statement.</td></tr>
<tr><td colspan="2">Q28. Absolute Pattern 2: Summary Question Summarizing a sentence, or an entire paragraph
Question Pattern: In lines 71-76, the author's allusions include all of the followings EXCEPT</td></tr>
<tr><td>A) Historical allusion
B) Scientific allusion
C) Medicinal allusion
D) Literary allusion</td><td>A) Allusion means a brief reference in a work of literature, explicit or indirect, to a person, place, event or to another literary work or passage.

(B) <u>It demystified gravity.</u> (C) <u>It has kept doctor after doctor away.</u>
(D) <u>It almost killed Snow White,</u></td></tr>
<tr><td colspan="2">Q29. Absolute Pattern 9: Relationships Question
Finding relations between the cause-effect, characters, and ideas including a Paired Passage.
Question Pattern: The author of Passage 2 would most likely regard "the American officials" (line 16, passage 1) are</td></tr>
<tr><td>A) essentially knowledgeable for their expectation
B) consistent with the trade restrictions
C) fearful to American angry farmers
D) less concerned about invasive pests than trade unbalance</td><td>D) <u>the USDA</u> initially barred Chinese apples <u>because they carry invasive pests</u> like the Oriental fruit fly that could destroy entire crops of American apples. <u>These dangers, unlike the government's attitude towards them, haven't changed.</u>

"unlike" leads the contradicting statement. It always gives the answer.</td></tr>
<tr><td colspan="2">Q30. Absolute Pattern 11: Textual Evidence Question Finding evidence for the previous question
Question Pattern: Which choice provides the best evidence for the answer to the previous question?</td></tr>
<tr><td>A) Lines 45-46 (Apple … phone.)
B) Lines 57-60 (This is all...America.)
C) Lines 67-69 (These dangers...haven't changed)
D) Lines 69-70 (The integrity...apple trade.)</td><td>C) Please refer to the above question</td></tr>
<tr><td colspan="2">Q31. Absolute Pattern 12: Informational Graphs
Finding facts described in the graphs or relations between the passage and the graph
Question Pattern: The graph most directly supports for which idea in the passage?</td></tr>
<tr><td>A) American officials in lines 15-16
B) President, Todd Fryhover in lines 24-28
C) The author's analysis in line 37-41
D) USDA expectation in lines 57-60</td><td>C) That means starting this month, China—the world's largest producer of apples—can freely enter American markets, selling cheap and low-quality fruit in direct competition with our nation's harvest.
The author is negative about the apple importation
A), B), D) are all positive about importing apples from China or opposite to the author's argument.</td></tr>
<tr><td colspan="2">The graph displays low importation of U.S. apples from China and high exportation of Chinese apples into U.S.</td></tr>
</table>

Questions 32-41 are based on the following passage.

Two Saturdays ago, a 7.8 magnitude earthquake ripped through Nepal, resulting in widespread damage to infrastructure, irreparable harm to historical sites, and, most tragically, the deaths of thousands and thousands of human beings. Such an event should inspire mourning and contemplation—sorrow for the people who lost their lives and gratitude for the lives that we still have.

Instead, in the aftermath of the tremors, a different sort of behavior rose up from the rubble. News outlets ran reports of individuals—some tourists and some Nepalese citizens—stopping in front of destroyed buildings for quick selfies. Here was one sort of earthquake response: Survey the tragic scene, take a smiling photo, and then skip off in the opposite direction. (32A& 33C) **If social media glorifies life—capturing our most intimate moments and recording our funniest jokes—then it does the opposite for death.**

To a certain degree, you can blame the photographers. A tactful person should have enough respect to avoid behavior that reduces a death into a tagged detail.

(Q34C)**Yet a larger, and more disconcerting, criticism of the selfie-behavior that emerged out of the Nepal earthquake has to do with the nature of social media itself**. Against a background of party photos and emojis, mortality loses all of its defining gravitas. The deceased become abject and even absurd—they simply cannot coexist with this sepia-tinted world in which every comment is an inside joke. Put it this way: There is nothing more unsettling than the Facebook profile of a dead teenager. I think the uneasy feeling derives from the lightheartedness of the content that dominates any social media platform. There are airy "lol" comments; there are witty photo captions. There is rarely, if ever, a reminder that this person—this very same smiling person—is fragile enough to die. (37A & 39C) **How can you reconcile social media's giddy artificiality with death's** stone-cold reality?

How can you connect a corpse to a profile picture? There is the illusion of popularity, the illusion of philanthropy, and the illusion of substance. In some ways, however, (35D &36D) **I think that the mortality-defying effects of social media are the most illusory and therefore the most dangerous.**

The easiest recommendation is to unplug your life and spend more time (38C) **appreciating the fragile beauty of real things. The fact that something—a season, a flower, or a person—is temporary, essentially makes that something more valuable.**

But realizing that everyone, myself included, needs social media for practical life purposes, a more realistic suggestion revolves around mindfulness. "Mindfulness"—this may sound like an empty word, but I believe that it encapsulates the overarching message that I've tried to drive home throughout a semester of column writing. The Internet is powerful, practical, and practically powerful. You need to use it for these reasons. However, you need to use the Internet well, which requires significant reflection. Think hard before you click to open a new tab; philosophize as you sign into Facebook. Everything about the Internet (40A) **conspires to sweep you away** into an arcade world of images and sounds, but you must resist in order to maintain your identity and willpower.

After all, your humanity is based in this resistance—and in the wonderful freedom that follows.

The major time spend on Facebook 2012 vs.2016

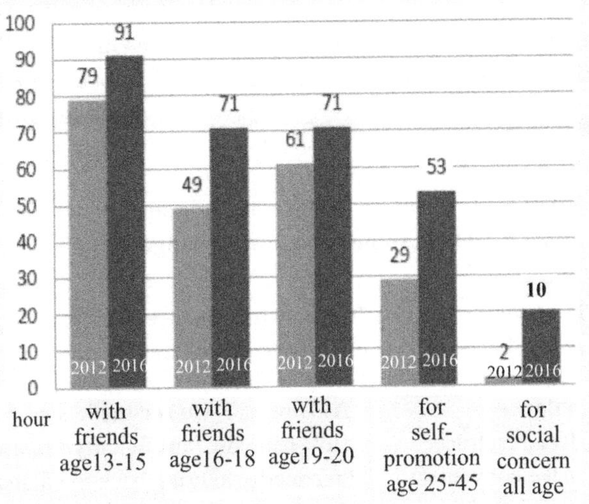

Q32. **Absolute Pattern 1: Main Idea Question** Finding the main idea of the entire passage or the paragraph **Question Pattern:** The author mentions **social media primarily encourage people to view death** as	
A) a medium to disrespect human tragedy B) an opportunity to increase followers **C)** a source of psychological pain D) a condition to be dealt with an emotional level	A) If social media glorifies life—capturing our most intimate moments and recording our funniest jokes—then it does the opposite for death. (C),(D) become positive aspect of social media, which are direct opposite to the author's tone and argument. (B) is minor example

Q33. **Absolute Pattern 11: Textual Evidence Question** Finding evidence for the previous question **Question Pattern:** Which choice provides the best evidence for the answer to the previous question?	
A) Lines 6-9 (Such an event...we still have.) B) Lines 10-11 (Instead,...from the rubble.) **C) Lines 17-20 (If social media...opposite for death)** D) Lines 21-22 (To a certain degree...photographers.)	C) Please refer to the above question

Q34. **Absolute Pattern 4: Example Question** Understanding example sentence and the true purpose behind a specific name or idea. **Question Pattern:** From the author's view, **the photographers** mentioned in line 22 are	
A) the main culprits who exploit Social media B) tactful people who know how to reduce a death into a tagged detail **C) less to be criticized** D) professionals to deserve enough respect	C) **To a certain degree, you can blame** the photographers, ... **Yet** a larger, and more disconcerting, criticism of the selfie-behavior that emerged out of the Nepal earthquake has to do with the nature of social media itself. 1) "To a certain degree" implies the author's mild concession to the photographers; therefore, less to be criticized. "Yet a larger…" indicates the social media is to be more criticized.

Q35. **Absolute Pattern 2: Summary Question** Summarizing a sentence, or an entire paragraph **Question Pattern:** The aspect of the social media that the **author condemns most is the illusion of**	
A) substance B) popularity C) philanthropy **D) defying human mortality**	D) How can you connect a corpse to a profile picture? There is (B) the illusion of popularity, (C) the illusion of philanthropy, and (A) the illusion of substance. In some ways, however, I think that (D) **the mortality-defying** effects of social media **are the most illusory and therefore the most dangerous**.

Q36. **Absolute Pattern 11: Textual Evidence Question** Finding evidence for the previous question **Question Pattern:** Which choice provides the best evidence for the answer to the previous question?	
A) Lines 21-22 (To a certain degree... photographers.) B) Lines 35-37 (I think...media platform.) C) Lines 45-47 (There is the illusion...substance) **D) Lines 47-49 (In some ways,...most dangerous.)**	D) Please refer to the above question

Q37. **Absolute Pattern 5: Word-In-Context Question** **Question Pattern:** In line 41, **"reconcile"** most nearly means	
A) balance B) declare a truce C) make convenient D) make available	A) How can you **reconcile** social media's giddy **artificiality** with death's stone-cold **reality**? How can you + artificiality= reality. In other words, how can balance them? *reconcile (to bring back to balance or compare)

<table>
<tr><td colspan="2">Q38. Absolute Pattern 4: Example Question
Understanding example sentence and the true purpose behind a specific name or idea.
Question Pattern: In lines 52-54, "a season, a flower, or a person" conveys the author's opinion that these are</td></tr>
<tr><td>A) temporary, therefore less valuable
B) universal, therefore easy to understand
C) ephemeral, but reveal the profound truth
D) neither realistic nor practical</td><td>C) The fact that something—a season, a flower, or a person—is temporary, essentially makes that something more valuable.
*Ephemeral means temporary
All three options are opposite perception in one way or another.
Please refer to incorrect choice pattern # 2</td></tr>
<tr><td colspan="2">Q39. Absolute Pattern 3: Inference Question Finding an indirect suggestion (or guessing)
Question Pattern: The author's perspective on Facebook is that of</td></tr>
<tr><td>A) an unsympathetic outsider
B) an appreciative user
C) a lamentable observer
D) an angry protestor</td><td>C) <u>How can you connect a corpse to a profile</u> picture?
Throughout the passage, the author observes lamentable effects of social media.

A), B) are Opposite D) "angry protestor" is Too extreme word
Please refer to incorrect choice pattern # 2, 12.</td></tr>
<tr><td colspan="2">Q40. Absolute Pattern 5: Word-In-Context Question
Finding a clue word and the keyword from the sentence in question
Question Pattern: In line 68, "conspires" most nearly means</td></tr>
<tr><td>A) intrigue
B) connive
C) collaborate
D) combine</td><td>A) Everything about the <u>Internet conspires</u> to <u>sweep you away</u> into an arcade world of images and sounds, <u>but you must resist</u>
*intrigue means to fascinate. *connive means secretly allow. *collaborate means work together
(B) is too weak (C), (D) are unrelated words</td></tr>
<tr><td colspan="2">Q41. Absolute Pattern 12: Informational Graphs
Finding facts described in the graphs or relations between the passage and the graph.
Question Pattern: Which claim about Facebook is supported by the graph?</td></tr>
<tr><td>A) All age groups are very responsive to social concerns
B) 13-15 age group represents the users for the practical life purposes in line 56
C) All age groups concern the least on social concerns
D) All age groups prioritize self-promotion than spending time with friends</td><td>C) All age groups spent 2 to 10 % to social concerns, least than other issues.

(A),(B) are direct opposite.</td></tr>
</table>

Questions 42-52 are based on the following passage.

Brain Research through Advancing Innovative Neurotechnologies (BRAIN) Initiative has (45B) **the potential to do for neuroscience what the Human Genome Project did for genomics** by supporting the development and application of innovative technologies that can create (42B&43A&44C) **a dynamic understanding of brain function. It aims to help researchers uncover the mysteries of brain disorders,** such as Alzheimer's and Parkinson's diseases.

(48D) **These technologies will shed light on the complex links between brain function and behavior.** For instance, by combining advanced genetic and optical techniques, scientists can now use pulses of light to determine how specific cell activities in the brain affect behavior. **While** these technological innovations have contributed substantially to our expanding knowledge of the brain, (46A) **significant breakthroughs** in how we treat neurological and psychiatric disease will require a new generation of tools to enable researchers to record signals from brain cells in much greater numbers and at even faster speeds. (47A) **That's where the BRAIN Initiative comes in.**

A Scientific Vision, which articulates the (47A) **scientific goals** of The BRAIN Initiative at the NIH charts (49D) **a multi-year scientific plan for achieving these goals, including timetables, milestones, and cost estimates. and focused effort across the agency.** (51D) **Once completed,** with Neuro-adaptive technology program, Systems-Based Neurotechnology for Emerging Therapies (SUBNETS) can measure and modulate, with the first set of **preliminary model** closed-loop medical devices, networks of neurons with intractable psychiatric illness and (50A) **alleviate severe symptoms** of diseases such as post-traumatic stress disorder and major depression.

BRAIN Initiative and Related Funding
(budget authority in millions of dollars)

Program/ ACCOUNT	FY 2014 Actual	FY 2015 Actual	FY 2016 Actual	FY 2016 Actual	Percent Change pres.	FY15
NSF Understanding the Brain	**93**	**106**	**144**	**147**	**2.1%**	**38.0%**
Specific to BRAIN Initiative	**23**	**48**	**72**	**72**	**0.0%**	**47.6%**
Natl Institutes of Health	**40**	**65**	**135**	**150**	**11.1%**	**130.8%**
DAPRA: Biomedical Technology	**121**	**160**	**114**	**114**		

Q42. **Absolute Pattern 1: Main Idea Question** Finding the main idea of the entire passage or the paragraph
Question Pattern: The **primary purpose of the BRAIN Initiative** is to help researchers

A) advance Human Genome Project
B) understand brain function and disorder
C) sequence the human genome
D) develop better human brain

B) It aims to help researchers uncover the mysteries of brain disorders,
The answer for this question was found from the amplifier, starting with "It". (BRAIN) Initiative... (A), (C) are unrelated issue

Q43. **Absolute Pattern 9: Relationships Question**
Question Pattern: Which choice provides the best evidence for the answer to the previous question

A) Lines 1-6 (Brain Research...brain function.)
B) Lines 16-23 (While these technological...faster speeds.)
C) Lines 23-24 (That's where...comes in.)
D) Lines 25-29 (A Scientific Vision...across the agency.)

A) Please refer to the above question

Q44. **Absolute Pattern 3: Inference Question** Finding an indirect suggestion (or guessing) **Question Pattern:** The **"mysteries" in line 7 implies** that at **the current stage,** the research of brain disorders	
A) is dynamically improving B) is expected to be unlocked pretty soon **C) is still at understanding level** D) has seen mysterious breakthrough recently	C) a dynamic **understanding of brain function**. It aims to help researchers uncover the mysteries of **brain disorders,..**

Q45. **Absolute Pattern 9: Relationships Question** Finding relations between the cause-effect, comparison-contrast, characters, and ideas **Question Pattern:** The author mentioned **Human Genome project in line 3** mainly to	
A) celebrates what it did to genomics **B) compare what BRAIN Initiative can do to neuroscience** C) introduce neurotechnology D) present achievement of BRAIN Initiative	B) Initiative has **the potential to do for neuroscience what the Human Genome Project did for genomics** by supporting the development

Q46. **Absolute Pattern 8: Understanding True Purpose** Finding the true purpose of statement, sentences, or the entire paragraph **Question Pattern:** The author uses **"While these...of brain,"** (lines 16-18) to make which of the following points?	
A) BRAIN Initiatives is even more pivotal B) BRAIN Initiative may succeed without these technological innovations C) These technological innovations are outmoded D) These technological innovations are role models	**A) While** these technological innovations have contributed substantially to our expanding knowledge of the brain, **significant breakthroughs** in how we treat...**That's where the BRAIN Initiative comes in.**
*"While," is used the same way as 'however,' 'although, or 'but.' It cancels out the previous phrase and gives more importance to the following clause. The answer is most likely placed within this 'while' clause.	

Q47. **Absolute Pattern 8: Understanding True Purpose** **Question Pattern:** In line 25, the author mentions "**A Scientific Vision**" mainly to	
A) present scientific goals of the BRAIN Initiative B) voice doubt about its undertaking C) raise budget surplus issue in a single project D) celebrate goals of BRAIN that are achieved	A) A Scientific Vision, which articulates the **scientific goals** of The BRAIN B), C) are negative, while the passage is positive tone. D) is the future prediction that can't be known yet.

Q48. **Absolute Pattern 4: Example Question** Understanding example sentence and the true purpose behind a specific name or idea **Question Pattern:** The author mentions the significance of **optical techniques** in line 13 because	
A) it is the state-of-the-art technology B) it will cure brain disorders such as Alzheimer's C) it allows to combine advanced genetics **D) it is a part of technologies that BRAIN can use**	D) **These technologies will shed light on the complex links between brain function and behavior.** For instance,
Keep in mind that you will never find the answer from the example sentence itself. The answer should be located right before or right after the example sentence in question. "For instance" is a signal for example sentence. Please refer to incorrect choice pattern # 11.	

Q49. **Absolute Pattern 2: Summary Question** Summarizing a sentence or entire passage **Question Pattern:** Which of the following objectives is **committed by BRAIN Initiative?**	
I. Multi-year scientific plan for the Working Group **I. Financial estimates for the research** II. Developing medicines for the brain disorder A) I only B) II only C) III only **D) I and II only**	D) The BRAIN Initiative at the NIH charts **a multi-year scientific plan** for achieving these goals, including timetables, milestones, and **cost estimates.** II. Is not stated. Please refer to incorrect choice pattern # 4

Q50. **Absolute Pattern 5: Word-In-Context Question** Finding a clue word and the keyword from the sentence in question **Question Pattern:** In line 34 **"alleviate"** most nearly means	
A) make less severe B) make dull C) reduce temper D) improve vitality	A) BRAIN Multi-Council Working Group's investments aim to leverage brain function research to alleviate the **burden of illness** and injury and provide novel The clue words are "burden of illness" (B), (C) are unrelated word usage (D) is too extreme word usage

Q51. **Absolute Pattern 3: Inference Question** Finding an indirect suggestion (or guessing) **Question Pattern:** The passage suggests that **Systems-Based Neurotechnology for Emerging Therapies** (line 30)	
A) is being conducted by medical institutions as the proven closed-loop medical devices B) is being widely applied to treat post-traumatic stress disorder C) is currently focusing on psychiatric illness **D) is only a prototype and not being practically applied yet.**	D) Once completed, with Neuro-…Systems-Based Neurotechnology for Emerging Therapies (SUBNETS) can measure and modulate, with the first set of preliminary closed-loop medical. Preliminary model," means prototype", which is not completed yet. "Once completed" means it is not developed yet. Therefore, all the other choices are incorrect.

Q52. **Absolute Pattern 12: Informational Graphs** Finding facts described in the graphs or relations between the passage and the graph. **Question Pattern:** Which of the following statements best **reflects the chart** after the passage?	
A) Specific to BRAIN Initiative reveals some funding issues over the past years B) Specific to BRAIN Initiative programs reduced its research areas in 2016 compared to 2015 C) The role of Biomedical technology in BRAIN Initiative has increased in 2016 **D) Understanding the Brain played the second most significant role in 2016 in terms of funding**	D) $147 vs. $150
Over 70% of graph questions requires little information from the reading passage. However superficial statement in question (e.g., "Based on information in the passage, the graph….?") always ask you to read the passage.	

SAT
Writing and Language Section
Answer Explanations
&
Pattern Analyses
for Test 1

Test 1 starts with the Answer Explanations

Please understand each question according to the Patterns

There's No Time Limit for this Practice.

ALL THE LOGIC AND RULES BEHIND EVERY SINGLE SAT QUESTION

Test 1 Writing & Language Section Patterns

Questions 1-11 are based on the following passage.

BREXIT

The United Kingdom European Union membership referendum, also known as the EU referendum and the Brexit [1] referendum, which a referendum that took place on Thursday 23 June 2016 in the United Kingdom to [2] gauge support for the country's continued membership in the European Union. The referendum result was not legally binding.

The result was split [3] with the constituent countries of the United Kingdom, with a majority in England and Wales voting to leave, and a majority in Scotland and Northern Ireland, voting to remain. To start the process to leave the [4] EU, which is expected to take several years, the British government will have to invoke Article 50 of the Treaty on European Union. The UK government has announced formal process of leaving the EU [5] although revoking the vote might be possible.

Membership of the EU had long been a topic of debate in the United Kingdom. [6] The country joined the European Economic Community (EEC, or "Common Market") in 1973.

Britain Stronger in Europe was the official group campaigning for the UK to remain in the EU and was led by the Prime Minister David Cameron and Chancellor George Osborne. [7] Other campaign groups, political parties, businesses, trade unions, newspapers and prominent individuals were also involved, and each side had supporters from across the political spectrum.Financial markets [8] were reacted negatively in the immediate aftermath of the result. Investors in worldwide stock markets lost more than the [9] equivalent of 2 trillion United States dollars on 24 June 2016, making it the worst single-day loss in history. The market losses amounted to 3 trillion US dollars by 27 June.

The value of the pound sterling against the US dollar fell to a 31-year low. The UK's and the EU's sovereign debt credit rating was also lowered by Standard & Poor's. By 29 June, the markets had returned to growth and the value of the pound had begun to rise.

Immediately after the result, the Prime Minister [10] David Cameron had announced he would resign, having campaigned unsuccessfully for a "remain" vote on behalf of Britain Stronger in Europe and HM Government. He was succeeded by Theresa May on 13 July.

Q1. Absolute Pattern 21: Subject-Verb, Pronoun, Noun Agreement

The United Kingdom European Union membership referendum, ***also known as the EU referendum and the Brexit [1] referendum,*** *which* is a referendum that took place on Thursday 23 June 2016 in the United Kingdom to gauge support for the country's continued membership in the European Union.

	A) NO CHANGE	**'which'** should be removed. "is" should be "was"
	B) referendum, are a referendum	Two errors: using the plural verb and the present tense.
	C) referendum, as a referendum	Verb is missing.
√	**D) referendum, was** a referendum	Uses the singular, past tense verb correctly

Finding the Main Subject and the Main Verb is the fundamental step to solve almost all questions.
When confronting confusing sentence like above, we can remove inessential context like this:

The United Kingdom European Union membership referendum, ~~***also known as the EU referendum and the** Brexit referendum*~~, *which* is a referendum that took place on Thursday....

D) The subject is singular "the United Kingdom European Union membership **referendum,**"
The non-restrictive modifier (quick interjection) "also known as....the Brexit referendum," is offset by a pair of commas because it is inessential information. We can forget—by intentionally not reading it—about the phrase within the pair of commas, and find the main verb right after the second comma.
Through this process we can see that "that took place on Thursday 23 June 2016" requires the main verb.

Q2. Absolute Pattern 10: Logical Expression		
... took place on Thursday 23 June 2016 in the United Kingdom to [2]gauge support for the country's continued membership in the European Union.		
Question: Which of the following alternatives would NOT be appropriate?		
A) check B) measure C) see D) alter		
√	**D) alter**	"alter" means 'to change.' and it changes the original meaning.
A), B), C) are all synonym to gauge.		

Q3. Absolute Pattern 15: Prepositional Idiom		
The result was split [3] with the constituent countries of the United Kingdom, with a majority in England and Wales ***voting to leave***, **and** a majority in Scotland and Northern Ireland, ***voting to remain***.		
	A) NO CHANGE	C) "Between ~and" is an irreplaceable idiomatic phrase. Ex) **between** apple **and** tomato. Easy is finding a pair of prepositional idiom pattern. However, when the former part of the idiom is capped in, while the latter one is disclosed, the question becomes harder one. When multiple choices throw only clueless prepositions, search if there's any structural similarity in the sentence. In this question, the parallel structure *'voting to remain.' and 'voting to leave'* gives a clue. * You can always ignore pronoun like person's name or country name.
	B) into	
√	**C) between**	
	D) in	

Q4. Absolute Pattern 12: Modifier Placement Error		
To start the process to leave the [4] EU, ***which is expected to take several years,*** the British government will have to invoke Article 50 of the Treaty on European Union.		
√	**A) NO CHANGE**	**"which is...years,"** the non-restrictive modifier (inessential information), must be offset by a pair of commas that modifies "To start the process to leave the [4] EU"
	B) EU expects	It sounds as if "EU expects..."
	C) EU, expecting	It should be passive "expected," not active "expecting." Or "EU" becomes the subject.
	D) EU and to expect	It changes the original meaning.

Q5. Absolute Pattern 1: Adding, Revising, Deleting, Retaining Information		
The UK government has announced formal process of leaving the EU [5] although revoking the vote might be possible.		
Which choice provides a **supporting example** that emphasizes the main point of the sentence?		
	A) NO CHANGE	B) The exact date of leaving emphasizes the previous portion of the sentence.
√	**B) ,confirming the due date by March 2019.**	A) "although" cancels out the previous portion of the sentence, rather than emphasizing it and creates contradiction C) Redundant error: "official process and formal process" D) any new information should be considered an unrelated information.
	C) ,confirming Brexit was driven by the official process	
	D) ,using the term "hard Brexit" rather than "soft Brexit."	

Q6. Absolute Pattern 1: Adding, Revising, Deleting, Retaining Information

Question: If the writer were to delete the underlined portion (adjusting the capitalization as needed), the sentence would primarily lose:

Membership of the EU **had long been a topic** of debate in the United Kingdom.
[6] The country joined the European Economic Community (EEC, or "Common Market") in **1973.**

	A) the meaning of EEC	C) The information adds more historical credibility that supports the previous sentence. A) "EEC" is mentioned for the first time in this sentence and there's nothing to lose. B) it was discussed already in the previous sentence. D) The BREXIT is the voting process to leave the E.U because UK believes E.U. and EEC is not important.
	B) the formal step to leave E.U. after the referendum.	
√	**C) the description of historical overview**	
	D) the importance of EEC to the United Kingdom.	

Q7. Absolute Pattern 1: Adding, Revising, Deleting, Retaining Information

At this point, the author wishes to **add** the following information. Should the author make this addition here?

Vote Leave was the official group campaigning for the UK to leave the EU and was fronted by the Conservative MPs Boris Johnson and Michael Gove.

	A) Yes, because it provides added information about the history of conflicts.	B) The previous sentence discusses the group backing the UK to remain in the EU. The following sentence, illustrating the opposite group, is an ideal addition. A) simply repeats the previous sentence. D) It's opposite.
√	**B) Yes, because it connects with the previous sentence.**	
	C) No, because it is mentioned in the following sentences.	
	D) No, because it is not persuasive enough.	

Q8. Absolute Pattern 21: Subject-Verb, Pronoun, Noun Agreement

Financial markets [8] were reacted negatively in the immediate aftermath of the result.

	A) NO CHANGE	D) is Active and Concise. A), B): Passive voice is illogical in this sentence. and is unnecessarily wordy. Find the Shortest One. C) is not a verb. "reacted by" is used as an adjective phrase to support the subject "Financial markets"
	B) were in great reaction	
	C) reacted by	
√	**D) reacted**	

Q9. Absolute Pattern 10: Logical Expression

Question: Which of the following alternatives would NOT be appropriate?

√	**A) equivocal to**	**equivocal means unclear**	C) almost	almost means equivalent
	B) equal to	equivalent means the same.	D) nearly	nearly means equivalent

Q10. Absolute Pattern 24: Verb Tense / Voice Error	
[10] **Immediately after the result**, the Prime Minister David Cameron **had announced** he would resign, having campaigned unsuccessfully for a "remain" vote on behalf of Britain Stronger in Europe and HM Government.	
Which choice expresses **the underlined sentence** most effectively?	
	A) NO CHANGE — 'had announced' is the past perfect. The tense is reversed.
	B) David Cameron followed the result, Cameron announced he would resign, after he campaigned
√	C) David Cameron **announced he would resign, having campaigned**
	D) David Cameron, by announcing that he would resign, having campaigned

C) "Immediately after the result," (or immediately after the result **was given)** points out that both 'the result' and 'the announcement' occurred at the same time. "having campaigned,."—meaning after he had campaigned— correctly displays the past perfect tense that occurred before the announcement.

A) "had announced" is the past perfect, illustrating that the announcement occurred before the result was given, which is opposite and the impossible situation.
B) Comma splice error + a redundant error ("Cameron" is written two times in one sentence, a redundant error)
D) No verb.

Q11. Absolute Pattern 9: Informational Graphs	
In **reference to the passage**, which choice offers an accurate interpretation of the table on the left ?	
√	**A)** The **table results** reflect **the cause** of the former Prime Minister David Cameron's **leaving the office**.
	B) The referendum result was legally binding**.**
	C) As the referendum confirmed, United Kingdom will start the formal process of leaving the EU immediately.
	D) As the referendum confirmed, the Leave group will leave the EU, and the Remain group will remain in EU.

A) The final paragraph describes that the Prime Minister would leave the office.
B) The first paragraph indicates it is not legally binding. C) The paragraph indicates that leaving the EU will take several years. D) Remain group cannot remain in EU.

Questions 12-22 are based on the following passage.

Are we alone?

{ Paragraph 1 }

Many scientists believe we are not alone in the universe. It's probable, they say, that life could have [12] rise on at least some of the billions of planets thought to exist in our galaxy alone -- just as it did here on planet Earth. This basic question about our place in the Universe is one that may be answered by scientific investigations. (A)

{ Paragraph 2 }

Experts from NASA and its partner institutions addressed this question on July 14, at a public talk held at NASA Headquarters in Washington.

[13] They outlined NASA's roadmap to the search for life in the [14] universe, it was an ongoing journey that involves a number of current and future telescopes. Sometime in the near future, people will be able to point to a star and say, 'that star has a planet like Earth'," says Sara Seager, professor of planetary science and physics at the Massachusetts Institute of Technology in Cambridge, Massachusetts. [15] However, the impression of how common planets are in the Milky way adversely creates backlash among scientists.(B)

{ Paragraph 3 }

NASA's quest to study planetary systems around other stars started with ground-based observatories, then moved to space-based assets like the Hubble Space Telescope, the Spitzer Space Telescope, and the Kepler Space Telescope. Today's telescopes can look at many stars and tell if they have one or more orbiting planets. (C)

16] However, they can determine if the planets are the right distance away from the star to have liquid water, the key ingredient to life as we know [17] it. { **Paragraph 4** } The NASA roadmap will continue with the launch of the Transiting Exoplanet Surveying Satellite TESS) in 2017 and the James Webb Space Telescope. These upcoming telescopes [18] would find and characterize [19] a host of new exoplanets— those planets that orbit other stars—expanding our knowledge of their atmospheres and diversity. The Webb telescope and WFIRST-AFTA will lay the groundwork, and future missions will extend the search for the nearby planets that are similar to Earth in size and mass, a key step in the search for life. (D)	["This technology we are using to explore exoplanets is real," said John Grunsfeld, astronaut and associate administrator for NASA's Science Mission Directorate in Washington. "The James Webb Space Telescope and the next advances are happening now. These are not dreams -- this is what we do at NASA." [20] After its launch in 2009, Kepler has dramatically changed what we know about exoplanets, finding most of the more than 5,000 potential exoplanets, of which more than 1700 have been confirmed. The Kepler observations have led to estimates of billions of planets in our galaxy, and shown that most planets within one astronomical unit are less than three times the diameter of Earth. Kepler also found the first Earth-size planet to orbit in the "habitable zone" of a star, the region where liquid water can pool on the surface.

Q12. Absolute Pattern 24: Verb Tense / Voice Error

Many scientists believe we are not alone in the universe. It's probable, they say, that life **could have** [12] rise on at least some of the billions of planets thought to exist in our galaxy alone -- just as it did here on planet Earth.

	A) NO CHANGE	Rise means emerge. Rise is base verb.
	B) raise	Raise means to move upward
√	**C) arisen**	"could have" requires the past participle. "arisen" (rise=> rose => arisen)
	D) arouse	Arouse means evoke feeling

Q13. Absolute Pattern 17: Pronoun Error

Experts from NASA and its partner institutions addressed this question on July 14, at a public talk held at NASA Headquarters in Washington. [13]They outlined NASA's roadmap to the search for life in the [14]universe.

√	**A) NO CHANGE**	A) "Experts" is the subject, which is plural and requires plural pronoun 'They'. B) 'He' is singular C) 'It' is singular. NASA itself can't outline NASA's roadmap. Only human can. D) "Those" is used as either the possessive pronoun like 'those cars' or an Indicative object like ' I like those too,' none of which works in this sentence.
	B) He	
	C) It	
	D) Those	

Q14. Absolute Pattern 16: Precision, Concision, Style

They outlined NASA's roadmap to the search for life in the universe,[14] it was an ongoing journey that involves a number of current and future telescopes.

	A) NO CHANGE	Pattern: Always Pick the Shortest One from the Multiple Choices! Making incorrect choice by reducing information is not easy. Adding a few words to make incorrect choice is a piece of cake. D) follows the precision and concision rule without adding any unnecessary conjunction. The shortest choice is always the answer. (A) comma splice
	B) and an ongoing journey	
	C) because it was an ongoing journey	
√	**D) an ongoing journey**	

Q15. Absolute Pattern 1: Adding, Revising, Deleting, Retaining Information

Which choice emphasizes the anticipation of some scientists' belief of the existence of planet like Earth.

	A) However, the impression of how common planets are in the Milky way adversely creates backlash among scientists.	All the other options are Negative and can't be an anticipation.
√	**B) There are just too many planets out there in our Milky Way galaxy**	
	C) Astronomers have currently discovered the evidential proof that there is no chance for Venus to sustain life.	
	D) Astronomers acknowledge that under the current technology there are many obstacles to materialize our space safari project.	

One of the major tricks applied in the Reading Section is to relying on the Positive-Negative value. That is, if the passage is Positive, the answer choice should never be Negative, vice versa. This simple rule is applied in Writing Section too and solves many difficult questions instantly.

B) The topic and the previous paragraph are all Positive, at least not necessarily Negative.
Also, the question is positive; therefore, it is seeking a positive answer

Q16. Absolute Pattern 23: Transition Words for Supporting Detail, Contrast, and Consequence

Today's telescopes can look at many stars and tell if they have one or more orbiting planets. [16] However, **they can determine** if the planets are the right distance away from the star to have liquid water

	A) NO CHANGE	C) 1> The adverb "even more" amplifies the preceding sentence. 2> The original sentence is positively paralleling with the following sentence, requiring "Even more."
	B) You bet!	
√	**C) Even more,**	A) Conjunctive adverb "however" cancels out the previous sentence. B) "You bet!" is informal colloquial language that should be avoided. D) 'Therefore' is used for consequence, making the previous sentence a premise.
	D) Therefore,	

Q17. Absolute Pattern 16: Precision, Concision, Style

Even more, **they can determine** if the planets are the right distance away from the star to have liquid water, the key ingredient to life as we know [17] it.

√	**A) NO CHANGE**	The pronoun "it" is correctly used to summarize the information.
	B) liquid water is essential to sustain life	(B), (C), (D) All three options are redundant as they repeat the previous sentence without adding any new information.
	C) water can be used to form life.	
	D) that the planets' distance is a way to understand whether liquid water exists or not.	

Q18. Absolute Pattern 24: Verb Tense / Voice Error

These **upcoming** telescopes [18] **would** find and characterize [19] a host of new exoplanets—

	A) NO CHANGE	'would' is past tense. The word 'upcoming' signals the future tense.
√	**B) will find**	"These upcoming" hints that the future tense "will find" is required.
	C) have to find	Change of meaning. "have to" is an interrogative that forces someone to do.
	D) that find	No verb.

Q19. Absolute Pattern 10: Logical Expression		
These upcoming telescopes will find and characterize [19] a host of new exoplanets		
Which choice most dramatically emphasizes the **massive scale** of upcoming discovery using the telescope observation projects?		
√	**A) NO CHANGE**	Quantity vs. Quality A) "host" means a lot or massive. The keyword in the question is "the massive scale," which quantifies the size of the future discovery project. B) and C) are quality that cannot be quantified. D) is not related issue to the question.
	B) more reliable data of	
	C) groundbreaking discovery of	
	D) the actual photographs of	

Q20. Absolute Pattern 23: Transition Words for Supporting Detail, Contrast, and Consequence		
[20] After its launch in 2009, Kepler **has dramatically changed** what we know about exoplanets, finding most of the...		
	A) NO CHANGE	'after' cannot replace 'since.'
	B) Having followed	'Having followed' means "After it (had) followed," illogical time frame and wordy error.
	C) With	change of original meaning. The question uses "After" that indicates a specific time frame. NEVER change the original meaning!
√	**D) Since**	The present perfect tense (have/has + p.p) requires "since."

Q21. Absolute Pattern 1: Adding, Revising, Deleting, Retaining Information		
Suppose the writer's primary purpose has been to describe the **possibility of searching for life**. Would this essay accomplish that purpose?		
	A) Yes, because it tells about a variety of challenges the scientists face along with their searching for life in exoplanets.	B) "the telescopes," the main apparatus appears in this passage, focus on searching for life in the universe. A) and D) are negative, while the passage maintains the positive tone. C) The passage introduces both the present and the future project.
√	**B) Yes, because it focuses primarily on scientists' application of new types of telescopes and other methods**	
	C) No, because it focuses mainly on the projects to be undertaken in the future.	
	D) No, because it focuses on the limited applications within the scope of modern technology in finding life in the universe	

Q22. Absolute Pattern 1: Adding, Revising, Deleting, Retaining Information		
Question: The writer wants to add the following sentence to the essay: What are the next steps to finding life elsewhere? The sentence would most logically be placed at Point:		
√	**A) A in Paragraph 1**	This basic question about our place in the Universe is one that may be answered by scientific investigations. (A)
	B) B in Paragraph 2	However, the impression of how common planets are in the Milky way adversely creates backlash among scientists. (B) is Negative and is not coherent with the question.
	C) C in Paragraph 3	Today's telescopes can look at many stars and tell if they have one or more orbiting planets.(C) is the body paragraph about the telescopes.
	D) D in Paragraph 4	The Webb telescope and WFIRST-AFTA will lay the groundwork, and future missions will extend the search for the nearby planets that are similar to Earth in size and mass, a key step in the search for life. (D) is the example that further details paragraph 3.
A) The following sentence starts with "This basic question," implying "this basic question" was the response to the previous question. Therefore, the previous sentence should very likely to be asking this question.		

Questions 23-33 are based on the following passage.

Black ice

Black [23] ice, sometimes called clear ice, refers to a thin coating of glaze ice on a surface, especially on roads. The ice itself is not black, but visually transparent, [24] allowing the often black road below to be seen through it. The typically low level of noticeable ice pellets, snow, or sleet [25] surrounds black ice means that areas of the ice are often practically invisible to drivers or people stepping on it. [26] Their is, thus, a risk of skidding and subsequent accidents due to the unexpected loss of traction. The term *black ice* in the United States is often incorrectly used to describe any type of ice that forms on roadways, even when standing water on roads turns to ice as the temperature falls below freezing. Correctly defined, black ice is formed on relatively dry roads, rendering it invisible to drivers. It occurs when in the textures present in all pavements very slightly below the top of the road surface contain water or moisture, thereby presenting a dry surface to tires until that water or moisture freezes and expands; drivers then find they are riding above the road surface on a honeycombed invisible sheet of ice.

Because it represents only a thin accumulation, black ice is highly transparent and thus difficult to see as compared with snow, frozen slush, or thicker ice layers. [27] In addition, it often is interleaved with wet pavement, which is nearly identical in [28] appearance, this makes driving, cycling or walking on affected surfaces extremely dangerous.

Deicing with salt (sodium chloride) is effective to down temperatures of about −18 °C (0 °F). At below −18 °C, black ice can form on roadways when the moisture from automobile exhaust condenses on the road surface. Such conditions caused multiple accidents in Minnesota when the temperatures dipped below −18 °C for a prolonged period of time in December 2008. [29] With salt's ineffectiveness at melting ice at these temperatures compounds the problem. Black ice may form even when the ambient temperature is several degrees above the freezing point of water 0 °C (32 °F), [30] if the air warms suddenly after a prolonged cold spell that has left the surface of the roadway well below the freezing point temperature. On December 1, 2013, heavy post-Thanksgiving weekend traffic encountered black ice on the westbound I-290 expressway in Worcester, Massachusetts. A chain reaction series of crashes resulted, involving three tractor-trailers and over 60 other vehicles. The ice [31] had formed suddenly on a long downward slope, [32] surprising drivers coming over the crest of a hill, who could not see crashed vehicles ahead until it was too late to stop on the slick pavement. Bridges and overpasses can be especially dangerous. Black ice forms first on bridges and overpasses because air can circulate both above and below the surface of the elevated roadway, causing the bridge pavement temperature to drop more rapidly.

Q23. Absolute Pattern 18: Punctuation Error

Which of the following alternatives to the underlined portion would **NOT be acceptable?**

	A) ice, sometimes called clear ice, refers	C) "sometimes called clear ice" is a quick-interjection that further describes the subject, 'Black ice.' This modifier is inessential information called the 'unrestrictive modifier.' Because the phrase is inessential to the sentence structure, it should be offset by a pair of commas on both sides to indicate that it's not a part of the main sentence. (C) misses one comma after "ice". B) and D) function as the same way as (A) a pair of comma.
	B) ice—sometimes called clear ice—refers	
√	**C) ice, sometimes called clear ice refers**	
	D) ice (sometimes called clear ice) refers	

Q24. Absolute Pattern 1: Adding, Revising, Deleting, Retaining Information

If the writer were to delete the underlined portion of the sentence, it would primarily lose:

The ice itself is not black, but visually transparent, [24] allowing the often black road below to be seen through it.

√	**A) an idea that emphasizes the reason for an optical illusion**
	B) a statement that introduces the main focus of the following paragraph.
	C) an unnecessary detail that contradicts information presented earlier in the paragraph.
	D) a clear image that conveys what most observers want to find out behind the black ice.

A) The preceding portion of the sentence is the reason that "allows (or allowing)" black road to be seen through it" **(the effect)** C) It is a necessary detail.

Q25. Absolute Pattern 21: Subject-Verb, Pronoun, Noun Agreement

The typically low **level** of noticeable ice pellets, snow, and sleet [25] surrounds black ice means that areas of the ice are often practically invisible to drivers or people stepping on it.

	Choice	Explanation
	A) NO CHANGE	When two verbs are shown in the question, the latter one becomes the main verb, and the former becomes either adjective or adverb.
	B) surrounding black ice meaning	C) properly use the verb "means" to describe the subject "level" and uses "surrounding" as an adjective phrase.
√	**C) surrounding black ice means**	A) uses both "surrounds" and "means" as the verb.. B) has no verb by using both "surrounding" and "meaning" as the adjective
	D) surrounding black ice mean	phrase. D) The subject is "level"; the singular; therefore, the verb has to be "means"

Q26. Absolute Pattern 21: Subject-Verb, Pronoun, Noun Agreement

[26] Their is, thus, **a risk of skidding and a subsequent accident** due to the unexpected loss of traction

	Choice	Explanation
	A) NO CHANGE	D) Plural subjects "a risk of skidding" and "a subsequent accidents" require plural verb "are."
	B) Their have been	
	C) There is	A), B) "Their" is possessive pronoun. (e.g., Their house is smaller than his.) C) "is" should be "are"
√	**D) There are**	

Key point: Some students may think that the subject is "a risk,' a singular noun that comprises "**a risk of** (skidding and a subsequent accident). That concept is incorrect because we have two subjects "a risk" and "a subsequent accident" that prove plural subject, which requires plural verb. If, however, there were no "a" before "subsequent," the answer should be (C)

Q27. Absolute Pattern 23: Transition Words for Supporting Detail, Contrast, and Consequence

Because it represents only a thin accumulation, black ice is highly transparent and thus difficult to see as compared with snow, frozen slush, or thicker ice layers. [27] In addition, it often is interleaved with wet pavement, which is nearly identical in [28] appearance, this makes driving, cycling or walking on affected surfaces extremely dangerous.

	Choice	Explanation
√	**A) NO CHANGE**	A) 'In addition' is used to support the previous subordinating clause "Because." The following sentence adds information by further elaborating its appearance.
	B) On the contrary,	
	C) Consequently,	B), D) drive the explanation to the opposite direction.
	D) In spite of such a thin accumulation,	C) The consequence has already been mentioned using the because-clause. ("black ice is highly transparent…")

Q28. Absolute Pattern 12: Modifier Placement Error

In addition, it often is interleaved with wet pavement, which is nearly identical in [28] appearance, this makes driving, cycling or walking on affected surfaces extremely dangerous.

Question: Which of the following alternatives to the underlined portion would **NOT** be acceptable?

	Choice	Explanation
	A) appearance, which makes	D) is a comma splice error.
	B) appearance, making	A) "which makes" or B) ",making" efficiently describe the effect of appearance.
	C) appearance. This makes	C) starting with a new sentence is an alternative
√	**D) appearance, this makes**	

Q29. Absolute Pattern 14: Possessive Determiners and Possessive Noun Error		
[29] With salt's ineffectiveness at melting ice at these temperatures **compounds** the problem.		
	A) NO CHANGE	B) The sentence needs a subject, "Salt's ineffectiveness." "compounds" is the main verb. A) "With" is a preposition, carrying a prepositional phrase, not a subject C), D) have to be a possessive form to link the following subjective noun ineffectiveness.'
√	**B) Salt's**	
	C) Salt	
	D) Sodium Chloride	

Q30. Absolute Pattern 1: Adding, Revising, Deleting, Retaining Information	
[30] if the air warms suddenly after a prolonged cold spell that has left the surface of the roadway well below the freezing point temperature.	
Question: In the preceding sentence, the clause " **if the air warms... freezing point temperature." primarily serves** to indicate:	
	A) that black ice phenomenon could occur in many southern states with the mild temperature.
	B) the strikingly complex characteristics of black ice
	C) that technique to prevent black ice has yet to be developed at present
√	**D) the atmospheric conditions that lead to Black Ice formation under the certain temperature.**
Pattern: Do Not Pick Any New Information that is Not Mentioned in the Passage or in the paragraph! D) The previous and the following clauses are Cause-and-Effect relation. The main clause states that even in the ambient weather, Black Ice forms. The reasons for the phenomenon are then described: "the surface of the roadway keeps below the freezing point temperature for a while." A), C) The passage does not mention about southern states or technique. New Info. is Always Incorrect. B) "complex characteristics" does not directly reflects the cause-effect relations.	

Q31. Absolute Pattern 24: Verb Tense / Voice Error		
The ice [31] had formed suddenly on a long downward slope, [32] **surprising drivers** coming over the crest of a hill, who could not see crashed vehicles ahead until it was too late to stop on the slick pavement.		
	A) NO CHANGE	Pattern: When multiple choices include different verb tenses, look for other verbs in the paragraph, identify the tense, and stick to the same tense. D) "suddenly" is the key point in this sentence. The word "suddenly" indicates immediate occurrence; therefore, we should use the simple past tense to show the situation occurred at the same time. A) The past perfect is incorrect tense. B) Redundant error C) The present perfect is incorrect.
	B) formed suddenly in a matter of seconds	
	C) has formed suddenly	
√	**D) formed suddenly**	

Q32. Absolute Pattern 10: Logical Expression		
The ice formed suddenly on a long downward slope, [32] **surprising drivers** coming over the crest of a hill, who could not see crashed vehicles ahead until it was too late to stop on the slick pavement.		
√	**A) NO CHANGE**	"The ice formed suddenly" indicates the situation with a brief moment in time that the drivers' reaction has to be seen instantaneously by using the "ing" form.
	B) surprised	"surprised" is a verb and can't be used because "crashed" the main verb, is already there.
	C) surprisingly alarmed	'surprising' and 'alarmed' are synonyms, a redundant error.
	D) cautioning	changes the original meaning. "surprise" and "caution" are antonym.

Q33. Absolute Pattern 1: Adding, Revising, Deleting, Retaining Information	
Suppose the writer's primary purpose has been to write an essay summarizing the **road trip safety education** in winter. Would this essay accomplish that purpose?	
	A) Yes, because it discusses the complete road trip safety measures in winter driving
	B) Yes, because it demonstrates the National Transportation Safety Board's effort to educate the dangers of black ice.
√	**C) No, because it focusses instead on what the Black Ice is, and how it forms.**
	D) No, because it focuses instead on describing the method of distinguishing Black Ice from White Ice.
Pattern: Do Not Pick Any New Information that is Not Mentioned in the Passage or in the paragraph! C) Road trip safety education isn't mentioned at all. D) White ice is not the main point.	

Questions 34-44 are based on the following passage.

9 TO 5 GROUP

In 2005 Brad Neuberg used "coworking" to describe a physical space which he originally called a "9 to 5 group". Neuberg organized a co-working [34] site called the "Hat Factory" in San Francisco, a live-work loft that was home to three technology workers, and open to others during the day. Brad was also one of the founders of Citizen Space, the first "Work Only" co-working space. Now, co-working places exist worldwide, with over 700 locations in the United States alone. Since 2006 a few studies have shown the number of co-working spaces and available seats have roughly doubled each year, [35] incrementing nearly as much as two times within twelve-month cycle.

San Francisco continues to have a large presence in the co-working community [36] and being home to a growing number of co-working places including RocketSpace, Sandbox Suites, and Citizen Space.

.The New York co-working community has also been evolving rapidly in places like Regus and Rockefeller Group Business Center. [37] The demand for co-working in Brooklyn neighborhoods is almost never ending. [38] Despite of the rise in the Millennials workforce, nearly one in 10 workers in the Gowanus area work from home that adds the reason for high demand. The industrial area of Gowanus, Brooklyn is seeing a surge in new startups like Co-workers, which are redesigning old buildings into new co-working spaces.

Some co-working places were developed by nomadic Internet entrepreneurs [39] lured by an enormous financial interest. A 2007 survey showed that many employees worry about feeling isolated and losing human interaction if they were to telecommute. Roughly a third of both private and public-sector workers also reported that they didn't want to stay at home during work.As of 2012, the U.K. is among the most responsive European country to the idea of collaborative working, with a special focus on London.

The city leads the co-working market not only for the large number of co-working places it offers but also for the [40] variety of places that exist to fit the differing needs among start-ups, entrepreneurs and freelancers, who avoid the existing office structure. Camden Collective is a regeneration project in London [41] that re-purposes previously vacant and underused properties, and opened its first 'wire-less wall-less' co-working space in 2009.

In March 2012 Google along with several local partners opened a co-working place in the heart of East London. Campus London is located in Tech City and helps multiple start-ups to grow under the same roof, by mentoring them and giving them the chance to learn more through the events that run everyday, [42] through which Campus London assists many startups. In June 2013, the U.K. Government announced it would be applying co-working principles to a new pilot scheme for its 'One Public Sector Estate' strategy covering 12 local authorities in England which will encourage councils to work with central government departments and other bodies so that staff share buildings. Co-working is also becoming more common in continental Europe, with the startup metropolis Berlin being a major booster for this development.

[43] This kind of working environment is not exclusive to big cities. Also smaller urban areas with many young and creative people and especially university cities may offer coworking places, with *Cowork Greifswald* in Germany being one example. Cooperations between co-working spaces and academic environments are focused.

Q34. Absolute Pattern 20: Restrictive Modifier (Essential Information)		
Neuberg organized a co-working [34] site the "Hat Factory" in San Francisco, a live-work loft that was home to three technology workers, and open to others during the day.		
√	**A) NO CHANGE**	"Hat Factory" should not be offset by a pair of commas.
	B) site, the "Hat Factory,"	No pair of commas is necessary for essential information.
	C) site, the "Hat Factory"	No comma in the front of "the"
	D) site the "Hat Factory,"	No comma after "Factory"
The sentence is restrictive. That is, "Hat Factory" is essential information, because the author wants to identify that it isn't any co-working site, but the co-working site named "Hat Factory" is.		

Q35. Absolute Pattern 19: Redundant Error		
Since 2006 a few studies have shown the number of co-working spaces and available seats have roughly **doubled each year**, [35] incrementing nearly as much **as two times** within **twelve-month** cycle.		
	A) NO CHANGE	Always Pick the Shortest One from the Multiple Choices! D) should be deleted to avoid redundancy. A), C): redundant error (doubled each year) B) redundant error (doubled) redundant error (each year)
	B) almost reaching 200 percent.	
	C) impressively expanding its numbers every twelve-month	
√	**D) delete the underlined portion**	

Q36. Absolute Pattern 21: Subject-Verb, Pronoun, Noun Agreement		
San Francisco continues to have a large presence in the co-working community, [36] and being home to a growing number of co-working places including RocketSpace, Sandbox Suites, and Citizen Space.		
	A) NO CHANGE	It changes to passive voice. *please do not choose 'being.' Using it is good for nothing.
	B) homing to	Colloquialism error. "homing" sounds unidiomatic and non-standard.
	C) and has home to	"**has** home to" should be "**is** home to"
√	**D) and is home to**	"and **(San Francisco) is** home to …." is the correct parallel structure.

Q37. Absolute Pattern 1: Adding, Revising, Deleting, Retaining Information		
The New York co-working community has also been evolving rapidly in places like Regus and Rockefeller Group Business Center. [37]		
Question: The writer is considering **adding** the following sentence: Several new startups like WeWork have been **expanding** all over the city. Should the writer make this addition here?		
√	**A) Yes, because it connects the paragraph's point about the rapid expansion of co-working community in the certain region.**	A) "has also been evolving rapidly" and " expansion" link up the two sentences and the main focus. B) The main theme is not startup companies, but the proliferation of co-working facilities. C) is only one of the startups mentioned in the first paragraph. D) is not stated in the passage.
	B) Yes, because it explains the significant number of startup business in New York	
	C) No, because it should focus on one main coworking company "the Hat Factory"	
	D) No, because it deviates from the paragraph's focus on major building like Rockefeller Group Business Center	

Q38. Absolute Pattern 23: Transition Words for Supporting Detail, Contrast, and Consequence

[38] Despite of (Cause) the rise in the Millennials work- (Effect) force, nearly one in 10 workers in the Gowanus area work from home that adds the reason for high demand.

	A) NO CHANGE	The change of meaning error. despite of = not affected by
√	**B) Due to**	due to = because of (**the cause**)
	C) For example,	'for example' and 'in addition to' are used to add up information to the previous sentence.
	D) In addition to	

The sentence is the cause-effect structure. Therefore, it needs 'due to.'

Q39. Absolute Pattern 1: Adding, Revising, Deleting, Retaining Information

Some co-working places were developed by **nomadic** Internet entrepreneurs [39] lured by an enormous financial interest

Question: Which choice maintains the essay's positive tone and most strongly support the main theme of the essay?

	A) NO CHANGE	B) "nomadic" means wondering from place to place. The modifier "seeking an alternative..." supports the needs of nomadic internet entrepreneurs. A) ":lured by" is negative word, not positive. the entire passage is about the positive effect of co-working. C) Co-working place is not a residence. D) is negative term.
√	**B) seeking an alternative to working in coffee shops and cafes, or to isolation in independent or home offices.**	
	C) wanting to find a place both to live and work	
	D) who were often dripped away from the main stream of the industry.	

Q40. Absolute Pattern 10: Logical Expression

The city leads the co-working market not only for the large number of co-working places it offers but also for the [40] variety of places that exist **to fit the differing needs among start-ups, entrepreneurs and freelancers, who avoid the existing office structure.**

Question: Which of the following alternatives to the underlined portion would **NOT be acceptable**?

	A) mobile	C) is antonym to the Bold faced phrase in the sentence. The very purpose of the co-working facilities is to avoid conventional place and find a new place.
	B) unique	
√	**C) conventional**	A), B), D) : All of them fit into the requirements for the co-working space described in the sentence.
	D) non-traditional	

Q41. Absolute Pattern 1: Adding, Revising, Deleting, Retaining Information

Question: If the writer were to delete the underlined portion of the sentence, the essay would primarily lose details that:

√	**A) illustrate some of the Camden collective Project's features that transformed old buildings**
	B) hint Google's considerable contribution
	C) support the essay's claim that London has become the hub of the co-working community in the world
	D) clarify the unfamiliar term "Camden collective Projects"

A) "re-purpose" = transformed; "previously vacant" = old, features, buildings
The underlined portion shows how the project transformed the old building into the co-working facilities.
B) Hardly is this passage related with Google. C) Co-working community in the world is not discussed.
D) Understanding the term 'Camden Collective Projects' does not provide any significance.

Q42. Absolute Pattern 19: Redundant Error			
Campus London is located in Tech City and **helps multiple start-ups** to grow under the same roof, **by mentoring them** and giving them the chance to learn more **through the events that run everyday**, [42] through which Campus London assists many startups.			
	A) NO CHANGE	The underlined portion is redundant	D) should be deleted to avoid redundant error.
	B) whereby startups receive valuable mentoring		A), B), C) contain very similar information to the previous portion of the sentence without adding extra information.
	C) through which Campus London provides daily events		
√	**D) Delete the underlined portion**		

Q43. Absolute Pattern 23: Transition Words for Supporting Detail, Contrast, and Consequence		
Co-working is also becoming more common in continental Europe, with the startup metropolis Berlin being a major booster for this development. [43] This kind of working environment is not exclusive to big cities.		
√	**A) NO CHANGE**	A) The sentence develops its issue by itself, and no additional transitional word is needed.
	B) For example, this kind	
	C) Generally speaking, this kind	
	D) Commonly, this kind	

Q44. Absolute Pattern 1: Adding, Revising, Deleting, Retaining Information	
Suppose the writer's primary purpose has been to **explain how co-working environment has become new trends** throughout North America and Europe. Would this essay accomplish that purpose?	
	A) Yes, because it describes the architectural design of New York co-working places.
√	**B) Yes, because it enumerates a number of events that successfully transformed old buildings and incubate startup entrepreneurs**
	C) No, because it focuses more on the major startup supporters like Google or Rockefeller Group Business Center.
	D) No, because it focuses on positive prospects only, while there are plausible negatives.
The main theme of the essay is the proliferation of co-working environment and facilities that help incubate startups. In that sense, it fulfills its purpose. A) The Architectural design of New York is not mentioned. C) The startup supporters like Google was only remotely mentioned. D) Negative points are not mentioned.	

SAT

Reading & Writing Practice

Test 1

ALL THE LOGIC AND RULES
BEHIND THE EVERY SINGLE
SAT QUESTION

Reading Test 1

65 MINUTES, 52 QUESTIONS

The passages below are followed by questions based on their content; questions following a pair of related passages may also be based on the relationship between the paired passages. Answer the questions on the basis of what is stated or implied in the passages and in any introductory material that may be provided.

Questions 1-10 are based on the following passage.

This passage is from Sense and Sensibility by Jane Austen

The family of Dashwood had long been settled in Sussex, where, for many generations, they had lived in so respectable a manner as to engage the general good opinion of their surrounding acquaintance.

The old Dashwood was a single man, who lived to a very advanced age, and who for many years of his life, had a constant companion and housekeeper in his sister. But her death, which happened ten years before his own, produced a great alteration in his home; for to supply her loss, he invited and received into his house the family of his nephew Mr. Henry Dashwood, the legal inheritor of the Norland estate, and the person to whom he intended to bequeath it.

But by his own marriage Mr. Henry added to his wealth. To him therefore the succession to the Norland estate was not so really important as to his Sisters, and could be but small.

He was neither so unjust, nor so ungrateful, as to leave his estate to Mr. Henry Dashwood on such terms as destroyed half the value of the bequest to his Sisters.

He meant not to be unkind, however, and, as a mark of his affection for the three girls, he left them a thousand pounds a-piece.

Mr. Dashwood's disappointment was, at first, severe; but his temper was cheerful and sanguine; and he might reasonably hope to live many years, and by living economically, lay by a considerable sum from the produce of an estate already large, and capable of almost immediate improvement.

But the fortune, which had been so tardy in coming, was his only one twelvemonth. He survived his uncle no longer; and ten thousand pounds, including the late legacies, was all that remained for his widow and daughters.

His son was sent for as soon as his danger was known, and to him Mr. Dashwood recommended, with all the strength and urgency which illness could command, the interest of his mother-in-law and sisters.

Mr. John Dashwood had not the strong feelings of the rest of the family; but he was affected by a recommendation of such a nature at such a time.

1

According to paragraph 2 (lines 6-15), the old Dashwood invited Mr. Henry Dashwood for

A) he had a contemptuous feeling to Mr. Henry

B) Mr. Henry had some financial issue

C) he had more than one reason

D) he needed to repent his wrongdoings

2

Which choice provides the best evidence for the answer to the previous question?

A) Lines 11-15 (for to supply…bequeath it)

B) Lines 16-17 (But by his own...his wealth.)

C) Lines 17-19 (To him therefore...but small.)

D) Lines 20-23 (He was neither … to his sister)

3

According to paragraph 1 and 2, all of the following correctly describe the Old Dashwood EXCEPT

A) he lived in the parents' house

B) his family was well respected from the neighbors

C) he did not have a wife

D) he lived all alone as a single man

CONTINUE

1 1

4

Which word best summarizes the description of the old Dashwood in the second paragraph (lines 6-15)?

A) acquisitive

B) uneducated

C) respectful

D) practical

5

To Mr. Henry, the succession to the Norland estate mentioned in line 17 was

A) significant

B) a gift to strengthen distinctive family tie

C) important to satisfy his greed

D) insignificant

6

The primary function of the passage is to

A) define a legal custom related to inheritance

B) emphasize the benefits of having good neighbors

C) introduce the settings of the story

D) show a prolonged family feud

7

It can be inferred from line 23 that the "Sisters"

A) had amassed great wealth

B) had some difficulties with the Old Dashwood

C) were not the legal inheritors

D) were preferred inheritors to Mr. Henry Dashwood

8

It can be inferred from lines 20-23 that in his will, the Old Dashwood tried to?

A) balance and appease every heir

B) condescend every heir

C) defend his estate from every heir

D) remove Mr. Henry from his family

9

In lines 27-32 (Mr. Dashwood's disappointment… immediate improvement.), the author characterizes Mr. Henry Dashwood as

A) a maverick

B) a dilettante

C) a charlatan

D) an optimist

10

Mr. John Dashwood's attitude in lines 45-48 (Mr. John Dashwood...such a time) can be best characterized as

A) appreciation

B) reluctance

C) ambivalence

D) frustration

CONTINUE

1

Questions 11-21 are based on the following passage.

Obama's Disillusioned Doctrine Hope and change, by any means necessary By Shubhankar Chhokra, Harvard University © The Harvard Crimson
Reprinted with Permission

Goldberg's piece lays out The Obama Doctrine, the organizing principle behind the momentous foreign policy of a man whose unlikely rise to the American presidency often overshadows his far more unlikely rise to the seat of Commander in Chief. Here's a man who went from being the Illinois State Senator to the commander of our armed forces in a mere four years—quite a remarkable feat.

No less remarkable a feat than Goldberg's essay itself, "The Obama Doctrine" is not conjecture from historians poring through State of the Union transcripts decades later, but rather the words of a sitting president. The gravity of this essay cannot be overstated. In it, we see Obama reflect on specific decisions—not striking Assad, pivoting to Asia, intervening in Libya—only in order to make broader claims about his presidency, to situate himself historically among the liberal interventionists, the internationalists, the isolationists, and the realists.

Out of these schools, Obama says he is closest to the realists, believing that "we cannot, at any given moment, relieve all the world's misery." He says, "We have to choose where we can make a real impact." That is why, he says, he stood quietly as Putin invaded Crimea in 2014, a core interest for Russia but hardly one for the United States. That is why he reneged on his 2012 promise to intervene in Syria after Assad deployed chemical weapons on his own people.

Throughout the interview, one observes an insuperable level of disillusionment in our president. Obama deplores the Western allies who ride on American coat tails, a claim that would be understandable if he at least took part of the blame for his missteps. In perhaps the most irritating line of the entire interview, Obama comments on the failure to stabilize Libya: "When I go back and I ask myself what went wrong, there's room for criticism, because I had more faith in the Europeans, given Libya's proximity, being invested in the follow-up." "There's room for criticism because I had more faith in the Europeans"—no line better betrays this administration's gross misunderstanding of global power dynamics. In Brussels along with 34 civilians, in the deadliest act of terrorism in Belgian history. Obama claims that "ISIS is not an existential threat to the United States," rather "climate change is a potential existential threat to the entire world if we do not do something about it." This is jaded Obama at work—recklessly allowing his Weltschmerz to loud his judgment, choosing more romantic, less controversial battles like climate change and the favorite cause of his first term, the "pivot to Asia."

This is not to discount Obama's likely genuine belief that climate change demands our attention more than terrorism. But at the root of this claim is not logic, but a fatigue of the Middle East and a yearning for something new. Obama explains to Goldberg about why he prefers to talk about Asia more than ISIS, "They are not thinking about how to kill Americans," he says. "What they're thinking about is 'How do I get a better education? How do I create something of value?'"

David Frum's takeaway from Goldberg's final essay is that all of us have disappointed Barack Obama—that our Western allies are guilty of free-loading, that Americans are guilty of overestimating the threat of ISIS to the point that out fear devolves into <u>bigotry</u>, and that the entire world just needs to be more realistic. President Obama is probably not wrong about any of this, but he is certainly wrong in expecting others to sympathize with his disappointment.

11

The author's tone when he says "quite remarkable feat" in line 9 is

A) cynicism

B) limited approval

C) enthusiasm

D) appreciation

CONTINUE

1 1

12

In lines 19-22, the statement "to situate himself… realists" emphasizes the author's recognition of

A) Obama as the liberal interventionists
B) Obama as president who made spectacular efforts
C) Obama, not subject to any of the category
D) people's provocative reaction against Obama

13

The author mentions Russia and Syria (lines 29-31) to suggest the

A) difficulty of controlling foreign affairs
B) extent to which real impact cannot be reached
C) extended examples of world's misery
D) degree of disappointment Obama rendered

14

Which choice provides the best evidence for the answer to the previous question?

A) Lines 14-15(The gravity of this essay...overstated.)
B) Lines 23-24 (Out of these schools...the realists.)
C) Lines 33-35 (Throughout the interview...president)
D) Lines 50-51 (Obama claims that...United States.)

15

President's attitude toward the Western allies is best characterized as

A) open-minded
B) pragmatic
C) disillusioned
D) apathetic

16

Which choice provides the best evidence for the answer to the previous question?

A) Lines 10-14 (No less...sitting president.)
B) Lines 14-15 (The gravity...cannot be overstated.)
C) Lines 15-16 (In it,...specific decisions)
D) Lines 41-43 ("When I go back...faith in the Europeans,)

17

The author's purpose of mentioning "climate change" (line 52) is to display the

A) problem the nation will ultimately encounter
B) problem demands our attention more than terrorism
C) issue Obama exploited to gloss over other crisis
D) an important issue Obama failed to meet

18

The author mentions ISIS in lines 50 to

A) emphasize a naïve indifference of Obama
B) describe the trivial subject
C) elicit Obama's priority
D) explain the uncertainty of Middle East

19

As used in line 74, "bigotry" most nearly means

A) discrimination
B) impartiality
C) adherence
D) overlooked evaluation

20

The author mentions David Frum mainly to

A) de-emphasize Goldberg's argument
B) cast aspersions on Goldberg's final essay
C) parody the words used by Barack Obama
D) rail against Western allies

21

The author's attitudes toward Barak Obama and David Frum are respectively

A) disappointment and acceptance
B) indifference and mild concern
C) praise and staunch advocacy
D) refusal and veneration

CONTINUE

1 1

Questions 22-31 are based on the following passage.

The following passage describes How 'Bout Them Apples Recent fruit deregulation bears little fruit By Shubhankar Chhokra May 8, 2015 Harvard University © The Harvard Crimson Reprinted with Permission

Passage 1

Nothing would please me more than writing an article chronicling mankind's fixation with the apple. That says a lot about me. Fortunately for you though, the apple is even more important as a commodity than an artifact, so this is the story of how one fruit might just determine the future of American agriculture.

Earlier this week, the United States Department of Agriculture announced that it is lifting its import restrictions on fresh apples from China. That means starting this month, China—the world's largest producer of apples—can freely enter American markets, selling cheap and low-quality fruit in direct competition with our nation's harvest.

American officials are hoping this decision would persuade the Chinese—who only currently import red and golden delicious apples from a handful of states—to loosen their own trade restrictions in good faith. As China's consumption of American apples is definitely nontrivial, this expectation of requital makes sense.

Interestingly, according to President of the Washington Apple Commission Todd Fryhover, Chinese consumers are especially hungry for more Red Delicious apples because their rich, crimson hue represents good fortune in their culture.

But flooding American markets with Chinese apples in hope of the reverse is ultimately unfruitful triage for the more pressing problem, one that is closer to home: we just had the largest apple crop in American history and need foreign buyers to compensate for lackluster domestic demand. Even if they do, it won't amount to much. If you've been following the Chinese's apple purchasing closely for the past couple years (like, who hasn't?), you would notice that China doesn't really need American apples.

Passage 2

Apples are important. They are lodged in our throats and imprinted on our cell phones. They proxy in for the unspecified fruit Eve gave Adam, and pies made out of them are quintessentially American. My graduating class planted 14 trees of them at our high school, and 30 years from now, we hope to return with spouses and children, hungry for the fruits of our labor. And as I eat this apple, alternating bites with lines of prose, I savor all this historical, cultural, and personal significance even more than its sweet flavor.

This is all to say the USDA is either lying or kidding itself when it says that it expects China to contribute no more than 0.4% of apples consumed in America. There are reasons why we haven't welcomed Chinese apples in the past. China's atrocious food safety regulations and pollution problems pose a serious threat to American consumers. And the USDA initially barred Chinese apples because they carry invasive pests like the Oriental fruit fly that could destroy entire crops of American apples. These dangers, unlike the government's attitude towards them, haven't changed. The integrity of the American economy does not boil down to apple trade. But at its core, the apple is important. It demystified gravity. It has kept doctor after doctor away. It almost killed Snow White, for Christ's sake. And in a matter of months, it will be shipped by the ton from China to a supermarket near you, leaving an important American industry to rot.

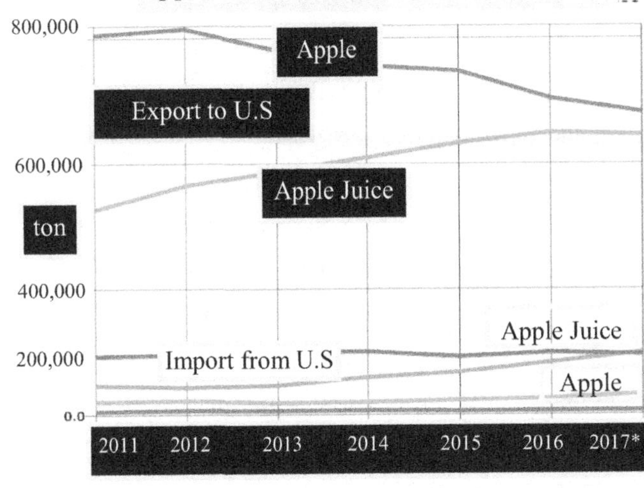

CONTINUE

1 1

22

In context, the author's tone in lines 1-15 ("Nothing … harvest") shifts from

A) awe to uncertainty
B) sadness to wonder
C) delight to concern
D) curiosity to frustration

23

According to the author, cheap fruits importation from China in lines 14 makes sense because

A) lifting its import restrictions on fresh apples from China prevents significant trade loss in other areas
B) fruit from China is different from ones the competitions produce in U.S.
C) Chinese to loosen their own trade restrictions can be guaranteed.
D) China's consumption of American apples in return will not be marginal

24

Which choice provides the best evidence for the answer to the previous question?

A) Lines 3-7 (Fortunately … agriculture.)
B) Lines 16-20 (American officials, … faith)
C) Lines 20-23 (As China's…senses)
D) Lines 37-41 (If you've…apples)

25

The statement in lines 24-29 indicates that Chinese consumers

A) value aesthetically pleasing fruit
B) savor rich taste of American apple
C) tend to relate crimson hue with culture
D) think Chinese apple has no crimson hue

26

In line 35, "lackluster" most nearly means

A) uninvolved
B) dwindling
C) lack of
D) diminishing

27

The parenthesis (like, who hasn't?) in line 39 in passage 1 primarily emphasizes

A) the importance of following the Chinese's apple purchasing trend
B) that everyone follows the Chinese's apple purchasing closely
C) the financial trade-off with China
D) tinged with humor to readers' reaction

28

In lines 71-76, the author's allusions include all of the followings EXCEPT

A) Historical allusion
B) Scientific allusion
C) Medicinal allusion
D) Literary allusion

29

The author of Passage 2 would most likely regard "the American officials" (line 16, passage 1) are

A) essentially knowledgeable for their expectation
B) consistent with the trade restrictions
C) fearful to American angry farmers
D) less concerned about invasive pests than trade unbalance

30

Which choice provides the best evidence for the answer to the previous question?

A) Lines 45-46 (Apple are important… cell phone.)
B) Lines 57-60 (This is all...America.)
C) Lines 67-69 (These dangers…haven't changed)
D) Lines 69-70 (The integrity...apple trade.)

31

The graph most directly supports for which idea in the passage?

A) American officials in lines 15-16
B) President, Todd Fryhover in lines 24-28
C) The author's analysis in line 37-41
D) USDA expectation in lines 57-60

CONTINUE

1

Questions 32-41 are based on the following passage.

The following passages describes about the A Death on Facebook How social media portrays mortality By Sam Danello May 4, 2015 Harvard University © The Harvard Crimson
Reprinted with Permission

Two Saturdays ago, a 7.8 magnitude earthquake ripped through Nepal, resulting in widespread damage to infrastructure, irreparable harm to historical sites, and, most tragically, the deaths of thousands and thousands of human beings. Such an event should inspire mourning and contemplation—sorrow for the people who lost their lives and gratitude for the lives that we still have.

Instead, in the aftermath of the tremors, a different sort of behavior rose up from the rubble. News outlets ran reports of individuals—some tourists and some Nepalese citizens—stopping in front of destroyed buildings for quick selfies. Here was one sort of earthquake response: Survey the tragic scene, take a smiling photo, and then skip off in the opposite direction. If social media glorifies life—capturing our most intimate moments and recording our funniest jokes—then it does the opposite for death.

To a certain degree, you can blame the photographers. A tactful person should have enough respect to avoid behavior that reduces a death into a tagged detail.

Yet a larger, and more disconcerting, criticism of the selfie-behavior that emerged out of the Nepal earthquake has to do with the nature of social media itself. Against a background of party photos and emojis, mortality loses all of its defining gravitas. The deceased become abject and even absurd—they simply cannot coexist with this sepia-tinted world in which every comment is an inside joke. Put it this way: There is nothing more unsettling than the Facebook profile of a dead teenager. I think the uneasy feeling derives from the lightheartedness of the content that dominates any social media platform. There are airy "lol" comments; there are witty photo captions. There is rarely, if ever, a reminder that this person—this very same smiling person—is fragile enough to die. How can you reconcile social media's giddy artificiality with death's stone-cold reality?

How can you connect a corpse to a profile picture? There is the illusion of popularity, the illusion of philanthropy, and the illusion of substance. In some ways, however, I think that the mortality-defying effects of social media are the most illusory and therefore the most dangerous.

The easiest recommendation is to unplug your life and spend more time appreciating the fragile beauty of real things. The fact that something—a season, a flower, or a person—is temporary, essentially makes that something more valuable.

But realizing that everyone, myself included, needs social media for practical life purposes, a more realistic suggestion revolves around mindfulness. "Mindfulness"—this may sound like an empty word, but I believe that it encapsulates the overarching message that I've tried to drive home throughout a semester of column writing. The Internet is powerful, practical, and practically powerful. You need to use it for these reasons. However, you need to use the Internet well, which requires significant reflection. Think hard before you click to open a new tab; philosophize as you sign into Facebook. Everything about the Internet conspires to sweep you away into an arcade world of images and sounds, but you must resist in order to maintain your identity and willpower.

After all, your humanity is based in this resistance—and in the wonderful freedom that follows.

The major time spend on Facebook 2012 vs.2016

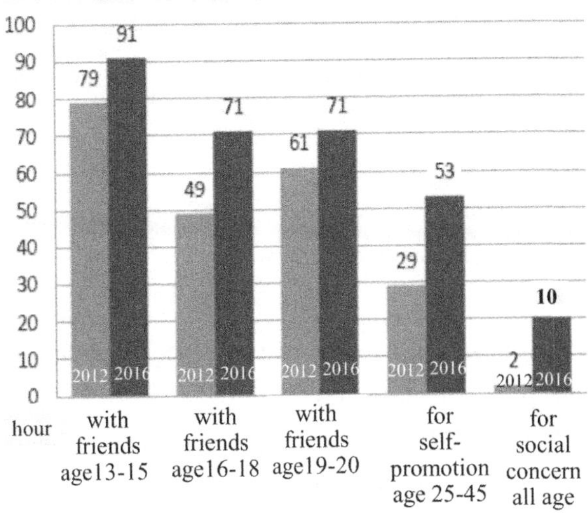

CONTINUE

1 1

32

The author mentions social media primarily encourage people to view death as

A) medium to disrespect human tragedy

B) an opportunity to increase followers

C) a source of psychological pain

D) a condition to be dealt with an emotional level

33

Which choice provides the best evidence for the answer to the previous question?

A) Lines 6-9 (Such an event...we still have.)

B) Lines 10-11 (Instead,...from the rubble.)

C) Lines 17-20 (If social media...opposite for death)

D) Lines 21-22 (To a certain degree...photographers.)

34

From the author's view, the photographers mentioned in line 22 are

A) the main culprits who exploit Social media

B) tactful people who know how to reduce a death into a tagged detail

C) less to be criticized

D) professionals to deserve enough respect

35

The aspect of the social media that the author condemns most is the illusion of

A) substance

B) popularity

C) philanthropy

D) defying human mortality

36

Which choice provides the best evidence for the answer to the previous question?

A) Lines 21-22 (To a certain degree... photographers.)

B) Lines 35-37 (I think...media platform.)

C) Lines 45-47 (There is the illusion...substance)

D) Lines 47-49 (In some ways,...most dangerous.)

37

In line 41, "reconcile" most nearly means

A) balance

B) declare a truce

C) make convenient

D) make available

38

In lines 52-54, "a season, a flower, or a person" conveys the author's opinion that these are

A) temporary, therefore less valuable

B) universal, therefore easy to understand

C) ephemeral, but reveal the profound truth

D) neither realistic nor practical

39

The author's perspective on Facebook is that of

A) an unsympathetic outsider

B) an appreciative user

C) a lamentable observer

D) an angry protestor

40

In line 68, "conspires" most nearly means

A) intrigue

B) connive

C) collaborate

D) combine

41

Which claim about Facebook is supported by the graph?

A) All age groups are very responsive to social concerns

B) 13-15 age group represents the users for the practical life purposes in line 56

C) All age groups concern the least on social concerns

D) All age groups prioritize self-promotion than spending time with friends

CONTINUE

1

Questions 42-52 are based on the following passages

The following passage discusses Brain Research through Advancing Innovative Neurotechnologies (BRAIN)

Brain Research through Advancing Innovative Neurotechnologies (BRAIN) Initiative has the potential to do for neuroscience what the Human Genome Project did for genomics by supporting the development and application of innovative technologies that can create a dynamic understanding of brain function. It aims to help researchers uncover the mysteries of brain disorders, such as Alzheimer's and Parkinson's diseases.

These technologies will shed light on the complex links between brain function and behavior. For instance, by combining advanced genetic and optical techniques, scientists can now use pulses of light to determine how specific cell activities in the brain affect behavior. While these technological innovations have contributed substantially to our expanding knowledge of the brain, significant breakthroughs in how we treat neurological and psychiatric disease will require a new generation of tools to enable researchers to record signals from brain cells in much greater numbers and at even faster speeds. That's where the BRAIN Initiative comes in.

A Scientific Vision, which articulates the scientific goals of The BRAIN Initiative at the NIH charts a multi-year scientific plan for achieving these goals, including timetables, milestones, and cost estimates. and focused effort across the agency. Once completed, with Neuro-adaptive technology program, Systems-Based Neurotechnology for Emerging Therapies (SUBNETS) can measure and modulate, with the first set of preliminary model closed-loop medical devices, networks of neurons with intractable psychiatric illness and alleviate severe symptoms of diseases.

BRAIN Initiative and Related Funding
(budget authority in millions of dollars)

Program/ ACCOUNT	FY 2014 Actual	FY 2015 Actual	FY 2016 Actual	FY 2016 Actual	Percent Change	
					pres.	FY15
NSF Understanding the Brain	**93**	**106**	**144**	**147**	**2.1%**	**38.0%**
Specific to BRAIN Initiative	**23**	**48**	**72**	**72**	**0.0%**	**47.6%**
Natl Institutes of Health	**40**	**65**	**135**	**150**	**11.1%**	**130.8%**
DAPRA: Biomedical Technology	**121**	**160**	**114**	**114**		

42

The primary purpose of the BRAIN Initiative is to help researchers

A) advance Human Genome Project

B) understand brain function and disorder

C) sequence the human genome

D) develop better human brain

43

Which choice provides the best evidence for the answer to the previous question

A) Lines 1-6 (Brain Research...brain function.)

B) Lines 16-23 (While these technological...faster speeds.)

C) Lines 23-24 (That's where...comes in.)

D) Lines 25-29 (A Scientific Vision...across the agency.)

1

CONTINUE

1

44

The "mysteries" in line 7 implies that at the current stage, the research of brain disorders

A) is dynamically improving

B) is expected to be unlocked pretty soon

C) is still at understanding level

D) has seen mysterious breakthrough recently

45

The author mentioned Human Genome project in line 3 mainly to

A) celebrates what it did to genomics

B) compare what BRAIN Initiative can do to neuroscience

C) introduce neurotechnology

D) present achievement of BRAIN Initiative

46

The author uses "While these...of the brain," (lines 16-18) to make which of the following points?

A) BRAIN Initiatives is even more pivotal

B) BRAIN Initiative may succeed without these technological innovations

C) These technological innovations are outmoded

D) These technological innovations are role models

47

In line 25, the author mentions "A Scientific Vision" mainly to

A) present scientific goals of the BRAIN Initiative

B) voice doubt about its undertaking

C) raise budget surplus issue in a single project

D) celebrate goals of BRAIN that are achieved

48

The author mentions the significance of optical techniques in line 13 because

A) it is the state-of-the-art technology

B) it will cure brain disorders such as Alzheimer's

C) it allows to combine advanced genetics

D) it is a part of technologies that BRAIN can use

49

Which of the following objectives is committed by BRAIN Initiative?

I. Multi-year scientific plan for the Working Group

I. Financial estimates for the research

II. Developing medicines for the brain disorder

A) I only

B) II only

C) III only

D) I and II only

50

In line 34, "alleviate" most nearly means

A) make less severe

B) make dull

C) reduce temper

D) improve vitality

51

The passage suggests that Systems-Based Neurotechnology for Emerging Therapies (line 30)

A) is being conducted by medical institutions as the proven closed-loop medical devices

B) is being widely applied to treat post-traumatic stress disorder

C) is currently focusing on psychiatric illness

D) is only a prototype and not being practically \ applied yet.

52

Which of the following statements best reflects the chart after the passage?

A) Specific to BRAIN Initiative reveals some funding issues over the past years

B) Specific to BRAIN Initiative programs reduced its research areas in 2016 compared to 2015

C) The role of Biomedical technology in BRAIN Initiative has increased in 2016

D) Understanding the Brain played the second most significant role in 2016 in terms of funding

STOP

If you finish before time is called,
you may check your work on this section.

Do not turn to the next section.

Writing and Language Test 1
35 MINUTES, 44 QUESTIONS

Each passage below is accompanied by a number of questions. For some questions, you will consider how the passage might be revised to improve the expression of ideas. For other questions, you will consider how the passage might be edited to correct errors in sentence structure, usage, or punctuation. A passage or a question may be accompanied by one or more graphics (such as a table or graph) that you will consider as you make revising and editing decisions.

Questions 1-11 are based on the following passage.

BREXIT

The United Kingdom European Union membership referendum, also known as the EU referendum and the Brexit [1] referendum, which a referendum that took place on Thursday 23 June 2016 in the United Kingdom to [2] gauge support for the country's continued membership in the European Union. The referendum result was not legally binding. The result was split [3] with the constituent countries of the United Kingdom, with a majority in England and Wales voting to leave, and a majority in Scotland and Northern Ireland, voting to remain.

To start the process to leave the [4] EU, which is expected to take several years, the British government will have to invoke Article 50 of the Treaty on European Union.

1

A) NO CHANGE

B) referendum, are a referendum

C) referendum, as a referendum

D) referendum, was a referendum

2

Which of the following alternatives would NOT be appropriate?

A) check

B) measure

C) see

D) alter

3

A) NO CHANGE

B) into

C) between

D) in

4

A) NO CHANGE

B) EU expects

C) EU, expecting

D) EU and to expect

CONTINUE

2 2

The UK government has announced formal process of leaving the EU [5] although revoking the vote might be possible.

Membership of the EU had long been a topic of debate in the United Kingdom. [6] The country joined the European Economic Community (EEC, or "Common Market") in 1973.

Britain Stronger in Europe was the official group campaigning for the UK to remain in the EU and was led by the Prime Minister David Cameron and Chancellor George Osborne. [7] Other campaign groups, political parties, businesses, trade unions, newspapers and prominent individuals were also involved, and each side had supporters from across the political spectrum.

5

Which choice provides a supporting example that emphasizes the main point of the sentence?

A) NO CHANGE

B) ,confirming the due date by March 2019.

C) , confirming Brexit was driven by the official process

D) , using term "hard Brexit" rather than "soft Brexit"

6

If the writer were to delete the underlined portion, the sentence would primarily lose:

A) The meaning of EEC

B) The formal step to leave E.U. after the referendum.

C) The description of historical overview.

D) The importance of EEC to the United Kingdom.

7

At this point, the author wishes to add the following information.

Vote Leave was the official group campaigning for the UK to leave the EU and was fronted by the Conservative MPs Boris Johnson and Michael Gove.

Should the author make this addition here?

A) Yes, because it provides added information about the history of conflicts.

B) Yes, because it connects with the previous sentence.

C) No, because it is mentioned in the following sentences.

D) No, because it is not persuasive.

CONTINUE

2 2

Financial markets [8] <u>were reacted</u> negatively in the immediate aftermath of the result. Investors in worldwide stock markets lost more than the [9] <u>equivalent of</u> 2 trillion United States dollars on 24 June 2016, making it the worst single-day loss in history. The market losses amounted to 3 trillion US dollars by 27 June. The value of the pound sterling against the US dollar fell to a 31-year low. The UK's and the EU's sovereign debt credit rating was also lowered by Standard & Poor's. By 29 June, the markets had returned to growth and the value of the pound had begun to rise.

Immediately after the result, the Prime Minister [10] <u>David Cameron had announced he would resign, having campaigned</u> unsuccessfully for a "remain" vote on behalf of Britain Stronger in Europe and HM Government. He was succeeded by Theresa May on 13 July.

8

A) NO CHANGE
B) were in great reaction
C) reacted by
D) reacted

9

Which of the following alternatives would NOT be appropriate?

A) equivocal to
B) equal to
C) almost
D) nearly

10

Which choice expresses the underlined sentence most effectively?

A) NO CHANGE
B) David Cameron followed the result, Cameron announced that he would resign, after he campaigned
C) David Cameron announced he would resign, having campaigned
D) David Cameron, by announcing that he would resign, having campaigned

CONTINUE

2

United Kingdom European Union membership referendum	
Should the United Kingdom remain a member of the European Union or leave the European Union?	
Location	United Kingdom Gibraltar
Date	23 June 2016

Results		
	Votes	**%**
Leave	**17,410,742**	**51.89%**
Remain	16,141,241	48.11%
Valid votes	33,551,983	99.92%
Invalid or blank votes	25,359	0.08%
Total votes	**33,577,342**	**100.00%**
Registered voters/ turnout	46,500,001	72.21%

11

In reference to the passage, which choice offers an accurate interpretation of the table on the left ?

A) The table results reflect the cause of the former Prime Minister David Cameron's leaving the office.

B) The referendum result was legally binding.

C) As the referendum confirmed, United Kingdom will start the formal process of leaving the EU immediately.

D) As the referendum confirmed, the Leave group will leave the EU, and the Remain group will remain in the EU.

CONTINUE

2 2

Questions 12-22 are based on the following passage.

Are we alone?

{ Paragraph 1 }

Many scientists believe we are not alone in the universe. It's probable, they say, that life could have [12] rise on at least some of the billions of planets thought to exist in our galaxy alone -- just as it did here on planet Earth. This basic question about our place in the Universe is one that may be answered by scientific investigations. (A)

{ Paragraph 2 }

Experts from NASA and its partner institutions addressed this question on July 14, at a public talk held at NASA Headquarters in Washington. [13] They outlined NASA's roadmap to the search for life in the [14] universe, it was an ongoing journey that involves a number of current and future telescopes. Sometime in the near future, people will be able to point to a star and say, 'that star has a planet like Earth'," says Sara Seager, professor of planetary science and physics at the Massachusetts Institute of Technology in Cambridge, Massachusetts. [15] However, the impression of how common planets are in the Milky way adversely creates backlash among scientists. (B)

12

A) NO CHANGE
B) raise
C) arisen
D) arouse

13

A) NO CHANGE
B) He
C) It
D) Those

14

A) NO CHANGE
B) universe, and an ongoing journey
C) universe because it was an ongoing journey
D) universe, an ongoing journey

15

Which choice emphasizes the anticipation of some Scientists' belief of the existence of a planet like Earth.

A) NO CHANGE
B) There are 100 billion planets in our Milky Way galaxy
C) Astronomers have currently discovered the evidential proof that there is no chance for Venus to sustain life.
D) Astronomers acknowledge that under the current technology, there are many obstacles to materialize our space safari project.

CONTINUE

2 2

{ **Paragraph 3** }

NASA's quest to study planetary systems around other stars started with ground-based observatories, then moved to space-based assets like the Hubble Space Telescope, the Spitzer Space Telescope, and the Kepler Space Telescope. Today's telescopes can look at many stars and tell if they have one or more orbiting planets.(C)
[16] However, they can determine if the planets are the right distance away from the star to have liquid water, the key ingredient to life as we know [17] it.

{ **Paragraph 4** }

The NASA roadmap will continue with the launch of the Transiting Exoplanet Surveying Satellite TESS) in 2017 and the James Webb Space Telescope. These upcoming telescopes [18] would find and characterize [19] a host of new exoplanets—those planets that orbit other stars—expanding our knowledge of their atmospheres and diversity. The Webb telescope and WFIRST-AFTA will lay the groundwork, and future missions will extend the search for the nearby planets that are similar to Earth in size and mass, a key step in the search for life.
(D)

16

A) NO CHANGE
B) Although at this phase,
C) Even more,
D) Therefore,

17

A) NO CHANGE
B) liquid water is the essential to sustain life.
C) water can be used to form life.
D) that the planets' distance is a way to understand whether liquid water exists or not.

18

A) NO CHANGE
B) will find
C) have to find
D) that find

19

Which choice most dramatically emphasizes the massive scale of upcoming discovery using the telescope observation projects?

A) NO CHANGE
B) more reliable data of
C) groundbreaking discovery of
D) the actual photographs of

CONTINUE

2 2

"This technology we are using to explore exoplanets is real," said John Grunsfeld, astronaut and associate administrator for NASA's Science Mission Directorate in Washington. "The James Webb Space Telescope and the next advances are happening now. These are not dreams -- this is what we do at NASA."

[20] After its launch in 2009, Kepler has dramatically changed what we know about exoplanets, finding most of the more than 5,000 potential exoplanets, of which more than 1700 have been confirmed. The Kepler observations have led to estimates of billions of planets in our galaxy, and shown that most planets within one astronomical unit are less than three times the diameter of Earth. Kepler also found the first Earth-size planet to orbit in the "habitable zone" of a star, the region where liquid water can pool on the surface.

20

A) NO CHANGE
B) Having followed
C) With
D) Since

21

Suppose the writer's primary purpose is to describe the possibility of searching for life.
Would this essay accomplish that purpose?

A) Yes, because it tells about a variety of challenges the scientists face along with their searching for life in exoplanets.
B) Yes, because it focuses primarily on scientists' application of a various types of telescopes and other methods in quest of searching for life in the universe.
C) No, because it focuses mainly on the projects to be undertaken in the future.
D) No, because it focuses on the limited applications within the scope of modern technology in finding life in the universe.

22

The writer wants to add the following sentence to the essay:

What are the next steps to finding life elsewhere?

The sentence would most logically be placed at point:

A) A in {Paragraph 1}
B) B in {Paragraph 2}
C) C in {Paragraph 3}
D) D in {Paragraph 4}

CONTINUE

2

Questions 23-33 are based on the following passage.

Black ice

Black [23] ice, sometimes called clear ice, refers to a thin coating of glaze ice on a surface, especially on roads. The ice itself is not black, but visually transparent, [24] allowing the often black road below to be seen through it. The typically low level of noticeable ice pellets, snow, or sleet [25] surrounds black ice means that areas of the ice are often practically invisible to drivers or people stepping on it. [26] Their is, thus, a risk of skidding and a subsequent accident due to the unexpected loss of traction. The term *black ice* in the United States is often incorrectly used to describe any type of ice that forms on roadways, even when standing water on roads turns to ice as the temperature falls below freezing. Correctly defined, black ice is formed on relatively dry roads, rendering it invisible to drivers. It occurs when in the textures present in all pavements very slightly below the top of the road surface contain water or moisture, thereby presenting a dry surface to tires until that water or moisture freezes and expands; drivers then find they are riding above the road surface on a honeycombed invisible sheet of ice.

23

Which of the following alternatives to the underlined portion would NOT be acceptable?

A) ice, sometimes called clear ice, refers
B) ice—sometimes called clear ice—refers
C) ice, sometimes called clear ice refers
D) ice (sometimes called clear ice) refers

24

If the writer were to delete the underlined portion of the sentence, it would primarily lose:

A) an idea that emphasizes the reason for an optical illusion
B) a statement that introduces the main focus of the following paragraph.
C) an unnecessary detail that contradicts information presented earlier in the paragraph.
D) a vivid image that most observers want to find out beneath the Black Ice.

25

A) NO CHANGE
B) surrounding black ice meaning
C) surrounding black ice means
D) surrounding black ice mean

26

A) NO CHANGE
B) Their have been
C) There is
D) There are

CONTINUE

2 2

Because it represents only a thin accumulation, black ice is highly transparent and thus difficult to see as compared with snow, frozen slush, or thicker ice layers. [27] In addition, it often is interleaved with wet pavement, which is nearly identical in [28] appearance, this makes driving, cycling or walking on affected surfaces extremely dangerous. Deicing with salt (sodium chloride) is effective to down temperatures of about −18 °C (0 °F).

At below –18 °C, black ice can form on roadways when the moisture from automobile exhaust condenses on the road surface. Such conditions caused multiple accidents in Minnesota when the temperatures dipped below –18 °C for a prolonged period of time in December 2008. [29] With salt's ineffectiveness at melting ice at these temperatures compounds the problem. Black ice may form even when the ambient temperature is several degrees above the freezing point of water 0 °C (32 °F), [30] if the air warms suddenly after a prolonged cold spell that has left the surface of the roadway well below the freezing point temperature.

27

A) NO CHANGE
B) On the contrary,
C) Consequently,
D) In spite of such a thin accumulation,

28

Which of the following alternatives to the underlined portion would NOT be acceptable?

A) appearance, which makes
B) appearance, making
C) appearance. This makes
D) appearance, this makes

29

A) NO CHANGE
B) Salt's
C) Salt
D) Sodium Chloride

30

In the preceding sentence, the underlined portion of if-clause primarily serves to indicate:

A) that black ice phenomenon could occur in many southern states with mild temperature
B) the strikingly complex characteristics of Black Ice
C) that technique to prevent black ice is not very well developed at present
D) the atmospheric conditions that lead to Black Ice formation under certain temperature.

CONTINUE

2 2

On December 1, 2013, heavy post-Thanksgiving weekend traffic encountered black ice on the westbound I-290 expressway in Worcester, Massachusetts. A chain reaction series of crashes resulted, involving three tractor-trailers and over 60 other vehicles. The ice [31] had formed suddenly on a long downward slope, [32] surprising drivers coming over the crest of a hill, who could not see crashed vehicles ahead until it was too late to stop on the slick pavement. Bridges and overpasses can be especially dangerous. Black ice forms first on bridges and overpasses because air can circulate both above and below the surface of the elevated roadway, causing the bridge pavement temperature to drop more rapidly.

31

A) NO CHANGE
B) formed suddenly in a matter of seconds
C) has formed suddenly
D) formed suddenly

32

A) NO CHANGE
B) surprised
C) surprisingly alarmed
D) cautioning

33

Suppose the writer's primary purpose has been to write an essay summarizing the road trip safety education in winter. Would this essay accomplish that purpose?

A) Yes, because it discusses the complete road trip safety measures in winter driving
B) Yes, because it demonstrates the National Transportation Safety Board's effort to educate the dangers of Black Ice.
C) No, because it focusses instead on what the Black Ice is, and how it forms.
D) No, because it focuses instead on describing the method of distinguishing Black Ice from White Ice.

CONTINUE

2 2

Questions 34-44 are based on the following passage.

9 TO 5 GROUP

In 2005 Brad Neuberg used "coworking" to describe a physical space which he originally called a "9 to 5 group". Neuberg organized a co-working [34] site the "Hat Factory" in San Francisco, a live-work loft that was home to three technology workers, and open to others during the day. Brad was also one of the founders of Citizen Space, the first "Work Only" co-working space. Now, co-working places exist worldwide, with over 700 locations in the United States alone. Since 2006 a few studies have shown the number of co-working spaces and available seats have roughly doubled each year, [35] incrementing nearly as much as two times within twelve-month cycle. San Francisco continues to have a large presence in the co-working community [36] and being home to a growing number of co-working places including RocketSpace, Sandbox Suites, and Citizen Space. The New York co-working community has also been evolving rapidly in places like Regus and Rockefeller Group Business Center. [37] The demand for co-working in Brooklyn neighborhoods is almost never ending.

34

A) NO CHANGE
B) site, the "Hat Factory,"
C) site, the "Hat Factory"
D) site the "Hat Factory,"

35

A) NO CHANGE
B) almost reaching 200 percent increase.
C) impressively expanding its numbers every twelve-month.
D) delete the underlined portion.

36

A) NO CHANGE
B) homing to
C) and has home to
D) and is home to

37

The writer is considering adding the following sentence:

Several new startups like WeWork have been expanding all over the city.

Should the writer make this addition here?

A) Yes, because it connects the paragraph's point about the rapid expansion of co-working community in the certain region.
B) Yes, because it explains the significant number of startup business in New York
C) No, because it should focus and address only one startup company and shouldn't include information about other startups.
D) No, because it deviates from the paragraph's focus on major building like Rockefeller Group Business Center

CONTINUE

2 2

[38] Despite of the rise in the Millennials workforce, nearly one in 10 workers in the Gowanus area work from home that adds the reason for high demand. The industrial area of Gowanus, Brooklyn is seeing a surge in new startups like Co-workers, which are redesigning old buildings into new co-working spaces.

Some co-working places were developed by nomadic Internet entrepreneurs [39] lured by an enormous financial interest.

A 2007 survey showed that many employees worry about feeling isolated and losing human interaction if they were to telecommute. Roughly a third of both private and public-sector workers also reported that they didn't want to stay at home during work.

As of 2012, the U.K. is among the most responsive European country to the idea of collaborative working, with a special focus on London. The city leads the co-working market not only for the large number of co-working places it offers but also for the [40] variety of places that exist to fit the differing needs among start-ups, entrepreneurs and freelancers, who avoid the existing office structure.

38

A) NO CHANGE

B) Due to

C) For example,

D) In addition to

39

Which choice maintains the essay's positive tone and most strongly supports the main theme of the essay?

A) NO CHANGE

B) seeking an alternative to working in coffee shops and cafes, or to isolation in index pendent or home offices.

C) wanting to find a place both to live and work

D) who were often dripped away from the mainstream of the industry.

40

Which of the following alternatives to the underlined portion would NOT be acceptable?

A) mobile

B) unique

C) conventional

D) non-traditional

CONTINUE

2

Camden Collective is a regeneration project in London [41] that re-purposes previously vacant and underused properties, and opened its first 'wire-less wall-less' co-working space in 2009. In March 2012 Google along with several local partners opened a co-working place in the heart of East London. Campus London is located in Tech City and helps multiple start-ups to grow under the same roof, by mentoring them and giving them the chance to learn more through the events that run everyday, [42] through which Campus London assists many startups. In June 2013, the U.K. Government announced it would be applying co-working principles to a new pilot scheme for its 'One Public Sector Estate' strategy covering 12 local authorities in England which will encourage councils to work with central government departments and other bodies so that staff share buildings.

41

If the writer were to delete the underlined portion of the sentence, the essay would primarily lose details that:

A) illustrate some of the Camden collective Project's features that transformed old buildings

B) hint Google's considerable contribution

C) support the essay's claim that London has become the hub of the co-working community in the world

D) clarify an unfamiliar term "Camden collective Projects"

42

A) NO CHANGE

B) whereby startups receive valuable mentoring

C) through which Campus London provides daily events

D) Delete the underlined portion

CONTINUE

2

Co-working is also becoming more common in continental Europe, with the startup metropolis Berlin being a major booster for this development. [43] This kind of working environment is not exclusive to big cities. Also smaller urban areas with many young and creative people and especially university cities may offer coworking places, with *Cowork Greifswald* in Germany being one example. Cooperations between co-working spaces and academic environments are focused.

43

A) NO CHANGE
B) For example, this kind
C) Generally speaking, this kind
D) Commonly, this kind

44

Suppose the writer's primary purpose has been to explain how co-working environment has become new trends throughout North America and Europe. Would this essay accomplish that purpose?

A) Yes, because it describes the architectural design of New York co-working places.
B) Yes, because it enumerates a number of events that successfully transformed old buildings and incubate startup entrepreneurs
C) No, because it focuses more specifically on the major startup supporters like Google or Rockefeller Group Business Center.
D) No, because it focuses on positive prospects only, while there exist plausible negatives.

STOP

If you finish before time is called,
you may check your work on this section.

Do not turn to the next section.

Chapter 1 Summary

Chapter Summary contains equal portions of

-12 Absolute Patterns for Reading Section

-20 Common Patterns for Incorrect Choices in Reading

-70 Absolute Patterns for Writing and Language Section

-24 Common Patterns for Incorrect Choices in Writing

You may study all at once to significantly improve your understanding and your scores.

Chapter 1

12 Absolute Patterns for the Reading Section

San: Do you know one of the worst mistakes that you can make while solving the reading questions, Jimin?

Nosediving into multiple choices even without knowing what the question is asking can cause a serious mistake. You should understand the question type by separating into two main parts: the pattern and the keywords.

Question Pattern never changes in the actual test,

while the keywords make each question unique.
The keywords are boldfaced here.

Q13. **Absolute Pattern 4: Example Question**
Understanding example sentence and the true purpose behind a specific name or idea.
Question Pattern: The author mentions **Russia and Syria** (lines 29-31) to suggest the

A) difficulty of controlling foreign affairs B) extent to which real impact cannot be reached C) extended examples of world's misery **D) degree of disappointment Obama rendered**	D) Russia and Syria issues are mere examples that support the main idea. The answer can be found not in the example but in the topic or concluding sentence that hosts the example because the author usually employs an example to emphasize his main idea.

Question Pattern is the main frame of the question, and the frame never changes. The number of these unchanging question patterns is very limited. In fact, there are only 12 of them. These patterns will appear in your test by slightly modifying some words-if not exactly written as shown in this book.
By understanding these 12 patterns, several advantages will reward you:

√ you will be familiar with tricky terms in the question so that you can save time in the actual test.
√ you will be able to guess what the question is basically seeking even without reading the passage.
√ you can avoid possible confusion or mistakes such as "EXCEPT" questions.

For instance, the above Q13 pattern "the author mentions" smells like example question that supports the purpose of the example.

Question Keywords make each question unique.
Test creators pick up some keywords from the passage and then plug those keywords into each question pattern to create each question.

Noun and verbs are the most common question keywords in the reading passage and each question.
Adjectives and adverbs seldom provide the Answer.
Understanding question alone, for example, knowing the tones in passage, can quite often solve the question.

Chapter 1

12 Absolute Patterns for the Reading Section

Category A: Content Question has six patterns:

San: The entire 52 questions in the reading section, both literary and informational passages, can be categorized into two parts:
Category A: Content Question;
Category B: Technique Question

12 Absolute Patterns—mostly one pattern per question —plus 20 Common Patterns for Incorrect Choices will be absolutely the most effective and systemic way to improve your scores.

Jimin: I sometimes don't even understand the meaning of the question. Can I be saved?

San: Your humble vocabulary could be one of the two reasons. Email me: satvancouver@gmail.com
I will give you the SAT ABSOLUTE Vocabulary with a picture book for FREE. But remember! I can't memorize them for you.

Category A: Content Question has six patterns:

▶ **Absolute Pattern 1: Main Idea Question**
Finding the main idea of the entire passage or the paragraph

▶ **Absolute Pattern 2: Summary Question**
Summarizing a sentence, or the entire paragraph

▶ **Absolute Pattern 4: Example Question**
Understanding example sentence and the true purpose behind a specific name or idea.

▶ **Absolute Pattern 5: Word-In-Context Question**
Finding clue words and keywords from the sentence in question

▶ **Absolute Pattern 8: Understanding the True Purpose**
Finding the true purpose of the statement

▶ **Absolute Pattern 11:** Textual Evidence Question
Finding evidence for the previous question

Chapter 1

12 Absolute Patterns for the Reading Section

Category A: Content Question has six patterns:

San: The Content question may also be called the local question.
Either with the line reference number (i.e., line 5) or without it, the content question normally asks localized, detailed information from only one or two sentences in the passage.

The question may ask explicitly stated keywords in the sentences, or, in more complex level, implicitly analogous (similar) situations within a sentence.

San: Neither of the cases requires the holistic understanding of the entire passage. Reading only the target sentence will save your precious time and mental horsepower.
Now. Let's talk about the Content Question Patterns.

Absolute Pattern 1: Main Idea Question

San: The main idea question asks either from the entire passage or a paragraph.

When question asks about the main idea of the entire passage, the answer is highly likely to be located in the concluding paragraph.—if not the last sentence.

To get the answer, the best way is to skip and save it for last until you have solved all the other questions because you might need to know the general idea of the entire passage).

For instance, if you found option (A) from the middle of the second paragraph while option (B) from the concluding paragraph (e.g., the fifth paragraph), the answer will be more likely (B) than (A) due to the unique characteristic of this question.

And also, the frequency does matter in the main idea question.

As an example, if option (A) has the keywords that appeared three times throughout the passage while option (B) five times, then (B) has the greater chance to be the answer because (B) appeared nearly twice more.

Chapter 2

12 Absolute Patterns for the Reading Section

Finally, there's a technique called "amplifier."
The amplifier is located right next to the sentence in question. The amplifier starts with a pronoun, such as "It" or "This"

The amplifier sentence often emphasizes—or de-emphasizes—the sentence in question, hence the answer. Also, pay special attention to the contrasting transitional conjunctions, transitional words or a phrase such as "because", "but", "however", "with all due respect", etc. They will always give you the answer either directly or indirectly.

Absolute Pattern 2: Summary Question

The basic technique to find the answer is almost the same as pattern 1: Main Idea Question.
The major difference, however, —especially in the literary passage—can be seen in its focusing on the manner of voice, tone, and the sentence style.
In literary passage, the answer often carries more subjective words, such as "criticize", "emphatic", "celebrate."

The summary question in informational passage (Science, History, and Social) is quite similar to the main idea question in that they both tend to apply broad and neutral tone in the keywords. That is, informational passage does not carry emotional tone like "blame," "criticize," or celebrates." Instead, it uses "approve" or disapprove."

Also, the Summary question in Informational passage looks like logic question. instead of relying heavily on the ambiguous context, it presents straightforward answer to those who are familiar with types of passages in natural science, history, social science.

70 Absolute Patterns for Writing Section

70 Absolute Patterns for Writing Section are created to introduce the most important grammar rules applied in the real SAT Writing and Language Test.

Question 1
Down the road from the school, my brother attend, Seven Eleven convenient store is always open, and some customers are always there.

A) NO CHANGE
B) school, my brother attends
C) school my brother attends
D) school, which is my brother attends,

RULE #1 Hint: Quick Interjection	**Restrictive Modifier** The correct answer is C. "the school" in sentence is not any schools in general but the only one where "my brother attends, which is located down the road near Seven Eleven convenient store" Therefore, it is an essential part of the sentence and needs to be considered as a part of the main sentence without offsetting (Be careful. It's not upsetting) with a pair of commas.

Question 2
It is comforting to see that the Seven Eleven store. And its customers are always there.

A) NO CHANGE
B) Seven Eleven store and that its customers
C) Seven Eleven store and its customers
D) Seven Eleven store that has the customers

RULE #2 Hint: That	**That-Clause as a Direct Subject** The correct answer is C. C) "that the Seven Eleven store and its customers" is the plural subject and completes the clause by using the plural verb "are." A) is incorrect because "that the Seven Eleven store" has no verb. B) is incorrect because of the same reason as (A). D) is incorrect because "are" is plural verb, while "the Seven Eleven store" is a singular, the subject-verb disagreement. The verb should be "is."

Question 3

The police's reasoning implied that, even if the robber was wearing a mask, it had enough knowledge to collect the evidence: such as the robber's height matching the suspect, weight, and foot size.

A) NO CHANGE
B) evidence; the height, weight, and foot size.
C) evidence, the height, weight, and foot size.
D) evidence: the height, weight, and foot size.

RULE #3
Hint:
Colon

The Usage of Colon

The correct answer is D.

D) The single most important purpose of colon is to introduce things.
It can introduce just about anything: a list of words, a list of phrases, and a list of clauses.
"...evidence: *the height, weight, and foot size.* "

A) is incorrect because colon means "such as." That is, they deliver basically the same function, and therefore one of them should be removed.

B) uses a semi-colon instead of colon. The colon and semicolon are very different. The primal purpose of the semicolon is to connect the following clause. It has no such a function to list information.

C) changes the original meaning by putting a comma after "evidence."

More Examples and Explanations

Colon can describe almost any form of statement.
-Monkey has only one desire on its mind: banana.
-Monkey has only one desire on its mind: a pile of banana.
-Monkey has only one desire on its mind: it wants to have a pile of banana.
-Monkey has three desires on its mind: finding banana trees, piling banana, eating a banana.

Now compare the following two sentences
-Apple corporation's cellphone beats its competitors specifically in the core area of waterproof functionality.

-Apple corporation's cellphone beats its competitors specifically in the core area: waterproof functionality.

As seen in the above comparisons, the main function of the colon is not only to introduce things but also to emphasize what the writer wishes to embolden.

If you are not sure whether to use a colon or not, just imagine a word "that is."
In other words, colon means "that is." You can write "that is" in place of a colon.

-Monkey has only one desire on its mind <that is> banana.
-Monkey has only one desire on its mind <that is> a pile of banana.

RULE #3
Hint: Colon

-Monkey has only one desire on its mind <that is> it wants to have a pile of banana.
-Monkey has three desires on its mind <that is:> finding banana trees, piling banana, eating a banana.

Colon, however, cannot be used in the middle of the incomplete sentence that obstructs the flow of the sentence.

Correct: Apple specializes in high-tech gadgets: cellphone, iPad, and computer.
Incorrect: Apple specializes in: high-tech gadgets such as cellphone, iPad, and computer

Question 4
However they choose their dormitory, college students at St. Johns are not entirely allowed to make their own decisions in choosing their roommates: as a result, many students choose an off-campus apartment.

A) NO CHANGE
B) roommates, as a result,
C) roommates; as a result,
D) roommates; and as a result,

RULE #4
Hint:
Semicolon

The Usage of Semi-colon

The correct answer is C.
C) The semicolon is used between two independent clauses. Semicolon functions as a conjunction. Therefore, it cannot be used together with other conjunctions such as *for, and, nor, but, or, yet, so.*

Transitional words/phrase such as "*accordingly*", "*consequently,*" "*for example,*" "*nevertheless,*" "*so,*" "*thus*" *etc. are all conjunctive adverbs that act like conjunctions.* Because they are not genuinely conjunction, however, a semicolon must be carried along to connect the following clause.

More example
Ex) Only the authorized Apple service center can replace the original Apple **parts;** an unauthorized service center can provide a repair service using generic parts.

As seen in the above examples, the semi-colon can be used when two opposite statements are presented in both sides.

Ex) The number of drunken drivers continues to **fall; consequently,** the police focus more on parking violations or speeding.

Ex) Some physicians' handwriting makes it extremely difficult to **read; accordingly,** all doctors' prescriptions for drugs are required to be recorded on the internet website that links between medical doctors and pharmacies in the country.

Question 5
As New York Times reported last year, Honda's airbag scandals have gone so far as to set up something of the comprehensive double-dealing; an intentional inspection report forgery and fraud from the board members—to inflate the sales, while avoiding critical industry standards test.

A) NO CHANGE
B) double-dealing, an intentional inspection report forgery and
C) double-dealing: with an intentional inspection report forgery and
D) double-dealing—an intentional inspection report forgery and

RULE #5
Hint: Dash

DASHES (—) + Guessing Based on the Meaning of the Keyword

The correct answer is D
D) The meaning "double-dealing" implies that two descriptions will follow, not one. Dashes are used to set off the interjection phrase between "and".

A) The original sentence uses a semicolon and a dash (—) combination, an impossible cocktail.
B) seems to be correct. The problem, however, is the change of original meaning. As introduced earlier, the word "double dealing along with the already presented second "dash" prove that this sentence is made of a double dashes.
C) It also uses a colon and dash combination. A dash after the conjunction "and" indicates another dash from the beginning .

Question 6
The secretary of internal affairs picked the house speaker Paul Ryan as a next candidate for the position—a dynamic colleague in Washington.

A) position—a dynamic colleague in Washington.
B) position; a dynamic colleague in Washington.
C) position, who is a dynamic colleague in Washington.
D) position with a dynamic colleague in Washington.

RULE #6
Hint: Dash

Dash

The correct answer is A.
A) One dash functions just the same way as the colon, and they are interchangeable.

B) is incorrect because a semicolon cannot be linked with a phrase.
C) is incorrect because of the misplaced modifier error. "who" is linked with the position, making ambiguous whether it refers to the secretary of internal affairs or the house speaker Paul Ryan.
D) is incorrect for the same reason as C.

Chapter1

24 Common Patterns for *In*correct Choices in Writing

1 Adding, Revising, Deleting, Retaining Information

This pattern contains a phrase such as 'If the author…'deleted / wish to add / support….would lose.., The multiple choices normally carries 'YES' 'NO' or 'Keep', 'Delete'.

Do not choose options with any new information. However tempting it may sound, insertion of new person, character, or specific information is outright wrong.

Any new conjunctions or conjunctive adverbs such as 'but,' 'because,' 'although,' 'since,' 'however,' 'Granted,' etc, steer the flow of sentences, paragraph, or the entire passage. Please be careful to those conjunction suddenly arising between the sentences.

2 Cause-Effect Relation Error

A sentence with a conjunction such as 'because,' 'if,' 'so,' or an adverb 'as a result,' 'consequently,' etc. presents the cause-effect relations, in which case you should find if the subordinating clause is correctly functioning.

Five key points associated with this pattern are (1) switching the cause and effect by flipping with a different conjunction, such as swapping 'because' with 'as a result'.

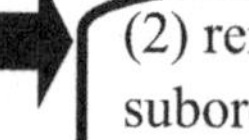

(2) removing a conjunction from the subordinating clause and creating comma splice error.

(3) adding another conjunction to a sentence that already has a conjunction (i.e., <u>although</u> I failed the test, <u>despite of this</u> failure I become invincible.)

(4) using a conjunction to a phrase, instead of a clause. (i.e., "<u>because</u> throwing a party secretively without telling him before his birthday.")

(5) using a preposition to a clause instead of a phrase. (i.e., "<u>because of</u> he wasn't advised in advance about his nomination, the candidate refused the acceptance.)

Chapter 1

24 Common Patterns for *In*correct Choices in Writing

3 Colloquialism (Nonstandard Language) Error

Colloquialism asks whether the word or phrase is following the formal (standard) written language.

Any options with the informal or casual language such as 'thing,' or 'plus,' or 'yellowish' is incorrect.

Putting an unidentified pronoun is also incorrect (i.e., "<u>they</u> say farmers should gorge during the bad harvest.")

Absolute spoken language such as "wanna" or "could of" is absolutely unacceptable.

4 Comparison Error

Comparison pattern asks broad range of comparisons, such as comparing the subjects, adjective, pronoun, phrase, or clause. Keep in mind "Apple to Apple."
You can't compare apple to orange.

When two things are compared, the exactly same parallel structure is required

For instance, it is easy to find a correlative conjunction error such as "not only ~but also."
Hard part is finding what's between them. (i.e., The country is famous **not only for** its natural resources **but also** <u>**by** processing</u> the resources.)

Another Important part to be remembered is a trick using a seemingly easy conjunction. If a question asks the latter portion of the conjunction, it becomes relatively easy.

However, if the former is missing, while the latter one appears, it won't be a piece-of-cake. (i.e., The country is famous <u>**for**</u> its natural resources <u>**but also** for processing</u> the resources.

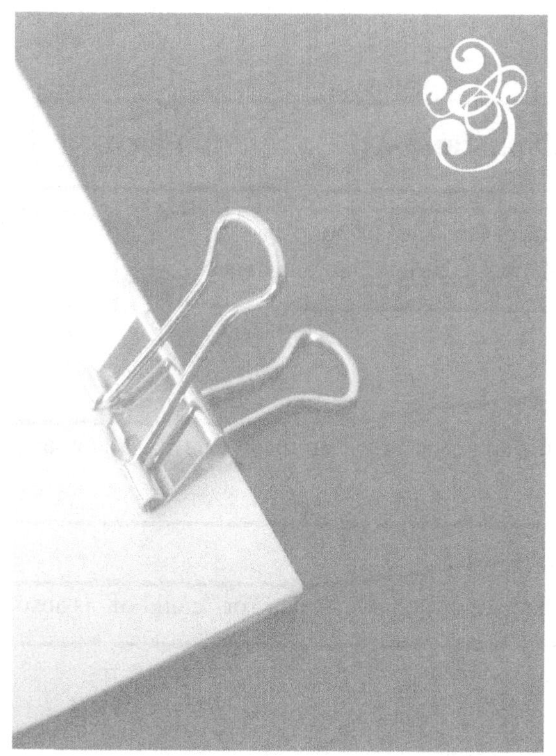

Chapter 2

1. **TEST 2**
2. **ANSWER EXPLANATIONS for TEST 2**
3. **CHAPTER SUMMARY**

SAT
Reading & Writing Practice
Test 2

ALL THE LOGIC AND RULES
BEHIND THE EVERY SINGLE
SAT QUESTION

Reading Test 2

65 MINUTES, 52 QUESTIONS

The passages below are followed by questions based on their content; questions following a pair of related passages may also be based on the relationship between the paired passages. Answer the questions on the basis of what is stated or implied in the passages and in any introductory material that may be provided.

Questions 1-10 are based on the following passage.

This passage is from Emma by Jane Austen.

Line Emma Woodhouse was the youngest of the two daughters. Her mother had died too long ago for her to have more than an indistinct remembrance of her caresses; and her place had been supplied by an excellent woman as governess, who had fallen little short of a mother in affection. Sixteen years had Miss Taylor been in Mr. Woodhouse's family, less as a governess than a friend.

Between *them* it was more the intimacy of sisters. The real evils, indeed, of Emma's situation were the power of having rather too much her own way, and a disposition to think a little too well of herself; these were the disadvantages which threatened alloy to her many enjoyments. Sorrow came--a happy sorrow. Miss Taylor married. It was on the wedding-day of this beloved friend that Emma first sat in mournful thought of any continuance.

The want of Miss Taylor would be felt every hour of every day. She recalled her past kindness--the kindness--how she had taught and how she had played with her from five years old—how she had devoted all her powers to attach and amuse her in health-and how nursed her through the various illnesses of childhood.

A large debt of gratitude was owing here followed Isabella's marriage, on their being left to each other, was yet a dearer, tenderer recollection. The evil of the actual disparity between Emma and Mr. Woodhouse in their ages (and Mr. Woodhouse had not married early) was much increased by his constitution and habits; for having been a valetudinarian all his life, without activity of mind or body, he was a much older man in ways than in years; and though everywhere beloved for the friendliness of his right way and never bangs it.

1

The relationship between Emma's family and Miss Taylor can be best summarized as that

A) Miss Taylor had been in romantic relations with Emma's father

B) Miss Taylor had a genuinely condescending view on Emma

C) Miss Taylor had a strong affinity to Emma

D) Miss Taylor had been a subservient governess

2

Which choice provides the best evidence for the answer to the previous question?

A) Lines 1-2 (Emma Woodhouse...two daughters.)

B) Lines 10-11 (Between them… sisters.)

C) Lines 11-14 (The real evils,...well of herself,)

D) Lines 30-33 (The evil...constitution and habits;)

3

Which of the following examples is most analogous to Emma's character described in lines 11-13 (The real evils...her own way)?

A) A girl bragging her cooking skills messes up the kitchen

B) A pizza delivery man grateful for a big tip

C) A store manager nonchalant about selling the goods

D) A teacher elated about one student who excelled on the test

CONTINUE

1 1

4

Line 7 ("happy sorrow") make use of which of the following literary devices?

A) Oxymoron

B) Onomatopoeia

C) Metaphor

D) Literary allusion

5

In line 20 "want" most nearly means?

A) Wish

B) Lack

C) Sympathy

D) Invoke

6

The author uses parallel structures in lines 22-26 (how…childhood) as part of a larger attempt to

A) convey the impact of separation

B) illustrate the joyful moments they shared

C) honor Miss Taylor's contribution

D) describe she won't have the same experiences in the future

7

After Isabella's marriage, both Emma and Miss Taylor realized

A) a strengthened unity after feeling abandoned

B) they were not real sisters and had no tender relations

C) a peculiar interest in marriage

D) Isabella left a large debt under their names

8

The primary purpose of the passage is to

A) highlight the contributions of Miss Taylor

B) describe the different characteristics between friends

C) illustrate the impact of an eventful moment to a character

D) reveal the reconciliation between friends

9

A) Lines 1-2 (Emma Woodhouse...two daughters.)

B) Lines 2-4 (Her mother had died...her caresses;)

C) Lines 7-9 (Sixteen years...than a friend)

D) Lines 17-21 (Miss Taylor married...every day.)

10

In line 33 "constitution" most nearly means?

A) Physical health

B) Principle

C) Wealth

D) Established legal relationships with others

CONTINUE

1 1

Questions 11-21 are based on the following passage.

This passage is about the impact of cyberbullying in United States.

Internet utopia begot carcinogenic diseases: cyberbullying. Some people see cyber-bullying as a form of cyberstalking, which involves more strategic and provoking intention than Internet trolling. A cyberbully may be anonymous and may solicit involvement of other people online who do not know the target. This is known as a "digital pile -on."

Cyberbullying has been defined as "when the Internet, cell phones or other devices are used to send or post text or images intended to hurt or embarrass another person." Cyberstalking has increased exponentially. Even police and prosecutors find themselves at risk, as gang members find out where they live — often to intimidate them into dropping a case." The FBI released the study "Stalking Victimization," which showed that one in four stalking victims had been cyberstalked as well. The Rape, Abuse and Incest National Network has released statistics that there are 3.4 million stalking victims each year. Of those, one in four reported experiencing cyberstalking.

According to Robin M. Kowalski, a social psychologist at Clemson University, cyberbullying has been shown to cause higher levels of anxiety for victims than normal bullying. Kowalksi states that this stems from the anonymity of the perpetrators, a common feature of cyberstalking. These include publishing lies and doctored photographs, threats of rape and other violence, posting sensitive personal information about victims, e-mailing damaging statements about victims to their employers, and manipulating search engines to make damaging material about the victim more prominent.

Victims frequently respond by adopting pseudonyms or going offline entirely. He added that more rigorous crackdown on hate crime—especially racial hate crime—can reduce growing number of victims by roughly 50%.

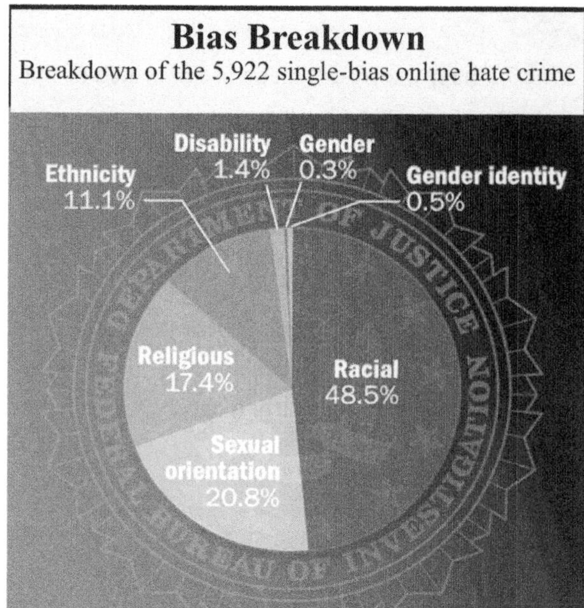

11

In describing cyberstalking in line 1-3, the author sees that

A) it usually glosses itself over with Internet utopia

B) it can cause carcinogenic diseases to its victims

C) it is usually associated with physical attack

D) it has provocative strategy than Internet trolling

12

Which of the following statements would LEAST likely support the cyberbullying in the mentioned passage?

A) sending an anonymous message to intimidate victims

B) fabricating a story and posting it on Facebook

C) repeatedly sending defaming text messages

D) repeatedly damaging the internet cable of the target

CONTINUE

1 1

13

Which statement resembles most the pattern of "digital pile-on" mentioned in line 7?

A) An illegal drug dealer hires innocent followers, who do not know they are committing a crime

B) A corrupt politician works with his staff silently to defame other candidates

C) An unknown high school student sends multiple text messages to a victim to spread rumors

D) An older brother suggests his sibling to post a classmate's family matter on Facebook

14

In line 13, the reference to "police and prosecutors" is used mainly to suggest

A) even law enforcement are using cyberbullying

B) the countermeasure is not very effective

C) some police are conniving with organized criminals

D) cyberstalking is pervasive crime

15

"one in four" in lines 18 and 22 show the relations between stalking and cyberstalking victims are

A) exactly identical victims

B) possible representative of general pattern

C) difficult to verify

D) negligible because 75% of stalking victims are not cyberstalking victims

16

According to Robin M. Kowalski in line 23, cyberbullying is different from normal bullying primarily in that normal bullying

A) is more pervasive in society

B) is committed by anticipated perpetrators

C) causes no challenging mental pains

D) causes more anxiety and depression to victims

17

The word "doctored" in line 29 most nearly means

A) prescribed

B) medicated

C) falsified

D) harassed

18

According to the passage, how would those who were victimized by cyberbullying respond to cyber attack

A) use the same measure of counterattack

B) change their identity

C) resort to law enforcement

D) evangelize social media users

19

Which choice provides the best evidence for the answer to the previous question?

A) Lines 16-19 (The FBI...cyberstalked as well.)

B) Lines 21-22 (Of those...cyberstalking)

C) Lines 24-26 (cyberbullying…normal bullying.)

D) Lines 36-37 (Victims … entirely.)

20

Which of the following statements most likely agrees with the pie chart?

A) Law enforcement should take more effort on reducing gender-bias hate crime

B) Tougher control on racial hate crime can reduce cyberbully victims possibly by half

C) Sexual-orientation hate crime is insignificant compared to religious hate crime

D) perpetrators are relatively generous to people with disability

21

Which choice provides the best evidence for the answer to the previous question?

A) Lines 9-12 (Cyberbullying … another person)

B) Lines 16-19 (The FBI ...cyberstalked as well.)

C) Lines 36-37 (Victims … entirely.)

D) Lines 37-39 (He added...victims.)

1 1

Questions 22-31 are based on the following passage.

The following passage describes about bee pollination

PASSAGE 1

Wherever flowering plants flourish, pollinating bees, birds, butterflies, bats, and other animals are hard at work, providing vital but often unnoticed services. But many pollinators are in serious decline. Some three-fourths of all native plants in the world require pollination most often by a native bee.

President Obama issued a memorandum establishing a Pollinator Health Task Force. The Strategy expands and adds to actions already being undertaken by Federal departments to reverse pollinator losses.

Although USDA has currently released the report showing a positive sign in that the number of managed honey bee colonies has been relatively consistent since 2014, the level of effort by the beekeeping industry to maintain these numbers has increased.

PASSAGE 2

Honey Bees are the most recognizable pollinators of hundreds of economically and ecologically important crops and plants in North America. These honey bees have been in serious decline for more than three decades in the United States. Starting in the 1940's when there were approximately 5.7 million colonies in the United States, the number of managed colonies used in honey production has declined to approximately 2.74 million colonies today. Sharp colony declines were seen following the introduction in 1987 of an external parasitic mite that feeds on honey bee hemolymph (blood).

Around 2006, a condition referred to as Colony Collapse Disorder (CCD) was first reported. Colonies diagnosed with CCD exhibit a rapid loss of adult worker bees, have few or no dead bees present in the colony, have excess brood and a small cluster of bees remaining with the queen bee, and have low Varroa mite and Nosema (fungal disease) levels. Colonies exhibiting CCD have insufficient numbers of bees to maintain the colony and these colonies eventually die.

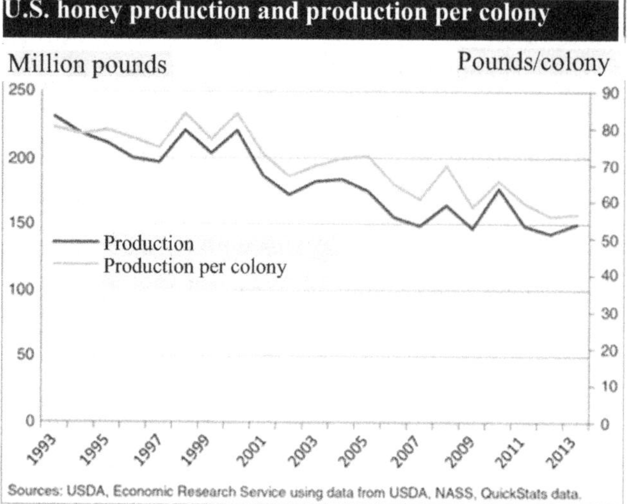

22

The discussion of honey bees in paragraph 1, Passage 1 indicates that

A) declining pollinators are mostly natives bees

B) other pollinators are often unnoticed

C) Colony Collapse Disorder is the major cause of the lose of honeybee

D) other pollinators are in fact increasing

23

Which choice provides the best evidence for the answer to the previous question?

A) Lines 1-4 (Wherever…services)

B) Lines 4-5 (But many pollinators...serious decline.)

C) Lines 5-7 (Some three-fourths...native bees)

D) Lines 8-9 (President Obama...Task Force.)

24

In passage 2, the known symptoms of Colony Collapse Disorder (CCD) include

A) loss of adult worker bees

B) sudden dead bees present in the colony

C) no signs of brood

D) sudden increase of Varroa mite

CONTINUE

1

25

Unlike passage 1, passage 2

A) tries to identify the syndrome from CCD

B) endorses the official view of losses of Honeybees

C) criticizes the underlying syndrome is overblown by the farmers

D) presents specific procedures to control CCD.

26

Which choice provides the best evidence for the answer to the previous question?

A) Lines 1-7 (Whenever flowering...a native bee.)

B) Lines 8-12 (President Obama...pollinator losses.)

C) Line s42-43 (Around 2006, ...first reported.)

D) Lines 49-51 (Colonies exhibiting CCD...eventually die.)

27

On the basis of information, Colony Collapse Disorder (CCD) was initially caused by

A) bloodsucking mite

B) excess brood and a small cluster of bees

C) honey bee hemolymph

D) toxic pesticide

28

It can be inferred from the passage that

A) most honey bees have completely disappeared

B) CCD was not known to outside until 2006

C) CCD symptoms did not exist before 2006

D) there is a slight correlation between CCD and the actual bee population decrease

29

In passage 2, the author mentions "the number of managed honey bees" in lines 15-16 primarily to

A) question CCD is the major cause

B) certify that the released report is official

C) testify the beekeeping industry's effort to maintain the proper level

D) show the consistent level of honey bee colonies

30

In line 10, "The Strategy expands …pollinator losses" suggests that the current strategy

A) is not as effective as it was initially planned

B) continues to appeal to many concerned beekeepers

C) is no more valid today

D) focuses not on immediate but on long-term changes

31

According to the passage, which of the following statements corresponds to the graph ?

A) U.S. honey production has dropped steadily since 2000.

B) In 2013, both production and production per colony increased roughly 30% compared to the output in 2009.

C) The increase in production between 2007 and 2008 proves that a Pollinator Health Task Force was effective

D) Abnormal production decline between 2000 and 2002 are closely related with CCD

CONTINUE

Questions 32-41 are based on the following passage.

The US Department of Transportation has pledged up to $40 million (funding subject to future appropriations) to one city to help it define what it means to be a "Smart City "and become the country's first city to fully integrate innovative technologies – self-driving cars, connected vehicles, and smart sensors – into their transportation network. San Francisco is one of the seven finalist cities. Here, the Bay Area has submitted the final report.

The San Francisco Bay Area has seen tremendous growth in the last few years and is expected to grow by an additional 25% in population and employment over the next two decades. The region's employment and output outpaced California's and the nation's. Here, employment is growing faster than population and the population faster than housing units.

Growth has posed enormous transportation challenges as it relates to the safety, mobility, environment and economic productivity. Some of the key trends noted in the Beyond Traffic document include current population growth, increase in number of older citizens and shift of people to mega-regions. These challenges are now impacting the citizens of San Francisco. Travel in the City is very time-consuming and expensive.

Problems will get worse. Freight demand is also on the rise. Increased deliveries in San Francisco have created safety conflicts, double parking, and blocked access with large trucks that are incompatible on the roads of a city like San Francisco.

To solve this issue, Incorporate Connected and Automated vehicle technology will be proven to be safe to further reduce travel costs, eliminate collisions and fatalities, and reduce parking demand sufficiently.

Once implemented, it will re-purpose parking facilities into affordable housing and other city amenities. In the world of transportation, we are no strangers to global firsts; San Francisco is a testbed of groundbreaking discoveries and trend-setting policies that get replicated globally.

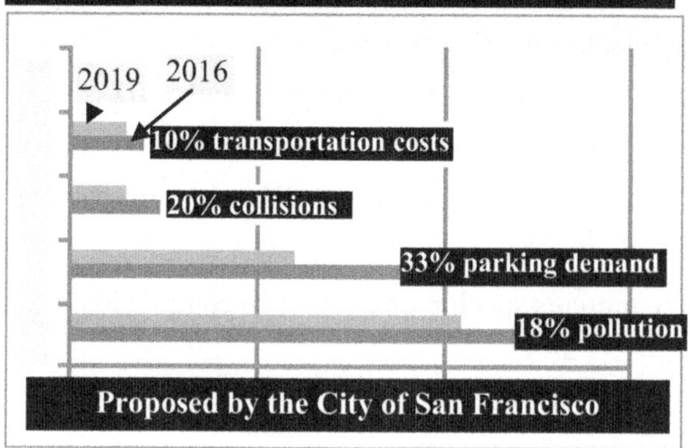

32

The author describes one of the advantages of San Francisco as?

A) growing number of older citizens

B) housing affordability

C) transportation system

D) the employment rate

33

Which choice provides the best evidence for the answer to the previous question?

A) Lines 1-2 (The San Francisco … last few years)

B) Lines 5-6 (The region's employment...the nation's.)

C) Lines 7-8 (Here, employment...housing units.)

D) Lines 12-15(Some of the key...mega-regions.)

34

"Currently, the biggest concern in San Francisco is probably

A) growing number of citizens

B) the number of housing units

C) employment output

D) transportation system

CONTINUE

1

35

The main purpose of the first paragraph (lines 1-8) is to

A) celebrate the current and the future growth of the city of San Francisco

B) present the city's irresolvable issues

C) indicate growing transportation challenge

D) emphasize the city's fascinating features

36

The author mentions "Some of the key trends" (line 12) in order to indicate

A) significant challenges in the city

B) short-term manageable problems

C) main factors that benefit the city

D) reasons for the tremendous growth of the city

37

Which of the following benefits can be expected from " Incorporate Connected and Automated vehicle technology in lines 25-26?

I. traveling cost efficiency

II. solution to parking demand

III. pollution elimination

A) I only

B) II, only

C) III only

D) I, II only

38

The freight demand issues include all of the following EXCEPT

A) mega-regions

B) delivery

C) safety

D) parking

39

Which of the following is the most accurate description of the organization in paragraphs 2,3,4,5 in lines 9-35 (Growth has posed enormous...get replicated globally.)?

A) A sequence of observations

B) A list of inferences drawn from prediction to facts

C) A statement of the main concerns, followed by specific examples that leads to a plan

D) A series of negative aspects to positive aspect that leads to outlook

40

In lines 33 "testbed" is closest in meaning to?

A) proven theory

B) platform

C) feasible facilities

D) convenient location

41

According to the benefits of Automated vehicle technology introduced in the last paragraph (lines 30-35), which choice is also supported best by the graph?

A) More affordable housing will be available

B) The biggest reduction can be anticipated from transportation costs

C) Compared to other factors, pollution reduction will benefit less

D) 20% reduction in collisions will also reduce fatalities by 20%

CONTINUE

1 1

Questions 42-52 are based on the following passages

The following two passages discuss about Artful Advertising *Fashion marketing moves from billboards to museum displays By Lily k. Alcagni November 20, 2015*
Harvard University ©The Harvard Crimson
Reprinted with Permission

Last October, LVMH allocated $143 million to found a private museum of contemporary art for its Louis Vuitton Foundation, and commissioned architect Frank Gehry to design and construct it in Paris's Bois de Boulogne. Even for the multinational conglomerate that runs Louis Vuitton, Moët, Hennessy, and 66 other luxury goods companies—all of which you've definitely heard of—this is a considerable investment worth investigating.

What merits a price tag of $143 million? In part, social capital. When prompted to explain why he wished to open the Louis Vuitton Foundation, Bernard Arnault, the CEO of LVMH, said, "We wanted to present Paris with an extraordinary space for art and culture, and demonstrate daring and emotion by entrusting Frank Gehry with the construction of an iconic building for the 21st century." Indeed, Arnault was able to successfully build his museum on a plot of land that had previously been denied to several other land developers. While these competitors wished to construct office buildings and business centers, Arnault was granted control of the land because his proposition was deemed to be a noble endeavor to create a public work.

But in a city that already boasts high concentrations of both art and culture, this was an ambitious—maybe even superfluous undertaking. It's clear to me that the goal of creating a rich, new ground for cultural discovery was only of secondary importance to Arnault. Though the museum has staged several provoking shows recently, in its opening weeks it showed nothing more than a condensed version of Arnault's private collection. Rather, Bernard Arnault invested almost $1.5 million in his own brand by reinvigorating the name of Louis Vuitton and thus claiming ownership of the art world in the name of high fashion.

It is no secret that newer fashion labels have begun to outmode Louis Vuitton, the oldest member of the LVMH conglomerate. In tying the brand's name to a new museum that is sleek, beautiful, and houses millions of dollars worth of art, Arnault intended to reposition and revive the label.

In fact, Arnault isn't alone in his ambitiously successful antics. And in the case of Miuccia Prada—the creative director behind the brands Prada and Miu Miu—the endeavor does not stem from a need to reposition her brands at all.

A long-time art collector and enthusiast, Prada's decision to open the Fondazione Prada museum derives simply from a confidence in her own taste in fine art as a designer of fine clothing.

The Metropolitan's Costume Institute, in tandem with Anna Wintour, mounts a humongous fashion exhibit each year that blurs the line between fashion and fine art in much the same way. In 2011, the museum launched its exhibit in honor of designer Alexander McQueen, and when the exhibit singlehandedly attracted more foot traffic than any other in the museum's history. Though I seriously believe that fashion belongs in museums, it seems that this is not the most effective marketing tactic. However, there does seem to be a way to create museums solely dedicated to clothes that is not alienating, but rather inviting. Valentino Garavani, owner and designer of the eponymous high-end label, has done so by founding a museum that won't cost him any overhead.

In 2011, Garavani and his partner Giancarlo Giammetti launched the Valentino Garavani Virtual Museum, a website and accompanying downloadable applet that provides viewers with unlimited, free access to 50 years of the label's haute coutue archives. Featuring cutting-edge, immersive 3-D, the virtual museum allows anyone to interactively explore over 5,000 dresses—their cut, materials, history, and production information. In comparison to the Louis Vuitton Foundation, Valentino's virtual gallery seems much more honest.

LVMH's new museum may indeed be a beautiful gift to the art world and a lovely amenity for Parisians, but as a surreptitious marketing attempt, it is ultimately nothing more than sponsored content. And while the Fondazione Prada purports only to add to its foundress's empire, I'm interested to see how its opening affects the revenue of the clothing brand that bears her name.

CONTINUE

1

42

In the first paragraph (lines 1-10), the author mainly does which of the following?

A) Speculates about a motivation
B) Describe outstanding achievement
C) Question practicality
D) Forecast failure

43

In line 24, the author describes that "Arnault was granted control of the land" because

A) the city of Paris valued Arnault's ownership of the art
B) Arnault intentionally misled his true intention
C) several other land developers didn't want the land
D) competitors prioritized arts and cultures

44

The author's tone in line 30 ("It is clear to me..) is?

A) Emphatic
B) Ambivalent
C) Ambiguous
D) Polemic

45

In lines 38 "reinvigorating" is closest in meaning to?

A) inviting
B) attracting
C) galvanizing
D) gathering

46

According to lines 53-56, the author views that Prada's decision to found a museum is based on

A) duplicity
B) art elitism
C) humanism
D) subversive intention

47

It can be inferred that the Metropolitan's Costume Institute in line 57 would undermine the author's argument by mentioning that Arnault and Prada's motivations are

A) inevitable because the line between fashion and fine art is in much the same way
B) necessary because the museum can attract more museumgoers
C) understandable because they are enjoying singular positions in fashion industry
D) inevitable because museum can be the most effective marketing tactic

48

The author's main purpose of referring Valentino Garavani in line 73 is to suggest that his museum

A) is more personally appealing
B) solely dedicates for sale, not for display
C) truly represents the cutting-edge technology
D) inspired Arnault and Prada's museums

49

Which choice provides the best evidence for the answer to the previous question?

A) Line 67-69 (However, there...inviting.)
B) Line 69-72 (Valentino Garavani...any overhead.)
C) Line 78-81 (Featuring cutting-edge...information)
D) Line 82-84 (In comparison...more honest.)

50

The main difference between Valentino Garavani museum and Arnault's and Prada's is that Valentino Garavani museum goers

A) can obtain affordable clothes displayed in it
B) can also access to virtual museum
C) can experience the state-of-the-art display
D) must visit virtual museum only

CONTINUE

1 1

51

Which choice provides the best evidence for the answer to the previous question?

A) Line 64-67 (Though…tactic)

B) Line 73-78 (In 2011, haute coutue archives.)

C) Line 82-84 (In comparison…honest)

D) Line 89-92 (And while the Fondazione…name)

52

The tone of the last paragraph (lines 85-92) is mainly

A) informative

B) appreciative

C) cynic

D) optimistic

STOP

If you finish before time is called,
you may check your work on this section.

Do not turn to the next section.

Writing and Language Test 2
35 MINUTES, 44 QUESTIONS

Each passage below is accompanied by a number of questions. For some questions, you will consider how the passage might be revised to improve the expression of ideas. For other questions, you will consider how the passage might be edited to correct errors in sentence structure, usage, or punctuation. A passage or a question may be accompanied by one or more graphics (such as a table or graph) that you will consider as you make revising and editing decisions.

Questions 1-11 are based on the following passage.

The World Digital Library

The World Digital Library (WDL) is an international digital library operated by UNESCO and the United States Library of Congress. The WDL [1] had stated that its mission is to [2] promoting international and intercultural understanding, expand the volume and variety of cultural content on the Internet, [3] provide resources for educators, scholars, and general audiences, and build capacity in partner institutions to narrow the digital divide within and among countries.

1

A) NO CHANGE
B) have stated
C) state
D) has stated

2

A) NO CHANGE
B) promotion of
C) promote and encourage
D) promote

3

A) NO CHANGE
B) by providing
C) to provide
D) which provides

CONTINUE

2 2

[4] Brown University is taking the major role among university participants.

The library intends to make available on the Internet, free of charge and in multilingual format, significant primary materials from cultures around the world, including manuscripts, maps, rare books, musical scores, recordings, films, prints, photographs, architectural drawings, and other significant cultural materials. [5]

After almost 20 years without participation, the United States [6] , which re-established its permanent delegation to the United Nations Educational, Scientific and Cultural Organization (UNESCO) in 2003.

4

Which choice best connects the sentence with the previous paragraph?

A) As written on the passage
B) It aims to expand non-English and non-western content on the Internet, and contribute to scholarly research.
C) It is a well-known fact that the Royal Library of Alexandria, Egypt, founded by Ptolemy, is considered to be the greatest ancient library in human civilization.
D) As the mode of modern information is becoming more digitized than paper-printed, the role of librarians is also shifting dramatically.

5

At this point, the author wishes to add the following information.

--encompassing materials obtained from many countries.

Should the author make this addition here?

A) Yes, because it provides added information of the materials.
B) Yes, because it connects well with the previous sentence.
C) No, because dash creates a punctuation error.
D) No, because it violates redundant error.

6

A) NO CHANGE
B) that re-established
C) by re-establishing
D) re-established

CONTINUE

2

Dr. James H. Billington, Librarian of Congress, was nominated as a commissioner of the U.S. National Commission to UNESCO and [7] has been invited to give a plenary speech at its inaugural conference in June 2005. [8] His speech entitled *A View of the Digital World Library*, which described a vision in which the rich collections that "institutions, libraries, and museums have preserved could be given back to the world free of charge and in a new form far more universally accessible than any forms that have preceded it."

7

A) NO CHANGE
B) had been
C) was
D) is

8

Which choice combines the underlined portion of the sentence most effectively?

A) NO CHANGE
B) His speech, entitled *A View of the Digital World Library*, described a vision in which the rich collections that "institutions, libraries, and museums have preserved
C) With his speech, entitled *A View of the Digital World Library*, described a vision in which the rich collections that "institutions, libraries, and museums have preserved
D) His speech, entitled *A View of the Digital World Library*, described a vision, the rich collections, institutions, libraries, and museums

CONTINUE

2

Google Inc. became the first partner of this public–private partnership and donated $3 million to support development of the World Digital Library in 2005.

The WDL opened with 1,236 items. As of late 2015, it lists more than 12,000 items from nearly 200 countries, dating back to 8,000 BCE.

At the National Commission's 2006 annual conference [9] ,which has been held every year since its establishment, Dr. John Van Oudenaren, Senior Advisor for the World Digital Library at the Library of Congress, outlined a project plan for bringing Dr. Billington's vision to fruition.

Foremost was the belief that the World Digital Library should engage partners in planning the four main project areas: technical architecture, selection, governance, and [10] garnering funding. This was achieved in December 2006, [11] that 45 national library directors, library technical directors, and cultural and educational representatives from UNESCO met in Paris to discuss the development of the World Digital Library.

9

A) NO CHANGE
B) ,held every year since its establishment,
C) that has been held yearly since its establishment
D) delete the underlined portion.

10

A) NO CHANGE
B) fund
C) funding
D) collecting working capital

11

A) NO CHANGE
B) in
C) in which
D) when

CONTINUE

2 2

Questions 12-22 are based on the following passage.

From Charles Darwin Autobiography

[12] German Editor, Gunter Schiller [13] having written to me for an account of the development of my mind and character with some sketch of my autobiography, I have thought that the attempt would amuse me, and might possibly interest my children or their children. [14] I had found no difficulty, for life is nearly over with me. I have taken no pains about my style of writing.

I was born at Shrewsbury on February 12th, 1809, and my earliest recollection goes back only to when I was a few months over four years old, when we went to near Abergele for sea-bathing, and I recollect some events and places there with some little distinctness.

My mother died in July 1817, when I was a little over eight years old, and [15] it is odd that I can remember hardly anything about her except her death-bed.

12

A) NO CHANGE
B) German Editor, Gunter Schiller,
C) German Editor Gunter Schiller,
D) German Editor Gunter Schiller

13

A) NO CHANGE
B) written
C) wrote
D) has written

14

A) NO CHANGE
B) Nor have I found difficulty,
C) Finding not difficulty,
D) Without finding difficulty,

15

A) NO CHANGE
B) its
C) it was
D) it had been

CONTINUE

2

In the spring of this same year I was sent to a day-school in Shrewsbury, where I stayed a year. I have been told that I was much slower in learning than my younger sister Catherine, and I believe that I was in many ways a naughty boy. Mrs. Darwin was a Unitarian and attended Mr. Case's chapel. But [16] both he and his brother were christened and intended to belong to the Church of England. My taste for natural history, and more especially for collecting, was well developed. I tried to make out the names of plants [17] and collected all sorts of things, shells, seals, franks, coins, and minerals. The passion for collecting which leads a man to be a systematic naturalist, a virtuoso, or a miser, was very strong in me, and was clearly innate, [18] as none of my sisters or brother ever had this taste.

16

A) NO CHANGE
B) both him and his brother
C) both his and brother
D) both he as well as his brother

17

At this point, the writer is considering adding the following sentence.

—Rev. W.A. Leighton brought a flower to school and taught us how by looking at the inside of the blossom the name of the plant could be discovered, which greatly roused my curiosity—

Should the writer make this addition here?

A) Yes, because it is consistent with the previous sentence and provides some added information.
B) Yes, because it enlightens us as well on how to find names of plants.
C) No, because it interrupts the paragraph's description of young Charles Darwin.
D) No, because Rev. W.A. Leighton is inessential character and is unnecessary to introduce.

18

A) NO CHANGE
B) but
C) and
D) moreover,

CONTINUE

2 2

I may here also confess that as a little boy I was much given to inventing deliberate [19] falsehoods, and this was always done for the sake of causing excitement. [20] Moreover, I once gathered much valuable fruit from my father's trees and hid it in the shrubbery, and then ran in breathless haste to spread the news that I had discovered a hoard of stolen fruit. I must have been a very simple little fellow when I first went to the school. ① A boy the name of Garnett took me into a cake shop one day, and bought some cakes for which he did not pay, as the shop man trusted him. ②When we came out I asked him why he did not pay for them, and he instantly answered, "Why, do you not know that my uncle left a great sum of money to the town on condition that every tradesman should give whatever was wanted without payment to anyone who wore his old hat and moved it in a particular manner?" and he then showed me how it was moved. ③He then went into another shop where he was trusted, and asked for some small article, moving his hat in the proper manner, [21] but he was such a naïve boy as I recall.

[22] When we came out he said, "Now if you like to go by yourself into that cake-shop (how well I remember its exact position) I will lend you my hat.

19

Which choice most effectively combines the sentences at the underlined portion?

A) NO CHANGE
B) falsehood, whereas
C) falsehood, indeed,
D) falsehood, consequently,

20

A) NO CHANGE
B) Thus,
C) For instance,
D) In the meantime,

21

Which choice most closely matches the stylistic pattern established earlier in the sentence?

A) NO CHANGE
B) , so that the tradesman could remember the remarks from the boy's uncle.
C) , and of course obtained it without payment.
D) , and mentioned about his uncle to the tradesman.

22

To make the passage most logical, the sentence should be placed

A) where it is now.
B) after sentence 1
C) after sentence 2
D) after sentence 3

CONTINUE

2 2

Questions 23-33 are based on the following passage.

The Greenhouse gas effects

Greenhouse gas concentrations in the atmosphere will continue to increase [23] unless the billions of tons of our annual emissions decrease substantially. Increased concentrations are expected to increase Earth's average temperature, influence the patterns and amounts of precipitation, reduce ice and snow cover, as well as permafrost, raise sea level, and increase the acidity of the oceans. [24]

Temperature [25] increases and other climate changes may directly impact our food and water supply, ecosystems, coasts, and human health. The bars in the bottom box indicate what temperatures and impacts are expected under the high and low emissions scenarios, which are determined by our actions.

23

Which choice offers the most logical information to support the entire passage?

A) NO CHANGE

B) although there is nothing we can do about it

C) , but some folks believe that it's an overblown media tactic.

D) ,which accumulate in our atmosphere

24

At this point, the author wishes to add the following phrases.

The mechanism is named after a faulty analogy with the effect of solar radiation passing through glass and warming a greenhouse. The way a green house retains heat is fundamentally different

Should the author make this addition here?

A) Yes, because it provides the added examples from the previous discussion.

B) Yes, because unlike the previous information, the addition brings more objective and mechanical function of the Greenhouse.

C) No, because some of the additions are redundant and unnecessarily wordy.

D) No, because it blurs the focus of the sentence

25

A) NO CHANGE

B) ,which increases fast

C) has been dramatically increased

D) increase

CONTINUE

2 2

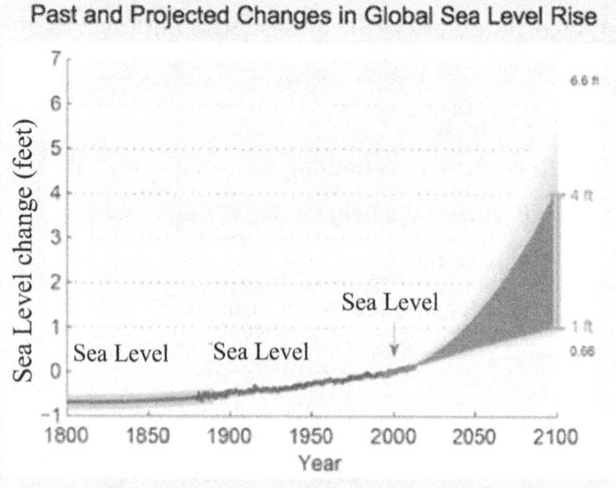

U.S. National Climate Assessment, 2014

The magnitude and rate of future climate change will primarily depend on many uncertain factors.

Among many noted estimates, the IPCC's "SRES" scenarios have been frequently used to make projections of future climate change.

<u>The SRES scenarios are "baseline" (or "reference") scenarios, which means that the current or future measures that limit GHG emissions are not to be rigidly defined</u>.[27]

Emissions projections of the SRES scenarios are [28] <u>comparable in range to the baseline emissions, which are broad in scenarios</u> that have been developed by the scientific community.

26

According to the information in the passage, which choice offers an accurate interpretation of the data in the chart?

A) Sea-level changes present the unclear relationship with the greenhouse

B) Thermal expansion in atmosphere is the direct effects of global warming but not the volume of water

C) The future sea level tells that drastic emission control won't make much difference.

D) The future sea level will be controlled within decades by our effort

27

Which choice supports the previously mentioned sentence?

A) They are, by far, the best, and therefore, should be employed as the most trusted guidelines

B) They forecast only up to 10 years of measurement.

C) They should never be practically applied.

D) They may function as a guideline.

28

A) NO CHANGE

B) comparable and relative to the baseline emissions scenarios broadly

C) broadly comparable to the baseline emissions scenarios

D) comparable to the baseline emissions scenarios, which are broad.

CONTINUE

2

Many greenhouse gases stay in the atmosphere for long periods of time. [29] As a result, even if emissions stopped increasing, atmospheric greenhouse gas concentrations would continue to increase and remain elevated for hundreds of years. Even if we stabilized concentrations and the composition of today's atmosphere, (which would require a dramatic reduction in current greenhouse gas emissions), surface air temperatures [30] will continue to warm. This is because [31] the oceans, which store heat, take many decades to fully respond to higher greenhouse gas concentrations. The ocean's response to higher greenhouse gas concentrations and higher temperatures will continue to [32] effect climate over the next several decades to hundreds of years.

Therefore, over the next several millennia, projections suggest that global warming [33] could affect the global economy.

Even if emissions were drastically reduced, global temperatures would remain close to their highest level for at least 1,000 years

29

A) NO CHANGE
B) But,
C) On the other hand,
D) Nonetheless,

30

A) NO CHANGE
B) would continue
C) are going to continue
D) are continuing

31

A) NO CHANGE
B) the oceans which store heat
C) the oceans, that store heat,
D) the oceans store heat

32

A) NO CHANGE
B) affect
C) endanger
D) push negatively

33

A) NO CHANGE
B) could be significantly reduced
C) could be possibly reversed
D) could be irreversible.

CONTINUE

2 2

Questions 34-44 are based on the following passage.

Café de Cat

Cat cafés are quite popular in Japan, with Tokyo being home to 58 cat cafés as of 2015. [34] Other forms of pet [35] rental such as rabbit cafés, are also common in Japan. [36] There are various types of cat café in Japan, some feature specific categories of cat such as black cats, fat cats, rare breed cats or ex-stray cats. Every cat café in Japan is required to obtain a license and comply with the strict requirements and regulations of the nation's Animal Treatment and Protection Law.

34

At this point, the author considers adding the following information,

The popularity of cat cafés in Japan is attributed to many apartments forbidding pets, and to provide cats relaxing companionship in what may otherwise be a stressful and lonely urban life.

Should the author add this information here?

A) Yes, because it establishes the psychological role cat can impart to its owner.
B) Yes, because it gives further explanations behind their popularity.
C) No, because such a detail doesn't fit in the introductory paragraph
D) No, because it mentions positive effects only to the place where side-effects should be presented.

35

A) NO CHANGE
B) rental, such as rabbit cafes,
C) rental, such as rabbit cafes
D) rental such as rabbit cafes

36

Which of the following choices would NOT be an alternate sentence?

A) Japan: some featuring specific categories of cat, such as black cats, fat cats, or ex-stray cats.
B) Japan, such as black cats cafe, fat cats cafe, or ex-stray cats cafe.
C) Japan, to name a few with black cats cafe, or ex-stray cats cafe.
D) Japan; which featuring specific categories of cat such as black cats, fat cats, or ex-stray cats.

CONTINUE

2 2

Japanese cat cafés feature strict rules to ensure cleanliness and animal welfare, in particular seeking to ensure that the cats are not disturbed by [37] excessive and unwanted attention, such as by young children or when sleeping. Many cat cafés also seek to raise awareness of cat's welfare issues, such as abandoned and stray cats.

Cat cafés have been spreading across North America [38] after 2014. The goal in North America generally is to help get cats adopted by partnering with local cat rescuers. ①The cat cafés across this region have come together to create The North American Cat Cafe Embassy. ②Saturday, October 17, 2015 saw the opening of Ontario's first cat café located in Guelph, Ontario. ③ The first cat café to open in North America was Le Café des Chats/Cat Café Montreal in Montreal, Canada, which opened its doors to the public in August 2014 [39] ,with 8 cats adopted from local shelters. ④ Catfe opened in Vancouver, British Columbia on December 14, 2015 and Kitty Cat Café and Pet Me Meow are both planning cafés for Toronto to open in 2015.

37

A) NO CHANGE
B) excessively
C) excess
D) excessed

38

A) NO CHANGE
B) in
C) by
D) since

39

Which of the following choices would NOT be an appropriate alternative phrase?

A) –having 8 cats adopted from local shelters.
B) ,which started with 8 cats adopted from local shelters.
C) , by home-staying 8 cats adopted from local shelters.
D) , 8 cats were adopted from local shelters.

40

To make this paragraph most logical, sentence ②Saturday, should be placed

A) Where it is now
B) Before sentence ①The cat
C) After sentence ③ The first
D) After sentence ④ Catfe

CONTINUE

2 2

Cat cafés in the United States differ from those in many other countries by their focus on adoptions. Hundreds of animals have been adopted through [41] their efforts. [42] Also, in United States, compliance with governmental food service regulations is required. The area where the cats are playing or being considered for adoption must be entirely separated from the area where food and drink are served. For example, a newly adopted cat must leave [43] without passing a food serving area through a separate door.

In May 2015, Grand Rapids, Michigan, announced Happy Cat Cafe will open sometime in 2016. They are hoping to partner with The Humane Society of West Michigan. The cafe raised $26,821 on Kickstarter with 549 backers.

In October 2015, the Blue Cat Cafe opened in Austin, Texas, [44] thereby partnering with the Austin Humane Society as a cafe and adoption center. It has live music for cats.

41

A) NO CHANGE
B) Catcafe
C) Its
D) Animal rescuers'

42

A) NO CHANGE
B) Consequently,
C) While,
D) Delete the underlined portion and change ' in the United States...' to "In the United States"

43

A) NO CHANGE
B) through a separate door, without passing a food serving area.
C) a food serving area through a separate door..
D) through a food serving area, without passing a separate door.

44

A) NO CHANGE
B) whereby it partners
C) in which it partners
D) partnering

STOP

If you finish before time is called,
you may check your work on this section.

Do not turn to the next section.

SAT Test 2 Answer Explanations & Pattern Analyses

If your Test 2 scores are unsatisfactory,

Test 3, 4, 5… won't be satisfactory either.

Please Practice the Answer Explanations and then come back to Test 2 again.

ALL THE LOGIC AND RULES BEHIND EVERY SINGLE SAT QUESTION

SAT Test 2

Reading Section Answer Explanations

&

Pattern Analyses

Questions 1-10 are based on the following passage.

<table>
<tr>
<td>Emma Woodhouse was the youngest of the two daughters. Her mother had died too long ago for her to have more than an indistinct remembrance of her caresses; and her place had been supplied by an excellent woman as governess, who had fallen little short of a mother in affection. Sixteen years had Miss Taylor been in Mr. Woodhouse's family, less as a governess than a friend.
(1C & 2B) Between them it was more the intimacy of sisters. The real evils, indeed, of Emma's situation were the power of having rather (3A) too much her own way, and a disposition to think a little too well of herself; these were the disadvantages which threatened alloy to her many enjoyments. (4A) Sorrow came--a happy sorrow. Miss Taylor married. It was on the wedding-day of this beloved friend that Emma first sat in mournful thought of any continuance.
(5B & 6A & 8C&9D) The want of Miss Taylor would be</td>
<td>felt every hour of every day.
She recalled her past kindness--the kindness--how she had taught and how she had played with her from five years old—how she had devoted all her powers to attach and amuse her in health-and how nursed her through the various illnesses of childhood.
A large debt of gratitude was owing here followed Isabella's marriage, on their being left to each other, (7A) was yet a dearer, tenderer recollection.
The evil of the actual disparity between Emma and Mr. Woodhouse in their ages
(10A) (and Mr. Woodhouse had not married early) was much increased by his constitution and habits; for having been a valetudinarian all his life, without activity of mind or body, he was a much older man in ways than in years; and though everywhere beloved for the friendliness of his right way and never bangs it.</td>
</tr>
</table>

<table>
<tr><td colspan="2">Q1. Absolute Pattern 9: Relationships Question
Finding relations between the cause-effect, comparison-contrast, characters, and ideas
Question Pattern: The relationship between Emma's family and Miss Taylor can be best summarized as that</td></tr>
<tr><td>A) Miss Taylor had been in romantic relations with Emma's father
B) Miss Taylor had a genuinely condescending view on Emma
C) Miss Taylor had a strong affinity to Emma
D) Miss Taylor had been a subservient governess</td><td>C) Between them it was more the intimacy of Sisters
B), D) Please refer to incorrect choice pattern #1 and #4</td></tr>
<tr><td colspan="2">Q2. Absolute Pattern 11: Textual Evidence Question Finding evidence for the previous question
Question Pattern: Which choice provides the best evidence for the answer to the previous question?</td></tr>
<tr><td>A) Lines 1-2 (Emma Woodhouse...two daughters.)
B) Lines 10-11 (Between them… sisters.)
C) Lines 11-14 (The real evils,...well of herself,)
D) Lines 30-33 (The evil...constitution and habits;)</td><td>B) Please refer to the above question</td></tr>
<tr><td colspan="2">Q3. Absolute Pattern 6: Analogy Question Finding a similar situation
Question Pattern: Which of the following examples is most analogous to Emma's character described in lines 11-13 (The real evils...her own way)?</td></tr>
<tr><td>A) A girl bragging her cooking skills messes up the kitchen
B) A pizza delivery man grateful for a big tip
C) A store manager nonchalant about selling the goods
D) A teacher elated about one student who excelled on the test</td><td>A) The real evils, indeed, of Emma's situation were the power of having rather too much her own way, and a disposition to think a little too well of herself; these were the disadvantages which threatened alloy to her many enjoyments</td></tr>
<tr><td colspan="2">A) This is analogy question. You may not find the exactly same wordings from the multiple choices. Instead, you should focus on logical relations between the reading passage and the multiple choices, such as positive vs. negative value / active vs. passive value / physical vs. mental value.
(C) nonchalant means not caring, which is opposite to the eagerness shown in Emma's character.
(D) has two people. The passage points out only one person "Emma". Counting the number of people or things involved in analogy question is very important factor.</td></tr>
</table>

<table>
<tr><td colspan="2">Q4. Absolute Pattern 5: Word-In-Context Question
Question Pattern: Line 7 ("happy sorrow") make use of which of the following literary devices?</td></tr>
<tr><td>A) Oxymoron
B) Onomatopoeia
C) Metaphor
D) Literary allusion</td><td><u>A) Sorrow came--a happy sorrow--</u>but not at all in the shape of any disagreeable consciousness. — Happy sorrow is an oxymoron. Oxymoron is a compressed paradox: a figure of speech in which seemingly contradictory terms appear side by side.
B) Onomatopoeia: the use of words which sound like what they mean. Sizzle sounds like bacon in a pan. C) Metaphor: a comparison between two things which are essentially dissimilar.
D) Literary allusion: a brief reference to a person, place, event</td></tr>
<tr><td colspan="2">Q5. Absolute Pattern 5: Word-In-Context Question
Question Pattern: In line 20 "want" most nearly means?</td></tr>
<tr><td>A) Wish
B) Lack
C) Sympathy
D) Invoke</td><td>B) lack (want) of Miss Taylor would be felt every hour of every day</td></tr>
<tr><td colspan="2">Q6. Absolute Pattern 10: Understanding the Structure of the Passage
Question Pattern: The author uses parallel structures in lines 22-25 (how she…childhood) as a part of larger attempt to</td></tr>
<tr><td>A) convey the impact of separation
B) illustrate the advent of cheerful moments
C) honor Miss Taylor's contribution
D) describe she won't have the same experiences in the future</td><td>A) The want of Miss Taylor would be felt every hour of every day. She recalled her past kindness--the kindness--how she had taught and how she had played with her from five years old—how she had devoted all her powers …
*The parallel structure is usually used to emphasize the true purpose, which is normally located right before/after the parallel structure.</td></tr>
<tr><td colspan="2">B), D) are future prediction. Please refer to incorrect choice pattern # #9
C) is true but does not the response to lines 22-25. Please refer to incorrect choice pattern # 8.
<u>Not all true statement can be the answer. The true statement must also reply to the question.</u></td></tr>
<tr><td colspan="2">Q7. Absolute Pattern 9: Relationships Question
Finding relations between the cause-effect, characters, and ideas including a Paired Passage.
Question Pattern: After Isabella's marriage, both Emma and Miss Taylor realized</td></tr>
<tr><td>A) a strengthened unity after feeling abandoned
B) they were not real sisters and had no tender relations
C) a peculiar interest in marriage
D) Isabella left a large debt under their names</td><td><u>A) Isabella's marriage</u>, on their being left to each other, was yet a dearer, tenderer recollection</td></tr>
<tr><td colspan="2">Q8 Absolute Pattern 1: Main Idea Question Finding the main idea of the entire passage or the paragraph
Question Pattern: The primary purpose of the passage is to</td></tr>
<tr><td>A) highlight the contributions of Miss Taylor
B) describe the different characteristics between friends
C) illustrate the impact of an eventful moment to a character
D) reveal the reconciliation between friends</td><td>C) The want of Miss Taylor would be felt every hour of every day.</td></tr>
<tr><td colspan="2">The keyword for the primary purpose question of this passage should be "Emma" as she is the narrator and the main character. Therefore, options A), B),D) should be eliminated in the first place.</td></tr>
</table>

Q9. **Absolute Pattern 11: Textual Evidence Question** Finding evidence for the previous question **Question Pattern:** Which choice provides the best evidence for the answer to the previous question?	
A) Lines 1-2 (Emma Woodhouse...two daughters.) B) Lines 2-4 (Her mother had died...her caresses;) C) Lines 7-9 (Sixteen years...than a friend) **D) Lines 20-21 (The want of Miss Taylor married...every day.)**	D) Please refer to the above question

Q10. **Absolute Pattern 5: Word-In-Context Question** Finding a clue word and the keyword from the sentence in question **Question Pattern:** In line 33 "**constitution**" most nearly means?	
A) Physical health B) Principle C) Wealth D) Established legal relationships with others	A) The evil of the actual disparity in their ages (and Mr. Woodhouse had not married early) was much increased by his constitution and habits; (A) 'ages' becomes a clue word to the answer

Questions 11-21 are based on the following passage.

Internet utopia begot carcinogenic diseases: cyberbullying. Some people see cyber-bullying as a form of cyberstalking, which involves (11D) **more strategic and provoking intention than Internet trolling**. (12D) **A cyberbully may be anonymous and may solicit involvement of other people online** (13A) **who do not know the target**. This is known as a "digital pile-on."

Cyberbullying has been defined as "when the Internet, cell phones or other devices are used to send or post text or images intended to hurt or embarrass another person." (14D) **Cyberstalking has increased exponentially**.
Even police and prosecutors find themselves at risk, as gang members find out where they live — often to intimidate them into dropping a case." The FBI released the study "Stalking Victimization," which showed that (15B) one in four stalking victims had been cyberstalked as well.

The Rape, Abuse and Incest National Network has released statistics that there are 3.4 million stalking victims each year. Of those, one in four reported experiencing cyberstalking.
According to Robin M. Kowalski, a social psychologist at Clemson University, cyberbullying has been shown to cause higher levels of anxiety for victims than normal bullying. Kowalksi states that this (16B) **stems from the anonymity** of the perpetrators, a common feature of cyberstalking. These include publishing (17C) **lies and doctored** photographs, threats of rape and other violence, posting sensitive personal information about victims, e-mailing damaging statements about victims to their employers, and manipulating search engines to make damaging material about the victim more prominent. (18B &19D) **Victims frequently respond by adopting pseudonyms or going offline entirely.** He added that more rigorous crackdown on hate crime—(20B & 21D) **especially racial hate crime—can reduce growing number of victims by roughly 50%.**

Q11. **Absolute Pattern 9: Relationships Question** **Question Pattern:** In describing **cyberstalking in line 1-3,** the author sees that	
A) it usually glosses itself over with Internet utopia B) it can cause carcinogenic diseases to its victims C) it is usually associated with physical attack **D) it has provocative strategy than Internet trolling**	D) cyberstalking, which involves **more strategic and provoking intention than Internet trolling** **Comparative conjunction or adverb such as "more than" always gives the answer.**

Q12. **Absolute Pattern 2: Summary Question** Summarizing a sentence or entire passage
Question Pattern: Which of the following statements would **LEAST likely support the cyberbullying**

A) sending an anonymous message to intimidate victims B) fabricating a story and posting it on Facebook C) repeatedly sending defaming text messages **D) repeatedly damaging the internet cable of the target**	D) A cyberbully may be (A) anonymous and may solicit involvement of other people online (C) who do not know the target. Cyberbullying ...used to send or (B) post text or images intended to hurt D) is physical, unrelated with the cyberbullying.

Q13. **Absolute Pattern 6: Analogy Question** Finding a similar situation
Question Pattern: Which statement resembles most the pattern of **"digital pile-on"** mentioned in line 7?

A) An illegal drug dealer hires innocent followers, who do not know they are committing a crime B) A corrupt politician works with his staff silently to defame other candidates C) An unknown high school student sends multiple text messages to a victim to spread rumors D) An older brother suggests his sibling to post a classmate's family matter on Facebook	**A) who do not know the target. This is** known as a "digital pile-on." **"This"** is called the amplifier. Amplifier plays a key role in finding the main issue.

Analogy question employs several well-established logic, one of which is "quantity-quality" logic.
For C), compared to the passage context and the other options, only one individual is committing a crime.
Counting how many people (activities) are involved is very important in all analogy questions.
Finding premise in the sentence is another critical concept.
A cyberbully may be anonymous (PREMISE) and may solicit involvement of other people online who do not know the target (CONCLUSION). This is known as a "digital pile-on." (A) and (D) apply this concept, but (D) brothers know each other.

Q14. **Absolute Pattern 4: Example Question**
Question Pattern: In line 13, the reference to **"police and prosecutors"** is used mainly to suggest

A) even law enforcement are using cyberbullying B) the countermeasure is not very effective C) some police are conniving with organized criminals **D) cyberstalking is pervasive crime**	D) (Main Idea) According to *Law Enforcement technology,* cyberstalking **has increased exponentially ...** (Example) Even police and prosecutors find themselves at risk, (B) is not mentioned.

Q15. **Absolute Pattern 3: Inference Question** Finding an indirect suggestion (or guessing)
Question Pattern: "one in four" in lines 18 and 22 show the relations between stalking and cyberstalking victims are

A) exactly identical victims **B) possible representative of general pattern** C) difficult to verify D) negligible because 75% of stalking victims are not cyberstalking victims	B) one in four stalking victims had been cyberstalked. one in four reported experiencing cyberstalking. "One in four" or 25% illustrates a possible representative of general pattern. The other choices are not stated.

Q16. **Absolute Pattern 9: Relationships Question**
Question Pattern: According to **Robin M. Kowalski** in line 23, cyberbullying is different from normal bullying primarily in that **normal bullying**

A) is more pervasive in society **B) is committed by anticipated perpetrators** C) causes no challenging mental pains D) causes more anxiety and depression to victims	B) cyberbullying has been shown to cause higher levels of anxiety for victims than normal bullying. Kowalksi states that this **stems from the anonymity** of the perpetrators. *The opposite of anonymity should be "anticipated".

<table>
<tr><td colspan="2">Q17. Absolute Pattern 5: Word-In-Context Question
Finding a clue word and the keyword from the sentence in question
Question Pattern: The word "doctored" in line 29 most nearly means</td></tr>
<tr><td>A) prescribed
B) medicated
C) falsified
D) harassed</td><td>C) These include publishing <u>lies</u> and <u>doctored</u> photographs,
(A), (B) are too literal implications (D) Too extreme
The clue word is "lies."
Please refer to incorrect choice pattern #12</td></tr>
</table>

<table>
<tr><td colspan="2">Q18. Absolute Pattern 2: Summary Question Summarizing a sentence, or an entire paragraph
Question Pattern: According to the passage, how would those who were victimized by cyberbullying respond to cyber attack</td></tr>
<tr><td>A) use the same measure of counterattack
B) change their identity
C) resort to law enforcement
D) evangelize social media users</td><td>B) Victims frequently respond by <u>adopting pseudonyms</u> or going offline entirely.</td></tr>
</table>

<table>
<tr><td colspan="2">Q19. Absolute Pattern 11: Textual Evidence Question Finding evidence for the previous question
Question Pattern: Which choice provides the best evidence for the answer to the previous question?</td></tr>
<tr><td>A) Lines 16-19 (The FBI released...cyberstalked as well.)
B) Lines 21-22 (Of those...cyberstalking)
C) Lines 24-26 (cyberbullying…normal bullying.)
D) Lines 36-37 (Victims … entirely.)</td><td>D) Please refer to the above question</td></tr>
</table>

<table>
<tr><td colspan="2">Q20. Absolute Pattern 12: Informational Graphs
Finding facts described in the graphs or relations between the passage and the graph
Question Pattern: Which of the following statements most likely agrees with the pie chart?</td></tr>
<tr><td>A) Law enforcement should take more effort on reducing gender-bias hate crime
B) Tougher control on racial hate crime can reduce cyberbully victims possibly by half
C) Sexual-orientation hate crime is insignificant compared to religious hate crime
D) perpetrators are relatively generous to people with disability</td><td>B) He added that more rigorous crackdown on hate crime—especially racial hate crime—can reduce growing number of victims.by roughly 50%

*48.5% is nearly half of the total victims
(A) Gender bias takes up only 0.3%, insignificant number.
(C) 20.8% (sexual) vs.17.4% (religious) are by far similar
(D) Not stated</td></tr>
</table>

<table>
<tr><td colspan="2">Q21. Absolute Pattern 11: Textual Evidence Question Finding evidence for the previous question
Question Pattern: Which choice provides the best evidence for the answer to the previous question?</td></tr>
<tr><td>A) Lines 9-12 (Cyberbullying … another person)
B) Lines 16-19 (The FBI released...cyberstalked as well.)
C) Lines 36-37 (Victims … entirely.)
D) Lines 37-39 (He added...victims.)</td><td>D) Please refer to the above question</td></tr>
</table>

Questions 22-31 are based on the following passage.

Passage 1	**Passage 2**
Wherever flowering plants flourish, pollinating bees, birds, butterflies, bats, and other animals are hard at work, providing vital but often unnoticed services. (22A & 23C) **But many pollinators are in serious decline. Some three-fourths of all native plants in the world require pollination most often by a native bee.** President Obama issued a memorandum establishing a Pollinator Health Task Force. The Strategy (30A) **expands and adds to actions already being undertaken** by Federal departments to reverse pollinator losses. (29C) **Although USDA has currently released the report showing a positive sign in that the number of managed honey bee colonies has been relatively consistent since 2014, the level of effort by the beekeeping industry to maintain these numbers has increased.**	Honey Bees are the most recognizable pollinators of hundreds of economically and ecologically important crops and plants in North America. These honey bees have been in serious decline for more than three decades in the United States. Starting in the 1940's when there were approximately 5.7 million colonies in the United States, the number of managed colonies used in honey production has declined to approximately 2.74 million colonies today. Sharp colony declines were seen following (Q27A) **the introduction in 1987 of an external parasitic mite** that feeds on honey bee hemolymph (blood). (25A &26C & 28B) **Around 2006, a condition referred to as Colony Collapse Disorder (CCD) was first reported.** Colonies diagnosed with CCD exhibit (24A) **a rapid loss of adult worker bees**, have few or no dead bees present in the colony, have excess brood and a small cluster of bees remaining with the queen bee, and have low Varroa mite and Nosema (fungal disease) levels. Colonies exhibiting CCD have insufficient numbers of bees to maintain the colony and these colonies eventually die.

Q22. **Absolute Pattern 2: Summary Question**
Question Pattern: The discussion of **honey bees in** passage 1 indicates

A) declining pollinators are mostly natives bees B) other pollinators are often unnoticed C) Colony Collapse Disorder is the major cause of the lose of honeybee D) other pollinators are in fact increasing	A) Some three-fourths of all native plants in the world require pollination **most often by a native bee.** B) is not responding to the question. C) is incorrect because the question asks the passage 1, not 2.

C) passage 1 and passage 2 are mutually exclusive. Please refer to incorrect choice pattern # 8

Q23. **Absolute Pattern 11: Textual Evidence Question** Finding evidence for the previous question
Question Pattern: Which choice provides the best evidence for the answer to the previous question?

A) Lines 1-4 (Wherever…services) B) Lines 4-5 (But many pollinators...serious decline.) **C) Lines 5-7 (Some three-fourths...native bees)** D) Lines 8-9 (President Obama...Task Force.)	C) Please refer to the above question

Q24. **Absolute Pattern 2: Summary Question**
Question Pattern: In Passage 2, the **known symptoms** of Colony Collapse Disorder (CCD) include

A) loss of adult worker bees B) sudden dead bees present in the colony C) no signs of brood D) overpopulation in the colony	**A) loss of adult worker bees** have **few or no dead bees** present in the colony, **have excess brood** and a **small cluster of bees remaining** with the queen bee, and have **low Varroa** mite and Nosema (fungal disease) levels. All the other choices are opposite from the passage.

Q25. **Absolute Pattern 10: Understanding the Structure of the Passage** **Question Pattern:** Unlike passage 1, **passage 2**	
A) tries to identify the syndrome from CCD B) endorses the official view of losses of Honeybees C) criticizes the underlying syndrome is overblown by the farmers D) presents specific procedures to control CCD.	A) This question limits your reading scope to passage 2 only. Therefore, options (A), (D) have a greater probability because they focus on "CCD" as it is the most visible word in passage 2. The last sentence in passage 2 ends with symptoms of CCD. Therefore D) is opposite.

Q26. **Absolute Pattern 11: Textual Evidence Question** Finding evidence for the previous question **Question Pattern:** Which choice provides the best evidence for the answer to the previous question?	
A) Lines 1-7 (Whenever flowering...a native bee.) B) Lines 8-12 (President Obama...pollinator losses.) **C) Lines 42-43 (Around 2006, ...first reported.)** D) Lines 49-51 (Colonies exhibiting CCD..eventually die)	C) a condition referred to as Colony Collapse Disorder (CCD) was first reported. A), B) are from passage 1. The answer should be in P2. D) is a part of symptoms description.

Q27. **Absolute Pattern 2: Summary Question** Summarizing a sentence, or an entire paragraph **Question Pattern:** On the basis of information, **Colony Collapse Disorder (CCD) was initially caused** by	
A) bloodsucking mite B) excess brood and a small cluster of bees C) honey bee hemolymph D) toxic pesticide	A) Sharp colony declines were seen following the introduction in 1987 of an external **parasitic mite** that feeds on honey bee hemolymph (blood) (B),(C) are the symptoms and what parasite mite feed on. (D) is Not stated

Q28. **Absolute Pattern 3: Inference Question** Finding an indirect suggestion (or guessing) **Question Pattern:** It can be **inferred** from the passage that	
A) most honey bees have completely disappeared **B) CCD was not known to outside until 2006** C) CCD symptoms did not exist before 2006 D) there is a slight correlation between CCD and the actual bee population decrease	B) **Around 2006,** a condition referred to as Colony Collapse Disorder (CCD) was **first reported.** * CCD was not known until 2006; it, however, doesn't mean it didn't exist before 2006. C) is incorrect because it could have existed without knowing it. A) is too extreme. D) is opposite.

Q29. **Absolute Pattern 8: Understanding True Purpose** **Question Pattern:** In passage 1, the author mentions "**the number of managed honey bees**" in lines 15-16 primarily to	
A) question CCD is the major cause B) certify that the released report is official **C) testify the beekeeping industry's effort to maintain the proper level** D) show the consistent level of honey bee colonies	C) the level of effort by the beekeeping industry to **maintain these numbers has increased**. B), D): The author's main point is not meant to praise USDA' report. In fact, it is opposite. Keep in mind that "although" clause cancels itself out in order to emphasize the main clause.

<table>
<tr><td colspan="2">Q30. Absolute Pattern 3: Inference Question Finding an indirect suggestion (or guessing)
Question Pattern: In line 10, "The Strategy expands ...pollinator losses" suggests that the current strategy</td></tr>
<tr><td>A) is not as effective as it was initially planned
B) continues to appeal to many concerned beekeepers
C) is no more valid today
D) focuses not on immediate but on long-term changes</td><td>A) The Strategy expands and adds to actions already being undertaken...
*"Expands and adds" implies the current strategy is not as effective as it was planned.</td></tr>
<tr><td colspan="2">B) is Opposite C) is Too Extreme. Please refer to incorrect choice pattern #12</td></tr>
<tr><td colspan="2">Q31. Absolute Pattern 12: Informational Graphs
Finding facts described in the graphs or relations between the passage and the graph
Question Pattern: According to the passage, which of the following statements corresponds to the graph ?</td></tr>
<tr><td colspan="2">A) U.S. honey production has dropped steadily since 2000
B) In 2013, both production and production per colony increased roughly 30% compared to the output in 2009.
C) The increase in production between 2007 and 2008 proves that a Pollinator Health Task Force was effective
D) Abnormal production decline between 2000 and 2002 are closely related with CCD</td></tr>
<tr><td colspan="2">A) This question does not require passage information.
Over 70% of graph/chart informational question does not require passage information. So, Please manage your time wisely.</td></tr>
</table>

Questions 32-41 are based on the following passage.

<table>
<tr><td>The San Francisco Bay Area has seen tremendous growth and is expected to grow by an additional 25% in population and (32D & 33B) employment. The region's employment and output outpaced the nation's. Here, employment is growing faster than population and the population faster than housing units.
Growth has posed (34D & 35C) enormous transportation challenges as it relates to the safety, mobility, environment and economic productivity. Some of the key trends include current population growth, increase in number of older citizens and shift of people to mega-regions. (36A) These challenges are now impacting the citizens of San Francisco. Travel in the City is very time-consuming and expensive.</td><td>Problems will get worse. Freight demand is also on the rise. (38A) Increased deliveries in San Francisco have created safety conflicts, double parking, and blocked access with large trucks that are incompatible on the roads of a city like San Francisco.
(39C) To solve this issue, Incorporate Connected and Automated vehicle technology will be proven to be safe to further reduce (37D) travel costs, eliminate collisions and fatalities, and reduce parking demand sufficiently.
Once implemented, (41A) it will re-purpose parking facilities into affordable housing and other city amenities. In the world of transportation, we are no strangers to global firsts; San Francisco is a (40B) testbed of groundbreaking discoveries and trend-setting policies that get replicated globally.</td></tr>
<tr><td colspan="2">Q32. Absolute Pattern 2: Summary Question Summarizing a sentence or entire passage
Question Pattern: The author describes one of the advantages of San Francisco as</td></tr>
<tr><td>A) growing number of older citizens
B) housing affordability
C) transportation system
D) the employment rate</td><td>D) The San Francisco Bay Area has seen tremendous growth and is expected to grow by an additional 25% in population and employment.

All the other choices are problems.</td></tr>
</table>

Q33. **Absolute Pattern 11: Textual Evidence Question** Finding evidence for the previous question **Question Pattern:** Which choice provides the best evidence for the answer to the previous question?	
A) Lines 1-2 (The San Francisco … last few years) **B) Lines 5-6 (The region's employment...the nation's.)** C) Lines 7-8 (Here, employment...housing units.) D) Lines 12-15(Some of the key...mega-regions.)	B) Please refer to the above question C) is negative factor.

Q34. **Absolute Pattern 2: Summary Question** Summarizing a sentence or entire passage **Question Pattern:** "Currently, **the biggest concern** in San Francisco is probably	
A) growing number of citizens B) the number of housing units C) employment output **D) transportation system**	D) Growth has posed **enormous transportation challenges** as it relates to the safety, mobility, environment and economic productivity A), B) are several factors that cause the biggest concern: Transportation. C) is advantage.

Q35. **Absolute Pattern 1: Main Idea Question** Finding the main idea of the entire passage, a specific paragraph, or sentences **Question Pattern:** The main purpose of the **first paragraph** (lines 1-8) is to	
A) celebrate the current and the future growth of the city of San Francisco B) present the city's irresolvable issues **C) indicate growing transportation challenge** D) emphasize the city's fascinating features	C) **enormous transportation challenges** as it relates to the safety, mobility, environment and economic productivity. Please pay special attention to the topic sentence in the following paragraph. When question asks the entire paragraph, it may ask the relationship between the paragraphs.
The first paragraph illustrates the examples of Paragraph 2, which starts with the growing challenges of transportation. B) is too extreme as the passage tries to offer a solution. D) is not the main purpose but only the secondary information	

Q36. **Absolute Pattern 8: Understanding the True Purpose** Finding the true purpose of statement **Question Pattern:** The author mentions "**Some of the key trends**" (line 12) in order to indicate	
A) significant challenges in the city B) short-term manageable problems C) main factors that benefit the city D) reasons for the tremendous growth of the city	A) Some of the key trends include current population growth, increase in number of older citizens and shift of people to mega-regions. **These challenges** are now impacting the citizens of San Francisco *"**These** challenges" is functioning as the amplifier.
B), C), and D) are direct opposite from the passage statement.	

Q37. **Absolute Pattern 2: Summary Question** Summarizing a sentence or entire passage **Question Pattern:** Which of the following **benefits** can be expected from " **Incorporate Connected and Automated vehicle technology** in lines 25-26?	
I. traveling cost efficiency **II. solution to parking demand** III. pollution elimination A) I only B) II, only C) III only **D) I, II only**	D) Incorporate Connected and Automated vehicle technology will be proven to be safe to further reduce **travel costs**, eliminate collisions and fatalities, and reduce **parking demand** sufficiently. III. Is nearly impossible.

Q38. **Absolute Pattern 2: Summary Question** Summarizing a sentence or entire passage
Question Pattern: The **freight demand issues include** all of the following **EXCEPT**

A) mega-regions B) delivery C) safety D) parking	A) Freight demand is also on the rise. Increased **deliveries** in San Francisco have created **safety conflicts, double parking, and blocked access** with large trucks. mega-regions is different issue: the population increase.

Q39. **Absolute Pattern 10: Understanding the Structure of the Passage**
Finding the structure of the entire passage or organizational relations between the paragraphs
Question Pattern: Which of the following is the most accurate description of the **organization in paragraphs 2,3,4,5** in lines 9-35 (Growth has posed enormous...get replicated globally.)?

A) A sequence of observations B) A list of inferences drawn from prediction to facts **C) A statement of the main concerns, followed by specific examples that leads to a plan** D) A series of negative aspects to positive aspect that leads to outlook	C) (Concern) Growth has posed enormous transportation challenges. -> (Specific Examples) Some of the key trends -> (The Plan) Using the Transport Platform model, D) it doesn't mention paragraphs 2,3,4 and also Paragraph 5 doesn't mention about negative aspects of the outlook.

Q40. **Absolute Pattern 5: Word-In-Context Question**
Finding a clue word and the keyword from the sentence in question
Question Pattern: In lines 33 "**testbed**" is closest in meaning to?

A) proven theory **B) platform** C) feasible facilities D) convenient location	B) San Francisco is a testbed of groundbreaking discoveries and trend-setting policies that get replicated globally. A) It's a city Policy, more than a theory. C) is Too Extreme as it implies physical facilities.

Q41. **Absolute Pattern 12: Informational Graphs**
Finding facts described in the graphs or relations between the passage and the graph.
Question Pattern: According to the benefits of Automated vehicle technology introduced in **the last paragraph** (lines 30-35), which choice is also **supported best by the graph**?

A) More affordable housing will be available B) The biggest reduction can be anticipated from transportation costs C) Compared to other factors, pollution reduction will benefit less D) 20% reduction in collisions will also reduce fatalities by 20%	A): reduce parking demand sufficiently to re-purpose parking facilities into affordable housing B): transportation costs will benefit 10%, the lowest reduction. C): pollution reduction will benefit more than transportation. D) is not stated.

This question is integrated type question that requires information from the passage.

Questions 42-52 are based on the following passage.

Last October, LVMH allocated $143 million to found a private museum of contemporary art for its Louis Vuitton Foundation, and commissioned architect Frank Gehry to design and construct it in Paris's Bois de Boulogne. Even for the multinational conglomerate that runs Louis Vuitton, Moët, Hennessy, and 66 other luxury goods companies—all of which you've definitely heard of—this is a considerable investment (42A)**worth investigating.**

What merits a price tag of $143 million? In part, social capital. When prompted to explain why he wished to open the Louis Vuitton Foundation, Bernard Arnault, the CEO of LVMH, said, "We wanted to present Paris with an extraordinary space for art and culture, and demonstrate daring and emotion by entrusting Frank Gehry with the construction of an iconic building for the 21st century." Indeed, Arnault was able to successfully build his museum on a plot of land that had previously been denied to several other land developers. While these competitors wished to construct office buildings and business centers, Arnault was granted control of the land (43B) **because his proposition was deemed to be a noble endeavor to create a public work.**

But in a city that already boasts high concentrations of both art and culture, this was an ambitious—maybe even superfluous—undertaking.

(44A) **It's clear to me** that the goal of creating a rich, new ground for cultural discovery was only of secondary importance to Arnault. Though the museum has staged several provoking shows recently, in its opening weeks it showed nothing more than a condensed version of Arnault's private collection. Rather, Bernard Arnault invested almost $1.5 million in his own brand by reinvigorating the name of Louis Vuitton and thus claiming ownership of the art world in the name of high fashion.

(45C) **It is no secret that newer fashion labels have begun to outmode** Louis Vuitton, the oldest member of the LVMH conglomerate. In tying the brand's name to a new museum that is sleek, beautiful, and houses millions of dollars worth of art, Arnault intended to reposition and revive the label.

In fact, Arnault isn't alone in his ambitiously successful antics. And in the case of Miuccia Prada—the creative director behind the brands Prada and Miu Miu—the endeavor does not stem from a need to reposition her brands at all.

(46B) **A long-time art collector and enthusiast,** Prada's decision to open the Fondazione Prada Museum derives simply from a confidence in her own taste in fine art as a designer of fine clothing.

The Metropolitan's Costume Institute, in tandem with Anna Wintour, mounts a humongous fashion exhibit each year that blurs the line between fashion and fine art in much the same way. In 2011, the museum launched its exhibit in honor of designer Alexander McQueen, and when (47B) **the exhibit singlehandedly attracted more foot traffic than any other in the museum's history.** Though I seriously believe that fashion belongs in museums, it seems that this is not the most effective marketing tactic. (48A & 49A) **However, there does seem to be a way to create museums solely dedicated to clothes that is not alienating, but rather inviting.** Valentino Garavani, owner and designer of the eponymous high-end label, has done so by founding a museum that won't cost him any overhead.

(50D & 51B) **In 2011, Garavani and his partner Giancarlo Giammetti launched the Valentino Garavani Virtual Museum, a website** and accompanying downloadable applet that provides viewers with unlimited, free access to 50 years of the label's haute coutue archives. Featuring cutting-edge, immersive 3-D, the virtual museum allows anyone to interactively explore over 5,000 dresses—their cut, materials, history, and production information.

(48A & 49A) **In comparison to the Louis Vuitton Foundation, Valentino's virtual gallery seems much more honest.**

LVMH's new museum may indeed be a beautiful gift to the art world and a lovely amenity for Parisians, but as a surreptitious marketing attempt, it is ultimately nothing more than sponsored content. (46B) **And while the Fondazione Prada purports only to add to its foundress's empire,** (52C) **I'm interested to see how its opening affects the revenue of the clothing brand that bears her name.**

Q42. **Absolute Pattern 2: Summary Question** Summarizing a sentence or entire passage
Question Pattern: In the **first paragraph** (lines 1-10), the author mainly does which of the following?

A) Speculates about a motivation B) Describe outstanding achievement C) Question practicality D) Forecast failure	A) Even for the multinational conglomerate ...this is a considerable investment worth investigating. (C) "question practicality" implies impracticality. The author warns of its too practical (money) approach, therefore opposite.

Q43. **Absolute Pattern 8: Understanding the True Purpose** Finding the true purpose of statement
Question Pattern: In line 24, the author describes that **"Arnault was granted control of the land" because**

A) the city of Paris valued Arnault's ownership of the art **B) Arnault intentionally misled his true intention** C) several other land developers didn't want the land D) competitors prioritized arts and cultures	B) Arnault was granted control of the land **because** his proposition **was deemed to be** a noble endeavor to create a public work. A) is incorrect because it becomes the favorable aspect of Arnault, whom the author criticizes.

Q44. **Absolute Pattern 5: Word-In-Context Question**
Finding a clue word and the keyword from the sentence in question
Question Pattern: The author's tone in line 30 **("It is clear to me..)** is?

A) Emphatic B) Ambivalent C) Ambiguous D) Polemic	A) It's clear to me that the goal of creating a rich, new ground for cultural discovery was only of secondary importance to Arnault. "It's clear" means Emphatic.

Q45. **Absolute Pattern 5: Word-In-Context Question**
Finding a clue word and the keyword from the sentence in question
Question Pattern: In lines 38 **"reinvigorating"** is closest in meaning to?

A) inviting B) attracting **C) galvanizing** D) gathering	C) Bernard Arnault invested almost $1.5 million in his own brand by reinvigorating the name of Louis Vuitton and thus claiming ownership of the art world in the name of high fashion. Reinvigorating means bringing back to life or galvanizing.

Q46. **Absolute Pattern 7: Understanding Attitude (Tone) Question**
Finding a tone such as positive-negative, active-passive, mental-physical, subjective-objective
Question Pattern: According to lines 53-56, the author views that **Prada's decision to found a museum is based** on

A) duplicity **B) art elitism** C) humanism D) subversive intention	B) A long-time art collector and enthusiast, Prada's decision to open the Fondazione Prada Museum derives simply from a confidence in her own taste in fine art as a designer of fine clothing. *Please note that 'art elitism' contains negative connotation. A) is true statement but does not respond to the question.

Q47. **Absolute Pattern 3: Inference Question** Finding an indirect suggestion (or guessing)
Question Pattern: It can be inferred that the **Metropolitan's Costume Institute** in line 57 would undermine the author's argument by mentioning that Arnault and Prada's motivation are

A) inevitable because the line between fashion and fine art is in much the same way **B) necessary because the museum can attract more museumgoers** C) understandable because they are enjoying singular positions in fashion industry D) inevitable because museum can be the most effective marketing tactic	B) "2011, the museum launched its exhibit...exhibit singlehandedly attracted more foot traffic than any other in the museum's history... (A), (C) are the author's statement in line 50 with pejorative connotation.

Q48. **Absolute Pattern 8: Understanding the True Purpose** Finding the true purpose of statement
Question Pattern: The author's main purpose of referring **Valentino Garavani** in line 73 is to suggest that his museum

A) is more personally appealing B) solely dedicates for sale not for display C) truly represents the cutting-edge technology D) inspired Arnault and Prada's museums	A) (Transition) **However**, there does seem to be a way to create museums solely dedicated to clothes. but rather inviting. (Example) Valentino Garavani,...has done so by founding a museum that won't cost him any overhead. A) "personally" can be understood as both the author herself and the public in general. B) is Opposite. It refers to Arnault and Prada C) is true statements but not the main purpose D) is Not Stated in the passage.

Q49. **Absolute Pattern 11: Textual Evidence Question** Finding evidence for the previous question
Question Pattern: Which choice provides the best evidence for the answer to the previous question?

A) Lines 67-69 (However, there...inviting.) B) Lines 69-72 (Valentino Garavani...any overhead.) C) Lines 78-81 (Featuring cutting-edge...information) D) Lines 82-84 (In comparison...more honest.)	A) Please refer to the above question

Q50. **Absolute Pattern 3: Inference Question** Finding an indirect suggestion (or guessing)
Question Pattern: The main difference between Valentino Garavani museum and Arnault's and Prada's is that **Valentino Garavani museum goers**

A) can obtain affordable clothes displayed in it B) can also access to virtual museum C) can experience the state-of-the-art display **D) must visit virtual museum only**	D) the Valentino Garavani Virtual Museum, **a website** and accompanying downloadable applet that provides viewers with unlimited, free access to 50 years of the label's haute coutue archives (A),(C) are not the main differences. (B) Physical museum doesn't exist.

Q51. **Absolute Pattern 11: Textual Evidence Question** Finding evidence for the previous question
Question Pattern: Which choice provides the best evidence for the answer to the previous question?

A) Lines 64-67 (Though…tactic) **B) Lines 73-78 (In 2011, haute coutue archives.)** C) Lines 82-84 (In comparison…honest) D) Lines 89-92 (And while the Fondazione…her name)	B) Please refer to the above question

Q52. **Absolute Pattern 7: Understanding Attitude (Tone) Question**
Finding a tone such as positive-negative, active-passive, mental-physical, subjective-objective
Question Pattern: The tone of the last paragraph (lines 85-92) is mainly

A) informative B) appreciative **C) cynic** D) optimistic	C) I'm interested to see how its opening affects the revenue of the clothing brand that bears her name. The author's tone in this sentence is clearly sardonic. Therefore, the answer should be the opposite from what it is written.

SAT Test 2

Writing and language Section Answer Explanations

& Pattern Analyses

Test 2 Writing & Language Section Patterns

Questions 1-11 are based on the following passage.

The World Digital Library

The World Digital Library (WDL) is an international digital library operated by UNESCO and the United States Library of Congress. The WDL [1] had stated that its mission is to[2] promoting international and intercultural understanding, expand the volume and variety of cultural content on the Internet, [3] provide resources for educators, scholars, and general audiences, and build capacity in partner institutions to narrow the digital divide within and among countries.[4] Brown University is taking the major role among university participants.

The library intends to make available on the Internet, free of charge and in multilingual format, significant primary materials from cultures around the world, including manuscripts, maps, rare books, musical scores, recordings, films, prints, photographs, architectural drawings, and other significant cultural materials. [5]

After almost 20 years without participation, the United States [6] , which re-established its permanent delegation to the United Nations Educational, Scientific and Cultural Organization (UNESCO) in 2003. Dr. James H. Billington, Librarian of Congress, was nominated as a commissioner of the U.S. National Commission to UNESCO and [7] has been invited to give a plenary speech at its inaugural conference in June 2005.

[8] His speech entitled *A View of the Digital World Library*, which described a vision in which the rich collections that "institutions, libraries, and museums have preserved could be given back to the world free of charge and in a new form far more universally accessible than any forms that have preceded it."

Google Inc. became the first partner of this public-private partnership and donated $3 million to support development of the World Digital Library in 2005. The WDL opened with 1,236 items. As of late 2015, it lists more than 12,000 items from nearly 200 countries, dating back to 8,000 BCE. At the National Commission's 2006 annual conference [9] ,which has been held every year since its establishment, Dr. John Van Oudenaren, Senior Advisor for the World Digital Library at the Library of Congress, outlined a project plan for bringing Dr. Billington's vision to fruition.

Foremost was the belief that the World Digital Library should engage partners in planning the four main project areas: technical architecture, selection, governance, and [10] garnering funding. This was achieved in December 2006, [11] that 45 national library directors, library technical directors, and cultural and educational representatives from UNESCO met in Paris to discuss the development of the World Digital Library.

Q1. Absolute Pattern 24: Verb Tense / Voice Error

The WDL [1] had stated that its mission is to [2] promoting international and intercultural understanding, expand the volume and variety of cultural content on the Internet,(3) provide resources for educators, scholars, and general audiences, and build capacity in partner institutions to narrow the digital divide within and among countries.

	Choice	Explanation
	A) NO CHANGE	A Demonstrative statement uses the present tense. D) This is a demonstrative statement that normally uses the simple present tense (e.g., The sun **rises.** William Shakespeare **is** the greatest playwright in history.) With no simple present tense in the options, the second best alternative should be D) the present perfect. B) and C): Subject-verb agreement error: the subject WDL is singular. "have" and "state" are plural verbs.
	B) have stated	
	C) state	
√	**D) has stated**	

Q2. Absolute Pattern 13: Parallel Structure

	Choice	Explanation
	A) NO CHANGE	D) 1> "its mission is" implies the future action. 2> To-infinitive clause performs the future action. 3> The above sentence is using "to-infinitive clause" in a parallel structure. 4> "to" can be dropped from the second to-infinitive clause, and use the only base verb: ***"to promote, (to) expand, (to) provide, and (to) build."*** A) "~ing" is used for on-going concern B) is noun C) "promote and encourage" is redundant
	B) promotion of	
	C) to promote and encourage	
√	**D) to promote**	

Q3. Pattern 13: Parallel Structure		
The WDL states that its mission is **to promote** international and intercultural understanding, **expand** the volume and variety of cultural content on the Internet,(3) **provide** resources for educators, scholars, and general audiences, and **build** capacity in partner institutions to narrow the digital divide		
√	**A) NO CHANGE**	A) As seen in the previous question, "provide" best meets the parallel structure. "to" can be dropped from the second to-infinitive clause by using only the base verb: ***"to promote, (to) expand, (to) provide, and (to) build."***
	B) by providing	
	C) to provide	
	D) which provides	

Q4. Absolute Pattern 1: Adding, Revising, Deleting, Retaining Information	
Question: Which choice best **connects the sentence with the previous paragraph?**	
[4] Brown University is taking the major role among university participants.	
	A) As written on the passage
√	**B) It aims to expand non-English and non-western content on the Internet, and contribute to scholarly research.**
	C) It is a well-known fact that the Royal Library of Alexandria, Egypt, founded by Ptolemy, is considered to be the greatest ancient library in human civilization.
	D) As the mode of modern information is becoming more digitized, the role of librarians is also shifting dramatically.

B) 1> The previous paragraph describes the international and intercultural promotion
2> The following paragraph describes the multilingual format.
3> Therefore, "the non-English content" is the most suitable topic.

Q5. Absolute Pattern 1: Adding, Revising, Deleting, Retaining Information		
At this point, the author wishes to add the following information. Should the author make this addition here? --**encompassing materials obtained from many countries.**		
The library intends to make available on the Internet, free of charge and in multilingual format, significant primary materials from cultures around the world, including manuscripts, maps, rare books, musical scores, recordings, films, prints, photographs, architectural drawings, and other significant cultural materials. [5]		
	A) Yes, because it provides added information of the materials.	D the phrase should not be added to avoid redundancy. A), B) The inclusion will only repeat the same information mentioned just earlier. C) There is no punctuation issue.
	B) Yes, because it connects well with the previous sentence.	
	C) No, because the usage of the dash is a punctuation error.	
√	**D) No, because it violates a redundant error.**	

Q6. Pattern 21: Subject-Verb, Pronoun, Noun Agreement		
After almost 20 years without participation, the United States [6] ,which re-established its permanent delegation to the United Nations Educational, Scientific and Cultural Organization (UNESCO) in 2003.		
	A) NO CHANGE	D) The sentence requires a verb. A), B) "which" and "that" technically function as a conjunction, creating the sentence without a verb. C) Missing verb
	B) that re-established	
	C) by re-establishing	
√	**D) re-established**	

Q7. Absolute Pattern 24: Verb Tense / Voice Error

Dr. James H. Billington, Librarian of Congress, was nominated as a commissioner of the U.S. National Commission to UNESCO and [7] has been invited to give a plenary speech at its inaugural conference in June 2005.

	Choice	Explanation
	A) NO CHANGE	C) 1> The previous clause uses the simple past tense. 2> The following clause contains "2005" that requires simple past tense.
	B) had been	
√	**C) was**	
	D) is	A) is present perfect and passive voice B) is the past perfect, passive D) is simple present

Q8. Absolute Pattern 16: Precision, Concision, Style

[8] His speech entitled *A View of the Digital World Library,* which described a vision in which the rich collections that "institutions, libraries, and museums have preserved could be given back to the world free of charge and in a new form far more universally accessible than any forms that have preceded it."

	Choice	Explanation
	A) NO CHANGE	Missing verb
√	B) **His speech**, entitled *A View of the Digital World Library*, **described** a vision in which the rich collections that "institutions, libraries, and museums have preserved	
	C) With his speech, entitled *A View of the Digital World Library*, described a vision in which the rich collections that "institutions, libraries, and museums have preserved	
	D) His speech, entitled *A View of the Digital World Library*, described a vision, the rich collections, institutions, libraries, and museums	

B) clears out the errors in the original sentence by
1>offsetting a pair of commas to the inessential information (unrestrictive modifier) "entitled...World library".
2> using the proper subject-verb arrangement (His speech...described)

C) has no subject. "With" should be deleted. D) changes the original meaning by creating an awkward sentence: "institutions, libraries, and museums could be given back..."

Q9. Absolute Pattern 19: Redundant Error

At the National Commission's 2006 annual conference [9],which has been held every year since its establishment,

	Choice	Explanation
	A) NO CHANGE	Always Pick the Shortest One from the Multiple Choices! D) "since its establishment" contains no meaningful information. The underlined portion is good for nothing.
	B) ,held every year since its establishment,	
	C) that has been held yearly since its establishment	A), B), C) are redundant. All of them repeat the word 'annual' only in a slightly different manner.
√	**D) delete the underlined portion.**	

Q10. Absolute Pattern 16: Precision, Concision, Style

Foremost was the belief that the World Digital Library should engage partners in planning the four main project areas : technical architecture, selection, governance, and [10]garnering funding.

	Choice	Explanation
	A) NO CHANGE	C) "Funding" maintains the parallel noun structure.
	B) fund	A) 'funding' itself contains the meaning 'garnering," redundancy. B) can be confused as a verb. D) is wordy
√	**C) funding**	
	D) collecting working capital	

Q11. Absolute Pattern 7: Conjunction Error		
This was achieved in December 2006, [11]that 45 national library directors, library technical directors, and cultural and educational representatives from UNESCO met in Paris to discuss the development of the World Digital Library.		
	A) NO CHANGE	'that' can't link the time clause. "that" should not be placed with a comma after "2006"
	B) in	'in' is a preposition that can't carry a clause
	C) in which	'in which' can be understood as 'where,' a place, not 'when.' "2006" is time, not a place.
√	**D) when**	Time-phrase should be linked by 'when'

Questions 12-22 are based on the following passage.

From Charles Darwin Autobiography

[12] German Editor, Gunter Schiller [13] having written to me for an account of the development of my mind and character with some sketch of my autobiography, I have thought that the attempt would amuse me, and might possibly interest my children or their children.

[14] I had found no difficulty, for life is nearly over with me. I have taken no pains about my style of writing.

I was born at Shrewsbury on February 12th, 1809, and my earliest recollection goes back only to when I was a few months over four years old, when we went to near Abergele for sea-bathing, and I recollect some events and places there with some little distinctness.

My mother died in July 1817, when I was a little over eight years old, and [15] it is odd that I can remember hardly anything about her except her death-bed. In the spring of this same year I was sent to a day-school in Shrewsbury, where I stayed a year.

I have been told that I was much slower in learning than my younger sister Catherine, and I believe that I was in many ways a naughty boy. Mrs. Darwin was a Unitarian and attended Mr. Case's chapel. But [16] both he and his brother were christened and intended to belong to the Church of England. My taste for natural history, and more especially for collecting, was well developed. I tried to make out the names of plants [17] and collected all sorts of things, shells, seals, franks, coins, and minerals.

The passion for collecting which leads a man to be a systematic naturalist, a virtuoso, or a miser, was very strong in me, and was clearly innate, [18] as none of my sisters or brother ever had this taste.

I may here also confess that as a little boy I was much given to inventing deliberate [19] falsehoods, and this was always done for the sake of causing excitement. [20] Moreover, I once gathered much valuable fruit from my father's trees and hid it in the shrubbery, and then ran in breathless haste to spread the news that I had discovered a hoard of stolen fruit. I must have been a very simple little fellow when I first went to the school. ① A boy the name of Garnett took me into a cake shop one day, and bought some cakes for which he did not pay, as the shop man trusted him. ②When we came out I asked him why he did not pay for them, and he instantly answered, "Why, do you not know that my uncle left a great sum of money to the town on condition that every tradesman should give whatever was wanted without payment to anyone who wore his old hat and moved it in a particular manner?" and he then showed me how it was moved. ③He then went into another shop where he was trusted, and asked for some small article, moving his hat in the proper manner, [21] but he was such a naïve boy as I recall.

[22] When we came out he said, "Now if you like to go by yourself into that cake-shop (how well I remember its exact position) I will lend you my hat.

Q12. Absolute Pattern 20: Restrictive Modifier (Essential Information)		
	A) NO CHANGE	D) 1> German Editor and Gunter Schiller is one person. 2> Gunter Schiller should be treated as an essential information. 3> In fact, to maintain the logical sentence, "Gunter Schiller (who)" is more important than "German Editor (what)" . 4> Therefore, The name should not be offset by a pair of commas
	B) German Editor, Gunter Schiller,	
	C) German Editor Gunter Schiller,	
√	**D) German Editor Gunter Schiller**	

Q13. Absolute Pattern 24: Verb Tense / Voice Error

German Editor Gunter Schiller [13] having written to me for an account of the development of my mind and character with some sketch of my autobiography, I **have thought** that the attempt would amuse me, and might possibly interest my children or their children.

	Choice	Explanation
√	**A) NO CHANGE**	The usage of 'having' A) German Editor Gunter should have written to Charles Darwin before Charles Darwin thought about it. Therefore, the answer should be "having written." (meaning after he wrote)
	B) written	
	C) wrote	
	D) has written	B) The participle 'written' is used to express a passive voice 'being written,' C) and D) are verb. However, the main verb—"have thought"— is already present, creating critical errors, such as comma splice, run-on, etc.

Q14. Absolute Pattern 23: Transition Words for Supporting Detail, Contrast, and Consequence

[14] I **had found** no difficulty, **for** life is nearly over with me. I **have taken** no pains about my style of writing.

	Choice	Explanation
	A) NO CHANGE	B) The previous portion should be the primary sentence that contains the subject and verb. It's because what's following is a subordinating clause "**for** life is nearly over with me" needs the primary clause. Therefore, it should be either A) or B).
√	**B) Nor have I found difficulty,**	
	C) Finding not difficulty,	
	D) Without finding difficulty,	A) The same storyline can't jumble with different tenses. A) "had found" is past perfect. The past perfect tense can't be used along with the present tense "have taken" in the following sentence. C) and D) aren't even sentences

Q15. Absolute Pattern 24: Verb Tense / Voice Error

My mother died in July 1817, when I was a little over eight years old, and [15] it is odd **that I can** remember hardly anything about her except her death-bed.

	Choice	Explanation
√	**A) NO CHANGE**	A) 1> This autobiography passage is a narrative form. 2> The present tense is the most ideal tense in narration. 3> The other non-underlined portion also uses the present tense.
	B) its	
	C) it was	B) 'its' is a possessive pronoun, and has no verb. C) is simple past D) is past perfect.
	D) it had been	

Q16. Absolute Pattern 15: Prepositional Idiom

But [16] both he and his brother were christened and intended to belong to the Church of England;

	Choice	Explanation
√	**A) NO CHANGE**	Correlative conjunction "both ~ and" A) The subjective pronoun 'he' should be used after the conjunction "But"
	B) both him and his brother	B) 'him' is objective pronoun.
	C) both his and brother	C) 'his' is possessive pronoun.
	D) both he as well as his brother	D) The idiom "both ~ and" can't be replaced with "both ~ as well as."

Q17. Absolute Pattern 1: Adding, Revising, Deleting, Retaining Information

At this point, the writer is considering adding the following sentence. Should the writer make this addition here?

—Rev. W.A. Leighton brought a flower to school and taught us how by looking at the inside of the blossom the name of the plant could be discovered, which greatly roused my curiosity—

√	A) Yes, because it is **consistent with the previous sentence** and provides some added information.
	B) Yes, because it enlightens us as well on how to find names of plants.
	C) No, because it interrupts the paragraph's description of young Charles Darwin.
	D) No, because Rev. W.A. Leighton is inessential character and is unnecessary to introduce.

A) The previous sentence introduces young Darwin's innate penchant for nature.
The following sentence further sketches his early curiosity for nature.
B) The reader is not mentioned and therefore unnecessary.
C), D) The added information makes the passage more descriptive.

Q18. Absolute Pattern 23: Transition Words for Supporting Detail, Contrast, and Consequence

The passion for collecting which leads a man to be a systematic naturalist, a virtuoso, or a miser, was very strong in me, and was clearly innate, [18] as none of my sisters or brother ever had this taste.

	A) NO CHANGE	B) Two clauses are contradicting to each other. Therefore, the conjunction "but" must be used.
√	**B) but**	
	C) and	A) 'as,' equalizes the idea. C) 'and' is used for a parallel structure.
	D) moreover,	D) 'moreover' is used to add or emphasize the previous sentence.

Q19. Absolute Pattern 23: Transition Words for Supporting Detail, Contrast, and Consequence

I may here also confess that as a little boy I was much given to inventing deliberate [19] falsehoods, and this was always done for the sake of causing excitement.

√	**A) NO CHANGE**	A) Conjunction "and" is required because the sentence flows as the parallel structure.
	B) falsehood, whereas	B) 'whereas' means 'on the contrary,' expressing an opposite view.
	C) falsehood, indeed,	C) and D) are incorrect because they are adverb, not a conjunction, and therefore can't tie the following clause.
	D) falsehood, consequently,	C) 'indeed' is used to emphasize the previous statement. D) "consequently" is used for the cause-and-effect relation.

Q20. Absolute Pattern 23: Transition Words for Supporting Detail, Contrast, and Consequence

[20]Moreover, I once gathered much valuable fruit from my father's trees and hid it in the shrubbery, and then ran in breathless haste to spread the news that I had discovered a hoard of stolen fruit.

	A) NO CHANGE	C) 1> 'For instance' adds details to the topic sentence. 2> The previous sentence sketches young Charles Darwin's childhood naivety.
	B) Thus,	
√	**C) For instance,**	A) 'Moreover' is used to add up another complementary statement B) 'Thus' is used to reveal the consequence.
	D) In the meantime,	D) 'In the meantime,' is used to show the different perspective from the previous statement

Q21. Absolute Pattern 1: Adding, Revising, Deleting, Retaining Information

He then went into another shop where he was trusted, and asked for some small article, moving his hat in the proper manner, [21] but he was such a naïve boy as I recall.

Which choice most closely **matches the stylistic pattern established earlier in the sentence**?

	A) NO CHANGE	C) flows well with the storyline.
	B) so that the tradesman could remember the remarks from the boy's uncle.	A) "naïve" doesn't fit in the description about the boy as he is a shoplifter
√	**C) and of course obtained it without payment.**	B) and D) are parts of lies the boy intrigued young Charles Darwin, not a true statement.
	D) while mentioning about his uncle to the tradesman.	

Q22. Absolute Pattern 1: Adding, Revising, Deleting, Retaining Information

When we came out he said, "Now if you like to go by yourself into that cake-shop (how well I remember its exact position) I will lend you my hat.

To make the passage most **logical, the sentence should be placed**

	A) where it is now.	D) The current position is correct. It is young Charles Darwin's turn to steal.
	B) after sentence 1	
	C) after sentence 2	
√	**D) after sentence 3**	

Questions 23-33 are based on the following passage.

The Greenhouse gas effects

Greenhouse gas concentrations in the atmosphere will continue to increase [23] unless the billions of tons of our annual emissions decrease substantially. Increased concentrations are expected to increase Earth's average temperature, influence the patterns and amounts of precipitation, reduce ice and snow cover, as well as permafrost, raise sea level, and increase the acidity of the oceans. [24] Temperature [25] increases and other climate changes may directly impact our food and water supply, ecosystems, coasts, and human health. The bars in the bottom box indicate what temperatures and impacts are expected under the high and low emissions scenarios, which are determined by our actions.

The magnitude and rate of future climate change will primarily depend on many uncertain factors. Among many noted estimates, the IPCC's "SRES" scenarios have been frequently used to make projections of future climate change.

The SRES scenarios are "baseline" (or "reference") scenarios, which means that the current or future measures that limit GHG emissions are not to be rigidly defined.[27] Emissions projections of the SRES scenarios are [28] comparable in range to the baseline emissions, which are broad in scenarios that have been developed by the scientific community.

Many greenhouse gases stay in the atmosphere for long periods of time. [29] As a result, even if emissions stopped increasing, atmospheric greenhouse gas concentrations would continue to increase and remain elevated for hundreds of years. Even if we stabilized concentrations and the composition of today's atmosphere, (which would require a dramatic reduction in current greenhouse gas emissions), surface air temperatures [30] will continue to warm. This is because [31] the oceans, which store heat, take many decades to fully respond to higher greenhouse gas concentrations. The ocean's response to higher greenhouse gas concentrations and higher temperatures will continue to [32] effect climate over the next several decades to hundreds of years.

Therefore, over the next several millennia, projections suggest that global warming [33] could affect the global economy. Even if emissions were drastically reduced, global temperatures would remain close to their highest level for at least 1,000 years

Q23. Absolute Pattern 1: Adding, Revising, Deleting, Retaining Information		
Which choice offers the most logical information to support the entire passage?		
√	**A) NO CHANGE**	A) The topic, the title, and the following passage are all about warning against the greenhouse gas emission. This sentence well presents the negative mood.
	B) although there is nothing we could do about it	
	C) , but some folks believe that it's an overblown media tactic.	B) is too regressive.
	D) ,which concentrates in our atmosphere	C) is opposite perception from the main view D) simply rewrites Greenhouse effect.

Q24. Absolute Pattern 1: Adding, Revising, Deleting, Retaining Information	
At this point, the author wishes to **add** the following phrases. Should the author make this addition here? *The mechanism is named after a faulty analogy with the effect of solar radiation passing through glass and warming a greenhouse. The way a green house retains heat is fundamentally different*	
	A) Yes, because it provides added examples of the previous discussion.
	B) Yes, because unlike the previous information, the addition brings more objective and mechanical function of the Greenhouse.
	C) No, because some of the additions are redundant and unnecessarily wordy.
√	**D) No, because it blurs the focus of the sentence**
D) 1> (The Previous Sentence) Earth's average temperature, influence the patterns and amounts of precipitation, reduce ice and snow cover, as well as permafrost, raise sea level, and increase the acidity of the oceans. [24] 2> (The Following Sentence) Temperature [25] increases and other climate changes may directly impact our food and water supply, ecosystems, coasts, and human health. Both previous and following sentences discuss the Earth temperature change caused by the Greenhouse. 3> The question asks whether the new sentence introducing the origin of the term "greenhouse" can be inserted in the middle. The answer is D) No.	

Q25. Absolute Pattern 21: Subject-Verb, Pronoun, Noun Agreement		
Temperature [25] increases and other climate changes **may directly impact** our food and water supply, ecosystems, coasts, and human health.		
	A) NO CHANGE	D) "Temperature increase and other climate changes" should be the subject, not a verb: we know this by looking at the verb "'may directly impact"
	B) ,which increases fast	
	C) has been dramatically increased	A), C) both use "increases" as a verb B) is wordy
√	**D) increase**	

Q26. Absolute Pattern 9: Informational Graphs	
According to the information in the passage, which choice offers an accurate interpretation of the data in the chart?	
	A) Sea-level changes present the unclear relationship with greenhouse effect
	B) Thermal expansion in atmosphere is the direct effects of Atlantic temperature anomaly
√	**C) The future sea level tells that drastic emission control won't make much difference.**
	D) The future sea level will be controlled within decades by our effort

(Topic Sentence): Greenhouse gas concentrations in the atmosphere will continue to increase unless the billions of tons of our annual emissions decrease substantially…. as well as permafrost, raise sea level.
(Concluding Sentence): Even if emissions were drastically reduced, global temperatures would remain close to their highest level for at least 1,000 years
C) is correct according to the graph and the passage.
A) is direct opposite to the first and the last sentences of the passage as well as to the graph.
B) "Thermal expansion in atmosphere" is not mentioned in the passage.
D) is direct opposite to the concluding sentence.

Q27. Absolute Pattern 1: Adding, Revising, Deleting, Retaining Information	
Among many noted estimates, the IPCC's "SRES" scenarios have been frequently used to make projections of future climate change. The SRES scenarios are "baseline" (or "reference") scenarios, which means that the current or future measures that limit GHG emissions are not to be rigidly defined. [27]	
Which choice **supports** the previously mentioned sentence?	
	A) SRES are, by far, the best, and therefore, should be employed as the most rigid guidelines
	B) SRES forecast only up to 10 years of measurement.
	C) SRES should never be practically applied.
√	**D) SRES may function as the guidelines.**

D) Based on the underlined portion of the sentence, only D) should be the answer.

A), C) are opposite to the statement. B) is not stated in the passage.

Q28. Absolute Pattern 16: Precision, Concision, Style		
Emissions projections of the SRES scenarios are [28] comparable **in range to** the baseline emissions, **which are broad in** scenarios that have been developed by the scientific community.		
	A) NO CHANGE	Always Pick the Shortest One from the Multiple Choices! C) is most succinct and precise.
	B) comparable and relative to the baseline emissions scenarios broadly	
√	**C) broadly comparable to the baseline emissions scenarios**	
	D) comparable to the baseline emissions scenarios, which are broad.	

A) "which are broad" is wordy and changes the original meaning.
B) "comparable" and "relative" are synonym.
D) "scenarios are broad" changes the meaning.

Q29. Absolute Pattern 2: Cause-Effect Relations

Many greenhouse gases stay in the atmosphere for long periods of time. [29] As a result, even if emissions stopped increasing, atmospheric greenhouse gas concentrations would continue to increase and remain elevated for hundreds of years.

√	**A) NO CHANGE**	A) The two sentences sitting between the adverb "As a result" clearly indicate the cause and effect.
	B) But,	B) cancels out the previous sentence.
	C) On the other hand,	C) suggests a different view.
	D) Nonetheless,	D) means despite what has been said and done.

Q30. Absolute Pattern 24: Verb Tense / Voice Error

Even **if we stabilized** concentrations and the composition of today's atmosphere, (which would require a dramatic reduction in current greenhouse gas emissions), surface air temperatures [30] will continue to warm.

	A) NO CHANGE	B) "if we stabilized" indicates that the verb in the main clause has to be the past tense.
√	**B) would continue**	A), C) are future. D) is present progressive tense .
	C) are going to continue	
	D) are continuing	

Q31. Absolute Pattern 22 : Non-Restrictive Modifier (Inessential Information)

This is because [31] the oceans, which store heat, take many decades to fully respond to higher green-house gas concentrations.

√	**A) NO CHANGE**	A) 'which store heat' is non-essential information. Therefore, it should be off-set by a pair of commas to separate it from the main clause.
	B) the oceans which store heat	B) hasn't got a pair of commas
	C) the oceans, that store heat,	C) "that" cannot be followed by a comma.
	D) the oceans store heat	D) "store" is a verb when he main verb "take" is already presented.

Q32. Absolute Pattern 6: Confusing Words

The ocean's response to higher greenhouse gas concentrations and higher temperatures will continue to [32] effect climate over the next several decades to hundreds of years.

	A) NO CHANGE	B) "affect" is normally used as a verb.
√	**B) affect**	A) "effect" is more often used as a noun
	C) endanger	C) and D) change the meaning.
	D) push negatively	

Q33. Absolute Pattern 10: Logical Expression

Therefore, over the next several millennia, projections suggest that global warming [33] could affect the global economy.

	A) NO CHANGE	D) Throughout the passage, the author's primary concern is the irreversible dire impact of the greenhouse. The author describes that the global warming trends will not change.
	B) could be significantly reduced	A) is new information, not supported by neither the previous nor the following sentence.
	C) could be possibly reversed	B) and C) are opposite perception
√	**D) could be irreversible**	

Questions 34-44 are based on the following passage. **Café de Cat** Cat cafés are quite popular in Japan, with Tokyo being home to 58 cat cafés as of 2015. [34] Other forms of pet [35] rental such as rabbit cafés, are also common in Japan. [36] There are various types of cat café in Japan, some feature specific categories of cat such as black cats, fat cats, rare breed cats or ex-stray cats. Every cat café in Japan is required to obtain a license and comply with the strict requirements and regulations of the nation's Animal Treatment and Protection Law. Japanese cat cafés feature strict rules to ensure cleanliness and animal welfare, in particular seeking to ensure that the cats are not disturbed by [37] excessive and unwanted attention, such as by young children or when sleeping. Many cat cafés also seek to raise awareness of cat's welfare issues, such as abandoned and stray cats. Cat cafés have been spreading across North America [38] after 2014. The goal in North America generally is to help get cats adopted by partnering with local cat rescuers. ① The cat cafés across this region have come together to create The North American Cat Cafe Embassy. ②Saturday, October 17, 2015 saw the opening of Ontario's first cat café located in Guelph, Ontario.	③ The first cat café to open in North America was Le Café des Chats/Cat Café Montreal in Montreal, Canada, which opened its doors to the public in August 2014 [39] ,with 8 cats adopted from local shelters. ④ Catfe opened in Vancouver, British Columbia on December 14, 2015 and Kitty Cat Café and Pet Me Meow are both planning cafés for Toronto to open in 2015. Cat cafés in the United States differ from those in many other countries by their focus on adoptions. Hundreds of animals have been adopted through [41] their efforts. [42] Also, in United States, compliance with governmental food service regulations is required. The area where the cats are playing or being considered for adoption must be entirely separated from the area where food and drink are served. For example, a newly adopted cat must leave [43] without passing a food serving area through a separate door. In May 2015, Grand Rapids, Michigan, announced Happy Cat Cafe will open sometime in 2016. They are hoping to partner with The Humane Society of West Michigan. The cafe raised $26,821 on Kickstarter with 549 backers. In October 2015, the Blue Cat Cafe opened in Austin, Texas, [44] thereby partnering with the Austin Humane Society as a cafe and adoption center. It has live music for cats.

Q34. Absolute Pattern 1: Adding, Revising, Deleting, Retaining Information

At this point, the author considers to add the following information, Should the author add this information here?

The popularity of cat cafés in Japan is attributed to many apartments forbidding pets, and to provide cats relaxing companionship in what may otherwise be a stressful and lonely urban life.

	A) Yes, because it establishes the psychological role cat can impart to its owner.
√	**B) Yes, because it gives further explanations behind their popularity.**
	C) No, because such a detail doesn't fit in the introductory paragraph
	D) No, because it mentions positive effects only to the place where side-effects should be presented.

A) The main theme is Cat Café, not a cat.
C) The degree of details in this sentence is necessary to support the topic sentence.
D) The overall essay is written from the positive point.

Q35. Absolute Pattern 18: Punctuation Error

Other forms of pet [35] rental such as rabbit **cafés, are** also common in Japan.

	A) NO CHANGE	C) "such as" phrase is not an essential part of the information in the sentence structure. Therefore, it should be separated from the main clause by a comma A) and D): Comma should separate "such as" from the main clause. B) Comma after "rabbit cafes" separates the verb from its main clause.
	B) rental, such as rabbit cafes,	
√	**C) rental, such as rabbit cafes**	
	D) rental such as rabbit cafes	

Q36. Absolute Pattern 18: Punctuation Error	
Question: Which of the following choices would **NOT be an alternate** sentence?	
	A) Japan: some featuring specific categories of cat, such as black cats, fat cats, or ex-stray cats.
	B) Japan, such as black cats cafe, fat cats cafe, or ex-stray cats cafe.
	C) Japan, to name a few with black cats cafe, or ex-stray cats cafe.
√	D) **Japan, which featuring** specific categories of cat such as black cats, fat cats, or ex-stray cats.

D) "which" must carry a clause. "featuring..." is a phrase, not a clause: either removing 'which' or fixing "which featuring" to "which features" is required.

A) A colon allows any type of statement. B) 'such as' presents a series of example
C) 'to name a few' presents a series of example.

Q37. Absolute Pattern 10: Logical Expression

Japanese cat cafés feature strict rules to ensure cleanliness and animal welfare, in particular seeking to ensure that the cats are not disturbed by [37] excessive and unwanted attention,

√	**A) NO CHANGE**	A) "excessive," an adjective, describes the following noun "attention"
	B) excessively	B) is an adverb and cannot modify noun.
	C) excess	C) means surplus D) is passive form of adjective "excess".
	D) excessed	

Q38. Absolute Pattern 15: Prepositional Idiom

Cat cafés have been spreading across North America [38] after 2014.

	A) NO CHANGE	D) 'since' should be used when the primary clause uses the present perfect or past perfect tense.
	B) in	A) 'after' and 'since' are not interchangeable. B) "in" and C) "by" can't replace 'since'
	C) by	
√	**D) since**	

Q39. Absolute Pattern 5: Comma Splice Error

The first cat café to open in North America was Le Café des Chats/Cat Café Montreal in Montreal, Canada, which opened its doors to the public in August 2014 [39] ,with 8 cats adopted from local shelters.

Which of the following choices would **NOT be an appropriate** alternative phrase?

	A) –having 8 cats adopted from local shelters.	D) Comma splice error.
	B) ,which started with 8 cats adopted from local shelters	A) A single dash emphasizes the following modifier. B) 'which' functions as a conjunction that allows the subordinating clause to follow
	C) , by home-staying 8 cats adopted from local shelters.	C) A preposition 'by' carries a gerund, 'home-staying, which is an ideal form of this sentence structure.
√	D) , 8 cats **were adopted** from local shelters.	

Q40. Absolute Pattern 11: Logical Sequence		
Question: To make this paragraph most logical, sentence 2 should be placed		
②Saturday, October 17, 2015 saw the opening of Ontario's first cat café located in Guelph, Ontario.		
	A) Where it is now	<1>.The cat cafés across this region have come together **to create The North American Cat Cafe Embassy.**
	B) Before sentence 1	<2> Saturday, **October 17, 2015** saw the opening of Ontario's first cat café located in Guelph, Ontario.
√	**C) After sentence 3**	<3> The first cat café to open in North America was Le Café des Chats/Cat Café Montreal in Montreal, Canada, which opened its doors to the public in **August 2014 ,** with 8 cats adopted from local shelters.
	D) After sentence 4	<4>. Catfe opened in Vancouver, British Columbia on **December 14, 2015** and Kitty Cat Café and Pet Me Meow are both planning cafés for **Toronto to open in 2015.**
Based on the chronological sequence above, sentence 2 should be located after sentence 3.		

Q41. Absolute Pattern 17: Pronoun Error		
Cat cafés in the **United States** differ from **those** in many **other countries** by **their** focus on adoptions. Hundreds of **animals** have been adopted through [41] **their** efforts.		
	A) NO CHANGE	A) ambiguity error. 1> The pronoun "their" indicates too many antecedents, blurring what it actually refers to: "their" could be "Cat cafes", "those" or other countries." Avoid using a pronoun when more than two nouns without clear distinctions are placed in one sentence
	B) Catcafe	B) The noun must be the possessive to connect "efforts."
	C) Its	C) The singular pronoun "Its" doesn't represent any word in the sentence.
√	**D) Animal rescuers'**	

Q42. Absolute Pattern 23: Transition Words for Supporting Detail, Contrast, and Consequence		
[42] Also, in United States, compliance with governmental food service regulations is required.		
√	**A) NO CHANGE**	A) The previous sentence, by focusing on adoption, introduces the different function of Catcafé in U.S. The following sentence further explores the regulations by using "Also."
	B) Consequently,	B) 'Consequently,' is used for cause-and-effect situation.
	C) While,	C) 'while' is mainly used for contradiction.
	D) Delete	

Q43. Absolute Pattern 12: Modifier Placement Error		
For example, a newly adopted cat must leave [43] without passing a food serving area through a separate door.		
	A) NO CHANGE	B)"leave through a door" is the correct modifier
√	B) **through a separate door**, without passing a food serving area.	A) It sounds as if "food serving area" is in a separate door.
	C) a food serving area through a separate door.	C) changes the meaning, "cat must leave a food serving area." (Are cats already there?)
	D) through a food serving area, without passing a separate door.	D) changes the meaning ("cat.. can't pass a separate door.")

Q44. Absolute Pattern 16: Precision, Concision, Style		
	A) NO CHANGE	D) 'partnering ~ ' is much more clear expression.
	B) whereby it partners	A), B), and C) all contain unnecessary conjunctive adverbs and the pronoun "it,"
	C) in which it partners	
√	**D) partnering**	

Chapter 2 Summary

Chapter Summary contains equal portions of

-12 Absolute Patterns for Reading Section

-20 Common Patterns for Incorrect Choices in Reading

-70 Absolute Patterns for Writing and Language Section

-24 Common Patterns for Incorrect Choices in Writing

You may study all at once to significantly

improve your understanding and your scores.

Chapter 2

12 Absolute Patterns for the Reading Section

Absolute Pattern 4: Example Question

Jimin : I think I can give a real shot for this kind of question. I love reading example sentences.

San: You love reading example sentences because it's easy to understand! Example sentences are supposed to be easy that helps the authors to clarify their main argument. Example sentences are almost certainly identifiable through a specific name or idea used in sentence. However...

...However, the example sentence itself rarely contains the answer in it. It merely supports the main idea.

The example sentence supports the main argument by illustrating the event or idea. Sometimes, it uses historical figures' speech or authorities' quotation, or analogy, etc. Since the example sentence is easier to understand than the main argument, folks try to find the answer by focusing on the example, but the example sentence betrays these folks' innocent wishes.

The answer should mostly be located right above or right below the example sentence. That's where the topic or the concluding sentences are.

Sometimes, the last sentence in a paragraph can be the example sentence. In that case, the topic sentence in the following paragraph can produce the answer because that's where the main idea starts, although many folks cut short reading the next paragraph, never imagining answer could possibly be there.

Chapter 2

12 Absolute Patterns for the Reading Section

Pattern 5: Word-in-Context Question

Jimin : Do I need to memorize tons of SAT vocabularies?

San: Yes. The Word-in-Context Pattern asks two types of questions: (1) Finding the precise meaning of the word—normally high-level SAT vocabulary. (2) Identifying the figurative meaning or the word usage in a unique situation.

I made those uninspiring vocabularies into pretty sexy ones. If you need them, let me know. Here's my email: satvancouver@gmail.com

(1) The words in multiple choices are literal meaning, NOT figurative: consider only the very first definition from the dictionary, not the second or third, or figurative one.
(2) When the word-in-context question asks the meaning of seemingly easy vocabulary, Never rely on your memory. I guarantee that you will miss this question if you undermine the easy word and do not review the passage.

The passage should provide clue words. Never skip finding a clue word from the passage.
The Word-in-Context question is not a piece-of-cake because it looks simple.
If you nosedive into the four multiple choices, you will be instantly trapped in. Game over! Everything will be confusing. So do not look at the multiple choices until you come up with a synonym for the question.
Real deal is to matching the synonym that you're guessing with the multiple choices.

Most importantly, you must distinguish between the clue word and the keyword in the multiple choices.
A clue word can be a flamboyant adjective or adverb, sitting pretty next to the plain answer that can be as simple as "it" (the singular pronoun).
Your job is to pick the keyword for the answer," not the pretty clue word.

Try this! What would you choose between
(A) foreboding relationship
(B) it.

Jimin: it's (B) now.
It looks pretty enough.

Chapter 2

12 Absolute Patterns for the Reading Section

Absolute Pattern 8: Understanding the True Purpose

To understand the true purpose of statement, indispensable is finding the main clause from the subordinating or conditional clause/phrase (i.e., although…., while…,).

in other words, you should distinguish the primary information from the secondary.

The trickiest part of this pattern is that it does not give you clear keywords, just like the inference question or analogy question.
Paradoxically, for this very reason, the exactly written statement in the multiple choices can be incorrect because that won't be the true purpose.

For example, if question sentence starts with "Much has been said about animal testing…,"
You should smell the Negative tone in the sentence. The true purpose behind the sentence forebodes a dire circumstance of animal welfare. Therefore, the answer choice should be Negative. It should never be positive, exactly because "much has been said" contains negative connotation.

Incorrect choice may use a bait such as keywords like "animal testing" with a positive tone. The correct answer may contain fuzzy words, but still it will be definitely negative tone. That's the beauty of finding answers without knowing exactly why.

The keywords in passage should be located at/near the:

√ coordinating conjunction "but (or similar perception), although/however, yet.

√ correlative conjunction such as "more ~ than"

√ transition words/phrase such as "on the other hand", in fact,", "Consequently," despite, notwithstanding.

70 Absolute Patterns for Writing Section

Question 7
That nickel-and-dime store where I used to buy stationery when I was only five-year-old kid was abandoned, leaving only a faded signage on the roof of the building.

A) NO CHANGE
B) That nickel and dime store where I used to buy stationery when I was only a five year old kid
C) When I was only a five year old kid, I used to buy stationary at that nickel-and-dime store
D) I used to buy stationery at that nickel-and-dime store when I was only five year old kid

RULE #7
Hint:
Hyphen

HYPHEN
The correct answer is A.
A) The hyphen is mainly used as an adjective by joining two or more words together.
The "nickel-and-dime" and "five-year-old" are the correct forms.
B), contrary to (A), has no hyphens. C) and D) are run-ons.

Example sentences using the hyphen as a compound adjective
-The employer is fed up with his do-nothing secretary.
-That thirteen-year-old girl got pregnant is not big news in some parts of Africa.
-We cannot give you with a money-back guarantee under this discount term.
-The newly introduced iPhone is not quite a state-of-the-art technology.

Question 8
The present interreligious conflicts in France which was ignited by the extreme Jihadist turned the entire Europe in turmoil.

A) NO CHANGE
B) France, that was ignited by the extreme Jihadist, turned
C) France, which were ignited by the extreme Jihadist turned
D) France, which were ignited by the extreme Jihadist, turned

RULE #8
Hint:
Punctuation

Double Commas for Non-restrictive Modifier (Inessential Information).

The correct answer is D.
D) Non-restrictive modifier means that some modifier is an inessential Information to understand and construct the entire sentence. It can be a short or long phrase or clause.
When placed in the middle of the independent sentence, it should be offset by a double commas acting as a parenthesis.
The present interreligious conflicts in France **(which was ignited by the extreme Jihadist)** turned the entire Europe in turmoil.
As seen above, the clause inside of the parenthesis "(which was...Jihadist)" is not necessary to construct the complete sentence or to understand it. It should be regarded as an inessential information and is called the Non-restrictive Modifier. Therefore, it should be offset by commas. Another error is "was." The subject is "conflicts," a plural.
A) is direct opposite to D.
B) is incorrect because "that" is normally used for a restrictive modifier. In other words, "that" should not be followed by a comma.

Continued

RULE #8
Hint:
Punctuation

B) is also subject-verb agreement error. The subject is conflicts"
C) has only one comma, creating a sentence fragment
The following examples illustrate appositive elements (a noun or noun phrase that describes the noun using double commas)

Ex1) The heart of Europe ***Paris*** is invaded by another terrorism.
Ex2) The heart of Europe***, Paris with more than 10% of Islam population,*** is invaded by another terrorism.
Ex3) The heart of Europe***, Paris that has proclaimed the war against terrorism,*** is invaded by another terrorism.

Other Non-restrictive Modifier Examples that require double commas.
Ex4) Chad's dream***, to become a national hockey player,*** is on the brink of a fiasco.
Ex5) Lynn***, the husband of the former Chairman in a big company,*** decided to buy an oil refinery company.

Question 9
The actor Tom Cruise established his own film company.

A) The actor Tom Cruise established
B) The actor, Tom Cruise, established
C) The acting film star, Tom Cruise, established
D) The actor who is Tom Cruise established

RULE #9
Hint:
Punctuation

Omitting Double Commas
The correct answer is A.
A) If the appositive and the word it modifies are so closely related (essential information), double commas should be omitted.
Without "Tom Cruise" the sentence will lose its original meaning and become very ambiguous because there are so many actors.

B) is incorrect because the double comma should not be used.
C) changes the meaning D) is wordy.

Question 10
The doctor recommended his patient take three pills a day.

A) his patient taking
B) his patient take
C) his patient takes
D) that his patient to take

RULE #10
Hint: Verb

Imperative Verb in Subjunctive Mood

The correct answer is B.
B) The imperative verb is used to give order or instruction.
When the imperative verb is used in a subjunctive mood—that you desire or imagine something is to be done or someone should do something, the model verb "should" can be dropped, and the only base verb is used.

Continued

RULE #10
Hint: Verb

Some typical imperative verbs are as follow: "ask", "demand", "determine", "insist", "move", "order", "pray", "prefer", "recommend", "regret", "request", "require", "suggest", and "wish".

The verb for the third person singular (he/she), in this process, drops the -s or -es.

A) is incorrect because "taking" is gerund used for going-concern.
C) is incorrect because, in an imperative situation, the verb must use the base verb, pretending that there was "should" before the base verb.
D) is incorrect because "to take" is not a verb.

Question 11
After I graduated high school, I have never been in a serious relationship with anyone.

A) NO ERROR
B) With my graduation from high school
C) Since I graduated high school
D) When I graduated high school

RULE #11
Hint: Verb

Since + The Present Perfect Tense

The correct answer is C.
C) "Since" always comes along with the present perfect tense.
A) "After" can't replace "since"
B) and D) are illogical sentences.

Question 12
While reading a detective novel, my cat was sleeping inside my arms.

A) my cat is sleeping inside my arms
B) I held my sleeping cat inside my arms
C) I fell asleep with my cat inside my arms
D) a sleeping cat was inside my arms

RULE #12
Hint:
Modifier

MODIFIER

The correct answer is B.

B) A typical question in dangling modifier is switching the rightful subject with something else. The original sentence—although it appears to be correct and clearly understood—is defective in that "my cat" can't read. The subject has to be human, who can read. Dangling Modifier means a disruption of descriptive clause.

Harder Example

Incorrect: Completely exhausted, the marathoner's uniform felt like wearing armor.
Correct: Completely exhausted, the marathoner in uniform felt as if he was wearing armor.

Question 13:
Jenkins, the professor, invited his international students on Thanksgiving day to serve a traditional turkey, wearing an old pilgrim costume.

A) NO CHANGE
B) after "Jenkins"
C) after "students"
D) after "Thanksgiving day"

RULE #13 Hint: Modifier	**Misplaced Modifier** The correct answer is B. B) Misplaced Modifier means the disruption of descriptive phrase, which should be placed after or before the thing or person it supposes to describe. The modifier "wearing an old pilgrim costumes" must be logically located after the person. C) is incorrect because "costume" is singular, but the "students" are plural, an impossible situation as if they all share a single clothe.

Question 14
Whatever the majority of the board decides does not reflect the employees' pay increase.

A) decides, reflect no pay increase of the employees.
B) decides, do not reflect the employees' pay increase.
C) makes on their decision do not reflect the employees' pay increase.
D) decides does not reflect the employees' pay increase.

RULE #14 Hint: Subject	**A Whole Package of Dependent Clause as a Subject** The correct answer is D. When the entire dependent clause acts as a subject, it should be treated as a single noun. The subject is " Whatever the majority of the board decides" The verb then should also be a singular "does not reflect" For this reason, all the other options are incorrect

Question 15
For the past year, every effort by Republican senators to topple Obama care considering embarrassing failure.

A) NO CHANGE
B) care considered embarrassing
C) care was considered embarrassingly
D) care was considering embarrassingly

RULE #15 Hint: Verb	**Sentence Fragment** The correct answer is C. Sentence fragment means that either subject or verb or both in a sentence are not in place; therefore, not functioning as an independent clause. C) maintains the correct passive verb "was considered" The sentence—based upon the meaning—requires a passive verb. Active voice options like B, D are wrong.

Chapter 2

24 Common Patterns for *In*correct Choices in Writing

5 Comma Splice Error

Comma splice appears when two independent sentences (clauses) are not joined by a conjunction but by a comma.

Comma splice error is one of the most frequently used incorrect option tricks. Just remember two clauses need one conjunction.

6 Confusing Words

This pattern asks the frequently confusing words (e.g., 'complement' and 'compliment')

7 Conjunction Error

There are three types of conjunctions: coordinating, subordinating, and correlative

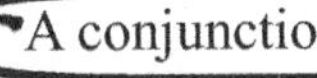

A conjunction connects two clauses.

Typical questions related with this pattern ask
(1) whether the statement is a clause or a phrase—a phrase should not be connected to a conjunction,
(2) whether a type of conjunction is properly used.

Three types of conjunctions are summarized in the appendix or all over in Google.

Chapter 2

24 Common Patterns for *In*correct Choices in Writing

8 Double Negative Error

Double negatives usually carry negative adverbs, such as 'hardly,' 'rarely,' 'seldom,' or 'without.'

One of these adverbs come together with 'not,' 'didn't,' or 'isn't,' creating a double negative error.

9 Informational Graphs

Informational graph questions are made of two types: (1) Independent question that requires no information from the passage
(2) Integrated question that require information from the passage.

Independent type appears more frequently, about 70 percent in SAT Official Test. You really do not have to waste your time peeking on the reading passage, even though the question indiscriminately asks you to read the passage.

This is what everyone in the College Board knows, except... you, maybe.

10 Logical Expression

This pattern borrows the technique from Word-In-Context in the reading passage.

Unlike that of reading section that focuses more on distinguishing literal meaning from figurative,

the logical expression in Writing section more often comes with the rules of syntax such as adjective, adverb, noun, and verb usage.

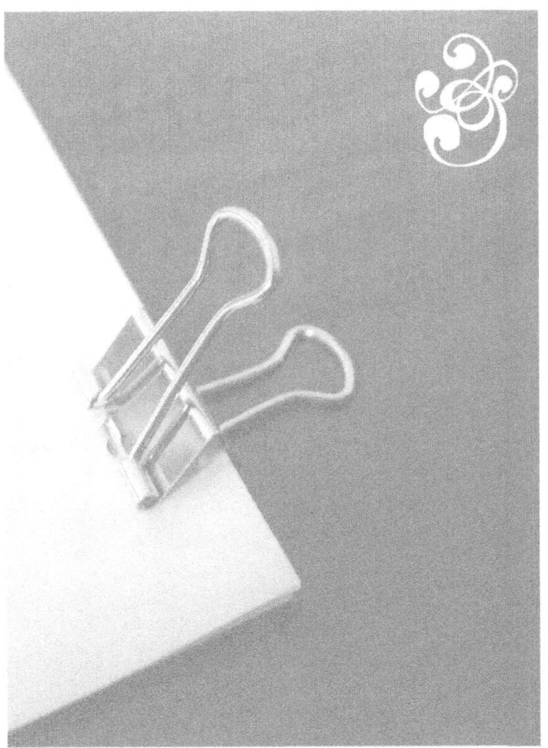

Chapter 3

1. TEST 3

2. ANSWER EXPLANATIONS for TEST 3

3. CHAPTER SUMMARY

SAT

Reading & Writing Practice

Test 3

ALL THE LOGIC AND RULES
BEHIND THE EVERY SINGLE
SAT QUESTION

Reading Test 3

65 MINUTES, 52 QUESTIONS

The passages below are followed by questions based on their content; questions following a pair of related passages may also be based on the relationship between the paired passages. Answer the questions on the basis of what is stated or implied in the passages and in any introductory material that may be provided.

Questions 1-10 are based on the following passage.

This passage is from Pride and Prejudice by Jane Austen Elizabeth visits Lady Catherine.

Mr. Collins's triumph was complete. The power of displaying the grandeur of his patroness to his wondering visitors, and of letting them see her civility towards himself and his wife, was exactly what he had wished for. ; and that an opportunity of doing it should be given so soon, was such an instance of Lady Catherine's condescension, as he knew not how to admire enough.

"I confess," said he, "that "I should not have been at all surprised by her ladyship's asking us on Sunday to drink tea. Who could have foreseen such an attention as this?" Lady Catherine will not think the worse of you for being simply dressed. She likes to have the distinction of rank preserved."

As the weather was fine, they had a pleasant walk. Every park has its beauty and its prospects, though she could not be in such raptures as Mr. Collins expected.

Lady Catherine was a tall woman. Her air was not conciliating, nor was her manner of receiving them such as to make her visitors forget their inferior rank. She was formidable by silence and was in authoritative tone.

1

Mr. Collins invited his visitors to Lady Catherine's place mainly to

A) build a new constructive relations with the visitors

B) allow the visitors to observe Lady Catherine's hospitality towards him

C) reconcile the visitors and Lady Catherine

D) find an opportunity to amass wealth

2

According to the passage Mr. Collins's persona can be seen as

A) cheerful

B) condescending

C) humble

D) ostentatious

3

Which of the following, if true, would be most in keeping with the main character trait of Mr. Collins?

A) Susan often uses an assumed name similar to that of rich people she knows to impress others

B) Max morally opposes the wrong doing of the rich people

C) Daniel lives in constant fear of running out of money and relies on the rich people

D) Cathy finds the condescending gesture of the rich people and advises her friends to ignore it

CONTINUE

1

4

Which choice provides the best evidence for the answer to the previous question?

A) Line 1 (Mr. Collins's triumph… complete)
B) Lines 2-5 (The power … his wife)
C) Lines 9-11 (I confess… drink tea)
D) Lines 20-23 (Lady Catherine was...inferior rank.)

5

The primary purpose of the passage is to

A) highlight the insightful characteristic of Mr. Collins
B) illustrate the supportive relationship between Mr. Collins and Lady Catherine
C) point out the major goal of Mr. Collins
D) demonstrate the societal status of Lady Catherine

6

Lady Catherine's role with Mr. Collins is most similar to that of

A) a confidant
B) an old friend
C) an abiding beneficiary
D) a condescending benefactor

7

In line 15 "preserved" most nearly means ?

A) Unviolated
B) Defended
C) Conserved
D) Acknowledge

8

The description in lines 17-19 (Every park has… Mr. Collins expected) suggests that Elizabeth

A) was not in such a joyful mood
B) was greatly inspired by the surroundings
C) was in such great rapture
D) was resentful to the other characters

9

Elizabeth observes that Lady Catherine as

A) a realistic and truly respectful person
B) a young and handsome person
C) a person hiding inferiority
D) a person creating superiority by lowering others

10

Which choice provides the best evidence for the answer to the previous question?

A) Line 1 (Mr. Collins's triumph… complete)
B) Lines 2-5 (The power … wished for;)
C) Lines 20 (Lady Catherine was a tall woman)
D) Lines 20-23 (Her air was...inferior rank.)

CONTINUE

1 1

Questions 11-21 are based on the following passage.

This passage is adapted from U.S. Food and Drug Administration Center for Drug Evaluation and Research Janet Woodcock, M.D. Director, Center for Drug Evaluation and Research January, 2016

Each year, CDER approves hundreds of new medications, most of which are variations of previously existing products, such as new dosage forms of already-approved products, or cost-saving generics. These new products contribute to quality of care, greater access to medication, more consumer choice that enhances affordability and public health.

However, products in a small subset of these new approvals, that we refer to as novel drugs, are among the more truly innovative products that often help advance clinical care to another level. Every year, CDER summarizes these new products.

The annual summary reports the quantity of novel drugs that it approved. However, it also focuses on the high quality of many of these new drugs, their contributions to enhanced patient care.

This year, we approved many new drugs to treat various forms of cancer, including myeloma, lung, skin, breast. This year's field also includes new drugs to treat reversal agent for a blood thinner.

For the first year, we approved more "orphan" drugs for rare diseases than any previous year in our history. In calendar year 2015, FDA's Center for Drug Evaluation and Research (CDER) approved 45 novel drugs, approved as new molecular entities (NMEs) under New Drug Applications (NDAs) or as new therapeutic biologics under Biologics License Applications (BLAs).

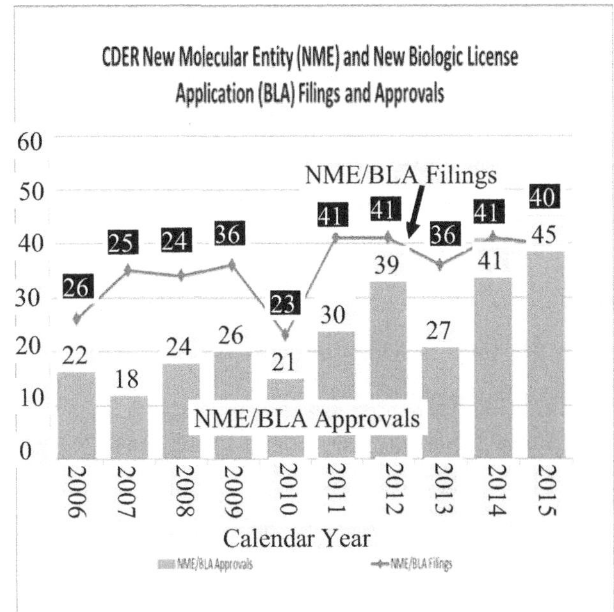

11

In describing new medications in line 1, the author emphasizes all of the followings EXCEPT

A) they will completely replace existing products

B) they will contribute to quality of care

C) they will allow greater accessibility to mediation

D) they will give more consumer choice

12

According to the 1st paragraph, which of the following medications would LEAST likely be approved by CDER?

A) Pills already-approved with new dosage forms

B) Cost-saving generic pills

C) Pills that allow greater access to the patients

D) Already-approved pills with more appealing name

13

Which of the following analogies most resembles "The annual summary" in line 15?

A) A boy reads over dozens of comics to kill time.

B) A respected physicist writes his autobiography

C) A chef buys over twenty boxes of only the highest quality tomatoes

D) A pianist renders music with a low quality piano

1 1

14

The main characteristics of Novel drug is that it is?

A) advanced and innovative

B) less expensive

C) more concerned with public health

D) little known previously

15

Which choice provides the best evidence for the answer to the previous question?

A) Lines 1-5 (Each year, ...cost-saving generics.)

B) Lines 5-8 (These new products...public health.)

C) Lines 9-12 (However, products...another level)

D) Lines 19-21 (This year,...skin, breast.)

16

The primary purpose of the passage is to

A) highlight the novel drugs approved by CDER

B) propose a change of the government regulations

C) distinguish between new medications and novel drugs

D) show the procedures CDER approves hundreds of new medications

17

Which choice provides the best evidence for the answer to the previous question?

A) Lines 1-5 (Each year, ...cost-saving generics.)

B) Lines 9-12 (However, products...another level)

C) Lines 19-21 (This year,...skin, breast.)

D) Lines 21-22 (This year's field...a blood thinner.)

18

In Line 23, "orphan" most nearly refers to

A) a drug for child without parent

B) a drug for rare diseases with a single purpose

C) an illegal drug without a name

D) a highly replicable and affordable drug

19

Paragraph 3 (lines 8—11) suggests that CDER has approved the new drugs available to the patients with or need of EXCEPT

A) multiple myeloma

B) skin cancer

C) lung cancer

D) a new blood thinner

20

Which of the following criteria is NOT expressed as the approval standards for new drug by CDER ?

A) The new molecular entities (NMEs)

B) New Drug Applications (NDAs)

C) World Health Organization Applications (WHO)

D) The Biologics License Applications (BLAs)

21

Which of the following statements most accurately interprets the graph following the passage ?

A) The filed numbers were highest in 2014

B) The approvals were lowest in 2010

C) The ratio of filed numbers vs. the approvals was highest in 2014

D) Nearly half of the filed numbers were approved in 2015

CONTINUE

1 1

Questions 22-31 are based on the following passage.

The Happiness Sale
By Marshall Zhang, Harvard University
© The Harvard Crimson
Reprinted with Permission

A. J. Maxwell's was an archetypal New York steakhouse on the corner of 48th and 6th in the heart of midtown Manhattan. There, a few weeks after my middle school graduation, my family splurged on a celebration of our first road trip to America. I distinctly remember the forty-dollar entrées that dotted the menu (the opulence of it all!), and sinking my teeth into a steak that the Old Spaghetti Factories I was used to could only dream of serving.

Today, A. J. Maxwell's is closed after years of poor reviews, with references to overpriced food and jerky-like steaks dating back to far before my visit. Though I can't say for certain, I suspect the steak I had eight years ago was not, in any particular way, noteworthy in the grand scheme of beef. But somehow that steak remains in my mind, more vividly than any steak I've had since, as close to perfection as a slab of meat can be. Diminishing marginal utility is one way to understand this seeming contradiction.

Loosely, this is the idea that the marginal (read: additional) utility (read: benefit) of extra stuff diminishes as we have more stuff to begin with: We would love an extra dollar if we only had ten dollars to our names, but could probably care less about the same dollar as millionaires.

For similar reasons, my very first fancy steak—though not incredible per se—was far more memorable than my tenth. The first let me peek into a whole new world of fine dining, while the tenth probably wasn't all that special next to the nine other fancy steaks before it.

As thoroughly broke college students who in the median will earn between $50,000 and $69,999 upon graduation and likely even more later in life, our marginal utility is high now relative to our expected marginal utility 20 years down the road. In other words, as we become older and richer, things and experiences that amaze us now will probably lose their luster.

We might understand this as a sale on happiness: Today, it would almost certainly take more than forty dollars to buy a steak as incredible to me as the one my 13-year-old self savored so dearly at A. J. Maxwell's. In more concrete terms, imagine we knew that, like the average American, we would be spending $55,000 every year by the middle of our lives (note, for the record, that the argument here works even if we're not planning on being a big future spender).

If we had the power to move a thousand dollars of that spending to today, we almost certainly would. Imagine if we had an extra grand today! Instead of a trip into Boston, we could take a once-in-a-lifetime trip to Paris.

It turns out that financial markets have created a way for us to move money through time in exactly this way: debt. We can borrow money from the bank today and pay it back with our higher incomes in the future, effectively taking out a loan from our richer, future self. The logic of introductory economics would say that we should squeeze every last penny out of the happiness sale in this way, borrowing large amounts of money to finance increased spending today until we could expect to consume roughly the same amount at every point in our lifetimes. But perfectly spreading out our consumption like this is impossible in practice and probably undesirable to boot.

Few banks would be willing to issue the large loans we would need, and we might be worried about the risk of being saddled with debt if we ended up earning less than we expected to. Furthermore, consumption is often positional, in the sense that what matters isn't necessarily how much we consume, but how much we consume relative to those around us. In other words, your 20-year class reunion might not be a lot of fun if you're paying down debt while your classmates are busy buying nice houses. We've been taught since childhood to spend when we know we'll have more and save precisely when we have little. Though this seems fairly reasonable, it certainly doesn't sound right to me those farmers who gorge themselves during good harvests and only attempt to store grain in bad harvests. Rather, they should be saving excess grain in good years so that they have more to eat in bad years.

But there will likely never be another time in our lives when happiness today can be found for so cheap relative to happiness tomorrow.

CONTINUE

1

22

The word "archetypal" in line 1 most nearly means

A) old

B) representative

C) ancient

D) very typical

23

In line 14-20 (Though I...meat can be.), the author feels that way because

A) his marginal utility was highest point that time

B) he wasn't aware of marginal utility that time

C) his appetite has changed since then

D) sales on happiness is just a concept

24

The author repeatedly uses the word "imagine" in lines 48 and 56 in order to

A) explain how depressing the reality is without marginal utility

B) qualify that marginal utility is only fancy idea

C) tell that we can do anything with marginal utility

D) show how fascinating the marginal utility is

25

Which of the following situations is most similar to marginal utility the author describes?

A) A church priest who restrains earthly desires

B) A rich entrepreneur who became an epicure

C) A film star who is fond of his first small role

D) A prolific writer who performs many roles other than writing

26

In discussing the marginal utility, the author addresses all of the following concerns EXCEPT

A) taking out a big loan against future income to spend now

B) earning less than we expected in the future

C) thinking that happiness today can be found for so cheap relative to happiness tomorrow

D) having the sense of how much others consume

27

Which choice provides the best evidence for the answer to the previous question?

A) Line 73-74 (Few banks...we would need)

B) Line 74-76 (we might be worried...we expected to)

C) Line 77-80 (Furthermore,...around us.)

D) Line 92-94 (But there will....happiness tomorrow.)

28

The passage is primarily concerned with

A) the problem of marginal utility

B) wide variety of consumption practice

C) emotional impact on a unique economic hypothesis

D) relationships between money and happiness

29

Which choice provides the best evidence for the answer to the previous question?

A) Lines 70-72 (But perfectly ...undesirable to boot.)

B) Lines 77-80 (Furthermore, ...those around us.)

C) Lines 83-85 (We've been taught...we have little)

D) Lines 92-94 (But there will be... tomorrow.)

30

The author's attitude toward the "farmers" in line 87 can be best described as

A) genuinely puzzled

B) solemnly respectful

C) condescendingly skeptical

D) generally indifferent

31

Which of the following persons would have the similar appreciation to the steak that the author once had at A. J. Maxwell's steakhouse?

A) we who become older and richer (line 40)

B) a bank lending money today (line 62)

C) yourself paying down debt (line 82)

D) farmers (line 87)

CONTINUE

1

Qustions 32-41 are based on the following passage.

The following passages describes about Virtual Reality and its consequences by Declan p. Garvey
April 18, 2014
Harvard University ©The Harvard Crimson
Reprinted with Permission

On Sunday morning Twitter user @Queen Demetriax_'s tweeted the following to the American Airlines corporate account:

> sarah@queendemetrizx@americanair
>
> Hellow my name's Ibrahim and I'm from Afghanistan. I'm part of Al Qaida and on June 1st I'm gonna do something really big bye. 10:37 am – 13 Apr 2014
>
> Within minutes, the company responded: @queendemetriax_ sarah, we take these threats very seriously. your IP address and details will be forwarded to security and the FBI.

Despite her frantic claims that she was "kidding," Dutch officials showed up at the Rotterdam native's house and arrested her on the spot, drawing to a close a news story that would have been completely fruitless had it not provided me a topic to write about. For that, you and I both have @QueenDemetriax's unreliable frontal lobe to thank. What this narrative seems to highlight however is not merely one girl's lapse in judgment (especially considering dozens of teenagers followed her lead), but a larger phenomenon in which Internet users fail to associate their online actions with real-world consequences. Senseless and shortsighted uses of the Internet have led to unemployment, pedophilia, robberies, political scandals, and arrests.

Older generations have always entertained at slight distrust of new technologies, fearing the limits of their privacy. And their kids have always gotten entertainment from that distrust. "No Grandpa, Gmail isn't asking for your birthday so they can steal your pension." "Yes, Mom, that's a webcam. No, Mom, the government can't watch you through it." Although...

But all kidding aside, maybe more Internet users need of figures like my dad reminding them that there is in fact a world that exists beyond the perimeters of their various screens.

One of the defining characteristics of our generation is our increasing technological proficiency and ability to master new platforms so quickly. But we've grown so accustomed to computers and social media that the magnitude of our online actions is forgotten. Despite what some privacy settings may claim, anything posted online is available to anyone at any time.

The novelty of these websites and applications has worn off, and for all intents and purposes, online postings are just as legitimate a form of communication as human interaction. Academics who study human behavior and the brain are just now beginning to understand the cognitive impact of social media on its 1.73 billion users worldwide. Significant levels of Internet usage can lead to loneliness, jealousy, suicidality, and memory deficiency. But the most fundamental change wrought by the Internet is our unprecedented need for constant and immediate affirmation. I'll be the first to admit, the number of likes I receive on a post has a direct impact on my mood in the short-run.

After accumulating 18 favorites on some stupid tweet over winter break, I spent the rest of the day parading around my house like a king. For those of you who dismiss the significance of this effect, I'll leave you with this. What else could have possibly motivated @QueenDemetriax_ to hit the send button? Was she testing American Airline's security procedures? Is she actually the worst terrorist of all time? No, and I don't think so. She hoped she could muster out a few favorites and maybe a retweet or two.

Well @QueenDemetriax, you got 10,000 of them, but they won't do much for you in jail. And maybe a retweet or two.

CONTINUE

1 1

32

In line 5-16, The author describes @Queen Demetriax' primarily to present

A) the extent to which a tweeter user can fabricate the story so easily
B) American Air's overreaction to one teenager's naivety
C) the main argument
D) one girl's lapse in judgment

33

Which choice provides the best evidence for the answer to the previous question?

A) Lines 24-26 (For that, ...frontal lob to thank.)
B) Lines 26-29 (What this...followed her lead),
C) Lines 29-31 (but a larger...consequences.)
D) Line 43-46 (But all kidding...various screens)

34

The author suggests that 'unconscious and abusive acts through internet can result in EXCEPT

A) political scandals
B) incarceration
C) removal from work
D) being bullied

35

The description in lines 47-55 (One of the...any time) emphasizes the author's feeling toward his generation that they

A) enjoy technology wholeheartedly
B) master new platforms in no time
C) find great difficulty in remembering online activities
D) are unaware of reckless online behavior

36

The author's attitude to younger generations' using social media is that

A) younger generation should be proud of proficiency
B) younger generation should be more attentive to what they are doing in social media
C) social media limits our privacy
D) older generation should resemble younger ones' technological proficiency

37

Which choice provides the best evidence for the answer to the previous question?

A) Lines 35-37 (Older generations... their privacy.)
B) Lines 47-50 (One of the...so quickly.)
C) Lines 51-53 (But we've....forgotten.)
D) Lines 53-55 (Despite what...any time)

38

In line 57, the discussion of "online postings as legitimate a form of communication" primarily serves to

A) emphasize the novelty of applications
B) explain that the online postings become as common as any other form of communications
C) trace the nature of online communication
D) give legal guidelines

39

Which best describes the primary function of the last sentence (lines 82-84)?

A) It offers a lighthearted behavior of an online user
B) It examines the role of online communication
C) It illustrates retweet won't do much in jail
D) It provides commentary about the consequence of malpractice

40

In line 80, "muster" most nearly means

A) necessitate
B) collect
C) brag
D) infiltrate

41

In lines 74-77 (What else … all time?), the author uses a series of rhetorical questions to emphasize

A) the author's belief that the young girl was naïve
B) that retweet is useful in a real world
C) the author's main concern
D) tougher security against terrorism is required

1

Questions 42-52 are based on the following passages

The following two passages discuss Islam and Democracy Empirically, numerically.
Harvard University Crimson©
Reprinted with Permission

Passage 1

Before the man was deposed, <u>Egyptian President</u> Mohamed Morsi was roundly derided for ramrodding through a new constitution that would have, as his critics charged, made Egypt into an illiberal theocracy.

Of special consternation was its second article, which declared that "Islam is the religion of the state and Arabic its official language. Principles of Islamic Sharia are the principal source of legislation." But when Egypt's next constitution, shepherded in by the military and ratified as Morsi stood trial, was found to contain nearly-identical language, the bells of discontent were not rung quite so small. Religious clauses in constitutions have abounded in Muslim countries, whether ruled by monarchs or mullahs, presidents or prime ministers, ever since Syria's 1950 post-colonial constitution declared Islamic jurisprudence to be the basis for legislation. Sharia can be described as "a principal source" of legislation.

Islam is either labeled as merely supreme or laws deemed repugnant to it are made explicitly invalid. So-called "repugnancy clauses," which invalidate laws judged contradictory to Islam and are perhaps the strongest endorsements of religion. Imagine if Goldilocks were to go constitution-picking. She would settle on something not too theocratic, not too secular. In the Muslim world, that may be just right.

Ranking Muslim Constitutions

Score on Islamic Constitution Index (ICI),2014 ICE SCORE

Country	Score (0–30)
Saudi Arabia	23
Iran	23
Iraq	15
Egypt	7
Malesia	5
Turkey	0
Indonesia	0

Source: D. Ahmed and A. Gouda *On a 0-30 scale, 30=most Islamic

Passage 2

Are democracy and constitutional Islam at odds? It is a complicated question, sure to be bandied about in the halls of the academy. But an empirical approach to this question can also be worthwhile.

One helpful measure is the Islamic Constitutions Index, developed by the academics Dawood I. Ahmed and Moamen Gouda, which assesses the degree of Islamic endorsement by constitutions on a scale from zero to 30 based on the demands made on public morality, rights and legislation, and the judiciary. Topping the chart, perhaps not unexpectedly, are regional rivals Iran and Saudi Arabia, the first a Shia theocratic quasi-democracy and the other a Sunni monarchy. But immediately following them is Pakistan, ally governed country with moderate civil rights protections—not quite as renowned for morality police or punishments like amputation and beheading. Avowedly secular Turkey is placed at the bottom.

On average, constitutions with higher measures of Islamic provisions in their constitutions are associated with worse scores in The Economist Intelligence Unit's democracy index, Freedom House's civil liberties ratings, the World Economic Forum's gender gap index, and the Pew Research Foundation's index of government restrictions on religion.

Does this analysis affirm the warning that "the elevation of Iranian-style theocrats," as one critical academic put it at the time, would undo the democratic order? (Here, the familiar chiding about correlation and causation need be remembered.) Meanwhile, Western nations were recently involved in rewriting the Iraqi and Afghanistan constitutions, both of which prominently enshrined the position of Islam that balances democracy. Between the high-minded sphere of constitutional design and actual, day-to-day impact on residents lies the apparatus of censors, judges, and policemen who modulate constitutional demands and translate them for the common man. What constitutions prescribe and what bureaucracies end up dealing out can be quite different.

CONTINUE

1 1

42

In line 11, "shepherded in" most nearly means

A) Sheep rearing
B) Herding
C) Directed
D) Pioneered

43

According to the passage 2, Saudi Arabia (line 41) is considered as the state where

A) constitutional Islam and democracy are mutually exclusive
B) Shia theocratic quasi-democracy is constantly evolving
C) democracy supersedes a Sunni monarchy
D) high Islamic endorsement is practiced by the constitutions

44

It can be inferred from lines 46-48 in passage 2 that morality police or punishments like amputation and beheading are

A) quite renowned in all Islamic states
B) not practiced in Pakistan
C) practiced more widely outside of Pakistan territory
D) not accepted under the civil rights protections in any Islamic states

45

The main purpose of both passages is

A) to study how Egypt strived to apply Islam to its governance.
B) to explore persistent religious conflicts in the Middle East
C) to opinion relations between democracy and religion in the world
D) to understand the constitutional Islam states in modern times

46

The examples cited in the third paragraph (lines 49-56) in Passage 2 are primarily intended to express the author's idea that

A) all Islamic states maintain relatively higher morality than other democratic nations
B) high Islamic provisions do not necessarily possess positive economic and civil rights
C) there is no democracy in Islamic states according to Freedom House's ratings
D) the government restrictions to religion in Islamic states need to be abolished

47

The parenthesis (Here… remembered.) in lines 60-62 in Passage 2 is mainly used to

A) qualify the previous remarks
B) emphasize the previous question
C) highlight the correlation between Islam and democracy
D) warn the elevation of Iranian-style theocrats

48

Which country in Passage 2 would the former Egyptian President Mohamed Morsi (line 1) in passage 1 probably attempt to resemble?

A) Iran (line 41)
B) Pakistan (line 44)
C) Turkey (line 48)
D) Iraq (line 63)

49

The reference to 'Goldilocks' in line 26, passage 1 conveys which of the following countries in Passage 2?

A) Saudi Arabia (line 41)
B) Pakistan (line 44)
C) Turkey (line 48)
D) Afghanistan (line 64)

CONTINUE

1 1

50

The author of Passage 1 would probably respond to lines 49-56 in Passage 2, (On average… religion.) by stating that

A) some index such as western gender laws are deemed to be repugnant to Islamic constitution

B) the Islamic states use a unique and different index

C) all the statistics are inaccurate

D) definitions of index are not easily identifiable among countries

51

Which choice provides the best evidence for the answer to the previous question?

A) Lines 1-5 (Before the man...illiberal theocracy.)

B) Lines 6-8 (Of special consternation...official language.)

C) Lines 10-14 (But when Egypt's next...so small.)

D) Lines 21-25 (Islam is either...endorsements of religion.)

52

Which of the following countries in the graph most likely agrees with the author's reference to 'Goldilocks' in line 26, passage 1

A) Iran

B) Saudi Arabia

C) Indonesia

D) Iraq

Writing and Language Test 3
35 MINUTES, 44 QUESTIONS

Each passage below is accompanied by a number of questions. For some questions, you will consider how the passage might be revised to improve the expression of ideas. For other questions, you will consider how the passage might be edited to correct errors in sentence structure, usage, or punctuation. A passage or a question may be accompanied by one or more graphics (such as a table or graph) that you will consider as you make revising and editing decisions.

Questions 1-11 are based on the following passage.

AIRBNB

Airbnb is an online marketplace that enables people to list, [1] browsing a place to stay temporarily, then rent vacation homes for a processing fee.

It has over 1,500,000 listings in 34,000 cities and 191 countries. Founded in August 2008 and [2] headquartered in San Francisco, California, the company is privately owned and operated. Shortly after moving to San Francisco in October 2007, Brian Chesky created the initial concept for AirBed & Breakfast. The original site offered short-term living quarters, breakfast, and a unique business networking opportunity for attendees who were unable to book a hotel in the saturated market.

1

A) NO CHANGE
B) find,
C) look for other people's house
D) searching for,

2

A) NO CHANGE
B) San Francisco as its headquarter
C) headquarter in San Francisco,
D) Airbnb has its headquarter in San Francisco

CONTINUE

2 2

At the time, roommates Chesky and Gebbia could not afford the rent for their loft in San Francisco. They made their living room into a bed and breakfast, accommodating three guests on air mattresses and providing homemade breakfast.

In February 2008, technical architect Nathan Blecharczyk joined as the third co-founder of Air Bed & Breakfast. During the company's initial stages, the founders focused on high-profile events where alternative lodging was [3] plenty.

The site Airbedandbreakfast.com officially launched on August 11, 2008.

To help fund the site, the founders created special edition breakfast cereals, with presidential candidates Barack Obama and John McCain as the inspiration for "Obama O's" and "Cap'n McCains". In two months, 800 boxes of cereal were sold at $40 each, [4] it has generated more than $30,000 for the company's incubation.

[5] With the website already built, they used the fund to fly to New York to meet users and promote the site. They returned to San Francisco with a profitable business model to present to West Coast investors.

3

A) NO CHANGE
B) not very close by
C) scarce
D) easily found

4

A) NO CHANGE
B) generating more than
C) that generated more than
D) thereby generating more than

5

Which choice best connects the sentence with the previous paragraph?

A) NO CHANGE
B) Hotel industries became wary of the company by that time.
C) Although the initial business plan seemed rosy, the reality waiting for them was the opposite.
D) Airbnb soon became the multibillion company

CONTINUE

2

In March 2009, the name Airbedandbreakfast.com was shortened to Airbnb.com, and [6] the site content expanded from air beds and shared spaces to a variety of properties including entire homes and apartments.

On May 25, 2011, [7] actor, and partner at A-Grade Investments Ashton Kutcher, announced a significant investment in the company and his role as a strategic brand advisor for the company.

6

A) NO CHANGE
B) the site contents
C) the content's site
D) the site's content

7

A) NO CHANGE
B) an actor and a partner
C) actor and partner
D) actor as a partner

CONTINUE

2 2

In July 2014, Airbnb revealed design revisions to their site and mobile app and introduced a new logo. Some considered the new icon to be visually similar to genitalia, [8] also a consumer survey by Survata showed only a minority of respondents thought this was the case.

[9] In the past, businesses were regulated by zoning laws, but Mayor Steven Fulop stated that the city does not have enough inspectors to deal the number of local units being rented out, approximately 300 of which rented through the service as of that date, and that rapid-evolving technology such as Airbnb made doing so impossible. Under the new legislation, Airbnb pays the city 6 percent hotel tax on the residential properties whose owners rent temporary living space to tourists for under 30 days, which is estimated to bring $1 million in revenue to the city, and expand tourist capacity beyond the city's 13 existing hotels.

8

A) NO CHANGE
B) but
C) nevertheless
D) moreover

9

At this point, the writer is considering adding the following sentence.

In October 2015, Jersey City, New Jersey became the first city in the New York metropolitan area to legalize Airbnb, and add it to their existing body of hotels and motels that pay taxes.

Should the writer make this addition here?

A) Yes, because it supports the main argument in the passage and one city Mayor's effort to expand business
B) Yes, because it provides a meaningful connection to the following sentences
C) No, because it should set up the argument for the benefit of the business
D) No, because this article focuses on the initial stage of the company

CONTINUE

2 2

Airbnb will also provide insurance protection to homeowners in the event damage done to their residence by renters. The new laws will not pre vent condominium associations from voting to prohibit use of Airbnb in [10] <u>them.</u>

[11] <u>Giving</u> the growth of international users, Airbnb opened 6 additional international offices in early 2012. These cities include Paris, Milan, Barcelona, Copenhagen, Moscow, and Sao Paulo.

10

A) NO CHANGE
B) it
C) those buildings.
D) their buildings.

11

A) NO CHANGE
B) Having given
C) After Airbnb was given
D) To give

CONTINUE

2 2

Questions 12-22 are based on the following passage.

NASA Confirms Evidence That Liquid Water Flows on Today

New findings from NASA's Mars Reconnaissance Orbiter (MRO) provides the strongest evidence yet that liquid water flows intermittently on present-day Mars.

Using an imaging spectrometer on MRO, [12] it detected signatures of hydrated minerals on slopes where mysterious streaks are seen on the Red Planet. These darkish streaks appear to ebb and flow over time. They darken and appear to flow down steep slopes during warm seasons, and then fade in cooler seasons. They appear in several locations on Mars when temperatures are above minus 10 degrees Fahrenheit (minus 23 Celsius) [13] but disappear at colder times.

[14] When we search for an extraterrestrial life, our quest on Mars has been to 'follow the water,' in our search for life in the universe, and now we have convincing science that validates what we've long suspected, said John Grunsfeld, astronaut and associate administrator of NASA's Science Mission Directorate in Washington.

12

A) NO CHANGE
B) they
C) researchers
D) Mars

13

A) NO CHANGE
B) and disappear
C) however, disappear
D) while disappearing

14

A) NO CHANGE
B) Because searching for an extra-terrestrial life is our goal,
C) As we search for an extraterrestrial life,
D) delete the underlined portion, and starts the sentence with "Our quest…".

CONTINUE

2 2

"This is a significant development, as it appears to confirm that water [15] —albeit briny—is flowing today on the surface of Mars."

These downhill flows, known as recurring slope lineae (RSL), often have been described as possibly related [16] to water.

The new findings of hydrated salts on the slopes point to what that relationship may be to these dark features. The hydrated salts would lower the freezing point of a liquid brine, [17] just as salt on roads here on Earth causes ice and snow to melt more rapidly. Scientists say it's likely a shallow subsurface flow, with enough water wicking to the surface to explain the darkening.

15

Which of the following alternatives would NOT be appropriate?

A) ,albeit briny,
B) (albeit briny)
C) although briny
D) ,though briny,

16

A) NO CHANGE
B) with potential liquid
C) with conceivable water
D) to water in some probability

17

At this point, the author wishes to delete the underlined phrase. Should the author proceeds to delete it or not?

A) Keep, because it confirms the same molecules of salts on Mars' surface and Earth.
B) Keep, because it helps visualize the process of melting ice
C) Delete, because it undermines the passage's central theory
D) Delete, because the description doesn't fit to the academic journal

CONTINUE

2 2

[18] They are hypothesized to be formed by flow of briny liquid water on Mars. The image is produced by draping an orthorectified (RED) image (ESP_031059_1685) on a Digital Terrain Model (DTM) of the same site produced by High Resolution Imaging Science Experiment (University of Arizona). Vertical exaggeration is 1.5."We found the hydrated salts only when the seasonal features were widest, [19] which suggests that either the dark streaks themselves and a process that forms them is the source of the hydration.

In either case, the detection of hydrated salts on these slopes means that water plays a vital role in the formation of these streaks," said Lujendra Ojha of the Georgia Institute of Technology (Georgia Tech) [20] in Atlanta, lead author of a report on these findings published Sept. 28 by Nature Geoscience. Ojha first noticed these puzzling features as a University of Arizona undergraduate student in 2010, using images from the MRO's High Resolution Imaging Science Experiment (HiRISE).

18

At this point, the writer is considering adding the following sentence in this new paragraph.

The dark streaks here are up to few hundred meters in length.

Should the writer make this addition here?

A) Yes, because a new paragraph cannot start with a pronoun.

B) Yes, because the exact measurement is an essential factor to determine the quality of briny liquid.

C) No, because the information is not directly related with the paragraph.

D) No, because the hypothesis is not fully confirmed to suggest the measurement.

19

A) NO CHANGE

B) which suggest that either the dark streaks themselves or a process that forms them is

C) suggested that either the dark streaks themselves or a process that forms them is

D) , suggesting that either the dark streaks themselves or a process that forms them are

20

A) NO CHANGE

B) in Atlanta lead

C) in Atlanta, leading

D) in Atlanta leads

CONTINUE

2 2

The new site study pairs HiRISE observations with mineral mapping by MRO's Compact Reconnaissance Imaging Spectrometer for Mars (CRISM).[21]

So far, HiRISE actually acquired 9137 images (Table 1), but from 2 to 3 times as much downlink data volume as expected, so the average image sizes are larger than previously expected. Ojha chose to acquire larger images rather than more images because it was operationally easier and because of a lifetime concern related to the number of on–off cycles to the FPS.

Table 1		
Image types acquired in the PSP.		
Number acquired in PSP		total % images
Total images	9137	100
Standalone small images	3465	38
Coordinated and ride-along images with other teams	5672	62
Stereo images / enhanced size	2064	23
Off-nadir observations	6839	75
Nadir observations including non-mineral zones	2298	25

Dwayne Brown / Laurie Cantillo
Headquarters, Washington
http://www.nasa.gov/press-release/nasa-confirms-evidence-that-liquid-water-flows-on-today-s-mars

21

At this point, the writer wants to further reinforce Ojhas research. Which choice most effectively accomplish this goal?

A) Using the HiRISE, he documented RSL at dozens of mineral sites on Mars.

B) Using the HiRISE, he was able to solve on-off cycles to the FPS.

C) Using the HiRISE, he acquired the average-size images.

D) Using the HiRISE, he chose to document more images as many as possible.

22

The writer wants the information in the passage to correspond as closely as possible with the information in the table.

Given that goal described in the passage would remain unchanged, on which research should Ojha conduct?

A) Standalone small images

B) Off-nadir observations

C) Stereo images with enhanced size

D) Nadir observations including non-mineral zones

CONTINUE

2 2

Questions 23-33 are based on the following passage.

Louis Armstrong

Louis Armstrong, nicknamed Satchmo or Pops, was an American trumpeter, composer, singer and occasional [23] actor. Luis Armstrong is considered as the most influential figures in jazz. His career spanned five decades, from the 1920s to the 1960s [24] ,different eras in jazz.

Coming to prominence in the 1920s as an "inventive" trumpet and cornet player, Armstrong [25] was not officially trained in jazz, shifting the focus of the music from collective improvisation to solo performance.

Armstrong was one of the first truly popular African-American entertainers to "cross over", whose skin color was secondary to his music in [26] likeminded fans' passion.

23

A) NO CHANGE
B) actor, and Luis Armstrong
C) actor
D) actor, who

24

Which of the following alternatives would NOT be appropriate?
A) , different eras in Jazz
B) –different eras in Jazz
C) : different eras in Jazz
D) ; different eras in Jazz

25

The writer wants to convey an attitude of genuine interest and respect to the later life of the musician. Which choice best accomplishes this goal?

A) NO CHANGE
B) was born when United States of America was severely experiencing racially the Divided States of America.
C) started his career by taking an unenviable position at the backstage.
D) was a foundational influence

26

Which choice most effectively sets up the contrast in the sentence and is consistent with the information in the rest of the passage?

A) NO CHANGE
B) the racially divided country.
C) the professional music industry
D) the society back in the 1930s.

CONTINUE

2 2

His artistry and personality allowed him socially acceptable to access the upper echelons of American society which [27] were highly open for black men of his era.

[28] ①Armstrong was born into a poor family in New Orleans, Louisiana, and was the grandson of slaves.

②He spent his youth in poverty, in a rough neighborhood known as "the Battlefield", which was part of the Storyville legal prostitution district.

③ His mother Mary "Mayann" Albert (1886–1927) then left Louis and his younger sister, Beatrice Armstrong Collins, in the care of his grandmother, Josephine Armstrong, and at times, his Uncle Isaac.

④At five, he moved back to live with his mother and her relatives. He attended the Fisk School for Boys, where he most likely had early exposure to music. He brought in some money [29] as a paperboy but also by finding discarded food and selling it to restaurants, but it was not enough to keep his mother from prostitution. He [30] often hang out in dance halls close to home, where he observed everything from licentious dancing to the quadrille.

27

A) NO CHANGE
B) appreciated
C) were accessible
D) were unapproachable

28

To improve the cohesion and flow of this paragraph, the writer wants to add the following sentence.

> His father, William Armstrong, abandoned the family when Louis was an infant and took up with another woman.

The sentence would most logically be placed after

A) sentence 1
B) sentence 2
C) sentence 3
D) sentence 4

29

A) NO CHANGE
B) working as a paperboy
C) not only as a paperboy
D) selling papers

30

A) NO CHANGE
B) was hang
C) often hung
D) was hanging

CONTINUE

2 2

After dropping out of the Fisk School at age eleven, Armstrong [31] joined a quartet of boys who sang in the streets for money. He also started to get into trouble. Cornet player Bunk Johnson said he taught Armstrong (then 11) to play by ear at Dago Tony's Tonk in New Orleans, [32] however in his later years Armstrong gave the credit to Oliver. Armstrong hardly looked back at his youth as the worst of times but drew inspiration from it instead: "Every time I close my eyes blowing that trumpet of mine—I look right in the heart of good old New Orleans... It has given me something to live for." [33]

31

A) NO CHANGE
B) had joined
C) has joined
D) was joined

32

A) NO CHANGE
B) in spite of
C) because
D) although

33

Which choice most effectively concludes the sentence and paragraph?

A) NO CHANGE
B) "Well...New Orleans indeed was such a beautiful land.
C) I regret things could have been better if I was a well-behaved kid.
D) Who knew I would be the king of music?

CONTINUE

2 2

Questions 34-44 are based on the following passage.

DRONE

An unmanned aerial vehicle (UAV), commonly known as a drone, as an unmanned aircraft system (UAS), or by several other names, is an aircraft without a human pilot aboard. The flight of UAVs may operate with various degrees of autonomy: either under remote control by a human operator, or under fully [34] and exhaustively by onboard computers. [35] Compared to manned aircraft, UAVs are often preferred for missions that are too [36] boring for humans. They originated mostly in military applications, although their use is expanding in commercial, scientific, recreational, agricultural, and other applications [37] such as, policing and surveillance, aerial photography, agriculture and drone racing. The term [38] ,more widely used by the public, "drone was given in reference to the resemblance of male bee that makes loud and regular sounds.

34

A) NO CHANGE
B) and categorically
C) and thoroughly
D) delete it

35

A) NO CHANGE
B) When you compare
C) Comparing
D) After the comparison

36

A) NO CHANGE
B) dangerous
C) theoretical
D) organized

37

A) NO CHANGE
B) , such as
C) ; such as,
D) such as:

38

The best placement for the underlined portion would be:

A) NO CHANGE
B) after "drone"
C) after "given"
D) after "bee"

CONTINUE

2

This term emphasizes the importance of elements other than the aircraft [39] ,indicating the significance of several elements of drone.

It includes several elements [40] ,such as ground control stations, data links, and other support equipment. Many similar terms are in use.

A UAV is defined as a powered, aerial vehicle that [41] do not carry a human operator, uses aerodynamic forces to provide vehicle lift, can fly autonomously or be piloted remotely, can be expendable or recoverable, and carry a lethal or nonlethal payload.

39

A) NO CHANGE
B) as it indicates the significance of several elements.
C) an indication of its term's significance.
D) delete the underlined portion.

40

Which of the following alternatives would NOT be appropriate?

A) , including ground control stations,
B) : ground control stations,
C) —ground control stations,
D) like ground control stations,

41

A) NO ERROR
B) does not carry a human operator, uses aero dynamic forces to provide vehicle lift, could fly autonomously or be piloted remotely, can be expendable
C) do not carry a human operator, uses aerodynamic forces to provide vehicle lift, fly autonomously or be piloted remotely, can be expendable
D) does not carry a human operator, uses aerodynamic forces to provide vehicle lift, can fly autonomously or be piloted remotely, expendable

CONTINUE

2 2

[42] Therefore, missiles are not considered UAVs because the vehicle itself is a weapon that is not reused, though it is also unmanned and in some cases remotely guided.

The relation of UAVs to remote controlled model aircraft is unclear. [43] Some jurisdictions base their definitions on size or weight; however, the US Federal Aviation Administration defines any unmanned flying craft as a UAV regardless of size.

[44] The UAV's global military market is dominated by United States and Israel. The US held a 60% military-market share in 2006. It operated over 9,000 UAVs in 2014. From 1985 to 2014, exported drones came predominantly from Israel (60.7%) and the United States (23.9%); top importers were the United Kingdom (33.9%) and India (13.2%).

42

A) NO CHANGE
B) Moreover,
C) For example,
D) Although,

43

At this point, the author wishes to delete the underlined phrase. Should the author proceeds to delete it or not?

A) Keep, because it provides a specific example of the previous sentence.
B) Keep, because it provides the reason for the inclusion of remote controlled model aircraft to UAV.
C) Delete, because it interrupts the flow of the paragraph by illustrating an unsettled decision
D) Delete, because it weakens the focus of the passage by shifting to remote controlled model aircraft.

44

Which of the following sentences is LEAST applicable as an alternate sentence?

A) The UAV's global market is dominated by United States and Israel.
B) As the related technology improves, there has been a huge expansion in the UAV's global military market in less than a decade.
C) UAV's global market, however, faces some serious privacy issues as it expands exponentially.
D) The U.S. Department of Defense has released a new statistics that shows Israel as the second largest market controller, next to the U.S.

SAT Test 3
Answer Explanations
&
Pattern Analyses

If your Test 3 scores are unsatisfactory,

Test 4, 5, 6… won't be satisfactory either.

Please Practice the Answer Explanations and then come back to Test 3 again.

ALL THE LOGIC AND RULES BEHIND EVERY SINGLE SAT QUESTION

SAT Test 3

Reading Section Answer Explanations

&

Pattern Analyses

Questions 1-10 are based on the following passage.

Mr. Collins's triumph was complete. (1B & 2D & 3A &4B & 5C) **The power of displaying the grandeur of** (6D) **his patroness to his wondering visitors,** (4B) **and of letting them see her civility towards himself** and his wife, was exactly what he had wished for. ; and that an opportunity of doing it should be given so soon, was such an instance of Lady Catherine's condescension, as he knew nothow to admire enough. "I confess," said he, "that "I should not have been at all surprised by her ladyship's asking us on Sunday to drink tea. Who could have foreseen such an attention as this?" Lady Catherine will not think the worse of you for being	simply dressed. She likes to have the distinction of (7A) **rank preserved.**" As the weather was fine, they had a pleasant walk. Every park has its beauty and its prospects, (8D) **though she could not be in such raptures** as Mr. Collins expected. Lady Catherine was a tall woman. (9D & 10D) **Her air was not conciliating, nor was her manner of receiving them such as to make her visitors forget their inferior rank.** She was formidable by silence and was in authoritative tone.

Q1. **Absolute Pattern 8: Understanding True Purpose** **Question Pattern:** According to the first paragraph, **Mr. Collins invited his visitors to Lady Catherine** mainly to	
A) build a new constructive relations with the visitors **B) let the visitors observe Lady Catherine's hospitality towards him** C) reconcile the visitors with Lady Catherine D) find an opportunity to amass wealth	B) The power of displaying the grandeur of his patroness to his wondering visitors, and of letting them see her civility towards himself

Q2. **Absolute Pattern 7: Understanding Attitude (Tone) Question** **Question Pattern:** According to the first paragraph, Mr. **Collins' persona** can be described as	
A) cheerful B) condescending C) humble **D) showy**	D) **The power of displaying** the grandeur of his patroness to his wondering visitors, and of letting them see her civility towards himself

Q3. **Absolute Pattern 6: Analogy Question** Finding a similar situation **Question Pattern:** Which of the following **analogies would be most in keeping with the main character trait of Mr. Collins?**	
A) Susan often uses an assumed name similar to that of rich people to impress others B) Max morally opposes rich people's wrongdoings C) Daniel lives in constant fear of running out of money and relies on rich people D) Cathy finds condescending gesture of rich people and advises her friends to ignore it	**A) The power of displaying** the grandeur of his patroness to his wondering visitors,...
B) is Opposite C) Mr. Collins is more active in taking his role than "Daniel"	

Q4. **Absolute Pattern 11: Textual Evidence Question** Finding evidence for the previous question **Question Pattern:** Which choice provides the best evidence for the answer to the previous question?	
A) Line 1 (Mr. Collins's triumph… complete) **B) Lines 2-5 (The power … wished for;)** C) Lines 9-11 (I confess…drink tea.) D) Lines 20-23 (Lady Catherine was...inferior rank.)	B) Please refer to the above question

Q5. **Absolute Pattern 1: Main Idea Question** Finding the main idea of the entire passage or the paragraph **Question Pattern:** The **primary purpose** of the passage is to	
A) highlight the insightful characteristic of Mr. Collins B) illustrate the supportive relationship between Mr. Collins and Lady Catherine **C) point out the major goal of Mr. Collins** D) demonstrate the societal status of Lady Catherine	C) Throughout the passage, the narrator reveals Mr. Collins's persona and his goal of displaying his patroness's grandeur. B), D) The keyword in the passage is definitely Mr. Collins, not anyone else.

Q6. **Absolute Pattern 9: Relationships Question** **Question Pattern: Lady Catherine's role** with Mr. Collins is of	
A) an aunt B) an old friend C) an abiding beneficiary **D) a condescending benefactor**	D) Mr. Collins' referring to "Lady Catherine" or "ladyship" shows the social rank; therefore, (A) and (B) are incorrect .C) is Opposite

Q7. **Absolute Pattern 5: Word-In-Context Question** Finding a clue word and the keyword from the sentence in question Question Pattern: In line 31 "**preserved**" most nearly means ?	
A) Unviolated B) Defended C) Conserved D) Acknowledge	A) Lady Catherine will not think the worse of you for being simply dressed. She likes to have the distinction of rank preserved. (unviolated)" "unviolated" is the closest meaning. For (D), "acknowledged" instead of "acknowledge" should have been used to be the answer.

Q8. **Absolute Pattern 7: Understanding Attitude (Tone) Question** Finding a tone such as positive-negative, active-passive, mental-physical, subjective-objective **Question Pattern:** The description in lines 17-19 **(Every park has... Mr. Collins expected) suggests that** Elizabeth	
A) was not in such a joyful mood B) was greatly inspired by the surroundings C) was in such great rapture D) was resentful to the other characters	A) Every park has its beauty and its prospects, though she could not be in such raptures as Mr. Collins expected.

Q9. **Absolute Pattern 7: Understanding Attitude (Tone) Question** **Question Pattern: Elizabeth observes that Lady Catherine** as	
A) a realistic and truly respectful person B) a young and handsome person C) a person hiding inferiority **D) a person creating superiority by lowering others**	D) Her air was not conciliating, nor was her manner of receiving them such as to make her visitors forget their inferior rank

Q10. **Absolute Pattern 11: Textual Evidence Question** Finding evidence for the previous question Question Pattern: Which choice provides the best evidence for the answer to the previous question?	
A) Lines 1-2 (Mr. Collins's triumph... complete) B) Lines 2-5 (The power ... wished for;) C) Lines 20 (Lady Catherine was a tall woman) **D) Lines 20-23 (Her air was...inferior rank.)**	D) Please refer to the above question

Questions 11-21 are based on the following passage.

<table>
<tr>
<td>Each year, CDER approves hundreds of new medications, most of which are variations of (11A) previously existing products, such as (12D) new dosage forms of already-approved products, or cost-saving generics. These new products contribute to quality of care, greater access to medication, more consumer choice that enhances affordability and public health.
(16A & 17B) However, products in a small subset of these new approvals, that we refer to as novel drugs, are among the more truly (14A & 15C) innovative products that often help advance clinical care to another level. Every year, CDER summarizes these new products.</td>
<td>The annual summary reports (13C) the quantity of novel drugs that it approved. However, it also focuses on the high quality of many of these new drugs, their contributions to enhanced patient care.
This year, we approved many new drugs to treat various forms of cancer, including myeloma, lung, skin, breast. This year's field also includes new drugs to treat (19D) reversal agent for a blood thinner.
For the first year, we approved more "orphan" drugs (18B) for rare diseases than any previous year in our history. In calendar year 2015, FDA's Center for Drug Evaluation and Research (CDER) approved 45 novel drugs, (20C) approved as new molecular entities (NMEs) under New Drug Applications (NDAs) or as new therapeutic biologics under Biologics License Applications (BLAs).</td>
</tr>
</table>

<table>
<tr><td colspan="2">Q11. Absolute Pattern 2: Summary Question Summarizing a sentence or entire passage
Question Pattern: In describing new medications in line 1, the author emphasizes all of the followings EXCEPT</td></tr>
<tr><td>A) they will completely replace existing products
B) they will contribute to quality of care
C) they will allow greater accessibility to mediation
D) they will give more consumer choice</td><td>A) most of which are variations of previously existing products

The other choices are all written in the passage.</td></tr>
</table>

<table>
<tr><td colspan="2">Q12. Absolute Pattern 2: Summary Question Summarizing a sentence or entire passage
Question Pattern: According to the 1st paragraph, which of the following medications would LEAST likely be approved by CDER?</td></tr>
<tr><td>A) Pills already-approved with new dosage forms
B) Cost-saving generic pills
C) Pills that allow greater access to the patients
D) Already-approved pills with more appealing name</td><td>D) new dosage forms of already-approved products, or cost-saving generics. These new products contribute to quality of care, greater access to medication, more consumer choice that enhances affordability and public health.</td></tr>
</table>

<table>
<tr><td colspan="2">Q13. Absolute Pattern 6: Analogy Question Finding a similar situation
Question Pattern: Which of the following analogies most resembles "The annual summary" in line 7?</td></tr>
<tr><td>A) A boy reads over dozens of comics to kill time.
B) A respected physicist writes his autobiography
C) A chef buys over twenty boxes of only the highest quality tomatoes
D) A pianist renders music with a low quality piano</td><td>C) The annual summary reports the quantity of novel drugs that it approved. However, it also focuses on the high quality of many of these new drugs,</td></tr>
<tr><td colspan="2">C) twenty boxes (quantity) and highest quality resemble the passage information.
A), comics are low (negative) quality.
B), D) The most important argument "quality" is not stated.</td></tr>
</table>

Q14. **Absolute Pattern 2: Summary Question** Summarizing a sentence or entire passage
Question Pattern: The main characteristics of Novel drug is that it is?

A) advanced and innovative B) less expensive C) more concerned with public health D) little known previously	A) we refer to as novel drugs, are among the more truly **innovative products**

Q15. **Absolute Pattern 11: Textual Evidence Question** Finding evidence for the previous question
Question Pattern: Which choice provides the best evidence for the answer to the previous question?

A) Lines 1-5 (Each year, ...cost-saving generics.) B) Lines 5-8 (These new products...public health.) **C) Lines 9-12 (However, products...another level)** D) Lines 19-21 (This year,...skin, breast.)	C) Please refer to the above question

Q16. **Absolute Pattern 1: Main Idea Question** Finding the main idea of the entire passage or the paragraph
Question Pattern: The **primary purpose** of the passage is to

A) highlight the novel drugs approved by CDER B) propose a change of the government regulations C) distinguish between new medications and novel drugs D) show the procedures CDER approves hundreds of new medications	A) "**However,** products in a small subset of these new approvals, that we refer to as **novel drugs,** are among the more truly innovative products

The word "novel" appears more than any other keywords in the rest of the options. Also, contradictory conjunction ("however" in this case) plays pivotal role to find the answer.

Q17. **Absolute Pattern 11: Textual Evidence Question** Finding evidence for the previous question
Question Pattern: Which choice provides the best evidence for the answer to the previous question?

A) Lines 1-5 (Each year, ...cost-saving generics.) **B) Lines 9-12 (However, products...another level)** C) Lines 19-21 (This year,...skin, breast.) D) Lines 21-22 (This year's field...a blood thinner.)	B) Please refer to the above question

Q18. **Absolute Pattern 5: Word-In-Context Question**
Finding a clue word and the keyword from the sentence in question
Question Pattern: In Line 11, "**orphan**" most nearly refers to

A) a drug for child without parent **B) a drug for rare diseases with a single purpose** C) an illegal drug without a name D) a highly replicable and affordable drug	B) orphan" drugs for **rare diseases** (A) is too literal implication. (C) and (D) are Unrelated words

Q19. **Absolute Pattern 2: Summary Question** Summarizing a sentence or entire passage
Question Pattern: Paragraph 3 (lines 8—11) suggests that **CDER has approved the new drugs** available to the patients with or need of EXCEPT

A) multiple myeloma B) skin cancer C) lung cancer **D) a new blood thinner**	D) We approved many new drugs..., (B) skin, breast, brain, colorectal, and other cancers. This year's field also includes (D) **reversal agent** for a commonly-used blood thinner.

Q20. **Absolute Pattern 2: Summary Question** Summarizing a sentence or entire passage **Question Pattern:** Which of the following criteria is **NOT expressed as approval** standards for new drug by CDER?	
A) The new molecular entities (NMEs) B) New Drug Applications (NDAs) **C) World Health Organization Applications (WHO)** D) The Biologics License Applications (BLAs)	C) FDA's Center for Drug Evaluation and Research (CDER) approved 45 novel drugs, approved as (A) new molecular entities (NMEs) under (B) New Drug Applications (NDAs) or as new therapeutic biologics under (D) Biologics License Applications (BLAs).

Q21. **Absolute Pattern 12: Informational Graphs** Finding facts described in the graphs or relations between the passage and the graph. **Question Pattern:** Which of the following statements most accurately interprets the **graph** following the passage ?
A) The filed numbers were highest in 2014 B) The approvals were lowest in 2010 **C) The ratio of filed numbers vs. the approvals was highest in 2014** D) Nearly half of the filed numbers were approved in 2015

Questions 22-31 are based on the following passage.

A. J. Maxwell's was an (22B) archetypal New York steakhouse on the corner of 48th and 6th in the heart of midtown Manhattan. There, a few weeks after my middle school graduation, my family splurged on a celebration of our first road trip to America. I distinctly remember the forty-dollar entrées that dotted the menu (the opulence of it all!), and sinking my teeth into a steak that the Old Spaghetti Factories I was used to could only dream of serving.

Today, A. J. Maxwell's is closed after years of poor reviews, with references to overpriced food and jerky-like steaks dating back to far before my visit. Though I can't say for certain, I suspect the steak I had eight years ago was not, in any particular way, noteworthy in the grand scheme of beef. But somehow that steak remains in my mind, more vividly than any steak I've had since, as close to perfection as a slab of meat can be. (23A) **Diminishing marginal utility is one way to understand this seeming contradiction.**

Loosely, this is the idea that the marginal (read: additional) utility (read: benefit) of extra stuff diminishes as we have more stuff to begin with: We would love an extra dollar if we only had ten dollars to our names, but could probably care less about the same dollar as millionaires.

For similar reasons, my very first fancy steak—though not incredible per se—was far more memorable than my tenth. The first let me peek into a whole new world of fine dining, while the tenth probably wasn't all that special next to the nine other fancy steaks before it.

As thoroughly broke college students who in the median will earn between \$50,000 and \$69,999 upon graduation and likely even more later in life, our marginal utility is high now relative to our expected marginal utility 20 years down the road. In other words, (25C) **as we become older and richer, things and experiences that amaze us now will probably lose their luster.** We might understand this as a sale on happiness: Today, it would almost certainly take more than forty dollars to buy a steak as incredible to me as the one my 13-year-old self savored so dearly at A. J. Maxwell's. In more concrete terms, imagine we knew that, like the average American, we would be spending \$55,000 every year by the middle of our lives (note, for the record, that the argument here works even if we're not planning on being a big future spender).

If we had the power to move a thousand dollars of that spending to today, we almost certainly would. (24D) **Imagine if we had an extra grand today!** Instead of a trip into Boston, we could take a once-in-a-lifetime trip to Paris.

It turns out that financial markets have created a way for us to move money through time in exactly this way: debt. (31B) **We can borrow money from the bank today and pay it back with our higher incomes in the future,** effectively taking out a loan from our richer, future self. The logic of introductory economics would say that we should squeeze every last penny out of the happiness sale in this way, borrowing large amounts of money to finance increased spending today until we could expect to consume roughly the same amount at every point in our lifetimes. But perfectly spreading out our consumption like this is impossible in practice and probably undesirable to boot.

Continued Next Page

Few banks would be willing to issue the large loans we would need, and we might be worried about the risk of being saddled with debt if we ended up earning less than we expected to. Furthermore, consumption is often positional, in the sense that what matters isn't necessarily how much we consume, but how much we consume relative to those around us. In other words, your 20-year class reunion might not be a lot of fun if you're paying down debt while your classmates are busy buying nice houses. We've been taught since childhood to spend	when we know we'll have more and save precisely when we have little. Though this seems fairly reasonable, (30C) **it certainly doesn't sound right to me those farmers who gorge themselves during good harvests and only attempt to store grain in bad harvests. Rather, they should be saving excess grain in good years so that they have more to eat in bad years.** (26C &27D & 28C &29D) **But there will likely never be another time in our lives when happiness today can be found for so cheap relative to happiness.**

Q22. **Absolute Pattern 5: Word-In-Context Question**
Finding a clue word and the keyword from the sentence in question
Question Pattern: The word **"archetypal"** in line 1 most nearly means

A) old **B) representative** C) ancient D) very typical	B) A. J. Maxwell's was an archetypal New York steakhouse in the heart of midtown Manhattan. *The prefix "arch" means representative. "heart" is the clue word.

Q23. **Absolute Pattern 7: Understanding Attitude (Tone) Question**
Question Pattern: In line 14-20 (**Though I...meat can be.), the author feels that way because**

A) his marginal utility was highest point that time B) he wasn't aware of marginal utility that time C) his appetite has changed since then D) sales on happiness is just a concept	A) But somehow that steak remains in my mind, more vividly than any steak I've had since, as close to perfection as a slab of meat can be. Diminishing marginal utility is one way to understand this seeming contradiction. **"Diminishing marginal utility"** implies the highest point that time.

Rule: Always Look for 'but,' or 'however' in the passage. That's where the answer is.
B) The author brings up the example to show the highest point of marginal utility in his youth to describe that diminishing marginal utility is one way to understand this seeming contradiction. In other words, his marginal utility was highest back then.

(C), (D) are unrelated words. They are all negative.
Please refer to incorrect choice pattern # 8, #1.

Q24. **Absolute Pattern 3: Inference Question** Finding an indirect suggestion (or guessing)
Question Pattern: The author repeatedly uses the word **"imagine"** in lines 48 and 56 in order to

A) explain how depressing the reality is without marginal utility B) qualify that marginal utility is only fancy idea C) tell that we can do anything with marginal utility **D) show how fascinating the marginal utility is**	D) imagine we knew that, we would be spending $55,000 every year. If we had the power to move a thousand dollars of that spending to today, we almost certainly would. Imagine if we had an extra grand today!

The word "imagine" is surrounded by the positive tone. Following this logic, A), B), and C), given Negative tone, should , however sounds similar to (D), be removed. Please refer to incorrect choice pattern # 12

Q25. **Absolute Pattern 6: Analogy Question** Finding a similar situation Question Pattern: Which of the following **situations is most similar to marginal utility** the author describes?	
A) A church priest who restrains earthly desires B) A rich entrepreneur who became an epicure **C) A film star who is fond of his first small role** D) A prolific writer who performs many roles other than writing	C) But somehow that steak remains in my mind, more vividly than any steak I've had since, as close to perfection as a slab of meat can be. Diminishing marginal utility is one way to understand this seeming contradiction. A film star (marginal utility) value his small role (present utility). (A),(B) are opposite of marginal utility

Q26. **Absolute Pattern 2: Summary Question** Summarizing a sentence, or an entire paragraph **Question Pattern:** In discussing the **marginal utility,** the author addresses all of the following **concerns EXCEPT**	
A) taking out a big loan against future income to spend now B) earning less than we expected in the future **C) thinking that happiness today can be found for so cheap relative to happiness tomorrow** D) having the sense of how much others consume	C) is the crux, Positive, concept of marginal utility (A) Few banks would be willing to issue the large loans...(B) the risk of being saddled with debt if we ended up earning less… but (D) how much we consume relative to those around us. to happiness tomorrow. All the others are Negative (concerns)

Q27. **Absolute Pattern 11: Textual Evidence Question** Finding evidence for the previous question **Question Pattern:** Which choice provides the best evidence for the answer to the previous question?	
A) Lines 73-74 (Few banks...we would need) B) Lines 74-76 (we might be worried...we expected to) C) Lines 77-80 (Furthermore,...around us.) **D) Lines 92-94 (But there will….happiness tomorrow.)**	D) Please refer to the above question

Q28. **Absolute Pattern 1: Main Idea Question** Finding the main idea of the entire passage or the paragraph Question Pattern: The passage is **primarily concerned** with	
A) the problem of marginal utility B) wide variety of consumption practice **C) emotional impact on a unique economic hypothesis** D) relationships between money and happiness	C) The main theme of the entire passage is marginal utility. The author's hypothesis is that we can borrow small bit of future income and spend it now to maximize our present happiness, called "marginal utility." A) is Opposite. B), D) are Too Broad concept

Q29. **Absolute Pattern 11: Textual Evidence Question** Finding evidence for the previous question **Question Pattern:** Which choice provides the best evidence for the answer to the previous question?	
A) Lines 70-72 (But perfectly ...undesirable to boot.) B) Lines 77-80 (Furthermore, ...those around us.) C) Lines 83-85 (We've been taught...we have little) **D) Lines 92-94 (But there will be… tomorrow.)**	D) Please refer to the above question

Q30. **Absolute Pattern 7: Understanding Attitude (Tone) Question** **Question Pattern:** The author's attitude toward the "**farmers**" in line 87 can be best described as	
A) genuinely puzzled B) solemnly respectful **C) condescendingly skeptical** D) generally indifferent	C) We've been taught since childhood... harvests. **Rather, they should be saving** excess grain in good years so that they have more to eat in bad years. The passage with personal anecdote using "I", normally has a strong subjective opinion—either positive or negative—and therefore, the answer will seldom be (D) "indifferent" or (A) "puzzled".

<table>
<tr><td colspan="2">Q31. Absolute Pattern 3: Inference Question Finding an indirect suggestion (or guessing)
Question Pattern: Which of the following persons would have the similar appreciation to the steak that the author once had at A. J. Maxwell's steakhouse?</td></tr>
<tr><td>A) we who become older and richer (line 40)
B) a bank lending money today (line 62)
C) yourself paying down debt (line 82)
D) farmers (line 87)</td><td>B) The steak the author had at steakhouse represents the marginal utility, which only bankers can lend by effectively taking out a loan from our richer, future self.
(A) as we become older, probably lose their luster.
(C) your 20-year class reunion might not be a lot of fun paying down debt (D) those who gorge themselves during good harvests.
A), C), D) are all Opposite and Negative concept to marginal utility.</td></tr>
</table>

Questions 32-41 are based on the following passage.

On Sunday morning Twitter user @Queen Demetriax_'s tweeted the following to the American Airlines corporate account:

> sarah@queendemetrizx@amfericanair
>
> Hello my name's Ibrahim and I'm from Afghanistan. I'm part of Al Qaida and on June 1st I'm gonna do something really big bye. 10:37 am – 13 Apr 2014
>
> Within minutes, the company responded: @queendemetriax_ sarah, we take these threats very seriously. your IP address and details will be forwarded to security and the FBI.

Despite her frantic claims that she was "kidding," Dutch officials showed up at the Rotterdam native's house and arrested her on the spot, drawing to a close a news story that would have been completely fruitless had it not provided me a topic to write about. For that, you and I both have @QueenDemetriax's unreliable frontal lobe to thank. (32C & 33C) **What this narrative seems to highlight however is not merely one girl's lapse in judgment (especially considering dozens of teenagers followed her lead), but a larger phenomenon in which Internet users fail to associate their online actions with real-world consequences.** (34D) **Senseless and shortsighted uses of the Internet have led to unemployment, pedophilia, robberies, political scandals, and arrests.**

Older generations have always entertained at slight distrust of new technologies, fearing the limits of their privacy. And their kids have always gotten entertainment from that distrust. "No Grandpa, Gmail isn't asking for your birthday so they can steal your pension." "Yes, Mom, that's a webcam. No, Mom, the government can't watch you through it." Although... But all kidding aside, maybe more Internet users need of figures like my dad reminding them that there is in fact a world that exists beyond the perimeters of their various screens.

(35D) **One of the defining characteristics of our generation is our increasing technological proficiency and ability to master new platforms so quickly.** (36B & 37C) **But we've grown so accustomed to computers and social media that the magnitude of our online actions is forgotten.** Despite what some privacy settings may claim, anything posted online is available to anyone at any time.

(38B) **The novelty of these websites and applications has worn off**, and for all intents and purposes, **online postings are just as legitimate a form of communication as human interaction.** Academics who study human behavior and the brain are just now beginning to understand the cognitive impact of social media on its 1.73 billion users worldwide. Significant levels of Internet usage can lead to loneliness, jealousy, suicidality, and memory deficiency. But the most fundamental change wrought by the Internet is our unprecedented need for constant and immediate affirmation. I'll be the first to admit, the number of likes I receive on a post has a direct impact on my mood in the short-run.

After accumulating 18 favorites on some stupid tweet over winter break, I spent the rest of the day parading around my house like a king. For those of you who dismiss the significance of this effect, I'll leave you with this. What else could have possibly motivated @QueenDemetriax_ to hit the send button? Was she testing American Airline's security procedures? Is she actually the worst terrorist of all time? (41C) **No, and I don't think so. She hoped she could** (40B) **muster out a few favorites and maybe a retweet or two.**

(39D) **Well @QueenDemetriax, you got 10,000 of them, but they won't do much for you in jail. And maybe a retweet or two.**

<table>
<tr><td colspan="2">Q32. Absolute Pattern 8: Understanding the True Purpose Finding the true purpose of statement
Question Pattern: In line 5-16, The author describes @Queen Demetriax' primarily to present</td></tr>
<tr><td>A) the extent to which a tweeter user can fabricate the story so easily
B) American Air's overreaction to one teenager's naivety
C) the main argument
D) one girl's lapse in judgment</td><td>C) however (D) is not merely one girl's lapse in judgment (C) but a larger phenomenon in which Internet users fail to associate their online actions with real-world consequences.</td></tr>
<tr><td colspan="2">Rule: Always Look for 'but,' or 'however' in the passage. That's where the answer is.
A), D) are not primary argument. Please refer to incorrect choice pattern # 5</td></tr>
</table>

<table>
<tr><td colspan="2">Q33. Absolute Pattern 11: Textual Evidence Question Finding evidence for the previous question
Question Pattern: Which choice provides the best evidence for the answer to the previous question?</td></tr>
<tr><td>A) Lines 24-26 (For that, ...frontal lob to thank.)
B) Lines 26-29 (What this...followed her lead),
C) Lines 29-31 (but a larger...consequences.)
D) Line 44-47 (But all kidding...various screens)</td><td>C) Please refer to the above question</td></tr>
</table>

<table>
<tr><td colspan="2">Q34. Absolute Pattern 2: Summary Question Summarizing a sentence, or an entire paragraph
Question Pattern: The author suggests that 'unconscious and abusive acts through internet can result in EXCEPT</td></tr>
<tr><td>A) political scandals
B) incarceration
C) removal from work
D) being bullied</td><td>D) Senseless and shortsighted uses of the Internet have led to (C) unemployment, (A) political scandals, and (B) arrests.</td></tr>
</table>

<table>
<tr><td colspan="2">Q35. Absolute Pattern 7: Understanding Attitude (Tone) Question
Question Pattern: The description in lines 47-55 (One of the...any time) emphasizes the author's feeling toward his generation that they</td></tr>
<tr><td>A) enjoy technology wholeheartedly
B) master new platforms in no time
C) find great difficulty in remembering online activities
D) are unaware of reckless online behavior</td><td>D) One of the defining characteristics of our generation is (A) our increasing technological proficiency and ability to (B) master new platforms so quickly. But we've... (D) our online actions is forgotten.
(A), (B) are true statements. However, they aren't what the author wants to emphasizes.</td></tr>
<tr><td colspan="2">Pattern: please be careful to true-but-inconsistent-with-the-question type of choice statement.
A), B) are not, though true, primary argument. Please refer to incorrect choice pattern # 5 (C) is too literal</td></tr>
</table>

<table>
<tr><td colspan="2">Q36. Absolute Pattern 7: Understanding Attitude (Tone) Question
Finding a tone such as positive-negative, active-passive, mental-physical, subjective-objective
Question Pattern: The author's attitude to younger generations' using social media is that</td></tr>
<tr><td>A) younger generation should be proud of proficiency
B) younger generation should be more attentive to what they are doing in social media
C) social media limits our privacy
D) older generation should resemble younger ones' technological proficiency</td><td>B) But we've grown...online actions is for gotten. The overall tone is against social media. Only (B) makes social media Negative within the same theme.

(C),(D) are true statements but neither consistent with the question nor the main theme of the passage.</td></tr>
</table>

Q37. **Absolute Pattern 11: Textual Evidence Question** Finding evidence for the previous question **Question Pattern:** Which choice provides the best evidence for the answer to the previous question?	
A) Lines 35-37 (Older generations... their privacy.) B) Lines 48-51 (One of the...so quickly.) **C) Lines 51-53 (But we've....forgotten.)** D) Lines 53-55 (Despite what...any time)	C) Please refer to the above question

Q38. **Absolute Pattern 8: Understanding the True Purpose** Finding the true purpose of statement **Question Pattern:** In line 57, the discussion of **"online postings as legitimate a form of communication"** primarily serves to	
A) emphasize the novelty of applications **B) explain that the online postings become as common as any other form of communications** C) trace the nature of online communication D) give legal guidelines	B) The novelty of these websites and applications has worn off, and for all intents and purposes, online postings are just as legitimate a form of communication as human interaction.
The author emphasizes widely accepted online communication and its impact to society. (A), (C) These two true statements are incorrect because these are not the primary idea.	

Q39. **Absolute Pattern 10: Understanding the Structure of the Passage** Finding the structure of the entire passage or organizational relations between the paragraphs **Question Pattern:** Which best describes the **primary function** of the last sentence (lines 82-84)?	
A) It offers a lighthearted behavior of an online user B) It examines the role of online communication C) It illustrates retweet won't do much in jail **D) It provides commentary about the consequence of malpractice**	D) Well @QueenDemetriax, you got 10,000 of them, but they won't do much for you in jail. And maybe a retweet or two. Make sure that the question is asking the function of the last sentence, not the context within it. The ending should function as a commentary about the main issue (the consequence of youth malpractice with their Social media.
(A) ,(C) are merely rephrasing sentences to support the main idea of the passage and therefore can't be the primary function of the last sentence of the passage. (B) is too broad in concept and doesn't fit with the lines in question.	

Q40. **Absolute Pattern 5: Word-In-Context Question** Finding a clue word and the keyword from the sentence in question **Question Pattern:** In line 79 **"muster"** most nearly means	
A) necessitate **B) collect** C) brag D) infiltrate	B) She hoped she could muster out a few favorites and maybe a retweet or two. Well @QueenDemetriax, you got 10,000 of them, but they won't do much Muster means to collect

Q41. **Absolute Pattern 8: Understanding the True Purpose** Finding the true purpose of statement
Question Pattern: In lines 74-77 (**What else … all time?),** the author uses a series of **rhetorical questions** to emphasize

A) the author's belief that the young girl was naïve B) that retweet is useful in a real world **C) the author's main concern** D) that tougher security against terrorism is required	C) The purpose of rhetorical question is not asking for the answer, but seeking the reader's agreement or emphasizing the author's main concern.

Passage 1 Questions 42-52 are based on the following passage.

Before the man was deposed, (Q48) **Egyptian President Mohamed Morsi was roundly derided for ramrodding through a new constitution that would have, as his critics charged, made Egypt into an illiberal theocracy.**

Of special consternation was its second article, which declared that "Islam is the religion of the state and Arabic its official language. Principles of Islamic Sharia are the principal source of legislation." But when Egypt's next constitution, (42C) **shepherded in by the military and ratified** as Morsi stood trial, was found to contain nearly-identical language, the bells of discontent were not rung quite so small. Religious clauses in constitutions have abounded in Muslim countries, whether ruled by monarchs or mullahs, presidents or prime ministers, ever since Syria's 1950 post-colonial constitution declared Islamic jurisprudence to be the basis for legislation.

(50A & 51D & 52D) **Islam is either labeled as merely supreme or laws deemed repugnant to it are made explicitly invalid. So-called "repugnancy clauses," which invalidate laws judged contradictory to Islam and are perhaps the strongest endorsements of religion.** Imagine (Q49) if **Goldilocks were to go constitution-picking. She would settle on something not too theocratic, not too secular. In the Muslim**

Ranking Muslim Constitutions

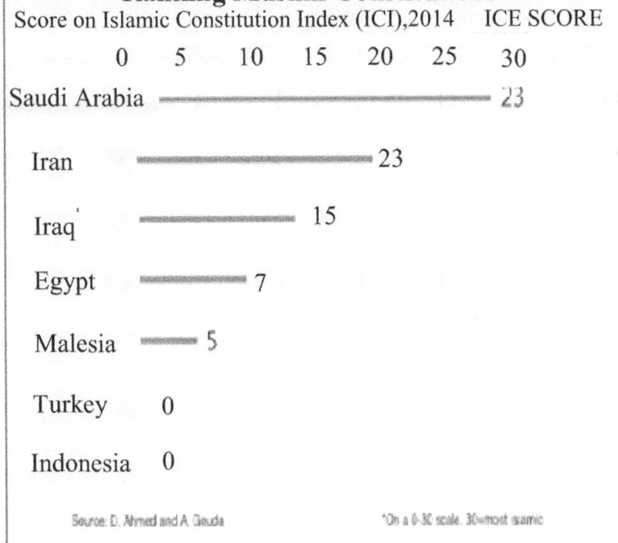

Score on Islamic Constitution Index (ICI),2014 ICE SCORE

0 5 10 15 20 25 30

Country	Score
Saudi Arabia	23
Iran	23
Iraq	15
Egypt	7
Malesia	5
Turkey	0
Indonesia	0

Source: D. Ahmed and A. Gouda *On a 0-30 scale, 30=most Islamic

Passage 2

(45D) **Are democracy and constitutional Islam at odds? It is a complicated question, sure to be bandied about in the halls of the academy. But an empirical approach to this question can also be worthwhile.**

One helpful measure is the Islamic Constitutions Index, developed by the academics Dawood I. Ahmed and Moamen Gouda, which assesses the degree of Islamic endorsement by constitutions on a scale from zero to 30 based on the demands made on public morality, rights and legislation, and the judiciary.

Topping the chart, perhaps not unexpectedly, are regional rivals (43D & 48A) **Iran and Saudi Arabia, the first a Shia theocratic quasi- democracy and the other a Sunni monarchy.** But immediately following them is Pakistan, the ally governed country with moderate civil rights protections—(44C) **not quite as renowned for morality police or punishments like amputation and beheading. Avowedly secular Turkey is placed at the bottom.**

(46B) **On average, constitutions with higher measures of Islamic provisions in their constitutions are associated with worse scores in** The Economist Intelligence Unit's democracy index, Freedom House's civil liberties ratings, the World Economic Forum's gender gap index, and the Pew Research Foundation's index of government restrictions on religion.

Does this analysis affirm the warning that "the elevation of Iranian-style theocrats," as one critical academic put it at the time, would undo the democratic order? (47A) **(Here, the familiar chiding about correlation and causation need be remembered.)**

Meanwhile, Western nations were recently involved in rewriting (49D & 52D) **the Iraqi and Afghanistan constitutions, both of which prominently enshrined the position of Islam that balances democracy.**

Between the high-minded sphere of constitutional design and actual, day-to-day impact on residents lies the apparatus of censors, judges, and policemen who modulate constitutional demands and translate them for the common man. What constitutions prescribe and what bureaucracies end up dealing out can be quite different.

<table>
<tr><td colspan="2">Q42. Absolute Pattern 5: Word-In-Context Question
Finding a clue word and the keyword from the sentence in question</td></tr>
<tr><td>A) Sheep rearing
B) Herding
C) Directed
D) Pioneered</td><td>C) But when Egypt's next constitution, shepherded in (directed) by the military and ratified as Morsi stood trial, bells of discontent were not rung quite so small.
A), B) are too literal meaning.</td></tr>
<tr><td colspan="2">Q43. Absolute Pattern 4: Example Question
Understanding example sentence and the true purpose behind a specific name or idea
Question Pattern: According to the passage 2, Saudi Arabia (line 41) is considered as the state where</td></tr>
<tr><td>A) constitutional Islam and democracy are mutually exclusive
B) Shia theocratic quasi-democracy is constantly evolving
C) democracy supersedes a Sunni monarchy
D) high Islamic endorsement is practiced by the constitutions</td><td>D) Iran and Saudi Arabia, the first a Shia theocratic quasi-democracy and the other a Sunni Monarchy.
(A) and (C) are Opposite (B) refers to Iran</td></tr>
<tr><td colspan="2">Q44. Absolute Pattern 3: Inference Question Finding an indirect suggestion (or guessing)
Question Pattern: It can be inferred from lines 46-48 in passage 2 that morality police or punishments like amputation and beheading are</td></tr>
<tr><td>A) quite renowned in all Islamic states
B) not practiced in Pakistan
C) practiced more widely outside of Pakistan territory
D) not accepted under the civil rights protections in any Islamic states</td><td>C) But Pakistan, —not quite as renowned for morality police or punishments like amputation and beheading.

In other words, they are more renown and frequently practiced outside Pakistan territory.
(A), (D) are opposite to the passage. (B) is incorrect because it's practiced a little</td></tr>
<tr><td colspan="2">Q45. Absolute Pattern 1: Main Idea Question Finding the main idea of the entire passage or the paragraph
Question Pattern: The main purpose of both passages is</td></tr>
<tr><td>A) to study how Egypt strived to apply Islam to its governance
B) to explore persistent religious conflicts in the Middle East
C) to opinion relations between democracy and religion around the world
D) to understand the constitutional Islam states in modern times</td><td>D) The focal points of both passages are Islam, constitutions, and the applications of Islamic constitutions in the present Islamic societies.
A) is applied to Passage 1 only.
C) religion around the world is not mentioned</td></tr>
<tr><td colspan="2">Q46. Absolute Pattern 4: Example Question
Understanding example sentence and the true purpose behind a specific name or idea.
Question Pattern: The examples cited in the third paragraph (lines 49-56) in Passage 2 are primarily intended to express the author's idea that</td></tr>
<tr><td>A) all Islamic states maintain relatively higher morality than other democratic nations
B) high Islamic provisions do not necessarily possess positive economic and civil rights
C) there is no democracy in Islamic states according to Freedom House's ratings
D) the government restrictions to religion in Islamic states need to be abolished</td><td>B) constitutions with higher measures of Islamic provisions in their constitutions are associated with worse scores in The Economist Intelligence Unit's democracy index,

(C), (D) are too extreme</td></tr>
</table>

<table>
<tr><td colspan="2">Q47. Absolute Pattern 10: Understanding the Structure of the Passage
Question Pattern: The parenthesis (Here… remembered.) in lines 60-62 in Passage 2 is mainly used to</td></tr>
<tr><td>A) qualify the previous remarks
B) emphasize the previous question
C) highlight the correlation between Islam and democracy
D) warn the elevation of Iranian-style theocrats</td><td>A) The main function of parenthesis is to: (1) define terms, (2) set the limit (3) add information.

Does this analysis affirm the warning...? (Here, the familiar chiding about correlation and causation need be remembered.)

(B), (D) are too extreme (C) "highlight" is opposite to "qualify"</td></tr>
<tr><td colspan="2">Q48. Absolute Pattern 9: Relationships Question
Question Pattern: Which country in Passage 2 would the former Egyptian President Mohamed Morsi (line 1) in passage 1 probably attempt to resemble?</td></tr>
<tr><td>A) Iran (line 41)
B) Pakistan (line 44)
C) Turkey (line 48)
D) Iraq (line 63)</td><td>A) Egyptian President Mohamed Morsi would have made Egypt into an illiberal theocracy. Topping the chart, , are regional rivals Iran and Saudi Arabia, the first a Shia theocratic quasi- democracy

*All three countries are maintaining low Islamic endorsement.</td></tr>
<tr><td colspan="2">Q49. Absolute Pattern 9: Relationships Question
Question Pattern: The reference to 'Goldilocks' in line 26, passage 1conveys which of the following countries in Passage 2?</td></tr>
<tr><td>A) Saudi Arabia (line 41)
B) Pakistan (line 44)
C) Turkey (line 48)
D) Afghanistan (line 64)</td><td>D) Imagine if Goldilocks were to go constitution-picking. She would settle on something not too theocratic, not too secular. In the Muslim world, that may be just right.

the Iraqi and Afghanistan constitutions, both of which prominently enshrined the position of Islam that balances democracy.
*Saudi Arabia, according to the passage, is leaning towards the extreme Monarchy; Pakistan and Turkey are two democratic states.</td></tr>
<tr><td colspan="2">Q50. Absolute Pattern 9: Relationships Question
Question Pattern: The author of Passage 1 would probably respond to lines 49-56 in Passage 2, (On average… religion.) by stating that</td></tr>
<tr><td>A) some index such as western gender laws are deemed to be repugnant to Islamic constitution
B) the Islamic states use a unique and different index
C) all the statistics are inaccurate
D) definitions of index are not easily identifiable among countries</td><td>A) " So-called "repugnancy clauses," which invalidate laws judged contradictory to Islam and are perhaps the strongest endorsements of religion…

On average, constitutions with higher measures of Islamic provisions in their constitutions are associated with worse scores in The Economist Intelligence Unit's democracy index,</td></tr>
<tr><td colspan="2">The Economist Intelligence Unit's democracy index is prepared from the view of Western that lacks Islamic perspective. Therefore, it could hints that some elements in the index can be a violation of the "repugnancy clauses"</td></tr>
</table>

Q51. **Absolute Pattern 11: Textual Evidence Question** Finding evidence for the previous question **Question Pattern:** Which choice provides the best evidence for the answer to the previous question?	
A) Lines 1-5 (Before the man...illiberal theocracy.) B) Lines 6-8 (Of special consternation...official language.) C) Lines 10-14 (But when Egypt's next...so small.) **D) Lines 21-25 (Islam is either...endorsements of religion.)**	D) Please refer to the above question

Q52. **Absolute Pattern 12: Informational Graphs** **Question Pattern: Which of the following countries** in the graph most likely agrees with the author's reference to **'Goldilocks' in line 26**, passage 1	
A) Iran B) Saudi Arabia C) Indonesia **D) Iraq**	Islamic endorsement in constitution: 30 /30 Islamic endorsement in constitution: 23 /30 Islamic endorsement in constitution: 0 /30 **D) Islamic endorsement in constitution: 15 /30**
D) Imagine if Goldilocks were to go constitution-picking. She would settle on something not too theocratic, not too secular. In the Muslim world, that may be just right. "15/30" = not too theocratic, not too secular. In the Muslim world, that may be just right.	

SAT Test 3

Writing and language Section Answer Explanations

&

Pattern Analyses

Test 3 Writing & Language Section Patterns

Questions 1-11 are based on the following passage.

AIRBNB

Airbnb is an online marketplace that enables people to list, [1] browsing a place to stay temporarily, then rent vacation homes for a processing fee.

It has over 1,500,000 listings in 34,000 cities and 191 countries. Founded in August 2008 and [2] headquartered in San Francisco, California, the company is privately owned and operated. Shortly after moving to San Francisco in October 2007, Brian Chesky created the initial concept for AirBed & Breakfast. The original site offered short-term living quarters, breakfast, and a unique business networking opportunity for attendees who were unable to book a hotel in the saturated market.

At the time, roommates Chesky and Gebbia could not afford the rent for their loft in San Francisco. They made their living room into a bed and breakfast, accommodating three guests on air mattresses and providing homemade breakfast.

In February 2008, technical architect Nathan Blecharczyk joined as the third co-founder of Air Bed & Breakfast. During the company's initial stages, the founders focused on high-profile events where alternative lodging was [3] plenty.

The site Airbedandbreakfast.com officially launched on August 11, 2008. To help fund the site, the founders created special edition breakfast cereals, with presidential candidates Barack Obama and John McCain as the inspiration for "Obama O's" and "Cap'n McCains". In two months, 800 boxes of cereal were sold at $40 each, [4] it has generated more than $30,000 for the company's incubation.

[5] With the website already built, they used the fund to fly to New York to meet users and promote the site. They returned to San Francisco with a profitable business model to present to West Coast investors.

In March 2009, the name Airbedandbreakfast.com was shortened to Airbnb.com, and [6] the site content expanded from air beds and shared spaces to a variety of properties including entire homes and apartments.

On May 25, 2011, [7] actor, and partner at A-Grade Investments Ashton Kutcher, announced a significant investment in the company and his role as a strategic brand advisor for the company. In July 2014, Airbnb revealed design revisions to their site and mobile app and introduced a new logo. Some considered the new icon to be visually similar to genitalia, [8] also a consumer survey by Survata showed only a minority of respondents thought this was the case.

[9] In the past, businesses were regulated by zoning laws, but Mayor Steven Fulop stated that the city does not have enough inspectors to deal the number of local units being rented out, approximately 300 of which rented through the service as of that date, and that rapid-evolving technology such as Airbnb made doing so impossible. Under the new legislation, Airbnb pays the city 6 percent hotel tax on the residential properties whose owners rent temporary living space to tourists for under 30 days, which is estimated to bring $1 million in revenue to the city, and expand tourist capacity beyond the city's 13 existing hotels. Airbnb will also provide insurance protection to homeowners in the event damage done to their residence by renters.

The new laws will not prevent condominium associations from voting to prohibit use of Airbnb in [10] them. [11] Giving the growth of international users, Airbnb opened 6 additional international offices in early 2012. These cities include Paris, Milan, Barcelona, Copenhagen, Moscow, and Sao Paulo.

Q1. Absolute Pattern 13: Parallel Structure

Airbnb is an online marketplace that enables people **to list**, [1] browsing a place to stay temporarily, then **rent** vacation homes for a processing fee.

	A) NO CHANGE	Always Pick the Shortest One from the Multiple Choices! Making incorrect choice by reducing information is not easy. Adding a few words, however, for the same purpose, is a piece of cake. B) maintains the parallel structure: "**to list, find, then rent.**" A), C), D) are all wordy that can be reduced to "find."
√	**B) find,**	
	C) look for other people's house	
	D) searching for,	

Q2. Absolute Pattern 13: Parallel Structure

It has over 1,500,000 listings in 34,000 cities and 191 countries. **Founded in** August 2008 and [2] **headquartered in San Francisco,** California, the company is privately owned and operated.

	Choice	Explanation
√	**A) NO CHANGE**	A) It starts with "founded in" Therefore, the same structure "headquartered in." should be the correct parallel structure.
	B) San Francisco as its headquarter	B) "California" should be linked to "San Francisco," instead of "its headquarter.
	C) headquarter in San Francisco,	C) "headquarter" is used as a noun, creating a new subject
	D) Airbnb has its headquarter in San Francisco	D) is a complete sentence, causing a comma splice.

Q3. Absolute Pattern 10: Logical Expression

During the company's initial stages, the founders focused on high-profile events where alternative lodging was [3] plenty

	Choice	Explanation
	A) NO CHANGE	C) New lodging company must find a place where rooms are scarce.
	B) not very close by	
√	**C) scarce**	A), D): customers wouldn't use the new lodging-offering company if there are plenty of rooms available.
	D) easily found	B) The sentence is not about lodging distance, but scarcity.

Q4. Absolute Pattern 12: Modifier Placement Error

In two months, 800 boxes of cereal were sold at $40 each, [4] it has generated more than $30,000 for the company's incubation.

	Choice	Explanation
	A) NO CHANGE	B) the modifier correctly describes the main clause.
√	**B) generating more than**	A) is a new sentence that creates a comma splice error.
	C) that generated more than	C) "that clause" cannot be followed by a comma as it normally carries a restrictive modifier.
	D) thereby generating more than	D) "thereby" is unnecessary.

Q5. Absolute Pattern 1: Adding, Revising, Deleting, Retaining Information

[5] With the website already built, they used the fund to fly to New York to meet users and promote the site.

Which choice best **connects the sentence with the previous paragraph**?

	Choice	Explanation
√	A) NO CHANGE	A) The startup company is still in the embryonic stage and the sentence reflects the initial stage of the company.
	B) Hotel industries became wary of the company by that time	B) changes the focus of the passage.
	C) Although the initial business plan seemed rosy, the reality waiting for them was opposite	C) Negative tone is incorrect because the overall tone in the passage is positive about Airbnb.
	D) Airbnb soon became the multibillion company	D) doesn't fit to the startup company description.

Q6. Absolute Pattern 14: Possessive Determiners and Possessive Noun Error

In March 2009, the name Airbedandbreakfast.com was shortened to Airbnb.com, and [6] the site's content expanded

	Choice	Explanation
	A) NO CHANGE	D) correctly connects two nouns.
	B) the site contents	A), B) Both "site" and "content" are noun, either one of which must be a possessive to the other noun.
	C) the content's site	C) The site should be the possessive, not the content.
√	**D) the site's content**	

Q7. Absolute Pattern 20: Restrictive Modifier (Essential Information)

On May 25, 2011, [7] actor, and partner at A-Grade Investments Ashton Kutcher announced a significant investment in the company and his role as a strategic brand advisor for the company.

	A) NO CHANGE
	B) an actor and a partner
√	**C) actor and partner**
	D) actor as a partner,

C) Actor and Ashton Kutcher is one individual and should not be separated by a comma.

B) "an" and "a" are considered as if an actor and a partner are different people.
D) 1> the comma after "a partner" severs the subject from the verb.
2> "as a partner" changes the original meaning as if the actor is limited to a partner.

Q8. Absolute Pattern 7: Conjunction Error

Some considered the new icon to be visually similar to genitalia, [8] also a consumer survey by Survata showed **only a minority** of respondents thought this was the case.

	A) NO CHANGE
√	**B) but**
	C) nevertheless
	D) moreover

B) Two sentences show the contrasting view with a single issue. Therefore, conjunction 'but' should be used.
A), C), D) are all conjunctive adverbs, not conjunctions. That is, they cannot connect the following clause without a semicolon. Therefore, incorrect regardless of their rhetorical meaning.

Q9. Absolute Pattern 1: Adding, Revising, Deleting, Retaining Information

At this point, the writer is considering adding the following sentence. Should the writer make this addition here

In October 2015, Jersey City, New Jersey became the first city in the New York metropolitan area to legalize Airbnb, and add it to their existing body of hotels and motels that pay taxes.

	A) Yes, because it supports the main argument in the passage and one city Mayor's effort to expand business
√	**B) Yes, because it provides a meaningful connection to the following sentences**
	C) No, because it should set up the argument for the benefit of the business
	D) No, because this article focuses on the initial stage of the company

B) The following sentence requires this added information as the topic sentence.
A) The Mayor tries to regulate the business, not "expanding it."
C): It's opposite. The following sentence provides the argument for the benefit of the city of New York
D) "No" should change to "Yes"

Q10. Absolute Pattern 24: Verb Tense / Voice Error

The new laws will not pre vent condominium associations from voting to prohibit use of Airbnb in [10] them.

	A) NO CHANGE
	B) it
	C) those buildings
√	**D) their buildings**

D) indicates the condominium associations' buildings.

A), B) are ambiguous as they could indicate many singular or plural nouns in the sentence.
C) 'those buildings' implies that the specific buildings have already been mentioned in the previous sentence.

Q11. Absolute Pattern 24: Verb Tense / Voice Error		
[11] Giving the growth of international users, Airbnb opened 6 additional international offices in early 2012.		
	A) NO CHANGE	B) "Having given" means After it had been given. The primary sentence shows that the company opened its new offices after it grew its users. A) The present progressive implies the simultaneous occurrence or on-going situation. Thus, the time sequence is reversed.
√	**B) Having given**	
	C) After Airbnb was given	
	D) To give	C) is passive. It should be active. It also uses "Airbnb" two times in one sentence, causing a redundant error. D) "To give" is the future tense.

Questions 12-22 are based on the following passage.

NASA Confirms Evidence That Liquid Water Flows on Today

New findings from NASA's Mars Reconnaissance Orbiter (MRO) provides the strongest evidence yet that liquid water flows intermittently on present-day Mars. Using an imaging spectrometer on MRO, [12] it detected signatures of hydrated minerals on slopes where mysterious streaks are seen on the Red Planet. These darkish streaks appear to ebb and flow over time. They darken and appear to flow down steep slopes during warm seasons, and then fade in cooler seasons. They appear in several locations on Mars when temperatures are above minus 10 degrees Fahrenheit (minus 23 Celsius) [13] but disappear at colder times.

[14] When we search for an extraterrestrial life, our quest on Mars has been to 'follow the water,' in our search for life in the universe, and now we have convincing science that validates what we've long suspected, said John Grunsfeld, astronaut and associate administrator of NASA's Science Mission Directorate in Washington.

"This is a significant development, as it appears to confirm that water [15] —albeit briny—is flowing today on the surface of Mars."

These downhill flows, known as recurring slope lineae (RSL), often have been described as possibly related [16] to water.

The new findings of hydrated salts on the slopes point to what that relationship may be to these dark features. The hydrated salts would lower the freezing point of a liquid brine, [17] just as salt on roads here on Earth causes ice and snow to melt more rapidly.

Scientists say it's likely a shallow subsurface flow, with enough water wicking to the surface to explain the darkening.[18] They are hypothesized to be formed by flow of briny liquid water on Mars. The image is produced by draping an orthorectified (RED) image (ESP_031059_1685) on a Digital Terrain Model (DTM) of the same site produced by High Resolution Imaging Science Experiment (University of Arizona). Vertical exaggeration is 1.5.

"We found the hydrated salts only when the seasonal features were widest, [19] which suggests that either the dark streaks themselves and a process that forms them is the source of the hydration.

In either case, the detection of hydrated salts on these slopes means that water plays a vital role in the formation of these streaks," said Lujendra Ojha of the Georgia Institute of Technology (Georgia Tech) [20] in Atlanta, lead author of a report on these findings published Sept. 28 by Nature Geoscience. Ojha first noticed these puzzling features as a University of Arizona undergraduate student in 2010, using images from the MRO's High Resolution Imaging Science Experiment (HiRISE).

The new site study pairs HiRISE observations with mineral mapping by MRO's Compact Reconnaissance Imaging Spectrometer for Mars (CRISM).[21] So far, HiRISE actually acquired 9137 images (Table 1), but from 2 to 3 times as much downlink data volume as expected, so the average image sizes are larger than previously expected. Ojha chose to acquire larger images rather than more images because it was operationally easier and because of a lifetime concern related to the number of on–off cycles to the FPS.

Q12. Absolute Pattern 17: Pronoun Error

Using an imaging spectrometer on MRO, [12] it detected signatures of hydrated minerals on slopes where mysterious streaks are seen on the Red Planet.

	A) NO CHANGE	
	B) they	
√	**C) researchers**	Only human (researchers) can use "an imaging spectrometer on MRO"
	D) Mars	

Q13. Absolute Pattern 13: Parallel Structure

They appear in several locations on Mars when temperatures are above minus 10 degrees Fahrenheit (minus 23 Celsius), [13] but disappear at colder times.

	A) NO CHANGE	Conjunction 'but' cancels out the previous clause.
√	**B) and disappear**	B): the Parallel structure in the sentence requires the conjunction "and."
	C) however, disappear	A) "but," C) "however", D) "while" are used to contradict or cancel out the preceding sentence.
	D) while disappearing	This sentence doesn't cancel each other out, but maintains the parallel structure.

Q14. Absolute Pattern 19: Redundant Error

[14] When we search for an extraterrestrial life, our quest on Mars has been to 'follow the water,' **in our search for life** in the universe, and now we have convincing science that validates what we've long suspected," said John Grunsfeld, astronaut and associate administrator of NASA's Science Mission Directorate in Washington.

	A) NO CHANGE	A), B), C) are all redundant with the following phrase in the same sentence.
	B) Because searching for an extra-terrestrial life is our goal,	
	C) As we search for an extraterrestrial life,	
√	**D) delete the underlined portion, and starts the sentence with "Our quest...."**	

Q15. Absolute Pattern 18: Punctuation Error

This is a significant development, as it appears to confirm that water [15] —albeit briny—is flowing today on the surface of Mars."

Which of the following alternatives would **NOT be appropriate**?

	A) NO CHANGE	Inessential Information should be separated from the main sentence using a punctuation.
	B) (albeit briny)	C) didn't use any punctuation as if 'although briny' is an essential information to construct the main sentence.
√	**C) although briny**	A) a pair of dashes, B) parenthesis, D) a pair of commas, all of which offset the inessential information from the main clause.
	D) ,albeit briny,	

Q16. Absolute Pattern 19: Redundant Error		
These downhill flows, known as recurring slope lineae (RSL), often have been described as **possibly** related [16] to water		
√	**A) NO CHANGE**	Pattern: Always Pick the Shortest One from the Multiple Choices! All the other choices are redundant to the word "possibly"
	B) with potential liquid	
	C) with conceivable water	
	D) to water in some probability	

Q17. Absolute Pattern 1: Adding, Revising, Deleting, Retaining Information		
At this point, the author wishes to delete the underlined phrase. Should the author proceeds to delete it or not? The hydrated salts would lower the freezing point of a liquid brine, [17] just as salt on roads here on Earth causes ice and snow to melt more rapidly.		
	A) Keep, because it confirms the same molecules of salts on Mars' surface and Earth.	B) "just as..." helps visualize the previous statement. A) The clause doesn't confirm it is the same molecules. C), D) Visualization neither undermines the theory nor unfits for the academic journal.
√	**B) Keep, because it helps visualize the process of melting ice**	
	C) Delete, because it undermines the passage's central theory	
	D) Delete, because the description doesn't fit to the academic journal	

Q18. Absolute Pattern 1: Adding, Revising, Deleting, Retaining Information	
Question: The dark streaks here are up to few hundred meters in length. Should the writer make **this addition** here?	
√	**A) Yes, because a new paragraph cannot start with a pronoun.**
	B) Yes, because the exact measurement is an essential factor to determine the quality of briny liquid.
	C) No, because the information is not directly related with the paragraph.
	D) No, because the hypothesis is not fully confirmed to suggest the measurement
A) The first sentence in a paragraph must not start with a pronoun. B) The description "the quality of briny liquid," isn't supported by or mentioned in the passage. C) The following sentence describes that there are relations between the sentences. D) The following sentence fully confirms the measurement.	

Q19. Absolute Pattern 21: Subject-Verb, Pronoun, Noun Agreement		
We found the hydrated salts only when the seasonal features were widest, [19]which suggests that **either** the dark streaks themselves **and** a process that forms them is the source of the hydration.		
	A) NO CHANGE	B) 1> "either...or" is the correct form of idiom 2> The subject is "a process," a singular; therefore, the verb, "is" required. C), D) 1> Tense error: "suggested," is past tense. 2> the verb, "are" is incorrect.
√	B) **which suggest** that either the dark streaks themselves **or a process** that forms them **is**	
	C) **suggested** that either the dark streaks themselves **or a process** that forms them **are**	
	D) **suggesting** that either the dark streaks themselves **or a process** that forms them **are**	

Q20. Absolute Pattern 22 : Non-Restrictive Modifier (Inessential Information)		
In either case, the detection of hydrated salts on these slopes means that water plays a vital role in the formation of these streaks," **said Lujendra Ojha of the Georgia Institute of Technology [20] in Atlanta, lead author** of a report on these findings published Sept. 28 by Nature Geoscience.		
√	**A) NO CHANGE**	A) The non-restrictive modifier should be separated by comma. "**,,,Atlanta, lead…**"
	B) in Atlanta lead	B) Without a comma, the modifier blurs the line between the main clause and the modifier, causing several errors such as change of meaning.
	C) in Atlanta, leading	C) 1> changes the original meaning 2> "leading author" sounds as if Lujendra Ojha is leading another author.
	D) in Atlanta leads	D) uses "leads" as a verb causing 1> change of meaning 2> comma splice error.

Q21. Absolute Pattern 1: Adding, Revising, Deleting, Retaining Information		
At this point, the writer wants to further reinforce Ojhas research. Which choice most effectively accomplish this goal?		
√	A) Using the HiRISE, he documented RSL at dozens **of mineral sites on Mars.**	A) "The new site study" and "mineral sites" correspond correctly to support each other's description.
	B) Using the HiRISE, he was able to solve on-off cycles to the FPS.	B) The passage didn't say he solved on -off cycles. It only hints that he was able to operate easily.
	C) Using the HiRISE, he acquired average-size images	C), D) are opposite to the passage.
	D) Using the HiRISE, he chose to document more images as many as possible.	

Questions 23-33 are based on the following passage.

Louis Armstrong

Louis Armstrong, nicknamed Satchmo or Pops, was an American trumpeter, composer, singer and occasional [23] actor. Luis Armstrong is considered as the most influential figures in jazz. His career spanned five decades, from the 1920s to the 1960s [24] ,different eras in jazz. Coming to prominence in the 1920s as an inventive" trumpet and cornet player, Armstrong [25] was not officially trained in jazz, shifting the focus of the music from collective improvisation to solo performance.

Armstrong was one of the first truly popular African-American entertainers to "cross over", whose skin color was secondary to his music in [26] likeminded fans' passion. His artistry and personality allowed him socially acceptable to access the upper echelons of American society which [27] were highly open for black men of his era. [28] ①Armstrong was born into a poor family in New Orleans, Louisiana, and was the grandson of slaves. ②He spent his youth in poverty, in a rough neighborhood known as "the Battlefield", which was part of the Storyville legal prostitution district.

③ His mother Mary "Mayann" Albert (1886–1927) then left Louis and his younger sister, Beatrice Armstrong Collins, in the care of his grandmother, Josephine Armstrong, and at times, his Uncle Isaac. ④At five, he moved back to live with his mother and her relatives. He attended the Fisk School for Boys, where he most likely had early exposure to music.

He brought in some money [29] as a paperboy but also by finding discarded food and selling it to restaurants, but it was not enough to keep his mother from prostitution. He [30] often hang out in dance halls close to home, where he observed everything from licentious dancing to the quadrille.

After dropping out of the Fisk School at age eleven, Armstrong [31] joined a quartet of boys who sang in the streets for money. He also started to get into trouble.
Cornet player Bunk Johnson said he taught Armstrong (then 11) to play by ear at Dago Tony's Tonk in New Orleans, [32] however in his later years Armstrong gave the credit to Oliver. Armstrong hardly looked back at his youth as the worst of times but drew inspiration from it instead: "Every time I close my eyes blowing that trumpet of mine—I look right in the heart of good old New Orleans... It has given me something to live for." [33]

Questions 34-44 are based on the following passage.

Q22. Absolute Pattern 9: Informational Graphs		
So far, HiRISE actually acquired 9137 images, but from 2 to 3 times as much downlink data volume as expected, so the average image sizes are larger than previously expected. **Ojha chose to acquire larger images rather than more images** because it was operationally easier and because of a lifetime concern related to the number of on–off cycles to the FPS.		
	A) Standalone small images	As described above, The on-going research will focus on C)
	B) Off-nadir observations	
√	**C) Stereo images with enhanced size**	
	D) Nadir observations including non-mineral zones	

Q23. Absolute Pattern 16: Precision, Concision, Style		
Louis Armstrong, nicknamed Satchmo or Pops, was an American trumpeter, composer, singer and occasional [23] actor. Luis Armstrong is considered as the most influential figures in jazz.		
	A) NO CHANGE	D) links the following clause while simplifying the entire sentence.
	B) actor, and Luis Armstrong	A), B) are redundant error. These options unnecessarily repeat Luis Armstrong, which can be avoided by linking with 'who.'
	C) actor	
√	**D) actor, who**	C) is run-on sentence.

Q24. Absolute Pattern 18: Punctuation Error		
Which of the following alternatives would **NOT be appropriate**?		
Passage: His career spanned five decades, from the 1920s to the 1960s [24], different eras in jazz.		
	A) , different eras in Jazz	D) 1> A semicolon requires a clause on both sides. 2> "different eras in Jazz" is not a clause., and therefore, cannot be used.
	B) –different eras in Jazz	
	C) : different eras in Jazz	A), B), C): comma, dash, and colon, all of which can carry a phrase.
√	**D) ; different eras in Jazz**	

Q25. Absolute Pattern 1: Adding, Revising, Deleting, Retaining Information		
Passage: Coming to prominence in the 1920s as an "inventive" trumpet and cornet player, Armstrong [25] was not officially trained in jazz, shifting the focus of the music from collective improvisation to solo performance.		
The writer wants to convey an attitude of genuine interest and respect **to the later life of the musician**. Which choice best accomplishes this goal?		
	A) NO CHANGE	D) is positive and expresses the author's respect to the **musician's later life success**.
	B) was born when United States of America was severely experiencing racially the Divided States of America.	A), C) are negative. B) is inconsistent with the question. It rather shows the back ground information.
	C) started his career by taking an unenviable position at the backstage.	C) is opposite. The question asks "the later life," not the starting career.
√	**D) was a foundational influence**	

Q26. Absolute Pattern 1: Adding, Revising, Deleting, Retaining Information

Passage: Armstrong was one of the first truly popular African-American entertainers to "cross over," whose skin color was secondary to his music in [26] likeminded fans' passion.

Which choice most effectively sets up the **contrast in the sentence** and is consistent with the information in the rest of the passage?

	Choice	Explanation
	A) NO CHANGE	B) sets up the direct contrast to racial issues introduced in the sentence. Other options are not necessarily related to racial issue.
√	**B) the racially divided country.**	
	C) the professional music industry	
	D) the society back in the 1930s.	

Q27. Absolute Pattern 10: Logical Expression

His artistry and personality allowed him socially acceptable to access the upper echelons of American society which [27] were highly open for black men of his era.

	Choice	Explanation
	A) NO CHANGE	D) only (D) is coherent to the sentence context.
	B) appreciated	A), B), C) are all opposite
	C) were accessible	
√	**D) were unapproachable**	

Q28. Absolute Pattern 11: Logical Sequence

To improve the cohesion and flow of this paragraph, the writer wants to add the following sentence.
His father, William Armstrong, abandoned the family when Louis was an infant and took up with another woman.
The sentence would most logically be placed after

	Choice	Explanation
	A) sentence 1	C) "His mother...then left" shows the chronological sequence.
√	**B) sentence 2**	A) and B) illustrate Armstrong's youth.
	C) sentence 3	D) Sentence 4 describes young Louis tapped into the world of his musical life.
	D) sentence 4	

Q29. Absolute Pattern 7: Conjunction Error

He brought in some money [29] either as a paperboy **but also** by finding discarded food and selling it to restaurants, but it was not enough to keep his mother from prostitution.

	Choice	Explanation
	A) NO CHANGE	C) "not only...but also" is a correlative conjunction that can't be replaced with other format.
	B) working as a paperboy	A) "either...but also" isn't the correct idiom
√	**C) not only as a paperboy**	B). D) can't reduce the first half of the "not only...but also" conjunction.
	D) selling papers	

Q30. Absolute Pattern 10: Logical Expression

Passage: He [30] often hang out in dance halls close to home, where he **observed** everything from licentious dancing to the quadrille.

	A) NO CHANGE	When multiple choices include different verb tenses, look for other verbs in the paragraph, identify the tense, and stick to it. C) Hung is the past tense of hang. The following verb "observed" suggests that we maintain the past tense. A) is present tense B), D) The progressive tense applies a short-continuing and repeating action.
	B) was hang	
√	**C) often hung**	
	D) was hanging	

Q31. Absolute Pattern 24: Verb Tense / Voice Error

After dropping out of the Fisk School at age eleven, Armstrong [31] joined a quartet of boys **who sang** in the streets for money

√	**A) NO CHANGE**	A) The entire passage uses the past tense. To maintain the parallel structure, this sentence must use the past tense as well. B) is past perfect. The situation is reversed. "Joining a quarter…" should come later. C) is present perfect. The overall passage uses the past tense. D) "he was joined by someone" is passive voice that doesn't make sense.
	B) had joined	
	C) has joined	
	D) was joined	

Q32. Absolute Pattern 7: Conjunction Error

Cornet player Bunk Johnson said he taught Armstrong (then 11) to play by ear at Dago Tony's Tonk in New Orleans, [32] however in his later years Armstrong gave the credit to Oliver.

	A) NO CHANGE	D) is coordinating conjunction for concessional statement. The statement provides an alternate explanations using "although. " A) The conjunctive adverb 'however,' requires a semicolon like ":however," B) is preposition and can't be used for a clause. C) is used for the cause-and-effect situation.
	B) in spite of	
	C) because	
√	**D) although**	

Q33. Absolute Pattern 1: Adding, Revising, Deleting, Retaining Information

Which choice most effectively concludes the sentence and paragraph?
It has given me something to live for." [33]

√	**A) NO CHANGE**
	B) "Well...New Orleans indeed was such a beautiful land.
	C) I regret things could have been better if I was a well-behaved kid.
	D) Who knew I would be the king of music?

A) The sentence does not require further conclusion.
B) It shifts its focus to New Orleans.
C) is negative. The entire passage is positive.
D) A self-congratulatory tone doesn't connect well with the previous sentence

Questions 34-44 are based on the following passage.

DRONE

An unmanned aerial vehicle (UAV), commonly known as a drone, as an unmanned aircraft system (UAS), or by several other names, is an aircraft without a human pilot aboard. The flight of UAVs may operate with various degrees of autonomy: either under remote control by a human operator, or under fully [34] and exhaustively by onboard computers.

[35] Compared to manned aircraft, UAVs are often preferred for missions that are too [36] boring for humans. They originated mostly in military applications, although their use is expanding in commercial, scientific, recreational, agricultural, and other applications [37] such as, policing and surveillance, aerial photography, agriculture and drone racing. The term [38] ,more widely used by the public, "drone was given in reference to the resemblance of male bee that makes loud and regular sounds. This term emphasizes the importance of elements other than the aircraft [39] ,indicating the significance of several elements of drone.

It includes several elements [40] ,such as ground control stations, data links, and other support equipment. Many similar terms are in use. A UAV is defined as a powered, aerial vehicle that [41] do not carry a human operator, uses aerodynamic forces to provide vehicle lift, can fly autonomously or be piloted remotely, can be expendable or recoverable, and carry a lethal or non-lethal payload.

[42] Therefore, missiles are not considered UAVs because the vehicle itself is a weapon that is not reused, though it is also unmanned and in some cases remotely guided.

The relation of UAVs to remote controlled model aircraft is unclear. [43] Some jurisdictions base their definitions on size or weight; however, the US Federal Aviation Administration defines any unmanned flying craft as a UAV regardless of size.

[44] The UAV's global military market is dominated by United States and Israel. The US held a 60% military-market share in 2006. It operated over 9,000 UAVs in 2014. From 1985 to 2014, exported drones came predominantly from Israel (60.7%) and the United States (23.9%); top importers were the United Kingdom (33.9%) and India (13.2%).

Q34. Absolute Pattern 10: Logical Expression

The flight of UAVs may operate with various degrees of autonomy: either under remote control by a human operator, or under fully [34] and exhaustively by onboard computers.

	Choice	Explanation
	A) NO CHANGE	A), B), C) are all synonym to "fully."
	B) categorically	
	C) thoroughly	
√	**D) delete it**	

Q35. Absolute Pattern 10: Logical Expression

[35] Compared to manned aircraft, UAVs are often preferred for missions that are too [36] boring for humans. The subject is 'UAVs', which is supported by its introductory modifier 'Compared to manned aircraft'. The original form of this sentence was "When UAVs are compared to manned aircraft,"

	Choice	Explanation
√	**A) NO CHANGE**	A) "Compared" is the contraction form of "(When UAVs are) compared to"
	B) When you compare	B) "you" changes the subject.
	C) Comparing	C) 1> The subject "UAVs" is non-human. 2> "comparing" is the contraction form of "When UAVs are comparing"
	D) After the comparison	D) is wordy.

Q36. Absolute Pattern 10: Logical Expression		
Compared to manned aircraft, UAVs are often preferred for missions that are too [36] boring for humans.		
	A) NO CHANGE	B) The storyline emphasizes the out-of-reach to human control. A), C), D) do not reflect the primary functions of the UAVs
√	**B) dangerous**	
	C) theoretical	
	D) organized	

Q37. Absolute Pattern 18: Punctuation Error		
They originated mostly in military applications, although their use is expanding in commercial, scientific, recreational, agricultural, and other applications [37]such as, policing and surveillance, aerial photography, agriculture and drone racing.		
	A) NO CHANGE	'Such as' phrase is an added information and not essential to complete the sentence. Thus, it must use a single comma to separate it from the main clause. B) Comma should be placed before "such as" A), C): Comma can't be placed after such as. D): A colon and 'such as' perform the same function and can't be placed simultaneously.
√	**B) , such as**	
	C) ; such as,	
	D) such as:	

Q38. Absolute Pattern 11: Logical Sequence		
The **term** [38] ,more widely used by the public, "**drone** was given in reference to the resemblance of male bee that makes loud and regular sounds.		
	A) NO CHANGE	Correct sentence: The **term drone**, more widely used by the public, was given ~. B) "The term" and "drone" can't be separated.
√	**B) after "drone"**	
	C) after "given"	
	D) after "bee"	

Q39. Absolute Pattern 19: Redundant Error		
This term emphasizes the importance of elements other than the aircraft [39] ,indicating the significance of several elements of drone.		
	A) NO CHANGE	Always Pick the Shortest One from the Multiple Choices! The underlined portion is redundant, and has to be removed.
	B) as it indicates the significance of several elements.	
	C) an indication of its term's significance.	
√	**D) delete the underlined portion.**	

Q40. Absolute Pattern 19: Redundant Error

Question: Which of the following alternatives would NOT be appropriate?

It **includes** several elements [40] ,such as ground control stations, data links, and other support equipment.

	Choice	Explanation
√	A) **, including** ground control stations,	A) "including" is repeating.
	B) : ground control stations,	B) "colon" [:]
	C) —ground control stations,	C) "dash" [—]
	D) like ground control stations,	D) "like" All the other options are used for the same function: introduce thing (s).

Q41. Absolute Pattern 21: Subject-Verb, Pronoun, Noun Agreement

A) A UAV is defined as a powered, aerial vehicle that [41] **do not** carry a human operator, **uses** aerodynamic forces to provide vehicle lift, **can fly** autonomously or be piloted remotely, can be expendable or recoverable, and carry a lethal or nonlethal payload.

	Choice
	B) does not carry a human operator, uses aerodynamic forces to provide vehicle lift, could fly autonomously or be piloted remotely, can be expendable
	C) do not carry a human operator, uses aerodynamic forces to provide vehicle lift, fly autonomously or be piloted remotely, can be expendable
√	D) **does** not carry a human operator, **uses** aerodynamic forces to provide vehicle lift, **can fly** autonomously or **be** piloted remotely, **expendable**

D) "does", "uses", "can fly", "*(can)* be", "*(can be)* expendable"

The correct sentence:
A UAV is defined as a powered, aerial **vehicle** that **does not** carry a human operator**, uses** aerodynamic forces to provide vehicle lift**, can fly** autonomously or (can) **be** piloted remotely, (can be) **expendable** or recoverable,…
* "(can)" and "(can be)" are removed to avoid redundancy and prevent the slow progression of expression.

A) 1> The subject in that-clause "Vehicle" is singular. 2> the singular verb "does" is required.
B) "could" is past tense, defying the present tense applied in the essay. C) "fly" is plural. => "flies"

Q42. Absolute Pattern 23: Transition Words for Supporting Detail, Contrast, and Consequence

	Choice	Explanation
	A) NO CHANGE	C) The following sentence describes the missiles that further specify what cannot be defined as UAV.
	B) Moreover,	
√	C) For example,	A) 'Therefore' is used to illustrate consequence. B) 'Moreover' is used to support the preceding information.
	D) Although,	D) 'Although' is used to illustrate the contrasting view

Q43. Absolute Pattern 1: Adding, Revising, Deleting, Retaining Information	
Question: At this point, the author wishes **to delete** the underlined phrase. Should the author proceeds to delete it or not?	
The relation of UAVs to remote controlled model aircraft is unclear. [43] Some jurisdictions base their definitions on size or weight; however, the US Federal Aviation Administration defines any unmanned flying craft as a UAV regardless of size.	
√	**A) Keep, because it provides a specific example of the previous sentence.**
	B) Keep, because it provides the reason for the **inclusion of remote** controlled model aircraft to UAV
	C) Delete, because it interrupts the flow of the paragraph by illustrating an unsettled decision.
	D) Delete, because it weakens the focus of the passage by shifting to remote controlled model aircraft.

A) The sentence must be kept as a supporting detail that backups the topic sentence.
B) The previous sentence (The topic) illustrates why the definition of UVAs is still unclear, Therefore, B) "the reason for the inclusion" is direct opposite statement.
C), D) both run counter to the central purpose of the previous sentence.

Q44. Absolute Pattern 1: Adding, Revising, Deleting, Retaining Information	
Question: Which of the following sentences is **LEAST applicable as an alternate** sentence?	
	A) The UAV's global market is dominated by United States and Israel.
	B) As the related technology improves, there has been a huge expansion in the UAV's global military market in less than a decade.
√	C) UAV's global market, however, faces **some serious privacy** issues as it expands exponentially.
	D) The U.S. Department of Defense has released a new statistics that shows Israel as the second largest market controller, next to the U.S.

C) Privacy issue has never been discussed. The negative tone also runs opposite to the overall positive tone of UAVs expansion in the passage.

A), B), and D): All of them share the positive aspects of UAVs expansion and connect well with the overall flow and tone of the preceding sentence.

Chapter 3 Summary

Chapter Summary contains equal portions of

-12 Absolute Patterns for Reading Section

-20 Common Patterns for Incorrect Choices in Reading

-70 Absolute Patterns for Writing and Language Section

-24 Common Patterns for Incorrect Choices in Writing

Chapter 3

12 Absolute Patterns for the Reading Section

Category B: Technique Question has six patterns:

Metaphorically speaking, if Category A: Content Question is about asking the interior of the building, Category B: Technique Question is about understanding the foundation and the skeletons of the building.

Category B: Technique Question has six patterns:

▶ **Absolute Pattern 3: Inference Question**
Finding an indirect suggestion (or guessing)

▶ **Absolute Pattern 6: Analogy Question**
Finding a similar situation

▶ **Absolute Pattern 7: Understanding Attitude (Tone) Question**
Finding a tone such as positive-negative, active-passive, mental-physical, subjective-objective

▶ **Absolute Pattern 9: Relationships Question**
Finding relations between the cause-effect, characters, and ideas including a Paired Passage.

▶ **Absolute Pattern 10: Understanding the Structure of the Passage**
Finding the structure of the entire passage or organizational relations between the paragraphs

▶ **Absolute Pattern 12: Informational Graphs**
Finding facts described in the graphs or relations between the passage and the graph.

Chapter 3

12 Absolute Patterns for the Reading Section

Absolute Pattern 3: Inference Question

Suppose you're a 2-year-old kid and very hungry. If you saw the McDonald's sign and points at it to your mom, what do you mean?
(A) I want to have that McDonald's signage (B) I want to have a hamburger.
That's the inference. Finding an indirect suggestion (or guessing)

The inference question usually sends us a signal in the question. It normally starts with "refers to...," "suggests..." "may think..." "implies..." etc.

The inference question seeks an indirect suggestion—hamburger, not the McDonald's signage—behind the reading passage. Therefore, whatever directly copied from the reading passage <u>should never be the answer</u> because the incorrect choice that you may choose—whether it is true statement or not—should belong to the content question, not inference.

For the inference question, you need to take a guess—an educated guess, based on the cause-and-effect reasoning.

As an example, we all know that a hammer is a tool to nail something.
If a question asked
"what does the hammer implies in the passage?"

The answer should never be "(A) to nail and secure something." Instead, you should pick the choice that implies hammer.

Chapter 3

12 Absolute Patterns for the Reading Section

Absolute Pattern 6: Analogy Question

Analogy question is pretty much similar to logic question.
It mainly asks finding a situational statement: the analogy question in reading section contains very well organized logic and premises.

Don't be shocked when multiple choices contain totally different information from the reading passage.

In analogy question,—unlike other questions—multiple choices do not use any statement or same words found in passage.
It suddenly asks (A) a school teacher (B) frogs (C) hardwood floor (D) Odyssey
They all have nothing to do with the passage content.

Instead, you should focus on the logical relation between the reading passage and the multiple choices.

Most common logic applied in Analogy question is as follow:
Positive vs. negative value
Active vs. passive value
Physical vs. mental value
Quantity-quality
A single person vs. two person involvement
Part vs. Whole comparison.
For example, if the passage contained a mother who lost her son during the war.
Your choice must contain
(1) Two-person involvement (mother, son)
(2) Negative (losing a son)
(3) External impact (war)

Chapter 3

70 Absolute Patterns for Writing and Language

Question 16
Cancun was not my first destination for vacation I found it too hot temperature there was unappealing at that time.

A) NO CHANGE
B) vacation; because I found
C) vacation because I found
D) vacation, found

RULE #16 Hint: Conjunction	**Run-on Sentence** The correct answer is C. The original sentence is a run-on. A run-on sentence contains multiple independent clauses without having a proper conjunction. "Because" connects and describes the cause-effect clause. B) has semicolon and "because" at the same time, one of which has to be dropped. Options A and D are run-on,

Question 17
The house that belongs to my tenant next to the backyard needs an additional repair.

A) NO CHANGE
B) The house that belongs to my tenant
C) The house of my tenant
D) My tenant's house

RULE #17 Hint: Wordiness	**Possessive Noun** The correct answer is D. A singular noun (human) + apostrophe + s is the way to make a singular possessive noun The original sentence and options B, C are unnecessarily wordy.

Question 18
The recent data sent by Voyager II further confirms Dr. Ray's theory whom argued about water molecules in the Mar's atmosphere.

A) NO CHANGE
B) ,in which he
C) , which
D) , who

RULE #18
Hint:
Pronoun

Antecedent for Pronoun

The correct answer is B.
The object in this sentence is 'theory', not Dr. Ray.

Therefore, both A) and D) are incorrect as "who" or "whom" refers to a human antecedent.
There's no human in the sentence, only "Dr. Ray's theory" is.

C) can't be correct because "which" ("theory") can't argue.

Question 19
<u>The passenger, who I saw yesterday,</u> crippling and begging on the Mall, is standing right next to me, flirting with a much younger girl.

A) NO CHANGE
B) The passenger that I saw yesterday
C) The passenger whom I saw yesterday
D) The passenger, what I saw yesterday,

RULE #19
Hint:
Pronoun

Who or Whom?

The correct answer is C.
If a noun (subject) follows right after either "whom" or "who" in the question, the answer should be "whom."

If a verb follows right after either "whom" or "who" in the question, the answer should be "who."

Question 20
The other side of the calculus that keeps the dark business humming is the crooked <u>police. They are paid handsome sums of the profits.</u>

A) NO CHANGE
B) police paying handsome sums of the profits.
C) police, who are paid handsome sums of the profits.
D) police, and they are paid handsome sums of the profits.

RULE #20
Hint:
Wordiness

Simplification

The correct answer is C.
C) connects the modifier correctly and concisely.

A) The original sentence employs two independent sentences unnecessarily.
B) changes the original meaning by saying that police are paying the profits.
D) uses an ambiguous "they"

Question 21

American athletes win most medals in the Olympics, whereby America has such great systems for preparing athletes.

A) NO CHANGE
B) because America has such great systems
C) moreover, America has such great systems
D) consequently, America has such great systems

RULE #21
Hint:
Conjunction

The Conjunction for Cause-Effect

The correct answer is B.
Be careful if the two clauses are pointing the cause-effect. The conjunction 'because' must be used.

A) "whereby" means "by which" to refer to means and method
C) "moreover" supports the preceding information
D) "consequently" refers to the effects.

Question 22

In a war against the Islamic State, women can be found in the ranks but also in command of guerrilla units.

A) NO CHANGE
B) not only in the ranks
C) by the ranks
D) more in the ranks

RULE #22
Hint:
Conjunction

Correlative Conjunction

The correct answer is B.
B) "but also" indicates the preceding conjunction must be "not only"

Following conjunctions represent similarity and emphasis
-Moreover / - just as / - likewise / - not only ...but also

Correlative conjunction cannot be used separately or replaced with other form.

Question 23

Some European industries have declined, and others are rising.

A) NO CHANGE
B) however,
C) since
D) but

RULE #23
Hint:
Conjunction

The Conjunction for Contrast

The correct answer is D.
The two clauses are contradicting. "but" is the conjunction for contradiction.
Following conjunctions (and conjunctive adverbs) represent contradiction

-However /-on the other hand / -but /-nevertheless /-aside from / -while or whereas
B) is incorrect because "however" requires semi-colon."

Question 24
The car making a squeaking noise as it veered to the right finally ran into the bakery.

A) NO CHANGE
B) made a squeaking noise, veering to the right, and
C) ,which was making a squeaking noise as it veered to the right,
D) , making a squeaking noise as it veered to the right,

RULE #24
Hint:
modifier

Restrictive Modifier

The correct answer is A.
The modifier should not be offset by a pair of commas if the clause requires it as a part of the essential information to understand the situation.
A) without the modifier, "The car" can be an ambiguous description and therefore requires this modifier as a part of the essential information.

B) not only changes the original meaning but also makes a parallelism error.
("made", "veering" and "ran")

C) and D) are non-restrictive modifiers, contrary to the original sentence.
C) is wordy too

Question 25
Some of the survivors in the refugee camps of Iraqi Kurdistan dominated by the heavily patriarchal system shows how strong the tradition influenced the war.

A) NO CHANGE
B) Iraqi Kurdistan; dominated by the heavily patriarchal system, shows
C) Iraqi Kurdistan, dominated by the heavily patriarchal system, show
D) Iraqi Kurdistan, dominated by the heavily patriarchal system show

RULE #25
Hint:
Modifier

Non-Restrictive Modifier

The correct answer is C
If the modifier merely putting an additional information, it should be offset by a pair of commas.

Chapter 3

24 Common Patterns for *In*correct Choices in Writing

11 Logical Sequence Error

This pattern is about finding the best sentence/ clause/ phrase sequence or placement.

Multiple choices normally carry statements such as (A) before sentence 1 (D) after sentence 4

One trick to find the best sequence (the answer) is to read the sentences from backward. The reasoning behind this technique is that identifying the conclusion is always easier than identifying the introduction or body sentence. To do that, follow the steps below:

Step 1. Find your best choice based on your understanding.

Step 2. Try to read your best choice from backward order (sentence 4-3-2-1), and see if "sentence 4" should be the conclusion.

12 Modifier (Placement) Error

A modifier must be placed immediately next to the word that it intends to modify.

In other words, a modifier should not be separated from the word that it owns the modifier.

Please consider the following sentence:
"Known as the great writer in U.S., *the brilliant skills of Mark Twain* are not from his education, but from intuition."

The modifier "the great writer" must describe a human Mark Twain not "the brilliant skills"

The correct answer for this dangling modifier error should be "*Mark Twain* developed his brilliant skills not from the education, but from intuition."

Chapter 3

24 Common Patterns for *In*correct Choices in Writing

13 Parallelism Error

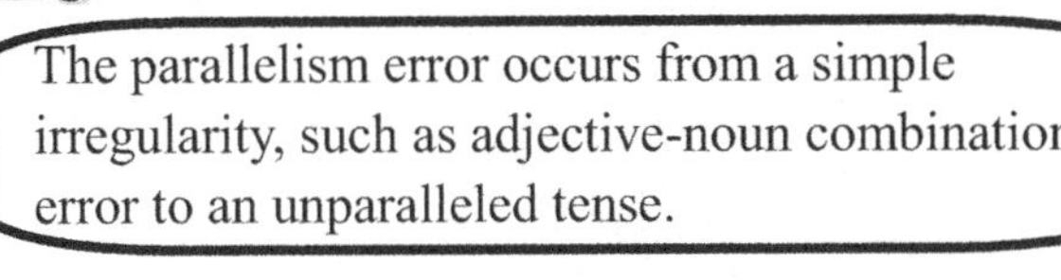

The parallelism error occurs from a simple irregularity, such as adjective-noun combination error to an unparalleled tense.

Idiom and prepositional idiom pattern asks the correct usage of preposition.

"The population of Kentucky is smaller than California" is incorrect because it compares the "population" to "California." Here's another example:
"Traffic accidents occur most frequently in New York than any other cities except in Seattle."

This sentence is incorrect too. "in Seattle" has to be corrected to "Seattle" because it compares to "any other cities" not the "accidents in New York."

14 Possessive Determiners and Possessive Noun Error

This pattern asks the possessive determiners ("its," "his," "their"), contractions (we're, you're) and adverbs ("there")

Add an apostrophe and s to a human, possessive, and singular noun

15 Prepositional Idiom Error

Idiom and prepositional idiom pattern asks the correct usage of preposition.

Ex) we cannot exist without drawing attention to the systems that define us, the systems [11] by which this world—our world, the world we share with all those around us—is **built.**

When confronting a complex sentence, simplifying the sentence is critical: look below:

systems by (on) which this world—~~*our world, the world we share with all those around us*~~—**is** built.

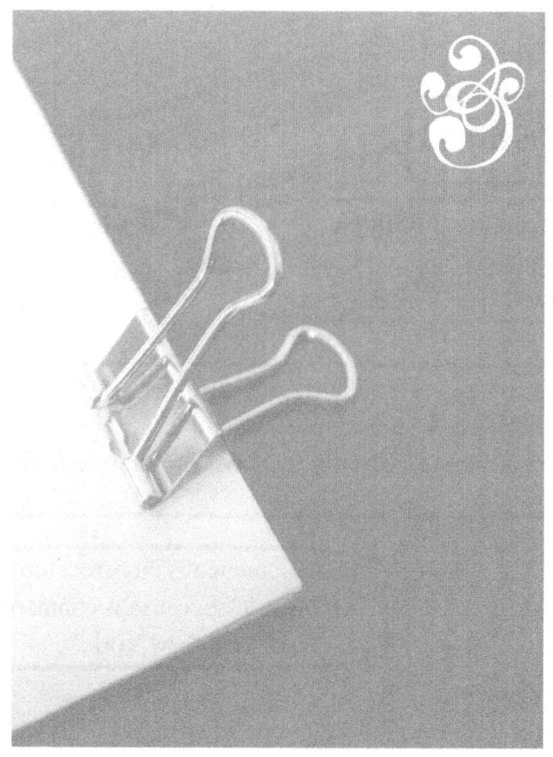

Chapter 4

1. TEST 4

2. ANSWER EXPLANATIONS for TEST 4

3. CHAPTER SUMMARY

SAT
Reading & Writing Practice
Test 4

ALL THE LOGIC AND RULES
BEHIND THE EVERY SINGLE
SAT QUESTION

Reading Test 4

65 MINUTES, 52 QUESTIONS

The passages below are followed by questions based on their content; questions following a pair of related passages may also be based on the relationship between the paired passages. Answer the questions on the basis of what is stated or implied in the passages and in any introductory material that may be provided.

Questions 1-10 are based on the following passage.

This passage is from The Count of Monte Cristo © 1844 by Alexandre Dumas.

The Count of Monte Cristo and Danglars are old friends.

About two o'clock the following day a calash, drawn by a pair of magnificent English horses, stopped at the door of Monte Cristo and a person, dressed in a blue coat and a quantity of black hair descending so low over his eyebrows as to leave it doubtful whether it were not artificial so little did its jetty glossiness assimilate with the deep wrinkles stamped on his features –a person desired to be taken for not more than forty, bent forwards from the carriage door and directed his groom to inquire at the porter's lodge whether the Count of Monte Cristo resided there, and if he were within.

"His excellency does reside here," replied the concierge; "but"—added he, glancing an inquiring look at Ali. Ali returned a sign in the negative. "But what?" asked the groom. His excellency does not receive visitors to-day."

"I never speak to his excellency," replied the concierge; "the valet de chamber will carry your message." The groom returned to the carriage. "Well?" asked Danglars. The man, somewhat crest-fallen by the rebuke he had received, repeated what the concierge had said. "Bless me," murmured Baron Danglars, "this must surely be a prince instead of a count by their styling him 'excellency,' and only venturing to address him by the medium of his valet de chamber. However, it does not signify, he has a letter of credit on me, so I must see him when he requires his money." "That fellow has a decidedly bad countenance, "said the count in a tone of disgust. Ali, cried he, striking at the same time on the brazen gong. Ali appeared.

"Summon Bertuccio,"said the count. Almost immediately Bertuccio entered the apartment.

"Did your excellency desire to see me?" inquired he. "I did, "replied the count.

1

The statement in lines 8-9 (a person desired...forty,) intends to

A) visualize an attractive imagery

B) show the character's mood

C) illustrate the humorous outfit

D) reveal the character's desire to look young

2

As used in line 8 "glossiness," the author views that the character attempts to

A) emphasize his shiny-wealthy feature

B) cover up the incongruity

C) show a form of attractive appearance

D) bring unaffected manner

3

Which of the following situations is analogous to the person's image in line 3-9 (a person....more than forty)

A) The police who restrain a violent criminal

B) The teacher performs a sophisticated experiment

C) The woman hides her donations to the charity

D) The criminal who pretends to be innocent at the scene of a crime

4

The purpose of Danglars' visit is to

A) meet his old friend, the Count

B) impress the Count

C) clear the debt he owed to the Count

D) prove his innocence

CONTINUE

1 1

5

Which choice provides the best evidence for the answer to the previous question?

A) Lines 1-3 (“About … Monte Cristo)

B) Lines 13-14 (His excellency...the concierge;)

C) Lines 15-16 (Ali returned ...ask the groom.)

D) Lines 28-30 (However, it does....his money.")

6

Which choice best describes what happened in the passage?

A) One character replies to another character’s surprising request

B) One character recalls a friendship with another character

C) One character criticizes another character’s inadvertent visit

D) One character carefully analyzes another character’s social and family status.

7

Which choice provides the best evidence for the answer to the previous question?

A) Lines 13-14 (His excellency...the concierge;)

B) Lines 15 (Ali returned...the negative.)

C) Lines 17 (His excellency...visitors today.)

D) Lines 31-34 (That fellow...appeared.)

8

“styling” in line 26 most nearly refers to

A) courtesy entitlement

B) the practice of tradition

C) ostentatious manner

D) similar to fashion

9

In the passage, the Count of Monte Cristo addresses Bertuccio with

A) appeal to mercy

B) shallow medium of expression

C) condescendingly addressing social status

D) condescendingly implying hierarchy

10

The character’s comment “countenance” in line 31 reveals

A) a disapproval of one character’s appearance

B) a deep hatred

C) reaction to the abrupt visit

D) an utter deference

CONTINUE

1 1

Questions 11-21are based on the following passage.

This passage is about how the industrialization and the Industrial Revolution affected the lives of the contemporary American women. – San

In the mid 1800's, hydraulic power performed diverse mechanical works that replaced workers' arduous labor, dawning the Industrial Revolution. Contemporary historians naively believed the industrialization in workplaces revolutionized the deprived lives of city dwellers.

During this time, observing girls and married women flowing into factories, Adam Togason, an English economist, cautioned that women without femininity would advent. Politicians such as Ruth Henry, or Smith Tyler, however, saw the phenomenon as an opportunity to liberate women from the socioeconomic submission.

Sociologists, adamantly questioned the early observers' beliefs. Their reasoning behind this was that such dramatic mechanical developments as spinning jenny, washing machine have not endowed better lives to women, although women's participation in industry has changed a lot since the Industrial Revolution.

Early twentieth century witnessed the increased numbers of married women taking men's jobs outside the home, but it had less to do with the industrialization or technological advancement smeared into the domestic work. Glass ceiling by gender, low pay jobs that usually require rudimentary skills gave little chance to women to advance in society, not unlike to that of the past 200 years..

Historical investigation concerning the Industrial Revolution needs serious revision in that Industrial Revolution did not necessarily revolutionize women's status in society. Rather, Industrial Revolution may even have failed to secure women from their conventional roles.

11

Ruth Henry in line 11 would most likely respond to Sociologists in line 14 as they are

A) misleading

B) realistic

C) absolutely correct

D) analytical

12

The author would most likely respond to Ruth Henry or Smith Tyler in lines 11 by

A) approving that industrialization would improve womanhood in American society

B) disapproving that industrialization would improve womanhood in America Society

C) approving that industrialization would degrade Womanhood

D) approving that industrialization would liberate black slavery

13

Which choice provides the best evidence for the answer to the previous question?

A) Lines 1-3 (In the mid-800's...Revolution.)

B) Lines 4-6 (Contemporary historians...city dwellers)

C) Lines 14-15 (Sociologists, adamantly ...belief.)

D) Lines 34-35 (Rather, industrial...conventional role)

14

Which of the following characteristics would LEAST likely be attributed to "phenomenon" mentioned in line 12?

A) Women living with the traditional pattern of female society

B) The employment of married women in industry

C) Married women flowing into factories

D) The usage of spinning jenny and washing machine

CONTINUE

1

15

The author's description in line 16 ("dramatic mechanical developments") serves primarily to illustrate

A) that with the right equipment, women could enjoy good living
B) how women's livelihood was stagnant
C) many steps involving industrialization
D) the importance of having good equipment for domestic work

16

Which choice provides the best evidence for the answer to the previous question?

A) Lines 1-3 (In the mid-800's...Revolution.)
B) Lines 4-6 (Contemporary historians...city dwellers)
C) Lines 10-13 (Politicians such as...submission.)
D) Lines 32-34 (Rather, industrial...conventional role)

17

In line 30, the author views historical investigation as

A) an erroneous theory
B) a revolutionary scholarly work
C) a quintessential guidebook for feminism study
D) a poorly drafted reference

18

It can be inferred that women's feelings toward the Industrialization may eventually have changed to that of

A) contemporary historians in line 4
B) Adam Togason in line 8
C) politicians in line 10
D) Ruth Henry in line 11

19

In line 25 "Glass ceiling" refers to

A) clear ties between male and female
B) unrealistically fragile working condition
C) substance of limitation
D) women's reality viewed through the glass

20

The author views line 29 ".past 200 years" with

A) total celebration
B) parallel in history
C) unprecedented development
D) somewhat unfair judgment

21

The author views married women's involvement into workforce during the industrialization in line 22 as

A) benefits from the industrialization
B) an inevitable fact generated by marriage trends
C) an emphatic example of gender equality
D) a side-effect of technological advancement

CONTINUE

1 1

Questions 22-31are based on the following passage.

This passage is about Sunspot activity

Sunspots are dark spots on the sun's photosphere. The first scientific periodicity of this phenomena is ascribed to an European observer, Galileo Galilei in 1610. Sunspots correspond to concentrations of magnetic field flux that inhibit convection and result in reduced surface temperature compared to the surrounding photosphere.

Although the records made by then Chinese naked- eye observers contradict it, Sun went through a period of inactivity in the late 17th century. This period is known as the Maunder Minimum. Without having a concrete evidence, the Maunder Minimum, from 1645 to 1715, is defined as the prolonged sunspot inactivity period.

The reason that the Maunder Minimum invites a special attention to scientists is because this period also corresponds to a climatic period called the "Little Ice Age."

Throughout the Maunder Minimum, terrestrial temperature was noticeably and abnormally cold at lower altitudes. Although sunspots themselves produce only minor effects on solar emissions, the magnetic activity that accompanies the sunspots can produce dramatic changes in the ultraviolet and soft x-ray emission levels.

These changes over the solar cycle have important consequences for the Earth's upper atmosphere. As revealed on the discrepancy between Chinese naked-eye observers and the later European scientists concerning the Maunder Minimum, whether sunspot activity is a transient phenomenon or long-lived feature due to unsustainable decomposition of the Sun's magnetic field remains elusive.

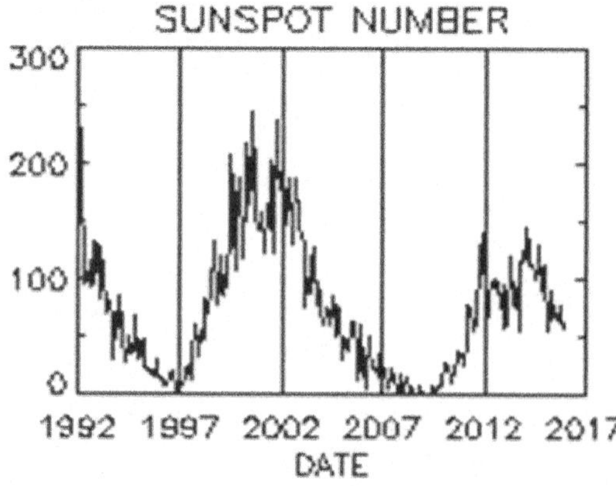

22

The passage defines solar activity cycle as

A) an enduring but not yet fully confirmed theory
B) significant to the modern global warming
C) transient phenomena and therefore insignificant
D) a mysterious supernatural phenomena

23

Which choice provides the best evidence for the answer to the previous question?

A) Lines 1 (Sunspots are...photosphere.)
B) Lines 19-21 (Throughout…altitudes.)
C) Lines 21-25 (Although sunspots..emission levels)
D) Lines 31-34 (whether sunspot…elusive.)

24

According to the last paragraph, which of the possible research projects would further ascertain the Sunspot activity is unsustainable feature of the Sun?

A) Finding relations between the sun's magnetic field decomposition and sunspot activity
B) Identifying whether the sun's magnetic field is sustainable or unsustainable
C) Confirming that the sunspot activity is a transient
D) Finding that the sunspot activity is related to the Maunder Minimum

25

Which choice provides the best evidence for the answer to the previous question?

A) Lines 15-18 (The reason...Little Ice Age.")
B) Lines 21-25 (Although sunspots..emission level)
C) Lines 26-28 (These changes...upper atmosphere)
D) Lines 31-34 (whether sunspot…elusive.)

26

The reference to the "Chinese naked-eye observers" (line 29) primarily serves to

A) solidify Maunder Minimum theory
B) respect the 16th century Chinese scientists
C) disqualify Maunder Minimum
D) provide a certain kind of zealotry

CONTINUE

1 1

27

"unsustainable" in line 33 most nearly means

A) unaccomplished
B) unassimilated
C) unabsorbed
D) abated

28

Why do scientists pay special attention to the Maunder Minimum?

A) because they know the Ice Age is coming
B) because the period is related with the Little Ice Age
C) because the sun's inactivity is related with it
D) because the single sunspot is as wide as the earth diameter that can threaten the earth

29

Understanding the ultraviolet and soft x-ray emission levels in line 24 is important because

A) they have significant consequences for the earth's upper atmosphere.
B) they bring the Ice Age
C) they decompose the sun's magnetic field fast
D) they affect the greenhouse and air quality

30

According to lines 29, the Chinese naked-eye observers

A) felt noticeably cold terrestrial temperature during the period
B) were mocked by later European scientists
C) experienced little temperature drop
D) observed a period of inactivity of the sun but not the temperature drop

31

The graph following the passage indicates the year that is most resemblance to Maunder Minimum in

A) 1992
B) 1997
C) 2002
D) 2012

CONTINUE

1

Questions 32-41 are based on the following passage.
The following passage describes coffee

Coffee is universal in its appeal. All nations do it homage. It has become recognized as a human necessity. People love coffee because of its two-fold effect--the pleasurable sensation and the increased efficiency in fashionable society, but it is also a favorite beverage of the men and women who do the world's work, whether they toil with brain or brawn.

No "food drink" has ever encountered so much opposition as coffee. Given to the world by the church and dignified by the medical profession, nevertheless it has had to suffer from religious superstition and medical prejudice. During the thousand years of its development it has experienced fierce political opposition, stupid fiscal restrictions, unjust taxes, irksome duties.

But coffee is something more than a beverage. It is one of the world's greatest adjuvant foods. Like all good things in life, the drinking of coffee may be abused. Indeed, those having an idiosyncratic susceptibility to alkaloids should be temperate in the use of tea, coffee, or cocoa.

In every high-tensioned country there is likely to be a small number of people who, because of certain individual characteristics, cannot drink coffee at all. These belong to the idiosyncratic minority of the human family.

Some people cannot eat strawberries; but that would not be a valid reason for a general condemnation of strawberries. One may be poisoned, says Thomas A. Edison, from too much food.

Trading upon the credulity of the hypochondriac and the caffeine-sensitive, in recent years there has appeared in America and abroad a curious collection of so-called coffee substitutes. They are "neither fish nor flesh, nor good red herring."

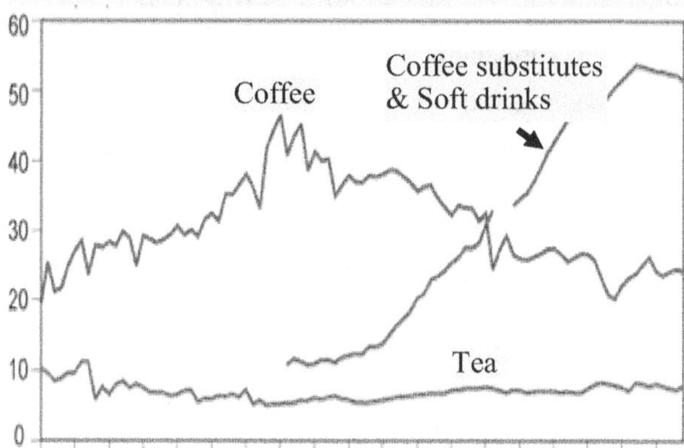

Sources: USDA, Economic Research Service using data on carbonated soft drinks from the Bureau of the Census for 1925-2015 and the Beverage Marketing Corporation for 1960-2015

32

In line 2, the word "homage" most nearly means

A) obey
B) surrender
C) appreciate
D) accept

33

The author mentions "men and women" in line 7 mainly to

A) pay the homage to those who do the world's work
B) celebrate coffee's commercial success as a drink
C) show that coffee has become people's necessity
D) emphasize coffee's delightful taste

34

Which choice provides the best evidence for the answer to the previous question?

A) Lines 2 (All nations...homage.)
B) Lines 2-3 (It has become...necessity)
C) Lines 3-6 (People love...society)
D) Lines 10-11 (No "food drink"...as coffee)

CONTINUE

1 1

35

In lines 32, the reference to Thomas A. Edison is used to emphasize the

A) pervasive historical evidence against coffee
B) argument that coffee is harmful
C) beneficial effect of coffee
D) authoritative tone against coffee

36

The analogy "neither fish nor flesh" in lines 38 serves to underscore the

A) unlikelihood that substitutes would replace coffee
B) increasing homogenization of coffee substitutes
C) universal availability of coffee substitutes
D) substitutes have their own merits

37

Which of the following person would most likely disagree with the author's view on coffee

A) men and women (line 7)
B) the medical profession (line 12)
C) those having a idiosyncratic susceptibility (line 21)
D) Thomas A. Edison (line 32)

38

Which choice provides the best evidence for the answer to the previous question?

A) Lines 6-7(but it is...men and women)
B) Lines 11-12 (Given to the world...medical profession)
C) Lines 21-23 (Indeed, those having...or cocoa.)
D) Lines 31-33 (one may be...too much food)

39

The author's tone concerning coffee substitute is

A) hopelessness
B) qualified approval
C) mild skepticism
D) celebration

40

The relationship between the first and second paragraph (lines 1~ 25) is that Paragraph 1?

A) offers an anecdote that paragraph 2 confirms
B) justifies the necessity of coffee, while paragraph 2 limits its justification
C) elaborates one-sided opinion, while paragraph 2 describes a popular misconception
D) offers pros, while paragraph 2 offers cons

41

Which statement best summarizes the description of coffee consumption between the author and the graph?

A) The author assumes that coffee's singular position is invincible; the graph supports the argument
B) The author believes that carbonated soft drink's popularity is only temporary; the graph indicates it is not
C) The author rejects the graph's methodology
D) The author and the graph may concede tea will eventually replace soft drinks and coffee

CONTINUE

1 1

Questions 42-52 are based on the following passage.

The following two passages discuss consumer spending. Mark Dooms, Chief Economist, U.S. Department of Commerce

PASSAGE 1

What Drives Consumer Spending?
First and foremost, income drives consumer spending; Today's release showed that income increased 0.3 percent and the gains in January. Recall that January's outsized gain was driven immediately by the lower tax withholdings called for by the Middle Class Tax Relief Act of 2010 (I certainly noticed a difference in my paycheck, and my local restaurants and bakeries were the primary beneficiaries).

Another factor in consumers' spending decisions is how wealthy they are. When consumers become wealthier, their spending goes up. Why is the stock market up, especially given the tumultuous events in North Africa, the Middle East, and Japan? Good question but no data.

A factor with no good data being one of the primary culprits. I'd like to think it's because folks have developed a more positive outlook on the U.S. economy, and indeed economic forecasts for growth in the U.S.

PASSAGE 2

The Theory of Economics does not furnish a body of settled conclusions immediately applicable to policy. It is a methodical speculation rather than a doctrine, an apparatus of the mind, a technique of thinking, which helps its possessor to draw correct conclusions. It is not difficult in the sense in which mathematical and scientific techniques are difficult; but the fact that its modes of expression are much less precise than these, renders decidedly difficult the task of conveying it correctly to the minds of learners.

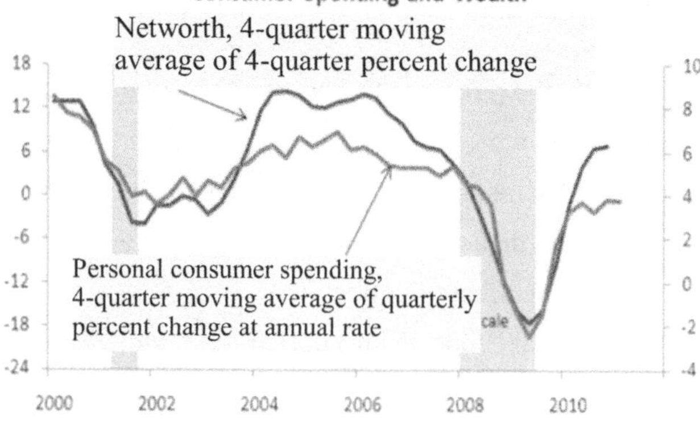

Source: Federal Reserve, BEA Note: Shading indicates recession

42

The author of Passage 1 responds to line 1, (what drive consumer spending?) with

A) emphatic confirmation

B) limited consent

C) ambivalence

D) analytical speculation

43

The author of Passage 1 shows that consumer spending is primarily driven by

A) the periodic income increase alone

B) the periodic spending habit

C) the government policy such as the Middle Class Tax Relief Act of 2010

D) the periodic income increase and individual abundance

44

The author of Passage 1 mentions his local restaurant and bakeries in line 9 in order to introduce

A) some major beneficiaries of Tax Relief Act

B) some people unaffected by Tax Relief Act

C) the middle class consumer's spending habits

D) alternative explanation for consumer spending habit

CONTINUE

1

45

In Passage 1, in 18 "culprit" most nearly means

A) crime

B) responsibility

C) misdeed

D) origin

46

Which aspect would probably be the great concern to the author of Passage 2 about Middle Class Tax Relief Act of 2010 in Passage 1?

A) Intentional tax policy would eventually undermine consumer savings in the long term

B) Complete unanimity of income and spending relationship cannot be established

C) How much consumer spending changes when wealth changes is still up for debate

D) An Economic policy can't be the conclusive facts for the application

47

Which choice provides the best evidence for the answer to the previous question?

A) Lines 26-28 (The Theory...a policy.)

B) Lines 28-31 (It is a methodical...conclusions.)

C) Lines 31-33 (It is not...are difficult)

D) Lines 33-36 (but the fact...minds of the learners.)

48

In Passage 2, in 29 "apparatus" most nearly means

A) readily applicable method

B) complex contraption

C) mechanical device

D) gear

49

The main difference between the author of Passage 1 and the author 2 is that the author 1

A) relies more on real economy and taxes, while the author 2 expounds the method and principle.

B) expounds the elements of method clearly, while the author 2 gathers relevant facts to apply economic principles

C) relates economics through tax policy, while the author 2 focuses more on consumer spending habit

D) relies more on the theory of micro economy, while the author 2, on macro economy

50

The author of Passage 2implies that mathematical technique in line 32 is

A) highly developed than the Theory of Economics

B) concerned more with the minds of learners

C) easier than the Theory of Economics

D) more precise in its modes of expression

51

The author seems to find the economic forecasts for growth in line 20 from

A) a factor with good data

B) the folks' more positive outlook on U.S. economy

C) the fact that the stock market went up

D) the direct impact of the Tax Relief Act of 2010

52

Which statement best summarizes the graph?

A) Wealth and consumer spending have been mostly synchronized over a 10-year period.

B) Wealth and consumer spending have not been synchronized over a 10-year period.

C) Consumer spending increased in 2005 when household net worth decreased

D) Consumer spending recovered faster than wealth in 2009

STOP

If you finish before time is called,
you may check your work on this section.

Do not turn to the next section.

Writing and Language Test 4
35 MINUTES, 44 QUESTIONS

Each passage below is accompanied by a number of questions. For some questions, you will consider how the passage might be revised to improve the expression of ideas. For other questions, you will consider how the passage might be edited to correct errors in sentence structure, usage, or punctuation. A passage or a question may be accompanied by one or more graphics (such as a table or graph) that you will consider as you make revising and editing decisions.

Questions 1-11 are based on the following passage.

WikiLeaks

WikiLeaks is an international [1] non-profitable journalistic organization that publishes secret information, news leaks, and classified media from anonymous sources, [2] mainly from organizations or individuals who do not disclose their names.

Its website, initiated in 2006 in Iceland by the organization Sunshine Press, claimed a database of more than 1.2 million documents within a year of its launch. Julian Assange, an Australian Internet activist, is generally described as its founder, editor-in-chief, and director. Hrafnsson is also a member of Sunshine Press Productions, [3] along with Assange, Hrafnsson and Gavin MacFadyen are the only known members outside.

1
A) NO CHANGE
B) non-profit journal organization
C) non-profitable journalism organization
D) non-profit journalistic organization

2
A) NO CHANGE
B) however, the origin of information is normally not disclosed.
C) —although the information is not readily verifiable.
D) DELETE IT.

3
A) NO CHANGE
B) in conjunction with,
C) together with Assange,
D) and with Assange

CONTINUE

2 2

The group has released a number of [4] significantly pivotal documents that have become front-page news items. Early releases included documentation of equipment expenditures and holdings in the Afghanistan war and a report informing a corruption investigation inKenya. In April 2010, WikiLeaks published gunsight footage from the 12 July 2007 Baghdad airstrike in which Iraqi journalists were among those killed by an AH-64 Apache helicopter, known [5] to be the *Collateral Murder* video. In July of the same **year,** WikiLeaks released [6] ,a compilation of more than 76,900 documents about the War in Afghanistan, Afghan **Diary** to the **world**.

WikiLeaks [7] relies on some degree on volunteers and previously described its founders as a mixture of Asian dissidents, journalists, mathematicians, and start-up company technologists from the United States.

4

A) NO CHANGE
B) significant and pivotal documents
C) significant documents, which is pivotal
D) significant documents

5

Which of the following alternatives to the underlined portion would NOT be acceptable?
A) to be
B) as
C) for
D) to

6

The best placement for the underlined portion would be:
A) NO CHANGE
B) After the word "year,"
C) After the word "Diary"
D) After the word "world"

7

A) NO CHANGE
B) reliance on some degree to
C) reliance to some degree on
D) relies to some degree on

CONTINUE

2 2

WikiLeaks progressively [8] adopt a more traditional publication model and no longer accepts either user comments or edits.

As of June 2009, the website had more than 1,200 registered volunteers and listed an advisory board comprising Assange, his deputy Jash Vora and seven other people, [9] some of them denied any association with the organization.

According to the WikiLeaks website, its goal is "to bring important news and information to the public. One of our most important activities is to publish original source material alongside our news stories, [10] for example, readers and historians alike can see evidence of the truth."

Another of the organization's goals is to ensure that journalists and whistleblowers are not prosecuted for emailing sensitive or classified documents. The online "drop box" is described by the WikiLeaks website as "[11] an innovative, security and anonymous way for sources to leak information to WikiLeaks journalists."

8

A) NO CHANGE
B) had adopted
C) is under the influence of drastic adoption with
D) adopts

9

A) NO CHANGE
B) some people
C) some of who
D) some of whom

10

A) NO CHANGE
B) so
C) because
D) moreover,

11

A) NO CHANGE
B) an innovative, secure, and anonymous
C) an innovatively secure and anonymous
D) an innovatively and securely anonymous

CONTINUE

2 2

Questions 12-22 are based on the following passage.

ISIS

The Islamic State of Iraq and Syria (ISIS) is a Salafi jihadist militant group that follows a fundamentalist, Wahhabi doctrine of Sunni Islam.

The [12] group adopted the name Islamic State and its idea of a caliphate have been widely criticized from the United Nations, [13] various governments refuted, and mainstream Muslim groups rejecting its statehood or caliphhood.

The group first began referring to itself as Islamic State or IS in June 2014, [14] which it proclaimed itself a worldwide caliphate and named Abu Bakr al-Baghdadi as its caliph. The group has been designated a terrorist organization by the United Nations. Over 60 countries are directly or indirectly waging war against ISIL. [15] Adopted at social media, ISIL is widely known for its videos of beheadings.

12

A) NO CHANGE
B) groups' adoption of
C) adoption of group
D) group's adoption of

13

A) NO CHANGE
B) along with various governments,
C) various governments,
D) both various governments

14

A) NO CHANGE
B) whom
C) that
D) when

15

A) NO CHANGE
B) Adept
C) Addicted
D) Annexed

CONTINUE

2 2

[16] The United Nations holds ISIL responsible for human rights abuses and war crimes, and Amnesty International has charged the group with ethnic cleansing on a "historic scale" in northern Iraq. Around the world, Islamic religious leadershave overwhelmingly condemned ISIL's ideology.

The United Nations [17] holds ISIS responsible for human rights abuses and war crimes, and Amnesty International has charged the group with ethnic cleansing on a "historic scale" in northern Iraq. Around the world, [18] ISIS gained prominence when it drove Iraqi government forces out of key cities in its Western Iraq and capturing Mosul.

16

In the preceding sentence, the writer is considering replacing " beheadings." with " beheadings: soldiers, civilians, journalists and aid workers

Should the writer make this revision?

A) Yes, because it fixes the incomplete sentence.

B) Yes, because it gives added information about the atrocity of the group.

C) No, because it unnecessarily lists examples that should be placed elsewhere.

D) No, because it is not proper to mention the occupations in this sentence.

17

A) NO CHANGE

B) hold

C) is held

D) are held

18

Which choice maintains the essay's negative tone and most strongly supports the writer at this point?

A) NO CHANGE

B) Islamic religious leaders have overwhelmingly condemned ISIS's ideology and actions.

C) ISIS has long argued that the group has the true path of true Islam and that its actions reflect the religion's real teachings or virtues.

D) Some extremists in countries like U.S. Russia, Israel, Turkey, Saudi Arabia hold the same opinion with the leaders in ISIS

CONTINUE

2 2

In June 2014, Saudi Arabia moved troops to [19] their borders with Iraq, after Iraq lost control [20] of, or withdrew from, strategic crossing points that then came under the control of ISIL, or tribes that supported ISIL.

In late January 2015, it was reported that ISIS members infiltrated the European Union and disguised themselves as civilian refugees who were emigrating from the war zones of Iraq.

An ISIS representative claimed that ISIS [21] had successfully smuggled 4,000 fighters, and that the smuggled fighters were planning attacks in Europe in retaliation for the airstrikes carried out against ISIS targets in Iraq and Syria.

[22] In the meantime, experts believe that this claim was exaggerated to boost their stature and spread fear, and acknowledged that some Western countries were aware of the smuggling.

19

A) NO CHANGE
B) there borders
C) it's border
D) its border

20

Which of the following alternatives to the underlined portion would NOT be acceptable?

A) of, or withdrew from, strategic
B) of (or withdrew from) strategic
C) of—or withdrew from—strategic
D) of, or withdrew from strategic

21

A) NO CHANGE
B) successfully smuggled
C) smuggled with success
D) had been successfully smuggled

22

A) NO CHANGE
B) Granted,
C) However,
D) Since

CONTINUE

2 2

Questions 23-33 are based on the following passage.

Quantum Physics

Quantum mechanics is a fundamental branch of physics concerned with processes [23] involving: for example, atoms and photons. <A> System such as these which [24] obey quantum mechanics can be in a quantum superposition of different states, [25] unlike classical physics. <B> Early quantum theory was profoundly reconceived in the mid-1920s. <C> The [26] reconceived theory is formulated in various specially developed mathematical formalisms. <D> Important applications of quantum theory include superconducting magnets, light-emitting diodes, and the laser transistor and semiconductors such as the microprocessor, medical and research imaging such as magnetic resonance imaging and electron microscopy, and explanations for many biological and physical phenomena.

23

A) NO CHANGE
B) involving; for example,
C) involving for example
D) involving, for example,

24

A) NO CHANGE
B) obeys quantum mechanics
C) abeyance of
D) have obeyed

25

A) NO CHANGE
B) unlike classical physics superposition
C) unlike that of classical physics
D) unlike in classical physics

26

Which of the following alternatives to the underlined portion would NOT be acceptable?

A) conceptualized
B) rehabilitated
C) redesigned
D) recalibrated

27

At this point, the writer wishes to introduce the practicality of Quantum mechanics.
Which sentence can be the best topic sentence for the new paragraph?

A) <A> System such as ...
B) <B> Early quantum theory...
C) <C> The reconceived...
D) <D> Important applications of...

CONTINUE

2 2

When quantum mechanics was originally formulated, it was applied to models [28] whose correspondence limit was non-relativistic classical mechanics. For instance, the well-known model of the quantum harmonic oscillator uses an explicitly non-relativistic expression for the kinetic energy of the oscillator, and is thus a quantum version of the classical harmonic oscillator. Early attempts to merge quantum mechanics [29] for special relativity has involved the replacement of the Schrödinger equation with a covariant equation. [30] For example, these theories were successful in explaining many experimental results, they had certain unsatisfactory qualities stemming from their neglect of the relativistic creation and annihilation of particles.
A fully relativistic quantum theory required the development of quantum field theory, which applies quantization to a field [31]—less than a fixed set of particles.
The first complete quantum field theory, quantum electrodynamics, provides a fully quantum description of the electromagnetic interaction.

28

A) NO CHANGE
B) whom
C) which
D) that

29

A) NO CHANGE
B) with special relativity involved
C) to special relativity had involved
D) into special relativity involves

30

A) NO CHANGE
B) While,
C) Due to
D) Moreover,

31

A) NO CHANGE
B) similar to
C) the same as
D) rather than

CONTINUE

2

The full [32] apparatus's of quantum field theory is often unnecessary for describing electrodynamic systems. A simpler approach, one that has been employed since the inception of quantum mechanics, is to treat charged particles as quantum mechanical objects being acted on by a classical electromagnetic field.

32

A) quantum field of apparatus
B) apparatus' quantum field
C) apparatus of quantum field
D) quantum field's apparatus

33

Suppose the writer's primary purpose had been to describe the difference between Quantum physics and classical physics.
Would this essay accomplish that purpose?

A) Yes, because it discusses both theories
B) Yes, because it focuses primarily on the early stage of Quantum theory that heavily depended on Classical Physics
C) No, because it focuses more on Classical Physics and its influence upon Quantum Physics
D) No, because it focuses more on Quantum Physics and its conceptual understanding.

CONTINUE

2 2

Questions 34-44 are based on the following passage.

Frankenstein, or the Modern Prometheus
By Mary Wollstonecraft Shelley

You will rejoice to hear that no disaster [34] accompany the commencement of an enterprise which you have regarded with such evil forebodings. Do you understand this feeling? This breeze, which has travelled from the regions [35] for which I am advancing, gives me a foretaste of those icy climes. Inspirited by this wind of promise, [36] what a fervent and vivid moment.

I try in vain to be persuaded that the pole is the seat of frost and [37] desolation, it ever presents itself to my imagination as the region of beauty and delight. There, Margaret, the sun is forever visible, [38] its broad disk just skirting the horizon and diffusing a perpetual splendor. There--for with your leave, my sister, I will put some trust in preceding navigators--there snow and frost are banished; and, sailing over a calm sea, we may be wafted to a land surpassing in wonders and in beauty every region hitherto discovered on the habitable globe.

34

A) NO CHANGE
B) had accompanied
C) is to be accompanied
D) has accompanied

35

A) NO CHANGE
B) to
C) towards
D) in

36

A) NO CHANGE
B) more fervent and vivid had my daydream become.
C) I have become more fervent and vivid
D) there has become more fervent and vivid in my daydream.

37

A) NO CHANGE
B) desolation; it ever
C) desolation that ever
D) desolation: it ever

38

A) NO CHANGE
B) it's
C) there is
D) there are

CONTINUE

2 2

I write a few lines in haste to say that I am safe--and well advanced on my voyage. This letter will reach England by a merchantman now on its homeward voyage from Archangel; more fortunate than [39] me, who may not see my native land, perhaps, for many years. I [40] am, however, in good spirits, my men are bold and apparently firm of purpose, nor do the floating sheets of ice that continually pass us, indicating the dangers of the region towards which we are advancing, [41] appearing dismay them. We have already reached a very high latitude; but it is the height of summer, and although not so warm as in England, the southern gales, which blow us speedily towards those shores which I so ardently desire to attain, breathe a degree of renovating warmth which I had not expected.

No incidents [42] has hitherto befallen us that would make a figure in a letter. One or two stiff gales and the springing of a leak are accidents which [43] experiencing navigators scarcely remember to record, and I shall be well content if nothing worse happen to us during our voyage.

39

A) NO CHANGE
B) myself
C) mine
D) I

40

A) NO CHANGE
B) am however in good spirits:
C) am, however, in good spirits:
D) am, however, in good spirits

41

A) NO CHANGE
B) appear to
C) appears to
D) that appear to

42

A) NO CHANGE
B) has hitherto befall
C) have hitherto befallen
D) have already befall

43

A) NO CHANGE
B) experienced
C) is experienced
D) experience

CONTINUE

2 2

So strange an accident [44] has happened to us and I cannot forbear recording it, although it is very probable that you will see me before these papers can come into your possession.

44

A) NO CHANGE
B) has happened to us that I
C) had happened to us and me
D) happened to us and I

STOP

If you finish before time is called,
you may check your work on this section.

Do not turn to the next section.

SAT Test 4
Answer Explanations
&
Pattern Analyses

If your Test 4 scores are unsatisfactory,

Test 4, 5, 6… won't be satisfactory either.

Please Practice the Answer Explanations and then come back to Test 4 again.

ALL THE LOGIC AND RULES BEHIND EVERY SINGLE SAT QUESTION

SAT Test 4

Reading Section Answer Explanations

&

Pattern Analyses

Questions 1-10 are based on the following passage.

About two o'clock the following day a calash, drawn by a pair of magnificent English horses, stopped at the door of Monte Cristo and a person, dressed in a blue coat, and a quantity of black hair descending so low over his eyebrows as to leave it (3D) **doubtful whether it were not artificial** so little did its jetty (2B) **glossiness assimilate** with the deep wrinkles stamped on his features –a (1D) **person desired to be taken for not more than forty**, bent forwards from the carriage door and directed his groom to inquire at the porter's lodge whether the Count of Monte Cristo resided there, and if he were within. "His excellency does reside here," replied the concierge; "but"—added he, glancing an inquiring look at Ali. Ali returned a sign in the negative. "But what?" asked the groom. (6C& 7C) **His excellency does not receive visitors to-day."** "I never speak to his excellency," replied the concierge; "the valet de chamber will carry your message." The groom returned to the carriage. "Well?" asked Danglars.	The man, somewhat crest-fallen by the rebuke he had received, repeated what the concierge had said. "Bless me," murmured Baron Danglars, (8A) **"this must surely be a prince instead of a count by their styling him 'excellency,'** and only venturing to address him by the medium of his valet de chamber. (4C & 5D) **However, it does not signify, he has a letter of credit on me, so I must see him when he requires his money."** (10B) **" That fellow has a decidedly bad countenance, "said the count in a tone of** disgust. Ali, cried he, striking at the same time on the brazen gong. Ali appeared. (9D) **"Summon Bertuccio,"said the count.** Almost immediately Bertuccio entered the apartment. "Did your excellency desire to see me?" inquired he. "I did, "replied the count.

Q1. **Absolute Pattern 3: Inference Question** Finding an indirect suggestion (or guessing)
Question Pattern: The statement in lines 8-9 **(a person desired...forty,)** intends to

A) visualize an attractive imagery B) show the character's mood C) illustrate the humorous outfit **D) reveal the character's desire to look young**	D) "Person desired to be taken ~ " implies the character's desire to look young.

Q2. **Absolute Pattern 3: Inference Question** Finding an indirect suggestion (or guessing)
Question Pattern: As used in line 8 **"glossiness,"** the author views that the character attempts to

A) emphasize his shiny-wealthy feature **B) cover up the incongruity** C) show a form of attractive appearance D) bring unaffected manner	B) as to leave it doubtful whether it were not artificial so little did its jetty glossiness assimilate with the deep wrinkles who, desired to be taken for not more than forty, The previous portion "doubtful, not assimilate" reveals the incongruity. This question employs two logics: Positive-Negative and Physical-Mental concept, two of the common logic in SAT.

Q3. **Absolute Pattern 6: Analogy Question** Finding a similar situation
Question Pattern: Which of the following situations is **analogous to the person's image** in line 3-9 (a person....more than forty)

A) The police who restrain a violent criminal B) The teacher performs a sophisticated experiment C) The woman hides her donations to the charity **D) The criminal who pretends to be innocent at the scene of a crime**	D) The logic should contain negative value. Only D) has this premise.

Q4. **Absolute Pattern 2: Summary Question** Summarizing a sentence, or an entire paragraph **Question Pattern:** The purpose of **Danglars' visit** is to	
A) meet his old friend, the Count B) impress the Count **C) clear the debt he owed to the Count** D) prove his innocence	C) **However,** it does not signify, he has a letter of credit on me, so I must see him when he requires his money."

Q5. **Absolute Pattern 11: Textual Evidence Question** Finding evidence for the previous question **Question Pattern:** Which choice provides the best evidence for the answer to the previous question?	
A) Lines 1-3 ("About … Monte Cristo) B) Lines 13-14 (His excellency...the concierge;) C) Lines 15-16 (Ali returned ...ask the groom.) **D) Lines 28-30 (However, it does....his money.")**	D) Please refer to the above question

Q6. **Absolute Pattern 10: Understanding the Structure of the Passage** **Question Pattern:** Which choice best describes **what happened** in the passage?	
A) One character replies to another character's surprising request B) One character recalls a friendship with another character **C) One character criticizes another character's inadvertent visit** D) One character carefully analyzes another character's social and family status.	C) "His excellency does not receive visitors to-day." The passage is Negative, the answer choice should never be Positive. It's best to find and pick the choice in negative tone. Please refer to incorrect choice pattern # 1, #5 D) is minor info., and "family" is not mentioned.

Q7. **Absolute Pattern 11: Textual Evidence Question** Finding evidence for the previous question **Question Pattern:** Which choice provides the best evidence for the answer to the previous question?	
A) Lines 13-14 (His excellency...the concierge;) B) Lines 15 (Ali returned...the negative.) **C) Lines 17 (His excellency...visitors today.)** D) Lines 31-34 (That fellow...appeared.)	C) Please refer to the above question

Q8. **Absolute Pattern 5: Word-In-Context Question** **Question Pattern: "styling"** in line 26 most nearly refers to	
A) courtesy entitlement B) the practice of tradition C) ostentatious manner D) similar to fashion	A) "Bless me," murmured Baron Danglars, "this must surely be a prince instead of a count by their styling him 'excellency,' and only venturing to address him by the medium of his valet de chamber. The clue word is "address him"

Q9. Absolute Pattern 3: Inference Question Finding an indirect suggestion (or guessing) **Question Pattern:** In the passage, the **Count of Monte Cristo addresses Bertuccio** with	
A) appeal to mercy B) shallow medium of expression C) condescendingly addressing social status **D) condescendingly implying hierarchy**	D) "Summon Bertuccio,"said the count. Almost immediately Bertuccio entered the apartment. "Did your excellency desire to see me?" inquired he. "I did, The conversation reveals that there's a hierarchy between the characters (A) The rank is reversed (B) It's not shallow, but emphatic (C) social status is not addressed

Q10. **Absolute Pattern 7: Understanding Attitude (Tone) Question** **Question Pattern:** The Character's comment "**countenance**" in line 31 reveals	
A) a disapproval of visitor's appearance **B) a deep hatred** C) reaction to the abrupt visit D) an utter deference	B) "That fellow has a decidedly bad countenance, "said the count in **a tone of disgust,** as he shut up his glass. "disgust" implies hatred. Inference question asks a hidden meaning behind the written statement. Therefore, (A), (C) are incorrect.

Questions 11-21 are based on the following passage.

In the mid 1800's, hydraulic power performed diverse mechanical works that replaced workers' arduous labor, dawning the Industrial Revolution. Contemporary historians naively believed the industrialization in workplaces revolutionized the deprived lives of city dwellers.

During this time, observing girls and married women flowing into factories, (18B) **Adam Togason, an English economist, cautioned that women without femininity would advent.** Politicians such as (11A) **Ruth Henry, or Smith Tyler, however, saw the phenomenon as an opportunity to liberate women from the socioeconomic submission.**

Sociologists, adamantly questioned the early observers' beliefs. Their reasoning behind this was that such dramatic mechanical developments as spinning jenny, washing machine (14A) **have not endowed better lives to women**, although women's participation in industry has changed a lot since the Industrial Revolution.

Early twentieth century witnessed the increased numbers of married women taking men's jobs outside the home, (21D) **but it had less to do with the industrialization or technological advancement** smeared into the domestic work. (14A&18B&19C&20B) **Glass ceiling by gender, low pay jobs that usually require rudimentary skills gave little chance to women to advance in society, not unlike to that of the past 200 years.**

(17A) Historical investigation concerning the Industrial Revolution **needs serious revision** in that Industrial Revolution did not necessarily revolutionize women's status in society.(12B & 13D&15B &16D) **Rather, Industrial Revolution may even have failed to secure women from their conventional roles.**

Q11. **Absolute Pattern 9: Relationships Question** **Question Pattern: Ruth Henry in line 11 would most likely respond to Sociologists** in line 14 as they are	
A) misleading B) realistic C) absolutely correct D) analytical	A) Ruth Henry, or Smith Tyler, however, saw the phenomenon as an opportunity to liberate women from the socioeconomic submission. Sociologists, adamantly questioned the early observers' beliefs *Ruth might have defended his position by saying the sociologists are misleading the situation.

Q12. **Absolute Pattern 9: Relationships Question** **Question Pattern: The author would most likely respond to Ruth Henry, or Smith Tyler** in line 5 by	
A) approving that industrialization would improve womanhood in American society **B) disapproving that industrialization would improve womanhood in American society** C) approving that industrialization would degrade womanhood D) approving that industrialization would liberate black slavery	B) Rather, Industrial Revolution may even have failed to secure women from their conventional roles" As described above, Ruth is the proponent of industrialization. The author is skeptical about its impact on womanhood. Therefore, he would disapprove Ruth Henry's argument.
A) is opposite B) is Not stated C) Ruth Henry favors Industrialization. Therefore, (C) is incorrect from Ruth's point of view. Please refer to incorrect choice pattern # 2.	

Q13. **Absolute Pattern 11: Textual Evidence Question** Finding evidence for the previous question **Question Pattern:** Which choice provides the best evidence for the answer to the previous question?	
A) Lines 1-3 (In the mid-800's...Revolution.) B) Lines 4-6 (Contemporary historians...city dwellers) C) Lines 14-15 (Sociologists, adamantly ...belief.) **D) Lines 34-35 (Rather, industrial...conventional role)**	D) Historical investigation concerning the Industrial Revolution needs serious revision in that Industrial Revolution did not necessarily revolutionize women's status in society.

Q14. **Absolute Pattern 2: Summary Question** Summarizing a sentence, or an entire paragraph **Question Pattern:** Which of the following characteristics would **LEAST likely be attributed to "phenomenon" mentioned in line 12?**	
A) Women living with the traditional pattern of female society B) The employment of married women in industry C) Married women flowing into factories D) The usage of spinning jenny and washing machine	A) dramatic mechanical developments as spinning jenny, washing machine have not endowed better lives to women. A), B), C) are parts of the phenomena

Q15. **Absolute Pattern 8: Understanding True Purpose** **Question Pattern:** The description in line 16 (**dramatic mechanical Developments) serves** primarily to illustrate	
A) that with the right equipment, women could enjoy good living **B) how women's livelihood was stagnant** C) many steps involving industrialization D) the importance of having good equipment for domestic work	B) dramatic mechanical developments as spinning jenny, washing machine have not endowed better lives to women. (Negative) Please refer to incorrect choice pattern # 1.

Q16. **Absolute Pattern 11: Textual Evidence Question** Finding evidence for the previous question **Question Pattern:** Which choice provides the best evidence for the answer to the previous question?	
A) Lines 1-3 (In the mid-800's...Revolution.) B) Lines 4-6 (Contemporary historians...city dwellers) C) Lines 10-13 (Politicians such as...submission.) **D) Lines 32-34 (Rather, industrial...conventional role)**	D) Historical investigation concerning the Industrial Revolution needs serious revision in that Industrial Revolution did not necessarily revolutionize women's status in society.

Q17. **Absolute Pattern 7: Understanding Attitude (Tone) Question** **Question Pattern:** In line 30, the **author views historical investigation** as	
A) an erroneous theory B) a revolutionary scholarly work C) a quintessential guidebook for feminism study D) a poorly drafted reference	A) Historical investigation concerning the Industrial Revolution needs serious revision in that Industrial ... Therefore, he would say it's an erroneous theory. A) "drafted reference." It's incorrect because it's more than a draft. The author argues it's misled history that needs investigation

Q18. **Absolute Pattern 9: Relationships Question** **Question Pattern:** It can be inferred that **women's feelings toward the Industrialization may eventually have changed** to that of	
A) contemporary historians in line 4 **B) Adam Togason in line 8** C) politicians in line 10 D) Ruth Henry in line 11	B) Adam Togason, an English economist, cautioned that women without femininity would advent. ... Rather, Industrial Revolution may even have failed to secure women from their conventional roles. (WOMEN) glass ceiling by gender, low pay jobs that usually require rudimentary skills gave little chance to women to advance in society.
A), C), D) all of them favored industrialization	

Q19. **Absolute Pattern 3: Inference Question** Finding an indirect suggestion (or guessing) **Question Pattern:** In line 25 "**Glass ceiling**" refers to	
A) clear ties between male and female B) unrealistically fragile working condition **C) substance of limitation** D) women's reality viewed through the glass	C) **Although** women's participation in industry has changed a lot since the Industrial Revolution, glass ceiling by gender, low pay jobs ...gave little chance to women to advance in society. "Glass ceiling" means invisible barriers (Negative). (A) is Positive. B), D) applied 'glass' too literally.

Q20. **Absolute Pattern 8: Understanding True Purpose** **Question Pattern:** The author views line 29 "**.past 200 years**" with	
A) total celebration **B) parallel in history** C) unprecedented development D) somewhat unfair judgment	B) **Although** women's participation in industry has changed a lot ...gave little chance to women to advance in society, **not unlike** to that of the past 200 years The main clause "not unlike 200 years.."., shows that the history is parallel (not changed, or opposite to (C). D) is Inconsistent with the question. It's not a degree of fairness.

Q21. **Absolute Pattern 4: Example Question** **Question Pattern:** The author views **married women's** involvement into workforce during the industrialization in line 22 as	
A) benefits from the industrialization B) an inevitable fact generated by marriage trends C) an emphatic example of gender equality **D) a side-effect of technological advancement**	D) "social issue", a negative effect of the industrialization, forced married women to work. Women's socioeconomic transformation had engendered unprecedented social issues such as married women being **forced into** hazardous factory operations (A), (C) are positive and opposite, (B) isn't the author's concern

Questions 22-31 are based on the following passage.

Sunspots are dark spots on the sun's photosphere. The first scientific periodicity of this phenomena is ascribed to an European observer, Galileo Galilei in 1610. Sunspots correspond to concentrations of magnetic field flux that inhibit convection and result in reduced surface temperature compared to the surrounding photosphere. (26C&30C) **Although the records made by then Chinese naked- eye observers contradict it, Sun** went through a period of inactivity in the late 17th **century. This period is known as the Maunder Minimum.** Without having a concrete evidence, the Maunder Minimum, from 1645 to 1715, is defined as the prolonged sunspot inactivity period. (28B) **The reason that the Maunder Minimum invites a special attention to scientists is because this period also corresponds to a climatic period called the "Little Ice Age."**	Throughout the Maunder Minimum, terrestrial temperature was noticeably and abnormally cold at lower altitudes. Although sunspots themselves produce only minor effects on solar emissions, the magnetic activity that accompanies the sunspots can produce dramatic changes in the ultraviolet and soft x-ray emission levels. (29A) **These changes over the solar cycle have important consequences for the Earth's upper atmosphere**. As revealed on the discrepancy between Chinese naked-eye observers and the later European scientists concerning the Maunder Minimum, (24A & 25D) **whether sunspot activity is a transient phenomenon or long-lived feature due to** (27D) **unsustainable decomposition of the Sun's magnetic field** (22A &23D) **remains elusive.**

Q22. **Absolute Pattern 2: Summary Question** Summarizing a sentence or entire passage **Question Pattern:** The passage defines **solar activity cycle** as	
A) an enduring but not yet fully confirmed theory B) significant to the modern global warming C) transient phenomena and therefore insignificant D) a mysterious supernatural phenomena	A) whether sunspot activity is a transient phenomenon or long-lived feature due to unsustainable decomposition of the Sun's magnetic field remains elusive. B) "global warming" is not stated. C) "insignificant" is opposite.

Q23. **Absolute Pattern 11: Textual Evidence Question** Finding evidence for the previous question **Question Pattern:** Which choice provides the best evidence for the answer to the previous question?	
A) Lines 1 (Sunspots are...photosphere.) B) Lines 19-21 (Throughout…altitudes.) C) Lines 21-25 (Although sunspots...emission levels) **D) Lines 31-34 (whether sunspot…elusive.)**	D) whether sunspot activity is a transient phenomenon or long-lived feature due to unsustainable decomposition of the Sun's magnetic field remains elusive

Q24. **Absolute Pattern 3: Inference Question** Finding an indirect suggestion (or guessing) **Question Pattern:** According to the last paragraph, which of the possible research projects would further **ascertain the Sunspot activity is unsustainable feature** of the Sun?	
A) Finding relations between the sun's magnetic field decomposition and sunspot activity B) Identifying whether the sun's magnetic field is sustainable or unsustainable C) Confirming that the sunspot activity is a transient D) Finding that the sunspot activity is related to the Maunder Minimum	A) The question asks "unsustainable feature." The sun's magnetic field will eventually become unsustainable. Hence the answer. B) is the status quo of the research C) will produce the opposite conclusion. D) is already known fact

Q25. **Absolute Pattern 11: Textual Evidence Question** Finding evidence for the previous question **Question Pattern:** Which choice provides the best evidence for the answer to the previous question?	
A) Lines 15-18 (The reason...Little Ice Age.") B) Lines 21-25 (Although sunspots...emission level) C) Lines 26-28 (These changes...upper atmosphere) **D) Lines 31-34 (whether sunspot…elusive.)**	D) If scientists identify the speed of the sun's magnetic field decomposition and its relations with sunspot activity, they will conclude that the sunspot activity is not transient phenomenon.

Q26. **Absolute Pattern 4: Example Question** Understanding example sentence and the true purpose behind a specific name or idea. **Question Pattern:** The reference to the "**Chinese naked-eye observers**" (line 29) primarily serves to	
A) solidify Maunder Minimum theory B) respect the 16th century Chinese scientists **C) disqualify Maunder Minimum** D) provide a certain kind of zealotry	C) "although the records made by then Chinese naked-eye observers contradict **it,** Sun went through a period of inactivity in the late 17th century. **This period** is known as the Maunder Minimum. (A) is opposite. (B), (D) are nonsensical
According to the passage, sun went through a period of inactivity in the late 17th century, the period known as the Maunder Minimum. However, Chinese naked-eye observers contradict it. In other words, they didn't observe a period of inactivity. Therefore, they would disqualify Maunder Minimum. "although" always gives the answer.	

Q27. **Absolute Pattern 5: Word-In-Context Question** Finding a clue word and the keyword from the sentence in question **Question Pattern:** "**unsustainable**" in line 33 most nearly means	
A) unaccomplished B) unassimilated C) unabsorbed **D) abated**	D) whether sunspot activity is a transient phenomenon or long-lived feature due to unsustainable decomposition of the Sun's magnetic field remains elusive. *Unsustainable means reducible or abated

Q28. **Absolute Pattern 9: Relationships Question**
Finding relations between the cause-effect, comparison-contrast, characters, and ideas
Question Pattern: Why do **scientists pay special attention to the Maunder Minimum**?

A) because they know the Ice Age is coming **B) because the period is related with the Little Ice Age** C) because the sun's inactivity is related with it D) because the single sunspot is as wide as the earth diameter that can threaten the earth	B) The reason that the Maunder Minimum invites a special attention to scientists is because this period also corresponds to a climatic period called the "Little Ice Age."

Q29. **Absolute Pattern 4: Example Question**
Understanding example sentence and the true purpose behind a specific name or idea
Question Pattern: Understanding the **ultraviolet and soft x-ray** emission levels in line 24 is important because

A) they have significant consequences for the earth's upper atmosphere. B) they bring the Ice Age C) they decompose the sun's magnetic field fast D) they affect the greenhouse and air quality	A) Although sunspots themselves produce only minor effects... changes in the ultraviolet and soft x-ray emission levels. These changes over the solar cycle have important consequences for the earth's upper atmosphere.

Q30. **Absolute Pattern 3: Inference Question** Finding an indirect suggestion (or guessing)
Question Pattern: According to lines 29, the **Chinese naked-eye observers**

A) felt noticeably cold terrestrial temperature during the period B) were mocked by later European scientists **C) experienced little temperature drop** D) observed a period of inactivity of the sun but not the temperature drop	C) As revealed on the discrepancy between Chinese naked-eye observers and the later European scientists concerning the Maunder Minimum, ...

(C) Maunder Minimum, as European scientists believed to have occurred, was not observed by Chinese observers. Chinese observers didn't experience sunspot inactivity (Maunder Minimum).
(D) Temperature must drop during the period of sun's inactivity

Q31. **Absolute Pattern 12: Informational Graphs**
Finding facts described in the graphs or relations between the passage and the graph.
Question Pattern: The graph following the passage indicates the year that is most resemblance to **Maunder Minimum** in

A) 1992 B) 1997 **C) 2002** D) 2012	**(C) 2002:** Sunspot number: 250 reveals the greatest number of sunspot or Maunder Minimum. (A) 1992: Sunspot number: 100 (B) 1997:Sunspot number: 0 (D) 2012: Sunspot number: 150

Questions 32-41 are based on the following passage.

Coffee is universal in its (32C) **appeal.**
All nations do it homage. (33C &34B) **It has become recognized as a human necessity.** People love coffee because of its two-fold effect--the pleasurable sensation and the increased efficiency in fashionable society, but it is also a favorite beverage of the men and women who do the world's work, whether they toil with brain or brawn.

(40C)**No "food drink" has ever encountered so much opposition as coffee.** Given to the world by the church and dignified by the medical profession, nevertheless it has had to suffer from religious superstition and medical prejudice. During the thousand years of its development it has experienced fierce political opposition, stupid fiscal restrictions, unjust taxes, irksome duties.

But coffee is something more than a beverage.
It is one of the world's greatest adjuvant foods.

Like all good things in life, the drinking of coffee may be abused. (37C&38C&39A) **Indeed, those having an idiosyncratic susceptibility to alkaloids should be temperate in the use of tea, coffee, or cocoa.** In every high-tensioned country there is likely to be a small number of people who, because of certain individual characteristics, cannot drink coffee at all. These belong to the idiosyncratic minority of the human family.

(35B) **Some people cannot eat strawberries; but that would not be a valid reason for a general condemnation of strawberries. One may be poisoned, says Thomas** A. Edison, from too much food.

Trading upon the credulity of the hypochondriac and the caffeine-sensitive, in recent years there has appeared in America and abroad a curious collection of (36A &Q39A) **so-called coffee substitutes. They are "neither fish nor flesh, nor good red herring.**
(41B) **"Sodas and substitutes have been shown by official government analyses to be sadly deficient in food value--their only alleged virtue.**

Q32. **Absolute Pattern 5: Word-In-Context Question**
Question Pattern: In line 2, the word "**homage**" most nearly means

A) obey B) surrender **C) appreciate** D) accept	C) Coffee is universal in its appeal. All nations do it homage D) When considering the original definition of "homage", meaning "great respect" and the overall tone of the author, (D) "accept" becomes too weak interpretation.

Q33. **Absolute Pattern 4: Example Question**
Finding the true purpose behind a specific name or idea within a sentence
Question Pattern: The author mentions "**men and women**" in line 8 mainly to

A) pay the homage to those who do the world's work B) celebrate coffee's commercial success as a drink **C) show that coffee has become people's necessity** D) emphasize coffee's delightful taste	C) It has become recognized as a human necessity. It is a favorite beverage of the men and women .

Q34. **Absolute Pattern 11: Textual Evidence Question** Finding evidence for the previous question
Question Pattern: Which choice provides the best evidence for the answer to the previous question?

A) Lines 2 (All nations...homage.) **B) Lines 2-3 (It has become...necessity)** C) Lines 4-6 (People love...society) D) Lines 9-10 (No "food drink"...as coffee)	B) Please refer to the above question

Q35. **Absolute Pattern 4: Example Question** **Question Pattern:** In line 32 the reference to **Thomas A. Edison** is used to emphasize the	
A) pervasive historical evidence against coffee **B) argument that coffee is harmful** C) beneficial effect of coffee D) authoritative tone against coffee	B) One may be poisoned, says Thomas A. Edison, from too much food. C) is opposite. Thomas A. Edison wasn't focusing on its benefits. Rather, he emphasizes that anything can be harmful from too much indulgence. (A) small number of people can't represent pervasive bias.

Q36. **Absolute Pattern 3: Inference Question** Finding an indirect suggestion (or guessing) **Question Pattern:** The analogy **"neither fish nor flesh"** in lines 38 serves to underscore the	
A) unlikelihood that substitutes would replace coffee B) increasing homogenization of coffee substitutes C) universal availability of coffee substitutes D) substitutes have their own merits	A) so-called coffee substitutes. They are "neither fish nor flesh, nor good red herring." "neither fish nor flesh." alludes that substitutes would not replace coffee.

Q37. **Absolute Pattern 9: Relationships Question** **Question Pattern:** Which of the following person would most likely **disagree with the author's view on coffee**	
A) men and women (line 7) B) the medical profession (line 12) **C) those having an idiosyncratic susceptibility (line 21)** D) Thomas A. Edison (line 32)	C) idiosyncratic susceptibility to alkaloids should be temperate in the use of tea, coffee, * Idiosyncratic, meaning abnormal, expands the author's claim for those who can't drink coffee.

Q38. **Absolute Pattern 11: Textual Evidence Question** Finding evidence for the previous question **Question Pattern:** Which choice provides the best evidence for the answer to the previous question?	
A) Lines 6-7(but it is...men and women) B) Lines 11-12 (Given to the world...medical profession) **C) Lines 21-23 (Indeed, those having...or cocoa.)** D) Lines 31-33 (one may be...too much food)	C) Please refer to the above question

Q39. **Absolute Pattern 7: Understanding Attitude (Tone) Question** **Question Pattern:** The **author's tone concerning coffee substitute** in line 11 is	
A) hopelessness B) qualified approval C) mild skepticism D) celebration	A) "neither fish nor flesh." alludes that substitutes would not replace coffee. The author's voice is so emphatic that it cancels out B) and C) because both "qualified" and "mild" contain some degree of Positive tone. C) is incorrect because of the word "mild."

Q40. **Absolute Pattern 10: Understanding the Structure of the Passage** **Question Pattern:** The relationship between the **first and second paragraph** (lines 1~17) is that paragraph 1?	
A) offers an anecdote that paragraph 2 confirms B) justifies the necessity of coffee, while paragraph 2 limits its justification **C) elaborates one-sided opinion, while paragraph 2 describes popular misconception** D) offers pros, while paragraph 2 offers cons	C) Coffee is universal in its appeal. All nations do it homage. **(elaborates a one-sided opinion,)** No "food drink" has ever encountered.... **(popular misconception)** *When two things (paragraphs, sentences, people) are compared, always focus on the SECOND one.

Q41. **Absolute Pattern 12: Informational Graphs** **Question Pattern:** Which statement best summarizes the **description of coffee consumption between the author and the graph?**	
A) The author assumes that coffee's singular position is invincible; the graph supports the argument **B) The author believes that carbonated soft drink's popularity is only temporary; the graph indicates it is not** C) The author rejects the graph's methodology D) The author and the graph may concede tea will eventually replace soft drinks and coffee	B) The author: "neither fish nor flesh." alludes that substitutes would not replace coffee. The graph: Coffee is declining, while soft drinks are increasing. C) is incorrect as it does not respond clearly to the author's main message about the issue.

Questions 42-52 are based on the following passage.

PASSAGE 1

What Drives Consumer Spending?

(42A) **First and foremost,** income drives consumer spending; Today's release showed that income increased 0.3 percent and the gains in January. (44A) **Recall that January's outsized gain was driven immediately by the lower tax withholdings called for by the Middle Class Tax Relief Act of 2010** (I certainly noticed a difference in my paycheck, and my local restaurants and bakeries were the primary beneficiaries).

(43D) **Another factor in consumers' spending decisions is how wealthy they are**. When consumers become wealthier, their spending goes up. Why is the stock market up, especially given the tumultuous events in North Africa, the Middle East, and Japan? Good question but no data.

(45B) **A factor with no good data being one of the primary culprits,** (Q51B) **I'd like to think it's because folks have developed a more positive outlook on the U.S. economy,** and indeed economic forecasts for growth in the U.S.

PASSAGE 2

(46D&47A&49A)**The Theory of Economics does not furnish a body of settled conclusions immediately applicable to policy. It is a methodical speculation rather than a doctrine,** an (48B) **apparatus of the mind**, a technique of thinking, which helps its possessor to draw correct conclusions. (Q50D) **It is not difficult in the sense in which mathematical and scientific techniques are difficult; but the fact that its modes of expression are much less precise than these,** renders decidedly difficult the task of conveying it correctly to the minds of learners.

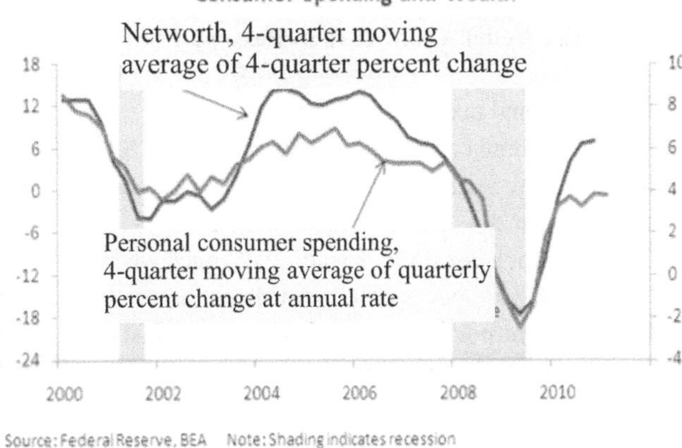

Q42. **Absolute Pattern 7: Understanding Attitude (Tone) Question** **Question Pattern:** The author of Passage 1 responds to line 1, (**what drive consumer spending**?) with	
A) emphatic confirmation B) limited consent C) ambivalence D) analytical speculation	A) First and foremost, income drives consumer spending. First and foremost,' reveals the author's emphatic tone of voice.

Q43. **Absolute Pattern 2: Summary Question** Summarizing a sentence, or an entire paragraph **Question Pattern:** The author of Passage 1 shows that consumer **spending is primarily driven by**	
A) the periodic income increase alone B) the periodic spending habit C) the government policy such as the Middle Class Tax Relief Act of 2010 **D) the periodic income increase and individual abundance wealth**	D) What Drives Consumer Spending? First and foremost, income drives consumer spending; "Another factor in consumers' spending decisions is how wealthy they are. Pattern: Always Search If There's a Second Statement. "First and foremost" indicates that there's another's coming.

Q44. **Absolute Pattern 4: Example Question** **Question Pattern:** The author of Passage 1 mentions his **local restaurant and bakeries** in line 9 in order to introduce	
A) some major beneficiaries of Tax Relief Act B) some people unaffected by Tax Relief Act C) the middle class consumer's spending habits D) alternative explanation for consumer spending habit	A) Parenthesis adds further information. Recall that January's outsized gain was driven largely by the Middle Class Tax Relief Act of 2010 (I certainly noticed a difference in my paycheck, and my local restaurants and bakeries were the primary beneficiaries). B) is Opposite. C) is Not Stated. D) There's no "alternative"

Q45. **Absolute Pattern 5: Word-In-Context Question** **Question Pattern:** In Passage 1, in 18 **"culprit"** most nearly means	
A) crime **B) responsibility** C) misdeed D) origin	B) A factor with no good data being one of the primary culprits, *culprit means one who is in responsible, only used a bit figurative in this context.

Q46. **Absolute Pattern 9: Relationships Question** Finding relations between the cause-effect, comparison-contrast, characters, and ideas **Question Pattern:** Which aspect would probably be the **great concern to the author of Passage 2 about Middle Class Tax Relief Act of 2010 in Passage 1?**	
A) Intentional tax policy would eventually undermine consumer savings in the long term B) Complete unanimity of income and spending relationship cannot be established C) How much consumer spending changes when wealth changes is still up for debate **D) An Economic policy can't be the conclusive facts for the application**	D) Passage 2: The Theory of Economics does not furnish a body of settled conclusions immediately applicable to policy. It is a methodical speculation. Passage 1: Recall that January's outsized gain was driven immediately by the lower tax withholdings called for by the Middle Class Tax Relief Act of 2010 Passage 2 focuses on the theory, rather than a policy. This is the only known information in Passage 2. A), B), and C) are all incorrect because, regardless whether the statements are true or false, they are all summaries of Passage 1.

Q47. **Absolute Pattern 11: Textual Evidence Question** Finding evidence for the previous question **Question Pattern:** Which choice provides the best evidence for the answer to the previous question?	
A) Lines 26-28 (The Theory...a policy.) B) Lines 28-31 (It is a methodical...conclusions.) C) Lines 31-33 (It is not...are difficult) D) Lines 33-36 (but the fact...minds of the learners.)	A) Please refer to the above question

<table>
<tr><td colspan="2">Q48. Absolute Pattern 5: Word-In-Context Question
Question Pattern: In Passage 2, in 29 "apparatus" most nearly means</td></tr>
<tr><td>A) readily applicable method
B) complex contraption
C) mechanical device
D) gear</td><td>B) It is a methodical speculation rather than a doctrine, an apparatus of the mind, a technique of thinking,... (mental concept)

Although the term, apparatus is commonly used for physical concept such as a gear or a device as in (C) or (D), the passage uses it with a figurative concept.

A) is incorrect because the author claims it isn't "readily applicable" but difficult</td></tr>
<tr><td colspan="2">Q49. Absolute Pattern 9: Relationships Question
Finding relations between the cause-effect, characters, and ideas including a Paired Passage.
Question Pattern: The main difference between the author of Passage 1 and the author 2 is that the author 1</td></tr>
<tr><td>A) relies more on real economy and taxes, while the author 2 expounds the method and principle.
B) expounds the elements of method clearly, while the author 2 gathers relevant facts to apply economic principles
C) relates economics through tax policy, while the author 2 focuses more on consumer spending habit
D) relies more on the theory of micro economy, while the author 2, on macro economy.</td><td>A)
P1 describes taxes and economy.
P2 describes theory and expression of economy

B) the order is flipped over.
C) is both referring to the passage 1
D) passage 1 refers both micro and macro.
Passage 2 refers on macro economics.</td></tr>
<tr><td colspan="2">Q50. Absolute Pattern 9: Relationships Question
Finding relations between the cause-effect, comparison-contrast, characters, and ideas
Question Pattern: The author of Passage 2implies that mathematical technique in line 32 is</td></tr>
<tr><td>A) highly developed than the Theory of Economics
B) concerned more with the minds of learners
C) easier than the Theory of Economics
D) more precise in its modes of expression</td><td>D) The Theory of Economics is not difficult in the sense in which mathematical and scientific techniques are difficult; but the fact that its modes of expression are much less precise</td></tr>
<tr><td colspan="2">Q51. Absolute Pattern 2: Summary Question Summarizing a sentence, or an entire paragraph
Question Pattern: The author seems to find the economic forecasts for growth in line 20 from</td></tr>
<tr><td>A) a factor with good data
B) the folks' more positive outlook on U.S. economy
C) the fact that the stock market went up
D) the direct impact of the Tax Relief Act of 2010</td><td>B) "I'd like to think it's because folks have developed a more positive outlook on the U.S. economy</td></tr>
<tr><td colspan="2">Q52. Absolute Pattern 12: Informational Graphs
Finding facts described in the graphs or relations between the passage and the graph.
Question Pattern: Which statement best summarizes the graph?</td></tr>
<tr><td>A) Wealth and consumer spending have been mostly synchronized over a 10-year period.
B) Wealth and consumer spending have not been synchronized over a 10-year period.
C) Consumer spending increased in 2005 when household net worth decreased
D) Consumer spending recovered faster than wealth in 2009</td><td>B) Opposite perception
C) Both moved in similar scale
D) Both moved in similar scale

This graph does not require passage information.,</td></tr>
</table>

SAT Test 4

Writing and language Section Answer Explanations

&

Pattern Analyses

Test 4 Writing & Language Section Patterns

Questions 1-11 are based on the following passage.

WikiLeaks

WikiLeaks is an international [1] non-profitable journalistic organization that publishes secret information, news leaks, and classified media from anonymous sources, [2] mainly from organizations or individuals who do not disclose their names. Its website, initiated in 2006 in Iceland by the organization Sunshine Press, claimed a database of more than 1.2 million documents within a year of its launch. Julian Assange, an Australian Internet activist, is generally described as its founder, editor-in-chief, and director. Hrafnsson is also a member of Sunshine Press Productions, [3] along with Assange, Hrafnsson and Gavin MacFadyen are the only known members outside.

The group has released a number of [4] significantly pivotal documents that have become front-page news items. Early releases included documentation of equipment expenditures and holdings in the Afghanistan war and a report informing a corruption investigation in Kenya.

In April 2010, WikiLeaks published gunsight footage from the 12 July 2007 Baghdad airstrike in which Iraqi journalists were among those killed by an AH-64 Apache helicopter, known [5] to be the *Collateral Murder* video. In July of the same year, WikiLeaks released [6] ,a compilation of more than 76,900 documents about the War in Afghanistan, Afghan Diary to the world.

WikiLeaks [7] relies on some degree on volunteers and previously described its founders as a mixture of Asian dissidents, journalists, mathematicians, and start-up company technologists from the United States.

WikiLeaks progressively [8] adopt a more traditional publication model and no longer accepts either user comments or edits. As of June 2009, the website had more than 1,200 registered volunteers and listed an advisory board comprising Assange, his deputy Jash Vora and seven other people, [9] some of them denied any association with the organization.

According to the WikiLeaks website, its goal is "to bring important news and information to the public. One of our most important activities is to publish original source material alongside our news stories, [10] for example, readers and historians alike can see evidence of the truth." Another of the organization's goals is to ensure that journalists and whistleblowers are not prosecuted for emailing sensitive or classified documents. The online "drop box" is described by the WikiLeaks website as "[11] an innovative, security and anonymous way for sources to leak information to WikiLeaks journalists."

Q1. Absolute Pattern 10: Logical Expression

WikiLeaks is an international [1]non-profitable journalistic organization

	Choice	Explanation
	A) NO CHANGE	D) only adjective can modify noun. Either "non-profit" or "not-for-profit" journalistic (adjective) organization (noun) can be the correct usage.
	B) non-profit **journal** organization	B) Both 'journal' and 'organization' are noun and can't be combined because they both are noun.
	C) non-**profitable** journalism organization	A), C) "non-profitable" is not a standard usage.
√	D) **non-profit journalistic** organization	

Q2. Absolute Pattern 19: Redundant Error

WikiLeaks is an international non-profit journalistic organization that publishes secret information, news leaks, and classified media from **anonymous sources**, [2] mainly from organizations or individuals who do not disclose their names.

	Choice	Explanation
	A) NO CHANGE	Always Pick the Shortest One from the Multiple Choices.
	B) however, the origin of information is normally not disclosed.	D) The underlined portion is redundant with the word anonymous source"
	C) —although the information is not readily verifiable.	A), B), and C) are repeating the information already written.
√	**D) DELETE IT.**	

Q3. Absolute Pattern 5: Comma Splice Error

Hrafnsson is also a member of Sunshine Press Productions, [3] along with Assange, Hrafnsson and Gavin MacFadyen are the only known members outside.

	A) NO CHANGE	D) "and" is conjunction "and" links the previous clause with the following clause.
	B) in conjunction with Assange,	
	C) together with Assange,	A), B), and C) "along with", "in conjunction with" and "together with" are—albeit seemingly conjunction— not a conjunction and can't connect the clause.
√	**D) and with Assange**	

Q4. Absolute Pattern 19: Redundant Error

The group has released a number of [4] significantly pivotal documents that have become front-page news items.

	A) NO CHANGE	D) is most concise and avoids redundancy.
	B) significant and pivotal documents	A), B), C): Redundant Error. "significantly" and "pivotal" are synonym, causing a redundancy.
	C) significant documents, which is pivotal	
√	**D) significant documents**	

Q5. Absolute Pattern 24: Verb Tense / Voice Error

Which of the following alternatives to the underlined portion would **NOT be acceptable**?

√	**A) to be**	A) "to be" is used for the future tense. "In April 2010." indicates the past.
	B) as	All the remaining options work well with the past tense.
	C) for	
	D) to	

Q6. Absolute Pattern 12: Modifier Placement Error

In July of the same year, WikiLeaks released [6] , a compilation of more than 76,900 documents about the War in Afghanistan, Afghan Diary to the world.

	A) NO CHANGE	C) The correct sentence: In July of the same year, WikiLeaks released Afghan War Diary, a compilation of more than 76,900 documents about the War in Afghanistan, to the world.
	B) After the word "year,"	
√	**C) After the word "Diary"**	A) The modifier "a compilation… Afghanistan" is so long that it separates the verb "released" from the object "Afghan Diary," blurring the original meaning.
	D) After the word "world"	

Q7. Absolute Pattern 15: Prepositional Idiom

WikiLeaks [7] relies on some degree to volunteers and previously described its founders as a mixture of Asian dissidents, journalists, mathematicians, and start-up company technologists from the United States.

	A) NO CHANGE	D) "to some degree" + "relies on" => "**relies** *to some degree* **on**"
	B) reliance on some degree to	B), C) 'Reliance' is noun. The sentence requires a verb, 'relies'
	C) reliance to some degree on	
√	**D) relies to some degree on**	

Q8. Absolute Pattern 24: Verb Tense / Voice Error

WikiLeaks progressively [8] adopt a more traditional publication model and no longer **accepts** either user comments or edits.

	Choice	Explanation
	A) NO CHANGE	D) 1> The simple past tense (adopted) should be ideal in this sentence. 2> However, having none in the options, the best alternative is to maintain the same present tense as used in the same sentence.
	B) had adopted	
	C) is under the influence of drastic adoption with	A) 1> Subject-verb agreement error. 2> "WikiLeaks" the title of the organization, is singular noun and therefore should use the singular verb.
√	**D) adopts**	B) 1> "had adopted" is past perfect tense. 2> the adjacent verb "accepts" is the present. 3> Tense can't jump from present to past perfect. C) is wordy

Q9. Absolute Pattern 7: Conjunction Error

As of June 2009, the website had more than 1,200 registered volunteers and listed an advisory board comprising Assange, his deputy Jash Vora and seven other people, [9] some of them denied any association with the organization.

	Choice	Explanation
	A) NO CHANGE	D) "whom" is used as a conjunction that links the previous clause.
	B) some people	A) and B) 1> Comma splice error. 2> No conjunction is used to link the subordinating clause "some of them..." or "some people"
	C) some of who	
√	**D) some of whom**	C) "of" is preposition. Therefore, "whom" must be used after the preposition. "who" is subjective.

Q10. Absolute Pattern 23: Transition Words for Supporting Detail, Contrast, and Consequence

According to the WikiLeaks website, its goal is "to bring important news and information to the public. One of our most important activities is to publish **original source material** alongside our news stories, [10] for example, readers and historians alike **can see evidence** of the truth."

	Choice	Explanation
	A) NO CHANGE	B) "so" means Therefore
√	**B) so**	C) 1> The "cause-clause" appeared already in the previous sentence. 2> It should use 'so', or 'therefore', or 'thus.' to show the consequence.
	C) because	D) is used to backup the consequence.
	D) moreover,	

Q11. Absolute Pattern 13: Parallel Structure

The online "drop box" is described by the WikiLeaks website as "[11] an **innovative**, **security** and **anonymous** way for sources to leak information to WikiLeaks journalists."

	Choice	Explanation
	A) NO CHANGE	B) innovative, secure, and anonymous = adjective, adjective, and adjective = The parallel structure.
√	**B) an innovative, secure, and anonymous**	
	C) an innovatively secure and anonymous	A) innovative (Adjective), security (Noun), and anonymous (Adjective) parallelism error.
	D) an innovatively and securely anonymous	C), D) change the meaning

Questions 12-22 are based on the following passage. **ISIS** The Islamic State of Iraq and Syria (ISIS) is a Salafi jihadist militant group that follows a fundamentalist, Wahhabi doctrine of Sunni Islam.. The [12] group adopted the name Islamic State and its idea of a caliphate have been widely criticized from the United Nations, [13] various governments refuted, and mainstream Muslim groups rejecting its statehood or caliphhood. The group first began referring to itself as Islamic State or IS in June 2014, [14] which it proclaimed itself a worldwide caliphate and named Abu Bakr al-Baghdadi as its caliph. The group has been designated a terrorist organization by the United Nations. Over 60 countries are directly or indirectly waging war against ISIL. [15] Adopted at social media, ISIL is widely known for its videos of beheadings. [16] The United Nations holds ISIL responsible for human rights abuses and war crimes, and Amnesty International has charged the group with ethnic cleansing on a "historic scale" in northern Iraq. Around the world, Islamic religious leadershave overwhelmingly condemned ISIL's ideology.	The United Nations [17] holds ISIS responsible for human rights abuses and war crimes, and Amnesty International has charged the group with ethnic cleansing on a "historic scale" in northern Iraq. Around the world, [18] ISIS gained prominence when it drove Iraqi government forces out of key cities in its Western Iraq and capturing Mosul. In June 2014, Saudi Arabia moved troops to [19] their borders with Iraq, after Iraq lost control [20] of, or withdrew from, strategic crossing points that then came under the control of ISIL, or tribes that supported ISIL. In late January 2015, it was reported that ISIS members infiltrated the European Union and disguised themselves as civilian refugees who were emigrating from the war zones of Iraq. An ISIS representative claimed that ISIS [21] had successfully smuggled 4,000 fighters, and that the smuggled fighters were planning attacks in Europe in retaliation for the airstrikes carried out against ISIS targets in Iraq and Syria. [22] In the meantime, experts believe that this claim was exaggerated to boost their stature and spread fear, and acknowledged that some Western countries were aware of the smuggling.

Q12. Absolute Pattern 14: Possessive Determiners and Possessive Noun Error

The [12] group adopted the name Islamic State and its idea of a caliphate ***have been widely criticized*** from the United Nations, various governments refuted, and mainstream Muslim groups rejecting its statehood ...

	A) NO CHANGE	D) "have been widely criticized " is the main verb. Therefore, "adopted" shouldn't be the verb. "The group's adoption of…" + "and its idea of a caliphate" make the plural subject
	B) groups' adoption of	
	C) adoption of group	A) uses "adopted" as the main verb. B) "groups" is incorrect usage. C) is flipped over. "group" and the following word "the name" simply don't link up.
√	**D) group's adoption of**	

Q13. Absolute Pattern 13: Parallel Structure

The group's adoption of the name Islamic State and its idea of a caliphate have been widely criticized from **the United Nations,** [13] **various governments** refuted, **and mainstream Muslim groups** rejecting its statehood or caliphhood.

	A) NO CHANGE	C) "the United Nations, various governments, and mainstream Muslim groups = Noun, Noun, and Noun = the parallel structure.
	B) along with various governments,	
√	**C) various governments,**	A) The verb 'refuted" should be deleted to make it the parallel structure. B), D) "along with" or "both" are unnecessary
	D) both various governments	

Q14. Absolute Pattern 7: Conjunction Error		
The group first began referring to itself as Islamic State or IS in June 2014, [14] which it proclaimed itself a worldwide caliphate and named Abu Bakral-Baghdadi as its caliph		
	A) NO CHANGE	D) "when" links up "June 2014"
	B) whom	A) "which" is ambiguous. B) is for a human precedent C) might work only were there no comma after '2014'
	C) that	
√	**D) when**	

Q15. Absolute Pattern 10: Logical Expression		
Passage: [15] Adopted at social media, ISIL is widely known for its videos of beheadings.		
	A) NO CHANGE	B) "Adept" means skillful.
√	**B) Adept**	A) Adopted = taking over someone's child C) addicted = obsessed D) annexed = to be combined
	C) Addicted	
	D) Annexed	

Q16. Absolute Pattern 1: Adding, Revising, Deleting, Retaining Information	
Adept at social media, ISIL is widely known for its videos of beheadings.	
Question: In the preceding sentence, the writer is considering replacing " beheadings." with " beheadings: soldiers, civilians, journalists and aid workers Should the writer make this revision?	
	A) Yes, because it fixes the incomplete sentence.
√	**B) Yes, because it gives added information about the atrocity of the group.**
	C) No, because it unnecessarily lists examples that should be placed elsewhere.
	D) No, because it is not proper to mention the occupations in this sentence.
B) By providing information of those who are victimized. The revised sentence emphasizes the organization's atrocity. A) There's no grammar error. C): It's not mentioned nowhere else. D): It is necessary to list explicitly who the victims were in order to arouse the reader's attention.	

Q17. Absolute Pattern 21: Subject-Verb, Pronoun, Noun Agreement		
The United Nations [17] holds ISIS responsible for human rights abuses and war crimes, and Amnesty International has charged the group with ethnic cleansing on a "historic scale" in northern Iraq.		
√	**A) NO CHANGE**	A) "The United Nations" is one entity, one organization, and. therefore. singular.
	B) hold	
	C) is held	B) is plural
	D) are held	C), D) are passive

Q18. Absolute Pattern 1: Adding, Revising, Deleting, Retaining Information

Around the world, [18] ISIS gained prominence when it drove Iraqi government forces out of key cities in its Western Iraq and capturing Mosul.

Question: Which choice maintains the essay's negative tone and most strongly supports the writer at this point ?

	Choice	Explanation
	A) NO CHANGE	B) is negative towards the ISIS and supports the writer's argument. A) is neutral narrative tone C) is positive towards the ISIS. D) is inconsistent with the question as it deviates from the question.
√	**B) Islamic religious leaders have overwhelmingly condemned ISIS's ideology and actions.**	
	C) ISIS has long argued that the group has the true path of true Islam and that its actions reflect the religion's real teachings or virtues.	
	D) Some extremists in countries like U.S. Russia, Israel, Turkey, Saudi Arabia hold the same opinion with the leaders in ISIS	

Q19. Absolute Pattern 14: Possessive Determiners and Possessive Noun Error

In June 2014, Saudi Arabia moved troops to [19] their borders with Iraq,

	Choice	Explanation
	A) NO CHANGE	D) 1> The subject "Saudi Arabia" is singular. 2> "its," singular possessive pronoun, connects "border." A) is possessive plural pronoun B) "there" is place adverb C) "It's" is the contraction for either it has or it is
	B) there borders	
	C) it's border	
√	**D) its border**	

Q20. Absolute Pattern 18: Punctuation Error

In June 2014, Saudi Arabia moved troops to its borders with Iraq, after Iraq lost control [20] of, or withdrew from, strategic crossing points that then came under the control of ISIL, or tribes that supported ISIL.

Which of the following **alternatives to the underlined portion would NOT be acceptable**?

Question: Which of the following alternatives to the underlined portion would NOT be acceptable?

	Choice	Explanation
	A) of, or withdrew from, strategic	D) uses only one comma. If a statement in a sentence simply adds extra information, it must be separated from the main clause using a necessary punctuation. A) a pair of commas, B) parenthesis, C) double dashes separate the interjected modifier from the main clause.
	B) of (or withdrew from) strategic	
	C) of—or withdrew from—strategic	
√	**D) of, or withdrew from strategic**	

Q21. Absolute Pattern 24: Verb Tense / Voice Error

	Choice	Explanation
√	**A) NO CHANGE**	A) "smuggle" should have occurred before the claim. "claimed" is past tense. "**had** successfully **smuggled**" is the past perfect. B) and C) are simple past, pointing that "claimed" and "smuggled" were occurring at the same time, an illogical situation. D) is passive voice. It sounds as if ISIS were the victims.
	B) successfully smuggled	
	C) smuggled with success	
	D) had been successfully smuggled	

Q22. Absolute Pattern 7: Conjunction Error

[22] In the meantime, experts believe that this claim was exaggerated to boost their stature and spread fear, and acknowledged that some Western countries were aware of the smuggling.

	Choice	Explanation
	A) NO CHANGE	C) 'however' cancels out the preceding sentence. The two sentences between the adverb "however" present the contrasting views A) 'In the meantime' means meanwhile B) 'Granted' means acknowledged D) 'since' means because
	B) Granted,	
√	**C) However,**	
	D) Since	

Questions 23-33 are based on the following passage.

Quantum Physics

Quantum mechanics is a fundamental branch of physics concerned with processes [23] involving: for example, atoms and photons. <A> System such as these which [24] obey quantum mechanics can be in a quantum superposition of different states, [25] unlike classical physics. <B> Early quantum theory was profoundly reconceived in the mid-1920s. <C> The [26] reconceived theory is formulated in various specially developed mathematical formalisms. <D> Important applications of quantum theory include superconducting magnets, light-emitting diodes, and the laser transistor and semiconductors such as the microprocessor, medical and research imaging such as magnetic resonance imaging and electron microscopy, and explanations for many biological and physical phenomena.

When quantum mechanics was originally formulated, it was applied to models [28] whose correspondence limit was non-relativistic classical mechanics.

For instance, the well-known model of the quantum harmonic oscillator uses an explicitly non-relativistic expression for the kinetic energy of the oscillator, and is thus a quantum version of the classical harmonic oscillator. Early attempts to merge quantum mechanics [29] for special relativity has involved the replacement of the Schrödinger equation with a covariant equation. [30] For example, these theories were successful in explaining many experimental results, they had certain unsatisfactory qualities stemming from their neglect of the relativistic creation and annihilation of particles.

A fully relativistic quantum theory required the development of quantum field theory, which applies quantization to a field [31]—less than a fixed set of particles.

The first complete quantum field theory, quantum electrodynamics, provides a fully quantum description of the electromagnetic interaction.
The full [32] apparatus's of quantum field theory is often unnecessary for describing electrodynamic systems.
A simpler approach, one that has been employed since the inception of quantum mechanics, is to treat charged particles as quantum mechanical objects being acted on by a classical electromagnetic field.

Q23. Absolute Pattern 18: Punctuation Error

Quantum mechanics is a fundamental branch of physics concerned with processes [23] involving: for example, atoms and photons.

	A) NO CHANGE	D) "for example" should be separated from the main sentence by offsetting with a pair of commas.
	B) involving; for example,	
	C) involving for example	A) a colon functions as "for example." Therefore, it cannot be used simultaneously B) a semi-colon carries a clause.
√	**D) involving, for example,**	C) lacks punctuation

Q24. Absolute Pattern 24: Verb Tense / Voice Error

System such as these which [24] obey quantum mechanics can be in a quantum superposition of different states,...

√	**A) NO CHANGE**	A) 1> "which obey" connects "these." Therefore, plural "obey" is required.
	B) obeys	B) "obeys" is singular.
	C) abeyance of	C) is noun D) 1> "have obeyed" is present perfect.
	D) have obeyed	2> Demonstrative statement like this passage should use the simple present tense as used in the surrounding sentences.

Q25. Absolute Pattern 4: Comparison		
System such as these which obey quantum mechanics can be in a quantum superposition of different states, [25] unlike classical physics.		
	A) NO CHANGE	Please read the following revised sentence. Unlike classical physics, system such as these obeys quantum mechanics. As seen above, "classical physics" is being compared with "system" Therefore, it requires "that" (system) to compare it correctly. B) "physics" and "superposition" are both nouns, so one of which should be a possessive form. D) "that" is missing as in (A).
	B) unlike classical physics superposition	
√	**C) unlike that of classical physics**	
	D) unlike in classical physics.	

Q26. Absolute Pattern 10: Logical Expression		
The [26]reconceived theory is formulated in various specially developed mathematical formalisms.		
Which of the following alternatives to the underlined portion would **NOT be acceptable?**		
	A) conceptualized	"Reconceived" means an idea taken into mind.
√	**B) rehabilitated**	B) means "to restore to healthy condition after imprisonment."
	C) redesigned	A), C), D) are all synonyms to reconceived. D) means recalculated
	D) recalibrated	

Q27. Absolute Pattern 11: Logical Sequence		
At this point, the writer wishes to introduce **the practicality** of Quantum mechanics. Which sentence can be the best topic sentence for the new paragraph?		
	A) <A> System such as ...	**Quantum mechanics is a fundamental branch** f physics concerned with processes involving: atoms and photons. <A> **System such as these** which obey quantum mechanics can be in a quantum superposition of different states, unlike classical physics. <B> **Early quantum theory** was profoundly reconceived in the mid-1920s. <C> **The reconceived theory** is formulated in various specially developed mathematical formalisms. <D> **Important applications of quantum theory** include .. D) Application means **practicality**.
	B) <B> Early quantum theory...	
	C) <C> The reconceived...	
√	**D) <D> Important applications of...**	

Q28. Absolute Pattern 14: Possessive Determiners and Possessive Noun Error		
When quantum mechanics was originally formulated, it was applied to models [28] whose correspondence limit was non-relativistic classical mechanics.		
√	**A) NO CHANGE**	A) 1> "whose" means 'of which' (of the models') or "of models' correspondence limit" 2> "whose" links up "models" to "correspondence limit (noun). B) "whom" is used only for human C), D) 'which' and 'that' are not possessive. Therefore, they can't link up another noun "correspondence"
	B) whom	
	C) which	
	D) that	

Q29. Absolute Pattern 24: Verb Tense / Voice Error

Early attempts to merge quantum mechanics [29] for special relativity has involved the replacement of the Schrödinger equation with a covariant equation.

	Choice
	A) NO CHANGE
√	**B) with special relativity involved**
	C) to special relativity had involved
	D) into special relativity involves

B) the past tense "involved," is required because the subject "Early attempts" implies the past activity.
A) "has involved" is present and singular.
C) 1> "had involved" is past perfect tense.
2> The past perfect tense can't be used independently.
3> It normally carries the simple past tense.
D) "involves" is the present tense.

Q30. Absolute Pattern 23: Transition Words for Supporting Detail, Contrast, and Consequence

[30] For example, these theories were successful in explaining many experimental results, they had certain unsatisfactory qualities stemming from their neglect of the relativistic creation

	Choice
	A) NO CHANGE
√	**B) While,**
	C) Due to
	D) Moreover,

B) 1> The sentence discusses the contradicting positions—"successful" and unsatisfactory."
2> "While", should be used in this contradictory circumstance.

A), D) are used to emphasize the previous statement.
C) is used for the cause-and-effect relation.

Q31. Absolute Pattern 4: Comparison

While these theories were **successful** in explaining many experimental results, they had **certain unsatisfactory** qualities stemming from their neglect of the relativistic creation and annihilation of particles. **A fully relativistic quantum theory required the development of quantum field theory, which applies quantization to a field** [31]—**less than** a fixed set of particles.

	Choice
	A) NO CHANGE
	B) similar to
	C) the same as
√	**D) rather than**

D) 1> The previous sentence discusses a sort of disappointment.
2> The following sentence diagnoses the problems and provides the solution.
3> That is, the scientists needed "the quantization to a field, where neither the relativistic creation can be neglected nor annihilation of particles be created.
4> Therefore, "rather than" is the correct answer.

Q32. Absolute Pattern 14: Possessive Determiners and Possessive Noun Error

The full [32] apparatus's of quantum field theory is often unnecessary for describing electrodynamic systems.

	Choice
	A) quantum field of apparatus
	B) apparatus' quantum field
√	**C) apparatus of quantum field**
	D) quantum field's apparatus

C) "quantum field" links up the following word "theory," creating the correct "quantum field theory"

A), D) 1> There's no "apparatus theory" 2> Apparatus means tool or system.
B), D) "apparatus" or "field" is non-human object. Therefore, they can't be "apparatus' " or "field's" It should use "of" for the possessive determiner.

Q33. Absolute Pattern 1: Adding, Revising, Deleting, Retaining Information	
Question: Suppose the writer's primary purpose had been to describe the difference between Quantum physics and classical physics. Would this essay accomplish that purpose?	
	A) Yes, because it discusses both theories
	B) Yes, because it focuses primarily on the early stage of Quantum theory that heavily depended on Classical Physics
	C) No, because it focuses more on Classical Physics and its influence upon Quantum Physics
√	**D) No, because it focuses more on Quantum Physics and its conceptual understanding.**

D) The main theme is Quantum Physics, not Classical Physics as the title stated.

Questions 34-44 are based on the following passage.

Frankenstein, or the Modern Prometheus

You will rejoice to hear that no disaster [34] accompany the commencement of an enterprise which you have regarded with such evil forebodings. Do you understand this feeling? This breeze, which has travelled from the regions [35] for which I am advancing, gives me a foretaste of those icy climes. Inspirited by this wind of promise, [36] what a fervent and vivid moment.

I try in vain to be persuaded that the pole is the seat of frost and [37] desolation, it ever presents itself to my imagination as the region of beauty and delight. There, Margaret, the sun is forever visible, [38] its broad disk just skirting the horizon and diffusing a perpetual splendor.

There--for with your leave, my sister, I will put some trust in preceding navigators--there snow and frost are banished; and, sailing over a calm sea, we may be wafted to a land surpassing in wonders and in beauty every region hitherto discovered on the habitable globe. I write a few lines in haste to say that I am safe--and well advanced on my voyage.

This letter will reach England by a merchantman now on its homeward voyage from Archangel; more fortunate than [39] me, who may not see my native land, perhaps, for many years.

I [40] am, however, in good spirits, my men are bold and apparently firm of purpose, nor do the floating sheets of ice that continually pass us, indicating the dangers of the region towards which we are advancing, [41] appearing dismay them. We have already reached a very high latitude; but it is the height of summer, and although not so warm as in England, the southern gales, which blow us speedily towards those shores which I so ardently desire to attain, breathe a degree of renovating warmth which I had not expected.

No incidents [42] has hitherto befallen us that would make a figure in a letter. One or two stiff gales and the springing of a leak are accidents which

[43] experiencing navigators scarcely remember to record, and I shall be well content if nothing worse happen to us during our voyage. So strange an accident [44] has happened to us and I cannot forbear recording it, although it is very probable that you will see me before these papers can come into your possession.

Q34. Absolute Pattern 24: Verb Tense / Voice Error		
You will rejoice to hear that no disaster [34] accompany the commencement of an enterprise which **you have regarded** with such evil forebodings.		
	A) NO CHANGE	D) 1> The narration and the subordinating clause (have regarded) indicate the past experience. 2> The closest tense should then be the present perfect.
	B) had accompanied	
	C) is to be accompanied	A) is plural. It should be singular because the subject 'disaster' is singular. B) 1> "had accompanied" is past perfect. The past perfect must be supported by the simple past tense in the same sentence or clause. 2> Tense can't jump from present to past perfect. C) is for the future.
√	**D) has accompanied**	

Q35. Absolute Pattern 15: Prepositional Idiom

This breeze, which has traveled from the regions [35] <u>for</u> which I am **advancing,** gives me a foretaste of those icy climes.

	Choice	Explanation
	A) NO CHANGE	D) <u>"towards" is used to describe the movement to a certain destination</u> (e.g., advancing towards San Francisco.)
	B) to	
√	**C) towards**	
	D) in	

Q36. Absolute Pattern 12: Modifier Placement Error

Inspired by this wind of promise, [36] <u>what a fervent and vivid moment</u>.

	Choice	Explanation
	A) NO CHANGE	C) 1> <u>The sentence begins with the modifier "inspired by"</u> 2> Only human subject can be "inspired."
	B) more fervent and vivid had my daydream become.	
√	C) **I** have become more fervent and vivid	
	D) there has become more fervent and vivid in my daydream.	

Q37. Absolute Pattern 18: Punctuation Error

I try in vain to be persuaded that the pole is the seat of frost and [37] <u>desolation, it ever</u> presents itself to my imagination as the region of beauty and delight.

	Choice	Explanation
	A) NO CHANGE	B) <u>Only semicolon can link up another clause with contradiction</u>. (e.g., John is a realtor; he can't sell his own house.) A) is comma splice error. When two clauses are combined, there must be a connector, either conjunction or semicolon. C) 1> Given that two clauses are contradicting, 2> "that" can't represent the contradictory clause. D) uses a colon. The colon is used to introduce things, not to contradict.
√	**B) desolation; it ever**	
	C) desolation that ever	
	D) desolation: it ever	

Q38. Absolute Pattern 5: Comma Splice Error

There, Margaret, the sun is forever visible, [38] <u>its</u> broad disk just skirting the horizon and diffusing a perpetual splendor.

	Choice	Explanation
√	**A) NO CHANGE**	A) 1> <u>The primary clause "the sun is forever visible," ends with the comma.</u> 2> which means the following statement should be a phrase. 3> Were it a clause like B), C) or D), it will be a comma splice error. 4> only (A) is phrase. B), C), D) are all clauses with verbs, causing a comma splice error.
	B) it's	
	C) there is	
	D) there are	

Q39. Absolute Pattern 17: Pronoun Error

This letter will reach England **by a merchantman** now on its homeward voyage from Archangel; more fortunate than [39] <u>me</u>, who may not see my native land, perhaps, for many years.

	Choice	Explanation
	A) NO CHANGE	D) <u>"I" is subjective pronoun that compares with a merchantman.</u> To illustrate, the original sentence can be divided into two parts: "**A merchantman** is more fortunate." and "**I am** less fortunate." that can be combined into "A merchantman is more fortunate than I (am)." A) is objective: "**A merchantman is** more fortunate." and "<u>**me am**</u>." is incorrect sentence. B) "myself" can't be used alone; it should come along with I. C) is a possessive
	B) myself	
	C) mine	
√	**D) I**	

Q40. Absolute Pattern 18: Punctuation Error

I [40] am, **however,** in good **spirits; my men** are bold and apparently firm of purpose, nor do the floating sheets of ice that continually pass us, indicating the dangers of the region towards which we are advancing,

√	**A) NO CHANGE**	A) 1> "however" should be offset by a pair of commas when inserted in the middle of the clause like (A) or (D). 2> "my men are bold…" is another clause that requires either conjunction or semicolon. B), C), and D) don't follow the standard punctuation described above.
	B) am however in good spirits:	
	C) am, however; in good spirits:	
	D) am, however, in good spirits,	

Q41. Absolute Pattern 21: Subject-Verb, Pronoun, Noun Agreement

I am, however, in good spirits; my men are bold and apparently firm of purpose, **nor do the floating sheets of ice** *that continually pass us, indicating the dangers of the region towards which we are advancing,* [41] appearing dismay them.

	A) NO CHANGE	B) 1> The conjunction "nor" signals the subordinating clause will follow. 2> "the floating sheets" is the subject in the subordinating clause. 3> *"that continually….advancing,"* is a quick interjection modifying the ice. 4> The quick interjection above is offset by a pair of commas, indicating that the subordinating clause is not completed yet and still waits for the verb. 5> "appear" (plural) corresponds to the subject "the floating sheets." (plural) A) is adjective C) 1> The subject "the floating sheets" is plural. 2> "appears to" is singular. D) should drop 'that'
√	**B) appear to**	
	C) appears to	
	D) that appear to	

Q42. Pattern 21: Subject-Verb, Pronoun, Noun Agreement

No incidents [42] has hitherto befallen us that would make a figure in a letter.

	A) NO CHANGE	C) The subject "incidents" (plural) requires the plural verb "have + befallen." Hitherto= so far.
	B) has hitherto befall	
√	**C) have hitherto befallen**	A) and B) "has" is singular; therefore incorrect. B) and D) "befall" has to be 'befallen' (the participle of befall) D) The adverb 'already' should be deleted because it changes the meaning..
	D) have already befall	

Q43. Absolute Pattern 10: Logical Expression

One or two stiff gales and the springing of a leak are accidents **which** [43] experiencing **navigators scarcely remember** to record, and I shall be well content if nothing worse happen to us during our voyage.

	A) NO CHANGE	B) should be "experienced navigators" who is experienced, not experiencing.
√	**B) experienced**	C) is verb. The verb "remember" is already given. D) is noun and can't link to the following noun "navigator."
	C) is experienced	
	D) experience	

Q44. Absolute Pattern 7: Conjunction Error

So strange an accident[44] has happened to us and I cannot forbear recording it, although it is very probable that you will see me before these papers can come into your possession.

	A) NO CHANGE	B) "So-that" clause (a cause-effect) is evident in this sentence. If you see "so" in a sentence, the answer could be either "that" clause or "as" phrase in the choice.
√	**B) has happened to us that I**	
	C) had happened to us and me	A) "and" can't replace "that" in "so-that" clause. C) is past perfect and also uses the incorrect pronoun "and me cannot..." D) is simple past, disregarding the same tense in the surrounding sentences.
	D) happened to us and I	

Chapter 4 Summary

Chapter Summary contains equal portions of

-12 Absolute Patterns for Reading Section

-20 Common Patterns for Incorrect Choices in Reading

-70 Absolute Patterns for Writing and Language Section

-24 Common Patterns for Incorrect Choices in Writing

Chapter 4

12 Absolute Patterns for the Reading Section

Absolute Pattern 7: Understanding Attitude (Tone)

Emulating the same feeling with the tone and attitude in reading passage is crux of the matter.
Let say the tone of the character in question is gloomy. Then, you must choose the one with the negative keyword or at least the one without positive tone. No matter how impressive the choice is to you, you don't pick the one with positive.

The author, narrator, or character in passage should give a certain impression to reader or to the other characters.
You should figure out the tone underneath his/her expression.
This attitude pattern often contains subjective tone such as positive-negative, active-passive, mental-physical tone

Keep in mind that (1) SAT passage can be divided into literature and informational.
In literature passage the answer is often subjective, clear in voice or attitude.

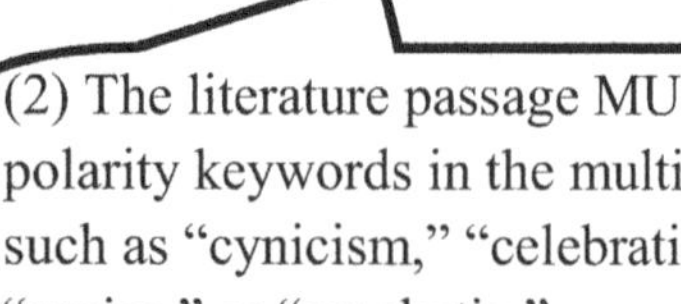

(2) The literature passage MUST contains polarity keywords in the multiple choices such as "cynicism," "celebration," "praise," or "emphatic."

(3) If the multiple choices in the literature passage do not contain such an emotional word, they're highly likely incorrect because the nature of the passage is supposed to be emotional.

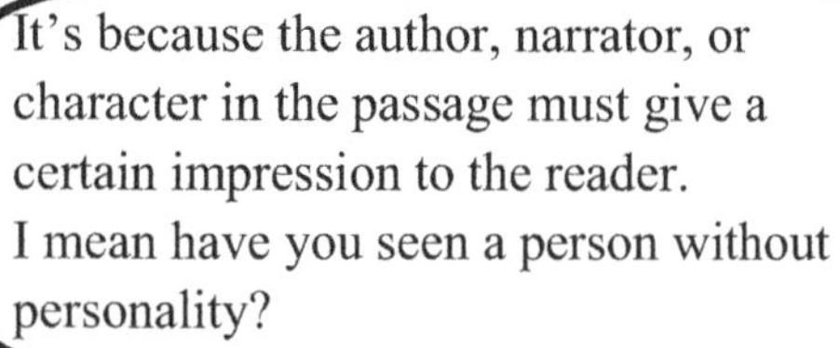

It's because the author, narrator, or character in the passage must give a certain impression to the reader.
I mean have you seen a person without personality?

(4) In Informational passage (history, science, social) the answer usually do not contain emotional keywords. The tone is ambiguous and neutral such as "express," "view," or "analyze."

You can solve tons of questions using this tone pattern.

Chapter 4

12 Absolute Patterns for the Reading Section

Absolute Pattern 9: Relationship Question

This pattern asks many different types of relations within a passage

(1) The relationships between the cause-effect situation: pay Attention to subordinating conjunctions such as "because, since, for, as, etc…"

(2) The relationships within a comparison-contrast: flagged by "more", "better", "never", often" ,"if." The answer may also carry comparison adverb.

(3) The relationships between historical or certain events (4) The relationships between characters, ideas, and arguments.

And finally, (5) the relationship between a paired passages.

Reciprocal Ideas in Paired Passages.

In a paired passages, multiple options (A), (B), (C), (D) should not be shared between the passages.

For example, if choice (A) statement is from the passage 1 but uses keywords taken from passage 2, then (A) has little chance to be the answer because information between two passages should be mutually exclusive.

It means, although we read both passages, two authors (passages) do not know each other's arguments.

In almost all cases in SAT, Passage 2 views the same issue from the bigger picture and yields more concerns than Passage 1.Therefore, the answer is pretty much already decided.

The reasoning behind this logic comes from the origin of two passages. In most cases, the source contexts in both Passage 1 and Passage 2 come from a single article. Passage 1 places intro. and the first half of the article; second half of the article including conclusion goes into Passage 2. Hence, Passage 1 reveals more general concept while Passage 2 presents more reservation.

Passage 2 always presents more limitations, concerns, counterarguments, opposition.

Common mistakes in this pattern!

When question asks

"~~compared to the paragraph~~ 1, paragraph 2…is?"

A very effective way to avoid such a mistake is to crossing out irrelevant information using your pencil.

Chapter 4

12 Absolute Patterns for the Reading Section

Absolute Pattern 10: Understanding the Structure

This question has little to do with the content in the passage.
A Typical question is something like "What is the primary function of the first paragraph?"

If you have two competing choices: e.g.,
(A) to argue harmful impact of mutation to protein in 70% of molecules,
(B) to introduce certain scientific analysis
the answer should be (B) because the major function of the first paragraph is to introduce things.
It will be nonsense to ask some detail information like (A) by questioning the function of the paragraph.

The question may also ask the role of partial information.
For example, the question may ask the function of although-clause, however-clause, but-clause, or the reason for saying "it seems" in the clause, or "the author's statement when he said "they may," etc.
You need to know the function (what it basically does), not the specific detail information in the statement.
As an example, "it seems" suggests "inconclusive situation".

Overall structural relationships question is the most complex type in this pattern.

The question normally asks relationships between paragraphs.
Therefore, the answer presents two significant distinctions between the paragraphs.
(e.g., "(A) paragraph 2 shows the critic's argument, while paragraph 3 shows the author's analyses that opposes the critic's argument")

70 Absolute Patterns in Writing and Language

Question 26
For decades the paleontologists had assumed that the Ice Age killed the dinosaurs, and their views changed quickly when the most massive meteorite crater was found in Yucatan.

A) NO CHANGE
B) but their views had changed
C) however, their views changed
D) but their views changed

Rule #26
Hint:
Conjunction

"But" should be used to contrast idea. "And" should be used to Paralleling idea.

The correct answer is D.
Use the conjunction 'but' to cancel out the previous sentence when two contrasting ideas are presented.

A): 1> The keywords "views changed quickly"
2> Two clauses between "and" are conflicting each other.
3> This is called "Misused AND"
B) is incorrect because "had changed" (the past perfect)" means that their views had changed before the crater was found, an impossible situation.
C) is incorrect because 'however' requires a semicolon (; however,)

Question 27
Although the new discoveries suggest otherwise, they claim that there are other versions of the Old Testaments.

A) NO CHANGE
B) the discoveries
C) theologians
D) it

Rule #27
Hint:
Pronoun

No Pronoun Can Be Used Independently Without Having Its Antecedent.
The correct answer is C.
In this sentence, the subject "they" in the main clause refers to "the new discoveries, which cannot "claim." Because it is illogical to say "the new discoveries claim", we should make (find) one that can claim. Theologians are the experts in Bible, who can claim.

A) is incorrect because it has unknown antecedent for pronoun "
* Please remember that it's colloquial error to write "they" out of the blue

Question28
The guest was entertained extravagant by the mayor of the city of North Vancouver, whose city has a strong tie to the guest's company.

A) NO CHANGE
B) with extravagance
C) extravagantly
D) extravagance

RULE #28

Hint: Adverbs

Adjective Cannot Modify Verb, But Adverb Can.
The correct answer is C.
By simply adding "-ly" at the end of the adjective, it will switch adjective "extravagant" to adverb "extravagantly" that modifies a verb.

Question 29
The New York Times chief editor has decided requiring all articles to be submitted at least one hour before the deadline.

A) NO CHANGE
B) to require
C) requesting
D) to requiring

RULE #29
Hint: Idiom

Prepositional Idioms that Imply the Future Action
The correct answer is B.

Any verb that implies "the future action" must use the preposition "to." (e.g., "wish to," "hope to," "expect to," "want to," "like to," 'plan to," "supposed to,")

Question 30
Forty-two years after the Apollo astronauts landed on the moon, new technology was not developed to initiate the same task any easier.

A) NO CHANGE
B) has not been developed
C) has not developed
D) had not been developed

RULE #30
Hint: Verb

Guessing the Verb Tense

The correct answer is B.
"Forty-two years" indicates something happened in the past. "after" also implies that the main clause describes the on-going event. Therefore, it should be present tense.
B) is the present perfect tense that complete the time sequence.
C) should be passive. D) is the past perfect, an event that occurred before the past.

Please refer to the following tense chart

Present Tense	Simple present Present continuous Present perfect	Jason works. Jason is working. Jason has worked.
Past Tense	Simple past Past continuous Past perfect	Jason worked. Jason was working. Jason had worked.
Future Tense	Future Future continuous Future perfect	Jason will work. Jason will be working. Jason will have worked.

HARDER EXAMPLE
Incorrect: I suspect the Olympic Council has a two-tiered vision for the future games: first, it had tried to replace the current exclusive sponsorship; second, it is wanting to add as much capacity to its operation as possible to have more multiple partners.

Correct: I **suspect** the Olympic Council **has** a two-tiered vision for the future games: first, it ***tries*** to replace the current exclusive sponsorship; second, it ***wants*** to add as much capacity to its operation as possible to have more multiple partners.

Question 31
Recent research has shown that Artificial Intelligence learns a natural algorithm as if a human being at a surprisingly a fast speed.

A) NO CHANGE
B) a humankind
C) a human being does
D) as fast as human being learns

RULE #31 Hint: If-clause	**"If" is a Conjunction that Requires a Subject and a Verb.** The correct answer is C The conjunction "If" carries the subject and verb properly. D) is incorrect because "as fast as" can't link to "as if"

Question 32
In a utopian socialism labeled by Henri de Saint-Simon, both rulers and subjects define themselves as the leader of the society.

A) NO CHANGE
B) like the leaders of the society
C) as the leading people of the society

RULE #32
Hint:
Agreement

The Antecedent Agreement

The correct answer is D.
'leader' has to be plural 'leaders' to modify "the rulers and subjects."
C) is wordy error "leading people" => "leaders"

Question 33
Meticulous analysis as well as the clinical researches of Parkinson's disease reveal that the parts of the symptoms are markedly similar to Down syndrome.

A) reveal that parts of the symptoms are markedly similar to that of
B) have revealed that the parts of the symptoms are markedly similar to
C) has revealed that the parts of the symptoms are markedly similar to
D) reveals that the parts of the symptoms are markedly similar to those of

RULE #33
Hint:
Agreement

As well as/ Together with / Along with Are Not A Conjunction

The correct answer is D.
The subject is "analysis, not "analysis as well as the clinical researches."
Since "analysis" is a singular, the verb has to be a singular "reveals."

A), C) The original sentence compares "the parts" with the "Down syndrome."
"the parts of the symptoms" should be compared to those of (the parts of) "Down syndrome."

Question 34
Of the two pictures, neither the main underground reservoir in the upper valley nor the five auxiliary reservoirs on the ground level are built completely satisfactory.

A) are built completely satisfactorily.
B) is built completely satisfactorily.
C) are built completely with satisfaction.
D) is built completely with satisfaction.

RULE #34
Hint:
Correlative Conjunction

In "Neither ~ Nor," The Subject Is Placed After "Nor."

The correct answer is C.
If a subject after nor is singular, the verb has to be singular. Do not concern about a noun after "neither."

"the main underground reservoir" is not the subject, but "the five auxiliary reservoirs" is.

A) is incorrect because adverb "completely" cannot modify another adverb "satisfactorily"

Chapter 4

24 Common Patterns for *In*correct Choices in Writing

16 Precision, Concision, Style Error

This pattern asks the shortest, precise style and economic expression.

Ether too choppy or unreasonably detailed and separated clause that uses an unnecessary conjunction is incorrect.

As long as it puts all the information together into a clear sentence, the shorter choice always becomes the answer. That is, a concise sentence shouldn't contain unnecessary conjunction or dependent clause, or reduce a clause to a phrase.

Redundancy should be the number one reason to blame the incorrect choice

17 Pronoun Error

Pronoun error asks whether the sentence inappropriately changes pronoun (e.g., from 'there' to 'their', or 'he' to 'they').

This pattern also put an ambiguous pronoun on the table. (i.e., "While Jason and John were walking, he hit him." The second pronoun must be identified.

18 Punctuation Error

Punctuation pattern mainly asks if the punctuation usage (e.g., colon, semicolon, dashes, super comma, and a pair of commas) correctly represents the sentence.

Chapter 4

24 Common Patterns for *In*correct Choices in Writing

19 Redundant Error

Redundant error can be easily identified when redundancy—in either meaning or word—is made within a short proximity.

The more complex question uses an unnecessary modifier that repeats the sentence.

This type of question also asks whether a clause repeats information from the previous paragraph.

20 Restrictive Modifier (Essential Information)

Essential information should be free from commas, dashes, or parentheses that separate the main sentence.

Identify whether the modifier is restrictive (essential information) or non-restrictive (inessential information).

Please consider the following sentence:
"The great U.S. writer, *Mark Twain,* did not take official education, but wrote with intuition."

To do that, consider whether the question sentence can stand alone without needing any additional information. If the sentence is complete, the modifier—supporting phrase or clause—is non-restrictive (inessential) modifier and therefore should be offset by the punctuation.

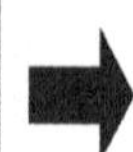

If, however, the statement in question, as in the above sentence without "Mark Twain," is ambiguous and incomplete, then the phrase or word is restrictive (essential) modifier and should be free from any punctuation.

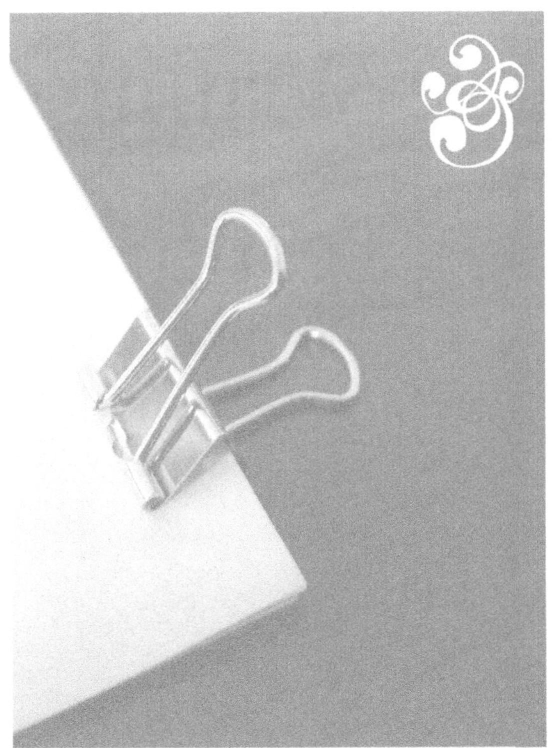

Chapter 5

1. TEST 5

2. ANSWER EXPLANATIONS for TEST 5

3. CHAPTER SUMMARY

SAT
Reading & Writing Practice
Test 5

ALL THE LOGIC AND RULES
BEHIND THE EVERY SINGLE
SAT QUESTION

Reading Test 5
65 MINUTES, 52 QUESTIONS

The passages below are followed by questions based on their content; questions following a pair of related passages may also be based on the relationship between the paired passages. Answer the questions on the basis of what is stated or implied in the passages and in any introductory material that may be provided.

Questions 1-10 are based on the following passage.

Black Girl, White Mother
Harvard University 2016 The Harvard Crimson, Inc.
Reprinted with permission.

I watched Michael Brown's mother speak to the press for the first time with my two best friends. We sat in silence, tears rolling down our cheeks, turning over the question of how this could have happened in our minds.

A year later, I held the hands of the same two girls, while we watched Tamir Rice's mother make an all too similar speech. A year before, none of us would have thought we'd be in the same position. We thought seeing and hearing one mother's overwhelming grief would be enough for this country to understand.

I should have known better, because we've seen mother after mother stand before us and try to make sense of how their babies ended up dead so early and so unfairly. It goes all the way back to Mamie Till, Emmett Till's mother, who's heartbreak was so profound that she left the casket of her 14 year old son's mutilated body open for the world to see.

We see a black mother crying about her dead child every other day.

Every time I watch the familiar hunched over body, see the bloodshot and teary eyes, hear the shaky and shallow breaths, I think of my mother. I imagine her standing in front of the hundred microphones, trying to hold it together as she thinks about her dead black baby.

I could easily be the next person considered too threatening by the police. My 5-foot-10-inch stature, pigmented skin, and smart mouth could intersect at the wrong time and wrong place and leave me bleeding out in the street.

My mother is different though.

Unlike Geneva Reed-Veal, or Sybrina Fulton, or Lucy McBath, my skin does not match that of my mother. Her skin shows bright and white, complimented by blonde hair and green eyes. I'm brown, coffee, or caramel colored.

My white mother has shaped every single part of my life. The simplest things—from how I take care of my hair, to what my ideal Thanksgiving meal looks like—are because of her. Her values, her language, her culture—they made me into the woman I am today. Her white skin gave me my lightness. It gave me my loose curls. It gave me my comfort in living and existing in the white world.

Her whiteness has characterized my life. And I don't doubt it would characterize my death too. My mother would stand in front of the nation, and cry about me, and people would listen. People would see her pain; they'd feel it twisting in their guts. Her words would carry a weight that would extend beyond a week of protest. Her words would reach beyond just the black community.

I know this because I've seen the difference having a white mother makes. I've seen it with my high school's administration, who rarely listened to my black classmates' black mothers, but always had ears for my mother. I've seen it in walking into stores and being immediately greeted versus being glanced at and ignored. I've seen it sitting on the curb, two cops in front of me, being giving the option of being escorted home instead going to the precinct after they spoke with her. After being caught red-handed breaking the law, my mother's conversation with that police officer is what prevented me from spending the night in a cell.

CONTINUE

1 1

1

"I should...known better" (line 13) implies that the author's experience in the past and present is characterized respectively as

A) conflicts to annoying
B) easily overlooked to enlightenment
C) enlightenment to conflicts
D) annoying to realization

2

The author's statement in lines 23-28 (Every time… baby.) is best characterized as

A) ironic
B) dramatic
C) nostalgic
D) celebratory

3

In lines 29-34(I could easily...different though), the author's statement conveys senses from

A) foreboding to vitality
B) adventure to justification
C) presentiment to relief
D) melancholy to absurdity

4

It can be inferred that the author's mother in lines 40-48

A) represents true vestige of humanity
B) gives more effort to protect her daughter
C) let the author dwell in normal white world
D) has a race value markedly different from other white or black people

5

The people's reaction in Lines 51-57 (My mother ...black community) highlights how people

A) are susceptible to institutional authority
B) fear their children would get killed by the police
C) should fight institutional authority when encounter injustice
D) would react differently to the same reality

6

As used in line 67, "red-handed" most nearly means

A) misconduct
B) bleeding hand
C) difficult situation
D) humiliation

7

The author repeats the word "my mother" throughout the passage in order to

A) intensify the symbols of white supremacy
B) fear of punishment for being black girl
C) mock the attitude of people
D) criticize institutional authority

8

The main purpose of the passage is to

A) defend black people's interest
B) mock the double-standards
C) search for justice
D) discover the merits of being white people

9

The author suggests that as a black woman, she

A) is exposed to higher degree of mortality
B) is proud of having a white mother
C) needs to restrain black identity
D) should pressure authority and social injustice

10

Which choice provides the best evidence for the answer to the previous question?

A) Lines 3-5 (We sat…our minds.)
B) Lines 10-12 (We thought…understand.)
C) Lines 29-30 (I could...the police)
D) Lines 40-41 (My white mother…my life.)

CONTINUE

1

Questions 11-21 are based on the following passage.

This passage is about Dichlorodiphenyltrichloroethane (DDT) and in relation to cancer and prevention pathways

Dichlorodiphenyltrichloroethane (DDT) is a colorless, tasteless, and odorless organochlorine known for its insecticidal properties. DDT has been formulated in multiple forms including smoke candles and lotions.

DDT is a persistent organic pollutant that is readily adsorbed to soils and sediments, which can act both as sinks and as long-term sources of exposure affecting organisms. Depending on conditions, its soil half-life can range from 22 days to 30 years. Routes of loss and degradation include runoff, volatilization, photolysis and aerobic and anaerobic biodegradation.

Due to hydrophobic properties, in aquatic ecosystems DDT and its metabolites are absorbed by aquatic organisms and adsorbed on suspended particles, leaving little DDT dissolved in the water. Its breakdown products and metabolites, DDE and DDD, are also persistent and have similar chemical and physical properties. DDT and its breakdown products are transported from warmer areas to the Arctic by the phenomenon of global distillation, where they then accumulate in the region's food web. Because of its lipophilic properties, DDT can bio accumulate, especially in predatory birds. DDT, DDE and DDD magnify through the food chain, with apex predators such as raptor birds concentrating more chemicals than other animals in the same environment. They are stored mainly in body fat.

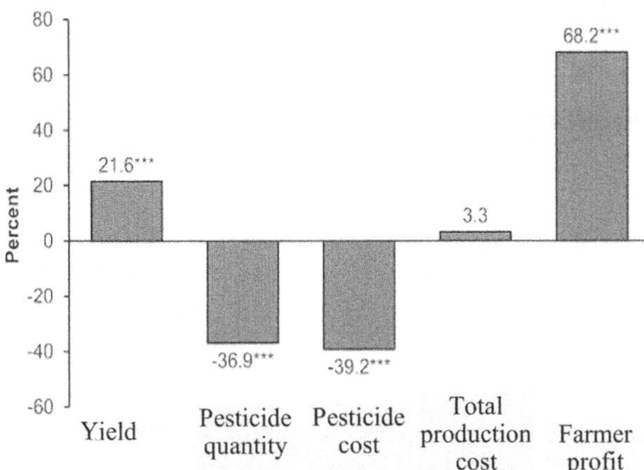

Is the Pesticide Control Helping Agricultural Productions Output?

11

The primary focus of the first two sentences (lines 1-5) is on

A) some characteristics of DDT and its usage as a product

B) a brief overview of DDT's beneficial application

C) scientific theories related with DDT

D) why DDT is not beneficial?

12

Which of the following statements about DDT is accurate?

A) Once exposed, soil's half-life of DDT may persist for over a quarter century

B) Depending on types of agricultural products, DDT may not cause damage to the produce

C) DDT, with conscionable application, may not affect human health

D) DDT's chemical property is observable

13

Which choice provides the best evidence for the answer to the previous question?

A) Lines 1-3 Dichlorodiphenyltrichloroethane ...properties.)

B) Lines 6-9 (DDT is a ....affecting lotions.)

C) Lines 10-11 (Depending on...30 years.)

D) Lines 11-14 (Routes of loss...biodegradation.)

14

According to the passage, if 10 grams of DDT insecticide absorbed in soil have undergone half-life, the original amount of DDT applied must have been

A) 20 grams applied 11 days ago.

B) 10 grams applied 22 days ago

C) 14 grams applied 22 years ago

D) 20 grams applied 30 years ago

CONTINUE

1 1

15

Which choice provides the best evidence for the answer to the previous question?

A) Lines 6-9 (DDT is a persistent…organisms.)

B) Lines 10-11 (Depending on…30 years.)

C) Lines 15-19 (Due to hydrophobic...in the water.)

D) Lines 19-22 (Its breakdown...physical properties)

16

In lines 15-19, the author suggests that the studies attempting to understand the impact of DDT on environment will produce the evidence of

A) relatively large amount of DDT residues in the contaminated water

B) DDT affected aquatic organisms in warmer areas but not in the Arctic.

C) DDT affected aquatic organisms in the Artic, but not in warmer area.

D) almost no DDT residue in the water

17

As used in line 15, "hydrophobic" most nearly means

A) suffering from an aquatic organism

B) repellant to mix with water

C) easily combined with non-aquatic organisms

D) incapable of working with fishery

18

Which of the following statements is true to lipophilic properties (line 26) ?

A) It affects relatively little to human

B) It affects almost all bird species equally

C) It prevents DDT from its accumulation

D) It affects eagle species most severely

19

According to lines 27-32, banning DDT application is important to bird species because

A) it transfers toxic substance to human

B) it magnifies toxic level in the marine animal

C) it is stored in bird's body fat

D) it can be fatal to some bird species

20

The graph presents which of the true statements?

A) When pesticide quantity decreases, farmer's profit necessarily decreases

B) Stable total production cost greatly affects the famer's profit

C) Decrease in pesticide quantity is not relevant factor to decrease in pesticide cost

D) There should be an alternative for higher yield without increasing pesticide usage

21

Which of the following statements is true about DDT?

A) DDT is toxic substance but DDE, and DDD are not

B) DDT was once used for people's skin care product

C) DDT residue inside the aquatic organisms is reduced through metabolism

D) DDT is relatively recent chemical compounds made for insecticide

CONTINUE

1 1

Questions 22-31 are based on the following passage.

The following passage is from Demian
by Hermann Hesse

I cannot tell my story without reaching a long way back. Novelists when they write novels tend to take an almost godlike attitude toward their subject, pretending to a total comprehension of the story, a man's life, which they can therefore recount as God Himself might. I am as little able to do this as the novelist is, even though my story is more important to me than any novelist's is to him for this is my story; it is the story of a man, not of an invented, or possible, or idealized, or otherwise absent figure, but of a unique being of flesh and blood.

If we were not something more than unique human beings, if each one of us could really be done away with once and for all by a single bullet, storytelling would lose all purpose. I have been and still am a seeker, but I have ceased to question stars and books; I have begun to listen to the teachings my blood whispers to me.

Each man carries the vestiges of his birth--the slime and eggshells of his primeval past--with him to the end of his days. Some never become human, remaining frog. We all share the same origin, our mothers; all of us come in at the same door. But each of us--experiments of the depths--strives toward his own destiny.

Two Realms, dark and well-lighted, I shall begin my story with an experience I had when I was ten and attended our small town's Latin school. The sweetness of many things from that time still stirs and touches me with melancholy: (alleys, houses and towers, chimes and faces, rooms rich and comfortable, warm and relaxed, rooms pregnant with secrets. Everything bears the scent of warm intimacy, servant girls, household remedies, and dried fruits. It was a realm of brilliance, clarity, and cleanliness, gentle conversations, washed hands, clean clothes, and good manners.

22

According to the passage, the thematic focus of the author's story will be

A) gaining a total comprehension of his subject
B) finding an alter ego in unique circumstance
C) finding an ultimate meaning in every detail
D) recounting man's life from God's view

23

Which choice provides the best evidence for the answer to the previous question?

A) Lines 1-2 (I cannot tell...way back.)
B) Lines 2-6 (Novelists when ...God Himself might.)
C) Lines 9-12 (for this is...flesh and blood.)
D) Lines 13-16 (If we were...all purpose.)

24

In the first paragraph (lines 1-12), the author likens his story as

A) a great artwork
B) a novel without fabrication
C) a story of any other novelist's writing
D) a novel between God and human

25

In the second paragraph (lines 13-26), the author believes other novelists' story

A) has to go a long way back in memories
B) is more like a single bullet storytelling
C) tries to assimilate with the will of nature
D) searches for the unique world's phenomena

26

In the first paragraph (lines 1-12), the author's description of his book conveys a sense of

A) adventure
B) relief
C) melancholy
D) true-to-life

CONTINUE

1 1

27

Which choice provides the best evidence for the answer to the previous question?

A) Lines 1-2 (I cannot tell...way back.)

B) Lines 2-6 (Novelists when ...God Himself might.)

C) Lines 6-9 (I am as little...is my story)

D) Lines 9-12 (it is the story...flesh and blood.)

28

The description of stars and books line 18 highlights how the author

A) wants his reader to be imbued with his life lesson

B) sees the external wonders are not as profound as introspection

C) realized books and stars contribute less to his life

D) regrets the pursuit of earthly desire

29

"frogs" in line 24 and "mothers" in line 25 probably imply between

A) qualification and generalization

B) stupid and smart

C) amphibian and mammal

D) cause and effect

30

The author's description of "Two Realms" in line 27 is defined as

A) juxtaposition

B) paradox

C) irony

D) literary allusion

31

Which of the following situations can be the other realm compared to the description of one realm in lines 27-39?

A) A world where murderer, ghost, and all the wild things happen

B) A class in which a kid is being rewarded

C) An alcove in a house where two siblings find a good hiding place

D) A mother reading a serial killer incidents from the Newspaper

Questions 32-41 are based on the following passage. The following passage is excerpted from President John Kennedy's Rice Stadium Moon Speech

No man can fully grasp how far and how fast we have come, but condense, if you will, the 50,000 years of man's recorded history in a time span of but a half-century. Stated in these terms, we know very little about the first 40 years, except at the end of them advanced man had learned to use the skins of animals to cover them. Then, only last week did we develop television, and now if America's new spacecraft succeeds in reaching Venus, we will have literally reached the stars before midnight tonight.

This is a breathtaking pace, and such a pace cannot help but create new ills as it dispels old, new ignorance, new problems, new dangers. Surely the opening vistas of space promise high costs and hardships, as well as high reward. So it is not surprising that some would have us stay where we are a little longer to rest, to wait.

But why, some say, the moon? Why does Rice play Texas? We choose to go to the moon not because they are easy, but because they are hard. We have seen facilities greatest and most complex exploration in man's history: Saturn C-1 booster rocket, generating power equivalent to 10,000 automobiles, each one as powerful as all eight engines of the Saturn combined, as tall as a 48 story structure, as wide as a city block. My fellow citizens, we shall send to the moon and then return it safely to earth, re-entering the atmosphere at speeds of over 25,000 miles per hour, causing heat about half that of the temperature of the sun--almost as hot as it is here today. I'm the one who is doing all the work, so we just want you to stay cool for a minute.

NASA R& D Budget and Its Allocations

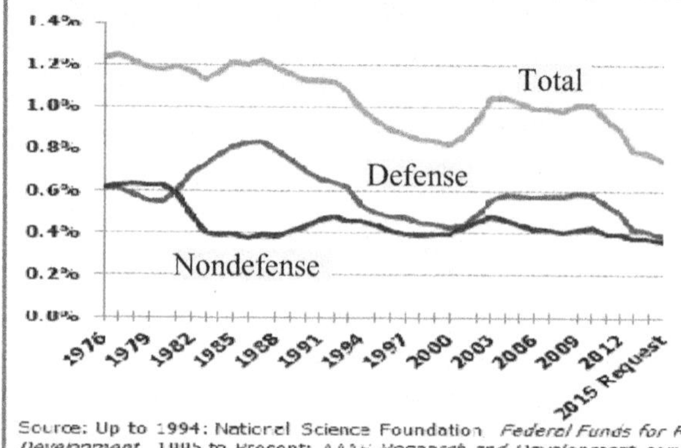

source: NASA adjusted to 2015 values

1

32

In his speech "50,000 years ..before midnight tonight," (lines 3-12) Kennedy intends to allude Kennedy alludes to the audience

A) a support for the space program
B) a precondition for public approval of the program
C) reasons for the low level of public awareness
D) some limitations that block space program

33

In the second paragraph (lines 12-18), Kennedy mentions despite of rapid advancement in space program certain obstacles should be overcome EXCEPT

A) demand from some people to delay the project
B) ignorance due to lack of information
C) high expenditure
D) restrictive government policy

34

The primary function of the first paragraph (lines 1-11) is to

A) show some of the impressive scientific achievement in human history
B) show human history through condensed time
C) introduce the speaker's main speech
D) educate some dramatic history to the audience

35

The tone of Kennedy in line 33 (so we just…for a minute) is

A) anger
B) humorous
C) didactic
D) profound

36

According to Kennedy, Rice wouldn't play Texas if

A) Texas were less challenging
B) Texas were more challenging
C) Texas were not assertive in sports
D) Texas were less progressive

37

Which choice provides the best evidence for the answer to the previous question?

A) Lines 1-2 (No man…we have come,)
B) Lines 2-4 (but condense,...a half century)
C) Lines 19 (But why, some say, the moon?)
D) Lines 20-21 (We choose...they are hard.)

38

In lines 22-27 (We have seen...a city block), Kennedy mainly describes the space project's

A) undetermined persistence
B) immensity
C) probable challenges
D) impact on society

39

In the last paragraph (lines 19-34), President Kennedy makes which of the following assumptions?

A) the local job creation
B) the old history of the city
C) the future projection
D) the size of annual income

40

Which choice provides the best evidence for the answer to the previous question?

A) Lines 19-20 (But why,...Texas?)
B) Lines 20-21 (We choose….they are hard.)
C) Lines 27-33 (My fellow citizens, …here today)
D) Lines 33-34 (I'm the one...for a minute)

41

The graph following the passage describes that

A) Defense R& D budget has continued to increase since 1976
B) Nondefense R&D budget has never exceeded defense budget since 1976
C) When nondefense budget was highest, defense budget was also highest.
D) When nondefense budget was lowest, defense budget was also lowest

CONTINUE

Questions 42-52 are based on the following passage.

Passage 1 is Excerpted from Til Death Do Us Part *Why marriage is right for me*
Harvard University (C) 2016 The Harvard Crimson, Reprinted with permission.

Passage 2 is from National Vital Statistics System

PASSAGE 1

We've all heard the statistics: Nearly half of first marriages end in divorce, women tend to be less happy in their marriages than men, bad marriages lead to heart disease, emotional suffering, etc. In fact, we've become so familiar with this scientific discourse that it seems these statistics have led to another: According to the Pew Research Center, 25 percent of millennials will "never get married." Although I'm skeptical to believe every "new study" I hear about the status of modern relationships, this one seems to be strikingly reflected in my own peer circles. Now more than ever, I hear friends happily discussing their rejection of marriage, and had taken for granted for their parents' separation.

Lately this paradigm shift in relationships has me questioning my own views: Perhaps believing in an institution that is trending toward the obsolete is foolish. After all, most of us are well aware that marriage can be a patriarchal institution intent on reinforcing and reaffirming certain backwards gender stereotypes. It is also an inherently exclusionary tradition that prohibits many loving couples from gaining certain legal protections and benefits. It seems we still value marriage as an institution.

There are many explanations for why this may be. Part of it is historical—marriage is a time-honored tradition of affirming a romantic relationship. Part of it is political—marriage accords a legal legitimacy to a relationship that allows for numerous social and financial benefits. And yet another part of it is religious or cultural. But what if we were to wash away. I am still inclined to believe that there's value in marriage beyond any of the social or financial benefits it offers. Unlike some of my peers, I look forward to the day when I can stand before my family and friends and say, "This is the person I choose.

PASSAGE 2

Divorce is associated with diminished psychological well-being in children and adult offspring of divorced parents, including greater unhappiness, less satisfaction with life, weaker sense of personal control, anxiety, depression, and greater use of mental health services. A preponderance of evidence indicates that there is a causal effect between divorce and these outcomes.

A study found that children living with just one parent after divorce suffer from more problems such as headaches, stomach aches, feelings of tension and sadness than those whose parents share custody.

Children of divorced parents are also more likely to experience conflict in their own marriages, and are more likely to experience divorce themselves. They are also more likely to be involved in short-term cohabiting relationships, which often dissolve before marriage.

There are many studies that show proof of an intergenerational transmission of divorce or staying single over prolonged period of time after the adulthood, especially when marriage was not bound by financial or religious foundation, but solely on brief romantic emotion to the partner. This doesn't mean that having divorced parents will absolutely lead a child to divorce.

There are two key factors that make this transmission of divorce more likely. First, inherited biological tendencies or genetic conditions may predispose a child to divorce as well as the "model of marriage" presented by the child's parents. At any age divorce can be difficult to handle emotionally. Everyone reacts differently and not everyone is a statistic, but the way they handle it can be shown in may different ways and it may turn out that "divorce tends to intensify the child's dependence and it tends to accelerate the adolescent's independence" pulling from the psychology article written by Carl E Pickhardt Ph.D. which is very true on the fact that divorce accelerates the rate of independence.

CONTINUE

1

42

In lines 12, the author of Passage 1 uses the word "my own peer circles." to suggest that the trend is

A) very recognizable

B) known to the author's peer circles

C) atypical

D) outdated

43

The author of Passage 1 finds marriage is still valued for all the reasons EXCEPT

A) Political

B) Monetary

C) Romantic

D) Cultural

44

The author of Passage 2 may view the author's friends in line 12 (my own peer circles) as they are

A) responding to intergenerational transmission conditions

B) defying patriarchal custom

C) experiencing excessive emotional suffering

D) one example of a quarter of millennials' view on marriage

45

Which choice provides the best evidence for the answer to the previous question?

A) Lines 40-46 (Divorce is …health services.)

B) Lines 47-49 (A preponderance of...outcomes.)

C) Lines 50-54 (A study found…share custody.)

D) Lines 62--65 (There are many…the adulthood.)

46

Unlike Passage 2, the author of Passage 1 develops an argument by relying on

A) personal contemplation

B) psychological observation

C) scientific evidence

D) citation from other source

47

How would the author of the Passage 2 respond to the author's statement in lines 34-36 (I am...it offers)?

A) Women should accept marriage is a patriarchal institution

B) Short-term cohabiting relationships is one way to find true love

C) For long-term relationships, love is not the only factor in marriage.

D) Feeling loving is the surest way to secure marriage

48

Which choice provides the best evidence for the answer to the previous question?

A) Lines 50-54 (A study found…parents share custody.)

B) Lines 62--68 (There are many…to the partner.)

C) Lines 68-70 (This doesn't mean...a child to divorce)

D) Lines 71-72 (There are two...more likely.)

49

The word "preponderance" in line 48 most nearly means

A) greater quality

B) limited

C) greater quantity

D) serious

50

Which of the following analogies best <u>refute</u> the author's assertion about "cohabiting" in line 60?

A) A shopkeeper speculates to be the owner of the shop

B) A mathematician formulates a simple theory in the same realm with the big theory, which he proves it later with the simple one.

C) A dog practices sheep herding into a pen before sold to a new owner who is sheep herder.

D) A boy tried to save allowance to buy a robot but ends up spending all.

1

1 1

51

Which of the following statements would both authors agree?

A) genetic conditions may predispose a person to divorce

B) love is a primary factor to maintain strong marriage

C) divorce affects a great deal on child's psychological development

D) psychological suffering is evident after divorce

52

The author of Passage 2 refers the adolescent's independence (line 81) in order to illustrate

A) an effective way to develop youth's independence

B) some paradoxical outcome of divorce

C) the reason divorce can't be tolerated to adolescents

D) a way to destroy the youth's independence

STOP

If you finish before time is called,
you may check your work on this section.

Do not turn to the next section.

Writing and Language Test 5
35 MINUTES, 44 QUESTIONS

Each passage below is accompanied by a number of questions. For some questions, you will consider how the passage might be revised to improve the expression of ideas. For other questions, you will consider how the passage might be edited to correct errors in sentence structure, usage, or punctuation. A passage or a question may be accompanied by one or more graphics (such as a table or graph) that you will consider as you make revising and editing decisions.

Questions 1-11 are based on the following passage.

Let's Engage the Silent Majority

I didn't expect Donald Trump to be President of the United States. I hoped and prayed he would lose. Throughout the election cycle, I tried to remain detached from the endless fear and bigotry that seemed to spew out of the Trump political machine. For me, my parents, and my community, this election was too personal, even though I tried to be detached from this fear. [1]

I am an undocumented [2] immigrant, one of the many directly under threat in Donald Trump's plan to deport all 11.5 million undocumented immigrants in the United States.

1

The author is thinking of deleting the underlined clause "even though...this fear" from the preceding sentence. Should he make this decision?

A) Yes, because this clause is unnecessary.

B) Yes, because the sentence is more focused without this clause.

C) No, because this clause describes the author's subconscious anxiety.

D) No, because this clause provides unidentified new information without evidence.

2

A) NO CHANGE

B) immigrant. One

C) immigrant, who is one

D) immigrant; one

CONTINUE

2 2

In addition, I am a visa-overstayer—one of about 4.6 million **that** he would prioritize [3] Trump has said in his deportation **campaign**. I'm terrified of my place in this country and am crippled by the seeming inevitability of the sweeping actions on immigration Trump has promised to the American people. He says he will cancel DACA, cancel funding to sanctuary cities, [4] and deport me, my parents, and members of my community. But in the face of uncertainty and overwhelming despondency, I refuse to be silenced.

President Trump directly threatens the physical and emotional wellbeing of me and all other undocumented people living in the US. [5] His presidency is built on a fundamental misunderstanding of the immigration system, on the notion that the nation's supposed vulnerability is the fault of undocumented immigrants, Muslims, and Latinos.

I don't write to concede defeat in the face of bigotry—our community will not be silent as our families are separated and our livelihoods dismantled. [6] You may write to ask for Donald Trump's pity or compassion when it comes to immigration.

3

The best placement for the underlined portion would be:

A) NO CHANGE
B) after the word In addition
C) after the word that
D) after the word campaign.

4

The author is thinking of removing the underlined portion. If he removes it, the paragraph would lose:

A) A shift in the mood from concern to reality
B) Overall summary of the paragraph
C) A shift in the mood from general to personal
D) A signal of hope

5

Which choice most efficiently introduces the description that follows in this sentence?

A) NO CHANGE
B) Members of my community support Trump,
C) Latinos attribute this consequence to Muslims,
D) His new immigration policy will not make immediate impact on the immigration system,

6

A) NO CHANGE
B) If I have time and courage, I will
C) I will not proclaim to
D) Neither do I

CONTINUE

2 2

I speak to my fellow undocumented Americans [7]directly and unswervingly, but my message is for everyone: Let us begin a dialogue with those who seek to suppress and deport us. For many who celebrate Trump, this election is a reassertion of their belief that undocumented immigrants do not deserve a place in this country. It is counterproductive (and impossible) to insulate ourselves from these voices, especially now that their views have been legitimized by the President himself. [8] We will be deported soon anyway. As undocumented immigrants, [9] I cannot crave to be part of U.S. citizens right away. Our immigration status is [10] fortunately tied up in our identity, so that we cannot exist without drawing attention to the systems that define us, the systems [11] by which this world—our world, the world we share with all those around us—is built. Just by living and breathing in America, we create pressure, we force reexamination, and therefore we are seen as a threat. Perhaps the hardest part of being undocumented is understanding that our futures depend on the worldviews and political leanings of other people.

7

A) NO CHANGE
B) directly,
C) directly based upon unswervingness
D) in direct motion

8

Which one best illustrates the author's emotional state?

A) NO CHANGE
B) We must engage.
C) We must accept the reality and respect Trump's decision.
D) The only way that we can legitimate ourselves is to leave the country.

9

A) NO CHANGE
B) exploiting politics is beyond our reach.
C) to raise political voice is next to impossible
D) we don't choose to be political

10

A) NO CHANGE
B) unexpectedly
C) undoubtedly
D) inextricably

11

A) NO CHANGE
B) on which
C) through which
D) from which

CONTINUE

2 2

Questions 12-22 are based on the following passage.

Oil Spill

An oil spill is the release of a liquid petroleum hydro-carbon into the environment, especially marine areas, [12] due to human activity, and is a form of pollution. The term is usually applied to marine oil spills, where oil is released into the ocean or coastal waters, but spills may also occur on land.

[13] Crude oil spill release from tankers offshore platforms, drilling rigs and wells, and spills of refined petroleum products (such as gasoline, diesel) and their by-products—[14] many such oil spills damage our environment to the irreversible point.

Oil spills penetrate into the structure of the plumage of birds and the fur of mammals, reducing its insulating ability, and making them more vulnerable to temperature fluctuations [15] but much less buoyant in the water.

12

Which of the following alternatives is NOT acceptable?

A) because of

B) because

C) result of

D) caused by

13

A) NO CHANGE

B) Crude oil spill release from tankers;

C) Crude oil spill release from tankers,

D) Crude oil spill release from tankers—

14

Which choice most effectively establishes threats to the environment?

A) NO CHANGE

B) oil spill removal process involves enormous work as expansive as the ocean, but it's by far the most effective solution.

C) it is irony that major oil refinery companies have cleanup companies, which generate revenue by the oil spills made by their parent company.

D) government policy has become strict enough to control the damage to the environment.

15

A) NO CHANGE

B) and

C) yet

D) resulting

CONTINUE

2 2

Cleanup and recovery from an oil spill are difficult [16] ,and depends upon many factors, including the type of oil spilled, the temperature of the water (affecting evaporation and biodegradation), and the types of shorelines and beaches involved.

[17] Technology that controls the ocean temperature to prevent evaporation and biodegradation is considered as state-of-the-art technology. Oil spills can have disastrous consequences for society [18] ; economically, environmentally, and socially.

16

A) NO CHANGE
B) and depend
C) , which depends
D) that depends

17

Which one provides details that best help the reader understand enormous tasks for oil clean up

A) NO CHANGE
B) Generally, over 70% of accidents occur in the ocean
C) Spills may take weeks, months or even years to clean up.
D) Over the last few decades, oil spill clean up technology has experienced dramatic advancement

18

A) NO CHANGE
B) : economically, environmentally, and socially.
C) ,environmentally economical and social.
D) economically, environmentally, socially.

CONTINUE

2

[19] As a result, oil spill accidents have initiated intense media attention and political uproar, bringing many together in a political struggle concerning government response to oil spills and [20] air pollution control in major cities in coastal area. Crude oil and refined fuel spills from tanker ship accidents have damaged vulnerable ecosystems in Alaska, the Gulf of Mexico, the Galapagos Islands, France, the Sundarbans, Ogoniland, and many other places.

19

A) NO CHANGE
B) In the meantime,
C) Then,
D) For example,

20

Which choice is most consistent with the previous portion of the sentence?

A) NO CHANGE
B) increase in budget to develop renewable energy source
C) what actions can best prevent them from happening.
D) energy conserving education to the public

21

Suppose the author's goal was to write a brief summary illustrating the hazardous impact of oil spills.
Would this summary fulfill the author's goal?

A) Yes, because the summary offers some of the consequences that oil spill creates
B) Yes, because the summary encourages establishing more strict government policy against oil spill prevention
C) No, because the summary focuses more on economic impact than on environmental impact
D) No, because the summary also represents struggles oil refinery companies experience to meet the government environment standards

CONTINUE

2 2

*Oil spill control guidelines for the surface area of shorelines				
Film thickness			Quantity spread	
Appearance	inches	mm	nm	gal/ sq. mi
Barely visible	0.0000015	0.0000380	38	25
Silvery sheen	0.0000030	0.0000760	76	50
First trace of color	0.0000060	0.0001500	150	100
Bright bands of color	0.0000120	0.0003000	300	200
Colors begin to dull	0.00004	0.0010000	1000	666
Colors are much darker	0.0000800	0.0020000	2000	1332

22

Please refer to the table and the passage.

In order to estimate quantity of oil spilled, all of following the variables must be available EXCEPT

A) Oil film thickness

B) Quantity spread

C) Total surface area

D) Direction of wind and current

CONTINUE

2 2

Questions 23-33 are based on the following passage.

An Advanced Practice Registered Nurse

An advanced practice registered nurse (APRN) [23] ,which is a nurse with post-graduate education in nursing. APRNs are prepared with advanced didactic and clinical education, knowledge, skills, and scope of practice in nursing.

<1>In 2004, It recommended that advanced practice registered nurses move the entry level degree to the doctorate level by 2015. <2>APRN defines a level of nursing practice [24] that utilizes extended and expanded skills in assessment, planning, diagnosis and evaluation of the care required. <3>Nurses practicing at this level are educationally prepared at the post-graduate level [25] upon completion of post-graduate programs. <4> It also defines the basis of advanced practice is the high degree of knowledge, skill, and experience that [27] apply to the nurse-patient/client relationship.

23

A) NO CHANGE
B) was
C) is
D) OMIT the underlined portion

24

Which of the following alternatives would NOT be acceptable?

A) ,which utilizes
B) utilizing
C) utilized
D) —utilizing

25

A) NO CHANGE
B) , once they are professionally ready.
C) if they are well-prepared in the post-graduate level programs.
D) OMIT the underlined portion.

26

Which of the following is most logical sequences of this paragraph?

A) NO CHANGE
B) <1>,<4>,<2>,<3>
C) <2>,<3>,<1>,<4>
D) <2>,<3>,<4>,<1>

27

A) NO CHANGE
B) are utilizable and applicable
C) is applied
D) are applied

CONTINUE

2 2

APRNs [28],who demonstrate effective integration of theory, practice and experiences [29] along with increasing degrees of autonomy in judgments and interventions. Intensive post-graduate education is designed to teach an APRN to use multiple approaches to decision-making, manage the care of individuals and groups, [30] to engage in collaborative practices with the patient or client to achieve best outcomes. Each nurse specialty, especially NPs, can have sub-specialties or concentrations in a specific field or patient population in healthcare, [31] each of them has a unique history and context, but shares the commonality of being an APRN.

28

A) NO CHANGE
B) ,which demonstrate
C) demonstrate
D) demonstrates

29

Which of the following alternatives to the underlined portion would NOT be acceptable?

A) together with
B) plus
C) as well as
D) in company with

30

A) NO CHANGE
B) engaging
C) engage
D) by engaging

31

A) NO CHANGE
B) each of which
C) each and every single NP
D) and each of which

CONTINUE

2 2

[32] Because education, accreditation, and certification are necessary components of an overall approach to preparing an APRN for practice, these roles are regulated by legislation and specific professional regulation. While APRNs are educated differently depending on their specific specialty, all APRNs are now trained at the graduate level and are required to attain at least a master's degree.

[33] International Council of Nurses established such regulations only in 1977.

32

Which alternative word is NOT acceptable?

A) For

B) As

C) Since

D) Although

33

Which choice provides an accurate and effective summary of this paragraph?

A) NO CHANGE

B) A registered nurse who has acquired the expert knowledge must maintain high work ethics.

C) An advanced practice registered nurse (APRN) is generally considered high paying job.

D) Generally, a Master of Science in Nursing is their field of concentration.

CONTINUE

2 2

Questions 34-44 are based on the following passage.

Black Cat By Edgar Allan Poe

From my infancy I was noted for the docility and humanity of my disposition. I was especially fond of animals, and was indulged by my parents with a great variety of pets. With these I spent most of my time, and never was so happy [34] when feeding and caressing them. To those [35],whom have cherished affection for a faithful and sagacious dog, I [36] need hardly be at the trouble of explaining the nature or the intensity of the gratification thus derivable. There is something in the unselfish and self-sacrificing love of a brute, which goes directly to the heart of him who has had frequent occasion to test the paltry friendship and gossamer fidelity of mere Man. I married early, and [37] in my wife was happy to **find** a **disposition** not uncongenial with my **own**.

34

A) NO CHANGE
B) as when
C) that when
D) than when

35

A) NO CHANGE
B) ; whom
C) , who
D) who

36

Which of the following alternatives would NOT be acceptable?

A) need scarcely
B) need not
C) hardly don't need to
D) don't need to

37

The best placement for the underlined portion would be:

A) NO CHANGE
B) after the word find
C) after the word disposition
D) after the word own

CONTINUE

2

[38] With my partiality for domestic pets being observed, she lost no opportunity of procuring those of the most agreeable kind. We had birds, gold fish, a fine dog, rabbits, a small monkey, and a cat.

This latter was a remarkably large and beautiful animal, entirely black, and sagacious to an astonishing degree. In speaking of his intelligence, my wife, who at heart was not a little tinctured with superstition, made frequent allusion to the ancient popular notion [39] that domestic pets owners reduce their mental depression up to 20%.

Pluto — this was the cat's name — was my favorite pet and playmate. I alone fed him, and he attended me wherever I went about the house. It was even with difficulty that I could prevent him [40] to following me through the streets.

Our friendship lasted, in this manner, for several years, [41] during which period my general temperament and character — through the instrumentality of the Fiend Intemperance — had (I blush to confess it) experienced a radical alteration for the worse.

38

A) NO CHANGE
B) Observing my partiality for domestic pets,
C) I gave partiality for domestic pets,
D) I gave partiality for domestic pets, which

39

Which one further illustrates the narrator's comments about ancient popular notion?

A) NO CHANGE
B) ,*which regarded* all black cats as witches in disguise.
C) that my parents used to tell me when I was young.
D) , which lingered in my mind always.

40

A) NO CHANGE
B) from
C) with
D) DELETE IT

41

A) NO CHANGE
B) during
C) and
D) however

CONTINUE

2 2

I suffered myself to use intemperate language at length, I even offered her personal violence. My pets, [42] of course, were made to feel the change in my disposition. I not only neglected, but ill-used them. For Pluto[43], however, I still retained sufficient regard to restrain me from maltreating him, as I made no scruple of maltreating the rabbits, the monkey, or even the dog, when by accident, or through affection, they came in my way. But my disease grew upon me — for what disease is like Alcohol! — and at length even Pluto, who was now becoming old, [44] additionally somewhat peevish — even Pluto began to experience the effects of my ill temper.

42

Which of the following alternatives would NOT be acceptable?

A) gradually,

B) naturally,

C) sadly,

D) affectionately,

43

A) NO CHANGE

B) ; however,

C) however,

D) however

44

A) NO CHANGE

B) consequently

C) basically

D) necessarily

STOP

If you finish before time is called,
you may check your work on this section.

Do not turn to the next section.

SAT Test 5
Answer Explanations
&
Pattern Analyses

If your Test 5 scores are unsatisfactory,

Test 6,7, won't be satisfactory either.

Please Practice the Answer Explanations and then come back to Test 7 again.

ALL THE LOGIC AND RULES BEHIND EVERY SINGLE SAT QUESTION

SAT Test 5

Reading Section Answer Explanations

&

Pattern Analyses

Questions 1-11 are based on the following passage.

I watched Michael Brown's mother speak to the press for the first time with my two best friends. We sat in silence, tears rolling down our cheeks, turning over the question of how this could have happened in our minds.

A year later, I held the hands of the same two girls, while we watched Tamir Rice's mother make an all too similar speech. A year before, none of us would have thought we'd be in the same position. We thought seeing and hearing one mother's overwhelming grief would be enough for this country to understand.

(1B) **I should have known better**, because we've seen mother after mother stand before us and try to make sense of how their babies ended up dead so early and so unfairly. It goes all the way back to Mamie Till, Emmett Till's mother, who's heartbreak was so profound that she left the casket of her 14 year old son's mutilated body open for the world to see.

We see a black mother crying about her dead child every other day.(2B) **Every time I watch the familiar hunched over body, see the bloodshot and teary eyes, hear the shaky and shallow breaths, I think of my mother**.

I imagine her standing in front of the hundred microphones, trying to hold it together as she thinks about her dead black baby. (3C&9A&10C) **I could easily be the next person considered too threatening by the police. My 5-foot-10-inch stature, pigmented skin, and smart mouth could intersect at the wrong time and wrong place and leave me bleeding out in the street.**

(7C) **My mother is different though.**

Unlike Geneva Reed-Veal, or Sybrina Fulton, or Lucy McBath, my skin does not match that of my mother. Her skin shows bright and white, complimented by blonde hair and green eyes. I'm brown, coffee, or caramel colored.

My white mother has shaped every single part of my life. The simplest things—from how I take care of my hair, to what my ideal Thanksgiving meal looks like—are because of her. Her values, her language, her culture—they made me into the woman I am today.

(4C) **Her white skin gave me my lightness. It gave me my loose curls. It gave me my comfort in living and existing in the white world.**

Her whiteness has characterized my life. And I don't doubt it would characterize my death too.

My mother would stand in front of the nation, and cry about me, and people would listen.

People would see her pain; they'd feel it twisting in their guts. Her words would carry a weight that would extend beyond a week of protest. Her words would reach beyond just the black community.

(5D&8B) **I know this because I've seen the difference having a white mother makes.** I've seen it with my high school's administration, who rarely listened to my black classmates' black mothers, but always had ears for my mother. I've seen it in walking into stores and being immediately greeted versus being glanced at and ignored. I've seen it sitting on the curb, two cops in front of me, being giving the option of being escorted home instead going to the precinct after they spoke with her. After being (6A) **caught red-handed breaking the law**, my mother's conversation with that police officer is what prevented me from spending the night in a cell.

Q1 **Absolute Pattern 2: Summary Question** Summarizing a sentence, or an entire paragraph
Question Pattern: The author's comment in line 13 (**I should...known better**) implies that the author's experience in the past and present is characterized respectively as

A) conflicts to annoying **B) easily overlooked to enlightenment** C) enlightenment to conflicts D) annoying to realization	B) We thought seeing and hearing one mother's overwhelming grief would be enough **(easily overlooked)** for this country to understand. I should have known better (**enlightenment**) C) is what she has realized now.

Q2. **Absolute Pattern 7: Understanding Attitude (Tone) Question**
Question Pattern: The author's statement in lines 23-28 (**Every time...baby.**) is best characterized as

A) ironic **B) dramatic** C) nostalgic D) celebratory	B) Every time I watch the familiar hunched over body, see the bloodshot and teary eyes, hear the shaky and shallow breaths, I think of my mother. I imagine her standing in front of the hundred microphones, trying to hold it together as she thinks about her dead black baby. (C) means homesickness D) is Opposite

Q3. **Absolute Pattern 7: Understanding Attitude (Tone) Question**
Question Pattern: In lines 29-34(**I could easily...different though**), the author's statement conveys senses from

A) foreboding to vitality B) adventure to justification **C) presentiment to relief** D) melancholy to absurdity	C) She believes that her mother's White identity is not going to let her get killed **(presentiment)** like other black children (**relief**).

Q4. **Absolute Pattern 3: Inference Question** Finding an indirect suggestion (or guessing)
Question Pattern: It can be inferred that the **author's mother** in lines 40-48

A) represents true vestige of humanity B) gives more effort to protect her daughter **C) let the author dwell in normal white world** D) has a race value markedly different from other white or black people	C) Her white skin gave me my lightness. ..It gave me my comfort in living and existing in the white world. *The author reveals her feeling through twisted sense of humor and sarcasm, which are different from (A) humanity, (B) protection, or (D) race value

Q5. **Absolute Pattern 3: Inference Question** Finding an indirect suggestion (or guessing)
Question Pattern: The **people's reaction** in lines 51-57 (**My mother...black community**) highlights how people

A) are susceptible to institutional authority B) fear their children would get killed by the police C) should fight institutional authority when encounter injustice **D) would react differently to the same reality**	D) I know this because I've seen the difference having a white mother makes. *Behind the author's statement are twisted with sarcasm, humor, melancholy, and sadness. How people would react to her white mother is not her true argument, but rather how people are biased, bigotry, and react differently.

Q6. **Absolute Pattern 5: Word-In-Context Question**
Question Pattern: As used in line 67, "**red-handed**" most nearly means

A) misconduct B) bleeding hand C) difficult situation D) humiliation	A) After being caught red-handed breaking the law, my mother's conversation with that police officer is what prevented me from spending the night in a cell. (B) is too literal implication. (C) is too weak, (D) is unrelated word

Q7. **Absolute Pattern 10: Understanding the Structure of the Passage**
Finding the structure of the entire passage or organizational relations between the paragraphs
Question Pattern: The author **repeats the word "my mother"** throughout the passage in order to

A) intensify the symbols of white supremacy B) fear of punishment for being black girl **C) mock the attitude of people** D) criticize institutional authority	C) The author is mocking the duplicity of the people. The essay is written by a black female who has a White mother. She betrays her feeling through sarcasm and satirical sketch pervade in society.

Q8. **Absolute Pattern 1: Main Idea Question** Finding the main idea of the entire passage or the paragraph
Question Pattern: The **main purpose** of the passage is to

A) defend black people's interest **B) mock the double-standards** C) search for justice D) discover the merits of being white people	B) I know this because I've seen the difference having a white mother makes. I've seen it... I've seen it in walking into stores...I've seen it sitting on... A) This question is also a part of inference question. If too literal, then disqualified.

Q9. **Absolute Pattern 2: Summary Question** Summarizing a sentence, or an entire paragraph **Question Pattern:** The author suggests that as **a black woman, she**	
A) is exposed to higher degree of mortality B) is proud of having a white mother C) needs to restrain black identity D) should pressure authority and social injustice	A) I could easily be the next person considered too threatening by the police. My 5-foot-10-inch stature, pigmented skin, and smart mouth could intersect at the wrong time and wrong place and leave me bleeding out in the street

Q10. **Absolute Pattern 11: Textual Evidence Question** Finding evidence for the previous question **Question Pattern:** Which choice provides the best evidence for the answer to the previous question?	
A) Lines 3-5 (We sat…our minds.) B) Lines 10-12 (We thought…understand.) **C) Lines 29-30 (I could...the police)** D) Lines 40-41 (My white mother…my life.)	C) Please refer to the above question

Questions 11-21 are based on the following passage.

Dichlorodiphenyltrichloroethane (DDT) is a colorless, tasteless, and odorless organochlorine known for its insecticidal properties. DDT has been formulated in multiple forms (11A& 21B) **including smoke candles and lotions.**

DDT is a persistent organic pollutant that is readily adsorbed to soils and sediments, which can act both as sinks and as long-term sources of exposure affecting organisms. (12A&13C&14D&15B) **Depending on conditions, its soil half-life can range from 22 days to 30 years.** Routes of loss and degradation include runoff, volatilization, photolysis and aerobic and anaerobic biodegradation.

Due to hydrophobic properties, in aquatic ecosystems DDT and its metabolites are absorbed by aquatic organisms and adsorbed on suspended particles, (16D&17B) **leaving little DDT dissolved in the water.** Its breakdown products and metabolites, DDE and DDD, are also persistent and have similar chemical and physical properties. DDT and its breakdown products are transported from warmer areas to the Arctic by the phenomenon of global distillation, where they then accumulate in the region's food web.

Because of its lipophilic properties, (18D&19D) **DDT can bio accumulate, especially in predatory birds. DDT, DDE and DDD magnify through the food chain, with apex predators such as raptor birds concentrating more chemicals than other animals in the same environment. They are stored mainly in body fat.**

Q11. **Absolute Pattern 2: Summary Question** Summarizing a sentence or entire passage **Question Pattern:** The **primary focus of the first two sentences** (lines 1-5) is on	
A) some characteristics of DDT and its usage as a product B) a brief overview of DDT's beneficial application C) scientific theories related with DDT D) why DDT is not beneficial?	A) colorless, crystalline, tasteless, and almost odorless...properties and environmental impacts. DDT has been formulated in multiple forms, including lotions... *The first half of the paragraph discusses DDT's characteristics and the second half, DDT as a product.

Q12. **Absolute Pattern 2: Summary Question** **Question Pattern:** Which of the following statements about **DDT is true?**	
A) Once exposed, soil's half-life of DDT may persist for over a quarter century B) Depending on types of agricultural products, DDT may not cause damage to the produce C) DDT, with conscionable application, may not affect human health D) DDT's chemical property is observable	A) the soil's half-life goes as long as 30 years. All other options are opposite and positive, which is contrary to the passage

Q13. **Absolute Pattern 3: Inference Question** Finding an indirect suggestion (or guessing) **Question Pattern:** Which choice provides the best evidence for the answer to the previous question?	
A) Lines 1-3 Dichlorodiphenyltrichloroethane…properties.) B) Lines 6-9 (DDT is a ….affecting lotions.) **C) Lines 10-11 (Depending on…30 years.)** D) Lines 11-14 (Routes of loss...biodegradation.)	C) , its soil half-life can range from 22 days to **30 years**

Q14. **Absolute Pattern 3: Inference Question** Finding an indirect suggestion (or guessing) **Question Pattern:** According to the passage, **if 10 grams of DDT insecticide absorbed in soil have undergone half-life, the original amount of DDT applied must have been**	
A) 20 grams applied 11 days ago B) 10 grams applied 22 days ago C) 14 grams applied 22 years ago **D) 20 grams applied 30 years ago**	D) Depending on conditions, its soil half-life can range from 22 days to 30 years. *10 grams of DDT undergone half-life should have originally been applied with appx. 20 grams between 22 days to 30 years ago

Q15. **Absolute Pattern 2: Summary Question** Summarizing a sentence or entire passage **Question Pattern:** Which choice provides the best evidence for the answer to the previous question?	
A) Lines 6-9 (DDT is a persistent…organisms.) **B) Lines 10-11 (Depending on…30 years.)** C) Lines 15-19 (Due to hydrophobic...in the water.) D) Lines 19-22 (Its breakdown...physical properties.)	B) Please refer to the above question

Q16. **Absolute Pattern 2: Summary Question** **Question Pattern:** In lines 15-19, the author suggests that the studies **attempting to understand the impact of DDT on environment will produce the evidence** of	
A) relatively large amount of DDT residues in the contaminated water B) DDT affected aquatic organisms in warmer areas but not in the Arctic. C) DDT affected aquatic organisms in the Artic, but not in warmer area. **D) almost no DDT residue in the water**	D) leaving little DDT dissolved in the water. DDE and DDD, DDT and its breakdown products are (B) transported from warmer areas to the Arctic

Q17. **Absolute Pattern 5: Word-In-Context Question** **Question Pattern:** As used in line 15, "**hydrophobic**" most nearly means	
A) suffering from an aquatic organism **B) repellant to mix with water** C) easily combined with non-aquatic organisms D) incapable of working with fishery	B) Due to hydrophobic properties, in aquatic ecosystems DDT and its metabolites are absorbed by aquatic organisms and adsorbed on suspended particles, leaving little DDT dissolved in the water. "hydro" means water and "phobic" means extreme fear. That is, DDT fears of water or simply does not mix with water. DDT leftover will be absorbed by animals or fish instead of residing in water.

Q19. **Absolute Pattern 2: Summary Question** Summarizing a sentence, or an entire paragraph **Question Pattern:** According to lines 27-32, **banning DDT application is important to bird** species because	
A) it transfers toxic substance to human B) it magnifies toxic level in the marine animal C) it is stored in bird's body fat **D) it can be fatal to some bird species**	D) DDT can bio accumulate, especially in predatory birds.

(A): The question asks relationship between bird species and DDT application. It asks why it is harmful to bird, not to human

(B): Bird does not transfer toxic substance to marine animals. It could be logical if the situation were reversed.

(C): is true statement, but it is a premise not the consequence. The passage warns DDT chemical is stored in body fat of bird species. The consequence is obvious. It can be fatal to the predatory species.

Q20. Absolute Pattern 12: Informational Graphs Finding facts described in the graphs or relations between the passage and the graph. Question Pattern: The graph presents which of **the true statements**?	
A) When pesticide quantity decreases, farmer's profit necessarily decreases B) Stable total production cost greatly affects the famer's profit C) Decrease in pesticide quantity is not relevant factor to decrease in pesticide cost **D) There should be an alternative for higher yield without increasing pesticide usage**	D) *It is logical to assume that there is an alternative to boost high yield because pesticide consumption decreased dramatically while increasing the yields. (A), (B), (C) are all opposite perception

Q21. **Absolute Pattern 2: Summary Question** Summarizing a sentence or entire passage **Question Pattern:** Which of the following statements is **true about DDT?**	
A) DDT is toxic substance but DDE, and DDD are not **B) DDT was once used for people's skin care product** C) DDT residue inside the aquatic organisms is reduced through metabolism D) DDT is relatively recent chemical compounds made for insecticide	B) DDT has been formulated in multiple forms **including smoke candles and lotions.** (A) Its breakdown products and metabolites, DDE and DDD, A) DDT, DDE, and DDD are all basically the same substances. C) is opposite. It won't reduce. D) DDT was introduced during WWII.

Questions 22-31 are based on the following passage.

<table>
<tr>
<td>I cannot tell my story without reaching a long way back. Novelists when they write novels tend to take an almost godlike attitude toward their subject, pretending to a total comprehension of the story, a man's life, which they can therefore recount as God Himself might. I am as little able to do this as the novelist is, even though my story is more important to me than any novelist's is to him-- (22B &23C&26D&27D) for this is my story; it is the story of a man, (24B) not of an invented, or possible, or idealized, or otherwise absent figure, but of a unique being of flesh and blood.
(25B) If we were not something more than unique human beings, if each one of us could really be done away with once and for all by a single bullet, storytelling would lose all purpose. I have been and still am a seeker, (28B) but I have ceased to question stars and books; I have begun to listen to the teachings my blood whispers to me.</td>
<td>Each man carries the vestiges of his birth--the slime and eggshells of his primeval past--with him to the end of his days. (29A) Some never become human, remaining frog. We all share the same origin, our mothers; all of us come in at the same door. But each of us--experiments of the depths--strives toward his own destiny.
Two Realms, (30A&31A) dark and well-lighted, I shall begin my story with an experience I had when I was ten and attended our small town's Latin school. The sweetness of many things from that time still stirs and touches me with melancholy: (alleys, houses and towers, chimes and faces, rooms rich and comfortable, warm and relaxed, rooms pregnant with secrets. Everything bears the scent of warm intimacy, servant girls, household remedies, and dried fruits. It was a realm of brilliance, clarity, and cleanliness, gentle conversations, washed hands, clean clothes, and good manners. .</td>
</tr>
</table>

<table>
<tr><td colspan="2">Q22. Absolute Pattern 2: Summary Question Summarizing a sentence or entire passage
Question Pattern: According to the passage, the thematic focus of the author's story will be</td></tr>
<tr><td>A) gaining a total comprehension of his subject
B) finding an alter ego in unique circumstance
C) finding an ultimate meaning in every detail
D) recounting man's life from God's view</td><td>B) for this is my story; it is the story of a man, not of an invented, or possible, or idealized.
A), C), and D) are direct opposite in that the author speaks about how other novelists write stories in line 1-5 .</td></tr>
<tr><td colspan="2">Q23. Absolute Pattern 11: Textual Evidence Question Finding evidence for the previous question
Question Pattern: Which choice provides the best evidence for the answer to the previous question?</td></tr>
<tr><td>A) Lines 1-2 (I cannot tell...way back.)
B) Lines 2-6 (Novelists when ...God Himself might.)
C) Lines 9-12 (for this is...flesh and blood.)
D) Lines 13-16 (If we were...all purpose.)</td><td>C) Please refer to the above question</td></tr>
<tr><td colspan="2">Q24. Absolute Pattern 2: Summary Question Summarizing a sentence or entire passage
Question Pattern: In the first paragraph (lines 1-12) the author likens his story is</td></tr>
<tr><td>A) a great artwork
B) a novel without fabrication
C) a story of any other novelist's writing
D) a novel between God and human</td><td>B) it is the story of a man not of an invented, or possible, or idealized.</td></tr>
</table>

<table>
<tr><td colspan="2">Q25. Absolute Pattern 2: Summary Question Summarizing a sentence or entire passage
Question Pattern: In the second paragraph (lines 13-26), the author believes other novelists' story</td></tr>
<tr><td>A) has to go a long way back in memories
B) is more like a single bullet storytelling
C) tries to assimilate with the will of nature
D) searches for the unique world's phenomena</td><td>B) if each one of us could really be done away with once and for <u>all by a single bullet, storytelling would lose all purpose.</u>

All the other choices are narrator's writing.</td></tr>
<tr><td colspan="2">Q26. Absolute Pattern 2: Summary Question Summarizing a sentence or entire passage
Question Pattern: In the first paragraph (lines 1-12), The author's description of his book conveys a sense of</td></tr>
<tr><td>A) adventure
B) relief
C) melancholy
D) true-to-life</td><td>D) it is the story of a man, <u>not of an invented</u> (true-to-life), or possible, or idealized, or otherwise absent figure, but of a unique being of flesh and blood.</td></tr>
<tr><td colspan="2">Q27. Absolute Pattern 11: Textual Evidence Question Finding evidence for the previous question
Question Pattern: Which choice provides the best evidence for the answer to the previous question?</td></tr>
<tr><td>A) Lines 1-2 (I cannot tell...way back.)
B) Lines 2-6 (Novelists when ...God Himself might.)
C) Lines 6-9 (I am as little...is my story)
D) Lines 9-12 (it is the story...flesh and blood.)</td><td>D) Please refer to the above question</td></tr>
<tr><td colspan="2">Q28. Absolute Pattern 4: Example Question
Question Pattern: The description of stars and books line 18 highlights how the author</td></tr>
<tr><td>A) wants his reader to be imbued with his life lesson
B) sees the external wonders are not as profound as introspection
C) realized books and stars contribute less to his life
D) regrets the pursuit of earthly desire</td><td>B) but I have ceased to question <u>stars and books</u>; I have begun to listen to the teachings my blood whispers to me.

<u>"Stars and books" refer to external wonders and "teaching my blood whisper" refers to introspection.</u></td></tr>
<tr><td colspan="2">Q29. Absolute Pattern 3: Inference Question Finding an indirect suggestion (or guessing)
Question Pattern: "frogs" in line 24 and "mothers" in line 25 probably imply between</td></tr>
<tr><td>A) qualification and generalization
B) stupid and smart
C) amphibian and mammal
D) cause and effect</td><td>A) <u>Some never become human, remaining frog</u> (limitation or qualification).
<u>We all share</u> (generalization) the same origin, our mothers</td></tr>
<tr><td colspan="2">Q30. Absolute Pattern 9: Relationships Question
Question Pattern: The author's description of "Two Realms" in line 27 is defined as</td></tr>
<tr><td>A) juxtaposition
B) metaphor
C) irony
D) literary allusion</td><td>A) <u>Two Realms,</u> dark and well-lighted, …
(A) Juxtaposition is a fact of two things being seen or placed close together with contrasting effect, especially with negative-positive tone.

Irony: using language that normally signifies the opposite, typically for humorous effect</td></tr>
</table>

<table>
<tr><td colspan="2">Q31. Absolute Pattern 3: Inference Question Finding an indirect suggestion (or guessing)
Question Pattern: Which of the following situations can be the other realm compared to the description of one realm in lines 27-39?</td></tr>
<tr><td>A) A world where murderer, ghost, and all the wild things happen
B) A class in which a kid is being rewarded
C) An alcove in a house where two siblings find a good hiding place
D) A mother reading a serial killer incidents from the Newspaper</td><td>A) The realms of dark and well-lighted.
*<u>The other realms should be where night lurks beneath the author's realms.</u>
All these options are "well-lighted, familiar" to the author's daily realms as described in lines 27-39</td></tr>
</table>

Questions 32-41 are based on the following passage.

<table>
<tr><td>(34C&35B) <u>No man</u> can fully grasp how far and how fast we have come, <u>but condense</u>, if you will, the 50,000 years of man's recorded history in a time span of but a half-century. Stated in these terms, we know very little about the first 40 years, except at the end of them advanced man had learned to use the skins of animals to cover them. Then, only last week did we develop television, and now if America's new spacecraft succeeds in reaching Venus, we will have literally reached the stars before midnight tonight.
(32A) This is a breathtaking pace, and such a pace cannot help but create new ills as it dispels old, (33D) new ignorance, new problems, new dangers. Surely the opening vistas of space promise high costs and hardships, as well as high reward. So it is not surprising that some would have us stay where we are a little longer to rest, to wait. <u>But why, some say, the moon? Why does Rice play Texas?</u></td><td><u>(36A&37D&39C&40B)</u><u>We choose</u> to go to the moon not because they are easy, but because they are hard.
<u>We have seen facilities</u> greatest and most complex exploration in man's history: Saturn C-1 booster rocket, (38B) generating power equivalent to 10,000 automobiles, each one as powerful as all eight engines of the Saturn combined, as tall as a 48 story structure, as wide as a city block. <u>My fellow</u> citizens, we shall send to the moon and then return it safely to earth, re-entering the atmosphere at speeds of over 25,000 miles per hour, causing heat about half that of the temperature of the sun--almost as hot as it is here today. <u>I'm the one</u> who is doing all the work, (35B) so we just want you to stay cool for a minute.</td></tr>
<tr><td colspan="2">Q32. Absolute Pattern 4: Example Question
Question Pattern: In his speech "50,000 years ..before midnight tonight," (lines 3-12) Kennedy intends to allude</td></tr>
<tr><td>A) a support for the space program
B) a precondition for public approval of the program
C) reasons for the low level of public awareness
D) some limitations that block space program</td><td>A) This is a breathtaking pace… <u>From the second paragraph Kennedy starts his main speech object: space program</u>.

<u>When the entire paragraph is in question, Pay close attention to the topic sentence of the following paragraph</u>.
B), C), D) are incorrect because the tone is Negative.</td></tr>
<tr><td colspan="2">Q33. Absolute Pattern 2: Summary Question
Question Pattern: In the second paragraph (lines 12-18), Kennedy mentions despite of rapid advancement in space program certain obstacles should be overcome EXCEPT</td></tr>
<tr><td>A) demand from some people to delay the project
B) ignorance due to lack of information
C) high expenditure
D) restrictive government policy</td><td>D) new <u>ignorance, new problems, new dangers</u>.
Surely the opening vistas of space promise <u>high costs and hardships, some would have us stay where we are a little longer to rest, to wait.</u>
D) is opposite because Kennedy administration supports the Program</td></tr>
</table>

Q34. **Absolute Pattern 10: Understanding the Structure of the Passage** Finding the structure of the entire passage or organizational relations between the paragraphs **Question Pattern:** The **primary function of the first paragraph** (lines 1-11) is to	
A) show some of the impressive scientific achievement in human history B) show human history through condensed time **C) introduce the speaker's main speech** D) educate some dramatic history to the audience	C) The Function of the first paragraph is to introduce the entire passage. The question asking the purpose of paragraph is not interested in the contents in the paragraph, but the structural form or contextual relations between the sentences. Therefore, all the other choices are—regardless if it is true or false—incorrect.

Q35. **Absolute Pattern 7: Understanding Attitude (Tone) Question** **Question Pattern:** The **tone of Kennedy in line 33 (so we just…for a minute) is**	
A) anger **B) humorous** C) didactic D) profound	B) almost as hot as it is here today. I'm the one who is doing all the work, so we just want you to stay cool for a minute. *Hot and cool juxtapose the situation that creates humor.

Q36. **Absolute Pattern 3: Inference Question** Finding an indirect suggestion (or guessing) **Question Pattern:** According to Kennedy, **Rice** (line 19) **wouldn't play Texas if**	
A) Texas were less challenging B) Texas were more challenging C) Texas were not assertive in sports D) Texas were less progressive	A) It is obvious that Rice is a way behind Texas in national college football ranking, so for Rice, Texas could be as daunting challenge as man shoots a rocket to the moon. The president's humorous tone once again drives the audience in light mood by alluding this fact.

Q37. **Absolute Pattern 11: Textual Evidence Question** Finding evidence for the previous question **Question Pattern:** Which choice provides the best evidence for the answer to the previous question?	
A) Lines 1-2 (No man…we have come,) B) Lines 2-4 (but condense,...a half century) C) Lines 19 (But why, some say, the moon?) **D) Lines 20-21 (We choose...they are hard.)**	D) Please refer to the above question

Q38. **Absolute Pattern 2: Summary Question** Summarizing a sentence or entire passage **Question Pattern: In lines 22-27 (We have seen...a city block)**, Kennedy mainly describes the space project's	
A) undeterred persistence **B) immensity** C) probable challenges D) impact on society	B) generating power equivalent to 10,000 automobiles, the F-1 rocket engines, each one as powerful as all eight engines of the Saturn combined, Saturn missile as tall as a 48 story structure, as wide as a city block.

<table>
<tr><td colspan="2">Q39. Absolute Pattern 2: Summary Question Summarizing a sentence, or an entire paragraph
Question Pattern: In the last paragraph (lines 19-34), President Kennedy makes which of the following assumptions?</td></tr>
<tr><td>A) The progress must be made in small, gradual steps
B) Had we tried earlier, the Moon would have been conquered already
C) We must welcome challenges
D) With the right equipment and audacity, any nations can tap the untried mission</td><td>C) <u>We choose</u> to go to the moon not because they are easy, but <u>because they are hard</u>.

(A) In the first paragraph he says how fast we've moved
(D) He says U.S. is the first in this mission</td></tr>
</table>

<table>
<tr><td colspan="2">Q40. Absolute Pattern 11: Textual Evidence Question Finding evidence for the previous question
Question Pattern: Which choice provides the best evidence for the answer to the previous question?</td></tr>
<tr><td>A) Lines 19-20 (But why,...Texas?)
B) Lines 20-21 (We choose....they are hard.)
C) Lines 27-33 (My fellow citizens, ...here today)
D) Lines 33-34 (I'm the one...for a minute)</td><td>B) Please refer to the above question</td></tr>
</table>

<table>
<tr><td colspan="2">Q41. Absolute Pattern 12: Informational Graphs
Finding facts described in the graphs or relations between the passage and the graph.
Question Pattern: The graph following the passage describes that</td></tr>
<tr><td>A) Defense R& D budget has continued to increase since 1976
B) Nondefense R&D budget has never exceeded defense budget since 1976
C) When nondefense budget was highest, defense budget was also highest.
D) When nondefense budget was lowest, defense budget was also lowest</td><td>A) Defense R&D budget experienced up-and-downs throughout the time span.
B) In the beginning, nondefense budget was higher than defense budget.
C) Non-defense budget was highest in 1976, but defense budget in 1976 was not. It was 1985.</td></tr>
</table>

Questions 42-52 are based on the following passage.

PASSAGE 1	PASSAGE 2
We've all heard the statistics: Nearly half of first marriages end in divorce, women tend to be less happy in their marriages than men, bad marriages lead to heart disease, (51D)**emotional suffering,** etc. In fact, we've become so familiar with this scientific discourse that it seems these statistics have led to another: According to the Pew Research Center, 25 percent of millennials will "never get married." Although I'm skeptical to believe every "new study" (42A&46A) **I hear about the status of modern relationships, this one seems to be strikingly reflected in my own peer circles. Now more than ever, I hear friends** happily discussing their rejection of marriage, and had taken for granted for their parents' separation. Lately this paradigm shift in relationships has me questioning my own views: Perhaps believing in an institution that is trending toward the obsolete is foolish. After all, most of us are well aware that marriage can be a patriarchal institution intent on reinforcing and reaffirming certain backwards gender stereotypes. It is also an inherently exclusionary tradition that prohibits many loving couples from gaining certain legal protections and benefits. It seems we still value marriage as an institution. There are many explanations for why this may be. Part of it is historical—marriage is a time-honored tradition of (43D) affirming a **romantic** relationship. Part of it is **political**—marriage accords a legal legitimacy to a relationship that allows for numerous social and **financial** benefits. And yet another part of it is religious or **cultural**. But what if we were to wash away. I am still inclined to believe that there's value in marriage beyond any of the social or financial benefits it offers. Unlike some of my peers, I look forward to the day when I can stand before my family and friends and say, "This is the person I choose.	(51D) **Divorce is associated with diminished psychological well-being** in children and adult offspring of divorced parents, including greater unhappiness, less satisfaction with life, weaker sense of personal control, anxiety, depression, and greater use of mental health services. (49C) A preponderance of evidence indicates that there is a causal effect between divorce and these outcomes. A study found that children living with just one parent after divorce suffer from more problems such as headaches, stomach aches, feelings of tension and sadness than those whose parents share custody. Children of divorced parents are also more likely to experience conflict in their own marriages, and are more likely to experience divorce themselves. (50B) **They are also more likely to be involved in short-term cohabiting relationships, which often dissolve before marriage.** (44A&45D) **There are many studies that show proof of an intergenerational transmission** of divorce or **staying single over prolonged period of time after the adulthood**, (47C&48B) **especially when marriage was not bound by financial or religious foundation, but solely on brief romantic emotion to the partner.** This doesn't mean that having divorced parents will absolutely lead a child to divorce. There are two key factors that make this transmission of divorce more likely. First, inherited biological tendencies or genetic conditions may predispose a child to divorce as well as the "model of marriage" presented by the child's parents. At any age divorce can be difficult to handle emotionally. Everyone reacts differently and not everyone is a statistic, but the way they handle it can be shown in may different ways and it may turn out that "divorce tends to intensify the child's dependence and (52B) **it tends to accelerate the adolescent's independence"** pulling from the psychology article written by Carl E Pickhardt Ph.D. which is very true on the fact that divorce accelerates the rate of independence.

42. **Absolute Pattern 4: Example Question**

Question Pattern: In line 12, the author of Passage 1 uses the word "**my own peer circles**." to suggest that the trend is

A) very pervasive B) known to the author's peer circles as well C) atypical D) outdated	A) I hear about the status of modern relationships, this one seems to be strikingly reflected in my own peer circles. Now more than ever, I hear friends .... "strikingly reflected" illustrates the degree of pervasiveness. B) is too weak implication.

Q43. **Absolute Pattern 2: Summary Question** Summarizing a sentence or entire passage **Question Pattern:** The author of Passage 1 finds **marriage is still valued for all the reasons EXCEPT**	
A) Political B) Monetary C) Romantic **D) Cultural**	D) Part of it is historical—(C) romantic relationship. Part of it is (A) political—or numerous social and (B) financial benefits.

Q44. **Absolute Pattern 9: Relationships Question** **Question Pattern:** The author of **Passage 2 may view the author's friends** in line 12 (my own peer circles) as they are	
A) responding to intergenerational transmission conditions B) defying patriarchal custom C) experiencing excessive emotional suffering D) one example of a quarter of millennials' view on marriage	A) There are many studies that show proof of an intergenerational transmission of divorce or staying single over prolonged period of time (C) is opposite (...hear friends happily discussing) (B), (D) are statements from P1.

Q45. **Absolute Pattern 11: Textual Evidence Question** Finding evidence for the previous question **Question Pattern:** Which choice provides the best evidence for the answer to the previous question?	
A) Lines 40-46 (Divorce is …health services.) B) Lines 47-49 (A preponderance of evidence… outcomes.) C) Lines 50-54 (A study found…parents share custody.) **D) Lines 62--65 (There are many…after the adulthood.)**	D) Please refer to the above question

Q46. **Absolute Pattern 9: Relationships Question** **Question Pattern:** Unlike Passage 2, the **author of Passage 1 develops an argument** by relying on	
A) personal contemplation B) psychological observation C) scientific evidence D) citation from other source	A) Unlike some of my peers, I look forward to the day when I can stand before my family and friends and say, "This is the person I choose. (B), (C), and (D) are found in both P1 and P2.

Q47. **Absolute Pattern 9: Relationships Question** **Question Pattern:** How would the author of the **Passage 2 respond** to the author's statement in lines 34-36 (I am...it offers)?	
A) Women should accept marriage is a patriarchal institution B) Short-term cohabiting relationships is one way to find true love **C) For long-term relationships, love is not the only factor in marriage.** D) Feeling loving is the surest way to secure marriage	C) especially when marriage was not bound by financial or religious foundation, but solely on brief romantic emotion to the partner. .. Passage 2 warns of marriage that is solely based on romance. (A) L20: patriarchal (Only in Passage 1) (B) L61: dissolve before marriage. (Opposite) (D) L67: but solely, brief romantic (Opposite)

Q48. **Absolute Pattern 11: Textual Evidence Question** Finding evidence for the previous question **Question Pattern:** Which choice provides the best evidence for the answer to the previous question?	
A) Lines 50-54 (A study found…parents share custody.) **B) Lines 62--68 (There are many…to the partner.)** C) Lines 68-70 (This doesn't mean...a child to divorce) D) Lines 71-72 (There are two...more likely.)	B) Please refer to the above question

Q49. **Absolute Pattern 5: Word-In-Context Question** **Question Pattern:** The word "**preponderance**" in line 48 most nearly means	
A) greater quality B) limited **C) greater quantity** D) serious	C) Preponderance (Pre + ponder + ance) =weighty. A preponderance of evidence indicates that there is number of quantifiable evidence. (A), (B), and (D) are quality perception. (B) is opposite

Q50. **Absolute Pattern 6: Analogy Question** Finding a similar situation **Question Pattern:** Which of the following analogies best **refute** the author's assertion about "**cohabiting**" in line 60?
A) A shopkeeper speculates to be the owner of the shop **B) A mathematician formulates a simple theory in the same realm with the big theory, which he later proves it with the simple one.** C) A dog practices sheep herding into a pen before sold to a new owner who is sheep herder. D) A boy tries to save allowance to buy a robot but ends up spending all.
B) They're also more likely to be involved in short-term cohabiting relationships, which often dissolve before marriage (B) A mathematician formulates a simple theory (**cohabiting practice**), grand theory (**marriage**), which he proves it (**successful marriage**) later with the simple one. This question uses two analogical logic: First, big vs. small concept; Second, success vs. failure concept . (A), (C) show no consequence (D) is true statement, not refutation

Q51. **Absolute Pattern 9: Relationships Question** **Question Pattern:** Which of the following statements would both **authors agree**?	
A) genetic conditions may predispose a person to divorce B) love is a primary factor to maintain strong marriage C) divorce affects a great deal on child's psychological development **D) psychological suffering is evident after divorce**	D) bad marriages lead to heart disease, mental pain, etc. L40: Divorce is associated with diminished psychological well-being in children and adult (A) Passage 2 only (B) Passage 1: Yes Passage 2: No (C) Passage 2 only

Q52. **Absolute Pattern 2: Summary Question** Summarizing a sentence or entire passage **Question Pattern:** The author of Passage 2 refers the **adolescent's independence** (line 81) in order to illustrate	
A) an effective way to develop youth's independence **B) some paradoxical outcome of divorce** C) the reason divorce can't be tolerated to adolescents D) a way to destroy the youth's independence	B) The author is sidestepping on divorce issue. Being dependent is surely a problem, but "being independent" is not. It's paradoxical, but positive outcome of divorce. (C) is incorrect because some adolescents became independent through the parents' divorce. **A technique called "setting aside" is difficult and confusing logic.** Setting aside" occurs when the author/narrator/character suddenly withdraws his/her argument or changes a topic.

SAT Test 5

Writing and language Section Answer Explanations

&

Pattern Analyses

Test 5 Writing & Language Section Patterns

Questions 1-11 are based on the following passage.

Let's Engage the Silent Majority

I didn't expect Donald Trump to be President of the United States. I hoped and prayed he would lose. Throughout the election cycle, I tried to remain detached from the endless fear and bigotry that seemed to spew out of the Trump political machine. For me, my parents, and my community, this election was too personal, even though I tried to be detached from this fear. [1]

I am an undocumented [2] immigrant, one of the many directly under threat in Donald Trump's plan to deport all 11.5 million undocumented immigrants in the United States. In addition, I am a visa-overstayer—one of about 4.6 million that he would prioritize [3] Trump has said in his deportation campaign. I'm terrified of my place in this country and am crippled by the seeming inevitability of the sweeping actions on immigration Trump has promised to the American people. He says he will cancel DACA, cancel funding to sanctuary cities, [4] and deport me, my parents, and members of my community. But in the face of uncertainty and overwhelming despondency, I refuse to be silenced. President Trump directly threatens the physical and emotional wellbeing of me and all other undocumented people living in the US. [5] His presidency is built on a fundamental misunderstanding of the immigration system, on the notion that the nation's supposed vulnerability is the fault of undocumented immigrants, Muslims, and Latinos. I don't write to concede defeat in the face of bigotry—our community will not be silent as our families are separated and our livelihoods dismantled. [6] You may write to ask for Donald Trump's pity or compassion when it comes to immigration.

I speak to my fellow undocumented Americans [7]directly and unswervingly, but my message is for everyone: Let us begin a dialogue with those who seek to suppress and deport us. For many who celebrate Trump, this election is a reassertion of their belief that undocumented immigrants do not deserve a place in this country.

It is counterproductive (and impossible) to insulate ourselves from these voices, especially now that their views have been legitimized by the President himself. [8] We will be deported soon anyway.

As undocumented immigrants, [9] I cannot crave to be part of U.S. citizens right away. Our immigration status is [10] fortunately tied up in our identity, so that we cannot exist without drawing attention to the systems that define us, the systems [11] by which this world—our world, the world we share with all those around us—is built. Just by living and breathing in America, we create pressure, we force reexamination, and therefore we are seen as a threat. Perhaps the hardest part of being undocumented is understanding that our futures depend on the worldviews and political leanings of other people.

Q1. Absolute Pattern 19: Redundant Error

Throughout the election cycle, **I tried to remain detached from the endless fear** and bigotry that seemed to spew out of the Trump political machine. For me, my parents, and my community, this election was too personal, **even though I tried to be detached from this fear.** [1]

Question: The author is thinking of deleting the clause "even though...this fear" from the preceding sentence. Should he make this decision?

√	**A) Yes, because this clause is unnecessary.**
	B) Yes, because the sentence is more focused without this clause.
	C) No, because this clause emphasizes the author's subconscious anxiety.
	D) No, because this clause provides unidentified new information without evidence.

A) It should be removed due to redundancy.

B) It is not the matter of focus, but the matter of redundancy.
C) The author's subconscious anxiety was explained in the preceding clause as well. Therefore, it is redundancy.
D) This clause is not new. It's redundant

Q2. Absolute Pattern 16: Precision, Concision, Style

I am an undocumented [2] immigrant, one of the many directly under threat in Donald Trump's plan to deport all 11.5 million undocumented immigrants in the United States.

√	**A) NO CHANGE**	Always Pick the Shortest One from the Multiple Choices! A) employs Precise and Concise modifier, sitting right next to the word it describes without requiring any conjunction like (C) or a semicolon like (D).
	B) immigrant. **One**	
	C) immigrant, **who** is one	B) can't be separated into two sentence because "One..." is a phrase, not a sentence. C) Unnecessary conjunction
	D) immigrant**; one**	D) Semicolon requires a clause; the following modifier is a phrase.

Q3. Absolute Pattern 12: Modifier Placement Error

In addition, I am a visa-overstayer—one of about 4.6 million **that he** would prioritize [3]Trump has said in his deportation campaign.

Question: The best placement for the underlined portion would be:

	A) NO CHANGE	C) 'that Trump had said he would...' is the correct placement.
	B) after the word In addition	A) is pronoun Error. The first sentence in a new paragraph can't start with a pronoun.
√	**C) after the word that**	B) Changes the original meaning. "Trump has said I am..."
	D) after the word campaign.	D) Change of original meaning. "the campaign Trump has said"

Q4. Absolute Pattern 1: Adding, Revising, Deleting, Retaining Information

Question: The author is thinking of removing the underlined clause. If he removes it, the paragraph would lose:

. He says he will cancel DACA, cancel funding to sanctuary cities, [4] and deport me, my parents, and members of my community.

	A) a shift in the mood from concern to reality	C) Retaining this information adds tension and drives the situation into more personal
	B) overall summary of the paragraph	
√	C) a **shift in the mood** from general to **personal**	A) The author already talks about the reality. B) The essay is not about his parents. Therefore, it loses no summary. D) "hope" is opposite word to use here.
	D) a signal of hope	

Q5. Absolute Pattern 1: Adding, Revising, Deleting, Retaining Information

Question: Which choice most efficiently introduces the description that follows in this sentence?

[5] His presidency is built on a fundamental misunderstanding of the immigration system, on the notion that the nation's supposed vulnerability is the fault of undocumented immigrants, Muslims, and Latinos.

√	**A) NO CHANGE**	A) Retaining this information adds clear cause-effect relations
	B) Members of my community support Trump,	
	C) Latinos attribute this consequence to Muslims,	B), D) are opposite perception. C) is not stated in the passage and inconsistent with the question
	D) His new immigration policy will not make immediate impact on the immigration system,	

Q6. Absolute Pattern 10: Logical Expression

I don't write to concede defeat in the face of bigotry—our community will not be silent as our families are separated and our livelihoods dismantled. [6] You may write to ask for Donald **Trump's pity or compassion** when it comes to immigration.

	Choice	Explanation
	A) NO CHANGE	D) is consistent with the preceding sentence
	B) If I have time and courage, I will	A), B) are positive that interrupts the negative tone of the passage C) "proclaim" is extreme, not a suitable word.
	C) I will not proclaim to	
√	**D) Neither do I**	

Q7. Absolute Pattern 19: Redundant Error

I speak to my fellow undocumented Americans [7] directly and unswervingly.

	Choice	Explanation
	A) NO CHANGE	Always Pick the Shortest One from the Multiple Choices!
√	**B) directly,**	B) is direct and concise. By removing a synonym, information becomes concise
	C) directly based upon unswervingness	
	D) in direct motion	A), C) "directly" and "unswervingly" are synonym D) is wordy

Q8. Absolute Pattern 1: Adding, Revising, Deleting, Retaining Information

Question: Which one best illustrates the author's emotional state?

	Choice	Explanation
	A) NO CHANGE	B) 1> The author wants to fight against Trump's decision.
√	**B) We must engage.**	2> Therefore, the answer should maintain the same active tone.
	C) We must accept the reality and respect Trump's decision.	3> The rest of the choices are ruled out simply because of their passive tone.
	D) The only way that we can legitimate ourselves is to leave the country.	

Q9. Absolute Pattern 17: Pronoun Error

As undocumented **immigrants,** [9] I cannot crave to be part of U.S. citizens right away.

	Choice	Explanation
	A) NO CHANGE	D) "As undocumented immigrants" (plural) modifies the following subject. Therefore, the subject must be the plural too: we (plural), and also human in plural form.
	B) exploiting politics is beyond our reach.	
	C) to raise political voice is next to impossible	A) 1> Pronoun error. 2> "immigrants" (plural) "I" (singular)
√	D) **we** don't choose to be political	B), C) "exploiting politics, "to raise political voice" cannot modify "undocumented immigrants" because they are non-human objects

Q10. Absolute Pattern 10: Logical Expression

Our immigration status is [10] fortunately tied up in our identity, so that we cannot exist without drawing attention to the systems that define us,

	Choice	Explanation
	A) NO CHANGE	'tied up' is negative word. "fortunately" is positive
	B) unexpectedly	"unexpectedly" dilutes the strong word "tied up"
	C) undoubtedly	"undoubtedly" dilutes the strong word "tied up"
√	**D) inextricably**	'inextricably' means complexly tied up.

Q11. Absolute Pattern 15: Prepositional Idiom

Passage: we cannot exist without drawing attention to the systems that define us, the systems [11] by which this world—our world, the world we share with all those around us—is **built.**

	A) NO CHANGE	'built on' is the correct prepositional idiom
√	**B) on which**	When confronting a complex sentence, simplifying the sentence is critical: look below:
	C) through which	systems **by which this world**~~—our world, the world we share with all those around us—~~**is built.**
	D) from which	

Questions 12-22 are based on the following passage.

Oil Spill

An oil spill is the release of a liquid petroleum hydro-carbon into the environment, especially marine areas, [12] due to human activity, and is a form of pollution. The term is usually applied to marine oil spills, where oil is released into the ocean or coastal waters, but spills may also occur on land. [13] Crude oil spill release from tankers offshore platforms, drilling rigs and wells, and spills of refined petroleum products (such as gasoline, diesel) and their by-products—[14] many such oil spills damage our environment to the irreversible point.

Oil spills penetrate into the structure of the plumage of birds and the fur of mammals, reducing its insulating ability, and making them more vulnerable to temperature fluctuations [15] but much less buoyant in the water.

Cleanup and recovery from an oil spill are difficult [16] and depends upon many factors, including the type of oil spilled, the temperature of the water (affecting evaporation and biodegradation), and the types of shorelines and beaches involved. [17] Technology that controls the ocean temperature to prevent evaporation and biodegradation is considered as state-of-the-art technology.

Oil spills can have disastrous consequences for society [18] ; economically, environmentally, and socially.
[19] As a result, oil spill accidents have initiated intense media attention and political uproar, bringing many together in a political struggle concerning government response to oil spills and [20] air pollution control in major cities in coastal area. Crude oil and refined fuel spills from tanker ship accidents have damaged vulnerable ecosystems in Alaska, the Gulf of Mexico, the Galapagos Islands, France, the Sundarbans, Ogoniland, and many other places.

Q12 Absolute Pattern 15: Prepositional Idiom

Which of the following alternatives is **NOT acceptable**?

Passage: An oil spill is the release of a liquid petroleum hydrocarbon into the environment, especially marine areas, [12] due to human activity,

	A) because of	B) 'because' is conjunction that connects the subordinating clause. 'because' cannot take on only a word or a short phrase like "human activity."
√	**B) because**	'because of' and 'because ' are not the same thing. "because of" is preposition.
	C) result of	
	D) caused by	C), D) are prepositions as well.

Q13. Absolute Pattern 13: Parallel Structure

[13] Crude oil spill release from **tankers** offshore **platforms,** drilling rigs and **wells,** and spills of refined petroleum products (such as gasoline, diesel) and their **by-products**—[14]**many such oil spills damage our environment** to the irreversible point.

	Choice	Explanation
	A) NO CHANGE	C) **"**tankers, platforms, wells, by-products**"** set the correct parallel structure. A) 'tankers' and 'offshore' should be separated by using a comma because "tankers" and "offshore platforms" are nouns and can't be tied together. B) Semicolon connects a clause. "offshore platforms" is not a clause. D) A pair of dashes makes it subject of the sentence.
	B) Crude oil from tankers;	
√	C) Crude oil spill release from **tankers,**	
	D) Crude oil spill release from tankers—	

1> The above boldface fonts (takers, platform, wells, by-products) show the parallel structure.
2> The main sentence hides all the way back, next to the "dash," "many such oil spills…."
3> The preceding phrases are modifiers that need to maintain parallelism.

Q14. Absolute Pattern 1: Adding, Revising, Deleting, Retaining Information

—[14]many such **oil spills damage our environment** to the irreversible point.

Question: Which choice most effectively establishes **threats to the environment**?

	Choice	Explanation
√	**A) NO CHANGE**	A) The question keywords "threats to the environment" suggest the answer should be negative. B), C), D) are all positive.
	B) oil spill removal process involves enormous work as expansive as ocean, but it's by far the most effective solution.	
	C) it is irony that major oil refinery companies have cleanup companies, which generate revenue by the oil spills made by their parent company.	
	D) government policy has become strict enough to control the damage to the environment.	

Q15. Absolute Pattern 7: Conjunction Error

and making them more vulnerable to temperature fluctuations [15] but **much less buoyant** in the water.

	Choice	Explanation
	A) NO CHANGE	B) 1> The preceding phrase "making them more vulnerable " and following "much less buoyant " indicate parallelism, requiring 'and'
√	**B) and**	
	C) yet	A), C) Contradictory conjunction 'but' or "yet" cancels out the preceding phrase.
	D) resulting	D) "resulting" is used for cause-effect relation.

Q16. Absolute Pattern 21: Subject-Verb, Pronoun, Noun Agreement

Cleanup and recovery from an oil spill **are** difficult [16] **and depends** upon many factors,

	Choice	Explanation
	A) NO CHANGE	B) The subject "cleanup and recovery" is plural, so is the verb "depend." "are difficult" hints that the following verb has to be plural.
√	**B) and depend**	A) 1> a punctuation error: when clauses share the same subject, a comma shouldn't be placed. 2> the subject-verb agreement error: "depends" is singular.
	C) , which depends	
	D) that depends	C), D) 1> the subject-verb agreement error 2> "which" or "that" are ambiguous as they don't specify which is being referred to.

Q17. Absolute Pattern 1: Adding, Revising, Deleting, Retaining Information

[17] **Technology** that controls the ocean temperature to prevent evaporation and biodegradation is considered as **state-of-the-art technology**.

Question: Which one provides details that best help the reader understand **enormous tasks for oil clean up**

	Choice	Explanation
	A) NO CHANGE	C) The question keywords 'enormous tasks' is the key. C) describes the enormous tasks.
	B) Generally, over 70% of accidents occur in the ocean	Choices A, B, D are all related to something else other than enormous tasks.
√	**C) Spills may take weeks, months or even years to clean up.**	
	D) Over the last few decades, oil spill clean up technology has experienced dramatic advancement	A), D) are quality, illustrating advanced skills

Q18. Absolute Pattern 18: Punctuation Error

Oil spills can have disastrous consequences for society [18] ; economically, environmentally, and socially.

	Choice	Explanation
	A) NO CHANGE	Semicolon error
√	**B) : economically, environmentally, and socially.**	Colon is used properly to introduce a list
	C) ,environmentally economical and social.	It changes the meaning
	D) economically, environmentally, socially.	Punctuation error

B) The purpose of 'colon' is straightforward: it introduces things. What to introduce wouldn't be a matter: a word, series of words, sentences, phrase, etc., are all acceptable after the colon.

A): semicolon functions as a conjunction that requires a clause to link to.
D) requires a comma before "economically" because the following three adverbs are non-restrictive (inessential elements) and, therefore, need to be separated from the main clause.

Q19. Absolute Pattern 23: Transition Words for Supporting Detail, Contrast, and Consequence

[19] As a result, **oil spill accidents have initiated intense media attention** and political uproar,

	Choice	Explanation
√	**A) NO CHANGE**	The preceding text explicitly suggests that the following sentence requires an adverb "As a result" to indicate a consequence.
	B) In the meantime,	'In the meantime' is used to contrast the information like 'while' or 'on the contrary'.
	C) Then,	'Then' is used to indicate the time sequence or concession.
	D) For example,	'For example' is used to support the preceding information.

The following adverbs are also used for consequence.

Correspondingly	Thus	In respect to	In that event
Subsequently	Hence	In consequence	Therefore

Q20. Absolute Pattern 1: Adding, Revising, Deleting, Retaining Information		
Which choice is most consistent with the previous portion of the sentence?		
bringing many together in a political **struggle concerning government response to oil spills** and [20] air pollution control in major cities in coastal area.		
	A) NO CHANGE	A), B), D) are all unrelated issues with oil spills.
	B) increase in budget to develop renewable energy source	
√	**C) what actions can best prevent them from happening.**	
	D) energy conserving education to the public	

Q21. Absolute Pattern 1: Adding, Revising, Deleting, Retaining Information	
Question: Suppose the author's goal was to write a **brief summary illustrating the hazardous impact** of oil spills. Would this summary successfully fulfill the author's goal?	
√	**A) Yes, because the summary offers some of the consequences that oil spill creates**
	B) Yes, because the summary encourages establishing more strict government policy against oil spill prevention
	C) No, because the summary focuses more on economic impact than on environmental impact
	D) No, because the summary also represents struggles oil refinery companies experience to meet the government environment standards
B), D) are not stated in the passage. C) is a minor issue.	

Q22. Absolute Pattern 9: Informational Graphs		
Question: In order **to estimate quantity of oil spilled**, all of the following variables must be available **EXCEPT**		
	A) Oil film thickness	film thickness is mentioned in the table
	B) Quantity spread	quantity spread is mentioned in the table
	C) Total surface area	total surface area can be calculated using the table
√	**D) Direction of wind and current**	Although an integral factor, wind direction is not mentioned in the passage.

Questions 23-33 are based on the following passage.

An Advanced Practice Registered Nurse

An advanced practice registered nurse (APRN) [23] ,which is a nurse with post-graduate education in nursing. APRNs are prepared with advanced didactic and clinical education, knowledge, skills, and scope of practice in nursing.

<1>In 2004, It recommended that advanced practice registered nurses move the entry level degree to the doctorate level by 2015. <2>APRN defines a level of nursing practice [24] that utilizes extended and expanded skills in assessment, planning, diagnosis and evaluation of the care required. <3>Nurses practicing at this level are educationally prepared at the post-graduate level [25] upon completion of post-graduate programs.

<4> It also defines the basis of advanced practice is the high degree of knowledge, skill, and experience that [27] apply to the nurse-patient/client relationship APRNs [28],who demonstrate effective integration of theory, practice and experiences [29] along with increasing degrees of autonomy in judgments and interventions.

Intensive post-graduate education is designed to teach an APRN to use multiple approaches to decision-making, manage the care of individuals and groups, [30] to engage in collaborative practices with the patient or client to achieve best outcomes.

Each nurse specialty, especially NPs, can have sub-specialties or concentrations in a specific field or patient population in healthcare, [31] each of them has a unique history and context, but shares the commonality of being an APRN.

[32] Because education, accreditation, and certification are necessary components of an overall approach to preparing an APRN for practice, these roles are regulated by legislation and specific professional regulation. While APRNs are educated differently depending on their specific specialty, all APRNs are now trained at the graduate level and are required to attain at least a master's degree. [33] International Council of Nurses established such regulations only in 1977.

Q23. Absolute Pattern 21: Subject-Verb, Pronoun, Noun Agreement

An advanced practice registered nurse (APRN) [23] ,which is a nurse with post-graduate education in nursing.

	A) NO CHANGE	",which" should be removed.
	B) was	The surrounding sentences use the present tense.
√	**C) is**	The subject 'APRN' requires the main verb 'is'
	D) OMIT	This option should be omitted from your selection.

Q24. Absolute Pattern 10: Logical Expression

APRN **defines** a level of nursing practice [24] that **utilizes** extended and expanded skills,

Question: Which of the following alternatives would **NOT** be acceptable?

	A) ,which utilizes	C) "utilized" becomes the verb in past tense; the main verb "defines" is already present.
	B) utilizing	A),B),D): all of them use the proper form of punctuations and conjunctions to function as a modifier.
√	**C) utilized**	
	D) —utilizing	

Q25. Absolute Pattern 19: Redundant Error

	A) NO CHANGE	Nurses practicing at this level are educationally prepared **at the post-graduate level** [25] upon completion of post-graduate programs. D) the underlined portion is redundant.
	B) once they are professionally ready.	
	C) if they are well-prepared in the post-graduate level programs.	
√	**D) OMIT the underlined portion.**	A), C) are redundant error, repeating the preceding clause. B) is comma splice error

Q26. Absolute Pattern 11: Logical Sequence

Question: Which of the following is most **logical sequences** of this paragraph?

	A) NO CHANGE	<2> **APRN defines a level of nursing practice** that utilizes extended and expanded skills, diagnosis and evaluation of the care required.
	B) <1>,<4>,<2>,<3>	<3> **Nurses practicing at this level** are educationally **prepared at the post-graduate level.**
	C) <2>,<3>,<1>,<4>	<4> **It also** defines **the basis of advanced practice** is the high degree of knowledge, skill and experience that apply to the nurse-patient/client relationship.
√	**D) <2>,<3>,<4>,<1>**	<1> In 2004, It **recommended that advanced practice** registered nurses

APRN defines a level -> at this level->It also defines->In 2004,
D): We know that <2> precedes <4> as a sequence should be followed by the words "defines" and "**also** defines"
We also know <4> precedes <1> because "advanced practice" should be placed before "move to the ...doctorate level"
Therefore, the answer should be in the order of <2><4><1>

Q27. Absolute Pattern 21: Subject-Verb, Pronoun, Noun Agreement

It also defines the basis of advanced practice is **the high degree** of knowledge, skill, and experience that [27] apply to the nurse-patient/client relationship.

	A) NO CHANGE	C) The verb "is applied" agrees with the subject "the high degree"
	B) are utilizable and applicable	A) The verb needs to be the passive voice because "the high degree " can't "apply by itself. B) "utilizable" and "applicable" are synonym, redundant error. The verb is plural.
√	**C) is applied**	
	D) are applied	

Q28. Absolute Pattern 21: Subject-Verb, Pronoun, Noun Agreement

APRNs [28], who **demonstrate** effective integration of theory, practice and experiences [29]along with increasing degrees of autonomy in judgments and interventions.

	A) NO CHANGE	C) The sentence does not have a verb. By simply removing 'who', we can make a verb.
	B) ,which demonstrate	A) ', who' should be removed. B) ',which' should be removed. D) The subject 'APRNs' is plural. "demonstrates" is singular.
√	**C) demonstrate**	
	D) demonstrates	

Q29. Absolute Pattern 3. Colloquialism (Nonstandard Language)

APRNs demonstrate effective integration of theory, practice and experiences [29]along with increasing degrees of autonomy in judgments and interventions.

Question: Which of the following alternatives to the underlined portion would **NOT** be acceptable?

	A) together with	B) "plus" is colloquial language and can't be used in writing.
√	**B) plus**	A), C), D) are all synonym and can be used in written form.
	C) as well as	
	D) in company with	

Q30. Absolute Pattern 13. Parallel Structure

Intensive post-graduate education is designed to teach an APRN **to use** multiple approaches to decision-making, **manage** the care of individuals and groups, [30] to engage in collaborative practices with the patient or client to achieve best outcomes;

	A) NO CHANGE	The above parallel structure should be: "to use~, (to) manage~, (to) engage~."
	B) engaging	C) 'To-infinitive' clause in parallel structure can drop 'to' from the second to-infinitive clause and use the base verb only.
√	**C) engage**	A) 'to' should be removed B), D) "engaging" is gerund.
	D) by engaging	

Q31. Absolute Pattern 7.Conjunction Error

Each nurse specialty, especially NPs, can have sub-specialties or concentrations in a specific field or patient population in healthcare, [31] each of **them** has a unique history and context, but shares the commonality of being an APRN.

	A) NO CHANGE	B) In order to link up these two clauses, we need to have a proper subordinating conjunction. "which" is used as a conjunction
√	**B) each of which**	
	C) each and every single NP	A) Comma splice error. "each of them~" does not have a conjunction to link the previous sentence.
	D) **and** each of **which**	C) Comma splice error. "each" and "every" are redundant. D) It has two conjunctions. "and" and "which".

Q32. Absolute Pattern 7.Conjunction Error

Which alternative word is **NOT acceptable**?

[32] Because education, accreditation, and certification **are necessary components** of an overall approach to preparing an APRN for practice, **these roles are regulated by legislation** and specific professional regulation

	A) For	D) We need a cause-effect conjunction. D) 'Although' is used for concessional clause. The clauses between the conjunction are arranged into the cause—effect.
	B) As	
	C) Since	'For', 'As', 'Since' are all synonym to 'Because'
√	**D) Although**	

Q33. Absolute Pattern 1: Adding, Revising, Deleting, Retaining Information

Which choice provides an accurate and effective **summary of this paragraph**?

While APRNs **are educated** differently depending on their specific **specialty,** all APRNs are now **trained at the graduate level** and are required to attain at least a **master's degree**.
[33] **International Council of Nurses** established such regulations only in 1977.

	A) NO CHANGE
	B) A registered nurse who has acquired the expert knowledge must maintain high work ethics.
	C) An advanced practice registered nurse (APRN) is generally considered high paying job.
√	**D) Generally, a Master of Science in Nursing is their field of concentration.**

A) "International" B) "work ethics" and C) "high paying job" are not mentioned in this paragraph

Questions 34-44 are based on the following passage. **Black Cat By Edgar Allan Poe** From my infancy I was noted for the docility and humanity of my disposition. I was especially fond of animals, and was indulged by my parents with a great variety of pets. With these I spent most of my time, and never was so happy [34] <u>when</u> feeding and caressing them. To those [35]<u>,whom</u> have cherished affection for a faithful and sagacious dog, I [36] <u>need hardly</u> be at the trouble of explaining the nature or the intensity of the gratification thus derivable. There is something in the unselfish and self-sacrificing love of a brute, which goes directly to the heart of him who has had frequent occasion to test the paltry friendship and gossamer fidelity of mere Man. I married early, and [37] <u>in my wife</u> was happy to find a disposition not uncongenial with my own. [38] <u>With my partiality for domestic pets being observed,</u> she lost no opportunity of procuring those of the most agreeable kind. We had birds, gold fish, a fine dog, rabbits, a small monkey, and a cat. This latter was a remarkably large and beautiful animal, entirely black, and sagacious to an astonishing degree. In speaking of his intelligence, my wife, who at heart was not	a little tinctured with superstition, made frequent allusion to the ancient popular notion [39] <u>that domestic pets owners reduce their mental depression up to 20%.</u> Pluto — this was the cat's name — was my favorite pet and playmate. I alone fed him, and he attended me wherever I went about the house. It was even with difficulty that I could prevent him [40] <u>to</u> following me through the streets. Our friendship lasted, in this manner, for several years, [41] <u>during which period</u> my general temperament and character — through the instrumentality of the Fiend Intemperance — had (I blush to confess it) experienced a radical alteration for the worse. I suffered myself to use intemperate language to at length, I even offered her personal violence. My pets, [42] <u>of course,</u> were made to feel the change in my disposition. I not only neglected, but ill-used them. For Pluto[43]<u>, however,</u> I still retained sufficient regard to restrain me from maltreating him, as I made no scruple of maltreating the rabbits, the monkey, or even the dog, when by accident, or through affection, they came in my way. But my disease grew upon me — for what disease is like Alcohol! — and at length even Pluto, who was now becoming old, [44] <u>additionally</u> somewhat peevish — even Pluto began to experience the effects of my ill temper.

Q34. Absolute Pattern 4: Comparison

With these I spent most of my time, and never was **so happy** [34] <u>when</u> feeding and caressing them.

	A) NO CHANGE	B) <u>"so…as" is correlative conjunction that always works as a pair</u>, and other alternatives cannot replace this form.
√	**B) as when**	
	C) that when	
	D) than when	

Q35. Absolute Pattern 17: Pronoun Error

To those [35]<u>,whom</u> **have cherished** affection for a faithful and sagacious dog, I [36] <u>need hardly</u> be at the trouble of explaining the nature or the intensity of the gratification thus derivable.

	A) NO CHANGE	D) <u>"who" is the subjective pronoun.</u> We know that <u>we need the subjective pronoun because the following word is the verb</u>, 'have.' (example) -I love wonder woman **WHO is** my heroin. -Wonder woman **WHOM I** loved married to Batman. A) and B) 'whom' is objective and should not be placed before verb. C) comma should not be used in restrictive (essential) modifier. "who have cherished…dog" is an essential modifier in the sentence.
	B) ;whom	
	C) ,who	
√	**D) who**	

Q36. Absolute Pattern 8: Double Negative Error		
To those who have cherished an affection for a faithful and sagacious dog, I [36] need hardly be at the trouble of explaining the nature		
Question:_ Which of the following alternatives **would NOT be acceptable**?		
	A) need scarcely	C) Double negative error: both 'hardly' and 'don't' are negative. Remove either one of them.
	B) need not	
√	**C) hardly don't need to**	
	D) don't need to	

Q37. Absolute Pattern 1: Adding, Revising, Deleting, Retaining Information		
I married early, and [37] in my wife was happy to find **a disposition** not uncongenial with my own.		
The **best placement** for the underlined portion would be:		
	A) NO CHANGE	B) "**I married early**, **and was happy** to find in my wife a disposition not uncongenial' is an ideal arrangement. A) Change of meaning: It appears to be ' I was happy with my wife' C) Change of meaning: in my **wife not uncongenial with my own** D)"...with my own in my wife" doesn't make sense.
√	**B) after the word find**	
	C) after the word disposition	
	D) after the word own	

Key point: choice C: 'not uncongenial' has to be compared with disposition, not wife.

Q38. Absolute Pattern 12: Modifier Error		
[38] With my partiality for domestic pets **being** observed, **she** lost no opportunity of procuring those of the most agreeable kind.		
	A) NO CHANGE	Wordiness error and passive. *do not choose 'being'
√	**B) Observing my partiality for domestic pets,**	"she" was observing my partiality
	C) **I** gave partiality for domestic pets,	comma splice
	D) **I** gave partiality for domestic pets, which	"which" is ambiguous and not needed

Q39. Absolute Pattern 1: Adding, Revising, Deleting, Retaining Information		
In speaking of his intelligence, my wife, who at heart was not a little tinctured with **superstition,** made frequent allusion to the **ancient popular notion** [39] that **domestic pets owners can reduce their mental depression up to 20%.**		
Question:_Which one further illustrates the narrator's comments about ancient popular notion?		
	A) NO CHANGE (The statement is more like modern one)	Inconsistent with the question
√	**B) , *which regarded* all black cats as witches in disguise.**	Most compatible with the ancient notion
	C) that my parents used to tell me when I was young.	Inconsistent with the question
	D) , which lingered in my mind always.	Too vague expression

Q40. Absolute Pattern 15: Prepositional Idiom

It was even with difficulty that I could **prevent** him [40] to following me through the streets.

A) NO CHANGE	B) from √	C) with	D) DELETE IT	B) "prevent something or someone from..." is the correct idiom

Q41. Absolute Pattern 7: Conjunction Error

Our friendship lasted, in this manner, for several years, [41], during which period my general temperament and character — through the instrumentality of the Fiend Intemperance — had (I blush to confess it) experienced a radical alteration for the worse.

√	A) NO CHANGE	"for several years, during which (period)" is the correct conjunction for time.
	B) during	"during" is preposition and can't carry the following clause.
	C) and	'and' is used for parallel structure. The primary and the dependent clause are not based on the parallel (equal) concept.
	D) however	'however' is an adverb and requires a semicolon to use it.

Q42. Absolute Pattern 15: Prepositional Idiom

Question: Which of the following alternatives would **NOT be acceptable**?

My pets, [42] of course, were made to feel the change in my disposition. I not only neglected, but ill-used them.

A) gradually,	B) naturally,	C) sadly,	**D) affectionately,** √

D) is Positive and contradicts to the sentence.
A) Negative (connotation) B) Negative (connotation) C) Negative

Q43. Absolute Pattern 18: Punctuation Error

For Pluto[43], however, **I still retained** sufficient regard to restrain me from maltreating him,

√	A) NO CHANGE	A) When 'however' is used in the middle of the sentence, it should have a pair of commas that offset 'however'.
	B) ; however,	Semicolon + however is used to connect the main and subordinating clause.
	C) however,	'however' cannot be used with a single comma in the middle of the sentence.
	D) however	'however' cannot be used without a punctuation

Q44. Absolute Pattern 15: Prepositional Idiom

But my disease grew upon me — for what disease is like Alcohol! — and at length even Pluto, who was now becoming old, [44] additionally somewhat peevish — even Pluto began to experience the effects of my ill temper.

A) NO CHANGE	**B) consequently** √	C) basically	D) necessarily	B) Aging causes Pluto becomes peevish **as a consequence**

Chapter 5 Summary

Chapter Summary contains equal portions of

-12 Absolute Patterns for Reading Section

-20 Common Patterns for Incorrect Choices in Reading

-70 Absolute Patterns for Writing and Language Section

-24 Common Patterns for Incorrect Choices in Writing

Chapter 5

12 Absolute Patterns for the Reading Section

Absolute Pattern 12: Informational Graphs

50~70 percent of graph questions require little information from reading passage.
The question, however, always demands our attention to the passage that only increase confusion.
(e.g., "Based on information in the passage, the graph....?").

The more you practice, the less will you be scared of solving the questions without reading the passage.

Absolute Pattern Summary for the Reading Section

Category A: Content Question

▶ Absolute Pattern 1: Main Idea Question
Finding the main idea of the entire passage, a specific paragraph, or sentences

▶ Absolute Pattern 2: Summary Question
Summarizing a sentence, or entire passage

▶ Absolute Pattern 4: Example Question
Understanding example sentence and the true purpose behind a specific name or idea within it.

▶ Absolute Pattern 5: Word-In-Context Question
Finding a clue word and the keyword from the sentence in question

▶ Absolute Pattern 8: Understanding the True Purpose
Finding the true purpose of statement

▶ Absolute Pattern 11: Textual Evidence Question

Category B: Technique Question

▶ Absolute Pattern 3: Inference Question
Finding an indirect suggestion (or guessing)

▶ Absolute Pattern 6: Analogy Question
Finding a similar situation

▶ Absolute Pattern 7: Understanding Attitude (Tone) Question
Finding a tone such as positive-negative, active-passive, mental-physical, subject-objective

▶ Absolute Pattern 9: Relationships Question
Finding relations between the cause-effect, characters, and ideas including a Paired Passage.

▶ Absolute Pattern 10: Understanding the Structure of the Passage
Finding the structure of the entire passage or organizational relations between the paragraphs

▶ Absolute Pattern 12: Informational Graphs
Finding facts described in graphs or relations between the passage and the graph.

Chapter 5

20 Common Patterns for *Inc*orrect Choices in Reading

1 Positive-Negative Tone (value)

This simple rule is the most powerful tool to isolate the incorrect options.
All you need is to identify the keywords—normally noun or verb—in each multiple choice.

Identify if the keywords in the multiple choices are positive or negative tone.

Then—based on positive-negative tone—match them with the reading passage's keywords, from the line you're supposed to read. Practically majority of the incorrect options are checked and axed down through this process.

2 Antonym or Opposite Perception

This pattern, next to the above Positive-Negative tone, appears most frequently.
The vast majority of incorrect choices, especially "EXCEPT", "NOT" questions apply this rule.

Almost all questions contain at least one antonym or opposite concept in multiple choices!

This type uses opposite tonality of voice, opposite character, or argument that are different from the reading passage, such as using a direct antonym or opposite logic. For instance, the graph shows increase while the passage is pointing downward.

Chapter 5

20 Common Patterns for *In*correct Choices in Reading

3 Active-Passive Value

Let's suppose we have two competing choices: A) sympathy B) sadness
Can you tell the difference? Not immediately, right?

Let's suppose you are watching a strange movie, where a female character is dying in bed. Would you feel sad? No! You will be sympathetic at most.

How about the dying person was in fact your baby sister in reality? Would you have the same sympathetic feeling? No! Very strong sadness will you have. This is the Active-Passive role.

As seen above, identifying whether it is active or passive tone/ attitude is very important. *Please note that this active-Passive is not the same thing as the active-passive voice in Grammar.

Here's another example!
Do you like ramen, Jimin?

Jimin: one of my favorites!

Let's suppose you are starving now. Your mom hurried to fix a bowl of hot ramen for you. But you found no egg in your ramen. You can't imagine ramen without eggs.
Now, how would you feel about the situation?
A) I'm disappointed because there's no egg in ramen B) It'll be great if I have an egg in ramen.

If you split them into a nanosecond,
A) should come first and B) should follow.

I would like to call it a sequential progression. Always choose what must come directly first.
B) is correct in statement but incorrect by disrupting the sequential progression that allows (A) first.

70 Absolute Patterns for Writing and Language Section

Question 35
Cindy cherished the moment of the day when her and her mother Caroline met the president of Walmart in recognition of the best employees of the year ceremony.

A) she and her mother Caroline met
B) her and her mother Caroline had met
C) she and her mother Caroline have met
D) her and her mother Caroline will meet

RULE #35
Hint:
Pronoun

"When" is Conjunction and should be Connected to a Subjective Pronoun.

The correct answer is A.

B)) and D) are incorrect because "her" is objective pronoun.
C) is incorrect because the tense in both clauses between "when" should be the same the past tense. "cherished" vs. "met."

Question 36

The disgruntled shopper had a tendency to claiming a refund for the goods he fully used, perhaps out of expectation at having to receive courtesy gift cards in the past.

A) NO CHANGE
B) tendency to claim
C) intention of claiming
D) intention to claim

RULE #36

Hint: Idiom

Noun that Must Use To-Infinitive Clause

The correct answer is B.
As introduced in Rule #4, the word "tendency" has the future concept. So the proper idiomatic preposition must be "to," which indicates the future action.'

A) is incorrect because "to+ base verb" is the right form, not "to+Verb~ing (gerund)"
D) is incorrect because it changes the meaning.

Question 37
Korean filmmaker Kim Sun Tak is similar to Alysia Syndayun in his use of ethnic backgrounds, but unlike his film, she dwells on the religious aspects of her film characters

A) NO CHANGE
B) but unlike him,
C) ; however, unlike his film,
D) but unlike the film he directed,

RULE #37
Hint:
Comparison

The Usage of Unlike for Comparison

The correct Answer is B
In the original sentence, "unlike his film is compared with "she.
"The sentence has two options to fix this issue: "unlike his film, her film" or "unlike him, she"

Question 38
Donald Trump has received many complaints about his recent Republican presidential nomination speech, which some audience condemn to be extreme.

A) to have been extreme
B) to be extremely
C) as extreme
D) as to have been extreme

RULE #38
Tense

The Past Tense for To-Infinitive Clause

The correct answer is A.
The main sentence indicates that Donald Trump has already received complaints. "to be" is used for a future action, which creates an impossible situation. The audience can only condemn to react to what already happened in the past, not the other way around. The past tense for 'To-infinitive' is "to have"

Question 39
The mutual relationship between the 2016 Brazil Olympic organizer and its sponsors are truly symbiotic, for neither can promote activities without each other.

A) is truly symbiotic
B) is based on a true symbiotic relation
C) are sincerely symbiotic
D) are nothing but truly symbiotic

RULE #39
Hint:
Agreement

Finding Subject

The correct answer is A
The "relationship" is the only subject, which is singular. Any word (s) that comes after the preposition—"between" in this sentence—is not a subject.
Therefore, the verb must be a singular "is."
B) is wordy and redundant.

Question 40
As the challenger throbbed in, the UFC heavyweight champion cringed, the challenger's blowing-out-punch more strong, and winding up the champ's last-ditch effort.

A) the challenger's blowing-out-punch more stronger
B) the challenger's blowing-out-punch more strongly
C) the challenger blew out punch stronger
D) the challenger blew out punch stronger

RULE #40 Hint: Modifier	**Modifier + Adverb** The correct answer is B With a one-syllable word or a word ending in -y or –ly, add the suffix -'er' to form a comparative phrase (e.g., cheap to cheaper). For more than one syllable, use 'more' to create the comparative phrase (e.g., expensive to more expensive). In this sentence, however, all the options contain comparative "more," which should have been "stronger," instead of "more stronger," leading us to think of something else. The only option available is to convert the adjective "strong" to the adverb "strongly." C), D) are incorrect because the preceding clause "the UFC heavyweight champion cringed" does not have a conjunction. To avoid the comma splice error, it should remain as a phrase like A or B.

Question 41
Clearly, the products will have been less appealing if the head designer had not tried to disperse the design concept in YouTube.

A) will be less appealing
B) would be less appealing
C) would have been less appealing
D) might be less appealing

RULE #41
Hint:
Tense

Past Perfect Tense for Conditional "If-Clause"

The correct answer C.
Because If-clause contains "had not tried", the past perfect tense, the main clause should also contain the past perfect "would have"

If clause (conditional clause)	Main clause (consequence)
If + past perfect (had + p.p)	Perfect conditional (would have/could have/ should have/must have/might have/ may have)
ex) If Jason had seen the accident,	He would have been fainted

Question 42
The amiable relation between Jason and I ended as soon as we each moved out on our own.

A) between Jason and me
B) between Jason and myself
C) between Jason and I
D) between Jason and me would

RULE #42
Hint:
Pronoun

Use Objective Pronoun after Preposition

The correct answer is A
The pronoun after the preposition "between" must be objective ("me" in this sentence), "Not Subjective "I".
D) is incorrect because the model verb "would," implies the repeated action in the past.

Question 43
Being canceled the job interview appointment that the company mailed to participate, Jason never canceled another job interview again.

A) Canceled
B) Canceling
C) Having canceled
D) After he made a cancellation on

RULE #43

Hint:
Tense

Having +pp for the Past Perfect Tense

The correct answer is C
The verb in the main sentence is past tense "canceled," and the subordinating clause indicates that Jason canceled a job interview before this job interview, showing a clear time sequence. In that case, the past perfect tense "Having + P.P" should be applied.
"Having canceled" means "After Jason had canceled."
D) "made cancellation" is wordiness error.

Question 44
In a world that the government has less and less control to terrorism, cold comfort has become a normal trend now.

A) in which the government has control less
B) where the government has less and less control
C) that the government has no control
D) that the government has significantly less and less control

RULE #44
Hint:
Place
Adverbial

Where vs. That
The correct answer is B

"where" and "that" should not be used interchangeably.

A), "in which" and "where" are interchangeable, which makes both of them correct. However, A) changes the original meaning by focusing on "controlling less to terrorism" than "less control."For options C and D, "that" can be used only when "a world" requires a modifier as a subject or object in the main clause.
In a situation when a context indicates a clear place adverbial phrase like "in a world" "where" should be used.

Chapter 5

24 Common Patterns for *In*correct Choices in Writing

21 Subject-Verb, Pronoun, Noun Agreement Error

Independent sentence must have subject, verb, and object or complement.

This pattern frequently asks a missing verb, some disagreement between a singular/plural or subjective-objective pronoun,
Ex) I'm better than (A) she (B) her.
(B) is incorrect.

22 Nonrestrictive Modifier (Inessential Information)

Nonrestrictive modifier (inessential information) should be offset by a pair of commas, dashes, or parentheses to separate it from the main clause.

Ex) My car, a special edition from Benz, needs a major repair.
", a special edition from Benz," is not an essential information.

23 Transition Words for Supporting Detail, Contrast, and Consequence

Transition words/phrase focus on words and phrases that support, contrast, or produce consequence.(e.g., 'for example' for supporting detail; 'As a result' for the consequence)

The most difficult one of this type is finding one that has unnecessary transition word where not needed.

24 Verb Tense/Voice Error

Verb tense question asks whether the verb inappropriately changes the tense (e.g., from past to past perfect).

Voice question asks whether the sentence inappropriately changes voice (e.g., from active to passive).

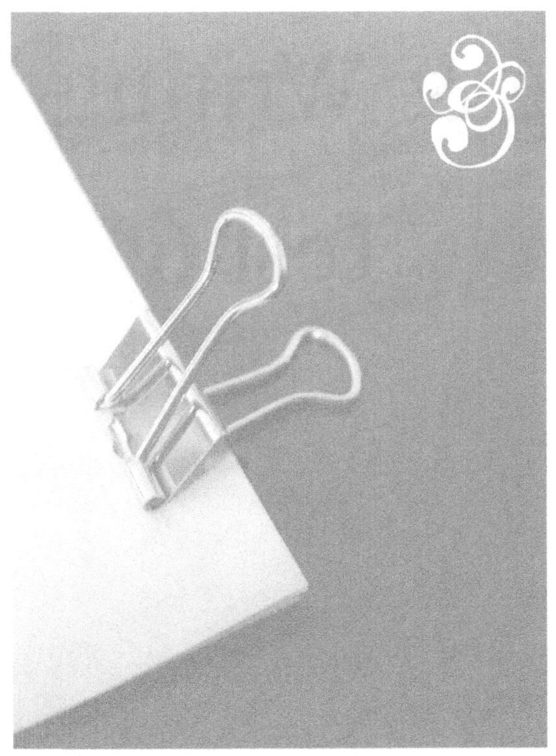

Chapter 6

1. TEST 6

2. ANSWER EXPLANATIONS for TEST 6

3. CHAPTER SUMMARY

SAT
Reading & Writing Practice
Test 6

ALL THE LOGIC AND RULES
BEHIND THE EVERY SINGLE
SAT QUESTION

Reading Test 6

60 MINUTES, 47 QUESTIONS

The passages below are followed by questions based on their content; questions following a pair of related passages may also be based on the relationship between the paired passages. Answer the questions on the basis of what is stated or implied in the passages and in any introductory material that may be provided.

Questions 1-10 are based on the following passage.

Between Fact and Fiction
Does history belong onstage?
Harvard University 2016 The Harvard Crimson,
Reprinted with permission.

It begins by falling in love with a name in a history book. Then comes the search for the details behind the name, then the gradual work to rebuild the world around it. Soon the name grows into a Person, someone I know but can never meet.

I chased my latest name (Margaret) to an archive in London. There were her letters—God, her handwriting!—and the first one, dated 1925, was to her friend Caroline and "completely private."

"Try + arrange that [it doesn't] get inserted in your biography," she wrote. She had penned the note nearly a century ago, but I flushed guiltily when I read it.

Historical research can be fascinating and beautiful and challenging and mysterious, but the first time I learned that wasn't in an archive. It was in a theater.

The play was Tom Stoppard's "Arcadia," in which two historians meet on an estate in the British countryside while researching the transition from the Enlightenment to Romanticism. Their historical subjects appear onstage too, not knowing their lives will be scrutinized 200 years later, revealing pieces of the historical puzzle as—or before—the historians discover it.

"Arcadia" mixed passionate love and the search for knowledge into beautiful disorder. In its famous final scene, the play's two time periods exist onstage simultaneously. Hannah Jarvis, one of the historians, sits within breathing distance of her historical actors when she solves the final piece of her historical puzzle, and none of them realize.

Professor Louis Menand described writing biography as molding a character. As you read more and more about your historical actor, he said, you continuously reshape your mental image of who they are.

Theater, I think, works in much the same way. Like archival material, a script can give only so much information. It is the theatermaker's responsibility to create, then tweak, a character whose actions and words match their echoes on the page. As in biography, the ultimate goal is to create a character who is as close to fully-realized as possible. But dramatizing history is a contentious topic, and historical characters can't always find a home onstage.

Historians have, time and time again, critiqued dramatic narratives for spreading Whig history—narratives of history which frame the past as a progression towards the inevitable present. Many contend that showing the public only the digestible versions of complex realities is destructive to understanding the past, present, and future. "Dump the destructive 'March of Progress' narratives!" historians call out. "Discard those presentist lenses of good and evil, truth and falsehood! People will think that's how life works!" So plays about history exist in a formal limbo.

They inhabit the shadowlands between fact and fiction, stretched taut between expectations that they will be both dramatic and instructive. But when fiction professes to deal in facts, the collateral damage can be serious.

That play embraces the ambiguity of the historical events it dramatizes. We don't know what really happened when Heisenberg and Bohr met in Copenhagen in 1941. In history, that ambiguity is a problem that needs to be solved.

CONTINUE

1

In Frayn's play, the ambiguity is the whole point." But is there only room for a historical play that is self-aware?

There can't be, and there mustn't be.

A play will not shape or destroy the academic discipline of history. Any play "based on a true story" remains just that. Audience members who take that fiction as truth are most likely also guilty of giving a Whig history of their morning.

So put history onstage, I say—sometimes, fictionalization is worth the risk. Stories are the way people and events embed themselves in public consciousness. You package moments in narratives so that people can remember them and think: yes, this still matters.

What did Lord Byron do that day, and why? the historian asks in chorus with the playwright. We are all asking the same questions, and answering them in different ways.

"It's wanting to know that makes us matter," Stoppard's Hannah Jarvis says, and the audience nods along.

The proper, footnoted history will always be more complex than its stage counterpart—lives are always messier than the ways we can communicate them.

But the stageplay reminds us to keep looking back: there is something there.

It reminds us to look to the past for the Persons, not just the names,; to remember that these were people who were made of flesh and blood, just like the actors now temporarily bearing their names."Come to me," the theater says, "and I will teach you to continue to want to know, to look to the past for that which is fascinating and beautiful and challenging and mysterious, and perhaps not as distant as it may seem."

1

The use of quotation mark in the context, "completely private." (line 11) is to

A) reveal a sudden sensation

B) criticize the author's misconduct on invading privacy

C) take an issue with Whig historian

D) reveal a sense of guilty for reading Margaret's letter without permission

2

The historians in line 54 would most likely criticize Whig history for its

A) precluding historical facts in the past based on the values of the present.

B) showing the public only the digestible versions of complex realities in history

C) using incorrect data to support a flawed conclusion.

D) severely overstating the history in the past

3

In lines 71-84, the author's attitude toward the Whig historian and theatermakers is best described respectively as

A) appreciative and deceitful

B) tentative and envious

C) skeptical and appreciative

D) condescending and furious

CONTINUE

1 1

4

The author suggests that stageplay should

A) not fictionalize the truth

B) tantalize the audience about history

C) reflect on how the past shapes the future

D) provide a room for history to be self-aware

5

Which choice provides the best evidence for the answer to the previous question?

A) Lines 77-79 (But is there...mustn't be)

B) Lines 80-81 (A play will...history.)

C) Lines 91-92 (What did...playwright.)

D) Lines 108-112 (Come to me...it may seem.)

6

As used in line 30, "disorder" most nearly means

A) chaos

B) confusing time and place

C) mystery

D) beautiful searching

7

The main purpose of the passage is to

A) appreciate stageplay

B) advance a theory of Whig history

C) note an impression of Whig historian

D) minimize erroneous assumption about historical play

8

The author reacts to stageplay with

A) appreciation as it emphasizes the present value

B) condemnation as it simplifies the complex nature of history

C) appreciation as it de-emphasizes the fact that history is made by names

D) condemnation as it justifies Whig historians' theory

9

Which choice provides the best evidence for the answer to the previous question?

A) Lines 72-74 (We don't know...in 1941)

B) Lines 74-75 (In history...to be solved.)

C) Lines 80-81 (A play ...discipline of history.)

D) Lines 104-108 (It reminds us...names.)

10

Which of the following most resembles the role of "play" to the academic discipline of history as described in lines 104-112 of the passage?

A) A kid learns math through games

B) A playwright writes a history book based on fact

C) A college professor teaches kindergarten kids for fun

D) A scientist values the present more than the past

CONTINUE

1 1

Questions 11-21are based on the following passage.

This passage is A Soldier of the Legion An Englishman's Adventures Under the French Flag in Algeria and Tonquin by George Manington

Most Englishmen, whose knowledge of the gay city of Paris is in the slightest degree superior to that of the ordinary summer tripper, are acquainted with the fine red stone building on the Boulevard St. Germaine, which is known as the Ministère de la Guerre, therefore it is unnecessary to give a lengthy description of this imposing edifice. It must, however, be explained why I, on the morning of the 26th February 1890, after pushing aside a big swing-door, found myself in the vestibule of this home of the supreme direction of one of the largest standing armies in the world.

I chanced one evening, to meet an Austrian gentleman, of old lineage and great wealth, who entertained us with the recital of his experiences during the Tonquin campaign of 1883-85. Owing to an affaire de coeur, he had enlisted in the Foreign Legion, had risen to the rank of sergeant-major, was twice wounded.

This narrative so excited my imagination and desire for adventure that I fell into slumber that night only after having decided on taking a similar course. Knowing that I should be likely to meet and mix with all conditions of men in the road I had chosen, on taking my decision I had determined to accept things as they were without complaint, so long as the life would bring me new experiences. The next morning I put my project into execution, and, as aforesaid, went to the fountain-head for information. Perhaps the officials may have had serious doubts as to whether I was in my right mind; and there was some excuse for them, for it is not every day that an individual comes to the Ministère, and in a matter-of-fact manner asks to enlist, in just such a way as one might ask for a room at an hotel. Whatever their thoughts may have been, they were exceedingly obliging, and informed me that I must go to the Rue St Dominique, the central recruiting office.

11

In lines 1-8 ("Most Englishmen,...edifice), the narrator's reference to Ministère de la Guerre is that the edifice

A) brought a sense of superiority to the narrator

B) required a special historical knowledge

C) called little attention

D) reflected other beautiful scenic places

12

The narrator's point of view in the passage is that of

A) a sympathetic man recalling early days in the foreign army

B) a sad observer of the Great War

C) an objective narrator presenting multiple characters

D) a wounded army veteran reflecting memorable events in the past

13

Which choice provides the best evidence for the answer to the previous question?

A) Lines 1-8 (Most Englishmen...imposing edifice)

B) Lines 8-13 (It must...in the world.)

C) Lines 14-17 (I chanced...1883-85.)

D) Lines 18-20 (Owing to an affaire...twice wounded.)

14

The narrator suggests that an Austrian gentleman in line 15 was

A) expressive

B) didactic

C) overbearing

D) puzzling

CONTINUE

1

15

In lines 32-33, "the officials have had serious doubts" suggests that they

A) thought the narrator's act was dubious
B) concerned about the narrator's decision
C) did not understand the narrator's language well
D) had no frequent requests similar to that of narrator

16

The officials in line 32 reacted to the narrator as if he were

A) heroic
B) crazy
C) serious
D) humorous

17

In developing the paragraphs 1-2 (lines 1-20), the narrator uses all of the following EXCEPT

A) prediction of his future
B) a recollection of conversation
C) reference to other person's background
D) generalization

18

The narrator's tone in describing his decision to joining the army is

A) argumentative
B) somber
C) decisive
D) laudatory

19

In lines 24-29, the narrator's assertion depends upon the premise that

A) imagination and desire should be parts of life
B) life must be associated with a new experience
C) narrative must excite the audience
D) man should be ready to mix well with all conditions in life

20

Which choice provides the best evidence for the answer to the previous question?

A) Lines 21-24 (This narrative…similar course)
B) Lines 24-26 (Knowing that…I had chosen)
C) Lines 28-29 (so long…new experience)
D) Lines 32-38 (Perhaps the officials...at an hotel)

21

Which statement best describes the interaction between the narrator and the officials in lines 32-41?

A) Both are attentive to say what they truly think should be done with the narrator's decision
B) Both realize that enlisting in the foreign army is foreboding of the Great War
C) Both misunderstand what the other is truly saying.
D) Both are reluctant to say any further about the narrator's decision

CONTINUE

1

Questions 22-31 are based on the following passage.

The following passage describes about Powerful media effects

From the early 20th century to 1930s, developing mass media technologies were credited with an almost irresistible power to mold an audience's beliefs, cognition and behaviors according to the communicators' will. The basic assumption of strong media effects theory was that audiences were passive and homogeneous. This assumption was not based on empirical evidence but on assumptions of human nature. There were two main explanations for this perception of mass media effects.

First, mass broadcasting technologies were acquiring a widespread audience, even among average households. Secondly, short term propaganda techniques were implemented during the war time by several governments as a powerful tool for uniting their people. "This propaganda exemplified strong, but ill-effect of communication" said the political scientist Harold Lasswell, who focused on the early media effects. Combing through the technological and social environment, early media effects theories stated that the mass media were all-powerful.

Hypodermic needle model, or magic bullet theory considers the audience to be targets of an injection or bullet of information fired from the pistol of mass media. The audience are unable to avoid or resist the injection or bullets.

Researchers uncovered mounting empirical evidence of the idiosyncratic nature of media effects on individuals and audiences. With these new variables added to research, it was difficult to isolate media influence that resulted in any media effects to an audience's cognition, attitude and behavior. As Berelson summed up in a widely quoted conclusion: "Some kinds of communication on some kinds of issues have brought to the attention of some kinds of people under some kinds of conditions have some kinds of effect."

The media play an indispensable role in the proper functioning of a modern democracy. Without mass media, openness and accountability are very tough to reach in contemporary democracies.

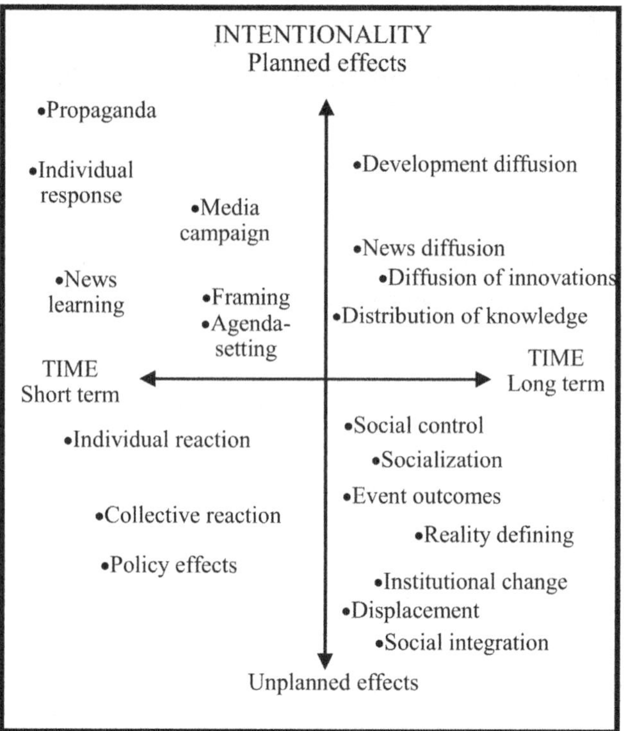

22

The author views media effects theory in line 6 as

A) evidence with plenty of data and statistics

B) a fundamental concept of media effects theory

C) a perception that cannot be proven

D) a familiar concept shared by several other theories

23

Which of the following assertions corresponds LEAST with the author's argument concerning the media effects theory?

A) Media communicator enjoys unilateral power to fabricate information

B) Communicators' will plays the dominant role

C) The audiences are believed to be all the same.

D) Government tries to avoid external impact such as war in order to unify internal consensus

CONTINUE

1 1

24

Which choice provides the best evidence for the answer to the previous question?

A) Lines 12-16 (Secondly, short term...their people.)
B) Lines 16-19 (This propaganda...early media effects.)
C) Lines 23-26 (Hypodermic needle...mass media.)
D) Lines 28-30 (Researchers…and audiences)

25

The word "pistol" in line 25 most nearly means?

A) information that viewers must absorb
B) news that the public can share
C) dangers felt by the audience
D) news from the gun control supporters

26

The quotation (lines 35-38) indicates that media effects

A) cannot be defined in a single term or value
B) can be determined by the degree of relationship between demographic attributes and social factors
C) show the even greater impact on individuals
D) remain as the most powerful influence to the public molding

27

Which statement would be most consistent with the mass media effects theory in lines 1-19?

A) German government banned its public from radio listening during the WWII
B) Terrorist organization utilizes YouTube for soldier recruitment
C) French people choose to read newspapers over radio to obtain quality news
D) British government often criticized the war propaganda

28

The author believes the role of media in modern democratic society serves chiefly to

A) mold public opinion
B) disclose reliable information
C) represent government propaganda
D) solidify selective transparency

29

Which choice provides the best evidence for the answer to the previous question?

A) Lines 16-19 (This propaganda...early media effects.)
B) Lines 23-26 (Hypodermic needle...mass media.)
C) Lines 28-30 (Researchers…and audiences)
D) Lines 41-43 (Without mass media democracies.)

30

The graph following the passage corresponds most consistently with the British government's media control during WWII in its

A) Short term planned effects
B) Long term planned effects
C) Short term unplanned effects
D) Long term unplanned effects

31

Harold Lasswell in line 18 may view "the communicators" in line 5 with?

A) respect
B) concern
C) analytical
D) naivety

CONTINUE

1 1

Questions 32-41 are based on the following passage.

The following passage is excerpted from Solar Panel Orientation and Positioning of Solar Panel

Solar panel refers to a panel designed to absorb the sun's rays as a source of energy for generating electricity or heating. The majority of modules use wafer-based crystalline silicon cells or thin-film cells. Most modules are rigid based on thin-film cells. Much of the incident sunlight energy is wasted by solar modules, and they can give far higher efficiencies if illuminated with mono-chromatic light. Therefore, another design concept is to split the light into different wavelength ranges and direct the beams onto different cells tuned to those ranges.

This has been projected to be capable of raising efficiency by 50%, with theoretical efficiencies being about 58% in cells with more than three junctions. Currently the best achieved sunlight conversion rate (solar module efficiency) is around 21.5% in new commercial products typically lower than the efficiencies of their cells in isolation. Research by Imperial College, London has shown that the efficiency of a solar panel can be improved by studding the light-receiving semiconductor surface with aluminum nanocylinders similar to the ridges on Lego blocks. Aluminum was found to have absorbed the ultraviolet part of the spectrum. The visible and near infrared parts of the spectrum were found to be scattered by the aluminum surface.

This, the research argued, could bring down the cost significantly and improve the efficiency as aluminum is more abundant and less costly than gold and silver. In 2013 solar generated less than 1% of the world's total grid electricity.

Yearly solar fluxes & human consumption[1]	
Solar	3,850,000
Wind	2,250
Biomass potential	~200

[1] Energy given in Exajoule (EJ) = 10^{18} J = 278 TWh
[2] Consumption as of year 2013

32

The primary function of the first paragraph is to

A) explore needs to change energy source from fossil fuel to solar energy

B) explain the current renewable energy technology

C) establish a brief introduction about solar panel

D) emphasize cost effectiveness of solar energy

33

Which of the following is true with modules described in paragraph 1?

A) modules must be flexible

B) Modules are often characteristically rigid

C) aesthetic approach is also important consideration

D) the thicker the film cell is, the better efficiency can be achieved

34

It can be inferred from the passage that the advanced solar panel in the future would most likely include higher functioning

A) mononchromatic light splitter

B) thick-film cells

C) rigid module

D) wafer-based crystalline silicon cells

35

Which choice provides the best evidence for the answer to the previous question?

A) Lines 7-10 (Much of the.....mono-chromatic light)

B) Lines 17-21 (Currently the best...cells in isolation.)

C) Lines 26-27 (Aluminum was found...the spectrum.)

D) Lines 28-30 (The visible and...aluminum surface)

CONTINUE

1 1

36

Which of the following sunlight conversion rates is consistent with the passage?

A) current rate: 22%, prototype development: 40%, in theory: 45%

B) current rate:58%, prototype development: 40%, in theory: 22%

C) current rate: 21.5%, prototype development: 45%, in theory: 58%

D) current rate: 21.5%, prototype development: 45%, in theory: 50%

37

By comparing the research result with Lego blocks, Imperial College researchers in line 22 primarily show

A) the efficiency of a solar panel

B) the flexibility of a solar panel

C) relatively convenient assembly method

D) cost-effective manufacturing approach

38

Which factor would be most consistent with the focus of future research on the solar panel?

A) Cost effective approach

B) Desirable location

C) Technical feasibility

D) Application of gold to the optimum level

39

Which choice provides the best evidence for the answer to the previous question?

A) Lines 17-21 (Currently the best...cells in isolation.)

B) Lines 26-27 (Aluminum was found...the spectrum.)

C) Lines 28-30 (The visible and...aluminum surface)

D) Lines 31-34 (This, the research...gold and silver)

40

According to the table and the last sentence (34-35), it can be inferred that the total grid electricity consumption in 2013 was

A) 400,000,000

B) 3,850

C) 2250

D) variable

41

Which of the following elements can increase the solar-generated electricity in the future?

A) Using aluminum

B) Achieving up to 21% of sunlight conversion rate

C) Public go-green campaign

D) Application of gold at the optimum level

CONTINUE

Questions 42-52 are based on the following passage.

Passage 1 is excerpted from the autobiography of Frederick Douglas, Passage 2 is from The Life and Work of Susan B. Anthony. The first part of the passage 2 is the public address by Susan Anthony at the temperance and teachers' conventions. The second part of the passage 2 is from The New York Sunday Times editorial after the conventions.

PASSAGE 1

In the early part of the year 1838, I became quite restless. I could see no reason why I should pour the reward of my toil into the purse of my master.

When I carried to him my weekly wages, he would, after counting the money, look me in the face with a robber-like fierceness, and ask, "Is this all?" He was satisfied with nothing less than the last cent. He would, however, when I made him six dollars, sometimes give me six cents, to encourage me. It had the opposite effect. I regarded it as a sort of admission of my right to the whole. My discontent grew upon me. I was ever on the look-out for means of escape; and I determined to try to hire my time, with a view of getting money with which to make my escape.

I got an opportunity, and applied to him to allow me to hire my time. He unhesitatingly refused my request, and told me this was another stratagem by which to escape. He exhorted me to content myself, and be obedient. He told me, if I would be happy, I must lay out no plans for the future.

PASSAGE 2

We believe that humanity is one in all those intellectual, moral and spiritual attributes out of which grow human responsibilities. Neither complexion nor sex is ever discharged from obedience to law, natural or moral, written or unwritten. We respectfully and earnestly pray that, in restoring the foundations of our nationality, all discriminations on account of sex or race may be removed; and that our government may be Republican in fact as well as form. Women and colored men are loyal, liberty-loving citizens, and we cannot believe that sex or complexion should be any ground for civil or political degradation.

--Response from The New York Sunday Times after the conventions

Susan B. Anthony, her Revolution was issued last Thursday as a sort of New Year's gift to what she considered a yearning public, and it is said to be "charged to the muzzle with literary nitre-glycerine." If Mrs. Stanton would attend a little more to her domestic duties and a little less to those of the great public, perhaps she would exalt her sex quite as much as she does by Quixotically fighting windmills in their gratuitous behalf. She might possibly set a notable example of world peace.

42

Frederick Douglas and Susan Anthony differ in their views of confinement in a way that Fredrick

A) views his goal as a self-liberation; Susan, as a whole society.

B) recognizes the difficulty of escaping from reality; Susan views womanhood can be ameliorated through equal education.

C) reminds the reader the importance of gender equality; Susan declares disobeying law offers no solutions.

D) finds money is a way to fulfill his desire; Susan warns gender inequality can be the ground of political degradation.

43

As presented in Passage 1, Frederick's desire to escape originates from

A) money

B) toiling work

C) moral and spiritual attributes

D) desire to liberate other slaves

CONTINUE

1 1

44

Master Thomas' response in lines 17-20 (He unhesitatingly...obedient) in Passage 1 implies that

A) Fredrick actually needs time for his own

B) Master Thomas sensed a similar experience in the past

C) Fredrick must be obedient in order to find contentment himself

D) Fredrick could go nowhere

45

Unlike Passage 1, Susan Anthony in Passage 2 presents the issue as

A) a way to satisfy individual desires

B) a process that can rectify the republic

C) a way to improve the entire humanity

D) a process requiring women's domestic duty

46

Which choice provides the best evidence for the answer to the previous question?

A) Lines 22-24 (We believe...human responsibility)

B) Lines 24-27 (Neither complexion...or unwritten)

C) Lines 27-31 (We respectfully...as well as form)

D) Lines 41-46 (If Mrs. Stanton...gratuitous behalf.)

47

As used in line 33, "complexion" is closest in meaning to?

A) unacceptable tradition

B) complex human nature

C) sophisticated social system

D) skin color

48

Master Thomas in Passage 1 and The New York Sunday Times in Passage 2 share their views in which of the following way?

A) Setting out the plan for the future is the road to unhappiness.

B) Woman should focus on domestic duties

C) Not all societal system is beautiful, but should be accepted in that way

D) Happiness can be obtained without leaving the current condition

49

The New York Sunday Times in Passage 2 would most likely respond to Master Thomas in lines 19-21 (He exhorted me...future) by

A) agreeing that domestic felicity can be achieved through obedience

B) disagreeing that the public affairs are more important than personal desire

C) conceding that slave can also obtain happiness

D) saying that women can't obtain enfranchisement, while black people can

50

Which choice provides the best evidence for the answer to the previous question?

A) Lines 22-24 (We believe...human responsibility)

B) Lines 27-31 (We respectfully...as well as form)

C) Lines 41-46 (If Mrs. Stanton...gratuitous behalf.)

D) Lines 46-47 (She might possibly...world peace.)

CONTINUE

1 1

51

The quotation in line 40 (“charged to nitre-glycerine) by The New York Sunday Times focuses Susan Anthony’s Revolution on its

A) spontaneity

B) magnitude

C) impracticality

D) novelty

52

The description in lines 31-34 ("Woman…degradation.) primarily serves to

A) suggest that women and black would be unlikely ever to consider entering politics

B) indicate woman and black play a pivotal role in society

C) show the adversities women and black had to overcome in society

D) imply some people's viewpoints are highly biased

STOP

If you finish before time is called,
you may check your work on this section.

Do not turn to the next section.

Writing and Language Test 6
35 MINUTES, 44 QUESTIONS

Each passage below is accompanied by a number of questions. For some questions, you will consider how the passage might be revised to improve the expression of ideas. For other questions, you will consider how the passage might be edited to correct errors in sentence structure, usage, or punctuation. A passage or a question may be accompanied by one or more graphics (such as a table or graph) that you will consider as you make revising and editing decisions.

Questions 1-11 are based on the following passage.

John Glenn and the Limits of Possibility

John Glenn, the first American to orbit the Earth [1] by circling the planet, a World War II veteran, and United States Senator for a tenure of 24 years, died on Thursday. He was 95.

[2] A native Ohioan who grew up in Ohio, I admired John Glenn. Glenn achieved an almost mythically larger-than-life status in American culture when he returned from space in 1962. From his journey in orbit on, Glenn continued to make Ohio and the United States proud. Both [3] because he achieved incredible feat and the way he handled himself with humility and plain-spoken grace, Glenn was an ideal role model.

1

A) NO CHANGE
B) circling the planet,
C) where he circled the planet
D) OMIT the underlined portion

2

A) NO CHANGE
B) Admiring a native Ohioan John Glenn, I grew up.
C) Admiring John Glenn as a native Ohioan, I grew up.
D) As a native Ohioan, I grew up admiring John Glenn.

3

A) NO CHANGE
B) because his incredible achievements as well as
C) because of his incredible achievements and
D) because of his incredible achievements and also because of

CONTINUE

2 2

He embodied so many characteristics teachers and parents want young people to learn about—and he was a homegrown legend. Having studied history for the last four years, [4] my perspective on why John Glenn is a hero has changed. My conviction that Glenn's legacy is important and my belief in the inspirational power of his life story [5] ; however, is unaltered. Glenn was a lionhearted warrior, an undaunted explorer, [6] and he was a judicious statesman.
<1>Glenn announced he would run for the Senate the day he retired from NASA in 1964, though he wasn't elected until 1974. <2>He was a fighter pilot in two wars, then a Navy and Marine test pilot, before being selected as one of the original "Mercury Seven" astronauts. <3>His famous orbit of earth was the culmination of twenty years of extraordinary feats of daring.
<4>In 1998, while still a sitting Senator, he returned to space at age 77, the oldest person ever to do so.

4

A) NO CHANGE
B) I changed my perspective on why John Glenn is a hero.
C) change of my perspective on why John Glenn is a hero has come upon me.
D) why John Glenn is a hero has changed.

5

A) NO CHANGE
B) however,
C) , however,
D) OMIT the underlined portion

6

A) NO CHANGE
B) who was a judicious statesman
C) and statesman who was judicious
D) and judicious statesman

7

For logic and sequence of this paragraph, sentence <1> should be placed:

A) NO CHANGE
B) after sentence <2>
C) after sentence <3>
D) after sentence <4>

CONTINUE

2 2

After officially retiring from the Senate, he helped found the John Glenn Institute for Public Service and Public Policy at The Ohio State University where he taught. <u>He continued to give lectures and visit schools until the end of his life</u>. [8]

John Glenn had one of the most impressive resumes in history. But accomplishments and accolades aside, [9] <u>sheer immensity that Glenn provided by devoting</u> to others—whether measured in time, energy, or personal risk—was itself heroic.

Glenn's passing is a reminder that an optimistic vision of America is possible. Without turning Glenn into a marble demigod or valorizing the cultural milieu from which he came, for that we be dishonest and a disservice to the man, I admire his human courage and his unwavering commitment to causes greater than himself. I respect the way he used his celebrity to create a platform from which he could unselfishly multiply his ability to do good.

8

The author is considering deleting the preceding sentence (He continued…).Should the author delete it?

A) Yes, because the sentence disrupts the paragraph's attention to John Glenn's career as a heroic astronaut.

B) Yes, because the sentence inappropriately shifts the focus of the paragraph from John Glenn, a hero to a philanthropist.

C) No, because the sentence is consistent with the paragraph's focus on the aspects of John Glenn's philanthropic activities after the retirement

D) No, because the sentence logically links the author's preference of Glenn as a philanthropist to astronaut.

9

A) NO CHANGE

B) the sheer immensity of Glenn's devotion

C) Glenn devoted with sheer immensity

D) Glenn devoted sheerly and immensely

CONTINUE

2

And I try to remember, without having lived through his most historic accomplishments myself, what it [10] was like to be inspired by a humble individual who dared to test the limits of possibility that transcends the limitations.[11]

10

A) NO CHANGE
B) will like to be
C) is like to be
D) DELTE IT

11

The author is considering deleting the underlined portion of the sentence. Should the author delete it?

A) Yes, because the portion shifts its focus from John Glenn as a heroic human being to just a human being.
B) Yes, because the portion does not deliver any meaningful information.
C) No, because the portion is emphasizing undaunted character John Glenn presented
D) No, because the portion logically concludes the essay.

CONTINUE

2 2

Questions 12-22 are based on the following passage.

Sarah Margaret Fuller Ossoli

Sarah Margaret Fuller Ossoli (1810 – 1850) [12] , is commonly known as Margaret Fuller, was an American journalist, critic, and women's rights advocate associated with the American transcendentalism movement. She was the first full-time American female book reviewer in journalism. Her book *Woman in the Nineteenth Century* is considered the first major feminist work in the United States. [13] Born in Cambridge, Massachusetts, [14] she was given a substantially early education by her father, Timothy Fuller.

She became **the first editor** (1) of the transcendentalist Journal ***The Dial*** (2) **in 1840** (3), before joining the New *York Tribune* **under Horace Greeley** (4) in 1844. [15]

12

A) NO CHANGE

B) ,commonly known as

C) ,was commonly known as

D) ,who is commonly known as,

13

If the author were to delete the preceding sentence, the paragraph would primarily lose information that

A) reveals social and racial bias Sarah Fuller encountered at that time it was published.

B) indicates the time and place the book was written

C) establishes the historic value of the book

D) describes the type of occupation Sarah Fuller worked

14

A) NO CHANGE

B) Sarah

C) it was Sarah Margarete Fuller who

D) this first major feminist in the United States

15

Which of the following information is not essential to understand the work and job of Sarah Fuller?

A) the first editor (1)

B) The Dial (2)

C) in 1840 (3)

D) under Horace Greeley (4)

CONTINUE

2 2

By the time she was in her 30s, Fuller [16] had earned a reputation as the best-read person in New England and became the first woman allowed to use the library at Harvard College. Her seminal work, *Woman in the Nineteenth Century*, was published in 1845. A year later, she was sent to Europe for the *Tribune* as its first female correspondent. She and her confidant Jane Kimberly soon became involved in the revolutions in Italy and she allied [17] her with Giuseppe Mazzini. She had a relationship with Giovanni Ossoli, [18] with whom she had a child. All three members of the family died in a shipwreck off Fire Island, New York, as they were traveling to the United States in 1850. Fuller's body was never recovered.

16

A) NO CHANGE
B) earned
C) has earned
D) had been earning

17

A) NO CHANGE
B) herself with Giuseppe Mazzini
C) with Giuseppe Mazzini
D) her being with Giuseppe Mazzini

18

A) NO CHANGE
B) with who
C) who
D) whose

CONTINUE

2 2

Many other advocates for women's rights and feminism, including [19] that of Susan B. Anthony, [20] cite Fuller as a source of inspiration. Many of her contemporaries ,however, were supportive, including her former friend Harriet Martineau. She said that Fuller was a talker [21] more than an activist. Shortly after Fuller's death, her importance faded; the editors who prepared her letters to be published, believing her fame would be short-lived, censored or altered much of her work before publication.

19

A) NO CHANGE
B) people such as Susan B. Anthony,
C) those of Susan B. Anthony,
D) Susan B. Anthony,

20

A) NO CHANGE
B) sighted
C) cited
D) site

21

A) NO CHANGE
B) less than
C) rather than
D) less then

22

Suppose the author's goal was to write a brief essay about the life of an early feminist.
Would this summary successfully fulfill the author's goal?

A) Yes, because the summary offers Susan Anthony's major events as a feminist
B) Yes, because the summary reveals social injustice Sarah Fuller encountered.
C) No, because the summary focuses more on the impact of Susan Anthony as her mentor
D) No, because the summary represents an early feminist' unfolded personal life rather than civil work.

CONTINUE

2 2

Questions 23-33 are based on the following passage.

A shape-memory ally

A shape-memory alloy (SMA) is an alloy that "remembers" its original shape and that when deformed returns to its pre-deformed shape [23] that heated. This material is a lightweight, solid-state [24] alternative to conventional actuators such as hydraulic, pneumatic, and motor-based systems. Shape-memory alloys have applications in robotics and automotive, aerospace and biomedical industries. The two main types of shape-memory alloys are copper-aluminum-nickel, and nickel-titanium (NiTi) alloys but SMAs can also be created [25] by alloy of zinc, and copper, and gold, and iron. Although iron-based and copper-based SMAs, such as Fe-Mn-Si, Cu-Zn-Al and Cu-Al-Ni, are [26] commercially available in the market and cheaper than NiTi, NiTi which bases SMAs are preferable for most applications [27] due to their stability, practicability and superior thermo-mechanic performance.

23

A) NO CHANGE
B) when
C) by
D) OMIT the underlined portion

24

Which of the following alternatives to the portion would NOT be acceptable?

A) replacement for
B) substitute for
C) enhancement to
D) equivalent to

25

A) NO CHANGE
B) with alloying zinc, copper, gold and iron.
C) with alloy of zinc, copper, gold and iron.
D) by alloying zinc, copper, gold and iron.

26

A) NO CHANGE
B) commercially available as a marketable product
C) commercial.
D) commercially available

27

Which of the following alternatives to the underlined portion would NOT be acceptable?

A) because their stability
B) because of their stability
C) owing to their stability
D) thanks to their stability

CONTINUE

2 2

NiTi alloys change from austenite to martensite upon cooling; M_f is the temperature at which the transition to martensite completes upon cooling. [28] Repeated use of the shape-memory effect may lead to a shift of the characteristic transformation temperatures (this effect is known as functional [29] fatigue, as it is closely related with a change of microstructural and functional properties of the material). The maximum temperature at which SMAs can no longer be stress induced is called M_d, where the SMAs are [30] permanently deformed.

28

Which one establishes a visual contrast to the image in the underlined sentence?

A) The first consumer commercial application was a shape-memory coupling for piping.

B) Intelligent Reinforced Concrete (IRC), which incorporates SMA wires embedded within the concrete can sense cracks and contract to heal macro-sized crack.

C) There have been, however, limited studies on using these materials in auto body.

D) During heating $A_s$and A_f are the temperature at which the transformation from martensite to austenite starts and finishes.

29

Which of the following alternatives to the underlined portion would NOT be acceptable?

A) exhaustion

B) weakness

C) stress

D) anxiety

30

Which of the following alternatives to the underlined portion would NOT be acceptable?

A) irrevocably

B) irreversibly

C) irreparably

D) forever

CONTINUE

2 2

The transition from the martensite phase to the austenite phase is only dependent on temperature and stress, not time, as most phase changes are, as there is no diffusion involved. Similarly, the austenite structure receives its name from steel alloys of [31] a similar and comparable structure. It is the reversible diffusion less transition between these two phases that results in special properties. [32] Martensite can be formed from austenite by rapidly cooling carbon-steel, this process is not reversible, so steel does not have shape-memory properties.

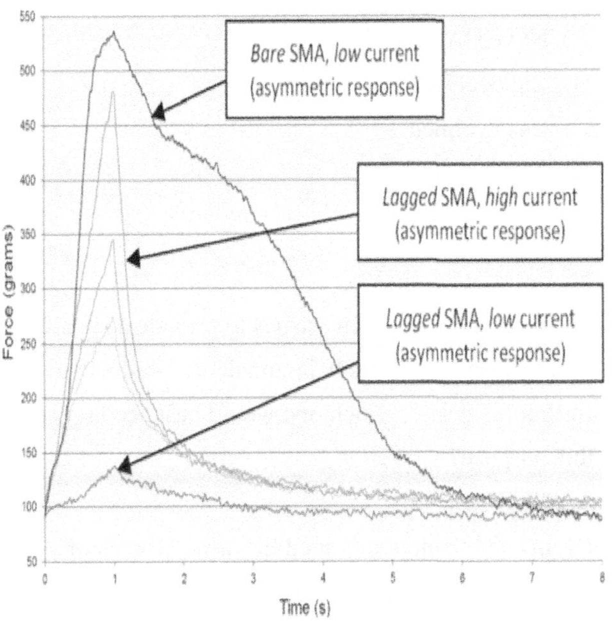

31

A) NO CHANGE
B) a comparable configuration and similar
C) a similar structure which is comparable.
D) similar

32

A) NO CHANGE
B) While martensite
C) With martensite
D) By martensite

33

The graph demonstrates the feasibility of SMA actuators that use conductive "lagging" method on which thermal paste is rapidly transferred from the SMA. Using this method, manufacturers can expect:

A) A significant reduction time in both Bare SMA low current and Lagged SMA, low current
B) A significant reduction time both Bare SMA low current and Lagged SMA, high current
C) A significant reduction time in Lagged SMA high current only.
D) A significant reduction time in Lagged SMA low current only.

CONTINUE

2 2

Questions 34-44 are based on the following passage.

Thomas Carmichael Hindman, Jr.

Thomas Carmichael Hindman, Jr. (January 28, 1828 – September 27, 1868) was a lawyer, United States Representative from the 1st Congressional District of Arkansas, [34] and he was a major general in the Confederate States Army during the American Civil War. After receiving his primary education in Ripley, he [35] had attended the Lawrenceville Classical Institute and graduated with honors in 1843. <1> Afterwards, he raised a company in Tippah County for the 2nd Mississippi regiment in the Mexican–American War. <2> Hindman served during the war as a lieutenant and later as a captain of his company. <3> He studied law, and was admitted to the state bar in 1851. <4>After the war, he returned to Ripley. He was elected as the Democratic Representative from Arkansas's 1st congressional district in the Thirty-sixth Congress from March 4, 1859, to March 4, 1861, but [36] had been declined to serve after the onset of the Civil War and Arkansas's secession from the Union. [37] Instead, Hindman waited wisely until war was over.

34

A) NO CHANGE
B) who was a major general
C) and was a major general
D) and *major general*

35

Which of the following is most logical sequences in this paragraph?

A) NO CHANGE
B) <1>,<2>,<4>,<3>
C) <1>,<2>,<4>,<3>
D) <4>,<1>,<2>,<3>

36

A) NO CHANGE
B) had declined
C) was declined
D) declined

37

At this point, the author wishes to provide a specific example on the efforts being made by Hindman to further his desire, which one would best accomplish this purpose?

A) NO CHANGE
B) Instead, Hindman joined the armed forces of the Confederacy.
C) Instead, Hindman sought peaceful resolution to end the Civil war.
D) Instead, Hindman moved to Mexican town of Carlota, where he engaged in coffee planting business and attempted to practice law.

CONTINUE

2

He commanded the Trans-Mississippi Department, and later raised and commanded "Hindman's Legion" for the Confederate States Army. After the war, Hindman avoided surrender to the federal government [38] by fleeing to Mexico City. After the execution of Maximilian I of Mexico, Hindman submitted a petition [39] to request for a pardon to President Andrew Johnson, but it was denied. Hindman, nonetheless, returned to his former life in Helena. He became the leader of the "Young Democracy" [40] , there he rebuilt a new political organization that was willing to accept the Reconstruction for the restoration of the Union. He was assassinated on September 27, 1868, at his Helena home. As the American Civil War approached, Hindman was a passionate voice for secession and was primarily Arkansas's most prominent Fire-Eater.

With war approaching, Hindman resigned from Congress and recruited a regiment at Helena, which was mustered into Confederate service. He requested the state government for muskets, clothing and ten days of rations [41] so that his men could "fight for our country".

38

A) NO CHANGE
B) into
C) towards
D) via

39

A) NO CHANGE
B) by officially requesting
C) and appealed to authority with respect
D) OMIT the underlined portion

40

A) NO CHANGE
B) , a new political organization
C) , it became a new political organization
D) ; a new political organization

41

A) NO CHANGE
B) so as
C) so as to
D) in order for

CONTINUE

2 2

He and his regiment were soon active participants in the disastrous Kentucky Campaign, followed soon after that by fierce fighting at the Battle of Shiloh in April 1862, [42] when he was slightly wounded. After his recovery, Hindman was promoted [43] to the rank of major general and was appointed commander of the Trans-Mississippi Department to prevent an invasion by the Union troops led by Samuel Curtis.

Events in Arkansas had taken a terrible turn for the worse. Most units had been stripped from the state for service east of the Mississippi River. When Hindman arrived in Little Rock, Arkansas, he found that his command was bare of soldiers, penniless, defenseless, [44] although no immediate threat was visible, Meantime, the Federal Army was approaching dangerously from the northwest.

42

Which of the following choices would NOT be acceptable?

A) NO CHANGE
B) where
C) but
D) a time that

43

Which one clearly adds objective and specific information that illustrates Hindman's army career?

A) NO CHANGE
B) to the envious rank
C) to rank that everyone aspires
D) to the rank that became critical in his army career

44

Which choice would most effectively maintain logical consistency?

A) NO CHANGE
B) consequently, Hindman attempted inevitable surrender .
C) and dreadfully exposed to its enemy.
D) but had a hope in politics that still called for him.

STOP

If you finish before time is called,
you may check your work on this section.

Do not turn to the next section.

SAT Test 6
Answer Explanations
&
The Pattern Analyses

If your Test 6 scores are unsatisfactory,

Test 7 won't be satisfactory either.

Please Practice the Answer Explanations and then come back to Test 6 again.

ALL THE LOGIC AND RULES BEHIND EVERY SINGLE SAT QUESTION

SAT Test 6

Reading Section Answer Explanations

&

The Pattern Analyses

Questions 1-11 are based on the following passage.

It begins by falling in love with a name in a history book. Then comes the search for the details behind the name, then the gradual work to rebuild the world around it. Soon the name grows into a Person, someone I know but can never meet.

I chased my latest name (Margaret) to an archive in London. There were her letters— (1A) **God, her handwriting!**—and the first one, dated 1925, was to her friend Caroline and "completely private."

"Try + arrange that [it doesn't] get inserted in your biography," she wrote. She had penned the note nearly a century ago, but I flushed guiltily when I read it.

(6C) **Historical research can be fascinating and beautiful and challenging and mysterious, but the first time I learned that wasn't in an archive. It was in a theater.**

The play was Tom Stoppard's "Arcadia," in which two historians meet on an estate in the British countryside while researching the transition from the Enlightenment to Romanticism. Their historical subjects appear onstage too, not knowing their lives will be scrutinized 200 years later, revealing pieces of the historical puzzle as—or before—the historians discover it.

"Arcadia" mixed passionate love and the search for knowledge into beautiful disorder. In its famous final scene, the play's two time periods exist onstage simultaneously. Hannah Jarvis, one of the historians, sits within breathing distance of her historical actors when she solves the final piece of her historical puzzle, and none of them realize.

Professor Louis Menand described writing biography as molding a character. As you read more and more about your historical actor, he said, you continuously reshape your mental image of who they are.

Theater, I think, works in much the same way. Like archival material, a script can give only so much information. It is the theatermaker's responsibility to create, then tweak, a character whose actions and words match their echoes on the page. As in biography, the ultimate goal is to create a character who is as close to fully-realized as possible.

But dramatizing history is a contentious topic, and historical characters can't always find a home onstage.

Historians have, time and time again, critiqued dramatic narratives for spreading Whig history—narratives of history which (2A) frame the past as a progression towards the inevitable present. Many contend that showing the public only the digestible versions of complex realities is destructive to understanding the past, present, and future"Dump the destructive 'March of Progress' narratives!" historians call out. "Discard those presentist lenses of good and evil, truth and falsehood! People will think that's how life works!" So plays about history exist in a formal limbo.

They inhabit the shadowlands between fact and fiction, stretched taut between expectations that they will be both dramatic and instructive. But when fiction professes to deal in facts, the collateral damage can be serious.

That play embraces the ambiguity of the historical events it dramatizes. We don't know what really happened when Heisenberg and Bohr met in Copenhagen in 1941. In history, that ambiguity is a problem that needs to be solved.

In Frayn's play, the ambiguity is the whole point." But is there only room for a historical play that is self-aware? **There can't be, and there mustn't be.** A play will not shape or destroy the academic discipline of history. Any play "based on a true story" remains just that. Audience members who take that fiction as truth are most likely also **guilty of giving a Whig history of their morning.**

(7A) **So put history onstage, I say—sometimes, fictionalization is worth the risk.** Stories are the way people and events embed themselves in public consciousness. You package moments in narratives so that people can remember them and think: yes, this still matters. What did Lord Byron do that day, and why? the historian asks in chorus with the playwright. We are all asking the same questions, and answering them in different ways.

"It's wanting to know that makes us matter," Stoppard's Hannah Jarvis says, and the audience nods along. The proper, footnoted history will always be more complex than its stage counterpart—lives are always messier than the ways we can communicate them.

(3C&4B) **But the stageplay reminds us to keep looking back: there is something there.** (8C&9D) **It reminds us to look to the past for the Persons, not just the names,;** (10A) **to remember that these were people who were made of flesh and blood, just like the actors now temporarily bearing their names.** "Come to me," the theater says, "and I will teach you to continue to want to know, (5D) **to look to the past for that which is fascinating and beautiful and challenging and mysterious,** and perhaps not as distant as it may seem."

Q1. **Absolute Pattern 7: Understanding Attitude (Tone) Question**
Finding a tone such as positive-negative, active-passive, mental-physical, subjective-objective
Question Pattern: The use of **quotation mark** in the context, "**completely private**." (line 11) is to

A) **reveal a sudden sensation** **B)** criticize the author's misconduct on invading privacy C) take an issue with Whig historian D) reveal a sense of guilty for reading Margaret's letter without permission	A) she must have felt sensation when she discovered the letter proven by the exclamation mark "God" in line 7. D) Where is the evidence that she felt guilty?

Q2. **Absolute Pattern 9: Relationships Question**
Finding relations between the cause-effect, characters, and ideas including a Paired Passage.
Question Pattern: The historians in line 54 would most likely **criticize Whig history** for its

A) precluding historical facts in the past based on the values of the present. B) showing the public only the digestible versions of complex realities in history C) using incorrect data to support a flawed conclusion D) severely overstating the history in the past	A) Whig history—narratives of history which *frame* the past as a progression towards the inevitable present. Frame means to limit or preclude. The author views Whig historians are bigotry. (A) is inconsistent with the question. (C) refers to dramatic narratives, not Whig history. (D) is opposite perception of the Whig historian.

Q3. **Absolute Pattern 7: Understanding Attitude (Tone) Question**
Question Pattern: In lines 71-84, the author's attitude toward the **Whig historian and theatermakers** is best described respectively as

A) appreciative and deceitful B) tentative and envious **C) skeptical and appreciative** D) condescending and furious	C) Audience members who take that fiction as truth are most likely also guilty of giving a Whig history...(**Negative**) But the stageplay reminds us to keep looking back: there is something there. It reminds us to look to the past for the Persons, not just the names (**Positive**) Not just in above sentences but in many places throughout the passage, the author criticizes Whig historians and praises theatermakers.

Q4. **Absolute Pattern 2: Summary Question** Summarizing a sentence or entire passage
Question Pattern: The author suggests that **stageplay should**

A) not fictionalize the truth **B) tantalize the audience about history** C) frame the present to shape the future D) provide a room for history to be self-aware	B) But the stageplay reminds us to keep looking back: there is something there. It reminds us to look to the past for the Persons, not just the names A) L86-fictionalization is worth...(Opposite) C) L55: Historians have critiqued frame the past (Opposite) D) L 79-But, historical play is self-aware? there can't be (Opposite)

Q5. **Absolute Pattern 11: Textual Evidence Question** Finding evidence for the previous question
Question Pattern: Which choice provides the best evidence for the answer to the previous question?

A) Lines 77-79 (But is there...mustn't be) B) Lines 80-81 (A play will...history.) C) Lines 91-92 (What did...playwright.) **D) Lines 108-112 (Come to me...it may seem.)**	D) Come to me," the theater says, "and I will teach you to continue to want to know, to look to the past for that which is fascinating and beautiful and challenging and mysterious, and perhaps not as distant as it may seem

<table>
<tr><td colspan="2">Q6. Absolute Pattern 5: Word-In-Context Question
Finding a clue word and the keyword from the sentence in question
Question Pattern: As used in line 30, “disorder” most nearly means</td></tr>
<tr><td>A) chaos
B) confusing time and place
C) mystery
D) beautiful searching</td><td>C) The clue word “beautiful” is the key to solve this question. “beautiful” is positive word. Therefore, the disorder must also be positive. In this process we can eliminate (A) and (B). Also, in line 14: Historical research can be fascinating and beautiful and challenging and mysterious,

D) is incorrect because it does not respond to the question. The question is seeking the meaning behind the word “disorder”, not “beautiful”</td></tr>
<tr><td colspan="2">Q7. Absolute Pattern 1: Main Idea Question Finding the main idea of the entire passage or the paragraph
Question Pattern: The main purpose of the passage is to</td></tr>
<tr><td>A) appreciate stageplay
B) advance a theory of Whig history
C) note an impression of Whig historian
D) minimize erroneous assumption about historical play</td><td>A) So put history onstage, Come to me,” the theater says, “and I will teach you to continue.
B), C) are minor info. D): The passage partially mentions about it but is only the element of (A).</td></tr>
<tr><td colspan="2">Q8. Absolute Pattern 2: Summary Question Summarizing a sentence or entire passage
Question Pattern: The author reacts to stageplay with</td></tr>
<tr><td>A) appreciation as it emphasizes the present value
B) condemnation as it simplifies the complex nature of history
C) appreciation as it de-emphasizes the fact that history is made by names
D) condemnation as it justifies Whig historians' theory</td><td>C) “It reminds us to look to the past for the Persons, not just the names,; to remember that these were people.

A), the present value vs. past value is the main concern of Whig history, not the stageplay.

B) and D) are incorrect because throughout the passage, the author favors stageplay.</td></tr>
<tr><td colspan="2">Q9. Absolute Pattern 11: Textual Evidence Question Finding evidence for the previous question
Question Pattern: Which choice provides the best evidence for the answer to the previous question?</td></tr>
<tr><td>A) Lines 73-74 (What really...in 1941)
B) Lines 74-75 (In history...to be solved.)
C) Lines 80-81 (A play ...discipline of history.)
D) Lines 104-108 (It reminds us...names.)</td><td>D) Please refer to the above question</td></tr>
<tr><td colspan="2">Q10. Absolute Pattern 6: Analogy Question Finding a similar situation
Question Pattern: Which of the following most resembles the role of “play” to the academic discipline of history as described in lines 104-112 of the passage?</td></tr>
<tr><td>A) A kid learns math through games
B) A playwright writes a history book based on fact
C) A college professor teaches kindergarten kids for fun
D) A scientist values the present more than the past</td><td>A) L108-112: “and I will teach you (KID) to continue to want to know, (LEARN MATH) to look to the past for that which is fascinating and beautiful and challenging and mysterious stageplay (through GAMES), ”

B) Opposite perception to stageplay
C) “Fun” can't be the goal of stageplay.
D) is describing Whig history</td></tr>
</table>

Questions 11-21 are based on the following passage.

Most Englishmen, whose knowledge of the gay city of Paris is in the slightest degree superior to that of the ordinary summer tripper, are acquainted with the fine red stone building on the Boulevard St. Germaine, which is known as the Ministère de la Guerre, (11C) **therefore it is unnecessary to give a lengthy description of this imposing edifice.** (12A) **It must, however, be explained why I, on the morning of the 26th February 1890, after pushing aside a big swing-door, found myself in the vestibule of this home of the supreme direction of one of the largest standing armies in the world.**

I chanced one evening, to meet an Austrian gentleman, of old lineage and great wealth, who entertained us with the recital of his experiences during the Tonquin campaign of 1883-85. Owing to an affaire de coeur, he had enlisted in the Foreign Legion, had risen to the rank of sergeant-major, was twice wounded. (14A) **This narrative so excited** my imagination and desire for adventure that **I fell into slumber that night** only after having decided on taking a similar course. Knowing that I should be likely to meet and mix with all conditions of men in the road I had chosen, (Q18C) **on taking my decision I had determined to accept things as they were without complaint,** (19B&20C) **so long as the life would bring me new experiences.** The next morning I put my project into execution, and, as aforesaid, went to the fountain-head for information. Perhaps the officials may have had serious doubts as to whether (16B) **I was in my right mind**; and there was some excuse for them, (15D) **for it is not every day that an individual comes to the _Ministère_, and in a matter-of-fact manner asks to enlist, in just such a way as one might ask for a room at an hotel.** (21D) **Whatever their thoughts may have been,** they were exceedingly obliging, and informed me that (13B) **I must go to the Rue St Dominique, the central recruiting office.**

Q11. **Absolute Pattern 2: Summary Question** Summarizing a sentence, or an entire paragraph
Question Pattern: In lines 1-8 ("Most Englishmen,…edifice), the **narrator's reference to Ministère de la Guerre is that the edifice**

A) brought a sense of superiority to the narrator
B) required a special historical knowledge
C) called little attention
D) reflected other beautiful scenic places

C) therefore it is unnecessary to give a lengthy description of this imposing edifice.

A) It's most Englishmen who felt superiority, not the narrator.
B) is Opposite D) is not stated.

Q12. **Absolute Pattern 7: Understanding Attitude (Tone) Question**
Finding a tone such as positive-negative, active-passive, mental-physical, subjective-objective
Question Pattern: The **narrator's point of view** in the passage is that of

A) a sympathetic man recalling early days in the foreign army
B) a sad observer of the Great War
C) an objective narrator presenting multiple characters
D) a wounded army veteran reflecting memorable events in the past

A) It must, however, be explained why I, on the morning of the 26th February 1890, …standing armies in the world.
B) and D) are Not Stated in the passage.

(C) Personal anecdote or essay is supposed to be subjective. This subjective perspective can be either positive or negative, but not objective like (C).

Q13. **Absolute Pattern 11: Textual Evidence Question** Finding evidence for the previous question
Question Pattern: Which choice provides the best evidence for the answer to the previous question?

A) Lines 1-8 (Most Englishmen...imposing edifice)
B) Lines 8-13 (It must...in the world.)
C) Lines 14-17 (I chanced...1883-85.)
D) Lines 18-20 (Owing to an affaire...twice wounded.)

B) is the best answer.
The other choices describe the background of the narrator, not of himself.

Q14. **Absolute Pattern 4: Example Question**
Understanding example sentence and the true purpose behind a specific name or idea.
Question Pattern: The narrator suggests that an **Austrian gentleman** in line 15 was

A) expressive B) didactic C) overbearing D) puzzling	**A)** This narrative so excited (EXPRESSIVE) my imagination and desire for adventure that I fell into slumber that night only after having decided on taking a similar course~

Q15. **Absolute Pattern 8: Understanding the True Purpose** Finding the true purpose of statement
Question Pattern: In lines 32-33, **"the officials have had serious doubts"** suggests that they

A) thought the narrator's act was dubious B) concerned about the narrator's decision C) did not understand the narrator's language well **D) had no frequent requests similar to that of narrator**	D) for it is not every day that an individual comes to the Ministère, and in a matter-of-fact manner asks to enlist.," (A), (B) are incorrect because the passage does not state whether the official thought that way.

Q16. **Absolute Pattern 7: Understanding Attitude (Tone) Question**
Finding a tone such as positive-negative, active-passive, mental-physical, subjective-objective
Question Pattern: The **officials in line 32 reacted** to the narrator as if he were

A) heroic **B) crazy** C) serious D) humorous	B) Perhaps the officials may have had serious doubts as to whether I was in my right mind" Please DO NOT choose the option that is opposite to the passage. Sometimes, SAT employs not quite an academic word such as "crazy" that defies our common sense. For instance, some reading passages criticize Martin Luther King Jr. or Abraham Lincoln. In that case, the answer choice can't be positive although they are beyond our reproach.

Q17. **Absolute Pattern 2: Summary Question** Summarizing a sentence or entire passage
Question Pattern: In developing the paragraphs 1-2 (lines 1-20), **the narrator uses all** of the following EXCEPT

A) prediction of his future B) a recollection of conversation C) reference to other person's background D) generalization	A) There is no prediction for the future in the paragraph. The narrator uses flashback. B) Line14: I chanced one evening… C) Line 14: Austrian, old lineage, wealth D) Line 1: Most Englishmen

Q18. **Absolute Pattern 7: Understanding Attitude (Tone) Question**
Finding a tone such as positive-negative, active-passive, mental-physical, subjective-objective
Question Pattern: The **narrator's tone** in describing his decision to joining the army is

A) argumentative B) somber **C) decisive** D) laudatory	C) on taking my decision I had determined to accept things as they were without complaint, so long as the life would bring me new experiences.

Q19. **Absolute Pattern 2: Summary Question** Summarizing a sentence, or an entire paragraph **Question Pattern:** In lines 24-29, **the narrator's assertion depends upon the premise** that	
A) imagination and desire should be parts of life **B) life must be associated with a new experience** C) narrative must excite the audience D) man should be ready to mix well with all conditions in life	B) Knowing that I should be likely to meet and mix with all conditions of men in the road I had chosen, on taking my decision I had determined to accept things as they were without complaint, **so long as** the life would bring me new experiences. **(Premise)** The key point is "so long as" alluding a "premise"
A) The word "imagination" came from the narrator's description about gentleman's narrative. D) "mix well" is his understanding, not the premise.	

Q20. **Absolute Pattern 11: Textual Evidence Question** Finding evidence for the previous question **Question Pattern:** Which choice provides the best evidence for the answer to the previous question?	
A) Lines 21-24 (This narrative...similar course) B) Lines 24-26 (Knowing that...I had chosen) **C) Lines 28-29 (so long...new experience)** D) Lines 32-38 (Perhaps the officials...at an hotel)	C) Please refer to the above question

Q21. **Absolute Pattern 9: Relationships Question** **Question Pattern:** Which statement best describes the **interaction between the narrator and the officials** in lines 32-41?	
A) Both are attentive to say what they truly think should be done with the narrator's decision B) Both realize that enlisting in the foreign army is foreboding of the Great War C) Both misunderstand what the other is truly saying. **D) Both are reluctant to say any further about the narrator's decision**	D) Perhaps the officials may have had serious doubts as to whether I was in my right mind;... Whatever their thoughts may have been C) is opposite because they communicated each other.

Questions 22-31 are based on the following passage.

From the early 20th century to 1930s, developing mass media technologies were credited with an almost irresistible power to mold an audience's beliefs, cognition and behaviors according to the communicators' will. The basic assumption of strong media effects theory was that audiences were passive and homogeneous. (22C) **This assumption was not based on empirical evidence but on assumptions of human nature.** There were two main explanation for this perception of mass media effect

First, (24A) **mass broadcasting technologies were acquiring a widespread audience,** even among average households. Secondly, (23D&Q27B) **short term propaganda techniques were implemented during the war time by several governments as a powerful tool for uniting their people.** (31B) **"This propaganda exemplified strong, but ill-effect of communication" said the political scientist Harold Lasswell, who focused on the early media effects.**

Combing through the technological and social environment, early media effects theories stated that the mass media were all-powerful.

Hypodermic needle model, or magic bullet theory considers the audience to be targets of an injection or bullet of information fired from the pistol of mass media. (25A)**The audience are unable to avoid or resist the injection or bullets.**

Researchers uncovered mounting empirical evidence of the idiosyncratic nature of media effects on individuals and audiences. With these new variables added to research, (26A) **it was difficult to isolate media influence that resulted in any media effects to an audience's cognition, attitude and behavior. As Berelson summed up** in a widely quoted conclusion: "

CONTINUED IN THE FOLLOWING PAGE

Questions 22-31 are based on the following passage.

"Some kinds of communication on some kinds of issues have brought to the attention of some kinds of people under some kinds of conditions have some kinds of effect."	The media play an indispensable role in the proper functioning of a modern democracy (28B&29D)**Without mass media, openness and accountability are very tough to reach in contemporary democracies.**

Q22. **Absolute Pattern 2: Summary Question** Summarizing a sentence, or an entire paragraph
Question Pattern: The author views **media effects** theory in line 6 as

A) evidence with plenty of data and statistics B) a fundamental concept of media effects theory **C) a perception that cannot be proven** D) a familiar concept shared by several other theories	C) This assumption was not based on empirical evidence but on the assumptions of human nature.

Q23. **Absolute Pattern 2: Summary Question** Summarizing a sentence or entire passage
Question Pattern: Which of the following assertions corresponds **LEAST** with the author's argument concerning **the media effects theory**?

A) Media communicator enjoys unilateral power to fabricate information B) Communicators' will plays the dominant role C) The audiences are believed to be all the same. **D) Government tries to avoid external impact such as war in order to unify internal consensus**	D) Secondly, short term propaganda techniques were implemented during the war time by several governments as a powerful tool for uniting their people. As seen above, (D) is direct opposite to the passage.

Q24. **Absolute Pattern 11: Textual Evidence Question** Finding evidence for the previous question
Question Pattern: Which choice provides the best evidence for the answer to the previous question?

A) Lines 13-16 (Secondly, short term...their people.) B) Lines 16-19 (This propaganda...early media effects.) C) Lines 23-26 (Hypodermic needle...mass media.) D) Lines 28-30 (Researchers…and audiences)	A) Please refer to the above question

Q25. **Absolute Pattern 3: Inference Question** Finding an indirect suggestion (or guessing)
Question Pattern: The word "**pistol**" in line 25most nearly means?

A) information that viewers must absorb B) news that the public can share C) dangers felt by the audience D) news from the gun control supporters	A) bullet of information fired from the pistol of mass media. The audience are unable to avoid... The word 'Pistol' is used figuratively to support the topic sentence "the propaganda"

Q26. **Absolute Pattern 3: Inference Question** Finding an indirect suggestion (or guessing)
Question Pattern: The **quotation** (lines 35-38) indicates that media effects

A) cannot be defined in a single term or value B) can be determined by the degree of relationship between demographic attributes and social factors C) show the even greater impact on individuals D) remain as the most powerful influence to the public molding	A) Researchers uncovered mounting empirical evidence of the idiosyncratic nature of media effects on individuals and audiences, identifying numerous intervening variables, A quotation is used as a part of example when author wants to backup or justify his idea. The answer should then be located right above or right below the quotation where the author's main point is described. D): albeit true statement, inconsistent with the question.

Q27. **Absolute Pattern 6: Analogy Question** Finding a similar situation
Question Pattern: Which statement would be most consistent with the mass **media effects theory** in lines 1-19?

A) German government banned its public from radio listening during the WWII
B) Terrorist organization utilizes YouTube for soldier recruitment
C) French people choose to read newspapers over radio to obtain quality news
D) British government often criticized the war propaganda

B) Secondly, short term propaganda techniques were implemented during the war time by several governments as a powerful tool

(A), (D) are Opposite. (C) is Inconsistent with the question as choosing the type of media is not an issue.

Q28. **Absolute Pattern 2: Summary Question** Summarizing a sentence or entire passage
Question Pattern: The author believes the **role of media in modern democratic** society serves chiefly to

A) mold public opinion
B) disclose reliable information
C) represent government propaganda
D) solidify selective transparency

B) Without mass media, openness and accountability **(Disclose reliable info.)** are very tough to reach in contemporary democracies.

Choice A and C describe the function of early mass media.
Choice D is opposite concept to the role of mass media in modern democratic society. "selective" should change to "all-inclusive".

Q29. **Absolute Pattern 11: Textual Evidence Question** Finding evidence for the previous question
Question Pattern: Which choice provides the best evidence for the answer to the previous question?

A) Lines 16-19 (This propaganda...early media effects.)
B) Lines 23-26 (Hypodermic needle...mass media.)
C) Lines 28-30 (Researchers…and audiences)
D) Lines 41-43 (Without mass media democracies.)

D) Please refer to the above question

Q30. **Absolute Pattern 12: Informational Graphs**
Finding facts described in the graphs or relations between the passage and the graph
Question Pattern: The graph following the passage corresponds most consistently with the British government's media control during WWII in its

A) Short term planned effects
B) Long term planned effects
C) Short term unplanned effects
D) Long term unplanned effects

A) As appeared on the graph, government propaganda is located in Short term Planned effects.

Secondly, short term propaganda techniques were implemented during the war time by several governments as a powerful tool for uniting their people…

Q31. **Absolute Pattern 9: Relationships Question**
Finding relations between the cause-effect, characters, and ideas including a Paired Passage.
Question Pattern: Harold Lasswell in line 18 may view "the communicators' will" in line 5 with?

A) respect
B) concern
C) analytical
D) naivety

B) "This propaganda exemplified strong, **but ill-effect of communication**" said the political scientist Harold Lasswell, who focused on the early media effects.

Questions 32-41 are based on the following passage.

(32C) **Solar panel refers to a panel designed to absorb the sun's rays as a source of energy for generating electricity or heating.**
The majority of modules use wafer-based crystalline silicon cells or thin-film cells. (33B) **Most modules are rigid** based on thin-film cells. Much of the incident sunlight energy is wasted by solar modules, and (34A&35A) **they can give far higher efficiencies if illuminated with mono-chromatic light. Therefore, another design concept is to split the light into different wavelength ranges and direct the beams onto different cells tuned to those ranges.**

(36D) **This has been projected to be capable of raising efficiency by 50%, with theoretical efficiencies being about 58% in cells with more than three junctions.** **Currently the best achieved sunlight conversion rate (solar module efficiency) is around 21.5%** in new commercial products typically lower than the efficiencies of their cells in isolation. (37A) **Research by Imperial College, London has shown that the efficiency of a solar panel can be improved by studding the light-receiving semiconductor surface with aluminum nanocylinders similar to the ridges on Lego blocks.** Aluminum was found to have absorbed the ultraviolet part of the spectrum, while the visible and near infrared parts of the spectrum were found to be scattered by the aluminum surface.

(38A&39D&41A) **This, the research argued, could bring down the cost significantly and improve the efficiency as aluminum is more abundant and less costly than gold and silver.** (40A) **In 2013 solar generated less than 1% of the world's total grid electricity.**

Q32. **Absolute Pattern 10: Understanding the Structure of the Passage**
Finding the structure of the entire passage or organizational relations between the paragraphs
Question Pattern: The **primary function** of the first paragraph is to

A) explore needs to change energy source from fossil fuel to solar energy B) explain the current renewable energy technology **C) establish a brief introduction about solar panel** D) emphasize cost effectiveness of solar energy	C) Solar panel refers to a panel designed to absorb the sun's rays as a source of energy for generating electricity or heating. A), B) are not stated in the passage. D) is not yet mentioned in the first paragraph.

Q33. **Absolute Pattern 2: Summary Question** Summarizing a sentence or entire passage
Question Pattern: Which of the **following is true with modules described in paragraph 1?**

A) modules must be flexible **B) Modules are often characteristically rigid** C) aesthetic approach is also important consideration D) the thicker the film cell is, the better efficiency can be achieved	B) Most modules are rigid A) is Too Extreme. C) is not stated. D) is Opposite statement.

Q34. **Absolute Pattern 3: Inference Question** Finding an indirect suggestion (or guessing)
Question Pattern: It can be inferred from the passage that the **advanced solar panel in the future** would most likely include higher functioning

A) mononchromatic light splitter B) thick-film cells C) rigid modules D) wafer-based crystalline silicon cells	A) they can give far higher efficiencies if illuminated with mono-chromatic light. Therefore, another design concept is to split the light into different wavelength ranges and direct the beams onto different cells tuned to those ranges. B), C), D) are all currently applied functions and configurations

<table>
<tr><td colspan="2">Q35. Absolute Pattern 11: Textual Evidence Question Finding evidence for the previous question
Question Pattern: Which choice provides the best evidence for the answer to the previous question?</td></tr>
<tr><td>A) Lines 7-10 (Much of the.....mono-chromatic light)
B) Lines 17-21 (Currently the best...cells in isolation.)
C) Lines 26-27 (Aluminum was found...the spectrum.)
D) Lines 28-30 (The visible and...aluminum surface)</td><td>A) Please refer to the previous question</td></tr>
<tr><td colspan="2">Q36. Absolute Pattern 9: Relationships Question
Question Pattern: Which of the following sunlight conversion rates is consistent with the passage?</td></tr>
<tr><td>A) current rate: 60%, prototype development: 80%, in theory: 100%
B) current rate:58%, prototype development: 40%, in theory: 100%
C) current rate: 21.5%, prototype development: 60%, in theory: 50%
D) current rate: 20%, prototype development: 50%, in theory: 60%</td><td>D) The Spectrolab scientists also predict that...more than 45% or even 50% in the future, with theoretical efficiencies being about 58% Currently, around 21.5% in new commercial...</td></tr>
<tr><td colspan="2">Q37. Absolute Pattern 4: Example Question
Question Pattern: By comparing the research result with Lego blocks, Imperial College researchers in line 22 primarily show</td></tr>
<tr><td>A) the efficiency of a solar panel
B) the flexibility of a solar panel
C) relatively convenient assembly method
D) cost-effective manufacturing approach</td><td>A) Research by Imperial College, ...shown that the efficiency of a solar panel can be improved by studding the light-receiving semiconductor surface with aluminum nanocylinders similar to the ridges on Lego blocks. …</td></tr>
<tr><td colspan="2">Q38. Absolute Pattern 2: Summary Question Summarizing a sentence or entire passage
Question Pattern: Which factor would be most consistent with the focus of future research on the solar panel?</td></tr>
<tr><td>A) Cost effective approach
B) Desirable location
C) Technical feasibility
D) Application of gold to the optimum level</td><td>A) This, the research argued, could bring down the cost significantly and improve the efficiency as aluminum is more abundant and less costly (D) than gold and silver.
C) is incorrect because the passage focuses on the cost that allows us to conjecture that technical feasibility is not a problem.</td></tr>
<tr><td colspan="2">Q39. Absolute Pattern 11: Textual Evidence Question Finding evidence for the previous question
Question Pattern: Which choice provides the best evidence for the answer to the previous question?</td></tr>
<tr><td>A) Lines 17-21 (Currently the best...cells in isolation.)
B) Lines 26-27 (Aluminum was found...the spectrum.)
C) Lines 28-30 (The visible and...aluminum surface)
D) Lines 31-34 (This, the research...gold and silver.)</td><td>D) Please refer to the above question</td></tr>
<tr><td colspan="2">Q40. Absolute Pattern 3: Inference Question Finding an indirect suggestion (or guessing)
Question Pattern: According to the table and the last sentence (lines 34-35), it can be inferred that the total grid electricity consumption in 2013 was</td></tr>
<tr><td>A) 400,000,000
B) 3,850
C) 2250
D) variable</td><td>A) In 2013 solar generated less than 1% of the world's total grid electricity.

Table shows solar generated 3,850,000 (less than 1%) of app. 400,000,000</td></tr>
</table>

Q41. **Absolute Pattern 3: Inference Question** Finding an indirect suggestion (or guessing) **Question Pattern:** Which of the following elements can **increase the solar-generated electricity in the future?**	
A) Using aluminum B) Achieving up to 21% of sunlight conversion rate C) Public go-green campaign D) Application of gold at the optimum level	A) This, the research argued, could bring down the cost significantly and improve the efficiency as aluminum is more abundant and less costly (D) than gold and silver. B) is currently available. C) is not mentioned. D) is opposite.

Questions 42-52 are based on the following passage.

PASSAGE 1	PASSAGE 2
In the early part of the year 1838, I became quite restless. (43A) **I could see no reason why I should pour the reward of my toil into the purse of my master.** When I carried to him my weekly wages, he would, after counting the money, look me in the face with a robber-like fierceness, and ask, "Is this all?" He was satisfied with nothing less than the last cent. He would, however, when I made him six dollars, sometimes give me six cents, to encourage me. It had the opposite effect. I regarded it as a sort of admission of my right to the whole. My discontent grew upon me. I was ever on the look-out for means of escape; and I determined to try to hire my time, with a view of getting money with which to make my escape. I got an opportunity, and applied to him to allow me to hire my time. He unhesitatingly refused my request, and (44B) **told me this was another stratagem by which to escape.** He exhorted me to content myself, and be obedient. (48D)He told me, if I would be happy, I must lay out no plans for the future.	(42A) **We believe that humanity is one in all those intellectual, moral and spiritual attributes out of which grow human responsibilities.** (47D) Neither **complexion** nor sex is ever discharged from obedience to law, natural or moral, written or unwritten. (45B&46C) **We respectfully and earnestly pray that, in restoring the foundations of our nationality, all discriminations on account of sex or race may be removed; and that our government may be Republican in fact as well as form.** (52D) **Women and colored men are loyal, liberty-loving citizens, and we can not believe that sex or complexion should be any ground for civil or political degradation.** --- --Response from The New York Sunday Times after the conventions Susan B. Anthony, her Revolution was issued last Thursday as a sort of New Year's gift to what she considered a yearning public, and it is said to be "charged to the muzzle with literary (51B) **nitre-glycerine."** (48D&49A&50C) **If Mrs. Stanton would attend a little more to her domestic duties and a little less to those of the great public, perhaps she would exalt her sex quite as much as she does by Quixotically fighting windmills in their gratuitous behalf. She might possibly set a notable example of world peace.**

Q42. **Absolute Pattern 9: Relationships Question** **Question Pattern: Frederick Douglas and Susan Anthony differ** in their views of confinement in a way that Fredrick
A) views his goal as a self-liberation; Susan, as a whole society. B) recognizes the difficulty of escaping from reality; Susan views womanhood can be ameliorated through equal education C) reminds the reader the importance of gender equality; Susan declares disobeying law offers no solutions. D) finds money is a way to fulfill his desire; Susan warns gender inequality can be the ground of political degradation.
A) Passage 1 is personal anecdote using the first person pronoun 'I,' while passage 2 uses 'We,' defining a goal for the society at large. (A) is the only option that illustrates this difference. (D) is incorrect because money was the motivation for escape, not the source of fulfillment. (B): P1 (correct), P2 (Not stated) (C): P1 (Incorrect), P2 (Incorrect) (D): P1(Incorrect), P2 (Correct)

Q43. **Absolute Pattern 2: Summary Question** Summarizing a sentence, or an entire paragraph
Question Pattern: As presented in Passage 1, **Frederick's desire to escape originates** from

A) money B) toiling work C) moral and spiritual attributes D) desire to liberate other slaves	A) sometimes give me six cents, to encourage me. It had the opposite effect. I regarded it as a sort of admission of my right to the whole. (C) is incorrect because it is a part of issue raised by Susan in passage 2.

Q44. **Absolute Pattern 3: Inference Question** Finding an indirect suggestion (or guessing)
Question Pattern: Master Thomas' response in lines 17-20 (**He unhesitatingly...obedient**) in Passage 1 implies that

A) Fredrick actually needs time for his own **B) Master Thomas sensed a similar experience in the past** C) Fredrick must be obedient in order to find contentment himself D) Fredrick could go nowhere	B) He unhesitatingly refused my request, and told me this was **another** stratagem by which to escape. * another means it happened before.

Q45. **Absolute Pattern 2: Summary Question** Summarizing a sentence, or an entire paragraph
Question Pattern: Unlike Passage 1, **Susan Anthony in Passage 2 presents the issue as**

A) a way to satisfy individual desires **B) a process that can rectify the republic** C) a way to improve the entire humanity D) a process requiring women's domestic duty	B) Please refer to the below question A) is for Passage 1 C) Susan promotes and focuses on the women's right. "entire humanity" must include "man" as well, therefore incorrect. D) is The view of New York Sunday Times, not Susan's

Q46. **Absolute Pattern 11: Textual Evidence Question** Finding evidence for the previous question
Question Pattern: Which choice provides the best evidence for the answer to the previous question?

A) Lines 22-24 (We believe...human responsibility) B) Lines 24-27 (Neither complexion...or unwritten) **C) Lines 27-31 (We respectfully...as well as form)** D) Lines 41-46 (If Mrs. Stanton...gratuitous behalf.)	C) We respectfully and earnestly pray that, in restoring the foundations of our nationality, all discriminations on account of sex or race may be removed; and that our government may be Republican in fact as well as form

Q47. **Absolute Pattern 5: Word-In-Context Question**
Question Pattern: As used in line 33, "**complexion**" is closest in meaning to?

A) unacceptable tradition B) complex human nature C) sophisticated social system **D) skin color**	D) Women and colored men are loyal, liberty-loving citizens, and we can not believe that sex or complexion should be any ground for civil or political degradation. As shown above, finding a clue word is pivotal in Word-in-Context question.

Q48. **Absolute Pattern 9: Relationships Question**
Question Pattern: Master Thomas in Passage 1 and **The New York Sunday Times** in Passage 2 **share their views** in which of the following way?

A) Setting out the plan for the future is the road to unhappiness. B) Woman should focus on domestic duties C) Not all societal system is beautiful, but should be accepted in that way **D) Happiness can be obtained without leaving the current condition**	D) Passage 1: He told me, if I would be happy, I must lay out no plans for the future. " Passage 2: When, she best honors her sex by leaving public affairs behind her, and endeavoring to show how happy she can make the little world. A), B) are from P2 only. C) is not mentioned in neither passage.

<table>
<tr><td colspan="2">Q49. Absolute Pattern 9: Relationships Question
Finding relations between the cause-effect, comparison-contrast, characters, and ideas
Question Pattern: The New York Sunday Times in Passage 2 would most likely respond to Master Thomas in lines 19-21 (He exhorted me...future) by</td></tr>
<tr><td>A) agreeing that domestic felicity can be achieved through obedience
B) disagreeing that the public affairs are more important than personal desire
C) conceding that slave can also obtain happiness
D) saying that women can't obtain enfranchisement, while black people can</td><td>A) If Mrs. Stanton would attend a little more to her domestic duties and a little less to those of the great public, perhaps she would exalt her sex quite as much...</td></tr>
<tr><td colspan="2">B) is Opposite statement from the passage
C), D): The Times focuses on womenhood only. Personal affair belongs to Passage 1, not 2</td></tr>
</table>

<table>
<tr><td colspan="2">Q50. Absolute Pattern 11: Textual Evidence Question Finding evidence for the previous question
Question Pattern: Which choice provides the best evidence for the answer to the previous question?</td></tr>
<tr><td>A) Lines 22-24 (We believe...human responsibility)
B) Lines 27-31 (We respectfully...as well as form)
C) Lines 41-46 (If Mrs. Stanton...gratuitous behalf.)
D) Lines 46-47 (She might possibly...world peace.)</td><td>C) Please refer to the above question</td></tr>
</table>

<table>
<tr><td colspan="2">Q51. Absolute Pattern 3: Inference Question Finding an indirect suggestion (or guessing)
Question Pattern: The quotation in line 40 ("charged to nitre-glycerine") by The New York Sunday Times focuses Susan Anthony's Revolution on its</td></tr>
<tr><td>A) spontaneity
B) magnitude
C) impracticality
D) novelty</td><td>B) Nitreglycerine is an explosive substance that makes bomb. Therefore, it describes the magnitude of the campaign.</td></tr>
</table>

<table>
<tr><td colspan="2">Q52. Absolute Pattern 3: Inference Question Finding an indirect suggestion (or guessing)
Question Pattern: The description in lines 31-34 ("Woman and colored...degradation.) primarily serves to</td></tr>
<tr><td>A) suggest that women and black would be unlikely ever to consider entering politics
B) indicate woman and black play a pivotal role in society
C) show the adversities women and black had to overcome in society
D) imply some people's viewpoints are highly biased</td><td>D) Women and colored men are loyal, liberty-loving citizens, and we can not believe that sex or complexion should be any ground for civil or political degradation.</td></tr>
<tr><td colspan="2">In this sentence Susan defends women and colored men against some people's viewpoints that are highly biased.
C) is true, but unrelated issue.</td></tr>
</table>

SAT Test 6

Writing and language Section Answer Explanations

&

The Pattern Analyses

Test 6 Writing & Language Section Patterns

Questions 1-11 are based on the following passage.

John Glenn and the Limits of Possibility

John Glenn, the first American to orbit the Earth [1] by circling the planet, a World War II veteran, and United States Senator for a tenure of 24 years, died on Thursday. He was 95.[2] A native Ohioan who grew up in Ohio, I admired John Glenn. Glenn achieved an almost mythically larger-than-life status in American culture when he returned from space in 1962. From his journey in orbit on, Glenn continued to make Ohio and the United States proud. Both [3] because he achieved incredible feat and the way he handled himself with humility and plain-spoken grace, Glenn was an ideal role model.

He embodied so many characteristics teachers and parents want young people to learn about—and he was a homegrown legend. Having studied history for the last four years, [4] my perspective on why John Glenn is a hero has changed. My conviction that Glenn's legacy is important and my belief in the inspirational power of his life story [5] ; however, is unaltered.

Glenn was a lionhearted warrior, an undaunted explorer, [6] and he was a judicious statesman. <1>Glenn announced he would run for the Senate the day he retired from NASA in 1964, though he wasn't elected until 1974. <2>He was a fighter pilot in two wars, then a Navy and Marine test pilot, before being selected as one of the original "Mercury Seven" astronauts. <3>His famous orbit of earth was the culmination of twenty years of extraordinary feats of daring. <4>In 1998, while still a sitting Senator, he returned to space at age 77, the oldest person ever to do so.

After officially retiring from the Senate, he helped found the John Glenn Institute for Public Service and Public Policy at The Ohio State University where he taught. He continued to give lectures and visit schools until the end of his life. [8] John Glenn had one of the most impressive resumes in history. But accomplishments and accolades aside, [9] sheer immensity that Glenn provided by devoting to others—whether measured in time, energy, or personal risk—was itself heroic.

Glenn's passing is a reminder that an optimistic vision of America is possible. Without turning Glenn into a marble demigod or valorizing the cultural milieu from which he came, for that we be dishonest and a disservice to the man, I admire his human courage and his unwavering commitment to causes greater than himself. I respect the way he used his celebrity to create a platform from which he could unselfishly multiply his ability to do good. And I try to remember, without having lived through his most historic accomplishments myself, what it [10] was like to be inspired by a humble individual who dared to test the limits of possibility that transcends our limitations.[11]

Q1. Absolute Pattern 19: Redundant Error

	Choice	Explanation
	A) NO CHANGE	Always Pick the Shortest One from the Multiple Choices! Making incorrect choice by reducing information is not easy. Adding a few words, however, for the same purpose, is a piece of cake. D) John Glenn, the first American to **orbit the Earth** [1] by circling the planet, A), B), and C) are redundant error
	B) **circling the planet,**	
	C) where he **circled the planet**	
√	**D) OMIT the underlined portion**	

Q2. Absolute Pattern 12: Modifier Placement Error

	Choice	Explanation
	A) NO CHANGE	D) correctly places the modifier before the subject "I" A) is redundant error. "A native Ohioan" and "grew up in Ohio" are basically the same meaning. B), C) "Admiring..." should be placed next to "I grew up." It sounds as if the author admires John because he is a native Ohioan.
	B) Admiring a native Ohioan John Glenn, I grew up.	
	C) Admiring John Glenn as a native Ohioan, I grew up.	
√	**D) As a native Ohioan, I grew up admiring John Glenn.**	

Key point: Choices A, B, C are all misplaced modifiers. Modifier should be placed right next to the one that it modifies. only D satisfies this arrangement.

Q3. Absolute Pattern 7: Conjunction Error

Both [3] because he achieved incredible feat and **the way** he handled himself with humility and plain-spoken grace, Glenn was an ideal role model.

	A) NO CHANGE	C) 1> "Both" is a preposition that carries a phrase. 2> "Glenn was an ideal role model" is the main clause. 3> The non-underlined portion "the way...plan-spoken grace" clearly shows the phrasal structure. 4> Therefore, the underlined portion should also be a phrase, and can't use a conjunction 'because'.
	B) because his incredible achievements as well as	
√	**C) because of his incredible achievements and**	
	D) because of his incredible achievements and also because of	

A), B) 1> "because" is a conjunction that links a clause. 2> It is a parallelism error that conflicts with the following phrase.
B) "as well as" and D) "also because of" should be replaced with "and"

Q4. Absolute Pattern 12: Modifier Placement Error

Having studied history for the last four years, [4] my perspective on why John Glenn is a hero has changed.

	A) NO CHANGE	B) 1> "Having studied ~" implies the subject has to be human. 2> The subject is human 'I' A) The subject 'my perspective' is non-human. C) "change" D) "why" are used as a subject and can't carry the modifier "having studied".
√	**B) I changed my perspective on why John Glenn is a hero.**	
	C) change of my perspective on why John Glenn is a hero has come upon me	
	D) why John Glenn is a hero has changed.	

Q5. Absolute Pattern 7: Conjunction Error

My conviction that Glenn's legacy is important and my belief in the inspirational power of his life story [5] ; however, is unaltered.

	A) NO CHANGE	C) a pair of commas should offset "however" when used in the middle of the sentence. A) semicolon + "however" is used when "however" carries a subordinating clause. (e.g., I am hungry; however, I have no money.) B) 'however' needs a pair of commas, not one. D) changes the original meaning
	B) however,	
√	**C) , however,**	
	D) OMIT the underlined portion	

Q6. Absolute Pattern 13: Parallel Structure

Glenn was a lionhearted **warrior,** an undaunted **explorer**, [6] and he was a **judicious statesman**.

	A) NO CHANGE	D) warrior, explorer, and judicious statesman are correct parallel structure. A), B), C) are all parallelism error
	B) **who was** a judicious statesman	
	C) **and statesman who was** judicious	
√	**D) and judicious statesman**	

Q7. Absolute Pattern 11: Logical Sequence

Question: **For logic and sequence of this paragraph**, sentence <1> should be placed:

	A) NO CHANGE	<2>He was a fighter pilot in two wars, then a Navy and Marine test pilot, before being selected as one of the **original "Mercury Seven" astronauts**. (Topic)
	B) after sentence <2>	<3>His **famous orbit** of earth was the **culmination of** twenty years of extraordinary feats of daring. (The supporting detail)
√	**C) after sentence <3>**	<1>Glenn announced he **would run for the Senate** the day **he retired from NASA in** 1964, though he wasn't elected until 1974. (Example)
	D) after sentence <4>	<4>In 1998, **while still a sitting Senator**, he returned to space at age 77, the oldest person ever to do so.

C) A sentence sequence question can easily be solved by reading the sentence from backward in 4,3,2,1 order, instead of 1,2,3,4. The reason behind this trick is that finding the conclusion is often easier than finding the introduction sentence.

Q8. Absolute Pattern 1: Adding, Revising, Deleting, Retaining Information

He **continued to give lectures** and visit schools until the end of his life. [8]

Question: The author is **considering deleting** the preceding sentence (He continued…).Should the author delete it?

	A) Yes, because the sentence disrupts the paragraph's attention to John Glenn's career as a heroic astronaut.
	B) Yes, because the sentence inappropriately shifts the focus of the paragraph from John Glenn, a hero to a philanthropist.
√	**C) No, because the sentence is consistent with the paragraph's focus on the aspects of John Glenn's philanthropic activities after the retirement**
	D) No, because the sentence logically links the author's preference of Glenn as a philanthropist to as an astronaut.

C) The previous sentence describes his later life after the retirement. Therefore, sentence 8 should not be deleted. For this reason, (A) and (B) are incorrect.
D) The author respects Glenn as a philanthropist as well as an astronaut

Q9. Absolute Pattern 10: Logical Expression

But accomplishments and accolades aside, [9] sheer immensity that Glenn provided by devoting to others—whether measured in time, energy, or personal risk—**was itself heroic.**

	A) NO CHANGE	B) "was itself heroic" is the verb that requires the subjective phrase, not another entire clause.
√	**B) sheer immensity of Glenn's devotion**	
	C) **Glenn devoted** with sheer immensity	A), C), and D) are all complete sentences and can't be used in the sentence that already has a verb.
	D) Glenn **devoted** sheerly and immensely	

Q10 Absolute Pattern 24: Verb Tense / Voice Error

And I try to remember, without **having lived** through his most historic accomplishments myself, what it [10]**was like to** be inspired by a humble individual who dared to test the limits of possibility that transcends our limits.[11]

√	**A) NO CHANGE**	'having lived,' meaning after he had lived (the past perfect situation), corresponds to the simple past "was" in the main verb.
	B) **will** like to be	'will' is used for the future tense
	C) **is** like to be	'is' is used for the present tense
	D) be	is' is used for the future tense

Q11. Absolute Pattern 19: Redundant Error	
...who dared to **test the limits of possibility** that transcends the limitations.[11]	
Question: The author is considering **deleting the underlined portion** of the sentence. Should the author delete it?	
	A) Yes, because the portion shifts its focus from John Glenn as a heroic human being to just a human being.
√	B) Yes, because the portion **does not deliver any meaningful information**.
	C) No, because the portion is emphasizing undaunted character John Glenn presented
	D) No, because the portion logically concludes the essay.
"test the limits of possibility" and "that transcends the limitations" are essentially identical phrases. It's best to delete it.	

Questions 12-22 are based on the following passage.

Sarah Margaret Fuller

Sarah Margaret Fuller Ossoli (1810 – 1850) [12] , is commonly known as Margaret Fuller, was an American journalist, critic, and women's rights advocate associated with the American transcendentalism movement. She was the first full-time American female book reviewer in journalism. Her book *Woman in the Nineteenth Century* is considered the first major feminist work in the United States. [13] Born in Cambridge, Massachusetts, [14] she was given a substantially early education by her father, Timothy Fuller.

She became the first editor (1) of the transcendentalist Journal *The Dial* (2) in 1840 (3), before joining the New *York Tribune* under Horace Greeley (4) in 1844. [15]

By the time she was in her 30s, Fuller [16] had earned a reputation as the best-read person in New England and became the first woman allowed to use the library at Harvard College. Her seminal work, *Woman in the Nineteenth Century*, was published in 1845. A year later, she was sent to Europe for the *Tribune* as its first female correspondent. She and her confidant Jane Kimberly soon became involved in the revolutions in Italy and she allied [17] her with Giuseppe Mazzini. She had a relationship with Giovanni Ossoli, [18] with whom she had a child.

All three members of the family died in a shipwreck off Fire Island, New York, as they were traveling to the United States in 1850. Fuller's body was never recovered. Many other advocates for women's rights and feminism, including [19] that of Susan B. Anthony, [20] cite Fuller as a source of inspiration. Many of her contemporaries, however, were supportive, including her former friend Harriet Martineau. She said that Fuller was a talker [21] more than an activist. Shortly after Fuller's death, her importance faded; the editors who prepared her letters to be published, believing her fame would be short-lived, censored or altered much of her work before publication.

Q12. Absolute Pattern 12: Modifier Error		
Sarah Margaret Fuller Ossoli (1810 – 1850) [12] *, is commonly known as Margaret Fuller,* **was** an American journalist, critic, and women's rights advocate associated with the American transcendentalism movement.		
	A) NO CHANGE	B) A pair of commas properly separates and offsets the modifier from the main clause. A) "is" should be removed because "was", the main verb, already exists. C) read (A) D) "who is" is not necessary because it simply functions as a complementizer.
√	**B) ,commonly known as**	
	C) ,**was** commonly known as	
	D) ,**who is** commonly known as	

Q13. Absolute Pattern 1: Adding, Revising, Deleting, Retaining Information

Her book *Woman in the Nineteenth Century* is considered the **first major feminist work** in the United States. [13]

Question: If the author were to **delete** the preceding sentence, the paragraph would primarily **lose** information that

	Choice	Explanation
	A) reveals **social and racial bias** Sarah Fuller encountered at that time it was published.	C) the first major feminist work will be lost from history.
	B) indicates the **time and place the book was written**	A) racial bias is not mentioned in the sentence B) can't be the primarily information D) her occupation is inconsistent with the sentence.
√	**C) establishes the historic value of the book**	
	D) describes the **type of occupation** Sarah Fuller worked	

Q14. Absolute Pattern 17: Pronoun Error

Born in Cambridge, Massachusetts, [14] **she** was given a substantially early education by her father, Timothy Fuller.

	Choice	Explanation
	A) NO CHANGE	B) 1> The topic sentence of each paragraph can't start with a pronoun. 2> The person's name must be given first before using the corresponding pronoun to avoid confusion.
√	**B) Sarah**	
	C) it was Sarah Margarete Fuller who	
	D) this first major feminist in the United States	A) Ambiguous pronoun C) Wordy D) Wordy + ambiguous

Q15. Absolute Pattern 1: Adding, Revising, Deleting, Retaining Information

She became the first editor (1) of the transcendentalist Journal *The Dial* (2) in 1840 (3), before joining the New *York Tribune* under Horace Greeley (4) in 1844. [15]

Question: Which of the following information is **not essential** to understand the work and job of Sarah Fuller?

	Choice	Explanation
	A) the first editor (1)	D) "under Horace Greeley" is not necessary information to understand the passage. .
	B) The Dial (2)	(A),(B),(C) are necessary information because they are directly related with Fuller.
	C) in 1840 (3)	
√	**D) under Horace Greeley (4)**	

Q16. Absolute Pattern 24: Verb Tense / Voice Error

By the time she was in her 30s, Fuller [16] **had earned** a reputation as the best-read person

	Choice	Tense	Explanation
√	**A) NO CHANGE**	past perfect	A) "By" refers to the completion of action in time adverbial phrase; therefore, the tense has to be perfect tense such as past perfect, present perfect, or future perfect.
	B) earned	simple past	
	C) has earned	present perfect	
	D) had been earning	progressive	C) The present perfect tense is incorrect because "she was~" indicates the past occurrence.

Q17. Absolute Pattern 17: Pronoun Error

She and her confidant Jane Kimberly soon became involved in the revolutions in Italy and she allied [17] her with Giuseppe Mazzini.

	Choice	Explanation
	A) NO CHANGE	B) The reflective pronoun 'herself' must be used with the corresponding subject. Therefore, herself clearly refers to Fuller.
√	**B) herself with Giuseppe Mazzini**	A) "she" and "her" are unclear. It could be Fuller or Jane.
	C) with Giuseppe Mazzini	C) "she" is unclear. It could be Fuller or Jane.
	D) her being with Giuseppe Mazzini	D) 'being' cannot be used. 'being' in multiple choices is good for nothing.

Q18. Absolute Pattern 17: Pronoun Error

She had a relationship with Giovanni Ossoli, [18] **with whom** she had a child.

	Choice	Explanation
√	**A) NO CHANGE**	A) Preposition "with" requires the objective relative pronoun: Preposition + Whom.
	B) with who	B) 'with' is a preposition that must carry an objective "whom".
	C) who	C) 'who' alone can't connect the following subject 'she.'
	D) whose	D) 'whose' is possessive that requires a noun.

Q19. Absolute Pattern 4: Comparison

Many other advocates for women's rights and feminism, including [19] that of **Susan B. Anthony**, cite Fuller as a source of inspiration

	Choice	Explanation
	A) NO CHANGE	'that of' is ambiguous and should be deleted.
	B) people such as Susan B. Anthony,	'such as' is redundant with 'including'
	C) those of Susan B. Anthony,	'those of' is ambiguous and should be deleted.
√	**D) Susan B. Anthony,**	**Many other advocates** "including Susan"'

Q20 Absolute Pattern 10: Logical Expression

	Choice	Explanation
	A) NO CHANGE	'cite' is present tense while other surrounding sentences are past tense.
	B) sighted	'sighted' means saw
√	**C) cited**	"cited" properly maintains the same tense with other surrounding sentences
	D) sited	site means a construction area

Q21. Absolute Pattern 4: Comparison

She said that Fuller was a talker [21] more than an activist

	Choice	Explanation
	A) NO CHANGE	The sentence is about the criticism Fuller received from other activists. Therefore, it has to be 'less than', instead of 'more than.'
√	**B) less than**	C) and D) both are using 'then', instead of 'than.' 'then' means by that time.
	C) rather then	
	D) less then	

Q22. Absolute Pattern 1: Adding, Revising, Deleting, Retaining Information	
Many other advocates for women's rights and feminism, including Susan B. Anthony cited Fuller as a source of inspiration.	
Question: Suppose the author's goal was to write a brief essay about the life of an **early feminist**. Would this **summary** successfully fulfill the author's goal?	
	A) Yes, because the summary offers Susan Anthony's major events as a feminist
√	**B) Yes, because the summary reveals social injustice Sarah Fuller encountered.**
	C) No, because the summary focuses more on the impact of feminism in general.
	D) No, because the summary represents an early feminist' unfolded personal life rather than civil work.
The keyword in the question is 'summary' that encourages us to read the concluding paragraph. A), C) are incorrect because the main character is Sarah Fuller, not Susan or feminism in general. D) The personal life story of Sarah Fuller is only briefly mentioned.	

Questions 23-33 are based on the following passage.

A shape-memory ally

A shape-memory alloy (SMA) is an alloy that "remembers" its original shape and that when deformed returns to its pre-deformed shape [23] that heated. This material is a lightweight, solid-state [24] alternative to conventional actuators such as hydraulic, pneumatic, and motor-based systems. Shape-memory alloys have Applications in robotics and automotive, aerospace and biomedicalindustries. The two main types of shape-memory alloys are copper-aluminum-nickel, and nickel-titanium (NiTi) alloys but SMAs can also be created [25] by alloy of zinc, and copper, and gold, and iron.

Although iron-based and copper-based SMAs, such as Fe-Mn-Si, Cu-Zn-Al and Cu-Al-Ni, are [26] commercially available in the market and cheaper than NiTi, NiTi which bases SMAs are preferable for most applications [27] due to their stability, practicability and . superior thermo-mechanic performance

NiTi alloys change from austenite to martensite upon cooling; M_f is the temperature at which the transition to martensite completes upon cooling. [28] Repeated use of the shape-memory effect may lead to a shift of the characteristic transformation temperatures (this effect is known as functional [29] fatigue, as it is closely related with a change of microstructural and functional properties of the material).

The maximum temperature at which SMAs can no longer be stress induced is called M_d, where the SMAs are [30] permanently deformed. The transition from the martensite phase to the austenite phase is only dependent on temperature and stress, not time, as most phase changes are, as there is no diffusion involved. Similarly, the austenite structure receives its name from steel alloys of [31] a similar and comparable structure. It is the reversible diffusion less transition between these two phases that results in special properties. [32] Martensite can be formed from austenite by rapidly cooling carbon-steel, this process is not reversible, so steel does not have shape-memory properties.

Q23 Absolute Pattern 7: Conjunction Error		
A shape-memory alloy (SMA) is an alloy that "remembers" its original shape and that **when deformed** returns to its pre-deformed shape [23] that heated.		
	A) NO CHANGE	when deformed ...[23] when heated.
√	**B) when**	B) 1> The original sentence was "**when** (its shape is) **heated**." 2> The preceding parallel structure also gives a clue "**when** (its original shape is) **deformed** returns to...." **when** (its deformed shape is) **heated**.
	C) by	A) 'that' is used as an indicative pronoun, which sounds as if "that heated shape"
	D) OMIT	C) "by" is a preposition. Preposition can't link the subordinating clause. D) omitting is not an option to link the 'shape' to 'heated.'

Q24. Absolute Pattern 10: Logical Expression

This material is a lightweight, solid-state [24] alternative to conventional actuators

Question: Which of the following alternatives to the portion would **NOT** be acceptable?

A) replacement for	B) substitute for	**C) enhancement to** √	D) equivalent to

C) "alternative" does not necessarily mean to make better or enhancement. The other options are all synonyms

Q25 Absolute Pattern 15: Prepositional Idiom

The two main types of shape-memory alloys are copper-aluminum-nickel, and nickel-titanium (NiTi) alloys but SMAs can also be created [25] by **alloy of** zinc, copper, gold, and iron.

	A) NO CHANGE	D) "by +~ing" is used to describe the means and method
	B) with alloying zinc, copper, gold and iron.	(A) "by alloy" should change to "by alloying" (B) "with" should be replaced to "by" (C) changes the meaning.
	C) with alloy of zinc, copper, gold and iron.	
√	**D) by alloying zinc, copper, gold and iron.**	

Q26. Absolute Pattern 19: Redundant Error

Although iron-based and copper-based SMAs, such as Fe-Mn-Si, Cu-Zn-Al and Cu-Al-Ni, are [26] commercially available **in the market** and cheaper than NiTi, NiTi which bases SMAs are preferable

	A) NO CHANGE	D) is succinct and precise.
	B) commercially available as a marketable product	Commercially available means marketable, causing a redundant error. A), B) are redundant error C) changes the meaning
	C) commercial	
√	**D) commercially available**	

Q27. Absolute Pattern 23: Transition Words for Supporting Detail, Contrast, and Consequence

Although iron-based and copper-based SMAs, such as Fe-Mn-Si, Cu-Zn-Al and Cu-Al-Ni, are commercially available and cheaper than NiTi, NiTi which bases SMAs are preferable for most applications [27] due to **their stability,** practicability and superior thermo-mechanic performance.

Question: Which of the following alternatives to the underlined portion would **NOT** be acceptable?

√	**A) because their stability**	A) 1> Although look alike, 'because' and 'because of' are different. 2> The former is conjunction that links up another clause, while the latter is preposition that links up a phrase, not a clause. 3> The underlined portion of the original sentence is a phrase, not a clause. 4> Therefore, 'because' should not be used. B), C), and D) are all prepositions that link the following phrase.
	B) because of their stability	
	C) owing to their stability	
	D) thanks to their stability	

Q28. Absolute Pattern 1: Adding, Revising, Deleting, Retaining Information	
NiTi alloys change from austenite to martensite upon **cooling;** M_f is the **temperature** at which the **transition** to martensite **completes upon cooling.** [28]	
Question: Which one establishes **a visual contrast** to the image in the underlined sentence?	
	A) The first consumer commercial application was a shape-memory coupling for piping.
	B) Intelligent Reinforced Concrete (IRC), which incorporates SMA wires embedded within the concrete can sense cracks and contract to heal macro-sized crack.
	C) There have been, however, limited studies on using these materials in auto body.
√	**D) During heating $A_s$and A_f are the temperatures at which the transformation from martensite to austenite starts and finishes.**

The question asks a visual contrast.
The preceding sentence has keywords such as **cooling, temperature, transition, complete upon cooling.**
D) has similar keywords that illustrate visual contrast such as **heating, temperatures, starts and finishes.**

To sum up, while the preceding clause shows the cooling process, the added information presents the heating process, which visualize its contrasting process.

Q29 Absolute Pattern 10: Logical Expression		
Repeated use of the shape-memory effect may lead to a shift of the characteristic transformation temperatures (this effect is known as **functional** [29] fatigue,		
Question: Which of the following alternatives to the underlined portion would **NOT** be acceptable?		
	A) exhaustion	D) "anxiety" is most likely used to human psychology, not to material in this category. A), B), C) are all synonyms that can alternately be used with fatigue. The keyword is "functional" right before fatigue.
	B) weakness	
	C) stress	
√	**D) anxiety**	

Q30. Absolute Pattern 10: Logical Expression		
The maximum temperature at which SMAs can no longer be stress induced is called M_d, where the SMAs are [30] permanently **deformed**.		
Question: Which of the following alternatives to the underlined portion would **NOT** be acceptable?		
	A) irrevocably	D) The keyword is "deformed." 'deformed forever' is nonsensical. "forever" is simply a synonym to the word permanent. A), B), C): All refer to the condition that is unable to recover.
	B) irreversibly	
	C) irreparably	
√	**D) forever**	

Q31 Absolute Pattern 19: Redundant Error		
Similarly, the austenite structure receives its name from steel alloys of [31] a similar and comparable structure.		
	A) NO CHANGE	D) is concise and direct.
	B) a comparable configuration and similar	A) "similar" and "comparable" are synonym
	C) a similar structure which is comparable	A), B), and C) are all redundant error
√	**D) similar**	

Q32. Absolute Pattern 5: Comma Splice Error		
[32] **Martensite can be formed** from austenite by rapidly cooling carbon-steel, **this process is not reversible**, so steel does not have shape-memory properties.		
	A) NO CHANGE	B) 1> The clause should start with a conjunction because the second clause starting with "this process is.." has no conjunction, acting as a main clause. 2>We should add a conjunction in the underlined portion, making as a subordinate clause 3> We can do this by putting "While" .
√	**B) While martensite**	
	C) With martensite	
	D) By martensite	A) The original sentence is a comma splice error, requiring a conjunction. C), D) Preposition cannot link up a clause.

Q33 Absolute Pattern 9: Informational Graphs	
Following chart demonstrates the feasibility of SMA actuators that use conductive "lagging" method on which thermal paste is rapidly transferred from the SMA. Using this method, manufacturers can expect:	
	A) a significant reduction time in both Bare SMA low current and Lagged SMA, low current
√	**B) a significant reduction time in both Bare SMA low current and Lagged SMA, high current**
	C) a significant reduction time in Lagged SMA high current only.
	D) a significant reduction time in Lagged SMA low current only.
Setting aside "Force," the graph shows a significant reduction time in both Bare SMA low current and Lagged SMA, high current	

Questions 34-44 are based on the following passage.

Thomas Carmichael Hindman, Jr.

Thomas Carmichael Hindman, Jr. (January 28, 1828 – September 27, 1868) was a lawyer, United States Representative from the 1st Congressional District of Arkansas, [34] and he was a major general in the Confederate States Army during the American Civil War.

After receiving his primary education in Ripley, he [35] had attended the Lawrenceville Classical Institute and graduated with honors in 1843. <1> Afterwards, he raised a company in Tippah County for the 2nd Mississippi regiment in the Mexican–American War. <2> Hindman served during the war as a lieutenant and later as a captain of his company.

<3> He studied law, and was admitted to the state bar in 1851. <4>After the war, he returned to Ripley.

He was elected as the Democratic Representative from Arkansas's 1st congressional district in the Thirty-sixth Congress from March 4, 1859, to March 4, 1861, but [36] had been declined to serve after the onset of the Civil War and Arkansas's secession from the Union. [37] Instead, Hindman waited wisely until war was over. He commanded the Trans-Mississippi Department, and later raised and commanded "Hindman's Legion" for the Confederate States Army. After the war, Hindman avoided surrender to the federal government [38] by fleeing to Mexico City. After the execution of Maximilian I of Mexico, Hindman submitted a petition [39] to request for a pardon to President Andrew Johnson, but it was denied. Hindman, nonetheless, returned to his former life in Helena.

He became the leader of the "Young Democracy" [40] , there he rebuilt a new political organization that was willing to accept the Reconstruction for the restoration of the Union. He was assassinated on September 27, 1868, at his Helena home. As the American Civil War approached,

Hindman was a passionate voice for secession and was primarily Arkansas's most prominent Fire-Eater.

With war approaching, Hindman resigned from Congress and recruited a regiment at Helena, which was mustered into Confederate service. He requested the state government for muskets, clothing and ten days of rations [41] so that his men could "fight for our country".

He and his regiment were soon active participants in the disastrous Kentucky Campaign, followed soon after that by fierce fighting at the Battle of Shiloh in April 1862, [42] when he was slightly wounded. After his recovery, Hindman was promoted [43] to the rank of major general and was appointed commander of the Trans-Mississippi Department to prevent an invasion	by the Union troops led by Samuel Curtis. Events in Arkansas had taken a terrible turn for the worse. Most units had been stripped from the state for service east of the Mississippi River. When Hindman arrived in Little Rock, Arkansas, he found that his command was bare of soldiers, penniless, defenseless, [44] although no immediate threat was visible. Meantime, the Federal Army was approaching dangerously from the northwest.

Q34. Absolute Pattern 13: Parallel Structure

Thomas Carmichael Hindman, Jr. (January 28, 1828 – September 27, 1868) was a **lawyer, United States Representative** from the 1st Congressional District of Arkansas, [34] **and** he was **a major general** in the Confederate States Army during the American Civil War.

	A) NO CHANGE	D) lawyer, United States Representative, and a major general = Noun, Noun, and Noun = Noun parallelism A) "and he was a major general" in the middle of the parallel structure creates parallelism error. B) "who" is a complementizer and unnecessary. C) 'was' is unnecessary.
	B) **who was** a major general	
	C) **and was** a major general	
√	**D) and *major general***	

Q35. Absolute Pattern 11: Logical Sequence

Passage: <1> Afterwards, he raised a company in Tippah County for the 2nd Mississippi regiment in the Mexican–American War.
<2> Hindman served during the war as a lieutenant and later as a captain of his company.
<3> He studied law, and was admitted to the state bar in 1851.
<4>After the war, he returned to Ripley.

Question: Which of the following is most **logical sequences in** this paragraph?

Answer Keywords: <1> Afterwards, he **raised a company** in Tippah County for the 2nd Mississippi regiment in the Mexican–American War. <2> Hindman served during the war as a lieutenant and later as **a captain of his company**. <4>**After the war, he returned** to Ripley. <3> **He studied law,** and was admitted to the state bar in 1851.

√	**B) <1>,<2>,<4>,<3>**	Once completed with your selection, try to read it backward: <3><4><2><1> as it will confirm your choice.

Q36. Absolute Pattern 24: Verb Tense / Voice Error

He **was elected** as the Democratic Representative from Arkansas's 1st congressional district in the Thirty-sixth Congress from March 4, 1859, to March 4, 1861, but [36] had been declined to serve after the onset of the Civil War and Arkansas's secession from the Union.

	A) NO CHANGE	D) 1> The past tense is used throughout the passage. 2> Therefore, this sentence should also use the simple past. A) is past perfect, passive. B) is past perfect. C) is passive.
	B) had declined	
	C) was declined	
√	**D) declined**	

Q37 Absolute Pattern 1: Adding, Revising, Deleting, Retaining Information	
He was elected as the Democratic Representative from Arkansas's 1st congressional district in the Thirty-sixth Congress from March 4, 1859, to March 4, 1861, but declined to serve after the onset of the Civil War and Arkansas's secession from the Union. [37]	
Question: At this point, the author wishes to provide **a specific example** of the efforts being made by Hindman to further his desire, which one would best accomplish this purpose?	
	A) Instead, Hindman waited wisely until war was over.
√	**B) Instead, Hindman joined the armed forces of the Confederacy**
	C) Instead, Hindman sought a peaceful resolution to end the Civil war.
	D) Instead, Hindman moved to Mexican town of Carlota, where he engaged in coffee planting business and attempted to practice law.

B) The previous and the following paragraphs describe his decision to serve in the army, which naturally connects (B). A), C), D) are, contrary to the rest of the paragraphs, all negative tone.

Q38. Absolute Pattern 15: Prepositional Idiom		
Hindman avoided surrender to the federal government [38] by fleeing to Mexico City.		
√	**A) NO CHANGE**	Preposition "by" describes the means or method
	B) into	'into' means getting inside.
	C) towards	"towards" is used for a direction.
	D) via	"via" is used for a direction.

Q39. Absolute Pattern 19: Redundant Error		
After the execution of Maximilian I of Mexico, Hindman submitted a petition [39] to request for a pardon to President Andrew Johnson, but it was denied. Hindman, nonetheless, returned to his former life in Helena.		
	A) NO CHANGE	The meaning "Petition" and options A), B), C) are Synonym; therefore, they should be deleted.
	B) by officially requesting	
	C) and appealed to authority with respect	
√	**D) OMIT the underlined portion**	D) is clear and concise

Q40. Absolute Pattern 16: Precision, Concision, Style		
He became the leader of the "Young Democracy" [40] , there **he rebuilt** a new political organization that was willing to accept the Reconstruction for the restoration of the Union.		
	A) NO CHANGE	B) is clear and concise. The simplification rule is the concept that makes the sentence concise without losing the original meaning.
√	**B) , a new political organization**	A), C) 1> Comma splice error. 2>"there he rebuilt" is a clause.
	C) , **it became** a new political organization	C) "it became" is a clause
	D) ; a new political organization	D) Semi-colon connects a clause, not a phrase.

Q41. Absolute Pattern 7: Conjunction Error		
Passage: He requested the state government for muskets, clothing and ten days of rations [41]so that **his men could fight** for our country		
√	**A) NO CHANGE**	A) Only 'so- that' carries a subordinating clause
	B) so as	B), C), D) are all prepositions and carry a phrase, not a clause.
	C) so as to	
	D) in order for	

Q42. Absolute Pattern 7: Conjunction Error		
He and his regiment were soon active participants in the disastrous Kentucky Campaign, **followed soon after that by fierce fighting at the Battle of Shiloh in April 1862**, [42]when he was slightly wounded.		
Which of the following choices would **NOT be acceptable**?		
	A) NO CHANGE	C) 1> Conjunction 'but' cancels out the previous clause. 2> The main clause and the following dependent clause are not conflicting.
	B) where	
√	**C) but**	B) 'where' connects the 'Kentucky Campaign.'
	D) a time that	A), D) try to connect ' in April 1862.'

Q43. Absolute Pattern 1: Adding, Revising, Deleting, Retaining Information		
After his recovery, Hindman was promoted [43] to the rank of major general and was appointed commander of the Trans-Mississippi Department to prevent an invasion by the Union troops led by Samuel Curtis.		
Which one clearly adds **objective and specific information** that illustrates Hindman's army career?		
√	**A) NO CHANGE**	A) Informing his rank illustrates Hindman's specific army career
	B) to the envious rank	B), C) are subjective information.
	C) to rank that everyone aspires	
	D) to the rank that became critical in his army career	D) only repeats the question.

Q44. Absolute Pattern 1: Adding, Revising, Deleting, Retaining Information		
[positive: Arkansas] [Negative: was bare of soldiers] When Hindman arrived in Little Rock, Arkansas, he found that his command **was bare of soldiers, penniless, defenseless,** [44] **although no immediate threat was visible,** and dreadfully exposed to its enemy. Meantime, the Federal Army was approaching **dangerously** from the northwest.		
Question: Which choice would most effectively **maintain logical consistency**?		
	A) NO CHANGE	C) is consistently negative with the previous description.
	B) consequently, Hindman attempted inevitable surrender.	A) and B) are opposite description.
√	**C) and dreadfully exposed to its enemy.**	A) There was immediate threat B) Hindman didn't surrender.
	D) but had a hope in politics that still called for him.	D) is inconsistent with other sentence

Chapter 6 Summary

Chapter Summary contains equal portions of

-12 Absolute Patterns for Reading Section

-20 Common Patterns for Incorrect Choices in Reading

-70 Absolute Patterns for Writing and Language Section

-24 Common Patterns for Incorrect Choices in Writing

Chapter 6

20 Common Patterns for *In*correct Choices in Reading

Not Stated in the Passage (incl. Future Prediction)

Some incorrect choices use words or statement that are not stated in the passage.

It just uses our familiar common senses, and we fall for it because our common sense whispers it's true.

New information, however tempting, is always incorrect.
Always find a clue words from the passage that must link up between the sentences.

5 Minor or Unrelated Example

This type appears frequently with the question Pattern 8: True Purpose Question.
For example, the answer for the main idea question in informational passage—say U.S. history—contains a relatively general and therefore neutral tone in keywords so that it could be fit into the general message being delivered by the passage, while maintaining the objective tone.

Contrary to this reasoning, were the keyword too specific and taken from some example sentence, it becomes a minor idea and therefore, incorrect choice.

Chapter 6

20 Common Patterns for *In*correct Choices in Reading

6 Insufficient Information

Do you sometimes feel two choices could be correct at the same time?

Jimin: No! not sometimes. Almost always. I do.

The truth is that those two choices could possibly be correct at the same time, but one is more correct than another.

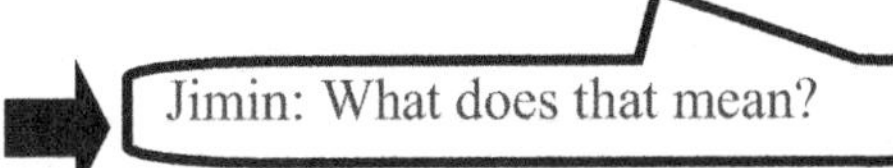

I'll tell you why.
If choice (A) contains one correct keyword while (B), two correct keywords, then choice (A) is incorrect because information is insufficient or only partially correct compared to (B).

7 Unrelated Word or Issue

In here I will focus on Pattern 5: Word-in-Context Question.
Common incorrect choices in this pattern usually employ the followings:
(1) Switching figurative meaning with the literal meaning (i.e. fire)

Jimin: What do you mean?

"Fire" has several different meanings: a chemical reaction fire is a literal description while "I'm on fire with you" is figurative.
The word in passage is most likely figurative. The words in the multiple choices must be literally understood by the dictionary's first definition.
Multiple choice keywords can't be figurative words.

(2) Placing an impressive flamboyant adverb or adjective right next to the plain keyword such as 'it' so that you can focus on unrelated pretty sexy bait instead of the keyword.

(3) Putting a difficult vocabulary that requires your handsome vocabulary knowledge. For this part, don't be shy. Email me for the Absolute Vocabulary: satvancouver@gmail.com

Chapter 6

20 Common Patterns for *In*correct Choices in Reading

8 Inconsistency with Question

This pattern employs the inconsistency trick. Some incorrect choices distract your attention by putting a true, but totally unrelated statement from the passage.

It is your job to limit the reading scope.

For instance, you should not find the answer from paragraph 2 when the question asks paragraph 1.

Let me explain further. Some sentence is very complex and long like 15 or 20 lines. If the question asks you to read lines 1-5, it really means lines 1-5, not lines 7 to 9.

9 Unknown Prediction

Some incorrect choices include a verb in future tense or adverb such as '<u>likely to be'</u> or regular verb or noun that contains the future meaning such as 'seem', 'will', 'anticipation'.

It is not your job to predict the future without having a logically written cause-effect situation in the passage. Even inference question is anchored in the cause-effect logic not the prediction.

Those unknown choices already have unknown congenital defects when they were born.

Chapter 7

20 Common Patterns for *In*correct Choices in Reading

10 Too Specific Example

Pattern 1: Main Idea Question should be a good example to explain. Main Idea does not seek out the answer from too specific example such as a specific person's name, place, thing, or event.

If you must choose the answer between Too General and Too Specific, choose the former.

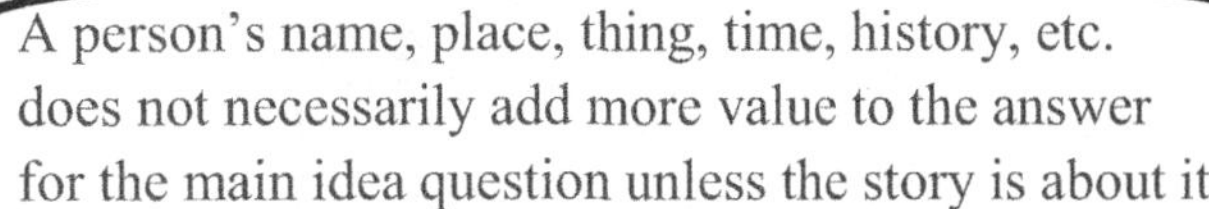

11 Too Objective Word Usage

This is the opposite pattern from the above one.
Let's take a look at Absolute Pattern 7: Understanding Attitude (Tone) as an example.

Some choices stop short at explaining the tone or attitude, making the choice too objective and vague.

We need a decisive tone with clear positive or negative value. For instance, in literary passage, the choice containing a word like "indifference" or "analyze" is almost always wrong without even reviewing the passage. It's because the nature of the literary passage is supposed to deliver a clear tone of the narrator or character. Too broad and objective word, therefore, can never be the answer choice.

Chapter 7

20 Common Patterns for *In*correct Choices in Reading

12 Extreme Word Usage

Incorrect choices using extreme words are relatively easy to rule out when they involve some obvious adverbs such as "always", "only", "never", etc.

Can you instantly compare the nature of the words like "dwindling" from "diminishing" and "compromise" from "accept?"

There's a distinctive dynamics between the synonyms or similar words. Compared to "dwindling," for example, "diminishing" is too extreme word. Let's suppose we use these words in animal extinction. Also, the word "accept" may sound too extreme to the defeated king if he thought of "compromise" from the political base of reasoning.

13 Shifting the Argument

Argument can change between paragraphs or within the passage.

For example, in paragraph 1, critics will argue with one thing, for which the author will oppose in paragraph 2 or 3.

In more complex passage, the author himself suddenly changes his opinion, making concession himself like in the form of repentance, or through realization, or with a sudden revelation...
This technique is called "side-stepping"

Side-stepping is quite confusing and it causes us to suspect our understanding of the entire passage. At this point, you'll get panic, thinking you're screwed with all the questions that you might have picked incorrect answers. The only way I can explain here is that there's a question asking about Side-stepping.
So, don't panic when you see one.

70 Absolute Patterns for Writing and Language Section

Question 45
Because airplane travels allow people to reach around the world drastically faster and more convenient, some have claimed the concept of borderline is radically different from earlier times.

A) NO CHANGE
B) is radically different from that in earlier times
C) is drastically and radically different than that of earlier times
D) is drastically different earlier times

RULE #45
Hint:
Comparison

In Comparison, Even a Tiny Insignificant Preposition should be Equally Compared

The correct answer is B.

"the concept of borderline" is compared with "the earlier times".

The correct sentence should be "the concept of borderline is radically different from that of (the concept of borderline) in earlier times

C) is incorrect because drastically and radically are redundant.
D) is incorrect because it changes the original meaning.

HARDER EXAMPLES
Incorrect: Some experts I spoke with said that a self-driving car population is closer at hand than one populated with trucks.
Correct: Some experts I spoke with said that the ***future populated with self-driving cars*** is closer at hand than ***one populated with trucks***.

Incorrect: Sometimes, the mysteries about Elvis Presley is more cryptic than Shakespeare.
Correct: Sometimes, the mysteries about Elvis Presley is more cryptic than ***those about*** Shakespeare.

Question 46
Ford's first vehicle Model A, which was first owned by Ernest Pfennig, a Chicago dentist, and capable of a top speed of five miles per hour.

A) and capability of
B) had a capability of
C) was capable of
D) was able to provide a capability of

RULE #46
Hint: Verb

Missing Verb

The correct answer is C
The original sentence does not contain the main verb.

B), D) are wordy. B) changes the verb form "are capable of" to a noun form "have a capability of" This is considered as a wordiness.
In a complex form, by simply covering up the non-restrictive modifier (inessential information offset by a pair of commas) you can drastically reduce the sentence complexity. That is, you can forget about ", which was first owned by Ernest Pfennig, a Chicago dentist," and try to deal with the subject and the verb only.

Question 47
When Clarence Anglin escaped the Alcatraz prison on a handcrafted rubber boat in June 11, 1962, with two other inmates John Anglin and Frank Morris, he had realized that he had left a note for a destination under his mattress.

A) NO CHANGE
B) Clarence had realized that Frank had left
C) he realized that John had left
D) Frank realized that John left

RULE #47
Hint
Pronoun
+
Tense

Ambiguous Pronoun + Tense

The correct answer is C.
When two or more people with the same gender are in one sentence, it is necessary to identify who the second person is.
In this sentence, choice C is correct because "he" in the main clause obviously indicates Clarence. Also, "had realized" is the past perfect, which means Clarence had realized even before the escape (the past tense "realized"), making an impossible situation.
A) and B) made this above error,

Question 48
That women and black people have to be given the enfranchisement were considered a radical idea in the eighteenth-century America.

A) have to be given the enfranchisement were
B) has to be given the enfranchisement were
C) have to be given the enfranchisement was
D) has to be given the enfranchisement was

RULE #48
Hint:
Verb

A Package Information "That-Clause."

The correct answer is C.
A package information using 'That-clause' is considered as a singular subject.
Therefore, the verb has to be singular.

Question 49
The concerned parents were anxious to see if their teenage children had drove the parents' vehicles recklessly.

A) had droven
B) had driven
C) have drove
D) drive

RULE #49 Hint: Verb	**Irregular Verb** The correct answer is B. Drive -> drove -> driven.

Question 50
Though the board members' criteria to select a new CEO for the company were both systemic as well as meticulous, the majority stockholders followed their own preference, thereby stifling the upcoming election.

A) NO CHANGE
B) was both systemic and
C) were both systemic as well as
D) were both systemic and

RULE #50 Hint: Conjunction	**Correlative Conjunction** The correct answer is D. The idiom "both ~ and" cannot be replaced with any other form. "Criteria" is plural of criterion. Therefore, the verb has to be the plural "were"

Question 51
Concerned that recruiting students was challenging last year, the university announced several scholarship plans in order to international students to be increased.

A) NO CHANGE
B) to increase international students.
C) for the international students to be increased.
D) to increase international students and remove their concern.

RULE #51 Hint: Simplification	**Choose an Active Voice instead of Passive.** The correct answer is B. A), C) are unnecessarily passive. Compared to the answer B, option D is wordy.

Question 52

Although the professor's promise " a completely open book test" suggested the final would be easy, students found it not that simple as they had expected.

A) not that simple
B) to be not that simple
C) not as simple
D) that simple

RULE #52
Hint:
Comparison

As ~ As

The correct answer is C.

"As...As" is an idiom and can't be replaced with "that...as"

Question 53

The staff favored the new stock option plan, a scheme the company's local divisions, rather than the reluctant head office, to decide how best to allocate profit equally.

A) NO CHANGE
B) that the company's local divisions, rather than the reluctant head office, decides
C) in which the company's local divisions, rather than the reluctant head office, decides
D) in which the company's local divisions, rather than the reluctant head office, decide

RULE #53
Hint:
Agreement

Subject-Verb Agreement

The correct answer is D.

In a complex form of statement like above, by simply covering up the non-restrictive modifier (inessential information offset by a pair of commas) you can drastically reduce the sentence complexity. That is, you can forget about ",rather than the reluctant head office, " and try to find the subject and the verb

"local divisions" (plural) cancels out options B and C, leaving A and D.

A) becomes a verb-less sentence.

Question 54

Results of the gloomy economic forecast in the upcoming fourth quarter sales, the CEO decided to sacrifice his perk, salary increase, and his merger plan.

A) NO CHANGE
B) Results by
C) Resulted by
D) Resulting in

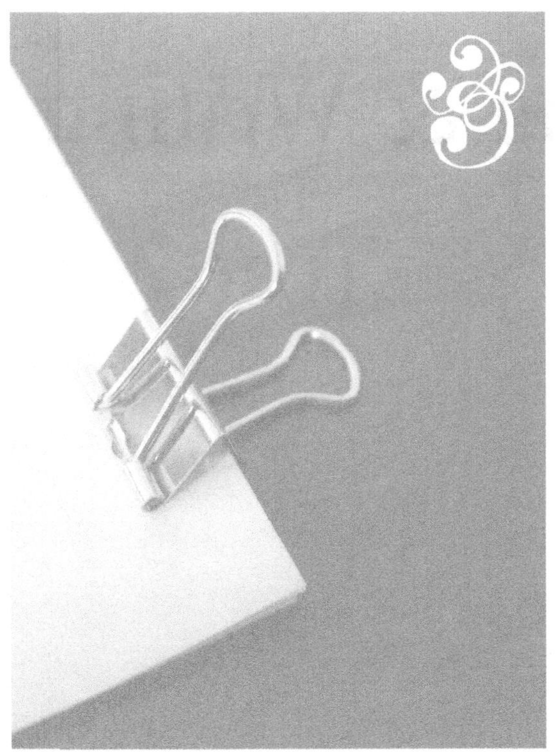

Chapter 7

1. TEST 7

2. ANSWER EXPLANATIONS for TEST 7

3. CHAPTER SUMMARY

SAT
Reading & Writing Practice
Test 7

ALL THE LOGIC AND RULES
BEHIND THE EVERY SINGLE
SAT QUESTION

Reading Test 7

65 MINUTES, 53 QUESTIONS

The passages below are followed by questions based on their content; questions following a pair of related passages may also be based on the relationship between the paired passages. Answer the questions on the basis of what is stated or implied in the passages and in any introductory material that may be provided.

Questions 1-10 are based on the following passage.
Don't Diss Ability
Harvard University 2016 The Harvard Crimson, . Reprinted with permission.

This summer was chock-full of new experiences. They were the kind of experiences that you read about in American road novels. Traveling worldwide and taking plane ride after plane ride reminded me of trashy teen romance films about travel, parentless escapades, and a reckless summer. As if I were living a Kerouac novel or an "Eat Pray Love"-sequel movie, I met people who played protagonists in their own lives, and fleeting co-stars in mine. In Manila, I met an artist who developed his own style of art and recently opened an art studio catered for people with autism. In Indianapolis, I met a budding public speaker who has delivered speeches at multi-million dollar fundraisers. That same weekend, I met an actress whose show ran for six seasons and won both Golden Globe and Emmy awards. What unifies all these people who crossed my path? It's not just their excellence. Rather, they all have intellectual and developmental disabilities (IDD).

In the United States, there are over 6.5 million individuals with IDD. There's been broader representation of people with IDD in popular media in recent years, and these long awaited representations have been slowly changing perceptions of people with disabilities. But even with the progress we've made, we still do not view people with IDD as full-members of our society. This is clearest when looking at the widespread lack of employment for people with IDD.

Unemployment rates for people with disabilities are at 85 percent—levels that for any other group of Americans would be unacceptable. Studies have shown that people with IDD aid in the general productivity of a work environment.

Employers also reported that the number of challenges faced by an employee with IDD were much fewer than those expected at the time the individual was hired. It turns out that the reason that people with IDD are not hired is not because they lack ability, but because people assume they lack ability. This insight highlights the main problem that this country has with people with disabilities.

Avenues to higher education for people with IDD are limited; for example, U.S., compared to Europe, lacks any sort of program for the mainstream education of students with IDD. But this is beside the point, because it's not the only way we can welcome people with IDD into the community. One of the simplest and most empowering things we can do is to hire individuals with IDD.

There is an abundance of jobs that individuals with disabilities have the ability to compete for. There's no reason I shouldn't run into workers with IDD in Library or when visiting a company. Our country can be better and hire a more diverse workforce. It's not a groundbreaking recommendation, but it may take time for employers to see it as a priority.

Doing our part to help create opportunities for people with IDD is critical, and employers must approach that task seriously, both here in our community and nationally. Waiting indefinitely for others to employ people with IDD would feel <u>disillusioning</u> to me, were it not for the fact that many people with IDD will hold positions of power once they make careers for themselves—roles in which who can directly open up opportunities to other people with IDD. At that point, as we sit behind mahogany desks with the responsibility of making hiring decisions, I hope we consider applicants who happen to have intellectual and developmental disabilities. We must shift our perspectives so that we see them as productive members of society, unlike the way they've been viewed for decades.

CONTINUE

1 1

1

In the opening paragraph the author primarily does which of the following?

A) compare the author's summer with road novels.
B) lay out the ways he traveled around the world
C) observe individuals with disability in a real world society
D) explain why people with disability appeal to the masses

2

The second paragraph, lines 21-30 (In the United States…IDD) can be best summarized as

A) individuals with IDD receive broader media attention
B) people's perceptions of the individuals with IDD are inflexible
C) the society is not aware that there are individuals with IDD
D) people's perceptions of the individuals with IDD have progressed and will continue

3

The author of the passage would agree that

A) individuals with IDD lack ability to be the part of workforce
B) people's perception is the major factor that preclude individuals with IDD from employment
C) the productivity of individuals with IDD at work is no less than that of normal employees
D) the employment rate of individuals with IDD is roughly only one-third.

4

Which choice provides the best evidence for the answer to the previous question?

A) Lines 21-22 (In the United States...IDD)
B) Lines 29-30 (This is…IDD)
C) Lines 31-33 (Unemployment...unacceptable)
D) Lines 39-42 (It turns out…ability.)

5

The author makes which of the following statements about the individuals with IDD

A) Unemployment rate is one example showing our perspective on people with IDD is changing for better.
B) U.S. provides better education chance than European countries.
C) Focusing more on these people's ability than disability depends on our perspectives.
D) Students with IDD have equal potential to learn

6

Which choice provides the best evidence for the answer to the previous question?

A) Lines 21-22 (In the United States...with IDD.)
B) Lines 39-42 (It turns...lack ability.)
C) Lines 45-48 (Avenues…students with IDD)
D) Lines 49-51 (But this is…the community.)

7

The author mentions library (line 57) in order to

A) encourage library to provide education to workers with IDD
B) acknowledge current limitation
C) criticize the inflexibility of employers
D) speculate better society for library workers

8

The main purpose of the passage is to

A) classify the unemployment rates of individuals with IDD
B) reminiscent his traveling experience with individuals with IDD
C) debunk the public misconception towards individuals with IDD
D) influence the reader to support the author's argument

CONTINUE

1 1

9

In line 72, the author refers to "mahogany desks" in order to

A) criticize employers who do not hire individuals with IDD
B) describe high quality desks
C) visualize appearance of those in power to hire individuals with IDD
D) mischaracterize individuals without IDD

10

As used in line 67, "disillusioning" most nearly means

A) false idea
B) imagination
C) untruth
D) evocation

Questions 11-21 are based on the following passage.

The following passage describes DNA mutation

In biology, a mutation is the permanent alteration. Mutations may or may not produce discernible changes in the observable characteristics of an organism. Mutations play a part in both normal and abnormal biological processes including: evolution. If a mutation changes a protein produced by a gene, the result is likely to be harmful, with an estimated two-thirds of amino acid polymorphisms that have damaging effects, and the remainder being either neutral or marginally beneficial.

Due to the damaging effects that mutations can have on genes, organisms have mechanisms such as DNA repair to prevent or correct mutations by reverting the mutated sequence back to its original state.

Natural selection within a population for a trait that can vary across a range of values, such as height, can be categorized into three different types. The first is directional selection, which is a shift in the average value of a trait over time—for example, organisms slowly getting taller.

Secondly, disruptive selection is selection for extreme trait values and often results in two different values becoming most common. This would be when either short or tall organisms had an advantage, but not those of medium height.

Finally, in stabilizing selection there is selection against extreme trait values on both ends, which causes a decrease in variance around the average value and less diversity. If selection would favor either one out of two mutations, but there is no extra advantage to having both, then the mutation that occurs the most frequently is the one that is most likely to become fixed in a population.

Mutations leading to the loss of function of a gene are much more common than mutations that produce a new, fully functional gene. But when selection is weak, mutation bias towards loss of function can affect evolution. For example, pigments are no longer useful when animals live in the darkness, and tend to be lost. This kind of loss of function can occur because of mutation bias. The speed at which loss evolves depends more on the mutation rate than it does on the effective population size, indicating that it is driven more by mutation bias than by genetic drift.

CONTINUE

1 1

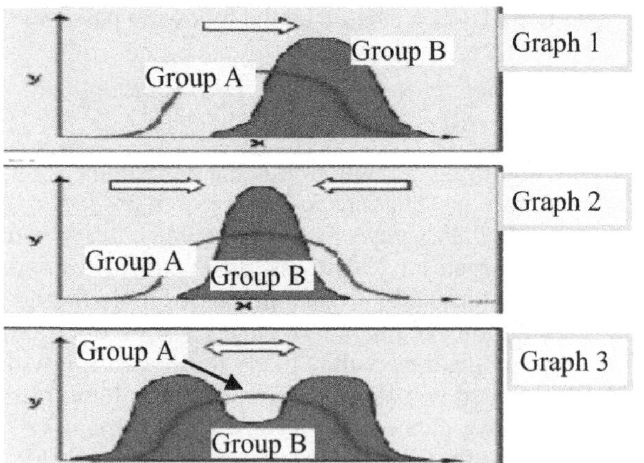

On each graph, Group A is the original population and Group B is the population after selection.

- Graph 1 shows directional selection, in which a single extreme phenotype is favored.
- Graph 2 shows stabilizing selection, where the intermediate phenotype is favored over the extreme traits.
- Graph 3 shows disruptive selection, in which the extreme phenotypes are favored over the intermediate

11

Paragraph 1 (lines 1-10) makes the points of mutation process as its EXCEPT

A) lasting effect on organism

B) largely benign biological processes

C) regular and irregular biological processes

D) observable changes

12

According to the passage, a mutation that alters a protein will ultimately

A) have no effect on the organism

B) produce damaging effects

C) benefit the organism

D) remain neutral permanently

13

Which choice provides the best evidence for the answer to the previous question?

A) Lines 1-2 (In biology…alternation.)

B) Lines 2-4 (Mutations may...an organism)

C) Lines 6-10 (If a mutation ..marginally beneficial)

D) Lines 11-15 (Due to the...original state)

14

According to paragraph 1 (lines 1-10), which pairing best represents the different ratios of harmful amino acid polymorphisms and the remainder respectively?

A) 10 percent and 30 percent

B) 50 percent and 50 percent

C) 70 percent and 30 percent

D) 90 percent and 10 percent

CONTINUE

1

15

According to paragraphs 3-4 (lines 16-34), if Leaf-eating deer migrates to Giraffe habitat, the deer must have undergone the natural selection of

I. Directional selection

II. Disruptive selection

III. Stabilizing section

A) I

B) II

C) III

D) I and III

16

Which choice provides the best evidence for the answer to the previous question?

A) Lines 19-21 (The first is directional...getting taller)

B) Lines 22-24 (Secondly, disruptive...most common.)

C) Lines 24-26 (This would be...medium height.)

D) Lines 27-30 (Finally, in stabilizing...less diversity.)

17

According to the last paragraph (lines 35-46), the most successful mutation bias depends on

A) genetic drift

B) proteins

C) evolution

D) frequency

18

According to the last paragraph (lines 35-46), which animal species would experience mutation bias that leads to loss of pigment?

A) Sloth

B) Duck

C) Bat

D) Frog

19

The author mentions “animals” in line 40 primarily to exemplify

A) the benefit of living in darkness

B) weak selection that causes mutation bias that ends up affecting evolution

C) a typical mutation bias

D) animals that cause our fear

20

As described in question 15, Leaf-eating deer that migrate to Giraffe habitat will be indicated in the chart

I. Chart 1

II. Chart II

III. Chart III

A) I

B) II

C) III

D) I and III

21

In the last paragraph, which of the following statements correctly describes "genetic drift"?

A) Genetic drift and natural selection are the same terms

B) Genetic drift mainly controls population size

C) Genetic drift does not at all contribute population size

D) Population size is affected more by mutation bias than by genetic drift

CONTINUE

1 1

Questions 22-31 are based on the following passage.

The following passage excerpted from U.S. President Lindon Johnson's address: The American Promise

I speak tonight for the dignity of man and the destiny of democracy. I urge every member of both parties, Americans of all religions and of all colors, from every section of this country, to join me in that cause. At times history and fate meet at a single time in a single place to shape a turning point in man's unending search for freedom. So it was at Lexington and Concord. So it was a century ago at Appomattox. So it was last week in Selma, Alabama.

Our lives have been marked with debate about great issues; issues of war and peace, issues of prosperity and depression. But rarely in any time does an issue lay bare the secret heart of America itself.

Rarely are we met with a challenge, not to our growth or abundance, our welfare or our security, but rather to the values and the purposes and the meaning of our beloved Nation.

There is no Negro problem. There is no Southern problem. There is no Northern problem. There is only an American problem. "Give me liberty or give me death." To apply any other test --to deny a man his hopes because of his color or race, his religion or the place of his birth--is not only to do injustice, it is to deny America and to dishonor the dead who gave their lives for American freedom. Many of the issues of civil rights are very complex and most difficult. But about this there can and should be no argument.

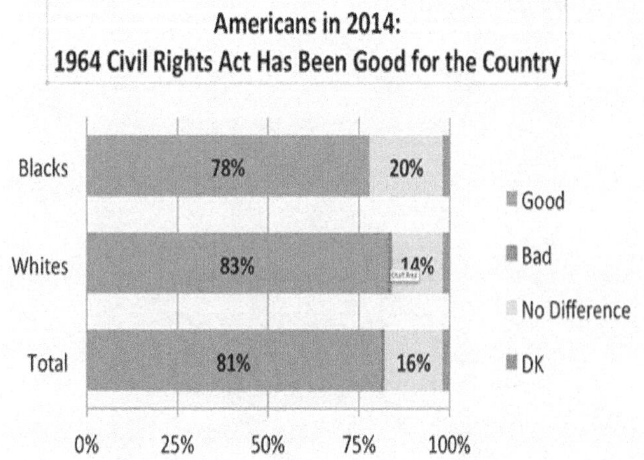

22

The president suggests that the cities mentioned in lines 8-10 were strongly influenced by

A) the police's biased control over racial discrimination

B) the lack pacifists' efforts

C) their own desire for freedom

D) his speech

23

The speaker's main concern when he addresses "I urge every member...that cause" (lines 2-5) is to

A) encourage the united participation

B) reveal the intensity of the problem

C) present the enjoyment of working together

D) urge the emotional responses

24

The phrase "a single time in a single place" in line 6 most directly implies that

A) a time to change has finally arrived

B) every American is anxious about unequal rights

C) man's unending search for freedom requires more time and place

D) the dignity of man hasn't been fully recognized yet

25

The speaker uses parallelism (There is no...American problem.) in lines 20-22 in order to

A) compare between actual problem and the secret heart of America

B) argue that there is no negro problem

C) list the least important problem to most important problem

D) generalize the issue as a single concern in society at large

CONTINUE

1

26

The tone of the president's comment in line 22 "give a liberty or give me death." can be characterized as

A) emphatic

B) inflexible

C) ambivalent

D) impressive

27

According to the passage, people in U.S. would most likely disagree with how to

A) improve the country

B) provide a better life to the people

C) protect the citizen

D) define the values of our nation

28

Which choice provides the best evidence for the answer to the previous question?

A) Lines 5-8 (At times...for freedom.)

B) Lines 16-17 (Rarely are we...our security,)

C) Lines 18-19 (but rather...beloved Nation.)

D) Lines 20-22 (There is no...American problem)

29

The word "test" in line 38 most nearly means

A) higher education entrance test

B) police interrogation

C) insecurity of nation

D) override of dignity

30

In line 28 "Many of the issues of civil rights", the president does which of the following?

A) Presents opposing viewpoints

B) Voices doubt about the nature of complexity

C) Issues a challenge to solve the complexity

D) Rationalizes inherent limitations

31

According to the graph, which statement is true about the poll in 2014 on 1964 Civil Rights Act

A) Blacks felt the Acts need to make more dramatic effect

B) Majority of Whites distasted the Acts

C) Whites women were more attentive with the Acts

D) Both Blacks and Whites contented enough with the Acts

CONTINUE

1

Questions 32--42 are based on the following passage.

The following passage is from Siddhartha by Herman Hesse

In the shade of the house, in the sunshine of the riverbank near the boats, in the shade of the Sal-wood forest, in the shade of the fig tree is where Siddhartha grew up, the handsome son of the Brahman, the young falcon, together with his friend Govinda, son of a Brahman.

The sun tanned his light shoulders by the banks of the river when bathing, performing the sacred ablutions, the sacred offerings. He already knew to feel Atman in the depths of his being, indestructible, one with the universe. In the mango grove, depths of shade poured into his black eyes.

Joy leapt in his father's heart for his son who was quick to learn; he saw him growing up to become great wise man and priest.

Love touched the hearts of the Brahmans' young daughters when Siddhartha walked through the lanes of the town with the luminous forehead, with the eye of a king, with his slim hips. But more than all the others he was loved by Govinda, his friend, the son of a Brahman. He loved Siddhartha's eye and sweet voice, he loved his walk and the perfect decency of his movements, he loved everything Siddhartha did and said and what he loved most was his spirit, his transcendent, fiery thoughts, his ardent will, his high calling.

Govinda wanted to follow Siddhartha and in days to come, when Siddhartha would become a god, when he would join the glorious, then Govinda wanted to follow him as his servant, his spear-carrier, his shadow. Siddhartha was thus loved by everyone. He was a source of joy for everybody, he was a delight for them all.

But he, Siddhartha, was not a source of joy for himself, he found no delight in himself. Dreams and restless thoughts came into his mind, flowing from the water of the river, sparkling from the stars of the night.

32

In line 9, “offerings” is closest in meaning to

A) giving

B) ritual

C) proposal

D) sacrifice

33

In the passage, Siddhartha is being described as

A) the one in the state of nirvana who realized the depth of universe

B) a great wise old man

C) a boy sees Atman inside some mango grove

D) a condescending and authoritative prodigy

34

Which choice provides the best evidence for the answer to the previous question?

A) Lines 1-4 (In the shade…grew up)

B) Lines 4-6 (the handsome son… a Brahman.)

C) Lines 7-9 (The sun tanned...the sacred offerings.)

D) Lines 9-11 (He already knew…the universe.)

35

Phrase “depths of his being” in line 10 and “depths of shade” in line 12 can represent respectively as

A) complexity and simplicity

B) darkness and innocence

C) spirituality and mentality

D) serious quality and deep distance

36

Paragraph 3 and 4 in lines 16-27 (Joy leapt in…his high calling.) suggests that Siddhartha

A) is in the state of nirvana that his family and friends have limited understanding of him

B) enjoys unchallenged position in society

C) encourages people to praise his holiness

D) is spiritually infused with and inspires his family

CONTINUE

37

In line 27, “high calling” is closest in meaning to

A) divine influence

B) arrogant voice

C) pitch of the voice

D) frequent talk

38

Lines 16-19 (Love touched....slim hips) mainly describes

A) Siddhartha’s sexual appeal

B) Siddhartha’s hot temperament

C) people’s applause to his fantastic slim hips

D) People’s reverence to the presence of Siddhartha

39

Govinda’s attitude towards Siddhartha could be best characterized as

A) confidence

B) submission

C) appreciation

D) friendship

40

Based on the last paragraph (lines 36-40), Siddhartha may eventually

A) get married to any girl and live happily ever after

B) live in the deep shade of mango grove

C) search for meaning in life

D) follow Govinda to understand life

41

Last paragraph (Lines 36-40) implies Siddhartha’s

A) desire to look cool

B) unwillingness to meet his family and friends’ wish

C) reluctance to take the current contentment

D) overindulgence to source of joy

Questions 42-52 are based on the following passage.

Sexist Science *The effect that implicit bias has on scientific research*

PASSAGE 1

Science is objective. The scientific process is rigorous, involving hard data and empirical observations. And, as a result, the conclusions are objectively factual. For example: Gravity exists. The Earth moves around the Sun. Evolution is the process by which different kinds of living organisms developed and diversified from earlier forms. Women are biologically inferior to men. Wait, what? Charles Darwin is well-known for developing the theory of evolution. He is a little bit less known for teaching that women are biologically inferior to women.

That can’t be right. Darwin was a reputable scientist, not just some sexist bigot. And yet, the same man who gave us the theory of evolution also gave us the insight that “the average standard of mental power in man must be above that of woman." How did hard, objective science lead Darwin to such a dangerously incorrect conclusion? It’s important to remember that Darwin lived in England from 1809 to 1882, during a time when women were not granted the same access and opportunities as men. For example, some doctors in 19th century Britain reported that studying "had a damaging effect on the ovaries, turning attractive young women into dried-up prunes."

As a result, even when Oxford and Cambridge eventually opened their doors to women, many families refused to let their daughters attend, for fear that they would no longer be marriageable. Gender norms in 19th century Britain simply did not allow women to achieve the same level of academic and professional success as their male peers.

Darwin was almost certainly influenced by the social and cultural norms of his time when he came to the conclusion that women are biologically inferior to men.

CONTINUE

PASSAGE 2

How objective is science? Scientists are socialized and influenced by the same societal pressures as the rest of us. As a result, even though the scientific process tries to be as objective as possible, scientists are human beings with implicit bias, just like everyone else. Therefore, science in this world and society is never purely objective—and it can even deliver sexually biased scientists.

Even though science involves numbers and data, it is all too easy for science to slide into the realm of subjectivity. For example, it is widely accepted in the scientific community that the egg passively sits in the bodies of women while sperm race towards it, eager to be the first to implant themselves. Yet, as anthropologist Emily Martin pointed out, this narrative does not represent the facts of biology. As a matter of fact, researches at Johns Hopkins University found that the mechanical force of the sperm's tail is not very great. Therefore, the egg isn't passively waiting for a sperm to penetrate it—the egg actually plays an active role in capturing a sperm with its own adhesive molecules.

Not everything in science is culturally constructed, but a good portion of it is. The parallels between cultural stereotypes of male and female behavior and the behavior of the egg and the sperm are too close to be coincidental. In science textbooks, the egg is often described as passively "sweeping" or "transporting" along the fallopian tube. The sperm, in contrast, is usually described as actively swimming or propelling itself forward.

Women More Likely Than Men to See Gender Discrimination

% saying there is a lot or some discrimination against women in our society today

42

The author's question mark in line 9 serves to demonstrate

A) abrupt resistance
B) feigned skepticism
C) measured receptivity
D) mild irritation

43

In lines 1-12 (Science...women.), the author expresses which of the following attitudes to Charles Darwin?

A) Amusement that such a respected scientist expressed over the supposedly trivial matter
B) Qualification that his view is compromised by societal conditioning
C) Annoyance that his view about women is solely based on women's incompetent physicality
D) Resignation about the impossibility of the theory of evolution

44

Lines 13-23 (That can't be right...as men) shifts the author's view from

A) a source of dismay to a complete acceptance
B) inevitable acknowledgement to logical assessment
C) vehement rejection to historical analyses
D) judicial assessment to resignation

45

The last paragraph (Darwin was almost...to man) in passage 1 primarily encourages reader to view Charles Darwin as

A) an intellectual misogynist
B) an opportunist in closed-society
C) a conditioned human being dealt with cultural myopia
D) unconscious patriarchist

CONTINUE

1 1

46

The author characterizes science and scientists in lines 40-48 as

A) any scientific theory can be promoted by subtle social pressure
B) valid scientific theory must be conducted only by those rigorous scientists
C) any scientific theory must be evaluated by the possible subjectivity
D) scientific theory should be objective and not be compromised by social influence

47

It can be inferred that scientists in passage 2 may believe that they

A) seek out scientific evidence that conforms society's preexisting beliefs
B) act as if they are only scientists, not human
C) are the victims of social bias
D) try to apply social subjectivity effectively as an opportunity

48

The author's purpose in lines 65-66 (Not everything…a good portion of it is) is to

A) defend diverse perspectives on scientists
B) discredit the view of culturally constructed science
C) note the acknowledgement that social conditioning is a factor in science
D) express there's value in cultural stereotype

49

It can be inferred that Charles Darwin in passage 1 might have responded to "societal pressures " in line 42 in passage 2 that

A) scientific study must be based on solemn detachment
B) social construction of the time reasonably affects scientific objectivity
C) women in scientific arena is inferior to man is my regretful speech, but truth is truth.
D) scientific objectivity reasonably affects social construction of the time

50

Which choice provides the best evidence for the answer to the previous question?

A) Lines 18-19 (How did...conclusion?)
B) Lines 23-27 (For example,...prunes.)
C) Lines 28-35 (As a result...peers.)
D) Lines 36-39 (Darwin...men)

51

Charles Darwin in Passage 1 might view the researches in lines 58 in Passage 2 as

A) the part of his theory of evolution
B) the work made by human being who couldn't escape from social influence
C) the work that egg tries to sneak away from the social influence
D) the work conducted by women scientists who influenced the results.

52

Which of the following analysis correctly represents the graph illustrated after the passage?

A) More women than men see gender inequality
B) Approximately 35% of women didn't respond
C) There are more men in "A lot" group than "Some" group
D) Fewer women responded "A lot" than men did.

STOP

If you finish before time is called,
you may check your work on this section.

Do not turn to the next section.

Writing and Language Test 7
35 MINUTES, 44 QUESTIONS

Each passage below is accompanied by a number of questions. For some questions, you will consider how the passage might be revised to improve the expression of ideas. For other questions, you will consider how the passage might be edited to correct errors in sentence structure, usage, or punctuation. A passage or a question may be accompanied by one or more graphics (such as a table or graph) that you will consider as you make revising and editing decisions.

Questions 1-11 are based on the following passage.

On leaving home

Harvard University 2016 The Harvard Crimson, Reprinted with permission.

I am well acquainted with my suitcase. After all, we've spent a lot of time together: [1] Its moved me back and forth between Canada and America, between my little hometown and a city where no one knows my name, between my parents' house and a college dorm and (most recently) a seedy summer apartment. I know that its wheels squeak at an uncomfortably high pitch. I know that its weight will bang into my calves at every other step [2] so that I skip and hobble in a particular way. canvas suitcase. I know that it exists to displace me—and for that I resent every durable green inch of [3] it for that reason. How tightly am I bound to my location?

1

A) NO CHANGE
B) It's
C) The suitcase
D) It was

2

A) NO CHANGE
B) unless
C) while
D) because

3

A) NO CHANGE
B) the suitcase.
C) it or that.
D) it.

CONTINUE

2 2

My life looks small [4] wraps in cardboard and canvas. Eventually, I can't look anymore.

I need to get out of this [5] used home. I grab my wallet and a map and, with pleasing randomness, decide to visit the Boston Harbor Islands. They seem far and inconvenient, and I am fed up with staying in one place.[6]

Two hours, two buses, and one subway ride later, I am standing inside the Boston Harbor Islands Ferry office. An older woman is in the process of closing the ticket kiosk, and seems annoyed by my presence. "The last ferry to the Islands left at one," she says curtly. Then, registering the look on my face, [7] we soften the atmosphere: "You could just catch the last ferry to Boston, though. There's a lot to do there."

First, I am bewildered. This isn't Boston?

Where am I? When did I leave my city? The woman informs me that we are in Hingham, but I've never heard of the town.

4

A) NO CHANGE
B) and wraps
C) wrapping
D) wrapped

5

A) NO CHANGE
B) used to be home.
C) use to-be home.
D) used-to-be home.

6

The author is considering deleting the preceding underlined sentence. Should he make this deletion?

A) Yes, because the sentence contradicts to the narrator's longing for homesickness.
B) Yes, because the sentence contains the word "inconvenient" that the narrator wishes to avoid.
C) No, because the sentence is informative and contributes the narrator's longing for new experience.
D) No, because the sentence sets up the new place other than the narrator's current apartment

7

A) NO CHANGE
B) soften voice whispers:
C) I was softened by the atmosphere:
D) she softens the atmosphere:

CONTINUE

2

In desperation, I pull out my map and look for [8] something—anything—that looks interesting. The only destination [9] marked Nantasket Beach **that** even remotely fits the **bill** is a little spot on the **coast**.

I trudge back to the heat-baked highway and wait for the next bus. It takes me another two hours and the advice of a series of strangers, but I eventually make it to my destination.

[10] The sand stretches down from a raised sidewalk in pale sun-bleached yellow dotted with pink and blue umbrellas. The waves froth high enough to sweep even adults off their feet. Shouting kids and screaming gulls and crashing surf produce a beach sound [11] so perfect ,and it feels slightly surreal.

8

A) NO CHANGE
B) something, anything that looks
C) something anything that looks
D) something or anything that looks

9

The best placement for the underlined portion would be:

A) NO CHANGE
B) after the words the bill is
C) after the word that
D) after the word coast

10

At this point, the author wishes to add the following statement:

I grew up in a small beach village.

Would this be a relevant addition here?

A) Yes, because it functions as a topic sentence that link to the following descriptions.
B) Yes, because it informs Nantasket Beach is idyllic.
C) No, because the sentence does not properly link to the following descriptions.
D) No, because it implies that the author's visit is premeditated.

11

A) NO CHANGE
B) as to feel
C) with it feels
D) that it feels

CONTINUE

2 2

Questions 12-22 are based on the following passage.

The new wave of British Heavy Metal

The new wave of British heavy metal (NWOBHM) was a nationwide musical movement that started in the United Kingdom in the late **1970s** and [12] have achieved international attention by the early 1980s. Journalist **Geoff Barton** in a May 1979 [13] coined the term issue of the British music **newspaper** *Sounds* to describe the emergence of new heavy metal bands in the late 1970s, during the period of punk rock's decline and the dominance of new wave music.

Although encompassing [14] variously diversified mainstream and underground styles, the music of the NWOBHM is best remembered for drawing on the heavy metal of the 1970s and infusing [15] it with the intensity of punk rock to produce fast and aggressive songs.

The DIY attitude of the new metal bands led to the spread of raw-sounding, self-produced recordings and [16] a proliferation of independent record labels. Song lyrics were usually about escapist themes such as mythology, fantasy, horror and the rock lifestyle.

12

A) NO CHANGE
B) achieved
C) has achieved
D) has been achieving

13

The best placement for the underlined portion would be:

A) NO CHANGE
B) after the word Geoff Barton
C) after the word newspaper
D) after the word 1970s,

14

A) NO CHANGE
B) diversified in various
C) diverse
D) DELET IT

15

A) NO CHANGE
B) them
C) NWOBHM
D) OMIT the underlined portion

16

A) NO CHANGE
B) independent record labels were proliferated.
C) a proliferation of independent record labels was followed.
D) record labels were proliferated independently.

CONTINUE

2 2

The NWOBHM began as an underground phenomenon growing in parallel to punk but largely ignored by the media. [17] The movement involved mostly young, white, male and working-class musicians and fans, who suffered the hardships brought on by rising unemployment for years after the 1973–75 recession. As a reaction to [18] <u>their</u> bleak reality, they created a community separate from mainstream society to enjoy each other's company and their favourite loud music.

The NWOBHM was heavily criticized for the excessive hype generated by local media in favour of mostly talentless musicians. [19] <u>Consequently,</u> it generated a renewal in the genre of heavy metal music and furthered the progress of the heavy metal subculture, whose updated behavioural and visual codes were quickly adopted by metal fans worldwide after the spread of the music to continental Europe, North America and Asia.

17

At this point, the author wants to add the following sentence:

> It was only through the promotion of rock DJ Neal Kay and *Sounds'* campaigning that it reached the public consciousness and gained radio airplay, recognition and success in the UK.

Would the author make this addition here?

A) Yes, because it provides an important link to the rest of the paragraph.

B) Yes, because it connects well with the previous sentence telling the reason for its unpopularity in the music industry.

C) No, because it strays from the main focus of the essay.

D) No, because it is directly contradicted to the previous sentence.

18

A) NO CHANGE

B) NWOBHM's

C) its

D) public's

19

A) NO CHANGE

B) Nonetheless,

C) For example,

D) Soon,

CONTINUE

2 2

The movement spawned perhaps a thousand metal bands [20] ; subsequently, only a few survived the advent of MTV and the rise of the more commercial glam metal in the second half of the 1980s. Among them, Iron Maiden and Def Leppard became international stars. Other groups, such as Diamond Head, Venom and Raven, remained underground, but were a major influence on the successful extreme metal subgenres of the late 1980s and 1990s.[21]

U.K. Album Sales by Genre (in millions)

	2014	2015	2016
Heavy Metal	29.79	27.82	24.23
Country	47.66	46.13	43.72
Electronic	-	-	8.74
Latin	25.13	16.5	12.35
R&B	77.01	69.89	57.87
Rock	139.6	124.16	103.71
Pop	233	266	299
Alternative	80.92	68.2	53.73
Classical	13.32	12.14	8.96
Jazz	11.79	11.78	8.78

20

A) NO CHANGE
B) ,however,
C) ,and
D) ,but

21

Which choice, if added here, would most effectively conclude the essay?

A) Many bands from the NWOBHM reunited in the 2000s and remained active through live performances and new studio albums.
B) Some critics in 1970s viewed NWOBHM as the significant exponent of the movement
C) Foreign hard rock acts, such as Kiss from the US, Rush from Scorpions from Germany, and especially AC/DC from Australia, climbed the British charts in the same period
D) Each of these bands was in crisis in the mid-to-late 1970s.

22

Given that all of the followings are true, which interpretation would most clearly reflect the passage and the table?

A) Heavy Metal, albeit active in the 2010s, is not getting a meaningful attention from industry.
B) Heavy Metal, albeit insignificant in sales, proved to be continuing to increase in sales
C) Heavy Metal, albeit not a major genre, was not the only one experienced decline in sales.
D) Critics, seeking the greatest benefit ,paid more attention on Pop than Heavy Metal

CONTINUE

2

Questions 23-33 are based on the following passage.

The Tower of Pisa

The Leaning Tower of Pisa *or simply the Tower of Pisa* is freestanding bell tower of the cathedral of the Italian city of Pisa [23] , and it is known worldwide for its unintended tilt. [24] Situated behind Pisa's cathedral and is the third oldest structure in the city's Cathedral Square. The tower's tilt began during construction, caused by an inadequate foundation on ground too soft on one side to properly support the structure's weight. [25] Galileo Galilei is said to have dropped two cannonballs of different masses from the tower to demonstrate that [26] its speed of descent was independent of their mass. However, the only primary source for this is the biography *Racconto istorico della vita di Galileo*, written by Galileo's secretary Vincenzo Viviani and published in 1717, long after Viviani's death.

23

A) NO CHANGE
B) which is known
C) , known
D) as known

24

A) NO CHANGE
B) It is situated
C) Being situated
D) The Tower of Pisa, situated

25

If the author wish to delete the underlined portion of the sentence, the paragraph would probably lose:

A) the fascinating feature that attracts tourists from around the world
B) a distinctive look that people talk about the tower
C) the main reason for its look
D) a specific detail of serious structural defects unknown until the repair was completed

26

A) NO CHANGE
B) their
C) it has
D) they have

CONTINUE

2 2

During World War II, the Allies discovered that the Germans were using the tower as an observation post. A U.S. Army sergeant sent to confirm the presence of German troops in the tower [27] which was impressed by the beauty of the cathedral, and thus refrained [28] to order an artillery strike, sparing it from destruction. Numerous efforts have been made to restore the tower to a vertical orientation or at least keep it from falling over. Most of these efforts [29] failed; some worsened the tilt.

On February 27, 1964, the government of Italy requested aid in preventing the tower from toppling. [30] Consequently, [31] these people considered important to retain the current tilt, due to the role that this element played in promoting the tourism industry of Pisa.

27

A) NO CHANGE
B) who was impressed
C) was impressed
D) impressed

28

A) NO CHANGE
B) that by ordering
C) from ordering
D) and ordered

29

A) NO CHANGE
B) failed: some worsened the tilt.
C) failed, some worsened the tilt.
D) failed with some worsened the tilt.

30

A) After all
B) However,
C) Nonetheless,
D) Moreover,

31

A) NO CHANGE
B) They were considered
C) It was considered
D) The Italian government considered

CONTINUE

2

A multinational task force of engineers, mathematicians, and historians gathered on the Azores islands to discuss the stabilization methods. <1> It was found that the tilt was increasing in combination with the softer foundations on the lower side. <2> Many methods were proposed to stabilize the tower, including the addition of 800 tones of lead counterweights to the raised end of the base. <3> The tower and the neighboring cathedral baptistery, and cemetery have been included in the Piazza del DuomoUNESCO World Heritage Site, which was declared in 1987. <4> The tower was closed to the public on January 7, 1990, after more than two decades of stabilization studies and spurred by the abrupt collapse of the Civic Tower of Pavia in 1989. The bells were removed to relieve some weight, and cables were cinched around the third level and anchored several hundred meters away. Apartments and houses in the path of the tower were vacated for safety. The solution chosen to prevent the collapse of the tower was to slightly straighten it to a safer angle by removing 38 cubic metres (1,342 cubic feet) of soil from underneath the raised end.

32

Which of the following sentences is diverting from the main issue in this paragraph?

A) <1>
B) <2>
C) <3>
D) <4>

33

Suppose the author's goal was to write a brief summary describing the timeline to stabilize the Tower of Pisa.
Would this summary accomplish his goal?

A) Yes, because it details the unique and effortful undertaking made by many scientists including Galilei Galileo
B) Yes, because it chronicles the important events of the project including some debates to stabilize the Tower.
C) No, because it focuses on the historical overview of the leaning Tower
D) No, because the historical figure like Galileo Galilei's experiment was the main concern.

CONTINUE

2 2

Questions 34-44 are based on the following passage.

Can Dark Knight Rise Again?

Entrepreneur Major Malcolm Wheeler founded National Allied Publications in autumn 1934. The company debuted with the tabloid-sized *New Fun: The Big Comic Magazine* #1 with a cover date of February 1935. The company's second title, *New Comics* #1, appeared in a size close to [34] what would become [35] comic books standard during the period fans and historians [36] call the Golden Age of Comic [37] Books with slightly larger dimensions than today's. That title evolved into *Adventure Comics*, which continued through issue #503 in 1983, becoming one of the longest-running comic-book series. In 2009 DC revived *Adventure Comics* with its original numbering.

34

A) NO CHANGE
B) that
C) which
D) ,which

35

A) NO CHANGE
B) comic's books standard
C) comic's books' standard
D) comic books' standard

36

A) NO CHANGE
B) calls
C) were calling
D) had called

37

A) NO CHANGE
B) Books: with slightly larger
C) Books, with slightly larger
D) Books; slightly larger

CONTINUE

2

In 1935, Joe Shuster, the future creators of Superman, created Doctor Occult, [38] who was the earliest DC Comics character to still be in the DC Universe. The themed anthology series would become a sensation with the introduction of Batman (May 1939). [39] By then, however, Wheeler-Nicholson had gone. In 1937, in debt to printing-plant owner [40] , Harry Donenfeld—who also published pulp magazines and operated as a principal in the magazine distributorship Independent News—Wheeler-Nicholson had to take Donenfeld on as a partner in order to publish *Detective Comics* #1.

Two DC limited series, *Batman: The Dark Knight Returns* by Frank Miller and *Watchmen* by Moore and artist Dave Gibbons, drew attention in the mainstream press for their [41] dark psychological complexity and promotion of the antihero. These titles helped pave the way for comics to be more widely accepted in literary-criticism circles and to make inroads into the book industry, with collected editions of these series as commercially successful trade paperbacks

38

A) NO CHANGE
B) whom was
C) which was
D) who is

39

A) NO CHANGE
B) Since then,
C) After then,
D) Later then,

40

A) NO CHANGE
B) Harry Donenfeld—who
C) , Harry Donenfeld, who
D) Harry Donenfeld who

41

A) NO CHANGE
B) dark psychology, complexity, and promotional
C) dark psychology, complex, and promotion
D) dark psychologically and complexly promotional

CONTINUE

2 2

The comics industry experienced a brief boom in the early 1990s, thanks to a combination of speculative purchasing [42] and several storylines which gained attention from the mainstream media.

DC's extended storylines in which Superman was killed, Batman was crippled, and superhero *Green Lantern* turned into the supervillain Parallax resulted in dramatically increased sales, but the increases were as temporary as the hero's replacements. Sales dropped off as the industry went into a major slump [43] , while manufactured "collectibles" numbering in the millions replaced [44] imagination and reality until fans and speculators alike deserted the medium in droves.

42

At this point, the author wishes to add the following true sentence:

(mass purchase of the books as collectible items, with intent to resell at a higher value as the rising value of older issues was thought to imply that *all* comics would rise dramatically in price)

Should he make this addition here?

A) Yes, because it clarifies what the speculative purchasing is.

B) Yes, because it describes one of consequences that the comics industry benefited from a brief boom in the early 1990s.

C) No, because it would distract readers from the main focus of the paragraph.

D) No, because it creates confusion with the following phrase "and several storylines media.

43

Which of the following alternatives is NOT an acceptable alternative?

A) , and

B) ; in the meantime

C) , but

D) , and simultaneously

44

A) NO CHANGE

B) imagination in reality

C) real imagination

D) imagination with reality

STOP

If you finish before time is called,
you may check your work on this section.

Do not turn to the next section.

SAT Test 7
Answer Explanations
&
The Pattern Analyses

If your Test 7 scores are unsatisfactory,

Practice the Answer Explanations and then solve the Actual Test 7 again.

ALL THE LOGIC AND RULES BEHIND EVERY SINGLE SAT QUESTION

SAT Test 7

Reading Section Answer Explanations

&

The Pattern Analyses

Questions 1-10 are based on the following passage.

This summer was chock-full of new experiences. They were the kind of experiences that you read about in American road novels. Traveling worldwide and taking plane ride after plane ride reminded me of trashy teen romance films about travel, parentless escapades, and a reckless summer. As if I were living a Kerouac novel or an "Eat Pray Love"-sequel movie, I met people who played protagonists in their own lives, and fleeting co-stars in mine. In Manila, I met an artist who developed his own style of art and recently opened an art studio catered for people with autism. In Indianapolis, I met a budding public speaker who has delivered speeches at multi-million dollar fundraisers. That same weekend, I met an actress whose show ran for six seasons and won both Golden Globe and Emmy awards. What unifies all these people who crossed my path? It's not just their excellence. Rather, they all have intellectual and developmental disabilities (IDD).

(1C) **In the United States, there are over 6.5 million individuals with IDD. There's been broader representation of people with IDD in popular media in recent years, and these long awaited representations have been slowly changing perceptions of people with disabilities.** (2B) **But even with the progress we've made, we still do not view people with IDD as full-members of our society.** This is clearest when looking at the widespread lack of employment for people with IDD.

Unemployment rates for people with disabilities are at 85 percent—levels that for any other group of Americans would be unacceptable. Studies have shown that people with IDD aid in the general productivity of a work environment.

Employers also reported that the number of challenges faced by an employee with IDD were much fewer than those expected at the time the individual was hired.

It turns out that the reason that people with IDD are not hired is not because they lack ability, (3B&4D) **but because people assume they lack ability. This insight highlights the main problem that this country has with people with disabilities.**

Avenues to higher education for people with IDD are limited; for example, U.S., compared to Europe, lacks any sort of program for the mainstream education of students with IDD. But this is beside the point, because it's not the only way we can welcome people with IDD into the community. One of the simplest and most empowering things we can do is to hire individuals with IDD.

(7B) **There is an abundance of jobs that individuals with disabilities have the ability to compete for. There's no reason I shouldn't run into workers with IDD in Library or when visiting a company.** Our country can be better and hire a more diverse workforce. It's not a groundbreaking recommendation, but it may take time for employers to see it as a priority.

Doing our part to help create opportunities for people with IDD is critical, and employers must approach that task seriously, both here in our community and nationally. (10D) **Waiting indefinitely for others to employ people with IDD would feel disillusioning** to me, were it not for the fact that many people with IDD will hold positions of power once they make careers for themselves—roles in which who can directly open up opportunities to other people with IDD. (9C) **At that point, as we sit behind mahogany desks with the responsibility of making hiring decisions, I hope we consider applicants who happen to have intellectual and developmental disabilities.** (5C&6B&8D) **We must shift our perspectives so that we see them as productive members of society, unlike the way they've been viewed for decades.**

Q1. **Absolute Pattern 1: Main Idea Question** Finding the main idea of the entire passage or the paragraph
Question Pattern: In the **opening paragraph the author** primarily does which of the following?

A) compare the author's summer with road novels.
B) lay out the ways he traveled around the world
C) observe individuals with disability in a real world society
D) explain why people with disability appeal to the masses

C) When one entire paragraph is being asked, the answer can often be found in the topic sentence of the following paragraph.

(A), (B) are mere examples.
(D) "But even with the progress we've made, we still do not view people with IDD as full-members of our society." As seen above, (D) is direct opposite. It should have been "why they do not appeal to masses. "

Q2. **Absolute Pattern 2: Summary Question** Summarizing a sentence, or an entire paragraph **Question Pattern:** The second paragraph, lines 21-30 (**In the United States...IDD**) can be best summarized as	
A) individuals with IDD receive broader media attention **B) people's perceptions of the individuals with IDD are inflexible** C) the society is not aware that there are individuals with IDD D) people's perceptions of the individuals with IDD have progressed and will continue	**B) But** even with the progress we've made, we still do not view people with IDD as full-members of our society (A) is incorrect because they do not receive attention (C): People are biased therefore are aware of. (D) is direct opposite .

Q3. **Absolute Pattern 2: Summary Question** Summarizing a sentence, or an entire paragraph **Question Pattern:** The **author of the passage would agree** that	
A) individuals with IDD lack ability to be the part of workforce **B) people's perception is the major factor that precludes individuals with IDD from employment** C) the productivity of individuals with IDD at work is no less than that of normal employees D) the employment rate of individuals with IDD is only one-third	B) the reason that people with IDD are not hired is (A) not because they lack ability, but because (B) people assume they lack ability. (C) The passage proves that they are better at work than they were initially thought. However, it doesn't mean people with IDD are equally productive to normal people.

Q4. **Absolute Pattern 11: Textual Evidence Question** Finding evidence for the previous question **Question Pattern:** Which choice provides the best evidence for the answer to the previous question?	
A) Lines 21-22 (In the United States...IDD) B) Lines 29-30 (This is...IDD) C) Lines 31-33 (Unemployment...unacceptable) **D) Lines 39-42 (It turns out...ability.)**	D) Please refer to the above question

Q5. **Absolute Pattern 2: Summary Question** Summarizing a sentence, or an entire paragraph **Question Pattern:** The author makes which of the following statements about the **individuals with IDD**	
A) Unemployment rate is one example showing our perspective on people with IDD is changing for better. B) U.S. provides better education chance than European countries. **C) Focusing more on these people's ability than disability depends on our perspectives.** D) Students with IDD have equal potential to learn	C) We must shift our perspectives so that we see them as productive members of society, unlike the way they've been viewed for decades. A), B) are direct opposite. unemployment rate is the major issue. D) is Too extreme.

Q6. **Absolute Pattern 11: Textual Evidence Question** Finding evidence for the previous question **Question Pattern:** Which choice provides the best evidence for the answer to the previous question?	
A) Lines 21-22 (In the United States...with IDD.) **B) Lines 39-42 (It turns...lack ability.)** C) Lines 45-48 (Avenues...students with IDD) D) Lines 49-51 (But this is...the community.)	B) Please refer to the above question

Q7. **Absolute Pattern 4: Example Question** Understanding example sentence and the true purpose behind a specific name or idea. **Question Pattern:** The author mentions **library (line 57) in order to**	
A) encourage library to provide education to workers with IDD **B) acknowledge current limitation** C) criticize the inflexibility of employers D) speculate better society for library workers	B) There is an abundance of jobs that individuals with disabilities have the ability to compete for.

Q8. **Absolute Pattern 1: Main Idea Question** Finding the main idea of the entire passage or the paragraph **Question Pattern:** The **main purpose** of the passage is to	
A) classify the unemployment rates of individuals with IDD B) reminiscent his traveling experience with individuals with IDD C) debunk the public misconception towards individuals with IDD **D) influence the reader to support the author's argument**	D) We must shift our perspectives so that we see them as productive members of society, (A),(B), (C) are all minor examples that support the main theme of the passage.

Q9. **Absolute Pattern 4: Example Question** Understanding example sentence and the true purpose behind a specific name or idea. **Question Pattern:** In line 72, the author refers to "**mahogany desks**" in order to	
A) criticize employers who do not hire individuals with IDD B) describe high quality desks **C) visualize appearance of those in power to hire individuals with IDD** D) condemn social bias, especially those rich employers	C) At that point, as **we** sit behind mahogany desks with the responsibility of making hiring decisions, **I hope we** consider applicants who happen to have intellectual and developmental disabilities. A), D) The author does not criticizes anyone at this point; rather urge them to hire people with IDD.

Q10. **Absolute Pattern 5: Word-In-Context Question** **Question Pattern: As** used in line 67, "**disillusioning**" most nearly means	
A) false idea B) imagination C) untruth **D) evocation**	D) Waiting indefinitely for others to employ people with IDD would **feel disillusioning** to me, **were it not for the fact** that many people with IDD will hold positions of power once they make careers for themselves. "were it not for the fact" is the conditional clause that implies the author's disillusionment or evocation.

Questions 11-21 are based on the following passage.

In biology, a mutation is the permanent alteration. Mutations may or may not produce discernible changes in the observable characteristics of an organism. Mutations play a part in both normal and abnormal biological processes including: evolution.
(11B&12B&13C) **If a mutation changes protein produced by a gene, the result is likely to be harmful,** (14C) **with an estimated two-thirds of amino acid polymorphisms that have damaging effects, and the remainder being either neutral or marginally beneficial.**

Due to the damaging effects that mutations can have on genes, organisms have mechanisms such as **DNA repair to prevent or correct mutations by reverting the mutated sequence back to its original state.**

Natural selection within a population for a trait that can vary across a range of values, such as height, can be categorized into three different types. (15A&16A&20A) **The first is directional selection, which is a shift in the average value of a trait over time—for example, organisms slowly getting taller.**

Secondly, disruptive selection is selection for extreme trait values and often results in two different values becoming most common.
This would be when either short or tall organisms had an advantage, but not those of medium height.

Finally, in stabilizing selection there is selection against extreme trait values on both ends, which causes a decrease in variance around the average value and less diversity. (16A) **If selection would favor either one out of two mutations, but there is no extra advantage to having both, then the mutation that occurs the most frequently is the one that is most likely to become fixed in a population.**

Mutations leading to the loss of function of a gene are much more common than mutations that produce a new, fully functional gene. (19B) **But when selection is weak, mutation bias towards loss of function can affect evolution.** (18C) **For example, pigments are no longer useful when animals live in the darkness, and tend to be lost.** This kind of loss of function can occur because of mutation bias. (17D&21D) **The speed at which loss evolves depends more on the mutation rate than it does on the effective population size, indicating that it is driven more by mutation bias than by genetic drift.**

Q11. **Absolute Pattern 2: Summary Question** Summarizing a sentence, or an entire paragraph
Question Pattern: Paragraph 1 (lines 1-10) makes the points of **mutation process** as its EXCEPT

A) lasting effect on organism **B) largely benign biological processes** C) regular and irregular biological processes D) observable changes	B) In biology, a mutation is (A) the permanent alteration . Mutations (D) may or may not produce discernible changes in the observable characteristics of an organism. Mutations play a part in (C) both normal and abnormal biological processes including: . If a mutation changes a protein produced by a gene, evolution, **(B)** the result is likely to be harmful

Q12. **Absolute Pattern 2: Summary Question** Summarizing a sentence, or an entire paragraph
Question Pattern: According to the passage, a **mutation that alters a protein** will ultimately

A) have no effect on the organism **B) produce damaging effects** C) benefit the organism D) remain neutral permanently	B) If a mutation changes a protein produced by a gene, the result is likely to be harmful,

Q13. **Absolute Pattern 11: Textual Evidence Question** Finding evidence for the previous question
Question Pattern: Which choice provides the best evidence for the answer to the previous question?

A) Lines 1-2 (In biology…alternation.) B) Lines 2-4 (Mutations may...an organism) **C) Lines 6-10 (If a mutation ..marginally beneficial)** D) Lines 11-15 (Due to the...original state)	C) Please refer to the above question

Q14. **Absolute Pattern 2: Summary Question** Summarizing a sentence, or an entire paragraph
Question Pattern: According to paragraph 1 (lines 1-10), which pairing best represents the different ratios of **harmful amino acid polymorphisms and the remainder respectively**?

A) 10 percent and 30 percent B) 50 percent and 50 percent **C) 70 percent and 30 percent** D) 90 percent and 10 percent	C) the result is likely to be harmful, with an estimated two-thirds of amino polymorphism that have damaging effects, and the remainder being either neutral or marginally beneficial.

Q15. **Absolute Pattern 2: Summary Question** Summarizing a sentence, or an entire paragraph
Question Pattern: According to paragraphs 3-4 (lines 16-34), **if Leaf-eating deer migrates to Giraffe habitat, the deer must have undergone the natural selection of**

I. Directional selection II. Disruptive selection III. Stabilizing section **A) I** B) II C) III D) I and III	A) The first is directional selection, which is a shift in the average value of a trait over time—for example, organisms slowly getting taller.

Q16. **Absolute Pattern 11: Textual Evidence Question** Finding evidence for the previous question
Question Pattern: Which choice provides the best evidence for the answer to the previous question?

A) Lines 19-21 (The first is directional...getting taller) B) Lines 22-24 (Secondly, disruptive...most common.) C) Lines 24-26 (This would be...medium height.) D) Lines 27-30 (Finally, in stabilizing...less diversity.)	A) Please refer to the above question

Q17. **Absolute Pattern 2: Summary Question** Summarizing a sentence or entire passage
Question Pattern: According to the last paragraph (lines 35-46), **the most successful mutation bias depends on**

A) genetic drift B) proteins C) evolution **D) frequency**	D) The speed at which loss evolves depends more on the mutation rate than it does on the effective population size, indicating that it is driven more by mutation bias than by genetic drift

Q18. **Absolute Pattern 9: Relationships Question**
Finding relations between the cause-effect, comparison-contrast, characters, and ideas
Question Pattern: According to the last paragraph (lines 35-46), which **animal species would experience mutation bias that leads to loss of pigment?**

A) Sloth B) Duck **C) Bat** D) Frog	C) For example, pigments are no longer useful when animals live in the darkness, and tend to be lost

Q19. **Absolute Pattern 3: Inference Question** Finding an indirect suggestion (or guessing) **Question Pattern:** The author mentions "**animals**" in line 40 primarily to indicate	
A) the benefit of living in darkness **B) weak selection that causes mutation bias that ends up affecting evolution** C) a typical mutation bias D) animals that cause our fear	B) But when selection is weak, mutation bias towards loss of function can affect evolution. For example, pigments are no longer useful when animals live in the darkness. C) is incorrect because the passage describes weak not a typical mutilation bias.

Q20. **Absolute Pattern 12: Informational Graphs** Finding facts described in the graphs or relations between the passage and the graph. **Question Pattern:** As described in question **15, Leaf-eating deer that migrate to Giraffe habitat will be indicated in the chart**	
I. Chart 1 II. Chart II III. Chart III **A) I** B) II C) III D) I and III	A) The first is directional selection, which is a shift in the average value of a trait over time—for example, organisms slowly getting taller.

Q21. **Absolute Pattern 2: Summary Question** Summarizing a sentence or entire passage **Question Pattern:** In the last paragraph, which of the following statements correctly describes **"genetic drift"**?	
A) Genetic drift and natural selection are the same terms B) Genetic drift mainly controls population size C) Genetic drift does not at all contribute population size **D) Population size is affected more by mutation bias than by genetic drift**	D) This kind of loss of function can occur because of mutation bias. The speed at which loss evolves depends more on the mutation rate than it does on the effective population size, indicating that it is driven more by mutation bias than by genetic drift.

Questions 22-31 are based on the following passage.

I speak tonight for the dignity of man and the destiny of democracy. (23A) **I urge every member of both parties, Americans of all religions and of all colors, from every section of this country, to join me in that cause.** At times history and fate meet at a single time in a single place to shape a (24A) **turning point** in (22C) **man's unending search for freedom.** So it was at Lexington and Concord. So it was a century ago at Appomattox. So it was last week in Selma, Alabama.

Our lives have been marked with debate about great issues; issues of war and peace, issues of prosperity and depression. But rarely in any time does an issue lay bare the secret heart of America itself.

Rarely are we met with a challenge, not to our growth or abundance, our welfare or our security, (27D&28C) **but rather to the values and the purposes and the meaning of our beloved Nation.**

There is no Negro problem. There is no Southern problem. There is no Northern problem. (25D)**There is only an American problem.** (26A) "**Give me liberty or give me death.**" To apply any other test--(29D)**to deny** a man his hopes because of his color or race, his religion or the place of his birth--is not only to do injustice, it is to deny America and to dishonor the dead who gave their lives for American freedom. (30D) **Many of the issues of civil rights are very complex and most difficult.** But about this there can and should be no argument.

Q22. **Absolute Pattern 4: Example Question**
Understanding example sentence and the true purpose behind a specific name or idea.
Question Pattern: The President suggests that **the cities mentioned** in lines 8-10 were strongly influenced by

A) the police's biased control over racial discrimination B) the lack pacifists' efforts **C) their own desire for freedom** D) his speech	C) At times history and fate meet at a single time in a single place to shape a turning point in man's unending search for freedom. (**Supporting details starts from here**) So it was at Lexington and Concord. So it was a century ago at Appomattox. So it was last week in Selma, Alabama. ... *The example sentence is surrounded by the topic and supporting details. When example sentence is in question, the answer is normally located right above or below the example sentence.

Q23. **Absolute Pattern 8: Understanding the True Purpose** Finding the true purpose of statement
Question Pattern: The speaker's main concern when he addresses **"I urge every member**..that cause" (lines 2-5) is to

A) encourage the united participation B) reveal the intensity of the problem C) present the enjoyment of working together D) urge the emotional responses	A) I urge every member of both parties, Americans of all religions and of all colors, from every section of this country, to join me in that cause.

Q24. **Absolute Pattern 3: Inference Question** Finding an indirect suggestion (or guessing)
Question Pattern: The phrase **"a single time in a single place"** in line 6 most directly implies that

A) a time to change has finally arrived B) every American is anxious about unequal rights C) man's unending search for freedom requires more time and place D) the dignity of man hasn't been fully recognized yet	A) At times history and fate meet at a single time in a single place to shape a turning point **(a time to change)** in man's unending search for freedom.

Q25. **Absolute Pattern 10: Understanding the Structure of the Passage**
Finding the structure of the entire passage or organizational relations between the paragraphs
Question Pattern: The speaker uses **parallelism (There is no...American problem.)** in lines 20-22 in order to

A) compare between actual problem and the secret heart of America B) argue that there is no negro problem C) list the least important problem to most important problem **D) generalize the issue as a single concern in society at large**	D) The repetition of "There is no" is used to claim as a single concern in society at large. (B): When president said that there is no "Negro problem", he tried to emphasize the issue as a single American problem.

Q26. **Absolute Pattern 7: Understanding Attitude (Tone) Question**
Finding a tone such as positive-negative, active-passive, mental-physical, subjective-objective
Question Pattern: The tone of the president's comment in line 22 **"give a liberty or give me death."** can be characterized as

A) emphatic B) inflexible C) ambivalent D) impressive	A) All men are created equal"..."give me liberty or give me death." Those words are a promise to every citizen that he shall share in the dignity of man. It's the reader who could be impressed, not the president himself. *Emphatic means decisive. B) is Negative

Q27. **Absolute Pattern 2: Summary Question** Summarizing a sentence, or an entire paragraph
Question Pattern: According to the passage, **people in U.S. would most likely disagree** with how to

A) improve the country B) provide a better life to the people C) protect the citizen **D) define the values of our nation**	D) Rarely are we met with a challenge, not to (A) our growth or abundance, our (B) welfare or (C) our security, (D) but rather to the values and the purposes

Q28. **Absolute Pattern 11: Textual Evidence Question** Finding evidence for the previous question
Question Pattern: Which choice provides the best evidence for the answer to the previous question?

A) Lines 5-8 (At times...for freedom.) B) Lines 16-17 (Rarely are we...our security,) **C) Lines 18-19 (but rather...beloved Nation.)** D) Lines 20-22 (There is no...American problem)	C) Please refer to the above question

Q29. **Absolute Pattern 5: Word-In-Context Question**
Finding a clue word and the keyword from the sentence in question
Question Pattern: The word **"test"** in line 23 most nearly means

A) higher education entrance test B) police interrogation C) insecurity of nation **D) override of dignity**	D) To apply any other test--**to deny** a man his hopes because of his color or race,.. **not only to do injustice**, Rarely, met, growth "test" is expressed as a challenge (override) to dignity.

Q30. **Absolute Pattern 8: Understanding the True Purpose** Finding the true purpose of statement
Question Pattern: In line 28 **"Many of the issues of civil rights,"** the president does which of the following?

A) Presents opposing viewpoints B) Voices doubt about the nature of complexity C) Issues a challenge to solve the complexity **D) Rationalizes inherent limitations**	D) Many of the issues of civil rights are very complex and most difficult. President acknowledges the complexity of issue. B) is Opposite C) is Too Extreme

Q31. **Absolute Pattern 12: Informational Graphs**
Finding facts described in the graphs or relations between the passage and the graph.
Question Pattern: According to the graph, which statement is true about the **poll in 2014 on 1964** Civil Rights Act

A) Blacks felt the Acts need to make more dramatic effect B) Majority of Whites distasted the Acts C) Whites women were more attentive with the Acts **D) Both Blacks and Whites contented enough with the Acts**	D) Blacks: 78%, Whites: 83% agreed (A) 78% contented (B) 83% supported (C) is Not stated in the graph

Questions 32-41 are based on the following passage.

<u>In the shade</u> of the house, in the sunshine of the riverbank near the boats, in the shade of the Sal-wood forest, in the shade of the fig tree is where Siddhartha grew up, <u>the handsome son</u> of the Brahman, the young falcon, together with his friend Govinda, son of a Brahman. <u>The sun tanned</u> his light shoulders by the banks of the river when bathing, performing the sacred ablutions, the (32B) **sacred** <u>offerings</u>. (33A&34D&35D) **<u>He already</u> knew to feel Atman in the <u>depths of his being,</u> indestructible, one with the universe. In the mango grove, depths of shade poured into his black eyes.** <u>Joy leapt in his father's heart for his son who was quick to learn; (36D)</u> **<u>he saw him growing up to become great wise man and priest.</u>** <u>Love touched</u> the hearts of the Brahmans' young daughters when Siddhartha walked through the lanes of the town with the luminous forehead, with (38D) **the eye of a king,** with his slim hips.	But more than all the others he was loved by Govinda, his friend, the son of a Brahman. He loved Siddhartha's eye and sweet voice, he loved his walk and the perfect decency of his movements, he loved everything Siddhartha did and said and what he loved most was his spirit, his transcendent, fiery thoughts, his ardent will, his (37A) **<u>high calling.</u>** **Govinda wanted to follow Siddhartha and in days to come, when Siddhartha would become a god,** when he would join the glorious, then Govinda wanted to follow him as (39B) **his servant**, his spear-carrier, his shadow. Siddhartha was thus loved by everyone. He was a source of joy for everybody, he was a delight for them all. (40C&41C) **But he, Siddhartha, was not a source of joy for himself, he found no delight in himself. Dreams and restless thoughts came into his mind, flowing from the water of the river, sparkling from the stars of the night.**

Q32. **Absolute Pattern 5: Word-In-Context Question**
Question Pattern: In line 9, **"offerings"** is closest in meaning to

A) giving **B) ritual** C) proposal D) sacrifice	B) The sun tanned his light shoulders by the banks of the river when bathing, performing the sacred ablutions, the <u>sacred offerings</u>. The word right before "offerings" is "sacred" meaning holy. So, we can infer that the word "offering" is prayer or ritual. (A), (C) are too literal implication

Q33. **Absolute Pattern 2: Summary Question** Summarizing a sentence or entire passage
Question Pattern: In the passage, **Siddhartha is being described** as

A) the one in the state of nirvana who realized the depth of universe B) a great wise old man C) a boy sees Atman inside some mango grove D) a condescending and authoritative prodigy	A) **He already knew to feel Atman in the depths of his being, indestructible, one with the Universe.** B) Siddhartha is being described as a boy D) is incorrect because the tone is Negative.

Q34. **Absolute Pattern 11: Textual Evidence Question** Finding evidence for the previous question
Question Pattern: Which choice provides the best evidence for the answer to the previous question?

A) Lines 1-4 (In the shade…grew up) B) Lines 4-6 (the handsome son… a Brahman.) C) Lines 7-9 (The sun tanned...the sacred offerings.) **D) Lines 9-11 (He already knew…the universe.)**	D) Please refer to the above question

Q35. **Absolute Pattern 3: Inference Question** Finding an indirect suggestion (or guessing)
Question Pattern: Phrase **"depths of shade" in line 10 and "depths of his being"** in line 12 can be understood respectively as

A) complexity and simplicity B) darkness and innocence C) spirituality and mentality **D) serious quality and deep distance**	D) feel Atman in the <u>depths of his being</u>, (**Mentality**) indestructible, one with the universe. <u>In the mango grove, depths of shade (**Physicality**)</u> poured into his black eyes. * The first "depth" describes inner quality, while the second "depth" describes physical depth of shadow

Q36. **Absolute Pattern 2: Summary Question** Summarizing a sentence, or an entire paragraph
Question Pattern: Paragraph 3 and 4 in lines 16-27 **(Joy leapt in…his high calling**.) suggests that Siddhartha

A) is in the state of nirvana that his family and friends have limited understanding of him B) enjoys unchallenged position in society C) encourages people to praise his holiness **D) is spiritually infused with and inspires his family**	D) Joy leapt in his father's heart for his son who was quick to learn; he saw him growing up to become great wise man and priest. A) is incorrect because "limited" is Negative word.

Q37. **Absolute Pattern 5: Word-In-Context Question**
Question Pattern: In line 27, "**high calling**" is closest in meaning to

A) divine influence B) arrogant voice C) pitch of the voice D) frequent talk	A) He loved Siddhartha's eye...he loved most was his spirit, his transcendent, fiery thoughts, his ardent will, his high calling. * Compared to the answer, (B), (C),(D) are all too literal Implications

Q38. **Absolute Pattern 2: Summary Question** Summarizing a sentence, or an entire paragraph
Question Pattern: Lines 16-19 (**Love touched....slim hips**) mainly describes

A) Siddhartha's sexual appeal B) Siddhartha's hot temperament C) People's applause to his fantastic slim hips **D) People's reverence to the presence of Siddhartha**	D) Love touched the hearts of the Brahmans' young daughters when Siddhartha walked through the lanes of the town with the luminous forehead, with the eye of a king, with his slim hips. *It reveals Siddhartha's spirituality

Q39. **Absolute Pattern 7: Understanding Attitude (Tone) Question**
Question Pattern: Govinda's attitude towards Siddhartha could be best characterized as

A) confident **B) submissive** C) appreciative D) friendly	B) He wanted to follow Siddhartha, the beloved, the splendid. And in days to come, when Siddhartha would become a god, when he would join the glorious, then Govinda wanted to follow him as his friend, his companion, his servant (**submissive)**

Q40. **Absolute Pattern 3: Inference Question** Finding an indirect suggestion (or guessing)
Question Pattern: Based on the last paragraph (lines 36-40), **Siddhartha may eventually**

A) get married to any girl and live happily ever after B) live in the deep shade of mango grove **C) search for meaning in life** D) follow Govinda to understand life	C) But he, Siddhartha, was not a source of joy for himself, he found no delight in himself * The passage doesn't describe what he will do next, but we can still infer that he would probably do (C) because he is described as the highest priest.

Q41. **Absolute Pattern 3: Inference Question** Finding an indirect suggestion (or guessing)
Question Pattern: Last paragraph (Lines 36-40) implies **Siddhartha's**

A) desire to look cool B) unwillingness to meet his family and friends' wish **C) reluctance to take the current contentment** D) overindulgence to source of joy	C) But he, Siddhartha, was not a source of joy for himself, he found no delight in himself. B) deviates the focus of the question.

Questions 42-52 are based on the following passage.

<table>
<tr><td>PASSAGE 1

Science is objective. The scientific process is rigorous, involving hard data and empirical observations. And, as a result, the conclusions are objectively factual. For example: Gravity exists. The Earth moves around the Sun. Evolution is the process by which different kinds of living organisms developed and diversified from earlier forms. (42A) Women are biologically inferior to men. Wait, what? Charles Darwin is well-known for developing the theory of evolution. He is a little bit less known for teaching that women are biologically inferior to women. (44C) That can't be right. Darwin was a reputable scientist, not just some sexist bigot. And yet, the same man who gave us the theory of evolution also gave us the insight that "the average standard of mental power in man must be above that of woman." How did hard, objective science lead Darwin to such a dangerously incorrect conclusion? (43B&44C&49B&51B) It's important to remember that Darwin lived in England from 1809 to 1882, during a time when women were not granted the same access and opportunities as men. For example, some doctors in 19th century Britain reported that studying "had a damaging effect on the ovaries, turning attractive young women into dried-up prunes."
As a result, even when Oxford and Cambridge eventually opened their doors to women, many families refused to let their daughters attend, for fear that they would no longer be marriageable. Gender norms in 19th century Britain simply did not allow women to achieve the same level of academic and professional success as their male peers.
(45C&50D) Darwin was almost certainly influenced by the social and cultural norms of his time when he came to the conclusion that women are biologically inferior to men.</td>
<td>PASSAGE 2

How objective is science?
(46A) Scientists are socialized and influenced by the same societal pressures as the rest of us. As a result, (47A) even though the scientific process tries to be as objective as possible, scientists are human beings with implicit bias, just like everyone else. Therefore, science in this world and society is never purely objective—and it can even deliver sexually biased scientists.
Even though science involves numbers and data, it is all too easy for science to slide into the realm of subjectivity. For example, it is widely accepted in the scientific community that the egg passively sits in the bodies of women while sperm race towards it, eager to be the first to implant themselves.
Yet, as anthropologist Emily Martin pointed out, this narrative does not represent the facts of biology. As a matter of fact, researches at Johns Hopkins University found that the mechanical force of the sperm's tail is not very great. Therefore, the egg isn't passively waiting for a sperm to penetrate it—the egg actually plays an active role in capturing a sperm with its own adhesive molecules.
(48C) Not everything in science is culturally constructed, but a good portion of it is.
The parallels between cultural stereotypes of male and female behavior and the behavior of the egg and the sperm are too close to be coincidental. In science textbooks, the egg is often described as passively "sweeping" or "transporting" along the fallopian tube. The sperm, in contrast, is usually described as actively swimming or propelling itself forward.</td></tr>
</table>

Q42. **Absolute Pattern 7: Understanding Attitude (Tone) Question**
Finding a tone such as positive-negative, active-passive, mental-physical, subjective-objective
Question Pattern: The author's **question mark** in line 9 serves to demonstrate

<table>
<tr><td>A) abrupt resistance
B) feigned skepticism
C) measured receptivity
D) mild irritation</td>
<td>A) Women are biologically inferior to men. Wait, what? Charles Darwin is well-known for developing the theory of evolution.

A) "mild" is Opposite feeling.
B) "feigned" is Opposite concept.</td></tr>
</table>

Q43. **Absolute Pattern 7: Understanding Attitude (Tone) Question**
Finding a tone such as positive-negative, active-passive, mental-physical, subjective-objective
Question Pattern: In lines 1-12 (Science...women.), the author expresses which of the following **attitudes to Charles Darwin?**

A) Amusement that such a respected scientist expressed over the supposedly trivial matter
B) Qualification that his view is compromised by societal conditioning
C) Annoyance that his view about women is solely based on women's incompetent physicality
D) Resignation about the impossibility of the theory of evolution

B) It's important to remember that Darwin lived in England from 1809 to 1882, during a time when women were not granted the same access and opportunities as men. (**Societal conditioning**)

(A) The author takes this matter seriously and "trivial" is opposite conception
(C) The statement implies that the author acknowledges women's physical inferiority.

Q44. **Absolute Pattern 7: Understanding Attitude (Tone) Question**
Finding a tone such as positive-negative, active-passive, mental-physical, subjective-objective
Question Pattern: Lines 13-23 (**That can't be right...as men) shifts the author's view** from

A) a source of dismay to a complete acceptance
B) inevitable acknowledgement to logical assessment
C) vehement rejection to historical analyses
D) judicial assessment to resignation

C) That can't be right. (**Rejection**) ...It's important to remember that Darwin lived in England from 1809 to 1882, during a time when women were not granted the same access and opportunities as men (A**nalyses)**

Q45. **Absolute Pattern 4: Example Question**
Understanding example sentence and the true purpose behind a specific name or idea
Question Pattern: The **last paragraph (Darwin was almost ...to man**) in passage 1 primarily encourages **reader to view Charles Darwin as**

A) an intellectual misogynist
B) an opportunist in a closed-society
C) a conditioned human being dealt with cultural myopia
D) unconscious patriarchist

C) The last paragraph points out that Darwin's view about women must be observed from social conditioning rather than his scientific assessment.

Q46. **Absolute Pattern 7: Understanding Attitude (Tone) Question**
Finding a tone such as positive-negative, active-passive, mental-physical, subjective-objective
Question Pattern: The author characterizes **science and scientists** in lines 40-48 as

A) any scientific theory can be promoted by subtle social pressure
B) valid scientific theory must be conducted only by those rigorous scientists
C) any scientific theory must be evaluated by the possible subjectivity
D) scientific theory should be objective and not be compromised by social influence

A) Scientists are socialized and influenced (**social pressure**) by the same societal pressures as the rest of us. even though the scientific process tries to be as objective as possible, scientists are human beings with implicit bias, just like everyone else.

(B) is missing the point and inconsistent with the question. The author's main argument is that scientists are prone to social influence. It's not about the quality (rigorousness) of scientists.
(C) "must be" should be changed to "could be or may be".
(D) This is direct opposite conception from (A), in which the author characterizes the inevitable limitation of scientists

Q47. **Absolute Pattern 3: Inference Question** Finding an indirect suggestion (or guessing)
Question Pattern: It can be inferred that **scientists in passage 2 may believe** that they

A) seek out scientific evidence that conforms society's preexisting beliefs B) act as if they are only scientists, not human C are the victims of social bias D) try to apply social subjectivity effectively as an opportunity	A) even though the scientific process tries to be as objective as possible, scientists are human beings As seen above, they will defend their work is objective within societal influence.

Q48. **Absolute Pattern 8: Understanding the True Purpose** Finding the true purpose of statement
Question Pattern: The author's purpose in lines 65-66 (**Not everything...a good portion of it is**.) is to

A) defend diverse perspectives on scientists B) discredit the view of culturally constructed science **C) note the acknowledgement that social conditioning is a factor in science** D) support there's value in cultural stereotype	C) Not everything in science is culturally constructed, but a good portion of it is. **(Acknowledgement of the societal factor)** "good portion of it" refers that a large percentage of

(A) is incorrect. The passage deals with only two perspectives—subjective and objective.
(B) "discredit" is opposite perception. (D) is Too extreme. It should be "acknowledge" instead of "support" at most.

Q49. **Absolute Pattern 3: Inference Question** Finding an indirect suggestion (or guessing)
Question Pattern: It can be inferred that **Charles Darwin in passage 1 might have responded to "societal pressures** " in line 42 in passage 2 that

A) scientific study must be based on solemn detachment **B) social construction of the time reasonably affects scientific objectivity** C) women in scientific arena is inferior to man is my regretful speech, but truth is truth. D) scientific objectivity reasonably affects social	B) England from 1809...a time when women were not granted the same access and opportunities as men. Only (B) corresponds to the statement of the author who represents Charles Darwin.

Q50. **Absolute Pattern 11: Textual Evidence Question** Finding evidence for the previous question
Question Pattern: Which choice provides the best evidence for the answer to the previous question?

A) Lines 18-19 (How did...conclusion?) B) Lines 23-27 (For example,...prunes.) C) Lines 28-35 (As a result...peers.) **D) Lines 36-39 (Darwin...men)**	D) Darwin was almost certainly influenced by the social and cultural norms of his time when he came to the conclusion that women are biologically inferior to men.

Q51. **Absolute Pattern 9: Relationships Question**
Question Pattern: Charles Darwin in Passage 1 might view the researches in line 58 in Passage 2 as

A) the part of his theory of evolution **B) the work made by human being who couldn't escape from social influence** C) the work that egg tries to sneak away from the social influence D) the work conducted by women scientists who influenced the results	B) It's important to remember that Darwin lived in England from 1809 to 1882, during a time when women were not granted the same access and opportunities as men. Only (B) corresponds to the author who represents Charles Darwin.

Q52. **Absolute Pattern 12: Informational Graphs**
Question Pattern: Which of the following analysis correctly represents the **graph** illustrated after the passage?

A) More women than men see gender inequality B) Approximately 35% of women didn't respond C) There are more men in "A lot" group than "Some" group D) Fewer women responded "A lot" than men did.	A) As shown in the graph.

SAT Test 7

Writing and language Section Answer Explanations

&

The Pattern Analyses

Test 7 Writing & Language Section Patterns

Questions 1-11 are based on the following passage.

On leaving home

I am well acquainted with my suitcase. After all, we've spent a lot of time together: [1] Its moved me back and forth between Canada and America, between my little hometown and a city where no one knows my name, between my parents' house and a college dorm and (most recently) a seedy summer apartment. I know that its wheels squeak at an uncomfortably high pitch. I know that its weight will bang into my calves at every other step [2] so that I skip and hobble in a particular way. canvas suitcase. I know that it exists to displace me—and for that I resent every durable green inch of [3] it for that reason. How tightly am I bound to my location?

My life looks small [4] wraps in cardboard and canvas. Eventually, I can't look anymore. I need to get out of this [5] used home. I grab my wallet and a map and, with pleasing randomness, decide to visit the Boston Harbor Islands. They seem far and inconvenient, and I am fed up with staying in one place.[6]

Two hours, two buses, and one subway ride later, I am standing inside the Boston Harbor Islands Ferry office. An older woman is in the process of closing the ticket kiosk, and seems annoyed by my presence. "The last ferry to the Islands left at one," she says curtly. Then, registering the look on my face, [7] we soften the atmosphere: "You could just catch the last ferry to Boston, though. There's a lot to do there." First, I am bewildered. This isn't Boston? Where am I? When did I leave my city? The woman informs me that we are in Hingham, but I've never heard of the town.

In desperation, I pull out my map and look for [8] something—anything—that looks interesting. The only destination [9] marked Nantasket Beach that even remotely fits the bill is a little spot on the coast. I trudge back to the heat-baked highway and wait for the next bus. It takes me another two hours and the advice of a series of strangers, but I eventually make it to my destination.

[10] The sand stretches down from a raised sidewalk in pale sun-bleached yellow dotted with pink and blue umbrellas. The waves froth high enough to sweep even adults off their feet. Shouting kids and screaming gulls and crashing surf produce a beach sound [11] so perfect ,and it feels slightly surreal.

Q1. Absolute Pattern 17: Pronoun Error

I am well acquainted with my suitcase. After all, **we've spent** a lot of time together: [1] Its moved me back and forth between Canada and America, between my little hometown and a city where **no one knows** my name, between my parents' house and a college dorm and (most recently) a seedy summer apartment.

	Choice	Explanation
	A) NO CHANGE	B) 1> It's = It has. 2> Because the overall tense (I am, we've spent, no one knows) surrounding the sentence is present tense, the answer should also be the present tense.
√	**B) It's**	
	C) The suitcase	A) "Its" is the singular possessive pronoun. Ex) My house is expensive; Its (my house) toilet bowl is made of gold.
	D) It was	C) is redundant error. D) "It was" is the past tense.

Q2. Absolute Pattern 23: Transition Words for Supporting Detail, Contrast, and Consequence

Passage: **I know that** its weight will bang into my calves at every other step [2] so that I skip and hobble in a particular way. canvas suitcase.

	Choice	Explanation
	A) NO CHANGE	B) 1> A conditional clause 'unless' shows an action will occur if another action doesn't follow. 2> Synonym to unless that carry conditional clause are: *But *Except *Saving *If not *Lest *Without *Unless
√	**B) unless**	
	C) while	A) [so that] is used to express the consequence in a cause-and-effect situation.
	D) because	C) [while] is used either in a concessional clause like "in the meantime" or synonym to 'during' (e.g.,) The poor see their income shrink while the rich see it rises. D) [because] is used in the cause-and-effect situation.

Q3. Absolute Pattern 19: Redundant Error		
Passage: I know that it exists to displace me—and **for that** I resent every durable green inch of [3] it for that reason. → redundancy ←		
	A) NO CHANGE	D) The pronoun "it" refers to the narrator's suitcase
	B) the suitcase.	A) "for that reason." is repeating. B) "the suitcase" repeating.
	C) it or that.	C) "that" is used as a demonstrative pronoun, making "that" unclear.
√	**D) it.**	

Q4. Absolute Pattern 10: Logical Expression		
Passage: My life looks small [4] wraps in cardboard and canvas.		
	A) NO CHANGE	D) My life looks small [4] *(as if My life is being)* **wrapped** in cardboard and canvas.
	B) and wraps	A) "wraps" is a verb. The main verb 'looks' is already stated.
	C) wrapping	B) "and wraps" becomes a verb after the conjunction 'and. C) "wrapping" is used for an on-going situation as if my life is wrapping...
√	**D) wrapped**	

Q 5. Absolute Pattern 18: Punctuation Error		
Passage: I need to get out of this [5] used home.		
	A) NO CHANGE	D) Hyphenation links up two or more words before a noun when they come as a single idea This is called a **compound adjective**.
	B) used to be home	
	C) used to-be home	A) [used home.] changes the original meaning. B) [used to be home.] by having no hyphens, all these words are acting independently. C) [used to-be home.] is missing one hyphen. Therefore, it changes the meaning.
√	**D) used-to-be home**	

Q6. Absolute Pattern 1: Adding, Revising, Deleting, Retaining Information	
Passage: They seem far and inconvenient, and I am fed up with staying in one place.[6]	
Question: The author is considering **deleting the preceding underlined** sentence. Should he make this deletion?	
	A) Yes, because the sentence contradicts to the narrator's longing for homesickness.
	B) Yes, because the sentence contains the "inconvenient" that the narrator wishes to avoid.
√	C) No, because the sentence contributes the **narrator's longing for new experience**.
	D) No, because the sentence sets up the new place other than the narrator's current apartment

C) "I need to get out of this used-to-be home. I grab my wallet and a map and, with pleasing randomness, decide to visit the Boston Harbor Islands. They seem far and inconvenient, and I am fed up with staying in one place."
The preceding sentence reveals the narrator's decision for a new experience.

A) "homesickness" is opposite because the author wishes to leave his place.
B) is opposite emotion. The author wishes to escape from his convenient used-to-be home.
D) The author isn't moving out. He just wants to travel.

Q7. Absolute Pattern 12: Modifier Placement Error

Then, registering the look on my face, [7] we soften the atmosphere: "

	Choice	Explanation
	A) NO CHANGE	D) Two people are conversing: the ticket counter clerk and the author. The preceding modifier and the following quote indicate that the clerk is looking at the author's face. A) The subject shouldn't be 'we' because one person is supposed to look on the other person's face. B) 1> The subject needs to be a human. 2> "a soften voice" isn't a human that can register. C) The subject, "I" can't be the same person in the modifier who is registering the look on his own face.
	B) soften voice whispers:	
	C) I was softened by the atmosphere:	
√	**D) she softens the atmosphere:**	

Q8. Absolute Pattern 18: Punctuation Error

In desperation, I pull out my map and look for [8] something—anything—that looks interesting.

	Choice	Explanation
√	**A) NO CHANGE**	A)1>The main function of dash is very simple and straightforward: It separates and emphasizes the word (s) in the middle of the statement. 2> In this manner, the pair of dashes functions similar to the pair of commas. 3>However, a dash is easy to identify so that it impresses the readers more than commas. 4> The dashes between 'anything,' impresses the reader, showing how desperate he is. B) The latter part of commas is missing. It should be a double-commas. C) 'anything' should be separated from the main sentence. D) changes the meaning
	B) something, anything that looks	
	C) something anything that looks	
	D) something or any thing that looks	

Q9. Absolute Pattern 12: Modifier Placement Error

Question: The best placement for the underlined portion would be:

	Choice	Explanation
	A) NO CHANGE	D) Placing the name right next to the coast can be the best way to modify and describe the coast. A) "marked" becomes a verb B) "bill" and "marked Nantasket Beach" become a phrase that are associated with each other. C) changes the original meaning.
	B) after the words the bill is	
	C) after the word that	
√	**D) after the word coast**	

Q10. Absolute Pattern 1: Adding, Revising, Deleting, Retaining Information

Question: At this point, the author wishes to **add** the following statement: Would this be a relevant addition here?

I grew up in a small beach village.

	Choice	Explanation
	A) Yes, because it functions as the topic that links to the following descriptions	C) The following sentences are all about Nantasket Beach and don't connect to the narrator's small beach. A) It can't function as the topic. B) is inconsistent with the question D) The author came to the beach by accident.
	B) Yes, because it informs Nantasket Beach is idyllic.	
√	**C) No, because the sentence does not link to the following descriptions.**	
	D) No, because it implies that the author's visit is premeditated.	

Q11. Absolute Pattern 23: Transition Words for Supporting Detail, Contrast, and Consequence

	Choice	Explanation
	A) NO CHANGE	D) so ~ that clause A) 1> so ~ that clause is a cause-and-effect clause 2> "and" can't replace "that" B) "so ~as" is used to connect a phrase, not a clause. 'to' is preposition for phrase. C) 'with' is preposition. Preposition can't link the following clause.
	B) as to feel	
	C) with it feels	
√	**D) that it feels**	

Questions 12-22 are based on the following passage.

The new wave of British Heavy Metal

The new wave of British heavy metal (NWOBHM) was a nationwide musical movement that started in the United Kingdom in the late 1970s and [12] have achieved international attention by the early 1980s. Journalist Geoff Barton in a May 1979 [13] coined the term issue of the British music newspaper.

Sounds to describe the emergence of new heavy metal bands in the late 1970s, during the period of punk rock's decline and the dominance of new wave music. Although encompassing [14] variously diversified mainstream and underground styles, the music of the NWOBHM is best remembered for drawing on the heavy metal of the 1970s and infusing [15] it with the intensity of punk rock to produce fast and aggressive songs.

The DIY attitude of the new metal bands led to the spread of raw-sounding, self-produced recordings and [16] a proliferation of independent record labels. Song lyrics were usually about escapist themes such as mythology, fantasy, horror and the rock lifestyle.

The NWOBHM began as an underground phenomenon growing in parallel to punk but largely ignored by the media. [17] The movement involved mostly young, white, male and working-class musicians and fans, who suffered the hardships brought on by rising unemployment for years after the 1973–75 recession. As a reaction to [18] their bleak reality, they created a community separate from mainstream society to enjoy each other's company and their favourite loud music.

The NWOBHM was heavily criticized for the excessive hype generated by local media in favour of mostly talentless musicians. [19] Consequently, it generated a renewal in the genre of heavy metal music and furthered the progress of the heavy metal subculture, whose updated behavioural and visual codes were quickly adopted by metal fans worldwide after the spread of the music to continental Europe, North America and Asia.

The movement spawned perhaps a thousand metal bands [20] ; subsequently, only a few survived the advent of MTV and the rise of the more commercial glam metal in the second half of the 1980s. Among them, Iron Maiden and Def Leppard became international stars. Other groups, such as Diamond Head, Venom and Raven, remained underground, but were a major influence on the successful extreme metal subgenres of the late 1980s and 1990s.[21]

Q12. Absolute Pattern 24: Verb Tense / Voice Error

The new wave of British heavy metal (NWOBHM) was a nationwide musical movement that started in the United Kingdom in the late **1970s** and [12] have achieved international attention **by** the early **1980s.**

	A) NO CHANGE	C) 1> "by…," when used in a time adverbial phrase, requires either the past perfect or the present perfect tense.
	B) achieved	2> In this sentence, using the present perfect is correct because "by the early 1980s" is being compared with "1970s," which is later than 1970s.
√	**C) has achieved**	3> Also, it should be "has achieved" because the subject "the new wave" is singular.
	D) has been achieving	B) 1970 and 1980 can't use the same tense. D) 'achieving' is a progressive tense.

Q13. Absolute Pattern 11: Logical Sequence

Journalist Geoff Barton **in a May** 1979 [13]coined the term **issue of the British music newspaper *Sounds*** to describe the emergence of new heavy metal bands in the late 1970s, during the period of punk rock's decline and the dominance of new wave music.

The **best placement** for the underlined portion would be:

	A) NO CHANGE	B) The correct sentence is: Journalist Geoff *Barton* *coined* the term in **a** May 1979 issue of the British music newspaper *Sounds* to describe the emergence of new heavy metal bands in the late 1970s,
√	**B) after the word Geoff Barton**	
	C) after the word newspaper	
	D) after the word 1970s,	A) 1> The original sentence is incorrect because it becomes "the term issue of…." or noun + noun 2> "**a**" in "in **a** May 1979" indicates the phrase is linked to "issue of the British music newspaper *Sounds*" C) newspaper and Sounds can't be separated. D) dangling modifier error

Q14. Absolute Pattern 19: Redundant Error

Although encompassing [14] variously diversified mainstream and underground styles, the music of the NWOBHM is best remembered for drawing on the heavy metal of the 1970s and infusing [15] it with the intensity of punk rock to produce fast and aggressive songs.

	A) NO CHANGE	C) "diverse," the adjective, describes the noun "mainstream".
	B) diversified in various	A), B) "variously" and "diversified" are synonym, creating a redundant error.
√	**C) diverse**	D) changes the meaning.
	D) DELETE IT	

Q15. Absolute Pattern 21: Subject-Verb, Pronoun, Noun Agreement

Although encompassing various mainstream and underground styles, the music of the NWOBHM is best remembered for drawing on the heavy metal of the 1970s and infusing [15] it with the intensity of punk rock to produce fast and aggressive songs

√	**A) NO CHANGE**	A) The pronoun 'it' refers to the music of the NWOBHM.
	B) them	B) The music of the NWOBHM is singular. "them' is plural
	C) NWOBHM	C) "NWOBHM" already took its position in the main clause and can't be written again in the subordinating clause that can cause a redundant error.
	D) OMIT the underlined portion	D) "Infusing" requires an object.

Q16. Absolute Pattern 13: Parallel Structure

The DIY attitude of the new metal bands led to the spread of **raw-sounding, self-produced recordings and** [16] **a proliferation** of independent record labels.

√	**A) NO CHANGE**	A) The sentence maintains the parallel structure. The original sentence is a series of phrases.
	B) independent record labels were proliferated.	B), C), D) are clauses, creating unnecessarily wordy expressions.
	C) a proliferation of independent record labels was followed.	
	D) record labels were proliferated independently.	

Q17. Absolute Pattern 1: Adding, Revising, Deleting, Retaining Information

At this point, the author wants to add the following sentence. Would the author make this addition here?

It was only through the promotion of rock DJ Neal Kay and *Sounds'* campaigning that it reached the public consciousness and gained radio airplay, recognition and success in the UK.

√	**A) Yes, because it provides an important link to the rest of the paragraph.**
	B) Yes, because it connects well with the previous sentence telling the reason for unpopularity in the music industry
	C) No, because it strays from the main focus of the essay.
	D) No, because it directly contradicts from the previous sentence.

A) The sentence begins with a negative tone, and then a concession follows, "it was only through"...
Finally, it further introduces how it positively affected a group of people in the society.
B) 1> The previous sentence is negative tone. 2> the added information is positive tone.
3> Therefore, the added information tells of popularity, instead of unpopularity.
C), D) are opposite explanations.

Q18. Absolute Pattern 21: Subject-Verb, Pronoun, Noun Agreement

As a reaction to [18] their bleak reality, **they** created a community separate from mainstream society to enjoy each other's company and their favorite loud music.

	Choice	Explanation
√	**A) NO CHANGE**	A) following "they" indicates the answer should be (A).
	B) NWOBHM's	B) calling its own name is illogical and unnatural.
	C) its	C) is singular pronoun
	D) public's	D) The sentence changes its meaning to "public's bleak reality"

Q19. Absolute Pattern 23: Transition Words for Supporting Detail, Contrast, and Consequence

[19] Consequently, it generated a renewal in the genre of heavy metal music and furthered the progress of the heavy metal subculture, whose updated behavioral and visual codes were quickly adopted by metal fans worldwide after the spread of the music to continental Europe, North America and Asia.

	Choice
	A) NO CHANGE
√	**B) Nonetheless,**
	C) For example,
	D) Soon,

B) 1> The previous sentence is negative "The NWOBHM was **heavily criticized** for the excessive hype…"
2> The following sentence is positive: "it generated a renewal in the genre of heavy metal"
3> "nonetheless" is concessional adverb that links up (-/+) clauses.

A) is used for cause-and-effect. C) is used to support the previous topic sentence.

D) 'soon' is for time.

The list of other concessional adverbs					
Nevertheless	However	Despite of	Though	Even so	Still

Q20. Absolute Pattern 23: Transition Words for Supporting Detail, Contrast, and Consequence

The movement spawned perhaps **a thousand metal bands** [20] ; subsequently, **only a few survived** the advent of MTV and the rise of the more commercial glam metal in the second half of the 1980s.

	Choice
	A) NO CHANGE
	B) ,however,
	C) ,and
√	**D) ,but**

D) Two clauses "perhaps…" and "only a few survived" are clear contradiction. Therefore, conjunction 'but'. should be used.

A) and C) are ruled out because 'subsequently' is used for a cause-and-effect situation.
C) 'and' is used in a parallel situation.
B) The correct form of 'however' is ;however,

Q21. Absolute Pattern 1: Adding, Revising, Deleting, Retaining Information

Question: Which choice, if added here, would most effectively **conclude the essay**?

	Choice
√	**A) Many bands from the NWOBHM reunited in the 2000s and remained active through live performances and new studio albums.**
	B) Some critics in 1970s viewed NWOBHM as the significant exponent of the movement
	C) Foreign hard rock acts, such as Kiss from the US, Rush from Canada, Scorpions from Germany, and especially AC/DC from Australia, climbed the British charts in the same period
	D) Each of these bands was in crisis in the mid-to-late 1970s.

A) follows the chronological sequence.
B) is too extreme for the underground.
C) The central theme of the passage is NWOBHM, the British underground musical bands, not a Foreign hard rock.
D) The overall tone of the passage is positive. Therefore, the final sentence can't be negative.

Q22. Absolute Pattern 9: Informational Graphs	
Given that all of the followings are true, which interpretation would most clearly reflect the passage and the table?	
	A) Heavy Metal, albeit active in the 2010s, is not getting a meaningful attention from music industry.
	B) Heavy Metal, albeit insignificant in sales, proved to be continuing to increase in sales
√	C) Heavy Metal, albeit not a major genre, was **not the only one** experienced decline in sales.
	D) Critics, seeking the greatest benefit ,paid more attention on Pop than Heavy Metal

C) All the rest musical genres except Pop experienced decrease in sales.
A) The sales record proves it got a decent attention.
B) It continued to decrease three years in a row.
D) Not stated in the table.

Questions 23-33 are based on the following passage.

The Tower of Pisa

The Leaning Tower of Pisa *or simply the Tower of Pisa* is freestanding bell tower of the cathedral of the Italian city of Pisa [23] , and it is known worldwide for its unintended tilt. [24] Situated behind Pisa's cathedral and is the third oldest structure in the city's Cathedral Square. The tower's tilt began during construction, caused by an inadequate foundation on ground too soft on one side to properly support the structure's weight. [25] Galileo Galilei is said to have dropped two cannonballs of different masses from the tower to demonstrate that [26] its speed of descent was independent of their mass. However, the only primary source for this is the biography *Racconto istorico della vita di Galileo*, written by Galileo's secretary Vincenzo Viviani and published in 1717, long after Viviani's death.

During World War II, the Allies discovered that the Germans were using the tower as an observation post. A U.S. Army sergeant sent to confirm the presence of German troops in the tower [27] which was impressed by the beauty of the cathedral, and thus refrained [28] to order an artillery strike, sparing it from destruction. Numerous efforts have been made to restore the tower to a vertical orientation or at least keep it from falling over. Most of these efforts [29] failed; some worsened the tilt.

On February 27, 1964, the government of Italy requested aid in preventing the tower from toppling. [30] Consequently, [31] these people considered important to retain the current tilt, due to the role that this element played in promoting the tourism industry of Pisa.

A multinational task force of engineers, mathematicians, and historians gathered on the Azores islands to discuss the stabilization methods. <1> It was found that the tilt was increasing in combination with the softer foundations on the lower side. <2> Many methods were proposed to stabilize the tower, including the addition of 800 tones of lead counterweights to the raised end of the base. <3> The tower and the neighboring cathedral baptistery, and cemetery have been included in the Piazza del DuomoUNESCO World Heritage Site, which was declared in 1987. <4> The tower was closed to the public on January 7, 1990, after more than two decades of stabilization studies and spurred by the abrupt collapse of the Civic Tower of Pavia in 1989.

The bells were removed to relieve some weight, and cables were cinched around the third level and anchored several hundred meters away. Apartments and houses in the path of the tower were vacated for safety. The solution chosen to prevent the collapse of the tower was to slightly straighten it to a safer angle by removing 38 cubic metres (1,342 cubic feet) of soil from underneath the raised end.

Q23. Absolute Pattern 16: Precision, Concision, Style

The Leaning Tower of Pisa *or simply the Tower of Pisa* is freestanding bell tower of the cathedral of the Italian city of Pisa [23] , and it is known worldwide for its unintended tilt.

	Choice	Explanation
	A) NO CHANGE	Always Pick the Shortest One from the Multiple Choices! C) is the clearest and most succinct.
	B) which is known	
√	**C) , known**	A) "and it is" is unnecessary, causing a wordiness error. B) 1> "which is" is unnecessary. 2> It is non-restrictive and requires comma before "which"
	D) as known	D) "as" is unnecessary and ambiguous.

Q24. Absolute Pattern 21: Subject-Verb, Pronoun, Noun Agreement

[24] Situated behind Pisa's cathedral **and is** the third oldest structure in the city's Cathedral Square.

	Choice	Explanation
	A) NO CHANGE	B) "and" is the conjunction that links the main clause. The previous portion of the sentence, however, is clearly not a clause. It should have a subject and verb to be called a clause.
√	**B) It is situated**	A) and C) have no subject and verb. D) has no verb.
	C) Being situated	
	D) The Tower of Pisa, situated	

Q25. Absolute Pattern 1: Adding, Revising, Deleting, Retaining Information

If the author wishes to **delete** the underlined portion of the sentence, the paragraph would probably lose:

The tower's tilt began during construction, caused by an inadequate foundation on ground too soft on one side to properly support the structure's weight. [25]

	Choice
	A) the fascinating feature that attracts tourists from around the world
	B) a distinctive look that people talk about the tower
√	**C) the main reason for its look**
	D) a specific detail of serious structural defects unknown **until the repair was completed**

C) The underlined portion of the sentence briefly introduces the reason for its tilt.
A) and B) are not mentioned, and inconsistent with the question
D) The passage states nothing about the completion of the repair

Q26. Absolute Pattern 17: Pronoun Error

Galileo Galilei is said to have dropped two cannonballs of different masses from the tower to demonstrate that [26] its speed of descent was independent of their mass.

	Choice	Explanation
	A) NO CHANGE	B) 'their' refers to the two cannonballs. *albeit this situation certainly did not happen in history.
√	**B) their**	A), C): "it", the singular pronoun, can't represent two cannonballs.
	C) it has	D) The verb, 'was' is already active in the sentence.
	D) they have	

Q27. Absolute Pattern 21: Subject-Verb, Pronoun, Noun Agreement

U.S. Army sergeant (who was) sent to confirm the presence of German troops in the tower [27] **which was impressed** by the beauty of the cathedral, and thus refrained [28] to order an artillery strike, sparing it from destruction.

	Choice	Explanation
	A) NO CHANGE	C) 1> When two verbs are shown in one sentence, the latter one is highly likely to be the real verb.
	B) who was impressed	2> In this sentence, "was impressed" is the main verb, not "sent"
√	**C) was impressed**	A) "which" needs to be omitted. B) "who" needs to be omitted.
	D) impressed	D) "by the beauty of the cathedral" indicates the verb should be passive

Q28. Absolute Pattern 15: Prepositional Idiom

Passage: A U.S. Army sergeant sent to confirm the presence of German troops in the tower was impressed by the beauty of the cathedral, and thus refrained [28] to order an artillery strike, sparing it from destruction.

	Choice	Explanation
	A) NO CHANGE	C) 'refrain ~ from' is the correct version.
	B) that by ordering	A) is the prepositional idiom error.
√	**C) from ordering**	B) 'that' carries a clause, not a phrase "by ordering." D) changes the meaning of the sentence
	D) and ordered	

Q29. Absolute Pattern 18: Punctuation Error

Most of these efforts [29] failed; some worsened the tilt.

	Choice	Explanation
√	**A) NO CHANGE**	A) The semicolon connects two alternate clauses.
	B) failed: some worsened the tilt.	This sentence is divided into two clauses: some effort failed while some got worsen.
	C) failed, some worsened the tilt.	B) The colon is used to introduce things.
	D) failed with some worsened the tilt	C) is comma splice error. D) "with" is preposition that can't carry another clause.

Q 30. Absolute Pattern 23: Transition Words for Supporting Detail, Contrast, and Consequence

On February 27, 1964, the government of Italy requested aid in preventing the tower from toppling. [30] Consequently, [31] these people considered important to retain the current tilt, due to the role that this element played in promoting the tourism industry of Pisa.

	Choice	Explanation
	A) After all	B) The sentence reveals people's conflicting view concerning the Tower. Therefore, 'However' must be used.
√	**B) However,**	
	C) Nonetheless,	A) 'consequently' and 'after all' are used for the cause-and-effect. C) 'Nonetheless' is used to a seemingly contradictory situation and then eventually emphasizes it.
	D) Moreover,	D) 'Moreover' is used to emphasize the previous statement.

Q31. Absolute Pattern 16: Precision, Concision, Style

	Choice	Explanation
	A) NO CHANGE	When multiple choices contain pronoun, it mainly asks ambiguity error.
	B) They were considered	D) The subject must be clearly identified like (D)
	C) It was considered	A) "these people," being used for the first time in this sentence, raise ambiguity for who "these people" are.
√	**D) The Italian government considered**	B) For the same reasoning as A) "They" can't be used. C) The verb "considered" needs to have an object.

Q 32. Pattern 11: Logical Sequence

A multinational task force of engineers gathered on the Azores islands to discuss the **stabilization methods.**
<1> It was found that **the tilt** was increasing. <2> Many methods were proposed to **stabilize the tower**.
<3> The tower has been included in the Piazza del DuomoUNESCO **World Heritage Site**.
<4> The tower was closed after more than two decades of **stabilization** studies.

Which of the following sentences **is diverting from the main issue** in this paragraph?

	A) <1>	Do Not Pick Any New Information that is Not Mentioned in the Passage or in the paragraph!
	B) <2>	C) 1> The keywords in surrounding sentences are the stabilization of the Tower. 2> UNESCO **World Heritage Site** is not a related issue at all .
√	**C) <3>**	
	D) <4>	

Q33. Absolute Pattern 1: Adding, Revising, Deleting, Retaining Information

Suppose the author's goal was to write a brief **summary describing the timeline to stabilize** the Tower of Pisa. Would this summary accomplish his goal?

	A) Yes, because it details the unique and effortful undertaking made by many scientists including Galilei Galileo
√	B) Yes, because it chronicles the important events of the project including **some debates to stabilize the Tower.**
	C) No, because it focuses on the historical overview of the Tower.
	D) No, because historical figure like Galileo Galilei's experiment was the main concern

B) The primary concern in this passage is about stabilizing the Tower of Pisa.
A), D): Galileo Galilei is not the related issue to the summary of the stabilization.
C) It describes only briefly about the historical overview of the Tower. An effort to stabilize the Tower takes up more than half of the passage. It is not a minor issue.

Questions 34-44 are based on the following passage.

Can Dark Knight Rise Again?

Entrepreneur Major Malcolm Wheeler founded National Allied Publications in autumn 1934. The company debuted with the tabloid-sized *New Fun: The Big Comic Magazine* #1 with a cover date of February 1935. The company's second title *New Comics* #1 appeared in a size close to [34] what would become [35] comic books standard during the period fans and historians [36] call the Golden Age of Comic [37] Books with slightly larger dimensions than today's.

That title evolved into *Adventure Comics*, which continued through issue #503 in 1983, becoming one of the longest-running comic-book series. In 2009 DC revived *Adventure Comics* with its original numbering.

In 1935, Joe Shuster, the future creators of Superman, created Doctor Occult, [38] who was the earliest DC Comics character to still be in the DC Universe.

The themed anthology series would become a sensation with the introduction of Batman (May 1939). [39] By then, however, Wheeler-Nicholson had gone. In 1937, in debt to printing-plant owner [40] , Harry Donenfeld—who also published pulp magazines and operated as a principal in the magazine distributorship Independent News—Wheeler-Nicholson had to take Donenfeld on as a partner in order to publish *Detective Comics* #1.

Two DC limited series, *Batman: The Dark Knight Returns* by Frank Miller and *Watchmen* by Moore and artist Dave Gibbons, drew attention in the mainstream press for their [41] dark psychological complexity and promotion of the antihero. These titles helped pave the way for comics to be more widely accepted in literary-criticism circles and to make inroads into the book industry, with collected editions of these series as commercially successful trade paperbacks

The comics industry experienced a brief boom in the early 1990s, thanks to a combination of speculative purchasing [42] and several storylines which gained attention from the mainstream media. DC's extended storylines in which Superman was killed, Batman was crippled, and superhero *Green Lantern* turned into the supervillain Parallax resulted in	dramatically increased sales, but the increases were as temporary as the hero's replacements. Sales dropped off as the industry went into a major slump [43] ,while manufactured "collectibles" numbering in the millions replaced [44] imagination and reality until fans and speculators alike deserted the medium in droves.

Q34. Absolute Pattern 17 : Pronoun Error

The company's second title *New Comics* #1 appeared in a size close to [34] what would become [35] comic books standard

√	**A) NO CHANGE**	A) 1> "what" is used to introduce the following statement "would become comic books standard." 2> "what" connects with and acting as a subject / object for "a size close to" B),C), D) cannot connect to "close to"
	B) that	
	C) ,which	
	D) which	

Q 35. Absolute Pattern 14: Possessive Determiners and Possessive Noun Error

The company's second title, *New Comics* #1, appeared in a size close to what would become [35] comic books standard during the period

	A) NO CHANGE	D) "Comic books' standard" is the correct possessive form A) "comic books" and "standard" are noun that requires a connector B) and C) apply the wrong possessive forms
	B) comic's books standard	
	C) comic's books' standard	
√	**D) comic books' standard**	

Q 36. Absolute Pattern 24: Verb Tense / Voice Error

The company's second title, *New Comics* #1, appeared in a size close to what would become comic books' standard during the period fans and historians [36] call the Golden Age

√	**A) NO CHANGE**	A) "call" can be either "would call" or "call," showing the people's reaction in the past as used in the demonstrative context. B) is singular C) is progressive tense, which is incorrect because it can only be used for a short continuous action. D) is past perfect tense
	B) calls	
	C) were calling	
	D) had called	

Q 37. Absolute Pattern 4: Comparison

The company's second title, *New Comics* #1, appeared in a size close to what would become comic books' standard during the period fans and historians call the Golden Age of Comic [37] Books with slightly large dimensions **than** today's.

	A) NO CHANGE	C) ",with slightly larger" uses the correct comparison. A) doesn't use the comparison, but it should for the sake of "than." B), D) Colon or semicolon can't be used along with the preposition 'with',
	B) Books: with slightly larger	
√	**C) Books, with slightly larger**	
	D) Books; slightly larger	

Q38. Absolute Pattern 7: Conjunction Error

In 1935, Joe Shuster, the future creators of Superman, created Doctor Occult, [38] who was the earliest DC Comics character to still be in the DC Universe.

	A) NO CHANGE	C) "Doctor Occult" is **a character** created by Joe Shuster. Therefore, it is non–human, and should be linked to "which."
	B) whom was	
√	**C) which was**	A) B) and D): "who" is used for a human precedent.
	D) who is	

Q39. Absolute Pattern 12: Modifier Placement Error

Passage: [39] By then, however, Wheeler-Nicholson **had gone.**

√	**A) NO CHANGE**	A) "By," in time adverbial phrase carries either the present perfect or the past perfect tense when two time-adverbial phrases are compared in a sentence.
	B) Since then,	
	C) After then,	B) 'Since then' is normally used with the present perfect tense C) and D) 'After than' and 'later then' are normally used with the simple past tense.
	D) Later then,	

Q40. Absolute Pattern 18: Punctuation Error

In 1937, in debt to printing-plant owner [40] , Harry Donenfeld—who also published pulp magazines and operated as a principal in the magazine distributorship Independent News—Wheeler-Nicholson had to take Donenfeld on as a partner in order to publish *Detective Comics* #1.

	A) NO CHANGE	B) 1> The subject "Wheeler" comes after the long modifier. 2> The sentence states that "the printing-plant owner" and "Harry Donenfeld" is the same person. 3> Therefore, a comma shouldn't separate this one person; otherwise, "Harry Donenfeld" will be the subject.
√	**B) Harry Donenfeld—who**	
	C) , Harry Donenfeld, who	
	D) Harry Donenfeld	A) and C) are incorrect for the above stated reason too. In this sentence, the modifier "who also published...News" is offset by a pair of dashes. D) is run-on sentence, conflicting with the following main clause and modifiers.

Q41. Absolute Pattern 10: Logical Expression

Two DC limited series, *Batman: The Dark Knight Returns* by Frank Miller and *Watchmen* by Moore and artist Dave Gibbons, drew attention in the mainstream press for their [41] dark psychological complexity and promotion of the antihero

√	**A) NO CHANGE**	A) complexity (noun), promotion (noun)
	B) dark psychology, complexity, and **promotional**	B) "promotional" is adjective. It should be a noun like the preceding noun to avoid a parallelism error.
	C) dark psychology, complex, and promotion	C) Noun (psychology), Adjective (complex), Noun (promotion) make a parallelism error.
	D) dark psychologically and complexly promotional	D) It changes the meaning by changing adjectives into adverbs, causing a parallelism error.

Q42. Absolute Pattern 1: Adding, Revising, Deleting, Retaining Information	
At this point, the author wishes to **add** the following true sentence: Should he make this addition here? mass purchase of the books as collectible items, with intent to resell at a higher value as the rising value of older issues was thought to imply that *all* comics would rise dramatically in price.	
√	A) Yes, because it **clarifies what the speculative purchasing** is.
	B) Yes, because it describes one of the consequences that the comics industry benefited from the brief boom
	C) No, because it would distract readers from the main focus of the paragraph.
	D) No, because it creates confusion with the following phrase "and several storylines…media."

A) This information describes what the speculative purchasing is.
B) It might be true statement but is inconsistent with this question.
C) and D) both are negative while the passage is positive.

Q43. Absolute Pattern 23: Transition Words for Supporting Detail, Contrast, and Consequence		
Sales dropped off as the industry went into a major slump[43] , while manufactured "collectibles" numbering in the millions replaced [44] imagination and reality until fans and speculators alike deserted the medium in droves.		
Which of the following alternatives is **NOT an acceptable** alternative?		
	A) , and	C) "but" cancels out the previous sentence.
	B) ; in the meantime,	Both clauses are negative, so they can't cancel each other out.
√	**C) , but**	A), B), D): All of them are used for the parallel structure
	D) , and simultaneously	

Q44. Absolute Pattern 15: Prepositional Idiom		
Sales dropped off as the industry went into a major slump, while manufactured "collectibles" numbering in the millions replaced [44] imagination and reality until fans and speculators alike deserted the medium in droves.		
	A) NO CHANGE	D) "replaced with" is the correct idiom and delivers the correct meaning of the statement.
	B) imagination **in** reality	
	C) real imagination	A), B), and C) change the original meaning awkwardly by using incorrect prepositions.
√	D) imagination **with** reality	

Chapter 7 Summary

Chapter Summary contains equal portions of

-12 Absolute Patterns for Reading Section

-20 Common Patterns for Incorrect Choices in Reading

-70 Absolute Patterns for Writing and Language Section

-24 Common Patterns for Incorrect Choices in Writing

Chapter 7

20 Common Patterns for *In*correct Choices in Reading

14 Repeating the Question

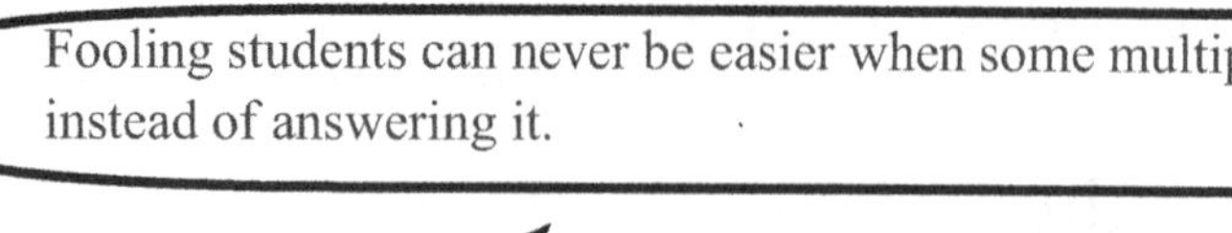

Fooling students can never be easier when some multiple choices paraphrase the question instead of answering it.

Some questions may look extremely easy at first sight because the choice you may pick paraphrases the question.

I remember that I pondered over one question for about 30 minutes until I realized there's capital letters "EXCEPT" at the tail of the question.

15 Synonym or Similar Perception

Virtually, the majority of correct answers rely on the synonym pattern.

However, some incorrect choices simply place opposite adjective or adverb right next to the synonym that eventually pollutes the meaning of the choice.

For example, can you distinguish between "acceptance" and "mild acceptance?" In fact, the former is Positive while the latter is Negative. Or, from "guarded approval" to "approval"? The former is Negative, the latter, Positive. All of these are different and only one—depending on situation—can be the answer.

Chapter 7

20 Common Patterns for *In*correct Choices in Reading

16 Concept Comparison

Absolute Pattern 3: Inference Question and Absolute Pattern 6: Analogy Question fundamentally ask Concept Comparison or Finding a Similar Situation

Concept comparison pattern normally presents one or two opposing concepts.

This concept can be subcategorized into, such as "Physical and Mental," "Negative and Positive," "Passive and Active," "Part and Whole," "A single individual involvement and Two individuals involvement", etc.

Without properly understanding the concept comparison and the mechanism within it, every choice may look extremely weird as none of those choices contains the info. from the passage.

17 Quantity-Quality Concept

Some keywords contain quantity concept, while others are quality.

As an example, the word "comics" inspires us a low quality, while "Mona Risa" inspires us high quality.

"One-fourth" tells us the measured-quantity, while "a lot of gold" or "king's decree" implies immensity (degree).

Chapter 7

20 Common Patterns for *In*correct Choices in Reading

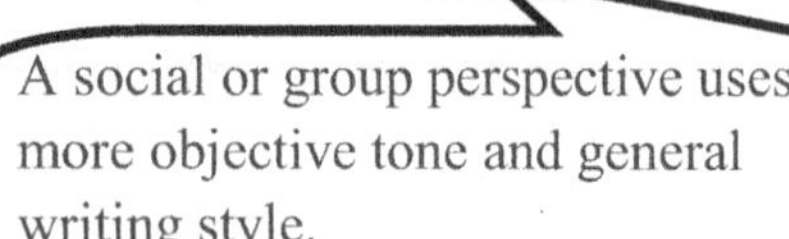

18 Personal-Group Perspective

Personal perspective is usually represented by the first person 'I'.

A social or group perspective uses more objective tone and general writing style.

Incorrect choices may confuse you between these two perspectives.
Therefore, it's critical to check if the passage is written by the first person perspective "I" or the third person in general.

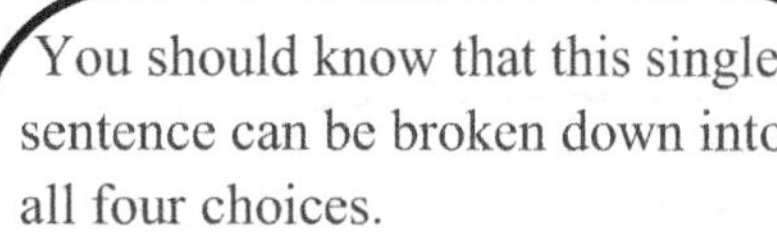

19 Part-Whole Relations

Imagine one paragraph (total of 15 lines) is made of a single long sentence.

You should know that this single sentence can be broken down into all four choices.
Please remember that you read only the lines assigned to you such as
(A) lines 1-2
(B) lines 3-5
(C) lines 6-10
(D) lines 11-12,
not the whole chunk of it.

Each choice, in this case, may contain a meaningful conjunction or conjunctive adverb such as 'although,' 'because,' 'yet,' etc.
Because of such a conjunction, the answer and incorrect choice may be distinguished.

Chapter 7

20 Common Patterns for *In*correct Choices in Reading

You should be ready to translate abstract concept.

Some keywords characterize the idea or material using our five senses (smell, hearing, touch, see, taste).

For instance, the answer, instead of using the word "onion," will describe it like "an edible bulb plant with a pungent taste and smell."

70 Absolute Patterns for Writing and language Section

RULE #54 Hint: Tense	**Tense in Modifier** The correct answer is C. The main sentence uses the past tense "decided." Therefore, the modifier must follow the same tense "resulted by"

Question 55
Without unanimity or no muted return, the UN security council in the meeting is entirely dependent upon the chairperson's final decision to send the UN peace corps to the conflicted region in Syria.

A) NO CHANGE
B) Neither unanimity as well as no
C) Neither unanimity or
D) Without unanimity or any,

RULE #55 Hint: Negative	**Double Negative** The correct answer is D. The preposition "without" is already negative. Having another negative "no" is a double negative error. It should be "Without...any." B) and C are both idiomatic error. "Neither ….nor" is the correct idiom.

Question 56
Working with new people along with re-organizing the old employees to a new branch, are always a daunting task, especially when there is little consensus about the products it carries.

A) NO CHANGE
B) is always
C) that is always
D) always have been

RULE #56 Hint: Verb	**Gerund as Subject** The correct answer is B. The gerund phrase is treated as a singular subject. *"along with" is not a conjunction. Therefore, whatever comes after "along with" is neither a subject affects the subject-verb agreement

Question 57
Those buyers who bought houses just before the subprime mortgage crisis in 2008 were either lucky or exceptional astute.

A) NO CHANGE
B) are neither lucky nor exceptionally astute
C) were not either lucky or exceptionally astute
D) were neither lucky nor exceptionally astute

RULE #57
Hint:
Idiom

Guessing Tone (Positive-Negative)

The correct answer is D.
The sentence must be negative tone because those buyers who bought houses before the crisis were far from lucky. Therefore, choice A is incorrect.
B) is using "are." It should be "were."
C) is wordy. "not either" can be reduced to "neither"

Question 58
Some of the glacial sediment deposits support the evidence that the Ice Age effected every continent except South America.

A) effected
B) was affected
C) affected
D) inflicted

RULE #58
Hint:
verb

Confusing word

The correct answer is C.
"affect" is commonly used as a verb, while "effect" is used as a noun.

Question 59
The radiation emitted by high-intensity-discharge microwave oven is very effective in activating molecules; foods inside the oven, much like the way of electromagnetic waves that zap through the air from TV or radio transmitters, are cooked or boiled safer and faster.

A) NO CHANGE
B) transmits, and cook or boil safer and faster.
C) is transmitted as cooked or boiled safely and fastly.
D) transmitters, cook or boil safer and faster.

RULE #59
Hint:
Agreement

Run-on

The correct answer is A.
Run-on sentence means a sentence that contains multiple independent clauses without having a proper conjunction
A) properly connects the subject "foods" and the verb "are cooked"
B) and C) use transmitter as a verb.
D) uses active verb "cooked," making "foods cooked"

Question 60

The Vancouver's Indian Reserves was located in the University of British Columbia.

A) NO CHANGE

B) Indian Reserves in Vancouver were

C) Vancouver Indian Reserves was

D) Indian Reserve's Vancouver was

RULE #60 Hint: possessive	**The Possessive Form Can't be used If the Noun Indicates the Title** The correct answer is C. The noun used as a title is considered as a singular and can't be used as a possessive determiner.

Question 61

The initial estimation of safely disposing of the toxic wastes is roughly ten times what the Du Pont spent to purchase it in its factory

A) for purchasing it

B) for the purchase of it

C) to purchase its own system

D) to purchase them

RULE #61 Hint: Pronoun	**Pronoun Without Antecedent** The correct answer is C. The pronoun "It" or "them" cannot be used without a preceding antecedent.

Question 62

Michael Jorden, Shaquille O'Neal, and Charles Barkley were hall of fame basketball players, each of these basketball players was awarded MVP more than once at the time they were playing.

A) NO CHANGE

B) each of which basketball players were awarded MVP more than once at the time they were playing

C) each of these basketball players was awarded MVP more than once at the time he was playing

D) each of which basketball players was awarded MVP more than once at the time each was playing

RULE #62 Hint: Pronoun	**Pronoun and Verb for "Each" and "Every"** The correct answer is D. The answer D "which" functions as a conjunction and it properly uses a singular verb "was" and a singular pronoun "each". Each or Every is singular; therefore, the proper pronoun should be "she/he" and should use a singular verb "was." Therefore, options A, B are incorrect. C) is a comma splice error.

Question 63
The theory of quantum mechanics that applies quantum correction compliments classic physics.

A) compliments classic physics
B) compliment that of classic physics
C) complements classic physics
D) complement that of classic physics

RULE #63
Hint: Words

Confusing Word: Complement vs. Compliment

The correct answer is C.
Complement = fill the gap   Compliment = praise

D) is incorrect for two reasons: first, the subject "the theory" is singular; however, the verb "complement" is plural; second, "that of" is not comparing anything in the sentence. It is ambiguous and unnecessary.

Question 64
Some of the hypotheses that Charles Darwin established to explain the origin of species were later rejected as inconsistent to convergent and divergent evolution theories.

A) lately rejected as inconsistent for
B) lately rejected as inconsistent with
C) later rejected as inconsistent with
D) later rejected as inconsistent to

RULE #64
Hint:
Words

Confusing Word: Later vs. Lately

The correct answer is C.
The correct idiom for the word "inconsistent" is "inconsistent with,"
"Lately" means recently.
The past tense "were" indicates the past occurrence, not the present. Therefore, options A and B are incorrect.

Question 65
For us, VIP customers are receiving extensive client care services seemed to be eagerly anticipating the courtesy programs at the mall.

A) NO CHANGE
B) For us, VIP customers receiving
C) For we VIP customers receiving
D) VIP customers who have received for us

RULE #65
Hint:
Pronoun

The Pronoun after Preposition

The correct answer is B.
Always use the objective pronoun "us" after the preposition.
A) "are receiving" is a verb. The verb "seemed to be" is already in place.
D) changes the original meaning.

Question 66
Fully automated vehicles are a work in progress, an autonomous vehicle that drives without any human interaction, parks parallel along a narrow girder, and they will even send an emergency signal to the driver when it is required.

A) NO CHANGE
B) is capable of sending an emergency signal to the driver
C) even sending an emergency signal to the driver will be accomplished
D) sends an emergency signal to the driver

RULE #66 Hint: Parallelism	**Parallelism** The correct answer is D. "that drives, parks, and sends" are the correct form of parallelism. Options A and C break the parallel structure by including an independent clause. B) is not only using the unnecessary word "is capable of" but also breaks the paralleling structure "that drives, parks, and is capable of"

Question 67
In the final exam, three identical questions had appeared that had been miscalculated in the midterm test.

A) NO CHANGE
B) three questions appeared
C) three identical questions had been appeared
D) three identical questions were appeared

RULE #67 Hint: Tense	Tense The correct answer is B. The midterm test should have been taken before the final. Therefore, the correct tense for "the final" should be past tense.

Question 68
Novelist George Orwell's accounts of all animals are equal, but some animals are more equal than others begin with the author's allegory of the Russian Revolution and culminated with his reminiscence of his past.

A) NO CHANGE
B) and culminates
C) , culminating
D) and culminate

RULE #68 Hint: Verb	**Parallel Present Tense in Descriptive (Narrative) Statement** The correct answer is D. A descriptive statement such as a natural phenomenon or announcement uses the simple present tense. The verb "begin" in non-underlined portion of the sentence indicates how the parallel structure should be maintained. A) is past tense. B) is incorrect because the subject "Orwell's accounts" is plural, while "culminates" is singular. C) changes the parallel structure.

Question 69
The maid at the hotel asked, "is the room temperature right for yourself and your family?"

A) for yours and your family?"
B) for you and your family?"
C) for yourselves ?"
D) for your and your family?"

RULE #69 Hint: Pronoun	**Reflective Pronoun "~SELF" Should Not Be Used Independently.** The correct answer is B. Reflective pronoun (self) cannot be used alone and must have its antecedent.

Question 70
Every summer my parents invite their relatives, those people come for a family reunion.

A) who come
B) the people came
C) they come
D) which are invited over and come

RULE #70 Hint: Redundancy	**Conjunction "Who"** The correct answer is A. B) and C) are comma splice error. D) Don't use "which" to people. It is also wordy.

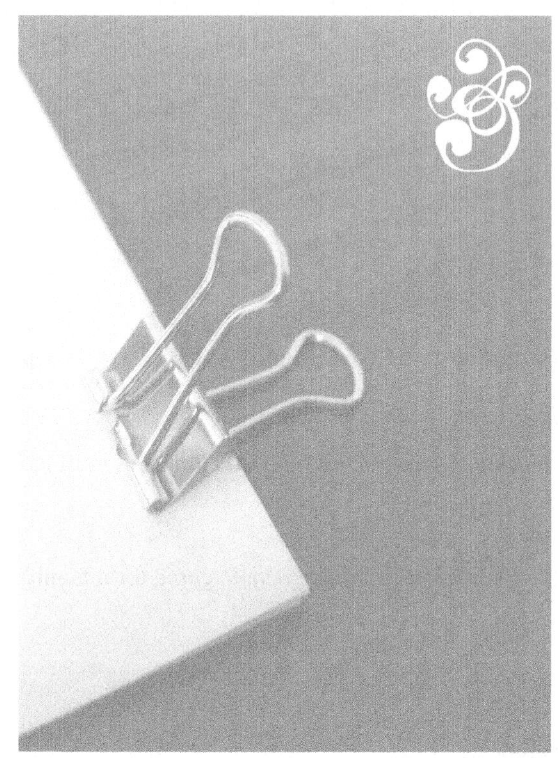

Chapter 8

COLLEGE BOARD PSAT PATTERN ANALYSES

COLLEGE BOARD SAT PATTERN ANALYSES

PSAT COLLEGE BOARD OFFICIAL TEST
PATTERN ANALYSIS

To download the test, please visit:
https://collegereadiness.collegeboard.org/pdf/psat-nmsqt-practice-test-1.pdf

To understand the full concept of this analysis, it is critical to study the previous chapters before proceed.

PSAT COLLEGE BOARD OFFICIAL GUIDE
READING SECTION PATTERNS

<table>
<tr><th colspan="3">Q1 . Absolute Pattern 1: Main Idea Question</th></tr>
<tr><td colspan="3">Question Pattern: main purpose</td></tr>
<tr><td>Step 1</td><td>Step 2</td><td>Step 3</td></tr>
<tr><td>Keywords from the Text</td><td>Keyword from answer</td><td>Tones / Concepts</td></tr>
<tr><td>L73: How as she to bear the change</td><td>(A) significant change</td><td>Sympathetic, Synonym</td></tr>
<tr><td colspan="3">Incorrect Choices & Their Common Patterns</td></tr>
<tr><td>Evidence</td><td>Incorrect keywords</td><td>Incorrect Patterns</td></tr>
<tr><td rowspan="3">The main character Emma appears more than any other characters. From this process, we can eliminate B) and D). (C) is ruled out because the overall tone of the passage is Positive.</td><td>(B) neighbor</td><td rowspan="3">B), C), D) are Unrelated example . Please refer to incorrect choice pattern #5</td></tr>
<tr><td>(C) personality flaws</td></tr>
<tr><td>(D) father</td></tr>
<tr><td colspan="3">B) and D) Please refer to incorrect choice pattern # 5: Minor or Unrelated Example
C) Identify tone of the passage: to do that, please read the concluding paragraph once again.
Literary genre like this passage, however, more often than not, does not have a clear-cut concluding paragraph.
In that case, it is pivotal to find some meaningful signals or transitional words, such as rhetoric question like line 73.
The overall tone—especially based on line 73—is sympathetic, which should be attributed to positive.
Therefore, (C) is incorrect because of its negative keyword “flaws.”
Please refer to incorrect choice pattern # 1: Positive-Negative Tone (Value)</td></tr>
</table>

<table>
<tr><th colspan="3">Q2 . Absolute Pattern 9: Relationships Question</th></tr>
<tr><td colspan="3">Pattern: best summarizes, first two paragraphs</td></tr>
<tr><td>Step 1</td><td>Step 2</td><td>Step 3</td></tr>
<tr><td>Keywords from the Text</td><td>Keyword from answer</td><td>Tones / Concepts</td></tr>
<tr><td>P1 Emma, handsome, comfortable;
P2: most affectionate daughter</td><td>(A) happily, loving</td><td>Both P1 & P2 depict Positive characteristics and environment of the main Character Emma.</td></tr>
<tr><td colspan="3">Incorrect Choices & Their Common Patterns</td></tr>
<tr><td>Evidence</td><td>Incorrect keywords</td><td>Incorrect Patterns</td></tr>
<tr><td rowspan="3">D) L8: “Her mother died too long ago” is a contradictory statement.</td><td>(B) governess, indifference</td><td rowspan="3">B), C) are not stated and also deviate from the main character descriptions in P1 and P2. Please refer to incorrect choice pattern #4 and #13.</td></tr>
<tr><td>(C) father’s wealth</td></tr>
<tr><td>(D) losing mother</td></tr>
<tr><td colspan="3">This question is also pretty much similar to the question #1, the main idea question.
The overall theme and tone of the first two paragraphs focus on the main character Emma, billowing full of sympathetic and positive tone For this reason, (B) and (C) become minor issues.
(D) is distraction because it rather focuses on “losing mother,” who in fact “died too long ago.”</td></tr>
</table>

Q3. Absolute Pattern 7: Understanding Attitude (Tone) Question		
Question Pattern: narrator indicates **Question Keyword (s):** nature, resulted in		
Step 1	Step 2	Step 3
Keywords from the Text	Keyword from answer	Tones / Concepts
L30: The real evils indeed of Emma's situation were the power of having rather too well of herself,	(B) self-satisfied	Negative / Active
Incorrect Choices & Their Common Patterns		
Evidence	Incorrect keywords	Incorrect Patterns
"power of having too well of herself" = self-satisfied. (A) is direct opposite perception from the passage context. (C) is Unrelated word usage. (D) is also Unrelated word usage. "inconsiderate" is more closely applied to a stupid person.	(A) despondent (C) friendless (D) inconsiderate	Negative / Passive Negative / Passive Negative / Passive

Q4. Absolute Pattern 11: Textual Evidence Question	
Question Pattern: best evidence **Question Keyword (s):** previous question	
C is the best answer	Please review the preceding question and answer explanations

Q5. Absolute Pattern 5: Word-in-Context Question		
Question Pattern: most nearly means **Question Keyword (s):** directed		
Step 1	Step 2	Step 3
Keywords from the Text	Keyword from answer	Tones / Concepts
L 26: Emma doing just what she liked; but directed chiefly **by her own.** Or guided by her instinct.	(C) guided	Active (Emma guides herself)
Incorrect Choices & Their Common Patterns		
Evidence	Incorrect keywords	Incorrect Patterns
*Please make sure who the agent is that controls the word-in-context. (A) Someone else should train Emma; (D) someone addresses for Emma (B) "aimed" is too literal expression, different from the figurative expression "directed"	(A) trained (B) aimed (D) addressed	Please refer to incorrect choice pattern #3 and #12
In WIC question, two patterns play the dominant roles: (1) Active-Passive (2) Figurative-Literal		

Q6. Absolute Pattern 5: Word-in-Context Question		
Question Pattern: most nearly means **Question Keyword (s):** want		
Step 1	Step 2	Step 3
Keywords from the Text	Keyword from answer	Tones / Concepts
L 54: want **(lack)** of Miss Taylor felt every hour ...	(B) lack	Negative / Passive
Incorrect Choices & Their Common Patterns		
Evidence	Incorrect keywords	Incorrect Patterns
The want of Miss Taylor would be felt every hour of every day. (B) "want" means lack or 'absence. (A),(C), (D) Antonym or opposite perception	(A) desire (C) requirement (D) request	Please refer to incorrect choice pattern #2 and #3.

Q7. Absolute Pattern Type 3: Inference Question		
Question Pattern: inferred **Question Keyword (s):** after Miss Taylor married she		
Step 1	Step 2	Step 3
Keywords from the Text	Keyword from answer	Tones / Concepts
L75: Emma was aware that great must be the difference between a Mrs. Weston only half a mile from them, and a Miss Taylor in the house; and with all her advantages, natural and domestic,	(B) fewer interaction	Negative/Physical concept. B) centers on Emma's Perspective
Incorrect Choices & Their Common Patterns		
Evidence	Incorrect keywords	Incorrect Patterns
Although this question asks Taylor's point of view, we should be Emma to understand the mood because Taylor doesn't explain her feeling, but Emma does. By calling Miss Taylor as "Mrs. Weston" we can observe how Emma feels isolated and separated from Miss Taylor.	(A) Mr. Woodhouse (C) more close friends (D) increased appreciation	A), C), D) describe Taylor's perspective, which is not stated at all in the passage.

Q8. Absolute Pattern 11: Textual Evidence Question
Question Pattern: best evidence Question Keyword (s): previous question
D is the best answer Please review the preceding question and answer explanations

Q9. Absolute Pattern Type 6: Analogy Question		
Question Pattern: situation, similar to **Question Keyword (s):** lines 83-91		
Step 1	Step 2	Step 3
Keywords from the Text	Keyword from answer	Tones / Concepts
L83: The evil of the actual disparity in their ages... his life, without activity of mind or body, he was a much older man	(B) younger one active	Physical
Incorrect Choices & Their Common Patterns		
Evidence	Incorrect keywords	Incorrect Patterns
(B) and Emma focus on physicality, younger and more active one. (A) "argument" is too extreme and mental concept. (C) focusing on the older scientist's superiority. (D) "enjoy same diversions" is direct opposite from Emma's situation.	(A) arguments (C) older, publish, more (D) enjoy same	Please refer to incorrect choice pattern #2. These are opposite concepts.

Q10. Absolute Pattern 5: Word-in-Context Question		
Question Pattern: most nearly means **Question Keyword (s):** plot		
Step 1	Step 2	Step 3
Keywords from the Text	Keyword from answer	Tones / Concepts
L9-Soviet people didn't plot building these networks	(C) plan	synonym/Mental concept
Incorrect Choices & Their Common Patterns		
Evidence	Incorrect keywords	Incorrect Patterns
In other words, Soviet people didn't plot (**think/conceive/plan**) of building these networks	(A) mark (B) form (D) claim	Please refer to incorrect choice pattern #12 and #17.

Words in the multiple choices in Word-in-Context question always apply the first definition from dictionary.
From this perspective, (A) and (B) become a one-, three-dimensional physical concept.
(C) is too extreme. The safe bet is not to choose any extreme word.

Q11. Absolute Pattern 4: Example Question		
Question Pattern: The references...primarily serve to **Question Keyword (s):** shoemaker		
Step 1	Step 2	Step 3
Keywords from the Text	Keyword from answer	Tones / Concepts
L30: They (new technologies) allow us to gain direct access to a worldwide community of others	(B) broad reach	Quantity
Incorrect Choices & Their Common Patterns		
Evidence	Incorrect keywords	Incorrect Patterns
B) "shoemaker," "programmer," and "apple farmer" are all parts of examples. The answer for the example question should normally be found in the right above/below the indicated lines in question. It's because that's where the topic sentence or the main purpose of the example is located.	(A) quality (C) trustworthy (D) limits	A), B) use Quality concept. D) uses Negative concept
*Please make sure the differences between (B) the degree of mass (quantity) and the degree of quality (A), (C), and (D). Please refer to incorrect choice pattern # 17: Quantity-Quality Concept		

Q12. Absolute Pattern 10: Understanding the Structure of the Passage		
Question Pattern: discussion primarily serves **Question Keyword (s):** 1960s		
Step 1	Step 2	Step 3
Keywords from the Text	Keyword from answer	Tones / Concepts
L6: Visitors to the Soviet Union in the 1960s...A vast informal economy driven by human relationships, dense networks of social connections through which people traded	(A) social networking	Positive
Incorrect Choices & Their Common Patterns		
Evidence	Incorrect keywords	Incorrect Patterns
1> The "social connections" is switched to "social networking" 2> This question asks the first sentence of the introduction paragraph, and asks how it primarily serves. Of course, it primarily serves (A) "to Introduce," "social connection (networking), " the main topic of the passage.	(B) technology (C) other countries (D) historical	Please refer to incorrect choice pattern #4 and #11.
As discussed in the previous question, the example sentence exists to support the topic or the main purpose of the paragraph found in the last sentence of the same paragraph.		

Q13. Absolute Pattern 5: Word-in-Context Question		
Question Pattern: most nearly means **Question Keyword (s):** post		
Step 1	Step 2	Step 3
Keywords from the Text	Keyword from answer	Tones / Concepts
L44: We can raise funds from individuals through websites that allow people to post descriptions of their projects	(A) publish	synonym
Incorrect Choices & Their Common Patterns		
Evidence	Incorrect keywords	Incorrect Patterns
Post = publish online All the other choices are not used as a synonym to "post online".	(B) transfer (C) assign (D) denounce	Please refer to incorrect choice pattern #7. Unrelated word

Q14. Absolute Pattern 5: Relationship Question		
Question Pattern: comparison, tended to **Question Keyword (s):** traditional organizations		
Step 1	Step 2	Step 3
Keywords from the Text	Keyword from answer	Tones / Concepts
L:71: previously large organizations perform, often efficiently, at lower cost	(D) more expensive	Negative
Incorrect Choices & Their Common Patterns		
Evidence	Incorrect keywords	Incorrect Patterns
Individual's technology empowered efficiency at lower cost, which was once more expensive in large organization. *It is pivotal to look at the argument from opposite perception. (B) "less regulation" is opposite to the line 71: "greater ease".	(A) innovative	Positive, Opposite
	(B) less regulation	Please refer to incorrect choice pattern #2.
	(C) less reliable	

Q15. Absolute Pattern 2: Textual Evidence Question	
Question Pattern: best evidence **Question Keyword (s):** previous question	
D is the best answer	Please review the preceding question and answer explanations

Q16. Absolute Pattern 8: Understanding Attitude (Point of View) Question [Category B]		
Question Pattern: author recognizes **Question Keyword (s):** counterargument		
Step 1	Step 2	Step 3
Keywords from the Text	Keyword from answer	Tones / Concepts
L85: Much has been written about how technology distances us ...I think those are important concerns.	(A) acknowledge risks	Primary concept
Incorrect Choices & Their Common Patterns		
Evidence	Incorrect keywords	Incorrect Patterns
"much has been written," forebodes the author's counterargument. This type of concession appears very often in the actual test. The answer to this type of tone should always be either (A) "acknowledge" or (B) "admitting."	(B) spend time	Please refer to incorrect choice pattern # 4,8.
	(C) 1960	
	(D) conceding	

Q17. Absolute Pattern 2: Textual Evidence Question	
Question Pattern: best evidence Question Keyword (s): previous question	
D is the best answer	Please review the preceding question and answer explanations

Q18. Absolute Pattern 10: Informational Graph Question	
Question Pattern: summarizes, the graph C is the best answer. This graph question does not require a reference from the reading passage.	
Incorrect Choices & Their Common Patterns	
Incorrect keywords	A) Unrelated word or Issue B) Incorrect value D) Future prediction cannot be the answer Many (70%) of the informational graph questions do Not require passage information. Please refer to incorrect choice pattern #4,7.
(A) computer, cell phone	
(B) tripled	
(D) likely to be	

Q19. Absolute Pattern 10: Informational Graph Question	
Question Pattern: graph **Question Keywords:** in 2012 D is the best answer. This graph question does not require a reference from the reading passage.	
Incorrect Choices & Their Common Patterns	
Evidence	Incorrect keywords
(A) Incorrect value	(A) out of proportion
(B) Incorrect value	(B) new upward
(C) Incorrect value	(C) peak

Q20. Absolute Pattern 10: Understanding the Structure of the Passage		
Question Pattern: passage is written **Question Keyword (s):** perspective, someone		
Step 1	Step 2	Step 3
Keywords from the Text	Keyword from answer	Tones / Concepts
Excerpt: This passage is adapted from Tina Hesman Saey, "Lessons from the Torpid." ©2012 by Society for Science & the Public. L75: but Fröbert hopes to find some protective molecule that could stave off hardened arteries in humans as well.	(C) knowledgeable	Primary concept
Incorrect Choices & Their Common Patterns		
Evidence	Incorrect keywords	Incorrect Patterns
1> Reading the excerpt is not waste of time but indispensable. Through the excerpt, we find that this informative passage is not likely written by someone who is not knowledgeable. Therefore, B) and D) are disqualified because even laymen could be a participant or an advocate. 2> When in doubt, read the conclusion. The very last sentence specifies that the passage focuses on human, not animal. Therefore, A) is incorrect.	(A) actively involved (B) cardiology (D) advocate, wildlife	Please refer to incorrect choice pattern # 4,6, and 9.

Q21. Absolute Pattern 8: Understanding the True Purpose		
Question Pattern: reasonable to conclude **Question Keyword (s):** main goal		
Step 1	Step 2	Step 3
Keywords from the Text	Keyword from answer	Tones / Concepts
L75: but Fröbert hopes to find some protective molecule that could stave off hardened arteries in humans as well.	(D) human diseases	Primary concept
Incorrect Choices & Their Common Patterns		
Evidence	Incorrect keywords	Incorrect Patterns
The above question explains this question too. Because the question asks "reasonable to conclude," we should also focus on the conclusion paragraph.	(A) squirrels (B) fat (C) exercise	Please refer to incorrect choice pattern #5

Q22. Absolute Pattern 11: Textual Evidence Question	
Question Pattern: best evidence	**Question Keyword (s): previous question**
A is the best answer	Please review the preceding question and answer explanations

Q23. Absolute Pattern 7: Understanding Attitude		
Question Pattern: tone	**Question Keyword (s):** quotations	
Step 1	Step 2	Step 3
Keywords from the Text	Keyword from answer	Tones / Concepts
L13: "You bring your own lunch with you."	(B) conversational	The tone is conversational and Positive
Incorrect Choices & Their Common Patterns		
Evidence	Incorrect keywords	Incorrect Patterns
All the other choices are negative tone.	(A) bleak (C) ominous (D) absurd	Please refer to incorrect choice pattern # 1

Q24. Absolute Pattern 5: Word-in-Context Question		
Question Pattern: most nearly means	**Question Keyword (s):** stores	
Step 1	Step 2	Step 3
Keywords from the Text	Keyword from answer	Tones / Concepts
L19: Bigger <u>fat stores</u> mean a greater chance of surviving	(B) reserves	Passive
Incorrect Choices & Their Common Patterns		
Evidence	Incorrect keywords	Incorrect Patterns
"store" has to be understood as a passive word because it is being stored. Nothing would actually store fat to bears. Given this conception, (A), (C), (D) are active and too literal	(A) preservatives (C) stacks (D) shelters	Please refer to incorrect choice pattern # 3

Q25. Absolute Pattern 2: Summary Question		
Question Pattern: What is hypothesis	**Question Keyword (s):** do not harden	
Step 1	Step 2	Step 3
Keywords from the Text	Keyword from answer	Tones / Concepts
L73: but the bears don't build up such artery-hardening streaks. "Our bears, they had nothing,"	(D) against hardened	Primary Concept
Incorrect Choices & Their Common Patterns		
Evidence	Incorrect keywords	Incorrect Patterns
<u>Transitional words or phrase such as "Not yet," or "but" always provide important clue, if not the answer.</u> A): it should change to "<u>despite of</u> increased plasma…" B) flipped over its cause-effect situation.	(A) increased plasma, flexible (B) pinches off hardening (C) exercise in short	Please refer to incorrect choice pattern # 8, 2, 4 respectively.

Q26. Absolute Pattern 11: Textual Evidence Question	
Question Pattern: best evidence	**Question Keyword (s): previous question**
D is the best answer	Please review the preceding question and answer explanations

Q27. Absolute Pattern 10: Informational Graph Question	
Question Pattern: graph **Question Keyword (s):** paragraph 10 A is the best answer. Keywords: Line 58: cholesterol high for humans This graph question require information from the reading passage.	
Line 58: Scandinavian brown bears spend the summer with plasma cholesterol levels considered high for humans; those values then increase substantially for hibernation	
Incorrect Choices & Their Common Patterns	
Incorrect keywords	Lines 58-62 point out several vocabularies used in the graph such as plasma cholesterol levels, high, humans, hibernation, etc. It also illustrates the graph situation. B), C), and D) Please refer to incorrect choice pattern #7
(B) zero exercise	
(C) sluggish circulation	
(D) heart attacks	

Q28. Absolute Pattern 10: Informational Graph Question	
Question Pattern: graph **Question Keyword (s):** hibernation effect on bears A is the best answer. Key point: only one, did not experience This graph question does not require information from the reading passage.	
Incorrect Choices & Their Common Patterns	
Incorrect keywords	
(B) only one, experienced	One bear did not show difference of plasma cholesterol during hibernation and active. B), C), and D) are all opposite to the graph. Please refer to incorrect choice pattern #2
(C) All	
(D) lowest	

Q29. Absolute Pattern 10: Understanding Structure of the Passage		
Question Pattern: structure	**Question Keyword (s):** first paragraph	
Step 1	Step 2	Step 3
Keywords from the Text	Keyword from answer	Tones / Concepts
L1: Problem of our age → L4: human life condition → L12: however, not to be deplored →	(B) position → Historical → advice →	Specific example is given Generalization is made Conclusion is presented
Incorrect Choices & Their Common Patterns		
Evidence	Incorrect keywords	Incorrect Patterns
The first paragraph starts with a specific example (the problem of our age), then it generalizes the issue (human life condition), and finally concludes with advice (not to be deplored)	(A) Personal (C) opposing, consensus (D) historical period	(A) No personal anecdote is presented (C) No opposing principle is presented (D) Insufficient Information Please refer to incorrect choice pattern # 6

Q30. Absolute Pattern Type 3: Inference Question		
Question Pattern: implies **Question Keyword (s):** ties of brotherhood		
Step 1	Step 2	Step 3
Keywords from the Text	Keyword from answer	Tones / Concepts
L1: problem of our age is the proper administration of wealth, that the ties of brotherhood may still bind together the rich and poor	(C) strained	Negative
Incorrect Choices & Their Common Patterns		
Evidence	Incorrect keywords	Incorrect Patterns
Line 1 describes the problem of our age (present) is that wealth administration between the rich and poor is NOT properly administered. In other words, it was better in the past. Therefore, (C) is the answer.	(A) fictitious (B) stronger (D) no longer	Please refer to incorrect choice pattern # 7,2,4 respectively.

Q31. Absolute Pattern 4: Example Question		
Question Pattern: as examples of **Keywords:** dwelling, dress		
Step 1	Step 2	Step 3
Keywords from the Text	Keyword from answer	Tones / Concepts
L9: there was little difference between the dwelling, dress, food, and environment of the chief and those of his retainers. . . .	(D) indications, differences	Primary concept
Incorrect Choices & Their Common Patterns		
Evidence	Incorrect keywords	Incorrect Patterns
The passage explicitly states the dwelling between the rich and the poor was little different in the past. The following sentence regrets such a situation still remains after the emergence of civilization, representing social division.	(A) more valued (B) necessities (C) all people entitled	(B), (C) the past only, not the present

Q32. Absolute Pattern Type 2: Inference Question		
Question Pattern: author describes as **Keywords:** houses of some		
Step 1	Step 2	Step 3
Keywords from the Text	Keyword from answer	Tones / Concepts
L16: It is essential, for the race that the houses of some should be homes for highest literature and the arts	(C) culture	Mental
Incorrect Choices & Their Common Patterns		
Evidence	Incorrect keywords	Incorrect Patterns
The passage states house (the physical concept) should provide a home for the arts (mental concept that preserve arts) "house" -the physical concept vs. "home"- mental concept.	(A) materials (B) size (D) guests	Please refer to incorrect choice pattern # 16

Q33. Absolute Pattern 2: Textual Evidence Question	
Question Pattern: best evidence Keywords: best evidence	
B is the best answer	Please refer to the preceding Answer explanations

Q34. Absolute Pattern 4: Example Question		
Question Pattern: author's uses phrase as an example of	**Keywords:** good old times	
Step 1	Step 2	Step 3
Keywords from the Text	Keyword from answer	Tones / Concepts
L20: Without wealth there can be no Maecenas. The "good old times" were not good old times.	(D) not share view	It summarize the author's point
Incorrect Choices & Their Common Patterns		
Evidence	Incorrect keywords	Incorrect Patterns
The author emphasizes the importance of wealth in modern times, betraying "good old times" has gone now. (A) "something said by people" refers to "good old times," for which Carnegie does not agree.	(A) advantage (B) replicates (C) division	Please refer to incorrect choice pattern # 7.

Q35 . Absolute Pattern 8: Understanding the True Purpose]		
Question Pattern: author's main point	**Keywords:** disadvantages, economic	
Step 1	Step 2	Step 3
Keywords from the Text	Keyword from answer	Tones / Concepts
L 66: <u>All intercourse between them is at an end. Rigid castes are formed, mutual ignorance breeds mutual distrust</u>	(C) divisions, categories	Negative, Mental
Incorrect Choices & Their Common Patterns		
Evidence	Incorrect keywords	Incorrect Patterns
The passage states the social division spawns neo-castes (hierarchy).	(A) culture (B) replicates (D) material	Please refer to incorrect choice pattern # 2,2,6 respectively.

Q36. Absolute Pattern 11: Textual Evidence Question	
Question Pattern: best evidence	**Keywords:** best evidence
D is the best answer	Please refer to the preceding Answer explanations

Q 37. Absolute Pattern 5: Word-in-Context Question [Category A: Content Question]		
Question Pattern: closest in meaning to	**Keywords:** in its train	
Step 1	Step 2	Step 3
Keywords from the Text	Keyword from answer	Tones / Concepts
L76~81: for it is, law...in development, ...brings improved conditions in its train.	(B) with	Primary Concept
Incorrect Choices & Their Common Patterns		
Evidence	Incorrect keywords	Incorrect Patterns
B) "in <u>its train" means process or with it</u>. <u>Some incorrect multiple options repeat the question instead of answering it</u>. (C), (D) repeat the question (A) is nonsensical	(A) before (C) anticipating (D) advancing	Please refer to incorrect choice pattern # 14

Q38. Absolute Pattern 2: Summary Question		
Question Pattern: The author suggests, **Keywords:** de-extinction...limited by		
Step 1	Step 2	Step 3
Keywords from the Text	Keyword from answer	Tones / Concepts
L 8: DNA may bring the animals back to life. Only species whose DNA is too old, such as dinosaurs.	(D) length, time	Synonym
Incorrect Choices & Their Common Patterns		
Evidence	Incorrect keywords	Incorrect Patterns
The author specifies the new tech. will be applicable to dinosaurs, for example; only the animal whose DNA is too old (A), (B), (C) Not stated in the passage	(A) scientists devote (B) contemporary (C) complexity	Please refer to incorrect choice pattern #4

Q39. Absolute Pattern 2: Textual Evidence Question	
Question Pattern: best evidence	**Keywords:** best evidence
B is the best answer	Please refer to the preceding Answer explanations

Q40. Absolute Pattern 5: Word-in-Context Question		
Question Pattern: most nearly means **Keywords:** deepest		
Step 1	Step 2	Step 3
Keywords from the Text	Keyword from answer	Tones / Concepts
L24: Just the thought of mammoths alive again invokes the wonder at its deepest level	(D) fundamental	Similar concept
Incorrect Choices & Their Common Patterns		
Evidence	Incorrect keywords	Incorrect Patterns
The author explains the undertaking is so sensational that it touches our emotional attachment (A), (B), (C): require practical, active, and direct involvement.	(A) engrossing (B) challenging (C) extensive	Please refer to incorrect choice pattern # 1and 2

Q41. Absolute Pattern 7: Understanding Attitude (Point of View) Question		
Question Pattern: The author primarily considers **Keywords:** shrinking biodiversity		
Step 1	Step 2	Step 3
Keywords from the Text	Keyword from answer	Tones / Concepts
L40: Species today are vanishing...that the trend has been called a sixth mass extinction, ...	(B) catastrophe	Negative
Incorrect Choices & Their Common Patterns		
Evidence	Incorrect keywords	Incorrect Patterns
Species, vanishing, great, mass extinction = catastrophe	(A) anomaly (C) curiosity (D) political	Please refer to incorrect choice pattern # 2 and 4.

Q42. Absolute Pattern 11: Textual Evidence Question	
Question Pattern: best evidence	**Keywords:** best evidence
A is the best answer	Please refer to the preceding Answer explanations

Q43 . Absolute Pattern 5: Word-in-Context Question		
Question Pattern: most nearly means **Keyword (s):** great		
Step 1	Step 2	Step 3
Keywords from the Text	Keyword from answer	Tones / Concepts
L37: Species today are vanishing great numbers—many from hunting	(C) large	Quantity
Incorrect Choices & Their Common Patterns		
Evidence	Incorrect keywords	Incorrect Patterns
This question simply asks **Quantity-Quality Concept** comparison Please refer to incorrect choice pattern # 17.	(A) lofty (B) wonderful (D) intense	All of them are quality.

Q44 . Absolute Pattern 4: Example Question		
Question Pattern: The reference serves mainly to **Keywords:** ferret, rhino		
Step 1	Step 2	Step 3
Keywords from the Text	Keyword from answer	Tones / Concepts
L 63: it could save endangered species. For example, extinct genes that lost a dangerous amount of genetic diversity, such as white rhino	(C) gene...compromised	Synonyms
Incorrect Choices & Their Common Patterns		
Evidence	Incorrect keywords	Incorrect Patterns
The passage uses these two animals as an example of species that have lost gene diversity or compromised. A) Unrelated issue B) Genetic diversity is the main issue, not the numbers of species	(A) extinct and living (B) dwindling numbers (D) new habitats	Please refer to incorrect choice pattern # 13

Q 45. Absolute Pattern 9: Relationships Question		
Question Pattern: between the two passages	**Question Keyword (s):** relationship	
Step 1	Step 2	Step 3
Keywords from the Text	Keyword from answer	Tones / Concepts
P1 (L7): Thanks, genetic P2 (L65): Such investigations, however	(B) P1: favorable P2: cautious	P1: Positive P 2: Negative
Incorrect Choices & Their Common Patterns		
Evidence	Incorrect keywords	Incorrect Patterns
L65: Such investigations, however,	(A) P1: political P2: advocate	P1:Not stated P2: Opposite
	(C) research study	P2: Opposite
	(D) P2: practical	P1: Positive P2: Positive

A paired passages in fact, more often than not, use a single article. SAT creators simply divide it by two passages: the first half of the passage including some introduction goes to Passage 1; some intro. with conclusion paragraph goes to Passage 2. Therefore, Passage 1 should always be more general and unilateral, while Passage 2 is more critical. Knowing this trick, the answer for this type of question tend to become quite straightforward.

Q46. Absolute Pattern 9: Relationships Question		
Question Pattern: author of passage 2 respond to 1	**Keyword (s):** prospect	
Step 1	Step 2	Step 3
Keywords from the Text	Keyword from answer	Tones / Concepts
(P1) L 22: profound news (P2) L59: lacks merit altogether	(C) concern, difficult problem	Passage 1 is Positive, while passage 2 is **Negative**
Incorrect Choices & Their Common Patterns		
Evidence	Incorrect keywords	Incorrect Patterns
In a paired passage question, passage 2 is almost always more serious, concerned, controversial, argumentative.	(A) approval	Opposite perception from the passage's tone
	(B) inevitable	This statement could be more close to P1, not P2
	(D) disdain	"Disdain" is improper language in informational passage like this one. Please refer to incorrect choice pattern # 12

Q47. Absolute Pattern 2: Textual Evidence Question	
Question Pattern: best evidence	**Keywords: best evidence**
A is the best answer	Please refer to the preceding Answer explanations

PSAT COLLEGE BOARD OFFICIAL GUIDE
WRITING AND LANGUAGE SECTION PATTERNS

Q1. Absolute Pattern 19: Redundant Error

Passage keywords: yearly, annually

	Choice	Explanation
	A) yearly, annually	Always Pick the Shortest One from the Multiple Choices! Not easy is making incorrect choice by reducing information. Adding a few words to make something wrong is a piece of cake. A), B), D) are all Redundancy error. Redundancy Error is harder than it may appear to be until looking at the answer. The easiest way to understand the Redundancy Error is to look for <u>the shortest one.</u>
	B) annually, each year	
√	**C) annually**	
	D) yearly, annually	

Q2. Absolute Pattern 4: Comparison

	Choice	Explanation
	A) big	(D) The meaning "primary" itself contains the superlative. 1> The phrase 'one of the' suggests the superlative is coming. (A) 'big' is not the superlative. (B), (C) 'things' is colloquial (a nonstandard language that can't be used) and also ambiguous.
	B) things	
	C) things	
√	**D) primary**	

Q3. Absolute Pattern 21: Subject-Verb, Noun, Pronoun Agreement

Passage keywords: American (singular)

	Choice	Explanation
	A) spend	C) The singular verb in the adjective clause 1> "the average American spend" modifies the subject "The hours," serving as an adjective clause. 2> Even though it is in the middle of the sentence working as an adjective for the main subject, it still needs to follow the subject-verb agreement. 4> "the average American" is singular (the singular subject in the adjective clause). 5> Therefore, the verb "spend" should be "spends." (the singular verb in the adjective clause) A) Plural B) The present perfect D) Passive
	B) have spent	
√	**C) spends**	
	D) are spent	

Q4. Absolute Pattern 7: Conjunction Error

Passage keywords: As long as, and

	Choice	Explanation
	A) As long as, and	Always find the main subject and the main verb no matter where they are! D) 'as long as' is subordinating conjunction. (e.g., as long as you stay) (D) the main subject "managers" connects with the following verb "should champion…"
	B) workers;	
	C) ,managers, should	
√	**D) workers,**	

<u>Finding an error that has no conjunction is easy, but an error having two conjunctions is paradoxically harder.</u>
(A) has two conjunctions: "as long as" and "and"
(B) A Semicolon functions as a conjunction, creating a double-conjunction error like (A)
(C) 1> The subject "manager" is separated from the verb "should" by a comma.
2> The subject and the verb can't be separated by a comma.

Q5. Absolute Pattern 11: Logical Sequence		
Passage keywords: [1] workers, lack of sleep [3] average American, 1970s [2] combat, problem [4] work efficiency		
Correct Sentence Sequence: [1] Topic (Main concern) => [3] Supporting details (Historical overview & Data) => [2] Analysis => [4] Solution		
	A) AS IT IS	[1] Topic (Main concern) => [2] Analysis => [3] Supporting details (Historical overview & Data) => [4] Solution
	B) before 1	[3] Supporting details (Historical overview & Data) => [1] Topic (Main concern) => [2] Analysis => [4] Solution
√	**C) after 1**	**Reviewing the sequence from backward is easier because identifying the conclusion is easier than identifying the introduction.**
	D) after 4	[1] Topic (Main concern) => [2] Analysis => [4] Solution => [3] Supporting details (Historical overview & Data)

*Finding Conclusion is always easier than finding introduction. Try to read backward (e.g., Sentence 4>3>2>1)

Q6. Absolute Pattern 1: Adding, Revising, Deleting, Retaining Information		
Passage keywords: adding (Positive)		
√	**A) benefit**	One of the major tricks applied in the Reading Section is to relying on the Positive-Negative value. That is, if the passage is Positive, the answer choice should never be Negative, vice versa. This simple rule is applied in Writing Section too and solves many difficult questions instantly. Only (A) is Positive B) Not stated in the passage (New info.) C), D): Negative
	B) methodology	
	C) No, not important	
	D) contradicts	

Q7. Absolute Pattern 1: Adding, Revising, Deleting, Retaining Information		
Passage keywords: long-term health		
	A) weekly attendance	In adding question, Always Pick the Choice with Very Specific, Not Generalized Neutral Words. Only B) is similar conception. A), D) Inconsistent with the question C) Not stated in the passage (New info.)
√	**B) lower risk, heart attack**	
	C) health, costs	
	D) employees, efficient	

Q8. Absolute Pattern 13: Parallel Structure		
Passage keywords: block, play, waking		
	A) waking	verb, verb, gerund
√	**B) wake**	Block (verb), play (verb), wake (verb) Always Pick the Shortest and the Simplest One!
	C) to wake	verb, verb, to-infinitive
	D) waking of	verb, verb, preposition

Q9. Absolute Pattern 15: Prepositional Idiom		
Passage keywords: "their workers" suggests more than three people		
	A) throughout	Extreme word usage. 'throughout means in every single part or person
√	**B) among**	**For more than three people/objects**
	C) between	For only two people/objects
	D) into	Preposition for direction (moving into somewhere or something)

Q10. Absolute Pattern 7: Conjunction Error		
Passage keywords: not only ~		
	A) and again	"not only ~ but also" cannot be replaced by any other combinations. * In more complex question, it changes or drops the preposition within the correlative conjunction. For example, (A) "not only to...but also" The correct form is "not only to...but also to..." (B) "not only to...but also in" (C) "not only...but also to" All of the above options are incorrect.
	B) but it	
	C) as also	
√	**D) but also**	

Q11. Absolute Pattern 1: Adding, Revising, Deleting, Retaining Information		
Passage keywords: successful leaders (positive)		
	A) AS IT IS	Do Not Pick Any New Information that is Not Mentioned in the Passage! Only D) is Positive. A) New information B), C): Inconsistent with the question
	B) overworked	
	C) employee schedules	
√	**D) embrace napping**	

Q12. Absolute Pattern 18: Punctuation Error		
Passage keywords: depends on, pollination, to increase		
	A) pollination—	"including honeybee pollination" is a quick interjection offset by a pair of commas. A) A comma and a dash combination is incorrect punctuation. B) A comma and a colon combination is incorrect punctuation. D) A comma and a semicolon combination is incorrect punctuation.
	B) pollination: this is	
√	**C) pollination,**	
	D) pollination;	

Q13. Absolute Pattern 21: Subject-Verb, Noun, Pronoun Agreement + 6: Confusing Words		
Passage keywords: importance (subject, singular)		
	A) highlights, affects	"The importance of bees" (the singular subject) + effect vs. affect B) The main subject is "importance" (singular), neither "bees" (plural) nor "The importance of bees" Therefore, the verb has to be singular "highlights" A) 'affect' is normally used as a verb, a double-verb error.
√	**B) highlights, effects**	
	C) highlight, effects	
	D) highlight, affects	

Q14. Absolute Pattern 17: Pronoun Error		
Passage keywords: 'They'		
	A) AS IT IS	B) The sentence starts with the modifier "known as ~." It introduces the main clause 'this Phenomenon....' A) is Pronoun error: New sentences in the new paragraph cannot start with a pronoun. A), C) created a new independent clause, unnecessary, ambiguous, and wordy. D) The noun "Colony" automatically becomes the subject, which is unacceptable as the main clause is following right after.
√	**B) known as**	
	C) **It is** known	
	D) Colony	

Rule #1: A Pronoun Cannot Start with the First Sentence in New Paragraph!
Rule #2: Always find the main subject and the main verb no matter where they are!

Q15. Absolute Pattern 9: Informational Graphs		
Passage keywords: exceeded 25%		
	A) exceeded 25%	70% of the Graph Questions Does Not Need a Passage Information 30% of the Graph Questions Needs a Passage Information All the graph questions in this PSAT Test required no passage information. B) This question does not need a reference from the passage.
√	**B) above, acceptable**	
	C) not changed	
	D) increased every year	A) 2011, Incorrect value (less than) C) Antonym or opposite perception D) Incorrect value (fluctuated every year)

Q16. Absolute Pattern 9: Informational Graphs		
Passage keywords: fell		*This question does not need a reference from the passage.
	A) fell	Antonym or opposite perception
	B) double	Incorrect value (less than double)
	C) acceptable	Incorrect value (more than acceptable)
√	**D) rose**	

Q17. Absolute Pattern 1: Adding, Revising, Deleting, Retaining Information		
Passage keywords: reasons that		
√	**A) reasons that**	A) This sentence functions as a topic sentence in this paragraph. (A) also correctly uses "reason ...that" idiom.
	B) and, there are	B) changes the original meaning by separating the original sentence using a conjunction 'and'
	C) reasons, why	
	D) delete	C) 1> Redundant error. 'reason' and 'why' are synonym. 2> As used in the original sentence, 'reason that' is the correct syntax. D) loses the topic sentence.

Q18. Absolute Pattern 1: Adding, Revising, Deleting, Retaining Information		
Passage keywords: neonicotinoids		
√	**A) support, previous sentence**	It applies the same keywords and add some more details to the previous sentence
	B) new idea	This sentence is not new as it repeats and further describes the previous sentence.
	C) place elsewhere	The sentence is the supporting details that is correctly located in here.
	D) contradict	It doesn't contradict the main idea

Q19. Absolute Pattern 10: Logical Expression			
A) scoffed	B) big deal	C) back burner	**D) ignored √**
(A), (B), (C) use colloquial (nonstandard or spoken) language			

Q20. Absolute Pattern 18: Punctuation Error + Pattern 16: Precision, Concision, Style		
Passage keywords: farmers, resorted (A complete sentence)		
	A) crops; when, being	Always pick the shortest one from the multiple choices! (C) 1> Always choose the most concise sentence from the options. 2> The most concise sentence means having no conjunction or dependent clause without losing the original meaning. 3> This is called simplification rule" 4> The option that usually starts with "an" is the answer under the simplification pattern.
	B) crops, this is	
√	**C) crops, an expensive**	
	D) crops; an expensive	
(A) has several errors: 1> a semicolon should carry a dependent clause, which is not applied to this sentence. 2> the subordinating conjunction 'when' cannot be used together with the semicolon. 3> the usage of 'being' suddenly changes from the active voice to the passive. (avoid an option that includes "being." Using "being" is good for nothing.) (B) 1> Comma splice 2> "this is" is ambiguous. (D) Semicolon error		

Q21. Absolute Pattern 14: Possessive Determiners and Possessive Noun Error		
Passage keywords: farmers (plural), dependence		
	A) they're	'they're' is the contraction of 'they are'
	B) there	'there' is an indicative pronoun to refer to a place
√	**C) their**	'their' is a plural possessive pronoun. 'their' indicates "other farmers" in the passage.
	D) its	'its' is a singular possessive pronoun

Q22. Absolute Pattern 1: Adding, Revising, Deleting, Retaining Information		
Passage keywords: CCD, decrease, pesticides.		
√	**A) CCD, decrease, pesticides**	The original sentence corresponds to the question's keyword 'future effort' positively. (A) 1> Positive 2> The question is seeking a positive prospect (B) Negative (C), (D) Not stated in the passage (New information) (D) focuses on Genetics. Also, they are not positive.
	B) devastating	
	C) other aspects	
	D) Genetic	

Q23. Absolute Pattern 18: Punctuation Error		
Passage keywords: Ferrua stood		
	A) stood,	A) A comma before "on the hillside" separates the subject 'Ferrur' from the verb 'stood,' B) semicolon C) dash make the same errors as (A) by creating an incomplete sentence.
	B) stood;	
	C) stood—	
√	**D) stood**	**stood on the hillside**

Q24. Absolute Pattern 15: Prepositional Idiom		
Passage keywords: dotted with		
√	**A) with**	'dotted with' is the correct idiom
B) inside C) for D) on		

Q25. Absolute Pattern 23: Transition Words for Supporting Detail, Contrast, and Consequence		
√	**A) for example**	A) <u>Look at the location of the question</u>. The question is placed right after the topic sentence, which normally functions as a supporting detail, which requires "for example."
	B) however,	
	C) by contrast	
	D) thereafter,	

Q26. Absolute Pattern 23: Transition Words for Supporting Detail, Contrast, and Consequence		
	A) Although	B) is grammatically correct by having a modifier before the main clause "a lunar guide…"
√	**B) Given that**	A) is used for concession or contrast.
	C) So	C) if "So" is used as a conjunction, the sentence should end with it. However, another sentence is following "a lunar guide…" Therefore, it is incorrect.
	D) delete	D) becomes incomplete sentence.

Q27. Absolute Pattern 1: Adding, Revising, Deleting, Retaining Information		
Passage keywords: First-century		
	A) Nature	The following sentence "First-century…" is a hint. The <u>topic sentence "not new"</u> can be used to describe the following <u>historical facts</u> and description. (A), (B), (D) are all unrelated words and issues
	B) all over the world	
√	**C) Farming... not new**	
	D) Talk of the Moon	

Q28. Absolute Pattern 1: Adding, Revising, Deleting, Retaining Information		
Question keywords: specific info. calendar		
	A) farm chores	<u>In adding information question, Always Pick the Choice with Very Specific Word, Not Generalized Neutral Words within the Existing topic.</u> (A), (B), (C) are too broad (vague).
	B) actions, farming	
	C) certain tasks	
√	**D) plant, weed, harvest**	Specific information

Q29. Absolute Pattern 14: Possessive Determiners and Possessive Noun Error		
	A) almanacs	<u>Noun cannot link another noun without a connector.</u> The original sentence "almanacs" and "editor" are both noun. (C) To link up, a possessive determiner an apostrophe and the letter '*s*' should be used.
	B) almanacs's	
√	**C) alamanac's**	
	D) almanacs'	

Q30. Absolute Pattern 19: Redundant Error

	Choice	Explanation
	A) skeptics, not sure	A), B), C) are all Redundancy error. 1> Redundancy Error is harder than it may appear to be until looking at the correct answer. 2> The easiest way to understand the Redundancy Error is to look from the sentence style: the most concise and precise statement. A), B), and C) literally write the definition of skeptics, which is not necessary at all.
	B) skeptics, yet convinced	
	C) skeptics—doubt	
√	**D) skeptics.**	

Q31. Absolute Pattern 17: Pronoun Error

Passage keywords: agriculture (subject, singular noun)

	Choice	Explanation
	A) their	D) "agriculture" is the only precedent for the pronoun that we can find from the preceding sentence. Therefore, A) and B) are removed. (D) is Singular possessive pronoun for agriculture
	B) those	
	C) it's	C) is contraction for 'it is'
√	**D) its**	

Q32. Absolute Pattern 1: Adding, Revising, Deleting, Retaining Information

Question keywords: reinforcing, also skepticism.

	Choice	Explanation
	A) supporters, wait verified	(D) Negative 1> The question is seeking a negative answer 2> The preceding and the following sentences are also negative. 3> Therefore, the options containing a positive tone, however related and tempting, should not be the answer. (A), (C) Positive (B) is redundant error. The same statement is already mentioned in the previous sentence.
	B) no sound, data	
	C) continue, farming	
√	**D) not fact**	

Q33. Absolute Pattern 1: Adding, Revising, Deleting, Retaining Information

Question keywords: importance, senses

	Choice	Explanation
√	**A) smell, fragrant**	Two keywords in (A) suggest the importance of senses
	B) photographs	B), C), D) are unrelated to the question 'supporting senses'
	C) takes, notes	
	D) soil preparation	

Q34. Absolute Pattern 1: Adding, Revising, Deleting, Retaining Information

Passage keywords: manuscript (Informative)

	Choice	Explanation
	A) detracts	Negative. The passage is not necessarily negative.
	B) No, previous sentence	It should not be deleted because it is informative to further support the previous sentence.
√	**C) defines term**	The underlined sentence further introduces the manuscript
	D) culinary artifact	Unrelated word or Issue

Q35. Absolute Pattern 23: Transition Words for Supporting Detail, Contrast, and Consequence		
Passage keywords: astonishing size (cause), challenge (effect)		
√	**A) because of**	'Because of' is used to relate cause and effect clauses
	B) regardless of	is used to contradict the previous text
	C) in contrast to	is used to contradict the previous text
	D) in addition to	is used to support the previous text

Q36. Absolute Pattern 19: Redundant Error		
	A) donation, University of Iowa	The phrase 'Because of...' emphasizes two elements: the size and the range of donation. (A), (B), (C) not only repeat the previously mentioned information — redundant errors—but also dilute the phrase emphasized by 'because of', eventually changing the original meaning
	B) donation, many culinary, artifacts	
	C) massive, donation, cookbooks	
√	**D) donations,**	

Q37. Absolute Pattern 7: Conjunction Error		
Passage keywords: happy to show, too delicate.		
	A) so	The conjunction for consequence
	B) for	The conjunction for cause-effect relations
	C) and	The conjunction for parallel structure
√	**D) but**	The conjunction for contrasting idea.

Q38. Absolute Pattern 17: Pronoun Error		
Passage keywords: volunteers (Third-person plural)		
	A) our	The precedent "volunteers" requires third-person plural form "their."
	B) his	
√	**C) their**	
	D) one's	

Q39. Absolute Pattern 10: Logical Expression		
The keyword in the passage: DIY		
	A) prosaic	Negative. Prosaic means boring
√	**B) simple**	The sentence requires a positive word.
	C) bare-bones	Negative. Colloquial (nonstandard) language
	D) protocols	Jargon. Unnecessarily special language considering the volunteers' simple tasks

Q40. Absolute Pattern 23: Transition Words for Supporting Detail, Contrast, and Consequence

Passage keywords: need, no expertise, puzzling

	A) moreover,	"easy" and "puzzling" show two sentences are contradicting to each other. Therefore, C) is the answer.
	B) therefore,	
√	**C) however,**	
	D) in short,	

Q41. Absolute Pattern 6: Confusing Words

	A) access of	
√	**B) access to**	'access to' is the correct form of idiom
	C) excess of	excess means extra
	D) excess to	

Q42. Absolute Pattern 24: Verb Tense / Voice Error

Passage keywords: recipes, don't (present), while

	A) had worked	B) 1> conjunction 'while' requires the same tense between the clauses. 2> Because the main clause is the present tense, the dependent clause should also use the present tense.
√	**B) work**	
	C) worked	(A) Past perfect tense (C) Past tense (D) is used to express possibility in the conditional clause
	D) could have worked	

Q43. Absolute Pattern 13: Parallel Structure

Passage keywords: three categories

√	**A) cheesecake, pie, pie,**	1> It uses the compound nouns 2> Under the compound noun, all the nouns should be considered as a single word without any interruption by a comma.
	B) almond, summer, mince,	
	C) cheesecake summer, mince	(B), (D) "almond" and "cheesecake" cannot be separated by a comma (C) "almond cheesecake" and "summer mince pie" should be separated by comma
	D) almond, cheesecake, summer, mince,	

Q44. Absolute Pattern Type 1: Adding, Revising, Deleting, Retaining Information

	A) after 1	The passage keywords: (A) library (B) cooking manuscript (C) 1800s (D) Fair, contestants
	B) after 2	
	C) after 3	The question keywords "the judges" and "delicious" match with the sentence sequence 1=> 2=> 3=> 4.
√	**D) after 4**	It is always essential to read from the backward order 4>3>2>1 because finding the concluding sentence is lot easier than finding the introduction sentence.

SAT COLLEGE BOARD OFFICIAL TEST
READING SECTION
PATTERN ANALYSIS

To download the test, please visit:
https://collegereadiness.collegeboard.org/pdf/sat-nmsqt-practice-test-1.pdf

The SAT Official Test is the property of the College Board.
Due to the copyright, the original text is extensively condensed and applied synonyms instead of using the original words.
To understand the full concept of this analysis, it is critical to study the previous chapters including the seven practice tests before you proceed.

Q 1. Absolute Pattern 10: Understanding the Structure of the Passage		
Question Pattern: what happens		
Step 1	Step 2	Step 3
Keywords from the Text	Keyword from answer	Tones / Concepts
Line 1. "came directly, breaking all…."	B) surprising request	Same tone
Incorrect Choices & Their Common Patterns		
Evidence	Incorrect keywords	Incorrect Patterns
1> This passage is literature genre. 2> The question "what happens," sounds like asking the main idea 3> that requires the holistic understanding of the entire passage. Therefore, we should focus on the conclusion and the topic. 4> The literature passage, however, does not provide a clear-cut conclusion. Therefore, we should focus on the introduction. 5> The four multiple choices in fact turn out to be asking the structure of the whole passage	A) argues C) reminisces D) criticizes	A), D) are Negative. C) the passage uses the present tense and describes present moment.

Please refer to incorrect choice pattern #1 and #5.
By observing the tone in the introduction, we can simply eliminate A) and D).
C): Focus on tone and the verb tense between the intro and the conclusion paragraphs to see if there's any monologue, flashback or tense shift.
Most of all, this question is the universal type question that requires a comprehensive understanding of the entire passage. It is best to save this question till the end and come back to it after solving all the other questions.

Q 2. Absolute Pattern 10: Understanding the Structure of the Passage		
Question Pattern: developmental pattern		
Step 1	Step 2	Step 3
Keywords from the Text	Keyword from answer	Tones / Concepts
Line 16: Who is it at this hour	B) encounter	Encounter between two main characters
Incorrect Choices & Their Common Patterns		
Evidence	Incorrect keywords	Incorrect Patterns
The question "developmental pattern" contains the neutral tone within. In other words, if the tone is too polarizing like C) or D), that would be only a part of developmental patterns. We should find more neutral keywords from the multiple choices that support the entire patterns.	A) analysis, traditional C) definitive D) cheerful	A) the term 'analysis' doesn't fit to literature genre. C), D) are too extreme word usage. Please refer to incorrect choice pattern #12

Q3. Absolute Pattern 5: Word-In-Context Question		
Question Pattern: most nearly means **Question Keywords:** directly		
Step 1	Step 2	Step 3
Keywords from the Text	Keyword from answer	Tones / Concepts
Line 65: ask directly because use of a go-between takes time	C) no mediation	Similar conception
Incorrect Choices & Their Common Patterns		
Evidence	Incorrect keywords	Incorrect Patterns
"go-between," in other words, Akira should have come through mediation (someone's help or indirectly). The context clarifies that the word "directly" is used as the synonym of without "go-between"	A) frankly B) confidently D) precision	A), B) , C) all interpret "directly" as a part of speech.

Q4. Absolute Pattern 9: Relationships Question		
Question Keyword: reaction, Akira fear		
Step 1	Step 2	Step 3
Keywords from the Text	Keyword from answer	Tones / Concepts
Line 1: breaking all tradition L57: Akira blushed. Depending on your response.	(A) proposal inappropriate	Akira's main concern is shown in P1.
Incorrect Choices & Their Common Patterns		
Evidence	Incorrect keywords	Incorrect Patterns
1> The question asks "Which reaction does "Akira" fear from Chie, not the other way around. 2> Therefore, we should focus on how the narrator mainly portrays the mindset of Akira, not Chie, for how he concerns about the reaction of Chie. 3> The tone of Akira, when asking for a marriage and his abrupt visit, is nothing but concern for his inappropriate appearance and marriage proposal.	(B) immaturity (C) unscheduled visit (D) underestimate sincerity	B), D) are what Chie said in lines 49-52 Please refer to the incorrect choice pattern #8, #13. C) is minor issue. Please refer to the incorrect choice pattern #5.

Q5. Absolute Pattern 11: Textual Evidence Question	
Question Pattern: best evidence	**Keywords:** best evidence
C is the best answer	Please refer to the preceding Answer explanations

Q6 . Absolute Pattern 7: Understanding Attitude (Tone) Question		
Question Keywords: Akira address Chie		
Step 1	Step 2	Step 3
Keywords from the Text	Keyword from answer	Tones / Concepts
L 1: breaking all tradition	(D) respect, deference	Please consider two characters' relation.
Incorrect Choices & Their Common Patterns		
Evidence	Incorrect keywords	Incorrect Patterns
Akira came to see Chie, the mother of his love Naomi. But he broke all tradition in a way to propose for marriage. Therefore, the attitude must be something between respect and deference.	(A) love (B) objectivity (C) mocking	A) Akira loves Chie's daughter. B) In literature genre Do Not Choose 'objective' tone, such as analysis or objectivity. C) is from Chie in line 49. Please refer to incorrect choice pattern #13

Q 7. Absolute Pattern 1: Main Idea Question		
Question Pattern: main purpose, first paragraph		
Step 1	Step 2	Step 3
Keywords from the Text	Keyword from answer	Tones / Concepts
Akira came directly, breaking all tradition. Was that it? Had he followed...receptive?	(D) reaction	Please be careful that the question centers on the narrator's view, not the character Akira.
Incorrect Choices & Their Common Patterns		
Evidence	Incorrect keywords	Incorrect Patterns
Akira's introspection in P1 is analyzed by the narrator, not the character Akira.	(A) culture (C) criticize (D) suggestion	A) is shifting the focus B), C) are not stated. Please refer to incorrect choice pattern #4 and #13.

Q 8. Absolute Pattern 5: Word-In-Context Question		
Question Pattern: form		
Step 1	Step 2	Step 3
Keywords from the Text	Keyword from answer	Tones / Concepts
Akira came directly, breaking all tradition. Was that it? Had he followed form..	(B) custom	Synonym
Incorrect Choices & Their Common Patterns		
Evidence	Incorrect keywords	Incorrect Patterns
The clue word is "tradition," which he did not follow by "breaking all tradition" The passage suggests he should have followed form or not breaking all tradition. (B) custom means tradition	(A) appearance (C) structure (D) nature	A), C), and D) are unrelated and too literal usage. Please refer to incorrect choice pattern # 7

Q 9. Absolute Pattern 2: Summary Question		
Question Keyword (s): matter of urgency		
Step 1	Step 2	Step 3
Keywords from the Text	Keyword from answer	Tones / Concepts
Line 39: I've received word of a position	(C) job	Synonym
Incorrect Choices & Their Common Patterns		
Evidence	Incorrect keywords	Incorrect Patterns
The passage is about Akira's marriage proposal. He describes the reason for his abrupt appearance due to the job offer he received.	(A) parents (C) someone else (D) Chie	A), C), and D) are not at all stated in the passage. Please refer to incorrect choice pattern #4.

Q10. Absolute Pattern 11: Textual Evidence Question	
Question Pattern: best evidence	**Keywords:** best evidence
B is the best answer	Please refer to the preceding Answer explanations

Q11. Absolute Pattern 4: Example Question.		
Question Pattern: the authors use the example to		
Step 1	Step 2	Step 3
Keywords from the Text	Keyword from answer	Tones / Concepts
Lines 1-9: Every day, millions, Last year, This frequent	(A) regularity	The keywords explains it.
Incorrect Choices & Their Common Patterns		
Evidence	Incorrect keywords	Incorrect Patterns
Every day, millions of shoppers.... Last year, Americans spent, holiday gifts, most people regularly buy... The question asks us to summarize the examples in lines 1-9. The answer for the example question is normally located right after/before the example sentences.	(B) recent increase (C) anxiety (D) number	Please refer to incorrect choice pattern #10. All the incorrect choices simply repeat the contexts from the example.

Q 12. Absolute Pattern 5: Word-In-Context Question		
Question Pattern: most nearly means	**Keyword:** ambivalent	
Step 1	Step 2	Step 3
Keywords from the Text	Keyword from answer	Tones / Concepts
L10: Many relish, At the same time, many dread	(B) conflicted	The keywords explains the conflict
Incorrect Choices & Their Common Patterns		
Evidence	Incorrect keywords	Incorrect Patterns
ambi (two) val (value) = conflicted or undecided.	(A) unrealistic (C) apprehensive (D) supportive	A), C) Please refer to incorrect choice pattern #12 D) Please refer to incorrect choice pattern #1.

Q13. Absolute Pattern 7: Understanding Attitude (Tone) Question		
Question Pattern: authors indicate	**Keywords**: people value gift-giving	
Step 1	Step 2	Step 3
Keywords from the Text	Keyword from answer	Tones / Concepts
Line 10: Many relish the opportunity, powerful means, stronger bonds.	(D) strengthen, relationship	The question is Positive. Therefore, it requires the positive answer.
Incorrect Choices & Their Common Patterns		
Evidence	Incorrect keywords	Incorrect Patterns
All the other choices are negative in one way or another that deviates from the question's positive tone "people value gift-giving"	(A) self-expression (B) inexpensive (C) requires, reciprocate	A), B), C) Please refer to incorrect choice pattern #1.

Q14. Absolute Pattern 11: Textual Evidence Question	
Question Pattern: best evidence	
A) is the best answer	Please refer to the preceding Answer explanations

Q15. Absolute Pattern 7: Understanding Attitude (Tone) Question		
Question Pattern: would likely describe as	Keywords: deadweight loss, social psychologists	
Step 1	Step 2	Step 3
Keywords from the Text	Keyword from answer	Tones / Concepts
L30: That is not surprising to social psychologists	(A) predictable	Synonym
Incorrect Choices & Their Common Patterns		
Evidence	Incorrect keywords	Incorrect Patterns
not surprising = predictable. Only (A) follows the same tone with the keyword "not surprising." All the other choices are moving to opposite direction.	(B) questionable (C) disturbing (D) unprecedented	B), C), D) Please refer to incorrect choice pattern #1 and #2.

Q16. Absolute Pattern 7: Understanding Attitude (Tone) Question		
Question Pattern: passage, indicates Keywords: assumption by gift-givers		
Step 1	Step 2	Step 3
Keywords from the Text	Keyword from answer	Tones / Concepts
L30: That is not surprising to social psychologists	(C) incorrect	Most logical and analytic tone
Incorrect Choices & Their Common Patterns		
Evidence	Incorrect keywords	Incorrect Patterns
In informational passage like this one, objective tone like (C) is almost always the answer. (A) and (B) are subjective and personal tone, therefore, incorrect. <u>The tone of line 30 betrays Objective and Negative.</u>	(A) insincere (B) unreasonable (D) substantiated	A), B) , Please refer to incorrect choice pattern #11 and #12 D) Please refer to incorrect choice pattern #2.

Q17. Absolute Pattern 11: Textual Evidence Question	
Question Pattern: best evidence **Keywords:** best evidence	
C is the best answer	Only C) describes (responds to) the gift-receiver's reaction. A), B), D) are about gift-givers.

Q 18. Absolute Pattern 5: Word-In-Context Question		
Question Pattern: most nearly means **Keyword:** convey		
Step 1	Step 2	Step 3
Keywords from the Text	Keyword from answer	Tones / Concepts
Line 54: Gifts convey stronger <u>signals of thoughtfulness</u>	(D) communicate	Similar mental conception
Incorrect Choices & Their Common Patterns		
Evidence	Incorrect keywords	Incorrect Patterns
<u>"signal" or "thoughtfulness" indicates "convey" is used as a mental conception</u> meaning sending or communicating, not a physical conveyance such as transport or exchange. B) is not even related to convey.	(A) transport (B) counteract (C) exchange	A), C) Please refer to incorrect choice pattern #16 B) Please refer to incorrect choice pattern #2

Q 19. Absolute Pattern 4: Example Question		
Question Pattern: authors, refer to, in order to **Keywords:** Camerer		
Step 1	Step 2	Step 3
Keywords from the Text	Keyword from answer	Tones / Concepts
According to Camerer	(A) offer, explanation	Bringing authorities has only one purpose: offering an explanation.
Incorrect Choices & Their Common Patterns		
Evidence	Incorrect keywords	Incorrect Patterns
To further explain or backup his argument, the author normally employs authorities such as scholars. <u>This type of question is very typical and (A) is always the answer.</u>	(B) argument (C) question (D) conclusion	B), C) Please refer to incorrect choice pattern #2 D) the sentence is located in the middle of the passage, not in the conclusion.

Q20. Absolute Pattern 12: Informational Graphs
Question Pattern: the graph **Keywords:** gift-givers, base prediction, appreciated on
B) is the best answer *This question is an independent type graph question and does not require passage information. Therefore, you don't need to waste time to re-read the passage.

Q 21. Absolute Pattern 12: Informational Graphs		
Question Pattern: represented in the graph **Keywords:** differences in gift-giver and recipient		
Step 1	Step 2	Step 3
Keywords from the Text	Keyword from answer	Tones / Concepts
Line 79: People spend hundreds of dollars, but somehow never learn	(A) inability, perspective	Similar mental conception
Incorrect Choices & Their Common Patterns		
Evidence	Incorrect keywords	Incorrect Patterns
When in doubt, read the conclusion, especially the last sentence of the passage to note the gist of a tone, clue words or essence. The last sentence describes people's inability to shift perspective.	(B) materialistic (C) opposition (D) misunderstanding	B), C) Please refer to incorrect choice pattern #4 and #16. D) Please refer to incorrect choice pattern #9. There's no "misunderstanding"

Q 22. Absolute Pattern 2: Summary Question Summarizing a sentence, or an entire paragraph		
Question Pattern: authors, to indicate **Keywords:** backbone		
Step 1	Step 2	Step 3
Keywords from the Text	Keyword from answer	Tones / Concepts
L3: Backbone, consists, regular, sugar and phosphate. Backbone is completely regular	(B) main structure, repeating	The passage focuses on "regulate" (regulation of) sugar and phosphate.
Incorrect Choices & Their Common Patterns		
Evidence	Incorrect keywords	Incorrect Patterns
A) focuses more on "organism," which is not stated in the passage. B): avoid Too extreme word choice. C) the passage focuses on sugar and phosphate	(A) organism (C) entirely (D) nitrogenous	A) Please refer to incorrect choice pattern #8 C) Please refer to incorrect choice pattern #12 D) Please refer to incorrect choice pattern #2

Q 23. Absolute Pattern 3: Inference Question Finding an indirect suggestion (or guessing)		
Keywords: nitrogenous bases pair randomly, contradicts		
Step 1	Step 2	Step 3
Keywords from the Text	Keyword from answer	Tones / Concepts
L27: A pair must be a purine and the other Pyrimidine, to bridge between the two.	(D) a pair must be	The key point is about how nitrogenous base pairs. D) describes the question's contradiction.
Incorrect Choices & Their Common Patterns		
Evidence	Incorrect keywords	Incorrect Patterns
A),B) focus more on "sugar" C) focuses on hydrogen bonds	(A) sugar (B) irregular (C) hydrogen bonds	A), B), C) Please refer to incorrect choice pattern #8

Q 24. Absolute Pattern 2: Summary Question Summarizing a sentence, or an entire paragraph		
Question Pattern: authors claim **Keywords:** biological interest		
Step 1	Step 2	Step 3
Keywords from the Text	Keyword from answer	Tones / Concepts
L14: Biological interest, consists not one, but two	(D) two chains	D) paraphrases the context
Incorrect Choices & Their Common Patterns		
Evidence	Incorrect keywords	Incorrect Patterns
The question and the answer (D) succinctly summarizes the passage.	(A) chemical formula (B) fiber (C) X-ray	A), B), C) Please refer to incorrect choice pattern #7. These are all unrelated words to the question.

Q 25. Absolute Pattern 4: Example Question		
Question Pattern: authors, main purpose **Keywords:** X-ray		
Step 1	Step 2	Step 3
Keywords from the Text	Keyword from answer	Tones / Concepts
L18: <u>However,</u> X-ray evidence, suggests, there are two.	(C) support authors, number of chains	The <u>author uses X-ray to support his argument</u> that presents the number of chains is two.
Incorrect Choices & Their Common Patterns		
Evidence	Incorrect keywords	Incorrect Patterns
Consider only B) or C) as possible answers. The question starts with "authors…supports…main purpose." <u>The question reveals itself the answer should be either **(C)** or (B).</u>	(A) DNA is molecule (B) alternate hypothesis (D) density of DNA	B) Please refer to incorrect choice pattern #8 A),D) Please refer to incorrect choice pattern #7. B) is exactly opposite perception A),D) are unrelated words usage

Q 26. Absolute Pattern 3: Inference Question Finding an indirect suggestion (or guessing)		
Question Pattern: implies that **Keywords:** if a pair, there wouldn't be room for it		
Step 1	Step 2	Step 3
Keywords from the Text	Keyword from answer	Tones / Concepts
L27: A pair must be a purine and the other Pyrimidine, to bridge between the two.	(B) purines, larger, than, purine, pyrimidine	The key point is about pairing purines and pyrimidine <u>to make room</u>.
Incorrect Choices & Their Common Patterns		
Evidence	Incorrect keywords	Incorrect Patterns
A),C), D) all do not mention about pairing between purines and pyrimidines. And they won't "make room."	(A) sugar (C) pyrimidines, purines (D) a pair of pyrimidines	A), C) Please refer to incorrect choice pattern #7. D) Please refer to incorrect choice pattern #2. D) is the direct opposite

Q 27. Absolute Pattern 2: Summary Question Summarizing a sentence, or an entire paragraph		
Question Pattern: authors, functions mainly to **Keywords:** exact, specific, complement		
Step 1	Step 2	Step 3
Keywords from the Text	Keyword from answer	Tones / Concepts
Lines 45-56: If the actual order, given, one could write down exact order, how duplicate itself	(D) emphasize, to be copied, replication	D) simply paraphrases the context
Incorrect Choices & Their Common Patterns		
Evidence	Incorrect keywords	Incorrect Patterns
The answer (D) and the passage are almost similar expression.	(A) confirm, sequences are known (B) counter the claim (C) authors' model	A), C) Please refer to incorrect choice pattern #7. They are unrelated words to the question B) Please refer to incorrect choice pattern #2. B) is direct opposite.

Q 28. Absolute Pattern 12: Informational Graphs		
Question Pattern: the table, the correct percentages **Keywords**: purines, yeast		
Step 1	Step 2	Step 3
Keywords from the Text	Keyword from answer	Tones / Concepts
Line 6: adenine and guanine, purines thymine and cytosine, pyrimidines	(C) 18.7%, 31.3%	(C) shows the exact numbers. Only the order is reversed to confuse.
(A) 17.1%, 18.7%	(B) 17.1%, 32.9%	(D) 31.3%, 32.9%

Q 29. Absolute Pattern 2: Summary Question Summarizing a sentence, or an entire paragraph		
Question Pattern: support the authors **Keywords:** pairing of bases in DNA		
Step 1	Step 2	Step 3
Keywords from the Text	Keyword from answer	Tones / Concepts
Line 6: adenine and guanine, purines thymine and cytosine, pyrimidines. Line 27: one member, must be purine, the other, pyrimidine	(A) Yes, adenine closest, thymine	Important point is that only certain pairs fit into the structure.
Incorrect Choices & Their Common Patterns		
Evidence	Incorrect keywords	Incorrect Patterns
B) is correct in responding "Yes" as is (A). However, the percentage of adenine should be closest to Thymine, and guanine to cytosine.	(B) adenine closest, guanine (C) No (D) No	C), D) incorrectly respond as "No. "

Q 30. Absolute Pattern 12: Informational Graphs		
Question Pattern: the table, the correct percentages **Keywords**: base percentages, sea urchin		
Step 1	Step 2	Step 3
Keywords from the Text	Keyword from answer	Tones / Concepts
Line 6: adenine and guanine, purines thymine and cytosine, pyrimidines	(A) 17.3%, 17.7%	(A) shows the exact numbers as described in lines 6-8 The other choices mixed up their pairings.
(B) 17.3%, 32.1%	(C) 17.3%, 32.8%	(D) 17.7%, 32.8%

Q 31. Absolute Pattern 2: Summary Question Summarizing a sentence, or an entire paragraph		
Question Pattern: table, authors, consistent with **Keywords:** percentage of adenine		
Step 1	Step 2	Step 3
Keywords from the Text	Keyword from answer	Tones / Concepts
Lines 41-45: long molecule many different permutations are possible	(D) It varies	D) ,by using a word "varies," corresponds to "many different" in the passage and only (D) states the reason.
Incorrect Choices & Their Common Patterns		
Evidence	Incorrect keywords	Incorrect Patterns
The question asks two things: whether each organism's DNA on the table has the same percentage of adenine (NO) and states the response as (D)	(A) The same (B) The same (C) Adenine, thymine	A), B) Please refer to incorrect choice pattern #2. They are directly opposite. B), C) discuss the relations between Adenine and Thymine, unrelated items.

Q 32. Absolute Pattern 1: Main Idea Question Finding the main idea of the entire passage or the paragraph		
Question Pattern: The main purpose of the passage		
Step 1	Step 2	Step 3
Keywords from the Text	Keyword from answer	Tones / Concepts
Line 48: very important questions, we have very little time. Line 57: the moment is short	(B) urgency of issue	As you can see, even the main purpose question relies heavily on tones. The last sentence emphasizes its tone by repeating the parallel sentence structure.
Incorrect Choices & Their Common Patterns		
Evidence	Incorrect keywords	Incorrect Patterns
Compared to incorrect choice (C), the answer (B) does not specify which "issue" is urgent, and by doing so avoids using incorrect words, yet still emphasizes the main point of the Passage.	(A) value of tradition (C) social divisions (D) question feasibility	A), D) Please refer to incorrect choice pattern #2. The author wants to sever tradition (patriarchy). The word "question" is direct opposite concept. (C) Please refer to incorrect choice pattern #6. "social divisions" is too broad, therefore, insufficient information to be the answer.

Q 33. Absolute Pattern 1: Main Idea Question Finding the main idea of the entire passage or the paragraph		
Question Pattern: the central claim of the passage		
Step 1	Step 2	Step 3
Keywords from the Text	Keyword from answer	Tones / Concepts
Line 48: they are very important questions; and we have very little time in which to answer them.	(A) women face a decision	A) corresponds the tone of urgency and the central claim of the passage.
Incorrect Choices & Their Common Patterns		
Evidence	Incorrect keywords	Incorrect Patterns
The question asks central claim of the passage which must include a word "women" and also "urgency."	(B) only if they give up (C) the male monopoly (D) transform positions	B),D) Please refer to incorrect choice pattern #4. (B), (D) are not stated info. C) doesn't mention about women. Please refer to incorrect choice pattern #6.

Q 34. Absolute Pattern 8: Understanding the True Purpose Finding the true purpose of statement		
Question Pattern: uses the word throughout the passage to **Keyword:** we		
Step 1	Step 2	Step 3
Keywords from the Text	Keyword from answer	Tones / Concepts
Line 72: Think we must. Let us think in …	(C) solidarity	C) "solidarity" corresponds to the main tone of the passage.
Incorrect Choices & Their Common Patterns		
Evidence	Incorrect keywords	Incorrect Patterns
Throughout the passage the author's tone is emphatic and urgent to emphasize "solidarity."	(A) friendliness (B) candor (D) respect	A), B), D) Please refer to incorrect choice pattern #7. All these words are not related to the tone in the passage.

Q 35. Absolute Pattern 3: Inference Question Finding an indirect suggestion (or guessing)		
Question Pattern: the setting **Keyword:** bridge		
Step 1	Step 2	Step 3
Keywords from the Text	Keyword from answer	Tones / Concepts
Line 1: a bridge over the River Thames, an admirable vantage ground for us to make a survey.	(B) provides a view	The contexts near bridge contain physical words like "vantage ground" or "make survey." These keywords imply that the author uses bridge as a physical concept.
Incorrect Choices & Their Common Patterns		
Evidence	Incorrect keywords	Incorrect Patterns
The cluewords "vantage ground" show how the word "bridge" is actually used here.	(A) fanciful (C) historic (D) legacy	A), C), D) Please refer to incorrect choice pattern #16. All these incorrect keywords allude mental conception.

Q 36. Absolute Pattern 3: Inference Question Finding an indirect suggestion (or guessing)		
Question keyword: procession		
Step 1	Step 2	Step 3
Keywords from the Text	Keyword from answer	Tones / Concepts
Line 23: trespassing along at the tail end of the procession, we go....	(D) less exclusionary	"trespassing" and "we go ourselves" = less exclusionary.
Incorrect Choices & Their Common Patterns		
Evidence	Incorrect keywords	Incorrect Patterns
Some questions like this one can be solved more easily by using the next textual evidence question.	(A) practical (B) celebrated feature (C) all richest, powerful	A),B) Please refer to incorrect choice pattern #1. The central tone of the passage is solemn. (A), (B) are positive tone. C) is not mentioned. Please refer to incorrect choice pattern #4.

Q37. Absolute Pattern 11: Textual Evidence Question Finding evidence for the previous question
Question Pattern: best evidence
C) is the best answer Please refer to the preceding Answer explanations

Q 38. Absolute Pattern 1: Main Idea Question Finding the main idea of the entire passage or the paragraph		
Question Pattern: Woolf (the author) characterizes the questions as		
Step 1	Step 2	Step 3
Keywords from the Text	Keyword from answer	Tones / Concepts
Line 53:For we have to ask ourselves, here and now (MOMENTOUS), do we wish to join or don't we? (PRESSING)	(C) momentous, pressing	C) completely summarizes using two words with grave tones.
Incorrect Choices & Their Common Patterns		
Evidence	Incorrect keywords	Incorrect Patterns
Line 48: And they are very important questions; and we have very little time in which to answer them.	(A) threatening (B) unanswerable (D) mysterious	A), B), D) Please refer to incorrect choice pattern #7. All these words are not related to the tone of the passage.

Q39. Absolute Pattern 11: Textual Evidence Question Finding evidence for the previous question
Question Pattern: best evidence
B) is the best answer Please refer to the preceding Answer explanations Choice C) is incorrect. Please refer to incorrect choice pattern # 6. (C) is less correct because info. is insufficient by answering only one answer, while (B) provides two answers.

Q 40. Absolute Pattern 3: Inference Question Finding an indirect suggestion (or guessing)		
Question Pattern: meaning, figurative **Keyword:** sixpence		
Step 1	Step 2	Step 3
Keywords from the Text	Keyword from answer	Tones / Concepts
Line 69: won us the right to our brand-new sixpence. how are we to spend six pence?	(C) opportunity	C) The main theme is women's opportunity. Six pence is used as a metaphor.
Incorrect Choices & Their Common Patterns		
Evidence	Incorrect keywords	Incorrect Patterns
The question asks central claim of the passage as well, which is women's opportunity that uses "six pence" as a metaphor	(A) Tolerance (B) knowledge (D) perspective	A), B), D) Please refer to incorrect choice pattern #7. All these words are not related to the tone of the passage.

Q 41. Absolute Pattern 1: Main Idea Question Finding the main idea of the entire passage or the paragraph		
Question Pattern: mainly serves to emphasizes		
Step 1	Step 2	Step 3
Keywords from the Text	Keyword from answer	Tones / Concepts
Line 72: Let us think in offices; in omnibuses, crowd, Shows, gallery, Courts, baptisms, marriages, funerals.	(B) pervasive	Pervasive = throughout and everywhere
Incorrect Choices & Their Common Patterns		
Evidence	Incorrect keywords	Incorrect Patterns
By using multiple places and situations, the author's tone draws emphatic, urgency, and also pervasiveness	(A) novel (C) complex (D) enjoyable	A), C), D) Please refer to incorrect choice pattern #7. All these words are not related to the tone of the passage.

Q 42. Absolute Pattern 4: Example Question		
Question Pattern: the author, primarily to	**Keyword:** several companies	
Step 1	Step 2	Step 3
Keywords from the Text	Keyword from answer	Tones / Concepts
Line 8: that are all working to make space mining a reality.	(B) growing interest	The example sentences themselves do not contain answer. The answer is located right before the example sentences where the author primarily suggests his concern
Incorrect Choices & Their Common Patterns		
Evidence	Incorrect keywords	Incorrect Patterns
D) although the example presents diverse companies and present many of their activities, this fact does not respond to the question: "primarily mention to"	(A) technological (C) profit (D) diverse ways	A), C) Please refer to incorrect choice pattern #4. D) Please refer to incorrect choice pattern #8.

Q 43. Absolute Pattern 2: Summary Question Summarizing a sentence, or an entire paragraph		
Question Pattern: the author of passage 1 indicates	**Keyword:** space mining, effect	
Step 1	Step 2	Step 3
Keywords from the Text	Keyword from answer	Tones / Concepts
Line 1: Follow money and you will end up in space.	(A) materials, economy	A) The central point of the passage is about generating money in space mining.
Incorrect Choices & Their Common Patterns		
Evidence	Incorrect keywords	Incorrect Patterns
The question asks central claim of the passage as well, which is how space mining generates economic gains.	(B) raise value (C) innovations (D) understanding	B), C), D) Please refer to incorrect choice pattern #5. All these words are minor concerns in the passage.

Q44. Absolute Pattern 11: Textual Evidence Question Finding evidence for the previous question	
Question Pattern: best evidence	
A) is the best answer	Please refer to the preceding Answer explanations

Q 45. Absolute Pattern 5: Word-In-Context Question		
Question Pattern: most nearly means	**Keyword:** demands	
Step 1	Step 2	Step 3
Keywords from the Text	Keyword from answer	Tones / Concepts
Line 19:firms maybe meeting earthly demands (NEEDS) for precious metals,	(D) desires	D) "demands" means "needs" or desire.
Incorrect Choices & Their Common Patterns		
Evidence	Incorrect keywords	Incorrect Patterns
All the other choices interpreted the word "demands" as some sort of questions.	(A) offers (B) claims (C) inquiry	A), B), C) Please refer to incorrect choice pattern #7. All these words are not related to the tone of the passage.

Q 46. Absolute Pattern 10: Understanding the Structure of the Passage		
Question Pattern: what function, serves	**Keyword:** water	
Step 1	Step 2	Step 3
Keywords from the Text	Keyword from answer	Tones / Concepts
Line 35: scenario, water mined from other worlds could become the most desired commodity	(C) offer examples, supporting, paragraph	"in this scenario" implies that the context is used to exemplify the previous statement.
Incorrect Choices & Their Common Patterns		
Evidence	Incorrect keywords	Incorrect Patterns
The question asks the structural relations between the example context (water) and the previous sentence.	(A) comparison (B) unexpected (D) outcome, proposal	A), B) D) Please refer to incorrect choice pattern #7. All these words are not related to the tone of the passage.

Q 47. Absolute Pattern 9: Relationships Question		
Question Pattern: central claim of passage 2,	**Keyword:** positive, but	
Step 1	Step 2	Step 3
Keywords from the Text	Keyword from answer	Tones / Concepts
Line 57: But its consequences requires, careful consideration.	(B) should be thoughtful	B) meets the central tone of the passage 2
Incorrect Choices & Their Common Patterns		
Evidence	Incorrect keywords	Incorrect Patterns
In almost all cases in SAT, Passage 2 views the same issue from the bigger picture and yields more concerns than P1.Therefore, B) is always the answer. The reasoning behind this logic...	(A) reckless (C) resources disappearing (D) commercial viability	A) Please refer to incorrect choice pattern #12. C) Please refer to incorrect choice pattern #4. D) Please refer to incorrect choice pattern #2

The reasoning behind this logic comes from the origin of passage. In most cases, the source contexts in both Passage 1 and Passage 2 are in fact a single article. Passage 1 places intro. and the first half of the article; second half of the article including conclusion goes into Passage 2. Passage 1 reveals more general concept while Passage 2 presents more reservation. Passage 2 always presents more limitations, concerns, counterarguments, opposition.

Q 48. Absolute Pattern 5: Word-In-Context Question		
Question Pattern: most nearly means	**Keyword:** hold	
Step 1	Step 2	Step 3
Keywords from the Text	Keyword from answer	Tones / Concepts
Line 67: History suggests those will be hard lines to hold (KEEP or MAINTAIN),	(A) maintain	A) "hold" is used as a positive sense
Incorrect Choices & Their Common Patterns		
Evidence	Incorrect keywords	Incorrect Patterns
All the other choices interpreted the word "hold" in the context as a negative sense	(B) grip	B), C), D) Please refer to incorrect choice pattern #1.
	(C) restrain	
	(D) withstand	

Q 49. Absolute Pattern 9: Relationships Question		
Question Pattern: relationship between passages		
Step 1	Step 2	Step 3
Keywords from the Text	Keyword from answer	Tones / Concepts
Line 57: But its consequences requires, careful consideration.	(D) reservations	This type of questions always makes the answer (D) even without reading the passages
Incorrect Choices & Their Common Patterns		
Evidence	Incorrect keywords	Incorrect Patterns
Please read the Q47 explanations.	(A) refutes	If you understand how these questions are made and passages are created, never will you miss this type of question. A), B), C) Please refer to incorrect choice pattern #6
	(B) more general	
	(C) practicality	

Q 50. Absolute Pattern 9: Relationships Question		
Question Pattern: the author of passage 2,	**Keyword:** future of space mining	
Step 1	Step 2	Step 3
Keywords from the Text	Keyword from answer	Tones / Concepts
Line 85: Without consensus, claims will be disputed,	(B) difficult, absence of regulation	When in doubt, read the conclusion.
Incorrect Choices & Their Common Patterns		
Evidence	Incorrect keywords	Incorrect Patterns
Although this question is paired with the following textual evidence question, Duel passages heavily rely on the conclusion as proven in this question.	(A) sustainable use, resource	A), C), D) Please refer to incorrect choice pattern #9. All the other choices use some prediction that is not stated in the passage.
	(C) without technologies	
	(D) Earth's economy	

Q51. Absolute Pattern 11: Textual Evidence Question Finding evidence for the previous question	
Question Pattern: best evidence	
D) is the best answer	Please refer to the preceding Answer explanations

Q 52. Absolute Pattern 9: Relationships Question		
Question Pattern: Passage 1 implicit, Passage 2, explicit **Keywords:** resources resources highly valued in space		
Step 1	Step 2	Step 3
Keywords from the Text	Keyword from answer	Tones / Concepts
Line 31: "In desert, what's worth more: gold or water?"	(A) different from Earth	Passage 1 is more persuasive and easier to understand than Passage 2
Incorrect Choices & Their Common Patterns		
Evidence	Incorrect keywords	Incorrect Patterns
Although the question asks two passages, question number 52, the last question in Reading Section, is usually very easy as this one and reading passage 1 is enough to find the answer.	(B) cheaply (C) precious (D) increase value	B), C), D) Please refer to incorrect choice pattern #2 and #4. None of these words corresponds to the question.

SAT COLLEGE BOARD OFFICIAL TEST
WRITING AND LANGUAGE SECTION
PATTERN ANALYSIS

To download the test, please visit:
https://collegereadiness.collegeboard.org/pdf/sat-practice-test-1.pdf

To understand the full concept of this analysis, it is critical to study the previous chapters before you proceed.

SAT COLLEGE BOARD OFFICIAL GUIDE
WRITING AND LANGUAGE SECTION PATTERNS

Q1. Absolute Pattern 10: Logical Expression

Passage keywords: Yogurt, advantages, drawbacks

	Choice	Explanation
	A) outdo	D) The clause "The advantages outweigh drawbacks" is the standardized expression. Since Yogurt is the host in this essay, the other options—normally applicable to human being—are inappropriate.
	B) defeat	
	C) outperform	
√	**D) outweigh**	

Q2. Absolute Pattern 1: Adding, Revising, Deleting, Retaining Information

Passage keywords: address/problem, a number of uses

	Choice	Explanation
	A) home, yogurt	This seemingly difficult question can easily be solved using parallelism. The previous sentence addresses the problem and then lists some solutions. 1> The previous sentence states "acid whey," which is difficult to dispose of. 2> the passage states "a number of uses (solutions)" starting with one example. 3> Therefore, the following sentence should present another example. 4> Only (B) contains the keywords relevant to another example of usage. A), C), D) are all unrelated issues: the context should discuss "acid whey.
√	**B) convert, into gas**	
	C) food additive	
	D) important diet	

Q3. Absolute Pattern 24: Verb Tense / Voice Error

Passage keywords: If it is,

	Choice	Explanation
√	**A) can, waterways**	When multiple choices include different verb tenses, look for another verb in the paragraph, identify the tense, and stick to it. 1> "If it is" is the present conditional clause. 2> Therefore, the main clause should follow the present tense: (A) B), D) "waterway's" is a possessive form that should carry another noun after that. C) "could have" is the past tense.
	B) can, waterway's	
	C) could have	
	D) waterway's	

Q4. Absolute Pattern 18: Punctuation Error

Passage keywords: and

	Choice	Explanation
	A) ; and	Noun, Noun, and Noun A series of items (nouns) must be listed as above. A semicolon in (A) or a colon in (B) can't be used amid a list of nouns. D) a comma should not be placed after "and"
	B) : and	
√	**C) , and**	
	D) , and ,	

Q5. Absolute Pattern 11: Logical Sequence

Passage keywords: difficult, dispose (Negative/the Main issue)=> If it is, pollute, deleting oxygen (Negative/ The supporting details)

	Choice	Explanation
	A) feed as supplement (sentence 4)	The Passage progresses as [1] The main concern => [2] The supporting details=> [3] The solution=> [4] the example for solutions=> **[5]The problem** Therefore, [5] should be relocated before [3]
	B) main problem (sentence 1)	
√	**C) produces larger, acid-whey (sentence 2)**	
	D) address the problem (sentence 3)	

Q6. Absolute Pattern 1: Adding, Revising, Deleting, Retaining Information		
Passage keywords: Though, these, methods, well worth effort (Positive)		
	A) Yes, not provide	One of the major tricks applied in the Reading Section is to relying on the Positive-Negative value. That is, if the passage is Positive, the answer choice should never be Negative, vice versa. This simple rule is nicely applied in Writing Section too and solves many difficult questions instantly. The topic and the previous paragraph are all Positive. (D) The description (the topic sentence) is positive. Therefore, the answer should be (D)
	B) Yes, fails	
	C) No, how, can be disposed	
√	**D) No, benefits**	
The sentence in question is Positive. Therefore, the answer should never be (A) or (B) because they are Negative. (C) The description is based on the previous paragraph.		

Q7. Absolute Pattern 15: Prepositional Idiom		
Passage keywords: it, digestive aid		
	A) to be	<u>"serving as" is the standardized form.</u> B) "as" is used to equalize two entities. (e.g., Tim serves as the captain of the team => Tim is the captain) A) is used for the future tense only. C) is used to compare two entities
√	**B) as**	
	C) like	
	D) for	

Q8. Absolute Pattern 13: Parallel Structure		
Passage keywords: "it is...serves, and (contains)		
	A) it contains	<u>The sentence parallels by using the list of verbs in simple present tense.</u> (A) "it" interferes the parallel structure. If the subject is one and only, it shouldn't be used again in the same sentence."
	B) containing	
√	**C) contains**	
	D) will contain	

Q9. Absolute Pattern 23: Transitions (Supporting Detail, Contrast, and Consequence)		
Passage keywords: healthy food, helping people stay		
√	**A) also**	Only (A) maintains the same positive tone. It gives more information about Greek yogurt as healthy food. B), C) The previous sentence and the sentence in question offer different benefits (low sugar, high protein). Therefore, (B) and (C) are incorrect. D) "for instance" is used to support the topic (main) statement. The previous sentence is not the topic sentence. In fact, it is located at the end of the paragraph, supporting its own topic sentence, Therefore, (D) is incorrect.
	B) in other words	
	C) therefore	
	D) for instance	

Q10. Absolute Pattern 10: Logical Expression		
Passage keywords: per serving		
√	**A) satiated**	<u>Words in question can be divided into Physical and Mental Concept.</u> A) is a physical concept. It means to supply food beyond desire. B), C), and D) are all mental concept that doesn't link to food .
	B) fulfilled	
	C) complacent	
	D) sufficient	

Q11. Absolute Pattern 7: Conjunction Error

Passage keywords: Because

	Choices	Explanation
	A) therefore farmers	B) Two clauses require only one conjunction. 1> "Because" is subordinating conjunction or simply a conjunction. 2> "therefore" is conjunctive adverb. or simply a conjunction. 3> Error is having two conjunctions (because, therefore) in two clauses. This sentence technically has no main clause but two subordinating clauses. 4> Therefore, the answer should be the one that has no conjunction.
√	**B) ,farmers**	
	C) ,so farmers	
	D) :farmers	

Easy is finding an error with the question that has No Conjunction.
Having Too Many Conjunctions is Equally Wrong and Harder to find what went wrong.
A) "therefore" and C) "so" are conjunctions (conjunctive adverbs) D) a colon also functions as a conjunction.

Q12. Absolute Pattern 9: Informational Graphs

The graph shows the average temperature can drop as low as (B) 12 degrees Fahrenheit.

Q13. Absolute Pattern 16: Precision, Concision, Style

Passage keywords: evidence, thawing

	Choices	Explanation
√	**A) following**	For this type of question, (A) should be the answer— almost always. You do not even need to re-read the passage. A) doesn't use conjunction "and" while all the other options do. (A) is concise and precise. B) and C) use "thawing" unnecessarily. D) uses "evidence" unnecessarily.
	B) thawing	
	C) thawing	
	D) evidence	

The quintessential concept of precision and concision is eliminating unnecessary words and keep the sentence simple.
B), C), D) are all Redundancy error.
1> Redundancy Error is harder than it may appear to be until looking at the correct answer.
2> The easiest way to understand the Redundancy Error is to look from the concision and precision of the sentence

Q14. Absolute Pattern 23: Transitions (Supporting Detail, Contrast, and Consequence)

Passage keywords: typically, late summer, entire ice, underwent, earliest date

	Choices	Explanation
	A) for example	B) 1> "however" cancels out the previous sentence in order to emphasize the following clause. 2> Two clauses between the transition word show a clear contradiction. 3> Therefore, it requires "however"
√	**B) however**	
	C) as such	
	D) moreover	

Q15. Absolute Pattern 22: Nonrestrictive Modifier (Inessential Information)

Passage keywords: an associate...

	Choices	Explanation
	A) Box, an associate...State	1> "an associate....State" is inessential information. 2> That is, even without having this information, the sentence is completely understood. 3> This is called a Nonrestrictive Modifier. 4> A Nonrestrictive Modifier needs to be offset (be careful. It's not upset) by a pair of commas. 5> Therefore, C) is the answer.
	B) Box an associate...State,	
√	**C) Box, an associate State,**	
	D) Box, geology, State	

Q16. Absolute Pattern 18: Punctuation Error		
Passage keywords: another factor added, thaw		
	A) thaw;	<u>The function of Colon is to Introduce Things</u> C) The preceding sentence invites the colon to introduce the name of the factor just like introducing a movie title. A) a semicolon doesn't have such a function. It only connects another clause. B) has two errors: (1) uses a semicolon and conjunction simultaneously (2) "and it was" is wordy. D) please don't choose "being." The choice with 'being' is almost always wrong.
	B) thaw; and it was	
√	**C) thaw:**	
	D) thaw: being	

Q17. Absolute Pattern 7: Conjunction Error		
Passage keywords: , some of it		
	A) of it	<u>If the choice contains "some of which" or "some of whom," that's the answer because the question asks the function of "which" as a conjunction that avoids comma splice error.</u> 1> The subject "tundra fires" and the verb "produced" make a complete independent sentence. 2> "Some of it" and "drifted" make it another clause. However, these two sentences are connected with a comma. This is called the Comma Splice error. 3> To avoid the comma splice error, the answer must contain a conjunction 4> Only (C) has the conjunction "which"
	B) soot	
√	**C) of which**	
	D) delete	

Q18. Absolute Pattern 24: Verb Tense / Voice Error		
Passage keywords: produced, drifted		
√	**A) fell**	When multiple choices include different verb tenses, look for another verb in the paragraph, identify the tense, and stick to it. A) The verbs "produced", "drifted" use the simple past 1> "2012," the time adverbial phrase, it requires the simple past tense. 2> Therefore, the following verb should also use the same past tense. B) is present C) is future D) is past perfect
	B) falls	
	C) will fall	
	D) had fallen	

Q19. Absolute Pattern 14: Possessive Determiners and Possessive Noun Error		
Passage keywords: snow and ice		
	A) it's	1> "ability," the word right next to the question is a noun. 2> Only possessive pronoun can link another noun. 3> Therefore, A) and C) are incorrect. B) there's no precedent that takes on "its" from the sentence.
	B) its	
	C) there	
√	**D) their**	

Q20. Absolute Pattern 1: Adding, Revising, Deleting, Retaining Information		
Passage keywords: absorbs, heat		Question keywords: self-reinforcing
	A) related, rising temp.	D) responds to the question keyword "self-reinforcing" A) and B) are basically repeating the question, instead of answering the question "self-reinforcing cycle." C) is opposite concept
	B) raises, temperature	
	C) cool	
√	**D) melting**	

Q21. Absolute Pattern 19: Redundant Error

Passage keywords: may, repeat, harmful

	Choice	Explanation
	A) again	A) "repeat" and "again" are redundant C) "with damage" and "harmful" are redundant D) "may" and "possibly" are redundant
√	**B) itself**	
	C) damage	
	D) possibly	

Q22. Absolute Pattern 11: Logical Sequence

Key concept: For PATTERN 11. Logical Sequence, it is always easier to find the answer by reviewing the sentences from backward order.

	Choice	Explanation
	A) As it is	<u>Conclusion is easier to understand than introduction. Therefore, reading backward is pivotal.</u> 1> Sentence 6 describes the public fund that helps organize his team's expedition. 2> Sentence 5 describes Box's team that travel to Greenland for sampling. 3> **Sentence 4 describes Box, currently organizing an expedition.** 4> Sentence 3 describes the harmful effect.
	B) after 1	
	C) after 2	
√	**D) after 5**	

As seen above, sentence 4 should be located right before sentence 6 for two reasons: (1) to connect the idea concerning the expedition. (sentence 4 => sentence 6) (2) to connect the idea concerning the harmful effect and finding the evidence through sampling. (sentence 3 => sentence 5)

Q23. Absolute Pattern 19: Redundant Error

Passage keywords: quickly

	Choice	Explanation
	A) soon	Always Pick the Shortest One from the Multiple Choices! A), B), and C) are all redundant error, repeating "soon and quickly."
	B) promptly	
	C) promptly	
√	**D) wore**	

Q24. Absolute Pattern 12: Modifier (Placement) Error

Passage keywords: Having, frustrated

	Choice	Explanation
	A) no colleagues	"Having frustrated" is what "I" experienced.
	B) colleagues	
	C) ideas	
√	**D) I**	

Q25. Absolute Pattern 15: Prepositional Idiom

Passage keywords: read

	Choice	Explanation
	A) into	"Read about" is the correct idiom.
√	**B) about**	
	C) upon	
	D) for	

Q26. Absolute Pattern 18: Punctuation Error		
Passage keywords: such as		
√	**A) ,such as**	"such as" needs a comma to separate itself from the main clause.
	B) ,such as:	B), C): Colon and 'such as' cannot be used simultaneously. D) a comma should not be placed after "such as".
	C) such as:	
	D) ,such as,	

Q27. Absolute Pattern 23: Transitions (Supporting Detail, Contrast, and Consequence)		
Passage keywords: office equipment		
	A) however	1> The paragraph begins with the benefits of the coworking space. 2> Generally, the following sentences support the topic sentence as a supporting detail. 3> The second sentence describes the use of equipment as one benefit. 4>The third sentence describes the space facilities as another benefit. 5> "In addition to" is, therefore, the most ideal transitional word.
√	**B) in addition to**	
	C) for these reasons	
	D) likewise	

Q28. Absolute Pattern 1: Adding, Revising, Deleting, Retaining Information		
Passage keywords: cost, co-working business		
	A) kept, provides details	Do Not Pick Any New Information that is Not Mentioned in the Passage! 1> The topic sentence focuses on the advantages that individual users can enjoy. 2> According to the topic sentence, the sentence in question becomes new information 3> New information is always wrong
	B) kept, main topic	
√	**C) deleted, blurs**	
	D) deleted, repeats	

Q29. Absolute Pattern 9: Informational Graphs		
	A) prevented	A) Negative—The paragraph's overall tone is positive C) misinterprets the numbers. 74% is the figure that individual users favored. D) has switched the numbers.
√	**B) 71, creativity**	
	C) 74, giving ideas	
	D) 12	

Q30. Absolute Pattern 17: Pronoun Error		
Passage keywords: are people		
	A) whom use	D) the relative pronoun that carries a verb must be a subjective form "who." A), B) "whom" is objective form and can't carry a verb. C) the verb "uses" should be "use."
	B) whom uses	
	C) who uses	
√	**D) who use**	

Q31. Absolute Pattern 11: Logical Sequence		
Question keywords: a quick tour, I took a seat		
	A) before 1: try to use coworking	Sentence [2] and the added information match with the context to each other. Sentence [3] illustrates the narrator's observation after he took a seat. Therefore, it should be located after [2] Sentence [3] and [4] are inseparable.
	B) after 1:	
√	**C) after 2:I chose, open work area**	
	D) after 3: more people appeared	

Q32. Absolute Pattern 18: Punctuation Error		
Passage keywords: I've gotten to know		
√	**A) colleagues:**	1> A colon does one thing and one thing only: it introduces things or brief information 2> No other punctuation can do the exactly same function as colon does. 3> Therefore, the answer is (A) as it introduces following "website developer, designer, a freelancer...
	B) colleagues;	
	C) colleagues,	
	D) colleagues	

Q33. Absolute Pattern 10: Logical Expression		
Passage keywords: help each other		
√	**A) share advice**	<u>Finding a logical expression is easy. Defining an illogical expression is less easy</u>. Illogical expressions are those with (1) too literal as in (B), (2) too extreme as in (C) (3) too formal as in (D)
	B) wisdom	
	C) proclaim	
	D) opine	

Q34. Absolute Pattern 23: Transitions (Supporting Detail, Contrast, and Consequence)		
Passage keywords: philosophy is the study		
√	**A) in broad terms,**	"philosophy is the study of...." describes the term.
	B) for example,	
	C) in contrast,	
	D) nevertheless,	

Q35. Absolute Pattern 16: Precision, Concision, Style		
√	**A) pragmatically,**	Compared to answer (A), all the other options are wordy, which, instead of adding a meaningful information, slows down the comprehension.
	B) programmatic way,	
	C) speaking in a way	
	D) speaking way	

Q36. Absolute Pattern 21: Subject-Verb, Pronoun, Noun Agreement		
Passage keywords: philosophy (subject)		
	A) teaching	B) is the only verb available among other choices.
√	**B) teaches**	
	C) to teach	
	D) and teaching	

Q37. Absolute Pattern 1: Adding, Revising, Deleting, Retaining Information		
Passage keywords: philosophy, useful tools, only 18 percent		
	A) consequently,	The following sentence is obviously Negative. 1> The answer for this question can be easily guessed by simply looking at the transition word "however." 2> The tone between two sentences moves from positive to negative. 3> "however" presents a clear contradiction.
	B) therefore,	
	C) notwithstanding...	
√	**D) however,**	

Q38. Absolute Pattern 23: Transitions (Supporting Detail, Contrast, and Consequence)		
Passage keywords: only 18 percent, 400, eliminated.		
	A) Therefore,	1> The tone is consistently negative between two sentences 2> Therefore, (C) is the answer. 3> Two sentences function as an example of the paragraph. 4> A) and B) are used in the conclusion.
	B) Thus,	
√	**C) Moreover,**	
	D) However,	

Q39. Absolute Pattern 16: Precision, Concision, Style		
√	**A) writing as**	Always Pick the Shortest One from the Multiple Choices! A) is most concise and precise without changing the meaning. B) and D) are wordy by adding no meaningful words like "these results" C) uses the word "also" as if there's another reason. However, "also" is already written in this sentence , implying that this very sentence itself is another reason. It is illogical to have another reason inside another reason.
	B) and these results can be	
	C) which can also be	
	D) when the results are	

Q40. Absolute Pattern 21: Subject-Verb, Pronoun, Noun Agreement		
Passage keywords: students (subject)		
	A) has	Always Start with the Main Subject and the Main Verb No Matter Where They Are! B) The subject "students" is plural that requires a plural verb. Choice A, and C are singular. Choice D is not a verb. It's a participle.
√	**B) have scored**	
	C) scores	
	D) scoring	

Q41. Absolute Pattern 12: Modifier (Placement) Error		
Passage keywords: have no intention		
	A) student's majoring	B) "students (who are) majoring" is the correct form of the adjective modifier. What is the adjective modifier? -It is a group of words that describes a noun, normally starting with "~ing" form. For choices A and D, "many" must have "students." "student's" is a singular possessive form, not a plural. C) "major" is used as a verb.
√	**B) students majoring**	
	C) students major	
	D) student's majors	

Q42. Absolute Pattern 1: Adding, Revising, Deleting, Retaining Information		
Passage keywords: students majoring, these skills are transferable Question keywords: ancient Greek philosopher Plato		
	A) Yes,	1> The paragraph describes the practicality of philosophy in modern education. It has nothing to do with Plato. 2> Therefore, it should simply be removed; D) it's not about 'undermine'
	B) Yes,	
√	**C) No, blurs**	
	D) No, undermine, passage claim	

Q43. Absolute Pattern 21: Subject-Verb, Pronoun, Noun Agreement		
Passage keywords: That		
	A) which	1> Here in this sentence that-clause acts as a subject. (e.g., **That I'm rich** is a lie.) 2> That is, when a sentence begins with "That", the verb must be singular because 'That' is singular. No matter how long 'That" clause is, it is singular . 3> A group of words that comes before the verb belongs to "that clause", which should be treated as a part of single subject "that." 4> It can be understood as "The fact that…." which requires a verb. 5> Therefore, the underlined portion should be deleted to make a verb.
	B) that	
	C) and	
√	**D) delete**	

Q44. Absolute Pattern 17: Pronoun Error		
Passage keywords: today's students		
	A) our	D) "their" refers to the subject "students"
	B) one's	
	C) his or her	
√	**D) their**	

ABSOLUTE PATTERN SERIES

SAT Absolute Patterns 7 Practice Tests

SAT 12 Absolute Patterns in Reading Section
The entire 52 questions in the Writing section, both literary and informational passages, can be categorized into three parts: Category A: Content Question; Category B:Technique Question; Category C: Integrated Question. These three categories can be subcategorized into eleven patterns.
Applying these 11 patterns—mostly one pattern per question —plus 20 incorrect choice patterns will be absolutely the most effective and systemic way to improve your scores.

SAT Absolute Patterns 12 Practice Tests Writing & Language

***70* Absolute Patterns in Writing & Language Section**
The entire Writing and Language Section uses these patterns.
CollegeBoard SAT creates questions based on these patterns.
Instead of solving each individual question endlessly without knowing the patterns and logic, assume that each question is made of a unique formula. For the perfect score, memorize 24 patterns in this book. Practice until every pattern becomes natural to you.

PSAT & SAT STARTER'S Absolute Patterns 3Practice

When you are entering SAT for the first time, you would probably rely heavily on your own strategy. Inside the mechanism of SAT, however, is just a little bit more complex so that it requires not only how much time you deal with the problems but also how systematically you can handle them.
To thoroughly understand the patterns, please solve one question at a time and check the answer using the step-by-step pattern explanations without a time limit.

SSAT Absolute Patterns Upper Level 7 Practice Tests

***SSAT* Hidden Patterns in Reading and Analogy Sections**
The entire Reading and Analogy Section use these Absolute Patterns.
The official SSAT creates the questions based on these patterns.
Instead of practicing each individual question endlessly without knowing the patterns and logic behind it, please work with these hidden patterns.

SSAT Absolute Patterns Middle Level 8 Practice Tests

15 and 10 Absolute Patterns in the Reading and Verbal Section
The entire 40 questions in the Writing section, both literary and informational passages, can be categorized into two parts: Category A: Content Question; Category B: Technique Question. These two categories can be subcategorized into 10 Absolute Patterns.
The 10 Absolute Patterns—mostly one pattern per question—will be absolutely the most effective and systemic way to improve your scores.

ABSOLUTE PATTERN SERIES

SSAT Absolute Patterns Elementary Level 8 Practice Tests
Absolute Patterns in Reading and Verbal Section

The entire 28 questions in the Writing section, both literary and informational passages, can be categorized into two parts: Category A: Content Question; Category B: Technique Question. These two categories can be subcategorized into 10 Absolute Patterns.

The 10 Absolute Patterns—mostly one pattern per question—will be absolutely the most effective and systemic way to improve your scores

ISEE Absolute Patterns Upper Level 7 Practice Tests

This book is designed to prepare students to succeed on ISEE upper Level. Absolute Patterns and over 1,000 practice questions with explanatory answers will prepare students to earn perfect scores!

ISEE Absolute Patterns Middle Level 8 Practice Tests

This book is designed to prepare students to succeed on ISEE Middle Level. Absolute Patterns and over 1,000 practice questions with explanatory answers will prepare students to earn perfect scores!

ISEE Absolute Patterns Lower Level 8 Practice Tests

This book is designed to prepare students to succeed on ISEE Lower Level. Absolute Patterns and over 1,000 practice questions with explanatory answers will prepare students to earn perfect scores!

About the author

San, for over 20 years of his career, worked in various educational industries. From college entrance consulting to teaching standardized tests such as SAT / ACT / IELTS / TOEFL / LSAT/ GRE, he has been helping numerous students to enter their top choice universities.

In fact, favoritism of College Board to high-level vocabularies and reading passages makes many high school students fearful and frustrated to SAT. But, despite of this fact, College Board most often than not follows unsurprising patterns—the patterns appear to be problematic and indeed are and will be an albatross around many, may students' necks—when they create SAT questions.

To create the questions and at the same time break the logics and patterns of SAT questions based on CollegeBoard's set-guidelines, San researched hundreds of Actual SAT tests released in the past 30 years.

Here, in this book, students can find how CollegeBoard exploits (?) SAT students by depending on a scenario remarkably similar to that of many questions for several decades.

San is currently living in North Vancouver, B.C. Canada, where he teaches—to further students' needs and realize their ambitions—and write books.

For enrollment through Skype lesson, please contact the author using his email: satvancouver@gmail.com

Dedicated to my wife, Eun Ju and my dog, Okong

Published in 2018 by Rockridge edu. enterprise & services. inc.

All inquiries should be addressed to:
Rockridge edu. enterprise & services inc.
869 SEYMOUR BLVD. NORTH VANCOUVER B.C. CANADA V7J 2J7
satvancouver@gmail.com

Made in the USA
Monee, IL
30 July 2022